INDIAN WARS OF M
CANADA AND THE UNIT
1812–1900

Drawing on anthropology and ethnohistory as well as the 'new military history', *Indian Wars of Mexico, Canada and the United States, 1812–1900* interprets and compares the way Indians and European Americans waged wars in Canada, Mexico, the USA and Yucatán during the nineteenth century. Fully illustrated with sixteen maps, detailing key Indian tribal domains and crucial battle sites, Bruce Vandervort rescues the New World Indian Wars from their exclusion from mainstream military history, and reveals how they are an integral part of global history.

Providing a thorough examination of the strategies and tactics of resistance employed by the Indian peoples of the USA, Vandervort contrasts their ways of war with those of the Métis (French Canadian-Indian peoples), their Canadian Indian allies, and the Yaqui and Mayan Indians of Mexico and Yucatán. Further, the book compares the Indian experience with that of concurrent resistance movements against European expansion in Africa, making it possible to isolate those aspects of resistance that seem unique to the Americas from those with broader implications. Vandervort also draws upon concepts employed in recent rewritings of the history of imperial warfare in Africa and Asia to identify more clearly those aspects of the way of war of the Indian-fighting army of the USA that are truly 'exceptional' and those that are merely generic.

This unique and fascinating study is a vital contribution to the field of military history but is also a valuable addition to the understanding of imperialism and attempts to resist it.

Bruce Vandervort is Professor of Modern European and African History at the Virginia Military Institute, USA. He is editor of *The Journal of Military History* and author of *Wars of Imperial Conquest in Africa, 1830–1914* (1998).

Warfare and History
General Editor
Jeremy Black
Professor of History, University of Exeter

Air Power in the Age of Total War
John Buckley

*The Armies of the Caliphs:
Military and Society in the
Early Islamic State*
Hugh Kennedy

*The Balkan Wars, 1912–1913: Prelude
to the First World War*
Richard C. Hall

English Warfare, 1511–1642
Mark Charles Fissel

*European and Native American Warfare,
1675–1815*
Armstrong Starkey

European Warfare, 1660–1815
Jeremy Black

European Warfare, 1494–1660
Jeremy Black

The First Punic War
J.F. Lazenby

*Frontiersmen: Warfare in Africa Since
1950*
Anthony Clayton

*German Armies: War and German
Politics, 1648–1806*
Peter H. Wilson

The Great War 1914–1918
Spencer C. Tucker

*The Irish and British Wars,
1637–1654. Triumph, Tragedy,
and Failure*
James Scott Wheeler

Israel's Wars, 1947–1993
Ahron Bregman

*The Korean War: No Victors,
No Vanquished*
Stanley Sandler

Medieval Chinese Warfare, 300–900
David A. Graff

Medieval Naval Warfare, 1000–1500
Susan Rose

Modern Chinese Warfare, 1795–1989
Bruce A. Elleman

*Modern Insurgencies and
Counter-insurgencies: Guerrillas
and their Opponents since 1750*
Ian F.W. Beckett

*Mughal Warfare: Imperial Frontiers and
Highroads to Empire 1500–1700*
Jos Gommans

Naval Warfare, 1815–1914
Lawrence Sondhaus

Ottoman Warfare, 1500–1700
Rhoads Murphey

The Peloponnesian War: A Military Study
J.F. Lazenby

*Samurai, Warfare and the State in
Early Medieval Japan*
Karl F. Friday

Seapower and Naval Warfare, 1650–1830
Richard Harding

The Soviet Military Experience
Roger R. Reese

Vietnam
Spencer C. Tucker

*The War for Independence and the
Transformation of American Society*
Harry M. Ward

*War and the State in Early Modern Europe:
Spain, the Dutch Republic and Sweden as
Fiscal–military States, 1500–1660*
Jan Glete

Warfare and Society in Europe, 1792–1914
Geoffrey Wawro

*Warfare and Society in Europe,
1898 to the Present*
Michael S. Neiberg

Warfare at Sea, 1500–1650
Jan Glete

*Warfare in Atlantic Africa, 1500–1800:
Maritime Conflicts and the
Transformation of Europe*
John K. Thornton

*Warfare, State and Society in the Byzantine
World, 565–1204*
John Haldon

*War in the Early Modern World,
1450–1815*
edited by Jeremy Black

*Wars of Imperial Conquest in Africa,
1830–1914*
Bruce Vandervort

*Western Warfare in the Age of
the Crusades, 1000–1300*
John France

*War and Society in Imperial Rome,
31 BC–AD 284*
Brian Campbell

Warfare and Society in the Barbarian West
Guy Halsall

War in the Modern World since 1815
edited by Jeremy Black

World War Two: A Military History
Jeremy Black

*War, Politics and Society in Early Modern
China, 900–1795*
Peter Lorge

*Warfare in the Ancient Near East,
to c. 1600 BC*
William J. Hamblin

*The Wars of the French Revolution and
Napoleon, 1792–1815*
Owen Connelly

INDIAN WARS OF MEXICO, CANADA AND THE UNITED STATES, 1812–1900

Bruce Vandervort

Routledge
Taylor & Francis Group
NEW YORK AND LONDON

First published 2006
by Routledge
270 Madison Ave, New York, NY 10016

Simultaneously published in the UK
by Routledge
2 Park Square, Milton Park, Abingdon, Oxon OX14 4RN

Routledge is an imprint of the Taylor & Francis Group

© 2006 Bruce Vandervort

Typeset in Bembo by Book Now Ltd
Printed and bound in Great Britain by
Antony Rowe Ltd, Chippenham, Wiltshire

All rights reserved. No part of this book may be reprinted or reproduced or utilised in any form or by any electronic, mechanical, or other means, now known or hereafter invented, including photocopying and recording, or in any information storage or retrieval system, without permission in writing from the publishers.

British Library Cataloguing in Publication Data
A catalogue record for this book is available from the British Library

Library of Congress Cataloging in Publication Data
Vandervort, Bruce.
Indian wars of Canada, Mexico, and the United States, 1812–1900/By Bruce Vandervort.
p. cm. – (Warfare and history)
Includes bibliographical references and index.
1. Indians of North America–Wars–1812–1815. 2. Indians of North America–Wars–1815–1875. 3. Indians of North America–Wars–1866–1895. 4. United States–Politics and Government–19th century. 5. Canada–Politics and government–19th century. 6. Mexico–Politics and government–19th century. I. Title. II. Series.

E83.812.V35 2005
973.04′97–dc22   2005016681

ISBN10: 0–415–22471–3 (hbk)
ISBN10: 0–415–22472–1 (pbk)

ISBN13: 9–78–0–415–22471–0 (hbk)
ISBN13: 9–78–0–415–22472–7 (pbk)

TO MY WIFE WENDY, FOR WHOSE MANY
TALENTS I HAVE THE GREATEST ADMIRATION
AND FOR WHOSE LOVE AND UNDERSTANDING
I AM DEEPLY GRATEFUL

CONTENTS

List of maps		x
Preface		xi

PART I 1

   Introduction 3
1 Worlds in motion 17
2 The New World in a century of small wars 38
3 World views and fighting faiths 66
4 Chiefs and warriors 80

PART II 103

   Introduction 105
5 The 'Great Clearance', 1815–42 107
6 Indian wars in Mexico, 1821–76 138
7 War on the plains, 1848–77 161
8 Conquest of Apachería, 1860–86 192
9 War on the Canadian prairies, 1870–85 211
10 Indian wars of the Porfiriato, 1876–1900 229
   Conclusion: Long shadows 243

Notes	249
Bibliography	302
Index	330

MAPS

1.1	Removal of the eastern US Indians to Indian Territory	26
5.1	First Creek War, 1813–14	117
5.2	Woodland Indian tribes of the eastern USA prior to removal	124
5.3	Second Seminole War, 1835–42	129
6.1	Yaqui homeland in the state of Sonora, Mexico	140
6.2	A terrain map of Yucatán, site of the Caste War of 1847–1900	150
6.3	Sites of importance in the Caste War in Yucatán, 1847–1900	153
7.1	Indian Tribes of the western USA in 1850	163
7.2	Sites of the US Indian wars, 1862–90	165
7.3	South Plains War against the Comanches and Kiowas, 1874-75	168
7.4	Great Sioux War, 1876–77	176
7.5	Battle of Little Bighorn, 25 June 1876	183
8.1	The Apache Wars, 1870–86	193
8.2	The Mexico–US borderlands	195
9.1	The creation of the Dominion of Canada, 1869–70	212
9.2	Campaigns of the North-West Rebellion, 1885	222

PREFACE

In an earlier book I made a plea for more 'cross-cultural comparative' studies in military history and gave as an example of what might be done James O. Gump's remarkable book *The Dust Rose Like Smoke: The Subjugation of the Zulus and the Sioux* (Lincoln: University of Nebraska Press, 1994).[1] In the book you have before you, I have tried to follow my own advice.

On one level I have undertaken to describe, interpret and compare the ways Indians and European Americans waged their nineteenth-century wars in the forests and swamps of the southeastern United States, on the plains and in the mountains of the American trans-Mississippi West, on the prairies of western Canada, in the mountain fastnesses and deserts of northern Mexico and, finally, in the semi-arid flatlands and rain forests of Yucatán.

Not only were the Indian wars of Canada, Mexico, the United States and Yucatán virtually simultaneous, linkages also existed between them. These manifested themselves in a number of concrete ways, all of which will be touched upon at some length in this book: (1) the importance to Indian insurgents throughout the 1815–90 period of cross-border sanctuaries (the Apaches in Mexico, the Sioux in Canada, the Yaquis in Arizona, the Mayas in British Honduras) and sources of supply; (2) fear on the part of the Canadians and Mexicans that the turmoil of Indian uprisings near their frontiers with the USA or use of those areas as sanctuaries by Indians might serve as a pretext for US invasion (the number one military priority for both countries during this period was defence against US attack); (3) growing realisation on the part of the three countries in the post-1865 era that international cooperation was required to bring the Indian wars to an end, by, for example, as far as the USA was concerned, getting Canadian authorities to discourage Indians from seeking asylum in Canada, gaining the right to cross the Mexican border in 'hot pursuit' of Apache raiders, and convincing the Mexican military to work closely with US troops in cornering and wiping out Apache war parties taking refuge in Mexico; (4) Mexican solicitation of US capital investment in development schemes in the state of Sonora intended to woo Yaqui dissidents into abandoning their demands for political autonomy and collective ownership of their land; (5) US mercenary involvement in the Caste War, the revolt of Mayan Indians in

PREFACE

Yucatán which began in 1847, and periodic US schemes to take over the country,[2] designs encouraged at one point by an expressed willingness of some prominent Yucatecans to make their country a US protectorate.[3]

But I believe there is scope for a second, much more ambitious sphere of comparison. Comparing the way the US military conducted its Indian wars from 1815 to 1890 with the practices followed over the same period, not only in neighbouring Canada and Mexico but also in the wider world of European imperial conquest, makes it possible to present the campaigns of the American Indian-fighting army in sharper relief and, at the same time, identify more clearly those aspects of the Indian wars of the USA that are truly 'exceptional' and those that are merely generic. The more global relationship, although no less important than the regional one, operated more at arm's length and on a more conceptual and theoretical plane. Its main elements were: (1) emulation by New World armies of European models of organisation and professional comportment (the French serving as models to the Americans and Mexicans, the British to the Canadians) in the first decades of New World independence, to a lesser degree later; in the case of the USA, the French model was applied in all land arms, through the adoption at the US military academy at West Point of the curriculum of the *École Polytechnique* in Paris, with its emphasis on engineering and gunnery, through the adoption of drill books translated from the French for use by both the infantry and cavalry, and, perhaps most importantly, through the imbibing of the Napoleonic 'ethos' of battle with its cult of the offensive, emphasis on decisive battle and stress on the attainment of 'glory' as the supreme goal of the individual soldier in war (though this ethos inspired infantry officers as well, its most ardent exponents were officers in the mounted arm). The curriculum of the Mexican national military academy, the *Colegio Militar*, also was based on that of the École Polytechnique, with the result that, like West Point and the École itself, it tended to graduate artillerymen and engineers; when the Mexican regular army finally became engaged in Indian fighting in the late nineteenth century, its proficiency in siege techniques, gunnery and military construction were its main contributions. Canada relied on the British army for defence until the 1870s and on British officers to train and lead its armed forces into the 1890s; even after the British presence was reduced, Canada's army remained British in everything from uniforms to weaponry and tactics, and the Canadians hankered after – and were gratefully given – a part in Britain's imperial wars down into the next century.

The comparative approach can reap the same dividends with respect to the Indian side of the story. Thus, a comparison of the strategies and tactics of resistance followed by the Indian peoples of the American West with those pursued by the *Métis* (French Canadian-Indian peoples) and their Indian allies in Western Canada and by the Mayas and Yaquis of Mexico, *and* with the experiences of African and Asian resistance movements against European expansion during the nineteenth century, makes it possible to isolate those aspects of resistance that seem to be unique to the Americas from those with broader implications.

Where possible, I have also tried to strengthen and enrich the narrative of the New World Indian wars by infusing it with insights from the traditional disciplines of anthropology and ethnohistory. Historians of the New World Indian wars need to come to grips not only with Indian 'ways of war', but also with the cultural, political, social, and religious contexts in which Indian warfare was so intrinsically embedded.

Last, but certainly not least, I have also made an effort to apply to the nineteenth century New World setting concepts that so far have been employed most fruitfully in revising accounts of imperial conquest in Africa and Asia. In 1976 Gary Nash wrote hopefully that '[American] Indian history stands poised on the edge of a new era of scholarship'. What heartened Nash was his belief that American history was 'turning away from the consensus school of historiography' whose smoothing over of class, ethnic and racial antagonisms had made it nearly impossible 'to focus on the experience of the Indian people in North America'. Nash thought that scholars who were engaged in the renewal of Indian history, particularly of the colonial era, would do well to 'borrow the methodologies and in some cases the conceptual models of African historians, who in the last two decades have brought the history of European–African relations and the ethnohistory of African societies to a position far in advance of the present state of Indian history'. While acknowledging the differences between the two historical experiences, Nash felt that 'the attitudes and strategies of colonisation that Europeans brought to North America and Africa, the patterns of trade and native responses, were in many situations similar enough to warrant a respectful consideration of the very rich recent work in African history'.[4]

I have followed Nash's lead here by taking on board the thesis of Ronald Robinson and John Gallagher, first set out in their path-breaking book, *Africa and the Victorians,* that imperial wars were often less a result of initiatives taken at the centre, in Western capitals, than of dynamism at the periphery that forced Western armies to attack and occupy.[5] Thus, in the New World setting, it can be argued that the frontier conflicts in which the armies of Canada, Mexico and the USA were engaged were occasioned as much by turmoil on the periphery as by plans for expansion made by governments. What makes the New World case different is the greater role of settler populations in precipitating the 'peripheral flux' that led to military intervention. One thinks here not only of the miners, railroad builders and homesteaders whose encroachments on Indian lands led to warfare in Canada and the Western USA, but also of the conflicts in Mexico and Yucatán which resulted from the designs of whites and mestizos on the lands of the Yaquis and Mayas. I believe that the concept of 'peripheral flux' functions better as an explanatory mechanism for what happened on the New World peripheries during the first six decades or so of the nineteenth century than for what took place during its remaining years. After the late 1860s the governments of Canada, Mexico and the USA became much more proactive and proved increasingly able to effectively use the manpower and resources at their disposal to defeat their Indian foes and place them on reservations or contain them in some other way.

Inherent in the 'peripheral flux' scenario is a second valuable concept drawn from new interpretations of the European 'Scramble' to occupy African territory, that of 'secondary imperialism' (or 'sub-imperialism'). This notion holds that there arose in Africa in the nineteenth century a number of polities which were engaged in an imperial expansion of their own and that the clash that eventually came was frequently not just a collision between Western imperial troops and tribal self-defence forces, but a contest between rival empires. It is further asserted that these indigenous empires owed their existence and capacity for expansion to a symbiotic relationship with their European rivals; formed to some extent as a response to European encroachment, they nonetheless owed much of their own dynamism to wealth and technology acquired through trade with these same European powers. This concept seems to apply to a number of wars between Africans and European invaders, for example, France's imperial wars in West Africa from 1850 to 1890 and the Italo–Ethiopian War of 1896.[6] In the North American context, a case can be made for the emergence of 'sub-imperial' forces in the American West, with the rise of the Sioux–Northern Cheyenne–Northern Arapaho confederacy on the northern Great Plains and the hegemony of the Comanche–Kiowa–Southern Cheyenne–Southern Arapaho alliance over much of the South Plains. Application of the term 'secondary empire' to the territorial domains of these two confederations seems justified, in that they were built around extensive trade with the whites and a military system, as we have seen, based on the gun and the horse, both of which came to them from European sources.

Finally, one area in which a comparative approach is particularly useful is in putting in perspective the human cost of the nineteenth century Indian wars in Canada, Mexico and the USA. Starting with the USA, figures for the period 1848–90 show 1,109 soldiers of the US Army killed and 1,061 wounded. Over the same period, US civilian losses totaled 461 dead and 116 wounded. Data on Indian losses only exist for the 1865–90 period and show dead and wounded together totaling 5,510, presumably including men, women and children.[7]

The wars against the Indians and Métis in western Canada were much less costly. The Red River Expedition to Manitoba in 1870 was able to complete its mission without losing a soldier or inflicting a single casualty upon the Métis enemy. The North-West Rebellion of 1885 in Saskatchewan would cost the Canadian armed forces only 40 dead and 115 wounded, while the Métis and Indians they were fighting suffered just 35 dead and 11 wounded.[8] A small number of settlers and North-West Mounted Police also died or suffered wounds in the fighting.

Mexico suffered far greater losses in her Indian wars than either Canada or

PREFACE

the USA. While there are no figures for losses on either side, there can be no doubt that the Yaqui-Mexican wars, which raged on with intervals of armed peace for the better part of one hundred years, from 1825 into the 1920s, cost the regular army and the militia and National Guard of the state of Sonora several thousands of dead and wounded. Thousands of Yaquis died and were wounded as well, including large numbers of women and children. But the wars against the Yaquis also incurred a high number of civilian casualties on the Mexican side, although, again, figures are not available. The losses in the Yaqui wars, however, pale in comparison to the long term Mexican losses at the hands of Indian raiders from the north, Apaches and Comanches. These raids, from the 1820s until the 1870s in the case of the Comanches and from the 1820s into the 1880s in the case of the Apaches, cost many thousands of lives, and led to the destruction of property worth millions of pesos and the carrying off of yet more thousands of Mexicans into captivity by the Indians. There is nothing in the annals of the much more highly publicised struggle between North American settlers and soldiers and their Indian foes that can compare with the travails experienced by their Mexican counterparts.

It is, however, Yucatán which must in terms of sheer human suffering seize our attention. The 1847–1900 Caste War between Mayan rebels and state and federal authorities may have cost some 200,000 to 300,000 lives, from a third to a half of the country's total population. In some areas of Yucatán, around 75 per cent of the population died in the fighting.[9]

These figures offer yet another demonstration of the hyperbole that has attended the Indian wars in North America. Proportionally, Mexico and Yucatán suffered far greater losses in blood and treasure than either Canada or the USA, yet their story is almost unknown in the Anglo-Saxon or broader European world. But there is another level of analysis that puts the small wars in nineteenth century North America into even sharper perspective.

The deaths incurred by the US Indian-fighting army from 1848 to 1890, 1,109 officers and other ranks, were less than those suffered by the British 24th Regiment of Foot in four hours of fighting against the Zulus at the battle of Isandlwana in South Africa on 22 January 1879. Zulu spears claimed 1,300 British and allied African soldiers, including more officers than died with Wellington at Waterloo. Although no accurate count was ever made, it is estimated that British rifles took the lives of some 3,000 Zulu warriors.[10] But even this 'last stand' of the 24th Foot, which has been compared to that of Custer's Seventh Cavalry at the Little Big Horn, pales in comparison to the hecatomb inflicted upon the Italian army by its Ethiopian enemies at the battle of Adowa in northern Ethiopia. From 6.10 in the morning till around three o'clock in the afternoon of 1 March 1896, this bloodiest single battle in all of the European colonial wars claimed the lives of 289 Italian officers and 4,600 other ranks, along with those of 2,000 of Italy's Eritrean and Tigrean allies.[11]

The approach taken in this study has forced me to be selective with respect to coverage of the Indian wars fought in the United States, perhaps more selective

PREFACE

than some readers will like. Thus, only passing reference is made here to, for example, the wars pitting the US Army against the various Indian peoples of California and the Pacific Northwest, the Navahos of New Mexico and the Utes of Colorado and Utah. Those who wish to know more about the conflicts I have not covered will find a number of volumes listed in the bibliography which give ample treatment to them.

A word may be in order about the organisation of this book. In the first four chapters I have tried to put in place the geopolitical and ideological/religious contexts in which the small wars of the New World occurred, as well as their more specifically military environment. I have sought to give even-handed treatment to the two sides in these conflicts and, where possible, have tried to draw comparisons between them. A short section has been inserted between this background material and the next six chapters, which are devoted to a narrative of the Indian wars of Mexico, Canada and the USA. The purpose of this introduction is to explain what I see as the crucial factor in determining the outcome of these wars: the resolution of internal conflicts and the subsequent consolidation of national power in the white settler states. The book concludes with an effort to trace the legacy of the Indian wars in the Indian and white communities and in the wider world.

I have written this book in such a way that it might be helpful to undergraduates and beginning graduate students as well as general readers. Thus, I have reduced its scholarly apparatus to a minimum, citing for the most part only sources of direct quotes or of factual information that might be in some dispute. I have also, however, supplied occasional bibliographical notes alerting readers to useful sources on topics under discussion in the text. The bibliography at the end of the volume will also provide students and general readers with ample suggestions of where to turn if this book should whet their appetites for further reading on the small wars of the New World.

Acknowledgements

My first and greatest debt as I bring this book to a close is to my family, both here and in Switzerland, for whom I have too often been a ghostly presence these past four years, when not absent altogether. To my dear wife Wendy, whose patience has been sorely tried by this undertaking, what I have brought together here as a work of scholarship is gratefully dedicated. The book is my second contribution to the 'Warfare and History' series at Routledge Publishers directed by Professsor Jeremy Black of the Department of History and Archaeology at Exeter University, whose many kindnesses and warm collegial support over the years have been greatly appreciated. The administration of the Virginia Military Institute (VMI) should know how grateful I am for its unstinting support for my research projects over the years. Friendship takes on a heightened importance in circumstances like these and I have been blessed with good friends. Space allows me to mention only a few here. Blair Turner has been a great and good friend and steady support since my first days at VMI in 1989. Larry Bland and I have been following the same road under the same star since my graduate school days at the University of Wisconsin more years ago than I care to remember. Two good friends from my days as a reporter in Geneva, Switzerland, died during the writing of this book and I very much regret that they did not live to read it. John Callcott and John Parry were at one and the same time worldly newsmen and English gentlemen of a now departed school. They and their kind are sorely missed.

I owe a special note of thanks to Head Librarian Don Samdahl and his staff at VMI's Preston Library. Over the years I have come to believe that if reference librarian Jan Holly can't find a book or article I'm looking for, it probably doesn't exist. Elizabeth Hostetter, who handled Preston Library's inter-library loan service for a number of years, was not just a close and valued accomplice in my scholarly endeavours but a personal friend. Her death last year after a long bout with cancer was a tragic loss.

Finally, some professional debts. To Dr. Bob Wooster, at the Corpus Christi branch of Texas A and M University, many thanks for suggesting that I expand my gaze in this book to encompass the Caste War in Yucatán. It was a grand idea and I hope I have capitalised on it. Alan C. Aimone, Senior Special Collections Librarian at the Library of the US Military Academy at West Point, N.Y., offered generous advice on printed sources and identified helpful contacts in the Indian wars scholarly community. Prof. Jeanne T. Heidler of the History Department at the US Air Force Academy in Colorado Springs, Colo., directed me to valuable sources on the Creek War of 1813–14. Finally, Dr. Victoria A.O. Smith of the History Department at the University of Nebraska–Lincoln was good enough to share with me her considerable expertise on the Yaqui Indians of Mexico. Of course, none of these generous souls is in any way responsible for the errors that will inevitably find their way into the text that follows.

Bruce Vandervort
Lexington, Virginia

PART I

INTRODUCTION

Beecher Island

It was just before dawn on 17 September 1868 when the Cheyenne cutting-out party swept down on the white scouts' camp on the banks of the Arickaree River in eastern Colorado Territory. There were only three or four of the raiders, young men who had defied their elders and gone off to steal the white men's horses despite threats of a beating.[1] They came from a big Cheyenne camp about twelve miles upstream, to which a few Brulé Sioux and Northern Arapahos had attached themselves. The raid didn't amount to much: only seven horses and two mules were driven off by the yipping, blanket-waving youths. But the commotion caused by the cutting-out party would make sure that the fifty-one scouts, who had slept on their arms that night, would be up and about when the big attack came a few minutes later.[2]

The men who now began moving about the camp, some saddling up to chase after the stolen horses, were not soldiers. Although commanded by an army officer and Civil War veteran, Major (Brevet Colonel) George A. 'Sandy' Forsyth, and looked after by an army surgeon, Dr. John G. Mooers, the scouts were civilians, 'first-class hardy frontiersmen' in the phrase of General Philip Sheridan, commander of the US Army's Division of the Missouri. Sheridan had ordered Forsyth to recruit the men in the summer of 1868, to fill in for the regulars who had been diverted from the frontier to Reconstruction duty in the South, and, one suspects, in part to appease local sentiment, which maintained that the army was doing a poor job of protecting the growing number of settlements from Indian raids and that their salvation lay in the raising of a large body of frontiersmen, 'children of the West', who could fight the Indians on their own terms. An editorial on 21 June 1867 in the Leavenworth, Kansas *Daily Times* had given shrill voice to the settler viewpoint:

> From the first alarm, up to the present moment, we have . . . urged the policy of hunting Indians by the Frontiersmen. They alone can do the work as it should be done. Regular troops are, in a great measure, the laughing stock of the Indians. . . . [But t]he border is in no humor for trifling. The howl of the savage comes too near to be musical.[3]

INTRODUCTION TO PART I

The fifty 'hardy frontiersmen' recruited on Sheridan's orders had all the trappings of an elite force. To begin with, they were handpicked from a large group of volunteers by Major Forsyth, with the aid of his second-in-command, Second Lieutenant Frederick Beecher, nephew of the well-known New England abolitionist, the Reverend Henry Ward Beecher. Pay was generous. Men who brought their own horses got $75 a month, men without horses $50. This at a time when Army privates were paid $15 a month (soon to be reduced to $13). The scouts also were well-armed. Each was issued with a Spencer seven-shot repeating rifle, a favourite of Union cavalrymen like Forsyth during the Civil War, an Army issue Colt revolver and a butcher's knife.[4] Forsyth's Scouts, as the force would be known, were expected to travel light so as to be able to intercept fast-moving Indian war parties before they fell upon the farmsteads which had begun to encroach upon Cheyenne hunting grounds in western Kansas. Rations and other supplies were kept to a minimum; ammunition made up most of the load carried by the scouts' four-mule pack train.[5]

Back on the Arickaree, Major Forsyth had not been slow to realise that the raid by the cutting-out party betokened the presence of a larger body of Indians, and had ordered scouts out to reconnoitre the low hills surrounding the camp. Minutes later, they came galloping back. Chief guide Abner 'Sharp' Grover seized Forsyth's arm and, pointing up the river valley, shouted, 'My God, Major, look at the Indians!'[6] There were a lot of them, five to six hundred, some Brulé Sioux along with a few Northern Arapahos, but for the most part Northern Cheyennes, many of whom belonged to the formidable Dog Soldier warrior fraternity.[7] The scout John Hurst recalled his first sight of the charging mass of warriors: '[T]he Indians were in full view, and such a view! All were mounted on their war horses, in war costume, with feathers and plumes flying, shouting war whoops, their horses running at full speed.'[8]

And they were very close. Forsyth invoked the classics to underscore just how close they were. 'Cadmus-like they appeared to spring full armed from the very earth', he wrote.[9] Teenage scout Sigmund Shlesinger, who had come West the year before from New York City, drew upon the Romantic novelist Sir Walter Scott to paint the scene. '[The Indians] seemed to spring from the ground like Roderick Dhu's Highland Scots', he said. Scots or Indians, Shlesinger was terrified by the onrushing warriors. 'I will frankly admit I was frightened almost out of my senses. I felt as if I wanted to run somewhere, but every avenue of escape seemed closed.'[10]

This was the scouts' dilemma. With the Indians so close, escape was impossible and a running fight would probably have ended in the loss of the entire command. The only real option available to the scouts was to make a defensive stand. Major Forsyth would later claim that it was he who hit upon the idea of making for the island – an overgrown sand bar, really – in a dry channel of the Arickaree just across from the camp.[11] Some of the scouts recalled the episode differently. One of them, George Washington Oaks, later insisted it was his comrades Thomas Murphy and Jack Stillwell who called out, 'Go on the island'.[12]

INTRODUCTION TO PART I

Whoever may have thought of it, the scouts' retreat to the island was no orderly withdrawal. '[W]e all made a grand rush for cover like a flock of scared quail', John Hurst recalled.[13] Nevertheless, the dawn raid on their camp by the wayward Cheyenne youths had alerted the white men to their danger and given them enough time to reach the island before the Indian mass descended upon them, although, as we will see, in their great haste they left behind supplies that would be sorely missed.

Having failed to overrun the scouts before they gained refuge on the island, the Cheyenne warriors and their allies now dismounted and, creeping through the tall river grass, proceeded to shoot down the scouts' horses. Their foe effectively immobilised, the Indians launched the first of a series of mass attacks on their position. Although John Hurst thought 'we were all going to be killed and scalped', the attacking warriors broke off their charge at the last moment, divided into two groups and veered around the sides of the island.[14] All, that is, except the half-Cheyenne, half-Sioux warrior Bad Heart, who 'counted coup' on the astonished scouts by riding over the island and back unscathed. The white men fired at the swirling mass of Indians from behind willow trees and brush and from rifle pits they scooped out for themselves with cups, plates, knives, anything that could be used to dig. There were two more large-scale attacks that first day, during the latter of which the great Cheyenne war leader, Roman Nose, was killed. Following a half-hearted assault early the next morning, the Indians gave up on mass attacks, and began a siege of the island. On 21 September, after three days of desultory sniping, the Cheyennes and their Sioux and Arapaho allies broke off the siege and rode away.

The departure of the Indian war party left Forsyth's men in possession of the field of battle. But their 'victory' had come at a heavy price. Already on the first day about a third of the scouts had been killed or wounded. The dead included the scouts' second-in-command, Lieutenant Beecher, and their doctor, the surgeon Mooers. The wounded included Major Forsyth, who was hit three times on the first day of the battle and was for all practical purposes unable to move. The death of Dr. Mooers only compounded what was already a looming medical crisis. In their hurry to escape to the sandbar, the scouts had left behind most of their medical supplies. This meant that wounds were never properly attended to and, as in the case of Major Forsyth, became infected. Equally troubling for the scouts was the lack of food. They had been almost out of rations the day before the Indian attack and had unwisely consumed what little was left for their evening meal. By the time the siege of the island came to an end, the scouts were living on decaying horse flesh, liberally seasoned with gunpowder to hide the taste, supplemented by the flesh of a coyote that had ventured too close and the fruit of the prickly pear that proliferated on the prairie nearby.

The scouts had realised the extent of their peril early on in the encounter and had taken desperate measures to bring a relief column to their rescue. Volunteers were found to slip through Indian lines at night and make their way across the prairie to get help from the army garrison at Ft. Wallace, some 85 miles away in Kansas. Although even the veteran guide 'Sharp' Grover believed it was a suicide mission, the volunteers managed to get through. On 26 September, nine days after their flight to the island in the Arickaree, now named Beecher Island after the slain lieutenant, Forsyth's Scouts were relieved by a detachment of 'Buffalo Soldiers', black troopers from the Tenth US Cavalry out of Ft. Wallace.

The scouts must have seemed a sorry sight. By the time the cavalry showed up, nearly half their number had been killed or wounded. All of their horses were dead. Many of the wounded were in parlous shape for lack of medical attention. One scout, whose leg wound had become gangrenous, died when the doctor with the relief column tried to amputate the limb. Major Forsyth, although he affected a Victorian stiff upper lip – his rescuers found him 'nonchalantly' reading a copy of *Oliver Twist* – was in serious condition.[15] He had been wounded in both legs, gangrene had set in and amputation was recommended. Forsyth had refused and, though he eventually recovered, it took two years before he could walk unaided. A head wound would produce mental aberrations later in life.

Thanks to the telegraph, the Forsyth Scouts' 'stand' on Beecher Island would become headline news across white America even before the Buffalo Soldiers rode to the rescue. The scouts who made their way across the Kansas prairie to Ft. Wallace had told their story to a reporter there on 24 September and the next day the plight of the force received prominent play on the front page of *The New York Times*. Almost immediately the scouts were acclaimed national heroes and their ordeal on Beecher Island began its quick passage from newspaper story to frontier legend.[16] Just six years later, no less a figure than the commander of the US Seventh Cavalry, Colonel George Armstrong Custer, was ready to accord the scouts pride of place in the Valhalla of the Indian-fighting army. Oblivious of course to how ironic his remarks would seem in just two years' time, Custer wrote that 'In all probability, there will never occur in our future hostilities with the savage tribes of the West a struggle ... equal [to it]'.[17]

The story of the September 1868 Battle of Beecher Island has been recounted here at great length, not only or even mainly because of its prominent place among the epic engagements of the North American Indian wars, but because of the insights it offers into the principal themes of this book.

Ways of war

The Battle of Beecher Island offers a classic demonstration of what anthropologists call the Horse and Gun Pattern of Plains Indian warfare. The Cheyenne, Sioux and Arapaho warriors who descended upon the scouts in the early morning hours of 17 September ranked among the American West's most famed practitioners of the fluid style of warfare developed by the Plains Indians with the advent of the horse. Horses had come to the Cheyennes in the eighteenth century, guns perhaps earlier. Lieutenant Beecher, in a reconnaissance of Indian camps in western Kansas before his secondment to Forsyth's Scouts, had come away convinced that the Cheyennes he and his comrades were destined to face were armed to the teeth – even the women and children – with top-of-the-range weapons, repeating rifles and Colt pistols. This was something of an exaggeration, it can be assumed, but the Indians who fought the scouts do appear to have been relatively well armed with gunpowder weapons.[18] This combination of horse and gun transformed Plains Indians like the Cheyennes and Sioux into what US Army officers were wont to describe as 'the best light cavalry in the world'.

The Forsyth Scouts, on the other hand, were something of an anomaly in the US Indian-fighting army. Irregulars like the white scouts had played a prominent role in Indian fighting in colonial days and on into the early national period, but, despite a revival during the manpower-scarce Civil War period, the trend from the War of 1812 onwards had been steadily in the direction of confining Indian fighting to the regular army. This tendency, strong though it might have been in official circles, still met with considerable hostility amongst the general public. There continued to be a deep distrust of professional armies in the Anglo-Saxon countries – not just the USA, but Canada as well – as sanctuaries for would-be gentry and handmaidens of tyranny. In Mexico, the regular army was feared by the population, and with reason, as an instrument of repression. People who felt like this reposed their trust in the people in arms, ordinary citizens in the militia or in ranger formations who would rise to the cause when needed and return to their homes when the crisis had passed. This sentiment waxed strong in Mexico, Canada and the USA during most of the 1800s, but especially in the first half of the century. But more to the point here, since colonial days large sections of the civilian population in the USA had argued that only frontiersmen, organised as rangers or scouts, men who could ride and shoot and 'knew' Indians and were able to fight them on their own terms, could protect settlers from Indian war parties. Many such critics would have agreed with this Kansas settler that it was the Army's very professionalism that made it unsuitable for fighting Indians. 'Talk about regulars hunting Indians!' he scoffed.

> They go out, and when night comes, they blow the bugle to let the Indians know that they are going to sleep. In the morning they blow the bugle to let the Indians know that they are going to get up. Between their bugle and their great [supply] trains, they manage to keep the redskins out of sight.[19]

This sort of complaint usually went hand in hand, as shown above, with demands for raising a force of frontiersmen to fight the Indians, men like the white scouts we have just followed to the Arickaree. Whatever else such demands might have represented, dislike for standing armies or contempt for what the Jacksonian tribune, Senator Thomas Hart Benton, called 'pothouse soldiers and schoolhouse officers', they also expressed a belief in a notion its supporters never would have articulated in these terms, a notion that today's military historians call 'symmetry'. To them, it was simply a matter of matching up plains-savvy frontiersmen with Plains Indian warriors. These critics would have been aware that the army thought it had taken the necessary step towards achieving 'symmetry' with Plains Indian opponents by making fighting them the almost exclusive province of its mounted arm. But these same critics would have been quick to reply that this was only a half step towards curbing the 'red devils' who raided settlements and impeded commerce on the prairies, that the cavalry (really mounted infantry) not only lacked the special skills needed to fight Indians, but also the mobility required to catch and destroy their fast-moving raiding parties before they vanished into the wilderness. Those damned bugles and long supply trains!

The Beecher Island scrap also demonstrates, however, that the belief of settlers in the West that 'symmetry' in Indian fighting could be achieved by replacing the 'yellow legs' of the US Army with their own kind was by and large an illusion. That Forsyth's Scouts were not the elite outfit the Kansas settlers and perhaps even General Sheridan expected them to be may come as a surprise to many American and European readers, brought up as they have been on a cinema and TV diet of tales of bold and intrepid frontiersmen, Daniel Boone, Davy Crockett, Buffalo Bill Cody and so on.

Though all of Forsyth's scouts had lived on or near the frontier, only a few qualified as 'frontiersmen' in the popular sense of the term, and while some were Civil War veterans (from both sides), not many had done any Indian-fighting. While it may not have been entirely the case that, as one recent historian has charged, what Forsyth got 'were a lot of young drifters who would turn their hand to anything' (including robbing stagecoaches),[20] it was nonetheless true that the majority lacked the skills normally associated with Plains scouting, the ability to live off the land, to 'read sign', and, especially, to 'think' like an Indian.[21]

But we should not single out Forsyth's Scouts for criticism. No frontier commander who was serious about fighting Indians really believed that white men, even 'hardy frontiersmen', could do as good a job of scouting Indians as other Indians could. General George Crook, who probably employed Indians as scouts (and combatants) more effectively than any soldier in the West, never used white scouts when he could help it. Few of them really knew the country, he said, and it was hard to get them to go out any distance. 'I always try to get Indian scouts', Crook wrote,

> Because with them scouting is the business of their lives. They learn all the signs of a trail as a child learns the alphabet; it becomes an instinct. With a white man the knowledge is acquired [later] in life.[22]

INTRODUCTION TO PART I

Perhaps the hardest thing about fighting Indians was *finding them*. For this, as a rule you needed Indian scouts. Close examination of the times when white soldiers were able to corner Indians will show clearly that it was Indian scouts who found the camps and led the soldiers to them. This was true of, for example, the discovery of the great Comanche village at Palo Duro Canyon on the Staked Plain of Texas, whose destruction brought the Red River War of 1874–5 to an end, and of the entrapment and slaughter by Mexican troops of Victorio's band of Apache raiders at Tres Castillos in Chihuahua in 1882. And, conversely, failure to use Indian scouts could cost troops dearly. Canadian forces went off to war against the Métis and Cree Indians in 1885 without much in the way of scouts of any kind, Indians or otherwise, and managed to get themselves ambushed and driven off in disarray by Crees at Cut Knife Hill in Saskatchewan.

But the inability of the Forsyth Scouts to cope with the Indian threat was not entirely their fault. They also lacked competent leadership. Indeed, the Beecher Island battle opens an instructive window onto the nature and functioning of nineteenth century military command, not only in the Indian-fighting armies of the New World but in those of imperial powers elsewhere as well. The Forsyth Scouts may not have been the 'hardy frontiersmen' they were advertised to be, but their commander was, if anything, more of a greenhorn than they were. Forsyth had been selected by General Sheridan to command the scouts not because of his Indian-fighting experience, of which he had none, but because he was a longstanding member of the general's circle of favourites, having served as his aide during the Civil War. Desperate for promotion, the major had badgered his patron relentlessly for some sort of field command and Sheridan had finally found the means to oblige. This kind of cronyism was not peculiar to General Sheridan and his bevy of acolytes, nor was 'Sandy' Forsyth's wire-pulling unusual in the nineteenth century US Army. Both were big blots on the escutcheon of the otherwise admirable General Crook, and combined with a colossal ego to mar the reputation of that other great US Indian fighter (and bitter Crook rival), General Nelson Miles. Nor were these faults limited to the New World commanders of the age. The late nineteenth century British Army was riven for two decades by an unedifying power struggle over everything from promotions to imperial grand strategy between the 'Ashanti Ring' of General Sir Garnet Wolseley and the (East) 'Indian Ring' gathered around General Sir Frederick Roberts.[23]

Apparently, neither Sheridan nor his protégé had any second thoughts about Forsyth's suitability for the role of commander of frontier scouts. Major Forsyth certainly doesn't seem to have thought that the job required any special talent. He scoffed at the notion that Indians could be 'a match for disciplined troops on the field of battle'; they were, he said, 'savages in all that the word implies'.[24] It was perhaps just as well for 'Sandy' Forsyth that he felt this way. Had he felt a need to 'bone up' on Indian fighting techniques, he almost certainly would have come up empty-handed. There was no body of doctrine on irregular warfare he could have pulled off a bookshelf to study or that his patron, General Sheridan, could have loaned him. The US Army never felt sufficient need for guidance of this sort to see that it got into print. As it was, Major Forsyth did what most of the officers in his situation were obliged to do. Ralph Andrist tells us that the major 'learned all he could by listening to experienced Indian fighters . . .'.[25] We do not know what Forsyth 'learned' from the veterans he talked to, but whatever it was, it was not much help to him, as the events that followed will reveal. The whole interlude casts doubt on the US Army's wisdom in assuming that its officers – and enlisted men – could learn Indian fighting on the job, or by taking advice from the old sweats.

Indeed, one wonders whether Major Forsyth listened to anything the veterans had to say. He told a fellow officer just before departing for the field that he was 'confident of being able to whip all the Indians he would meet on the plains with his select company of scouts'.[26] This was a common sentiment among Western soldiery off to shoulder the 'white man's burden'. In 1895, Lt. Colonel Paul-Louis Monteil of the French marines, back in civilisation after having spent three years traversing the Sahara, boasted that 'with ten armed men you can go all the way across Africa'.[27] A bit closer to home and forty years earlier, the young Lieutenant John L. Grattan, fresh out of West Point and placed in command of troops at Fort Laramie, Wyoming, was of the opinion, 'as expressed often and in earnest, that, with thirty men, he could whip the combined force of all the Indians of the prairie'. On 19 August 1854, Grattan got his chance. He led a detachment of 30 men to a nearby Sioux camp to demand the surrender of a warrior accused of stealing an immigrant's cow, managed to goad the Indians into a fight, and ended up getting himself killed along with his entire force.[28]

In any case, Forsyth's self-confidence does not seem to have reassured his scouts. Although they would ride into history bearing his name, the Forsyth Scouts do not seem to have been terribly impressed with their commander. Those among them who did know something about frontier scouting recognised Forsyth for the amateur he was. 'We knew for two days that we were biting off a chew that we could not get away with, and we urged Forsyth to give it up, but he went right on', a scout recalled.[29] Nor did the major ever give the sceptics much reason to change their minds. Early on in their foray into Indian country, he had ordered the scouts to charge a group of haymakers from a nearby fort, having mistaken them for Indians.[30] Then, when the troop did come upon the trail of Indians, not just a few raiders but from all indications a whole big village of them, and the men had thought it might be the better part of valour not to pursue them any further, Forsyth had questioned their fighting spirit and downplayed the danger they were in. 'That ended the discussion,' said John Hurst, 'but all the same, it did not convince us of the wisdom of the course.'[31] It was, of course, this large body of Indians which eventually turned on the scouts and came within a whisker of catching them in the open and wiping them out.

INTRODUCTION TO PART I

What seems to have convinced Major Forsyth that no special leadership qualities were required to defeat Indians, and to have assured the US Army hierarchy that no special doctrine needed to be formulated to overcome Indians (or any other irregulars, for that matter), was an unquestioning belief in what General Nelson Miles would refer to, in the context of the Apache wars of the 1880s, as the 'superior intelligence' of the white race and the 'modern appliances' its soldiers were able to bring to bear on the field of battle.[32] Those two assumptions lay at the very heart of the ethos that inspired the 'way of war' of the Indian-fighting armies of the New World and the European armies of imperial conquest. The first assumption, what the recent historian of New Zealand's Anglo-Maori wars, James Belich, has called the 'Victorian interpretation of racial conflict', held that the defeat of 'uncivilised' peoples was rendered inevitable by their lack of the 'higher mental faculties' that provided Europeans with seemingly unique powers 'to co-ordinate, to think strategically, and to innovate tactically and technically'.[33] If this belief among Western soldiers in the innate superiority of the white man seems to have abated somewhat over the last century, as the result of sobering experience, the belief in 'modern appliances' as the key to military prowess, if anything, has grown stronger with time.

General Miles's belief in the efficacy in the Apache wars of such 'modern appliances' as the heliograph is an early example of what we today call 'technological determinism', the notion that military technology, especially weaponry and the firepower it engenders, decides battles and wins wars. This belief undergirds what might be described as the 'Rorke's Drift interpretation' of military history. This view takes its name from another famous 'stand', in this case of British imperial infantry in January 1879, during the Anglo–Zulu War, at a place in South Africa called Rorke's Drift. The battle fought there has since been immortalised in the popular movie *Zulu*. The 'stand', which pits around 130 officers and men of the South Wales Borderers against some 4,000 Zulus, ends with the Zulus giving up and departing after a series of frontal assaults, much as the Cheyenne–Sioux–Arapaho war party did at Beecher Island. As the Zulus finally retire over the hill, crusty old regimental Colour Sergeant Bourne tells his commanding officer, Lieutenant John Rouse Merriott Chard, 'It's a miracle, sir'. Chard, an officer of Engineers, will have none of this mystical claptrap. 'If it's a miracle, Colour Sergeant, it's a short chamber Boxer Henry 4.5 calibre miracle', he snorts, referring to the cartridge fired by the Martini-Henry breechloading rifle his men carried at Rorke's Drift and used with such effect against the charging Zulu *impi*. Just as the people who made the film *Zulu* did their best to convince audiences that the 'miraculous' victory of the British soldiers at Rorke's Drift was the product of the killing power of their breechloading rifles (there are nearly as many close-ups of the Martini-Henry in the film as there are of Michael Caine), so American frontiersmen and soldiers at the time and historians since have tended to ascribe the Forsyth Scouts' deliverance at Beecher Island 11 years before to the Spencer carbine.

INTRODUCTION TO PART I

The scouts themselves clearly thought their Spencers had saved the day. 'Our bullets seemed to daze the Indians . . . who could not determine how we were able to load and fire so rapidly,' John Hurst wrote.[34] Most of the historians who have studied the fight on the Arickaree have tended to echo Hurst. Writing in 1963, a leading historian of the Buffalo Soldiers, William H. Leckie, credited the lever-action Spencer repeaters with 'handily' driving off the Indian attackers.[35] Ten years later, Robert M. Utley, the dean of scholars of the US Indian wars, attributed the scouts' salvation to 'disciplined volley fire from Spencer repeating carbines'.[36] Thirty years on, the verdict had not changed. Stan Hoig, an expert on the South Plains Indian wars, wrote that 'The Cheyennes had failed to wipe out the small force of embattled scouts, their mass charges proving ineffective against the firepower of the Spencer repeating rifles and Colt revolvers.'[37] Finally, the most recent historian of the Beecher Island battle, John Monnett, concludes that 'the effectiveness of the seven-shot Spencer carbines with which the scouts were armed saw them through the early crisis at Beecher Island.'[38] It takes more than a little chutzpah to swim against such a tsunami of expert witness, but a case can be made that there was more to the story of the scouts' escape from annihilation than the firepower of their Spencers. To find the other pieces of the puzzle, we need to look at what happened on the Arickaree from the perspective of the Indian attackers, from the vantage point, then, of *their* 'way of war'.

The Battle of Beecher Island provides a number of illuminating insights into Indian ways of war – and not only those of Plains Indians like the Cheyennes. Let us begin with Bad Heart's daring ride into the heart of the white scouts' defence. This was the sort of heroics that Plains Indians regarded as the ultimate test of manhood, against which the mere killing of an enemy fighter faded into insignificance. Feats of this sort were also thought to unnerve opponents and deprive them of the psychological edge so important to victory in war. The scout Jack Stillwell remembered gaping open-mouthed as the bold warrior went thundering past.[39] Although it is an exaggeration to argue as he does that war was just 'a great game' to Plains Indians like the Cheyennes and Sioux, the historian Ralph Andrist was surely correct in observing that the pursuit of individual glory by warriors could and often did disrupt the collective effort usually needed to win battles.[40] No better example of this can be given than the reckless cutting-out raid of the Cheyenne youths, which put the white scouts on their guard and probably saved them from being destroyed. For the indiscipline of the young Cheyennes denied their elders the kind of battle they wanted to fight, the kind of battle Plains Indians excelled at. 'We knew that we would be no match for that army of red men [out] in the open,' the scout John Hurst conceded.[41] What might have happened to the scouts was what did happen to some of General George Crook's soldiers at the battle of the Rosebud on 17 June 1876, on the eve of the Custer massacre. Troopers from Crook's Third Cavalry were caught strung out in pursuit of 'fleeing' Sioux warriors, who suddenly turned and overwhelmed them, charging bodily and rapidly through the soldiers, knocking them from their horses with lances and knives, dismounting and killing them, cutting the arms of several off at the elbows in the midst of the fight and carrying them away.[42]

As it was, the Cheyennes and their allies were forced to fight the sort of battle Indians everywhere most disliked and sought to avoid whenever possible: a frontal attack on a defensive position. So averse were they to battles of this sort that they frequently backed away from them even when they greatly outnumbered their opponents. Scout Louis McLoughlin couldn't understand why the Indians never pushed home their attacks on Beecher Island. 'Two or three times,' he said, 'if the Indians had kept on a minute or two longer, they would have got us, as sometimes we would hardly have a shot left when they broke [around the island].'[43] The reluctance of Indian warriors to strike home, as at Beecher Island, was not for lack of courage, as the great personal bravery of individuals like Bad Heart clearly demonstrates, but rather because of an unwillingness to incur heavy casualties. Even before the whites came on the scene, it was the kiss of death for an Indian leader, whether in the Eastern Woodlands or on the plains, in the mountains of the Southwest or on the Canadian prairies, to suffer big losses in battle. He would undergo censure by his people and would probably never get anyone to follow him to war again. This reluctance to fight pitched battles was only reinforced by the experience of war against the whites. Yes, the soldiers' firepower was daunting, but it was not only that. Indians had access to firearms as well, and sometimes took into battle more sophisticated weapons than their white opponents. Indian leaders over time had become acutely aware of how few their people were compared to their white enemies. Warriors who died in battle could not be replaced, unlike fallen bluecoats, whose places could be taken by soldiers drawn from seemingly endless reserves of men back home. And behind the regular army stood the hordes of white settlers, who were only too eager to take up the gun and go after Indians. In order to put the Cheyenne approach to the Battle of Beecher Island in perspective, it might be useful to compare it with the way Zulu warriors in South Africa eleven years later fought the battle of Isandlwana, another of the imperial era's famous 'stands', on the same day (22 January 1879) as the Rorke's Drift fight. The Zulu army launched a massive frontal attack on a British and allied African force of some 1,800 men in the opening phase of the battle, throwing one of its regiments head-on against the British lines, where it took ferocious punishment from those Martini-Henry rifles we have just heard about. Whilst this was going on, however, the two wings of the Zulu army managed to outflank and envelop the enemy, and in the general assault that followed killed 21 British officers and 581 other ranks, along with some 470 allied African soldiers. The Zulus paid dearly for their victory – an estimated 3,000 warriors were killed – but that same day, of course, they launched their epic attack on Rorke's Drift. The difference in tactics between the Zulus and

Cheyennes lies in large measure in the great demographic gap between the two peoples. There were about a quarter of a million Zulus in 1879. When the war with the British began, the Zulu paramount king, Cetshwayo, mobilised an army of at least 40,000 men. A little less than half of them were committed to battle at Isandlwana.[44] By contrast, there were only about 3,500 Cheyennes – men, women and children – roaming the Western plains in 1850, and probably even fewer by 1868.[45] A large portion of their warrior population thus was present at Beecher Island. The Cheyennes, and, by extension, most other Indian peoples, simply could not afford the kind of losses the Zulu king was willing to contemplate in order to achieve victory. Among the Indian peoples treated in this book, in fact, only the Mayas of Yucatán enjoyed a demographic edge over their enemies. The fate of the North American Indians, and the Yaquis of northwestern Mexico as well, to be outstripped demographically by their white foes, if not always outnumbered on the battlefield, is one of the striking anomalies of small wars in the New World.

And then there is the great Cheyenne war leader, Roman Nose.[46] His death on the first day of the Arickaree fight probably had as much to do with the Indian failure to bring the engagement to a successful conclusion as any other factor. And not for the reasons one might imagine. Although he was a famous warrior and a powerful presence, tall, athletic, recognisable even in the crush of battle because of his distinctive war bonnet, it was not only his prowess in war that had won him a devoted following among his people and a fearsome reputation amongst his white enemies. He was widely thought to possess particularly powerful 'medicine' and had given several demonstrations of its potency on the battlefield. In the course of a set-to with the troops of General Patrick Connor's command on the Powder River in Wyoming in September 1865, for example, Roman Nose 'rode close along the length of the army's ranks four times before his horse was shot from under him.'[47] The magic that protected him from the soldiers' guns resided in the war bonnet he wore, which was decked out with

> the skins of a barn swallow, a bat, and a kingfisher. The barn swallow flies close to the ground, and the bat darts up and down and is impossible to hit. When a person shoots at the wearer, the real person is not actually within the gun sights [but] is close to the ground like the barn swallow or darting high up in the air like the bat. The bat also flies at night, giving the wearer protection in battle at that time, and the kingfisher closed up bullet holes in the body because when the kingfisher dives into the water, the water closes over it.[48]

But the great medicine man Ice who made the war bonnet for Roman Nose warned him that its magic would be lost if he shook hands with anyone after he put it on, or ate food that had been served up with a metal utensil.[49] On the day before the attack on the scouts Roman Nose had eaten bread taken from the fire with a metal fork. To restore his lost 'medicine' would have required a lengthy process of ritual purification but, instead of doing this, he allowed himself to be badgered by his warriors into leading the third mass attack on the white men dug in on Beecher Island. Roman Nose led the charge and was shot in the back and killed.[50] His death demoralised the encircling warriors. Not only had they lost a great war leader but his 'medicine', which they had come to regard as a guarantee of success in battle, had been taken from them as well. This episode serves as a powerful reminder of the crucial impress of the spiritual upon Indian warmaking. Again and again in this book we will have occasion to observe the interconnectedness of war and religion in Indian life.

The 'technological determinism' explicit or implicit in so much of the historiography of the New World Indian wars and, indeed, of nineteenth-century imperial warfare in general, can at best offer only a partial explanation for the success of Western-style armies. We believe that the New World experience provides some of the best evidence we have for drawing alternative conclusions. Indeed, it will be argued here that superior military technology had almost nothing to do with the victory of European American armies in the New World Indian wars. There is something to be said for the impact of *non-military* technologies on the outcome of the Indian wars – the steamboats on the rivers, barbed wire, the telegraph, railroads – but these are greatly underplayed in the traditional accounts. These civilian innovations clearly were important, but the victories of the European Americans came largely because they could draw upon populations vastly greater than those of their adversaries; because they profited from enemy weaknesses, including a corrosive individualism like that exhibited by the Cheyenne cutting-out party at Beecher Island and abiding intra-tribal rivalries which allowed the white armies to divide their Indian opponents and use them against each other; and because they were able to deny Indian peoples access to vital food supplies, not just in the sense of the much remarked-upon slaughter of the North American buffalo herds, but, more generally, because of a progressive occupation by white settlers of Indian grazing and hunting lands and their use for mining, agriculture and the building of transportation networks.

The Indian wars in the Americas proceed in two phases, and the Battle of Beecher Island occurs on the cusp between the two. Prior to 1868, the New World passed through an era of considerable flux, marked by intense civil strife in the Canadas, Mexico and, especially, the USA. Although the era also produced powerful integrative and expansionist ideas – national self-determination in Canada, *La Reforma* in Mexico and Manifest Destiny in the USA – internal opposition impeded where it did not effectively stifle their realisation. The opposition to these movements in every case included Indian peoples, either acting alone or in collaboration with other protagonists. In Canada, Indian resistance to white rule by way of a more highly centralised nation-state would remain latent, manifesting itself only in the 1870s and '80s, but in the Mexican case it was at the very heart of opposition to the liberalising and centralising thrust of *La Reforma*, both in the 1850s and '60s and in its earlier incarnations. In the USA, meanwhile, the dream of one nation 'from sea to shining sea' failed in the first half of the nineteenth century, not only because of the rise of the Confederacy, but because of the growth beyond the Mississippi River of a kind of 'secondary imperialism', the forging of powerful Indian confederations led by the Comanches and the Sioux, and because of the continued sway of Apache raiders over the Mexico–US borderlands. But Indian efforts, arms in hand, to preserve the old free life on the plains and in the woodlands, mountains and deserts of the Americas would fail in the second half of the nineteenth century as new, more highly centralised governments finally proved capable of turning their considerable advantages in population and resources into victory, if not always on the battlefield then at least at the end of the day. This outcome would have been only dimly glimpsed, if at all, by the Forsyth Scouts as they chewed their putrid horsemeat on Beecher Island in the autumn of 1868. Just about eighteen months to the day before their ordeal began, another aggressive but inexperienced officer had led a detachment of soldiers into another bloody encounter with a large war party of Cheyennes, Sioux and Arapahos, this time near Fort Kearny, Wyoming. But Brevet Lt. Colonel William Fetterman's 80 troopers had no island to run to and perished to a man.[51] In the last months of 1868 it would have been difficult to sense the immense power of the new or reinvigorated European American nation-states building, as it were, behind the dam of natural obstacles and Indian opposition that had frustrated their designs in earlier years. But the power was there and in two short decades, a bit longer in the case of Mexico, it would burst through the restraints that had held it in check and bring the centuries-long age of Indian wars to a close.

1

WORLDS IN MOTION

Introduction

In Europe, the nineteenth century customarily is described as a century of peace, the calm surface of events being ruffled by only one quasi-global conflict (the Crimean War of 1854–6) and a succession of localised wars accompanying the national unification struggles in Germany and Italy and the long death agony of the Ottoman Empire. For the rest of the world, however, the century was anything but peaceful. From 1837 to 1901, the British Army fought over 400 battles in some 60 campaigns against enemies ranging from the Maori of New Zealand to, as we shall see, the *Métis* of western Canada. All this in the course of constructing an empire that by 1900 would encompass one quarter of the globe. Meanwhile, France, the second-ranking imperial power, had added Madagascar, Indochina, most of North Africa and much of West Africa to its domains, while newcomers Germany and Italy had managed to carve out empires of their own from the leavings of their more venerable predecessors.

Warfare in the Americas during this period paralleled in important ways the conflicts unleashed in Africa and Asia by the European imperial powers. To begin with, the scope and timing of European and American imperial advance are striking in their coincidence. Thus, over the first half of the nineteenth century, while the French were conquering Algeria and Senegal and Britain was bringing the rest of the Indian subcontinent under its sway, subduing the Burmese, establishing a sphere of influence in Afghanistan and bullying the Chinese into giving up Hong Kong, the USA managed to secure the withdrawal of Britain and Spain from disputed territory on its borders, to lay claim to vast new lands in the West (more than one million square miles) by way of the Louisiana Purchase from Napoleonic France, to defeat and evict or confine on reservations all of the Indian peoples east of the Mississippi River, and to take by force half of the territory of the Mexican Republic. Much of this, however, represented *potential* that would only be realised in the second half of the nineteenth century. In 1867, the USA purchased Alaska from Russia and in the next two decades completed its drive from 'sea to shining sea' by subduing the Indian tribes who inhabited the trans-Mississippi West. The new self-governing Dominion of Canada, meanwhile, had greatly increased its territory by purchasing the holdings of the Hudson's Bay Company in western Canada in 1869 and, in short, sharp wars in 1870 and 1885, defeated the Indians and Métis who resisted its takeover. Mexico, pretty much at the mercy of indigenous and invading Indian peoples during the first half of the nineteenth century, managed to quell both the Mayan and Yaqui insurgents within its borders and Apache and Comanche interlopers (with crucial help from the USA) from 1876 to 1901. These were, of course, the halcyon years of European imperialism, the period which saw every last Pacific island and all of Africa save for Ethiopia, Liberia and Morocco brought into the European grasp, completion of the French conquest of Indochina and the humbling and exploitation of China itself by the European powers.

Europeans saw all of these events as being of a piece. Indeed,

> In its spatial enormity and temporal brevity, the settlement of the [American] West was considered to be the most dramatic of the acts by which European dominion over the world had been established. Lord James Bryce noted in *The American Commonwealth* that nothing like it had occurred in human history since the Egyptian monarchy had been created along the Nile.[1]

To European statesmen like Lord Curzon, the powerful proconsul of the British Raj, the American West was simply the largest and most celebrated of the many 'voids' on the world map being filled by the headlong surge of European imperialism in the nineteenth century.[2] The completion in 1867 of the Union Pacific Railroad, linking the Atlantic and Pacific coasts of the USA, was an event of profound global consequence in the view of the Paris travel journal, *Le Tour du Monde*. It gave confirmation once again, wrote the journal's North American correspondent, of the 'mysterious law of history which requires that all people in their progressive march must always advance toward the West', but, 'More important, with the construction of this railroad, one can say that civilisation has made its trip around the world'.[3]

Even though their country had presumably turned inward to accomplish it, prominent nineteenth-century Americans gloried in the notion of the US Indian-fighting army as the spearhead of a European civilising mission. And when the time came to decide whether or not to continue that mission among America's 'little brown brothers' in Asia, following the Spanish–American War, Senator Henry Cabot Lodge, a leading proponent of American imperialism, told the US Congress in arguing for occupation of the Philippine Islands that 'the record of American expansions which closes with Alaska has been a long one, and today we do but continue the same movement. The same policy runs through them all'.[4]

Just as European statesmen were eager to include the Americans among the great imperial powers of the day, so were European soldiers quick to welcome the US Indian-fighting army into the imperial fraternity of arms. The dean of

British colonial warfare theorists, Colonel Charles E. Callwell, drew no distinctions between the British wars to subdue the Indian subcontinent, the French seizure of Algeria and the campaigns of the US cavalry against the 'Red Indians' of the western plains and deserts. In his classic primer, *Small Wars: Their Principles and Practice*, first published in 1896, Callwell lumped the North American Indian wars with European 'wars against nature' in Africa and Asia, wars in which the principal foes were not the indigenous inhabitants, but rather distance, climate, terrain and disease. The colonel consciously likened US cavalry tactics on the plains, principally the surprise descents on Indian villages that were an essential part of the Army's post-1865 Indian-fighting strategy, to the *razzia* or raids employed in Algeria in the 1840s by the horsemen and infantry of French Marshal Thomas-Robert Bugeaud, whom he called 'one of the greatest masters of irregular warfare'.[5] American contemporaries agreed with Callwell. US Army Captain Randolph B. Marcy had taken with him on campaign against the Comanches in Texas in the 1850s a copy of a French account of the Algerian conquest, and was struck, he would later write,

> with the remarkable similarity between the habits of the Arabs and those of the wandering tribes that inhabit our Western prairies. Their manner of making war is almost precisely the same, and a successful system of operations for one, will in my opinion, apply to the other.[6]

The captain was not alone in his musings. No less a figure than Marcy's superior, the Secretary of War Jefferson Davis, recommended that the US government look to the French system of large-scale aggressive patrolling in Algeria as the model for its posture vis-à-vis the Indian tribes of the trans-Mississippi West. Marcy, Davis and those who thought like them considered the French approach in Algeria much superior to the then current US system of static defence, in which troops were parcelled out among tiny garrisons sprinkled along the fringes of white settlement.[7]

Crucial as this debate might have been to US military affairs in the years before the Civil War, it is only one example of the extent to which the Indian wars of the United States and the other post-colonial states in the New World formed a natural and integral part of a global pattern of imperial conflict in the years 1815–90. That pattern manifested itself, on a regional level, in the inter-relatedness of the Indian wars that took place in Mexico, Canada and the USA, and, on a more universal level, in the conceptual and institutional links which bound the armies of the New World states to contemporary military establishments in Europe and to the imperial campaigns undertaken by European armies in Africa and Asia.

The US military took an interest in European methods of colonial warfare, especially in the pre-Civil War era, and not only with respect to whether or not frontier troops should remain on the defensive in static posts. The British, French and Russian use of 'native auxiliaries' in their colonial wars, in India,

West Africa, the Caucasus and Central Asia, was much studied and debated by US soldiers. While George McClellan and Jefferson Davis seemed to think that large Indian levies could play the role of 'cossacks' or *spahis* (North African Arab irregular cavalry in the French army), other US soldiers felt Indians could only be trusted as scouts and guides.[8] On a less cosmic scale, there was much copying in the New World of the uniforms and equipment of European colonial troops: the Zouave mania in the US on the eve of the Civil War; the adoption of the French képi as standard headgear in the US and Mexican armies; use by US Army officers on the frontier of the solar helmet from British India. Mention should also be made of the US Army's experiment in the 1850s with camels as beasts of burden. This experiment was undertaken on orders from the Secretary of War Jefferson Davis, who had been impressed with stories of Napoleon's use of camels in Egypt following the French invasion of 1798. Davis's decision to promote the employment of camels in the Indian wars in Texas and the Southwest was influenced by news that the French army had resumed using them in the Sahara.[9]

The tides of emulation were reversed to some extent after the US Civil War, with some European colonial officers expressing admiration for the US cavalry in suppressing the Indians. The US Army also fell out of love with the French in the aftermath of France's defeat in the Franco–Prussian War of 1870, transferring its affections to the victorious Prussians. Though there were tendencies in this direction in Mexico as well, the greater Mexican intellectual engagement with France kept the Mexican army more or less loyal to its French 'connection'. However, with the launch of an American overseas empire in 1898, the US once again began looking closely at the experiences of European imperial armies for lessons in how to fight 'small wars'. In 1900 Captain J.S. Herron of the US Second Cavalry toured European colonial outposts around the world on behalf of his country's War Department in search of information US troops could use in their own colonial wars. The US was then engaged, of course, in the 'pacification' of the Philippine Islands, just conquered from Spain.[10]

European American expansion

The newly independent (or self-ruling, as in the case of Canada) states in the Americas, with some exceptions, attracted large numbers of white settlers. And nowhere was this more the case than in North America, whose generally temperate climate, small indigenous population and abundance of good farmland acted as inducements to Old World immigrants, especially from Northern Europe. (Argentina, at the other end of the hemisphere but endowed with similar attributes, was also a popular destination for European immigrants, although they tended to be from Latin rather than Northern European origins.)

There were few other places in the emerging imperial world quite like the Americas in this regard. In Africa, most tropical colonies either proved unattractive to European settlers or were placed off-limits to settlement by their colonial masters. Only the two more or less temperate extremities of the continent, Algeria in the north and South Africa and the Rhodesias in the south, received large numbers of European settlers. Conditions there differed greatly from those that greeted emigrants to North America, however. In both regions, European emigrants found themselves heavily outnumbered by the indigenous population and would only be able to impose their will upon them by installing repressive minority regimes. In Algeria, French conquest had preceded European settlement and, somewhat like US professional soldiers in the West, the French army saw as one of its main tasks the protection of the 'natives' from a rapacious settler community. In fact, Algeria remained under military rule after the conquest, much to the consternation of the settlers, until the advent of the Third Republic in the 1870s.[11] In Southern Africa, meanwhile, the situation differed yet again. Here, as James O. Gump has pointed out, the aim of policy towards the indigenous population was not so much to put the 'natives' on reservations in order to get them out of the way of white settlement, as was the case in Canada and the USA, as to transform them into a cheap labour force for employment on white farms or down white mines.[12] To find situations where the pattern of white emigration and settlement resembles the North American experience, it is necessary to cross the Pacific Ocean, to New Zealand and Australia. Like Canada and the USA, both had relatively inviting climates and agricultural conditions (although the Australian outback was and is forbidding to settlement) and small indigenous populations. Warfare against the 'natives' also followed patterns similar to those in North America. White settlers in Australia, it would seem, demonstrated even less tolerance of the aboriginal population than their counterparts in the Americas. This had dire consequences for the indigenous peoples, especially after the British government permanently withdrew its troops and turned over Australian frontier defence to local militias in 1838, a step US authorities were never so reckless as to take.[13] The outcome was almost ceaseless conflict and a death toll of some 2,000–2,500 European settlers and an estimated 20,000 Aborigines during the period of settlement in the nineteenth century, losses considerably higher than those in the USA.[14] The New Zealand experience more closely resembles the American in that the business of dealing with indigenous opposition was for the most part entrusted to the (British) regular army and not the militia, with the result that the genocidal implications of the Australian system were avoided.[15]

Meanwhile, back in the New World, population movements of historic proportions were underway throughout the 1800s. In Canada, immigrants from Europe, particularly the British Isles, and the USA began to fill up available land in Upper Canada (Ontario Province) in the 1830s and '40s, some of it only recently obtained by treaty from its Indian inhabitants, and to swell the population of its burgeoning cities, especially Toronto. To the west, the Hudson's Bay Company had restricted settlement to the Red River Colony of Manitoba, leaving the rest of the vast prairie and parkland region to the fur trade and buffalo hunting. In the 1840s, some 1,000 settlers of European descent were living in the colony, along with around 6,000 French- and English-speaking Métis who had begun to make the Red River Colony their home after leaving their earlier centre at Pembina, just across the border in what had become Dakota Territory in the USA.[16] Most of the European settlers were farmers. The Métis also did some subsistence farming, but their preferred means of livelihood – and grand passion – was buffalo hunting on the Canadian and American plains. The sale of the Hudson's Bay Company's western lands to the new Dominion of Canada in 1869 opened up the whole region between Manitoba and British Columbia to white settlement. Before the deluge began, however, the government in Ottawa negotiated a series of treaties with the Indian tribes inhabiting the area, in which the Indians, some more reluctantly than others, agreed to settle on reserves in return for promises to assist them in making the transition from nomadic life to farming. A new constabulary, the North-West Mounted Police, was formed to implement these treaties and to generally 'civilise' the Canadian West. Despite all of these precautions, however, the process of transition from an unfettered life on the plains to life on restricted reserves did not proceed smoothly for many of the Indian peoples involved. The subsequent influx of settlers from eastern Canada and abroad led to friction with the region's Blackfoot and Cree Indian tribes and to armed showdowns on two separate occasions, 1870 and 1885, with the French-speaking Métis community.

In Mexico, meanwhile, the new republic (1821) made a bid to open up new lands for settlement by enshrining the concept of private property in the nation's constitution, which had the effect of rendering illegal Indian communal property-holding arrangements that had been tolerated, even in some cases encouraged, by the Spanish authorities, such as those in force among the Yaqui people in the northern state of Sonora. In the case of the Yaquis, the aim of the liberals who led the new Mexican republic was to make the tribe's fertile farmlands along the Yaqui River in the southern part of the state available for white and mestizo settlement. The encroachments of settlers on these Yaqui lands, with encouragement from the state and federal governments, met with fierce resistance and became a major factor in the almost constant warfare between the Yaquis and government forces during the nineteenth century. In Yucatán, meanwhile, pressure by *ladino* (Hispanic) planters and settlers on the lands of the Mayas also helped to spark conflict and was a contributing factor to the outbreak of the Caste War in 1847.

It was in the United States of America, however, that white settlement in the nineteenth century assumed the most dynamic proportions. By 1820, the whole of the country east of the Mississippi River had been divided up into states or territories and efforts were underway to remove what was left of the eastern Indian population to the west. Over the next three decades, waves of white settlers traversed the Father of Waters and occupied lands up to the 98th meridian, along the eastern boundary of Indian Territory (the new home of the eastern Indian tribes) and up to the bend of the Missouri River, where movement ceased for a time. This was the edge of what some contemporaries called 'The Great American Desert', a high plains zone where annual rainfall fell below that required for conventional farming. Not a few observers thought that a combination of climate and the fierce Indian nomads who roamed it would make this region permanently uninhabitable by white settlers. Bonaparte's Consul-General in the US from 1800 to 1814, M. Félix de Beaujour, offered a prescient, if overly pessimistic, view of what awaited white soldiers who dared to venture into this 'desert'. They would find in 'those vast solitudes', he wrote,

> a race of men, like the Tartars, hardened to the chase, indefatigable horsemen who would continually harass them, would cut off their convoys and end by destroying them in detail. They would have to carry on against such a people as these, the same species of warfare the Romans waged against the Parthians, and this war would be eternal, because there is no means of stopping a wandering people.[17]

The halt at the 98th meridian was broken, not by a change in the weather or a sudden conversion of the Indian nomads to peaceful agricultural pursuits, but by the Gold Rush of 1849 in California. The whole pattern of westward migration changed sharply, as great wagon trains of emigrants began heading out across the Great Plains, through passes in the Rocky Mountains and over the Great Basin to the Pacific shore. In the 1820s, American traders had opened a Santa Fe Trail from Missouri to the Mexican Southwest. After the Mexican–American War of 1846–8, emigrants would follow the same trail to New Mexico and Arizona, the new territories carved out by the victorious Americans. The Santa Fe Trail skirted yet another great area of white settlement in the 1840s and '50s, the Lone Star State of Texas. By 1860, there were 1.3 million white settlers in the West; over the next decade, the number rose by one million, and in 1880 stood at 4.9 m.[18] In the 1870s, the last areas still being fought over by white settlers and their indigenous inhabitants were the Rocky Mountains and the plains and prairies to the east of the mountains, bordered on the north by Canada and on the south by the Rio Grande River. This would be the main arena of conflict between the horse soldiers of the US Army and the plains tribes that Félix de Beaujour had equated with the Tartars and Parthians of old, and the scene of the last great stand of the plains warriors, the Sioux of Crazy Horse and Sitting Bull, the Cheyennes of Roman Nose and Dull Knife, the Comanches and Kiowas of Quanah Parker and Satanta. But there was another zone of confrontation that would prove even more difficult for the Americans, the mountains and deserts of Arizona, New Mexico and Old Mexico, the homelands of the Apache war parties that would occupy the bluecoat soldiers of Generals Crook and Miles, and their Mexican counterparts, well into the 1880s, nearly ten years after the last of the Sioux had returned from the Land of the Great Mother and laid down their arms.

PART I

Peripheral flux

Until fairly recently, European and North American historians tended to see the 'less-developed' world before contact with the West as static, timeless, inhabited by 'peoples without history', as in English historian H.R. Trevor-Roper's famous remark about African history. 'Perhaps in the future there will be some African history to teach,' he said in 1963. 'But at present there is none. There is only the history of Europeans in Africa. The rest is darkness . . . and darkness is not a subject of history.'[19] Now, four decades later, as a 'new' African history and a 'new' American Indian history, both firmly rooted in oral history and a multidisciplinary approach, take their places in the academic firmament, Trevor-Roper's Eurocentric worldview is likely to find few adherents. Historians today are more likely to agree with anthropologists Brian Ferguson and Neil Whitehead that 'all societies have the same amount of history behind them. European explorers only step into local history; they do not set it in motion'.[20]

It may be helpful to recall just how much 'in motion' the non-Western world was on the eve of the nineteenth century global 'Scramble' that brought so much of it under Western rule. As Philip Curtin has reminded us, in Africa 'the empire building of the pre-colonial century [from *c.* 1770 to 1870 and, in some cases, beyond] had been mainly African'.[21] The examples are numerous and impressive: the Zulu empire forged by Shaka in southern Africa; the jihad states of al-Hajj 'Umar, Ahmadu Seku and Samori in West Africa; the Mahdist theocratic state in the Sudan; the Sokoto empire of northern Nigeria; the resuscitated Solomonic empire in Ethiopia; the Ashanti kingdom in Ghana.[22]

There was also considerable flux in nineteenth-century Asia, a good deal of it brought on by European imperialist pressures, some of it internally generated. In China, for example, the weakness of the Qing dynasty in the face of multiple foreign provocations led to the kingdom-wide Taiping Rebellion (1850–64) which nearly overthrew the monarchy in favour of a utopian regime with strong primitive Christian overtones dedicated to sweeping land reform, the abolition of private property and equality for women, among other novelties. Although the Taiping uprising was crushed in the end, with help from Western mercenaries like General Charles George 'Chinese' Gordon, the upheaval so devastated the country – an estimated 20 million people lost their lives – that it doomed the ruling dynasty to eventual collapse, with consequences for the twentieth century that are well known.[23]

Something along the same lines was taking place in the New World at approximately the same time. Here, too, flux gripped indigenous peoples on the periphery of expanding white empires, sometimes as a result of pressures exerted by advancing white armies or encroaching white settlements, but as often as not because of the inherent dynamism of the indigenous peoples themselves.

In the Old Northwest of the United States, roughly today's Upper Middle West, the white encroachment which followed the French and Indian War (1756–63) and, especially, the American War of Independence, had forced

Indian peoples of the region to set aside longstanding differences and move towards greater cooperation. While a military alliance was the immediate object of this movement, as time went on and the pressure of white settlement increased, calls for some form of political confederation in defence of Indian lands began to be heard. By the time the War of 1812 broke out, this tendency would be articulated as pan-Indianism, and would boast followers among the Shawnee, Delaware, Ottawa, Potawatomi and Sauk and Fox peoples, to name only the larger tribes of the region.

From at least the heyday of the mid-nineteenth century American historian and chronicler of Manifest Destiny, Francis Parkman, until fairly recently, scholars in the English-speaking world have chosen to see the movement toward Indian confederation as the handiwork of its two presumed political 'leaders', first, the Ottawa war chief Pontiac (c. 1720–69) in the 1760s, and, second, the Shawnee warrior and statesman Tecumseh (1769–1813) in the early 1800s.[24] Important though the leadership of these men was, especially that of Tecumseh, it is now clear that the Parkmanesque obsession with the 'chiefs' served to obscure another equally crucial dimension of pan-Indianism: the growth and spread of nativist religions, or what one writer has called 'revitalisation movements'.[25] For these movements, primarily the one centered around the Delaware prophet Neolin in the 1760s,[26] and another around the brother of Tecumseh, Tenskwatawa (c. 1775–1836), widely known as 'The Prophet',[27] provided the vital spiritual undergirding for the Indian wars of resistance in the Old Northwest which began with what Parkman called the 'Conspiracy of Pontiac' in 1763–6 and concluded with the death of Tecumseh in 1813, fighting alongside the British in the War of 1812.[28] Although the confederation of Indian peoples sought by these political and spiritual movements never came to pass, their adherents killed during the War of 1812 or driven across the Mississippi River in the great Indian removal that followed, they nonetheless for a time posed a serious challenge to American expansionism and, even in defeat, gave strong evidence of an Indian capacity to evolve universal political and spiritual alternatives to physical domination and cultural extinction at the hands of the whites.

In the southeast of the USA, the great Creek Indian confederation contracted rather than expanded under first British and then American pressure, but by way of a process of ethnogenesis, inadvertently gave rise to a wholly new tribal entity, the Seminoles, who over time became the dominant indigenous force in Florida. These ethnic Creeks, disturbed by the approach of Anglo settlements in Georgia, had begun migrating into Spanish Florida in the early 1700s. There they had taken advantage of a weak Spanish presence to impose themselves, and a century later, their ranks swollen by an influx of escaped black slaves and the absorption of tribes native to the peninsula, had for the most part turned their backs on their origins and achieved recognition as an independent people.[29] They would subject the soldiers of the American Republic to the longest Indian war in its history, from 1835–42.

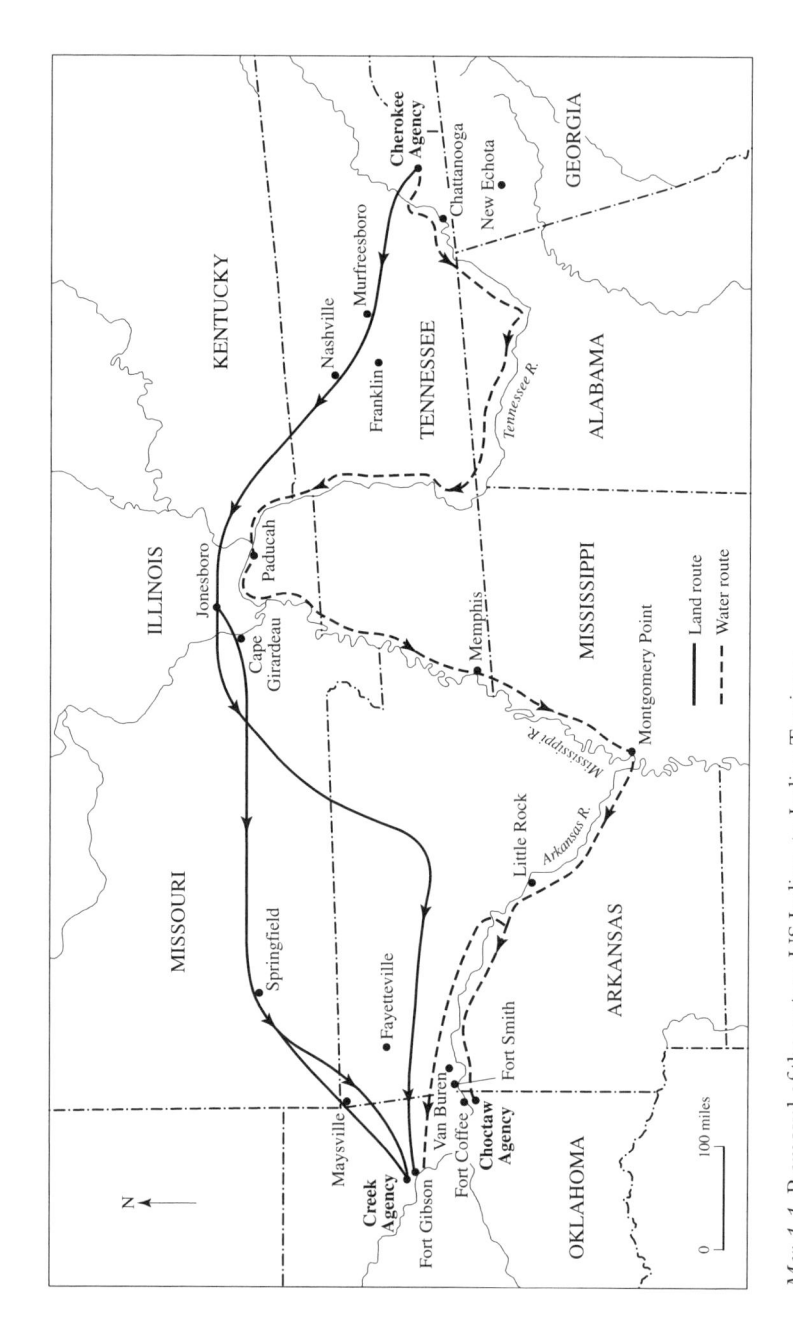

Map 1.1 Removal of the eastern US Indians to Indian Territory.

United States

Comanche and Sioux secondary empires

But the salient examples of indigenous expansionism in North America were not to come from the oak and pine forests of the Old Northwest or the pine barrens and cypress swamps of Florida, but, as in Africa, from its grassland expanses. Just as the most powerful of the indigenous empires in nineteenth-century Africa took shape behind Shaka Zulu's 'foot cavalry' on the veldt of southern Africa or Hausa and Tukolor paladins on the savannas of central and West Africa,[30] so their equivalents in North America came into being on the southern and northern Great Plains of the USA as a result of the exertions of the aggressive horsemen of the Comanche and Sioux confederations.[31]

The Comanches

In the early years of the nineteenth century, the hunting grounds of the Comanches, the 'Lords of the South Plains', extended east some 400 miles from the New Mexican settlements of Taos and Santa Fe to the area around present-day Austin and San Antonio, Texas, and south some 600 miles from the Arkansas River in northern Oklahoma to the Rio Grande River on the future border between the USA and Mexico. Although this vast plain, known as the *Comanchería* to neighbouring New Mexicans, turned arid in the hot summers, it was transformed into 'a sea of nutritious grass' when the rainy season came. This was the home of the great Southern buffalo herd, 'a paradise for nomads who lived by hunting'. The Comanches shared this 'paradise' with the Kiowas and their Kiowa-Apache allies after 1790 and the Southern Cheyennes and Southern Arapahos after 1840.[32]

By the mid-nineteenth century, the twelve bands that had comprised the Comanche people in the early 1700s when they separated from their Shoshone brethren in Montana and moved south onto the plains, had merged into five. Two of the bands stood out for their fighting reputations and hostility to white encroachment: the Yamparikas (Root Eaters), who roamed north central Texas, and the Kwahadis (Antelope Eaters), inhabitants of the high plains of the Texas Panhandle, a region known to Hispanics as the *Llano Estacado* and to Anglos as the Staked Plain.[33] The Comanches were never as numerous as their actual military power and, especially, their power over the imaginations of their Anglo and Hispanic enemies, might suggest. In one of the more remarkable flights of fancy in this regard, Major Robert Neighbors, the US government agent for the tribe in the 1850s, said that 'when all the [Comanche] bands assembled in council, and stretched out in encampment along a stream, it took a whole day to ride from one end of the camp to the other'.[34] The Comanches, even in their late eighteenth-century heyday, probably never numbered more than 20,000 people, and by the 1870s, their numbers reduced by war, hunger and smallpox and cholera epidemics, the 'Lords of the South Plains' may have numbered no more than some 5,000 men, women and children and perhaps as few as half that.[35]

The Sioux

In the mid-nineteenth century, the people the French had called the Sioux (a corruption of the Ojibwa word for 'enemies') were the most numerous of the trans-Mississippi Indian peoples. In 1870, on the eve of their last great contest with the bluecoat soldiers, the several branches of the Sioux totalled just under 32,000 members.[36] Historians believe the Sioux once inhabited the Ohio and Mississippi river valleys, but around 1650, French explorers, the first whites to make contact with them, found them living in the forests of northern Wisconsin and Minnesota. The Sioux of this early period were a semi-sedentary people who supported themselves through a mix of hunting and farming. Not long afterwards, they began to migrate in large numbers towards the plains. Until recently, it was thought that the move came as a result of pressure from their Cree and Ojibwa neighbours, who had been armed with gunpowder weapons by the French.[37] The current wisdom, however, holds that it was the pull of the plains and the buffalo herds that proliferated there rather than the push of Ojibwa and Cree aggression that propelled the Sioux onto the plains.[38]

Migration splintered the Sioux into three distinct groups: the sedentary Santee Sioux, who continued to occupy lands in southern Minnesota and who would rise up in a bloody revolt against their white settler neighbours in 1862[39]; the semi-sedentary Yankton and Yanktonais Sioux, who lived in northeastern South Dakota; and, finally, the seven branches of the Teton Sioux, who by the mid-1700s had acquired guns and horses and were following the buffalo on the Great Plains. The Tetons are the Sioux of legend, the fierce nomads who massacred the troops of Grattan, Fetterman, and, most famously, George Armstrong Custer before succumbing to *force majeure* and confinement on reservations in South Dakota. Of the seven recognised subdivisions of the Teton Sioux, the best known in the wider world were the Hunkpapas of Gall and Sitting Bull and the Oglalas of Crazy Horse and Red Cloud.[40]

The Teton Sioux were one of the most aggressive Indian peoples in North America, dominating the buffalo-rich heartland of the northern plains by force of arms for nearly a century. Perhaps the Indian world's supreme egoists, the Tetons called themselves 'Lakotas' or 'The Men' and

> They made no concessions, few alliances, and many enemies. They were hated by many and feared by most, and they boasted of this reputation. They were proud of their superiority and were vigilant in defending it.[41]

James O. Gump has not hesitated to describe the kind of hegemony these Lakotas exercised over their neighbours as a 'secondary empire'.[42] First, they terrorised the semi-sedentary peoples on the eastern edge of the plains into subjection: the Arikaras, Hidatsas, Mandans and Pawnees. Then it was the turn of the Crow buffalo hunters to the west, who found themselves pushed from eastern Montana into western Montana and Wyoming in the mid-nineteenth century. Along with their Northern Cheyenne and Northern Arapaho allies, the Sioux lorded it over a vast plain from the Black Hills of South Dakota to the Crow hunting grounds at the foot of the Rockies and from the edge of the Comanchería in the south to the home of the Plains Crees and Blackfeet far to the north in Canada.[43]

The explorers Lewis and Clark, decades before white eruption onto the plains, were the first Americans to take the measure of the expansionist Sioux. The Western Sioux were in the midst of building their 'secondary empire' on the plains when the two Virginians encountered them in 1804 in the Mandan country on the upper Missouri River. Haughty and truculent, the Sioux impressed Lewis and Clark as 'the vilest miscreants of the savage race', 'pirates of the Missouri', but for all that the most serious obstacle to US expansion on the northern plains. 'Unless these people are reduced to order by coercive measures . . . the citizens of the United States can never enjoy but partially the advantages which the Missouri presents,' they warned their superiors.[44]

Canada

The Plains Crees

As we have seen, until recently historians believed that the Sioux were routed out of their woodland habitat in the upper Midwest of the USA and pushed onto the plains by gun-toting Crees (and Ojibwas). Although that does not appear to have been the case, it nonetheless is true that the Crees, particularly after part of the tribe made its own transition to life on the plains, entered into more or less permanent conflict with the Sioux, fuelled largely by competition for buffalo and horse-raiding. Prior to that, from 1670 to 1790, Cree life had centred on the woodlands above Lake Superior and north of the western plains of Canada in an arc stretching toward the Rocky Mountains. During this phase of their existence, these Woodland Crees forged a close relationship with the Hudson's Bay Company, which supplied them with muskets to hunt beaver and other fur-bearing animals.[45] Large numbers of Crees clustered around the Hudson's Bay trading posts, much as Southwestern Indians gathered about the Spanish *presidios* and missions, where they constituted a kind of company militia, known as the 'Home Guards'. Cree ties with the company brought them the firearms they used to overawe their neighbours and, eventually, to trade for the horses that would enable many of them to shift over to life on the western Canadian plains. That transition, under way by the end of the 1700s, ultimately provided the Plains Crees with what one author has called 'a complete way of life based on Spanish horses, English muskets, and the North American bison'.[46]

PART I

The Cree transition to nomadic life on the plains of the Canadian West was facilitated by regional alliances with other tribes. Their relationship with the neighbouring Assiniboine people was virtually symbiotic almost from the start of the Cree years on the plains.[47] Although George F.G. Stanley, an early historian of the North-West Rebellion in Canada in 1885, calls the Blackfeet of central and southern Alberta 'sworn enemies' of the Crees, this was not always true.[48] From the late seventeenth century until the early 1800s, the Crees and Blackfeet remained enmeshed in what J.S. Milloy has called 'an alliance of convenience'. The Crees played the role of middlemen in the Blackfoot fur trade with the Hudson's Bay Company and provided their allies with the guns they needed to defeat their Shoshone enemies. The Cree–Blackfoot alliance began to fall apart when the Hudson's Bay Company decided to open trading posts in Blackfoot country, thus eliminating the need for Cree intermediaries in the fur trade in the region. The process of alienation was hastened when the Crees's traditional source of horses, the Hidatsa and Mandan villages in the Missouri River Valley, could no longer supply sufficient mounts and the Crees were forced to turn to the Crows of Montana. The price of Crow horses was a military alliance to fight the Blackfeet.[49]

The period from 1790 to the 1850s has been described as 'the golden years' of the Plains Crees, a time when the buffalo were still plentiful, contact with whites remained limited and Cree warriors were able to hold their own in battle with their Blackfoot and Sioux enemies.[50] But an acute observer at mid-century could have foreseen a rapid closure to this time of plenty and greatness. The buffalo herds were already beginning to dwindle noticeably and the Cree hunters were forced to move deeper into the plains to find them, in the process worsening yet further their relations with the Blackfeet.[51] The decade of the 1870s would bring a cascade of disasters down upon the Plains Crees. Canadian government envoys arrived after 1870 to negotiate treaties confining the Western Indians to reserves. Close on their heels came white settlers and railroad surveyors. At the same time there was an influx of American whisky traders, whose diluted product would wreak havoc on the Canadian tribes, along with a series of devastating cholera and smallpox epidemics. And, in 1879, the buffalo disappeared entirely from the Canadian plains.[52] Gerald E. Friesen, the historian of the Canadian prairie West, has described this period of rapid change in terms that bear repeating at some length. The changes that now began to press upon Cree life were unprecedented, he wrote, and they came with striking speed.

> A typical Cree youth might have been hunting buffalo and raiding for horses in the 1860s just as his grandfather had done sixty years before; in the 1870s he might have succumbed to the whisky trade or been struck by an epidemic; almost certainly he would have been removed to a reserve and perhaps even taught the rudiments of agriculture. In the 1880s, some of his children might have been attending school, and

he, having faced starvation for three or four years in succession, might have participated in the violence associated with the 1885 uprising.[53]

There are no good figures on the number of Plains Crees at any point in the period under consideration here. Gerald Friesen states that in 1870 there were 25–30,000 'Indians in the western interior' (along with some 10,000 Métis and just 2,000 Europeans or Canadians).[54] Desmond Morton finds that in 1884, on the eve of the North-West Rebellion, there were 26,000 Indians of all descriptions in the Canadian West.[55]

The Borderlands

The Apaches

The three-sided struggle in the Southwest borderlands between Americans, Mexicans and Apaches possessed an epic quality it has never lost. Raging intermittently for decades across immense distances, over some of the most hostile terrain in the New World, it ushered onto the stage figures who acquired not just a North American or Mexican but a worldwide fame: the Apache leaders Mangas Coloradas, Cochise, Victorio and Geronimo; the American generals George Crook and Nelson Miles; and the Mexican Indian fighters Colonel Lorenzo García and General Joaquin Terrazas. Over time, however, the lustre attached to the names of the individual leaders has faded (except, interestingly, in the case of the Apaches, especially Cochise and Geronimo[56]), whilst that adhering to the rank and file who fought the wars has, if anything, grown brighter. Little appreciated in their own day, the 'Buffalo Soldiers', the black troopers of the Ninth and Tenth Cavalry regiments who did so much of the fighting on the American side in the 1870s and '80s, are today the subjects of a spate of admiring books and at least one hit song. But it is the Apaches themselves, both as a people and as warriors, who have most clearly retained the interest of succeeding generations. In the time of their greatness, they were held up as international symbols of uncompromising resistance. The gangs of young working-class toughs who terrorised fin-de-siècle Paris were proud to be known as 'les Apaches'. That kind of reputation has endured, as Mark Cocker has pointed out. 'At once primitive and sophisticated, the Apaches were for Euro-Americans, the ultimate tribal stereotype,' he writes. 'Even today ... the word "Apache" retains a detonative quality matched only by those for the standard demons of the natural world, like the wolf, the tiger, the shark.'[57] Indeed, the greatest of the US Army's Apache fighters, General George Crook, once called the Chiricahua Apaches, the most feared branch of the tribe, the people of Mangas Coloradas, Cochise and Geronimo, 'the tigers of the human species'.[58]

For the Spanish, the first whites to make contact with them, the Apaches were the most fearsome of Indians because they proved to be the least amenable to Hispanic civilisation and the Christian faith, the ultimate *gente sin razón*. They did not welcome the friars as the Yaquis had done, or adopt European ways like the Opatas.[59] 'They hurl themselves at danger like a people that know no God nor that there is any hell,' a priest wrote around 1660.[60] Whether it was Apache refusal to accept Christianity and thus 'civilisation' or Spanish slaving expeditions into Apachería that precipitated it, Apaches and Spaniards were at each other's throats almost from the onset of Spanish penetration into the Southwest.[61]

Two centuries later, New Spain had given way to the Mexican Republic, but the attitude toward the Apaches had changed little. If anything, it was more virulent than in the past. One of Mexico's veteran Apache fighters, Colonel Lorenzo García, portrayed the struggle against the Apaches as an epic contest between the forces of barbarism and civilisation. Nothing was 'more noble', he wrote in the 1880s, 'than the campaign we have launched . . . against the sworn enemy of civilisation, against an avid vampire [who lies in wait to] draw the blood of humanity along the path of progress.'[62]

Apaches and the Hispanic population of Mexico had already been warring against each other for over 200 years before the first hostile encounter took place between Apaches and US troops. Although the Apaches had been raiding across northern New Spain since the late 1600s, there had been something of a hiatus toward the end of Spanish rule. Odie Faulk has written that the Spaniards typically approached the Apaches with a cross in their right hand and a sword in the left, and that when the Apaches rejected the cross, the Spaniards simply replaced it with the sword.[63] In the 1780s, the colonial regime sheathed the sword and inaugurated a programme whereby Apaches who settled around the presidios and missions would be issued rations as a substitute for the fruits of raiding. The viceroy who devised the new policy, Don Bernardo de Gálvez, admittedly took a rather cynical view of it, advising frontier officials to 'stimulate the consumption of alcohol [among the Indians] to the point where they can't get along without it'.[64] Still, the system of regular rations induced several hundred Apaches to settle down on what looked very much like forerunners of the Indian reservations set up in North America in the next century and, in the process, achieved the aim of fomenting divisions within the tribe between the so-called *Apaches de paz* and the 'wild' or *bronco* Apaches who refused to settle down. Providing rations also cost much less than New Spain's earlier 'forward policy', which had committed substantial numbers of Spanish troops and their indigenous allies to periodic sweeps of enemy territory.[65] 'It cost the Spanish eighteen to thirty thousand dollars per year, which they used to furnish the Apache with supplies in return for not raiding Hispano-American settlements'.[66]

With the coming of Mexican independence, however, the Apache troubles flared up again, and on a larger scale. This occurred in part because the new federal government in Mexico City, distracted by internal political struggles and, in any case, on the verge of bankruptcy, stopped distributing rations to the Apaches and simultaneously decided in the 1820s to reduce the number of frontier garrisons from 34 to 29. For beleaguered Mexican settlers in the frontier states of Sonora and Chihuahua, this was a catastrophic turn of events. In time, the role of the Mexican federal government in frontier defence declined to almost nothing, and state and local authorities were obliged to shoulder the burden of staving off the Indian raiders.[67] There was, however, another aspect of the problem. The southern branch of the Chiricahua Apaches had gradually made the Sierra Madre Mountains in Sonora its permanent home and the base for its attacks on Mexican ranches and towns. Equipped with modern firearms obtained over the border in the USA, their ranks periodically replenished with eager recruits from Apache bands across the frontier, the southern Chiricahuas, under the leadership of veteran raiders like Juh, constituted a virtual state-within-a-state in Sonora. Their enclave, by now home to the band of the legendary Geronimo, would only be eliminated in the mid-1880s when the US Army finally realised that there could be no peace on Apache reservations in the USA until the last of the bronco Apaches, the 'wild' southern Chiricahuas, were brought to heel.

Although no comprehensive figures for the various branches of the Apache people appear to be available, it has been estimated that in the two decades following the US Civil War the Chiricahua and Western Apache bands numbered around 6,000 men, women and children.[68]

Mexico

The Yaquis of Sonora

The Yaqui struggle for political autonomy and community in nineteenth-century Mexico cannot easily be understood without a grasp of what had transpired during the years of initial contact with Spanish civilisation, when the tribe voluntarily gave up its life in isolated villages or *rancherías* to live in towns – ultimately the Eight Towns, or eight 'sacred pueblos' – under Jesuit tutelage. The Jesuit credo that it was necessary to forge a compact community of believers around the mission churches and to build a psychological wall around the Yaqui country to isolate it from the secular colonial world, powerfully reinforced an already strong Yaqui sense of community and territoriality. A Yaqui myth was born out of the confluence of ancient belief and the new Christian teachings which held that in 1414 four Yaqui prophets, joined by a band of angels, 'walked the length and breadth of Yaqui territory, singing its boundaries. These boundaries were regarded as sacred. The land within them was given to the Yaquis by God.' The Yaqui domain thus consecrated encompassed the Yaqui River flowing out of the Sierra Madre Mountains southwest into the Gulf of California, the fertile fields interspersed with brushlands and thick mesquite forests in the bottomlands along the banks of the river and the 'black slopes and peaks' of the Bacatete Mountains to the north.[69]

The 'Singing of the Boundary' joined with an earlier myth, that of 'The

PART I

Talking Tree', to create in the Yaqui consciousness a feeling for community and place that was perhaps stronger than anywhere else in the Indian world. The 'Talking Tree' myth relates the prophesying of a coming 'new world' of foreign ways and beliefs to the ancestors of the Yaqui, a people known as the Surem. The myth describes the sudden appearance of a talking tree whose message can only be deciphered by the two daughters of a wise man. Through the girls, the tree foretells a coming time of baptisms, floods, famine, droughts and fabulous new inventions, and then falls silent. Some of the Surem are apprehensive and decide to leave the tribal homeland, some to wander in a northern land of many islands, others to make their homes beneath the sea or in the depths of the Bacatete Mountains, where they would continue to exist as an enchanted people. The rest of the Surem, it appears, 'decided to stay and to see these new things'. They would become the modern-day Yaquis and be known as the 'baptised ones'. The latter would remain, however, in perpetual communion with those ancestors who had become spirits in the mountain fastnesses and this communion would make the territory of the Yaqui doubly sacred and inviolable.[70]

The Yaquis' self-image as a 'special people' extended to the political sphere as well. Throughout their years as wards of the Jesuits and as more or less willing subjects of the Spanish crown, they had continued to practise a system of local self-government that vested ultimate political authority in an elected council of elders.[71] Spanish (or, later, Mexican) tampering with the internal democratic processes of the Eight Towns, by, for example, seeking to impose officials of their own choosing on the population, was an unfailing recipe for conflict between the Yaquis and Hispanic authorities. Yaquis proved equally loath to allow their own leaders to bypass the town councils, even in times of war. As we will see, even charismatic military chiefs like Juan Banderas or Cajeme found their positions threatened when they tried to assume dictatorial powers in wartime.

The Yaquis occupied a special place in the minds of the 80,000 or so whites and mestizos who inhabited the state of Sonora. They enjoyed a reputation among their Mexican neighbours, writes Edward Spicer, which 'seemed to overshadow that of any other living Indian group, except the Apaches'. The Mexican view of the Yaquis was frankly schizophrenic. On the one hand, they believed the Yaquis to be a particularly aggressive and warlike people and the catalyst of their troubles with other nearby Indian peoples: the Opatas and Pimas in northern and central Sonora; the Serís of the coastal plain and the offshore island of Tiburón; and, especially, the Mayos in the Mayo River valley to the south, fellow Cahita-speakers and close kin to the Yaquis.[72]

But this nagging fear coexisted with another, very different attitude toward the Yaquis. Thinly populated Sonora desperately needed labourers to work the mines, farms and ranches and Yaquis were reckoned to be among the state's best workers. Robert Hardy, a British traveller who toured Sonora in the 1820s, found Yaquis working everywhere. 'They are miners, gold-diggers, pearl-divers, agriculturalists and artisans,' he wrote.[73] Some sixty years later, in the midst of the bloodiest of the many wars between Yaquis and Mexicans, the Mexican historian Fortunato Hernández could still write that as workers the Yaquis were simply irreplaceable. No one else was so well suited for hard work in the unforgiving climate of Sonora, he said, recalling how he had seen Yaqui farm labourers harvesting wheat when it was 110 degrees F. in the shade.[74] Evelyn Hu-DeHart has convincingly demonstrated that it was a combination of Sonora's perpetual shortage of labour and the Yaquis' reputation for hard work and valuable skills that more than anything else shielded them against policies of extermination and deportation through most of the desperate years of the nineteenth century.[75]

Yaqui population figures, as recorded in the official censuses taken in Sonora, bear witness to the unhappy effects of Mexican independence upon the people of the tribe. While it is estimated that the total number of Yaquis remained what it had been under the Jesuits in the 1700s, some 30,000, now the majority increasingly felt obliged to leave the eight 'sacred pueblos' of their ancestors to find work elsewhere or refuge from government persecution. Thus, whereas Sonora state censuses found some 12,000 Yaquis residing in the eight towns in 1850 and again in 1873, by 1889, in the wake of the great revolt led by Cajeme, barely 1,000 remained. The rest were in hiding in the nearby mountains or dispersed from Los Angeles, California, to the silver mines of upland Sonora, working or avoiding the authorities.[76]

The Mayas of Yucatán

The Mayas who rose up in revolt against the white or ladino population of Yucatán in 1847 were, of course, descendants of the great Mayan civilisation which had once exercised hegemony over not only Yucatán and neighbouring parts of what is today Mexico but also over contemporary Belize, western Guatemala and northern Honduras. That Mayan empire, already in decline, was destroyed by Spanish conquistadors in the 1520s. Over the next three centuries, a fitful process of acculturation took place whereby the Mayas adopted Catholic Christianity (albeit in a markedly syncretic form), rudiments of the Spanish system of local government (the *cabildo*), and a Latin writing script. The Spanish Crown exercised a kind of indirect rule over Mayan communities, much as it did among the Yaquis in Sonora, converting local nobles (*batabs*) into royal governors and permitting the continuation of communal ownership of land in return for the payment of taxes. This limited autonomy was offered in exchange for submission to a labour regime in which many Mayas became peons on white farms or plantations or servants in white homes in the few cities in the region (e.g. the Yucatán capital, Mérida, ostentatiously built on the ruins of the Mayan city of Tiho). Despite the long Spanish rule, most Mayas never became hispanised in any fundamental sense. Most never learned any more than a few necessary words of Spanish and Mayan communities stoutly resisted sending their children to Spanish-speaking schools.

Mayan culture remained rooted in ancient traditions and Mayan society continued to revolve about longstanding kinship and lineage groups.[77]

The coming of Mexican independence in 1821 was not welcomed by the Mayan population any more than it was by the Yaquis. The Creoles who had engineered the expulsion of the Spanish from Yucatán, in a largely bloodless revolt, quickly made it known that, although they were prepared to grant Indians the right of citizenship, they did not intend to respect either Indian political autonomy or communal land ownership. As we have seen, this was pretty much in line with the outlook of the liberals who came to power elsewhere in Mexico after independence. What was different about the situation in Yucatán was the failure of its ladino ruling class to keep a later promise, made to win Mayan support for their 1839 bid for independence from Mexico City, to lower or even, in some cases, to abolish taxes. This unhonoured pledge, plus ladino pressures on Mayan land and meddling in local government, led to the uprising in 1847 known to history as the Caste War.[78] The two sides were unevenly matched in terms of numbers, with the advantage going to the Mayas by a large margin. This was an anomaly in the New World Indian wars. Although precise figures do not exist, it is estimated that Mayas accounted for around 80 per cent of the Yucatán population of some 506,000 when the war broke out.[79] Although other important issues were at stake, the struggle was portrayed by both sides as a race war. It was destined to be the bloodiest of all the indigenous uprisings and civil conflicts that plagued the history of nineteenth-century Mexico. It was also the most successful of the Indian wars to be discussed in this book, both in the sense that the Mayan rebels won significant victories over their ladino enemies, and that a portion of rebel territory remained unconquered down into the 1930s.

Conclusion

This, then, was 'Indian country' in the first half of the nineteenth century. It is not difficult to discern in the friction-laden atmosphere of this time the contours of an impending and decisive clash. The westering pressures of white settlement in the USA have already cleared the eastern half of the country of most of its remaining Indian population and deposited it west of the Mississippi River in Indian Territory (Oklahoma). By the time of the US Civil War, the tide of settlement will have begun lapping at the edges of the Great Plains and, by virtue of a leap forward inspired by the lure of gold, will have wrested California and the Pacific Northwest from their indigenous inhabitants. The final contest will come on the plains, where the horse and gun pattern of Indian warfare will be tested against the US Army, and in the mountains and deserts of the southwestern borderlands, where Mexican–US cooperation will be required to cope with elusive Apache raiders. On the northern plains, serious skirmishing has already begun with the formidable Sioux; on the southern plains, continuous frontier warfare pits the Comanche confederation against steadily encroaching Texans. In all of this, the US Army's role will be, by and large, a *reactive* one, foisted upon the soldiers by homesteaders, miners and railroad builders clamouring for protection from 'savage' raiders.

In Mexico, meanwhile, full-scale warfare has already erupted between Yaquis and the Hispanic population of Sonora and between the Mayas and ladinos of Yucatán. Much blood has already flowed, much more than will flow in all of the North American Indian wars, and there is much more to come. The fighting here is much more intense than on the other side of the border since the Indian peoples engaged are relatively more numerous and more inclined to engage the enemy in pitched battle. The Hispanic population also is at a disadvantage since its regular army remains aloof from the struggle and the burden of white 'defence' is borne by a citizen militia almost never adequate to the task.

Finally, Canada's transition to Dominion status within the British Empire has given impetus to a movement for national territorial consolidation, in large measure to ward off the attentions of the country's voracious southern neighbour. Rupert's Land, the vast western domain of the Hudson's Bay Company, will be incorporated into the Confederation of Canada and the government in Ottawa will move swiftly to secure the allegiance to the Crown of the region's Indian and mixed-blood population – by agreement if possible, by force if necessary. But, in the latter case, there will be no British Army to carry out the task of 'pacification'; a policy of imperial retrenchment in London will have repatriated by 1870 almost all of the British troops traditionally garrisoned in Canada. War with the indigenous peoples of Western Canada, if it comes, will have to be fought for the most part by the country's provincial militia, poorly-equipped, largely untrained, and officered by cast-offs of the British Army.

2

THE NEW WORLD IN A CENTURY OF SMALL WARS

Indian motives for war

The Indian view of warfare can be described as *existential*, i.e. that war was a natural human activity whose skilful practice opened the way to glory on this earth and eternal life in the hereafter. For those New World peoples who were of European descent or who had embraced European culture, on the other hand, war was (and is) viewed as *instrumental*, a means to an end.

Before the Europeans came to the New World, motives for war differed little between the woodland and plains tribes of North America. The Creeks and Shawnees, like the Sioux or Cheyenne, went to war for revenge, prestige and glory, and plunder, and, on occasion, to fight off invaders bent on taking over their hunting grounds. As white settlers stepped up their encroachments upon Indian lands, however, war became focused more and more narrowly on defending tribal territory.[1]

Although most Indian tribes drew a distinction between raiding and warfare, the Apaches who roamed the deserts and mountains of the American Southwest and northern Mexico appear to have drawn a sharper line than most. While Plains Indians, for instance, raided in order to acquire wealth, in horses particularly, or to win glory, the Apaches tended to lump raiding in with hunting and gathering as a means of sustaining themselves. Raiding thus took on the status of an economic activity and one which grew in scope and importance throughout Apache history. It first became an urgent necessity for Apaches in the eighteenth century when Plains tribes, particularly the Comanches, used their temporary advantage in gunpowder weapons to drive the Apaches off the plains. This not only cost the latter access to buffalo meat, but meant that, unlike the Plains peoples, they had no buffalo hides, meat or tallow to trade to other Indians or to whites for horses or guns, and were obliged to raid to get them. But raiding was also closely linked to hunting and gathering, as we have seen. As long as there was enough territory for these pursuits, Apaches could get along without seizing the goods of others. But as white settlements and mines spread in Apachería, raiding took on a much greater importance to the Apache economy and thus increased in volume.[2]

If raiding was seen as an economic activity, 'war was intended to bring physical harm to an enemy or enemies and only secondarily, if at all, to provide economic returns'. War was almost always for the purpose of revenge, usually for an Apache death during a raid. Whilst going to war could be a limited, once-off affair, sometimes it involved certain foes often enough that they acquired permanent enemy status. 'After many years, Mexicans and Comanches achieved such status for most Chiricahua bands. Americans also achieved this position with some bands but in a much shorter time.'[3]

Warfare between the Apaches and the Comanches, which had begun in competition for access to the plains buffalo herds, gradually became endemic. From time to time, the Comanches had joined forces with the Spanish and, later, the Mexicans to make war on the Apaches.[4] They also often lay in wait for Apache raiders coming back from forays into Mexico, to despoil them of their loot. 'We fought the ones in the buffalo head hats [Comanches] all the time', an Apache oldtimer told D.C. Cole. 'If they could catch us in the open, we were done for, but usually we could lead them into canyons where we took what they had.'[5]

Indian ways of war

Whether in the woodlands of the Eastern United States, on the prairies of the western US and Canada or in the deserts of the Southwestern borderlands, the main military formation of the North American Indians tended to be the 'war band', usually a relatively small body of fighting men who compensated for their sparse numbers by their consummate knowledge of terrain and their warrior skills and spirit, inculcated through a lifetime of practice. As conflict between Indians and whites intensified and white threats to Indian territory grew, war bands became bigger and tribes sometimes undertook to enter into alliances with other Indian peoples or even to form confederations to resist white encroachments. For the Creeks and Shawnees (and the Sioux and Comanches, but not the Apaches, as we shall see), fending off white settlers and the white soldiers sent to protect or clear the way for them meant fielding much larger armies, which in turn meant forming tactical alliances or even confederations with other Indian peoples (and seeking the help of sympathetic whites, where possible). Thus, whereas prior to the late 1700s or early 1800s sending out a war party of 100 men would have been an unusual undertaking for any of the Eastern woodland tribes, once settlers began pouring into the Old Northwest where the Shawnees lived or putting pressure on Creek lands in Georgia and Alabama, these Indian peoples began to send larger and larger forces into the field and to reach out to neighbouring tribes for help.[6] The same phenomenon can be observed on the western plains of the USA after 1865, as war parties of the Comanche and Sioux confederations of as many as 1,000 warriors begin to make their appearance.

PART I

Woodland warfare

The Creeks of the woodlands of the southeastern USA never moved into enemy territory without a large screen of scouts to the front and rear of their columns. Thus, their armies were seldom surprised, wrote the French adventurer Louis Leclerc Milfort, who claimed to have served as a chief on Creek campaigns from 1776 to 1795. It was not the Creeks but their enemies who had to worry about being ambushed, he said, 'and it is very dangerous for those who are not familiar with it'.[7]

Milfort's point was well illustrated by the blow dealt to Andrew Jackson and his Tennesseans at the battle of Enotachopco during the Creek War of 1813–1814. The Indian ambush at Enotachopco Creek was nicely timed, catching Jackson's retreating troops in the process of fording the stream, with his vanguard on one bank, a rearguard on the other, and his artillery in the water. 'Jackson immediately ordered the rear guard to engage the Indians; at the same time he called for the left and right columns to wheel around, recross the creek above and below the [Creeks] and surround them . . .'.[8] But, '[T]o my astonishment and mortification,' Jackson later reported to his commander in Charleston, South Carolina, General Thomas Pinckney, 'when the word had been given to Colo. [William] Carroll to halt and form . . . I beheld . . . the rear guard precipitately give way. This shameful retreat was disastrous in the extreme.' Although Jackson managed to drive enough troops back across the stream to hold off the Creeks long enough for the main body of his force to withdraw, it was a very close call.[9]

Plains warfare

The horse and gun pattern

What made the Indians of the Western United States and Canada such formidable warriors and, to people everywhere, the archetypal American Indians, was their adoption over two centuries (from roughly 1630 to 1830) of what the American anthropologist Frank R. Secoy called the 'Horse and Gun Pattern'.[10] For some Indians, mainly those in the Southwest and on the southern plains, the horse came first. In the north, on the plains of Western Canada and on the northern Great Plains of the USA, it was the gun that arrived first. Let us begin with the horse.

THE HORSE

The role of the horse in altering the cultures and economies – and ways of war – of the Plains Indians 'cannot be exaggerated'.[11] As one early student of the Comanches of the South Plains observed, 'The modifications in our own way of living incident to the invention of the steam railway and the automobile were not more far-reaching...'.[12] The anthropologist Bernard Mishkin, writing over 60 years ago, has given us one of the most trenchant analyses of the impact of the horse upon a Plains Indian people. 'So deeply embedded was the horse in every phase' of the life of the Kiowas, South Plains allies of the Comanches, that they claimed to have no memory of a time when they went about on foot. Mishkin's account of what the horse meant to the Kiowas is worth quoting in some detail. With the coming of the horse,

> The tempo of life was drastically accelerated, values completely revised. [T]he breadth of inter-tribal contact impregnating the culture with new ideas and new material traits, the dependence on swift and continuous movements for economic success, all depended for their development upon the horse.

In less abstract terms, the replacement of dogs by horses as beasts of burden meant that more buffalo meat could be carried away from the hunt, thus enhancing food supply. More commodious tipis were now possible, since horses could carry longer tipi poles and more skin covers. The advent of the horse also produced a new style of warfare, one featuring much greater speed and mobility. Weapons changed as well. Bows and lances were shortened, shields made smaller, to facilitate warfare on horseback. Horse raiding became a major preoccupation of Plains Indian warriors, as the size of one's horse herd became the principal marker of wealth and prestige in most Plains tribes.[13]

For all that, the advent of the horse did not change warfare among the Western Indians in quite the same ways or for quite the same reasons as has been surmised. Before the coming of the horse, a kind of heavy infantry, dressed in leather armour and carrying leather-embossed shields, was the Queen of Battles on the Plains. The foot soldiers drew up in lines and fired arrows or hurled spears at each other from behind a wall of shields. This exchange of missiles would continue until one or the other side got tired of it and decided to charge. The battle usually ended in a close quarters free-for-all. Acquisition of horses at first simply meant that the footsloggers became mounted infantry, clambering aboard their new steeds with their spears and war bows. Nor did Indians in the Southwest and on the South Plains discard their armour. For they had inherited from the Spaniards not only mounts but a system of mounted warfare: 'the heavy-cavalry tactics of the Spaniards, including mass shock attacks by leather-armoured horsemen'.[14] As late as the early nineteenth century, the Apaches were using large mixed forces of spear-toting cavalry and foot archers, both armoured, to fight the Spanish. In 1807 a Spanish officer told the American military explorer, Captain Zebulon Pike, about a recent battle in which a large force of Apache heavy cavalry, under counterattack by Spanish lancers, took shelter behind a screen of bowmen, who succeeded in driving off the Spaniards.[15] But this kind of mass shock warfare could only be sustained so long as horses were plentiful, and for most Indian peoples they would not be for some time. Losses of horses in battle reduced the capacity to hunt and threatened tribal well-being. The only way out of this conundrum was to replenish herds by raiding and this was best done by employing 'the light-cavalry tactics stereotypical of later Plains warfare'. This proved to be the thin end of the wedge in the transition from heavy to light cavalry war-making amongst the Plains Indians. Reinforcement of this process came with the introduction of firearms, which provided 'a long-range defense against the shock tactics of heavy cavalry and [emphasized] the value of light tactics'.[16] We need to remember that this transition was only a few decades old when the first Anglo-American horsemen ventured onto the Plains and thus that the superb light cavalry tactics they so often remarked upon amongst their Indian foes actually were of quite recent vintage and not the product of long experience in intertribal warfare, as seems to have been assumed.

The horse was much less important to the Mexican Indians featured in this study, the Yaquis and Mayas. Like other Indian tribes who fell under Spanish rule, they had been forbidden to ride or own horses and thus had come to appreciate their military value either very late, as in the case of the Yaquis, or not at all, as in the case of the Mayas.[17] It was only when Yaquis began serving in the armies of the great caudillos of northern Mexico during the political struggles of the mid-1800s that they learned the value of cavalry. Mayan disinterest in horses stemmed from the fact that they were of limited use in the dense rain forests of Yucatán.

Although the woodland Indian peoples of the eastern USA were familiar with horses from an early date, with few exceptions they seem not to have made much use of them in warfare before the end of the eighteenth century.[18] Some, in fact, never took to the horse, at least while they remained in their ancestral homelands. Although their white enemies, the frontiersmen of Tennessee, developed a formidable mounted infantry arm and used it to great effect during the war of 1813–14, the Creek Indians continued to wage war on foot. It is worth remarking, however, that once the woodland peoples who had shunned the horse were forced to remove beyond the Mississippi River, to the prairies of what is today Oklahoma, in the 1820s and '30s, they quickly took to mounted life and soon were competing with more established peoples for buffalo on the nearby Great Plains. Former woodland peoples – particularly the Delawares, Shawnees, Kickapoos and Potawatomis – also provided mounted scouts and irregular troops for the US cavalry and Mexican state militia units in the mid- to late nineteenth century.[19]

It was, however, among the Indian peoples of the Western USA and Canada that the horse truly came into its own as an instrument of war. Some distinctions need to be made here, however. The Apaches, formidable horsemen and prodigious horse thieves though they were, preferred to fight on foot, among the cliffs and boulders of their mountainous homeland, and saw horses only as a quick way of getting from one place to another. Even the Crow buffalo hunters of Wyoming and Montana preferred fighting on foot once engaged with an enemy.[20] And, as we will see, the ultimate test of courage amongst the Cheyenne Dog Soldier warrior fraternity was to fight to the death or victory on foot, one leg secured to the ground by a rope and picket pin.

Indian mounted warfare reached its highest degree of development among the tribes of Western Canada and the Northern and Southern Plains of the USA, the Blackfeet and Crees on the one hand, the Sioux and Cheyennes and the Comanches and Kiowas on the other. The soldiers who fought them were profuse in their praise of their mounted Indian foes, often but not always after the tribesmen in question had been safely ensconced on reservations. The soldiers' view was seconded by John D. Finerty, a *Chicago Times* reporter, who accompanied the troops of General George Crook during the Sioux War of 1876. Finerty believed that mounted Plains Indian warriors were more than the equal of elite European cavalry, even 'the Chasseurs d'Afrique of Macmahon [sic], with all their Arab horses'.[21]

But, for all the romanticism invested in the saga of the horse Indians by their contemporaries and modern-day writers, there is a darker side to the story that some recent historians have been at pains to point out. To begin with, as the historian Pekka Hämäläinen has demonstrated at great length, the impact of the 'horse revolution' was felt unevenly among the plains peoples, for largely environmental reasons. The conversion of the Crees of Western Canada to the horse and buffalo hunting on the plains remained something less than full-blown because of the long, intensely cold Canadian winters. A scarcity of winter forage routinely killed off Cree ponies and the short growing season limited the amount of grass available even in spring and summer. This perpetual shortage of horses made the Crees among the most inveterate horse thieves on the plains and, as we have seen, even provoked changes in the tribe's 'foreign policy'. Another result was that dogs continued to play an important role as beasts of burden among the Crees long after they adopted the horse.[22]

The Comanches at the other end of the Great Plains had to face up to the opposite problem: an embarrassment of riches. Their huge horse herds, the largest on the plains, had to be moved almost daily to find new grass; they began to compete for forage with the buffalo, whose numbers were already starting to dwindle from overhunting (by Indians; the often-described slaughter by white hunters in the 1870s simply finished the job). The upshot of this was periodic starvation among the Comanches, who found themselves forced to eat their horses and even, in some cases, to raise cattle for food.[23]

According to Hämäläinen, the only Plains Indians who made a genuine success of the transition to the horse culture were the Sioux. They enjoyed a less forbidding climate than the Crees and thus could count on relatively plentiful forage for their horse herds. It would also appear, however, that human agency played a role in the smoother adaptation of the Sioux. They seem to have consciously sought a balance between the size of their horse herds and the available grass.[24] Still, the Sioux situation was far from idyllic. As R.B. Hassrick pointed out some time ago, for the Sioux there could never be a 'resting on laurels'.[25] The steady increase in their numbers, something of an anomaly among western Indians, forced them to war constantly upon their neighbours to acquire new hunting grounds. In the process, they made many enemies, who allied with the whites against them and contributed significantly to their defeat in the 1870s.

THE GUN

By the nineteenth century, most Indian peoples not only had horses but also were fairly well acquainted with firearms. The tribes in the Eastern United States and Canada had been exposed to gunpowder weapons since the sixteenth or seventeenth centuries and had become proficient in their use. Most Eastern Indians knew how to mould lead shot for the muskets they carried, but gunpowder had to be purchased. This dependence on white suppliers was sometimes a crippling liability for Indian warriors. Some gun-toting Indians later learned to reload cartridges, to the great surprise of their white foes.

> Powder and lead [were] obtained by breaking up cartridges of another calibre that didn't fit [an Indian's] gun and using these to reload the shells – which worked about as well as the right shells would have, had he been able to obtain them. Some of the shell casings were reloaded as many as fifty times.[26]

In the Western USA and Canada, firearms came on the scene somewhat later than in the East. In areas under Spanish (and later Mexican) control, Indians, who often made up the majority of the population, were forbidden to possess gunpowder weapons out of a fear that they would use them to overthrow white rule. Elsewhere in the West, however, firearms gradually became available to Indian warriors, usually through the fur trade. French traders were the first to supply guns to Western Indians, not only the Crees, Ojibwas and Assiniboines of Western Canada, but also Texas tribes, such as the Comanches, who obtained muskets from traders from Louisiana. This for a while placed the Indians of the Hispanic Southwest, such as the Apaches, at a disadvantage in war.[27] This was overcome in time, however, by one of the particularities of prairie commerce, the tendency of the trade in horses to flow from south to north and the trade in guns to move in the opposite direction. Thus the Apaches eventually were able to overcome their deficiency in firearms by trading horses to tribes further north in exchange for guns.[28]

Penetration of the West by the Americans following the Louisiana Purchase and the War of 1812 added substantially to the weaponry available to Indian warriors. On the northern plains, American traders proferred muskets crafted especially for the Indian trade in a bid to take the commerce in furs and buffalo hides away from the British Hudson's Bay Company.[29] Even before the Mexican–American War of 1846–8, the southwest borderlands witnessed a lively trade in firearms between Indians and American traders. This trade would place the Mexican inhabitants of the Southwest and of Mexico proper at a considerable disadvantage *vis-à-vis* Apache and Comanche raiders and prompt charges that the Indians were being armed in order to pave the way for a Yankee takeover of northern Mexico.[30]

Indian insurgents in Mexico itself faced greater difficulties in obtaining gunpowder weapons. Because of the Spanish ban on selling arms to Indians, the Yaquis of the northwestern state of Sonora had no acquaintance with firearms before the 1820s, when they first rose up in revolt against the Mexican authorities. Most of the guns they acquired were either stolen or captured from the enemy until later in the nineteenth century, when they began to buy them in Arizona Territory. The bow probably remained the main weapon in the arsenal of these Indians longer than anywhere in the Americas outside the Amazon Basin. As late as the Mexican Revolution of 1910, some Yaquis were still fighting with bows and arrows.[31] The Mayas of Yucatán fared somewhat differently. When the state of Yucatán rebelled against the Mexican central government in 1839, the insurgents found themselves so short of troops that they began recruiting – and arming – Mayas. This considerable break with the past had near fatal consequences for the Hispanic minority of Yucatán. As a result of participation in the rebellion, the Mayas not only learned first-hand how the *blancos* fought but were issued firearms that they retained and put to good use in their own uprising in 1847.[32]

Firearms were not, however, the only weapon in Indian arsenals and the extent to which they displaced earlier arms should not be exaggerated. Although there are no recorded examples of American Indian peoples saying 'no' to the gun in the manner of the early modern Japanese or the Zulus in nineteenth-century South Africa, there are also no instances we know of where more venerable weapons were suddenly and totally discarded in favour of firearms. Until the advent of the repeating rifle, the bow continued to be the rapid-fire weapon par excellence among Indian warriors. An expert bowman could launch several arrows in the time it took a musketeer to reload his weapon. US Army Colonel Richard Dodge, a veteran Plains commander and a well-known sceptic about Indian fighting abilities, nonetheless 'said an Indian might grasp as many as ten arrows in his left hand and get rid of all ten before the first struck its target, each capable of inflicting a death wound at twenty or thirty yards'.[33] And, even when the use of firearms became widespread among Indian war bands, this did not mean that warriors left their bows and war clubs at home. As we have seen, the Yaqui Indians of northern Mexico were still using bows and arrows in the early twentieth century. Although the Mayas fielded large armies of foot soldiers armed with guns, the most formidable weapon in their arsenal remained the simple machete, extremely effective in close quarter fighting in the Yucatán bush and rainforests.[34]

Much has been written about how the combination of the horse and the gun transformed Plains Indian warriors into a superb light cavalry, what veteran

PART I

Indian campaigner and Custer subordinate Captain Frederick Benteen called 'great shots, great riders, the best fighters the sun ever shone on'.[35] This view, however, needs some qualification. The big advantage of gunpowder weapons over bows and arrows was their ability to kill or at least wound at a considerable distance. This ability was, of course, dependent upon accuracy, and this was notoriously difficult to achieve from the back of a horse, moving or otherwise. This was why cavalry dismounted when they wanted to engage in serious shooting. The muzzleloaders in use in the American West until the 1870s were particularly difficult to reload on horseback. Thomas Mails tells us that 'White authorities' marvelled at the Indian warriors' skill at reloading guns at full gallop on horseback, especially the antique trade muskets so many of them carried during the antebellum era.

> Racing full tilt, a warrior could fire and reload his muzzle-loader at will, shooting with one hand or both hands over the back or under the neck of his horse. Taking four or more balls in his mouth, he simply spit them into his gun's muzzle after first sloshing in an estimated charge of powder from his powder horn.

Mails claims that 'In this reckless manner a dozen warriors fighting at close range could send a deadly hail of fire toward an enemy'.[36] We might be permitted to add that with these sorts of reloading techniques the warriors would have to have been very close in order to hit anyone or to cause them serious harm if they did.

For some time after the appearance of guns on the plains, the bow retained its popularity for long-range fighting on horseback, for reasons that are obvious in the above account, while the optimum weapon for close-in work against other riders remained the lance or even the knife – provided you could get close enough to use them. All of this began to change, however, in the view of one veteran observer, with the advent of the 'breechloader revolution', which he saw favouring Indian warriors as much, perhaps more, than their bluecoat foes. General George Crook claimed that 'As long as the muzzle-loading arms were in use, we had the advantage of them and twenty men could whip a hundred, but once the breechloaders came into use it is entirely different; these they can load on horseback, and now they are a match for any man'.[37]

Captain Benteen aside, however, most US soldiers in the West tended to think that Indians were poor shots with guns. This may have been largely true, although some prominent exceptions can be noted: The Modocs in their 1873 war in Northern California and the Nez Percés in 1877 shot rings around their US Army opponents.[38] But most US soldiers were also poor shots well into the 1880s, and for the same reason that so many Indians were. Indians could rarely spare ammunition for target practice, while the US government refused until the Indians wars were nearly over to provide funds for firing ranges, on the grounds that it was a waste of money. Indifferent Indian marksmanship also may have stemmed in some cases from a greater interest in the pyrotechnic value of firearms than in their killing power. This was the case with some of Africa's most formidable indigenous armies, the nineteenth-century hosts of the king of Ashanti and of the Mahdi in the Sudan, for example.[39] Fascination with the noise and smoke of gunfire probably ebbed among the North American Indians after some years' experience of firearms, but continued to play an important role in Mayan warfare in Yucatán into the mid-nineteenth century. A major factor in the psychological warfare used by the Mayas to capture towns from their white opponents was 'the din of a heavy, constant gunfire (albeit uncertain and not very lethal)', according to a general who led troops against them in the 1860s.[40]

Plains warfare: the face of battle

Wallace and Hoebel's description of Comanche battle tactics below gives a good idea of the 'face of battle' when the Plains tribes came to grips with each other or with their new white enemies. Many of the 'moves' employed by the Comanches in this account also would have been familiar to cavalrymen who fought the Cheyennes or Sioux on the northern Plains. When the Comanches encountered an enemy determined to engage in pitched battle,

> the wedge-shaped mass of Comanches quickly assumed battle formation. The wedge turned into the shape of a huge ring or wheel without hub or spokes, whose rim consisted of one or more distinct lines of warriors. This ring, winding around with machinelike regularity and precision, approached nearer and nearer the enemy with each revolution. As a warrior approached the point on the circle nearest the enemy, he dropped into the loop around his horse's neck on the side opposite his target and discharged his arrows from beneath the neck of his horse while traveling at full speed.[41]

In cases where the Comanches found themselves on the defensive, they broke off action, to reform on the enemy's flanks. The aim was to get the foe to wear out his horses by charging futilely, at which point the Comanches would once again have the advantage. In the event of one of their number being killed or wounded, two men 'riding abreast, one on each side of the prostrate warrior, would reach down and take hold of [him] as they passed, either dragging him to safety or swinging him up beside one of them'.[42]

When Comanches on a raid or in a war party found themselves hard-pressed by a force too large to resist, they divided and subdivided their band until there were so many different tracks to follow that pursuers had to give up. The scattered warriors stayed in contact by signalling, by using the call of an owl or a coyote. In daylight, they would signal by using blankets to release smoke from campfires in columns; 'Different numbers of columns had different meanings'. Mounds of stones were arranged to show which route had been followed.[43]

PART I

On a retreat, Comanche warriors usually had sufficient fresh mounts along to keep moving quickly and relentlessly. Members of the group who couldn't keep up were left behind. Captives might be abandoned or killed. There were no stops to forage for food; horses might be killed and eaten. When water was scarce, warriors drank horses' blood.[44]

Indian logistics

The economic basis for war

The Indian tribes of the eastern USA tended to be sedentary agriculturalists, although the term 'sedentary' should be used with caution. Some of the crops they grew, maize in particular, wore out the soil quickly, making it necessary to move villages frequently. It should also be noted that the Creek and Seminole peoples of the southeastern USA were almost alone among North American Indians in owning large herds of cattle. Cattle had been introduced into their economies as a substitute for the wild deer, whose meat and hides had been a staple of Creek and Seminole existence. With the decline of deer herds due to overhunting, cattle were acquired from whites to fill the void. In time, possession of large herds of cattle became a marker of social distinction among these Indian peoples, much as it was among the Bantu peoples of southern Africa.[45]

The Plains Indians of the western USA, the Sioux and Cheyenne, for example, were nomads who followed the buffalo, and supplemented their meat diet by trading for beans, squashes and maize with the semi-sedentary tribes who lived on the eastern edge of the Plains. The Canadian tribes that concern us, the Plains Crees and Blackfeet, roamed the prairies of the present-day provinces of Manitoba, Saskatchewan and Alberta and the plains of the northern USA in pursuit of the buffalo.

In economic terms, the Mexican Indian peoples we will be treating in this book differed from the tribes further north in a number of ways. The Yaquis of the northwestern Mexican state of Sonora were a sedentary farming people, living in eight large towns and growing maize and other crops in the rich soil along the Yaqui River. They also herded cattle, goats and sheep and took jobs outside their homeland as labourers in the mines and on the haciendas of their Mexican neighbours. The Mayas of the state of Yucatán in the far southeast of Mexico were descendants of the great Indian civilisation of that region. Subdued by the Spanish in the 1500s, many of the Mayas had become peons, or agricultural labourers, on the estates of their conquerors. Others, burrowed deeper into the southern rainforest, never were brought into servitude and inhabited large villages from which they cultivated maize and other crops. Although sedentary farmers, they were also avid hunters and supplemented their diet with meat from deer hunted down with shotguns in the dense forests that surrounded their villages.[46]

Supply in the field

One of the advantages Indian peoples enjoyed in their wars with whites was a relative lack of logistical problems. Indian warriors in the field generally travelled light. Creeks went to war clad only in breechclout and moccasins and carried a blanket, cords for leading off stolen livestock and leather for repairing moccasins, in addition to their weapons.[47] On the plains, Comanche warriors customarily went off on raids bearing their arms, a lasso, a change of clothing and a robe in case the weather turned cold. Comanche war parties tended to carry more gear than raiding parties, however, as the 'Lords of the South Plains' liked to dress up for battle.[48] The Mayas of Yucatán, whose way of war most closely resembled that of their white adversaries, carried their personal effects in henequen bags, called *habucos*, slung over their shoulders and their ammunition in cartridge belts. Their 'uniform' consisted of a shirt and shorts of crude cotton, a straw hat and sandals of tanned leather or of woven fibres from the linden tree.[49]

Raiders and war parties tried to live off the land as far as possible, but also carried 'iron rations' that could be consumed in emergencies. There was always the worry that when in enemy territory, for example, cooking fires or wandering hunters might give the intruders away. Plains Indians like the Sioux or Crees tended to carry jerked buffalo or deer meat or *pemmican*, a mix of lean dried meat pounded fine and combined with melted fat and sometimes dried berries, to tide them over.[50] Apache warriors packed dried cakes made from the fruit of the prickly pear or mescal (century plant or agave), which they sometimes crumbled up and mixed with water.[51] The large Mayan armies often found it hard to live off the countryside and so carried supplies of parched corn with them on campaign.

The logistical advantage enjoyed by most Indians evaporated, however, when they were forced on the defensive. Whereas whites could draw upon a vast hinterland for supplies, Indians normally had only what they or their village had accumulated and once that had been destroyed by attackers, they were largely destitute. When catastrophes of this sort occurred outside the harvest or hunting season, the result could be death for warriors and their families. Indians who lived on the plains, where the winters were frigid and snow tended to accumulate in huge drifts, were the most vulnerable in this regard. This weakness proved to be a major Indian liability in the nineteenth century wars with the army.

European American ways of war

Small wars

In his classic primer on colonial warfare, the British colonel Charles Callwell described the Indian wars of the Americas as 'small wars', which he defined as including

PART I

> All campaigns other than those where both the opposing sides consist of regular troops. It comprises the expeditions against savages and semi-civilised races by disciplined soldiers; it comprises the campaigns undertaken to suppress rebellions and guerrilla warfare in all parts of the world where organised armies are struggling against opponents who will not meet them in the open field; and it thus obviously covers operations varying in their scope and in their conditions.[52]

The colonel went on to break down 'small wars' into three basic categories: (1) external campaigns of conquest or annexation; (2) expeditions launched internally to suppress lawlessness or sedition or to promote settlement of newly acquired territories; and (3) campaigns abroad to avenge wrongs or to eliminate a dangerous enemy.[53]

With a bit of judicious stretching (or shrinking), the New World Indian wars dealt with in this book would seem to fit into the categories set out above, as Colonel Callwell believed they did. The Creek War of 1813–14, covered in Chapter 5 below, was clearly an American campaign aimed at annexing the Creek homeland in Alabama and Georgia. But, if one accepts the legalisms deployed by the Mexican, Canadian and US governments to justify them, the great bulk of the Indian wars we will be examining here fall under Callwell's more benign heading of efforts to pacify or to promote the settlement of newly acquired territories. Thus, the Anglo-Canadian Red River Expedition of 1870, while clearly seen by its participants as a punitive expedition aimed at the region's French-speaking Métis population, was presented by Ottawa as intended to restore order in a new possession of the Dominion. The Mexican government, while it never hid a desire to take over at least part of the Yaqui patrimony for distribution to white or mestizo settlers, could still argue that since all Indians were citizens under the terms of the Mexican constitution, its interminable nineteenth-century wars against the Yaquis were in reality intended to suppress internal sedition. Similarly, the campaigns waged against the Plains and Apache Indians could be explained by the US government as constabulary operations intended to keep the peace and protect property in territories obtained by way of the Louisiana Purchase of 1803 and by the Treaty of Guadalupe Hidalgo in 1848 which brought the war between the US and Mexico to a close. It will require no powerful leap of the imagination to see how these legal frameworks have enabled New World nations to portray their Indian wars not as wars of imperial conquest like those engaged in by the armies of the Old World, but as police actions aimed at promoting law and order and a 'civilised' way of life.[54]

A major problem Western armies had to contend with in fighting these small wars, Callwell wrote, was the variety of foes they had to face.

> Strategy and tactics assume all manner of forms. It is difficult to conceive methods of combat more dissimilar than those employed

respectively by the Transkei Kaffirs, by the Zulus, and by the Boers, opponents with whom British troops successively came into conflict within a period of three years [1878–81] and in one single quarter of the African continent.[55]

Although New World armies may not have been obliged to face as many dissimilar opponents as those of the major imperial powers, such as Britain or France, soldiers in the Americas did have to cope with some substantial differences in ways of fighting. The prominent antebellum US cavalry officer, General William S. Harney, who will appear frequently in our story, served against Sauk and Fox warriors amongst the hills and dales of Illinois and Wisconsin in the 1830s and fought the Seminole Indians in the swamps of Florida in the 1830s and '40s before heading out west to take on the horsemen of the Sioux tribes on the plains of Nebraska.[56] General George Crook, who also features prominently in this account and whose career was taking off just as Harney's was coming to a close, learned his trade fighting Indians in the Pacific Northwest before the US Civil War, then in the early 1870s was assigned, much against his will, to battling Apaches in the mountains and deserts of Arizona. It was, ironically, in the Apache wars of the 1870s and '80s that Crook would stake out his reputation as perhaps the USA's greatest Indian fighter. When placed in command of one of the three columns converging on the Sioux in the ill-fated campaign of 1876, he proved incapable of adapting to plains warfare and twice had to withdraw in the face of the enemy.[57]

Taking up the constabulary function meant that the New World armed forces essentially were engaged in defending or pushing forward the frontiers deemed to exist between white 'civilisation' and Indian 'savagery'. In carrying out their task of frontier protection, most European American armies at one time or another found themselves faced with a choice between a strategy of static defence and one of movement. A close examination of the history of the Indian wars seems to indicate that this choice was most often manifest in the first half of the 1800s, when national governments and the armies that served them still lacked the purchase to behave as Callwell would have counselled them to do:'[T]he way to deal with Asiatics', he famously stated, is 'to go for them and cow them by sheer force of will'.[58] Callwell would have approved, however, of the campaigns conducted during the War of 1812 by the renowned American 'border captains', William Henry Harrison and Andrew Jackson, who carried fire and sword into Indian country and inflicted decisive defeats on their foes. This strategy succeeded as well as it did, however, not because the American invaders imposed themselves by 'sheer force of will' upon their Indian foes, but because the enemies they faced, like the Creek tribe of the southeastern US, were sedentary agriculturists who lived in large towns. And, the decision of the Creeks to resist Jackson's 1814 incursion into their country with a strategy of static defence, by forting up at Horseshoe Bend, led to one of the greatest disasters to befall an Indian people in the whole of the nineteenth century.

PART I

Although for some reason he does not comment on it, Callwell must have found it interesting, if difficult to understand, that once the theatre of the US Indian wars shifted to the plains of the trans-Mississippi West, where the enemy were wide-ranging nomadic hunters, the US Army gradually went over to a strategy of static defence. There was a sporadic effort to conduct a strategy of movement in the 1830s, when the first dragoon regiments were formed, but men and horses proved unequal to the task and it was abandoned in favour of defending the frontier by way of a string of forts. Although a debate about the wisdom of this course took place, with leading figures in the army and government championing adoption of a strategy of movement along the lines of the one that had been employed by the French in Algeria in the 1840s, no changes were made until after the Civil War. There seem to have been two main reasons for this. To begin with, the Congress never was convinced that a big army, certainly one big enough to wage a war of movement over the wide open spaces of the West, was needed to defeat the Indians, and refused to fund one. Anyway, forts were less expensive than a big army because they could be built by army labour from raw materials taken from the nearby wilderness. Also, settlers were keen to have a fort in their neighbourhood, even if its garrison was too small to stop Indian raids, as it almost always was, because the soldiers bought local goods and services, and they complained loudly to their elected officials whenever they heard that plans were being made to shut down forts.[59]

After Appomattox, the US military took a different tack. Once treaties were signed confining the more biddable Indians to reservations, the army was able to label those still roaming about as 'hostiles'. Treaty making also cut down on the number of potential combatants the military had to contend with, making it possible, but just barely, for the army to carry out its mission with the minuscule force Congress authorised, no more than 25,000 men for the whole of the West in the 1870s and '80s. A war of movement, sometimes referred to as 'total war', was mounted against these 'hostiles', usually employing converging columns and often attacking in winter when the Indians were shut up in their camps and their ponies were weak from lack of forage. This strategy was used to defeat the Comanche confederation in the Red River War of 1874–5 and the Sioux confederation in the Great Sioux War of 1876–7. An even more intensive and innovative war of movement, featuring collaboration between US and Mexican forces and employing large numbers of Indians as scouts and combatants, was required to bring the Apaches to heel in the 1880s.[60]

The new Mexican republic tried to defend its northern frontier by continuing the static defence strategy of the former colonial regime, which had been based on a line of *presidios* (forts) along the border, but this proved to be a failure. The Mexican national army's attention had turned to involvement in internal politics and repelling foreign invasions and, as a result, there were too few regulars to man the forts. Those that did serve were demoralised by low and infrequent pay and a general lack of proper military equipment. By the 1830s, the burden of frontier defence was for the most part being borne by the border communities themselves. But local militia and, after 1850, National Guard units lacked the resources and manpower to do an effective job of defending the frontier against Apache and Comanche raiders, much less mount punitive expeditions into Indian country.[61]

Wars against nature

One of the most widely known of Colonel Callwell's many observations on 'small wars' is his contention that, for the most part, they are 'campaigns against nature [rather] than against hostile enemies'.[62] In a recent book, British military historian Jeremy Black describes the United States as a 'relatively benign sphere for expansion' as compared, for example, to 'the cold of northeast Siberia' into which Russian expansionists plunged or 'the hostile (to westerners) disease environment in the tropics' well known to European armies operating in Africa or Asia.[63] Although the Wild West could not boast winters to compare with those of, say, Kolymskaya, it did sometimes get cold on the plains. In the late autumn of 1855, Colonel William S. Harney undertook to prove to Sioux 'hostiles' in the Dakotas that winter could not shield them from the wrath of the Great White Father. To that end, he marched a column of troops from Ft. Laramie, Wyoming to Ft. Pierre, Dakota Territory, in freezing cold and storms of sleet. When the soldiers finally got to their destination they quickly discovered that accommodations left something to be desired and that supplies were scarce. The cold was such that ink had to be heated on a stove before it could be used. Soldiers housed in tents in some cases had to have frozen feet and hands amputated. 'One soldier even lost his penis due to cold', having ventured outdoors to 'make water' in subzero weather. But Harney had made his point: The Sioux took to calling him 'Mad Bear' and did their best to stay away from him and his men.[64]

It also could get hot in the West. In 1834, on their first ever foray into Indian country, in this case western Oklahoma and northern Texas, the newly formed US First Dragoon Regiment had to endure several days of 105 degree F. temperatures. Water was scarce. Some two-thirds of Colonel Henry Dodge's men ended up on the sick list and some of them died, along with 100 horses. The dragoons' mission, to overawe Comanches and Kiowas who had been molesting American traders on the Santa Fe Trail, was not a success.[65]

European American armies

United States

Like other developing countries around the world, then and since, Mexico, Canada and the United States turned to the great military powers of the day for help in building up their armed forces. Thus, much like Mehemet Ali's Egypt in the 1820s and '30s, the United States from the early years of nationhood well into the succeeding century relied upon France, the era's acknowledged repository of the martial arts, for the material and technical assistance required to forge a national army. While it may go largely unrecognised today, it would be difficult to overestimate the influence of French military thought and practice upon the evolution of the US army, particularly in the antebellum period.[66] As Russell Weigley noted, 'all parties in the United States' regarded France as the leading military power of the age and turned to her for help and guidance in forging the military institutions of the new republic.

> Americans of the revolutionary military tradition admired France for the successes she had won with the bayonets of her armed citizens. Americans of the conservative military tradition noted that after her wars France reverted to an army of regulars, presumably retaining, however, the high standards which Napoleon had bequeathed to the officer corps.[67]

The French influence was at its most visible in the early decades of the new nation. Almost all of the coastal fortifications built to protect the country in the years of its greatest vulnerability to British attack were the work of French engineers or were designed along French lines. As Roger Kennedy has put it, 'From an architectural point of view, the Star-Spangled Banner first flew from a French fort, and the torpedoes damned by Admiral David Farragut emerged from apertures designed by Napoleon's former aide General Simon Bernard'.[68] Less visible but more influential in the long term was the French impact on the professional education of officers of the US Army. The curriculum and methods of instruction at the US Military Academy at West Point, source of some two-thirds of army officers by 1850, were closely modelled on those of the Ecole Polytechnique in Paris. Thus, the Enlightenment-inspired emphasis of the Ecole on the teaching of mathematics and science and on the training of engineers and artillerists was carried over wholesale into the West Point curriculum. And French, the language of war during this period, was the only foreign language taught at the Academy.

The shaping of West Point in the image of the École Polytechnique was largely the work of Sylvanus Thayer, superintendent of the Academy from 1819 to 1833, and Dennis Hart Mahan, Thayer's disciple and professor of engineering and military science at West Point down into the years of the Civil War. Thayer visited Europe in 1815 and brought back around 1,000 volumes on military subjects, mostly in French, for the library of the new Academy. Mahan, who had enrolled in the French School of Application for Engineers and Artillery at Metz, returned to the US in 1830 to teach the capstone course in engineering and tactics for graduating seniors at West Point. Mahan taught his course from 'his own translations of standard French works in various branches of military science'.[69] 'For the remainder of his career, he proclaimed to class after class that the modern soldier, to be a capable leader, had to study

Napoleonic tactics.'[70] And, of course, one is obliged to add: Napoleonic grand strategy, the quest for decisive battle, which could only be achieved, Bonaparte had taught, by pursuit of the offensive. These precepts were enshrined in the *Summary of the Art of War* by a Swiss-born former member of Bonaparte's staff, Baron Antoine-Henri Jomini, which constituted a veritable bible of military thought for the West Point-educated US Army officer and would guide the hand of American generals throughout the Civil War and, arguably, well beyond.

By the middle of the nineteenth century, the extent of congruence between the American and French militaries was considerable, as Major Alfred Mordecai of the US Army Ordnance Department reported following a fact-finding tour of European military establishments. 'The small arms in the French army having generally been taken as patterns for our own troops', he wrote, 'are so well known as to render unnecessary a description of them.' The same was true of French artillery. 'The "materiel" of the French system of field artillery being well known to us, a notice of the few modifications recently made in some of the details is all that is required here'.[71]

But there were elements of the French military system that the Americans did not choose to follow. One was the tradition established during the French Revolution, and extended by Napoleon, of recruiting officers in large numbers from the ranks. This system had its admirable side, observed Major Mordecai, once again. 'The French army may be said to possess a truly *republican* constitution,' he reported. This had positive effects on the army, since the son of the meanest peasant could reasonably hope to rise to the marshalate. Mordecai believed that 'The influence of such considerations in promoting good conduct, desire of instruction, and zealous performance of duty, is incontestably great'. Still, he concluded, this policy of 'careers open to talent' was one French innovation that the US Army probably would not want to emulate. For, too often, he sniffed, it led to the 'sacrifice of refinement of character and manners on the part of a portion of the officers'.[72]

But the 'shavetails' who emerged from the Point to take up commands on the frontier brought with them more Napoleonic baggage than simply an appreciation of the emperor's grand strategy or the tactics that had won the day for Bonaparte at Marengo or Austerlitz. They also carried with them the Napoleonic 'ethos of war', the belief that seeking battlefield glory is the ultimate quest of the soldier. Many of these young officers had imbibed their love of glory from Dennis Hart Mahan, once again, this time in his capacity as president of the 'Napoleon Club' which flourished at West Point down into the Civil War and membership of which was considered *de rigueur* for any aspiring officer.[73] Although more will be said on this matter later, it may be worthwhile to point out here that, while the Napoleonic 'ethos' would inspire officers in all the American combat arms, it would have a particularly profound impact on cavalrymen, who had primary responsibility for subduing the Indians in the west. The consequences of this outlook were not all positive.

PART I

Infantry did most of the fighting for the whites in the Eastern American Indian wars, although, as we will see, mounted riflemen played a greater role than they generally have been credited with. In the American West, however, the great distances and the nature of the enemy dictated that the mounted arm would predominate in the region's unfolding Indian wars. 'The great extent of our frontier and the peculiar service devolving on the troops render it indispensable,' wrote the Army commanding general Winfield Scott in 1850, 'that the *cavalry* element should enter largely into the composition of the army.'[74]

The mounted men who now assumed the main burden of Indian fighting in the West should not be perceived, however, as the true cavalry, wielders of the *arme blanche*, that so many of them yearned to be. As Richard Wormser has put it, the US cavalry 'suffered – the leaders, that is – from a strange two-headedness. They wanted to be cavalrymen, beaux sabreurs, in situations that called for gunmen, carabineers'.[75] And no wonder. The Napoleonic *esprit de guerre* so many of them had imbibed, most often though not exclusively, at West Point made it hard for them to accept what they had in fact become: dragoons or mounted infantry. To get a sense of the mental adjustment these cavalry officers had to make, it is worth quoting at some length from Dennis Hart Mahan, the West Point professor and head of the 'Napoleon Club', who taught so many of them. This was the description of cavalry warfare he left with his students.

> The *cuirassier sans peur* . . . careless and indifferent to the maddening strife around . . . with sabre raised, he rushes on his foe . . . like the tornado, [to] level all before him, and leave nothing of his task unfinished but the gathering of the wreck he leaves in his track. . . . The dashing bold hussar, that epitome of military impudence and insolence at the tavern, should present those qualities in a sublimated form on the field . . . careering with a falcon's speed and glance upon his quarry.[76]

In reality, if not always in the mind's eye of the horsemen themselves, troopers in the American West functioned as mounted infantry.[77] Sabres were gradually discarded, and cavalrymen learned to rely on carbines and, later, six-shot pistols as their main weapons. The cavalry refused, though, to part with its 'American' horses, the thoroughbreds brought in at considerable expense from the East. These were big horses, the sort that might have been in demand for shock warfare with sabre or lance. And they were good to look at, the kinds of beasts that would gladden a horse fancier's heart. If the US cavalry had been fighting a European enemy, the horses it prized so much might have done nicely, but warfare on the plains or in the mountains of the West was a different proposition. In that setting, the premium was on endurance, the capacity to cover a lot of ground and keep on doing it day after day, in pursuit of an elusive foe, and the 'American' horses the cavalry took such pride in lacked that kind of stamina.

By contrast, the Chasseurs d'Afrique, the French regular cavalry in Algeria, quickly adopted the smaller, hardier 'barb' horse used by their guerrilla foes, thus increasing their ability to stay in the field in spite of shortages of forage and water.[78]

Captain Richard S. Ewell of later Confederate army fame and 180 men of the First Dragoons teamed up with a body of infantry to chase Mescalero Apache raiders in New Mexico in early 1855. But 'because it was mid-winter and bitterly cold the dragoons' horses gave out and toward the end of the campaign, they could not keep up with the infantry'.[79] This was not an isolated incident. At the battle of Four Lakes during Colonel George Wright's campaign against the Spokane Indians and their allies in Washington Territory in 1858, dragoons had a rare opportunity to close with the enemy and do a bit of sabreing, but pursuit of the broken foe, cavalry's more important function, proved to be another matter. As Lieutenant Lawrence Kip reported, the dragoons' horses 'were too much worn out to allow them to reach the main body [of Indians, and the dragoons] were therefore obliged to halt when they reached the hillside, their horses being entirely blown'.[80]

Another major problem with the 'American' horses was feeding them. Unlike Indian ponies, they could not survive on prairie grass. Hay and grain were required to feed them and this made up a good portion of the load of the long wagon trains that accompanied US cavalry expeditions into the field. And when the hay and grain gave out, the results could be disastrous in the extreme. General Patrick Connor's Powder River Expedition in late 1865 ran into fierce storms and two of its three columns managed to get lost in the wilds of Wyoming. Nearly a thousand horses and mules died for lack of forage before the troops found their way back to 'civilisation'.[81]

This reliance upon mounted men to wage its Indian wars in the West put the US Army at odds with other colonial armies of the era. Despite Colonel Callwell's dictum that 'The moral effect of a charge of trained and disciplined horse upon a mob of irregular warriors is tremendous',[82] cavalry – even mounted riflemen – played less of a role in European wars of imperial conquest than on the plains of the Wild West. To begin with, many of the European campaigns were fought in the tropics, where conditions made the employment of cavalry impossible. In Africa, for example, the presence south of the Sahara of the tsetse fly, bearer of sleeping sickness (*trypanosomiasis*), ruled out the use of any hoofed animals, so that even supplies had to be carried on the backs or heads of humans. A similar situation prevailed in much of Asia. But, even where horsemen could be deployed, European colonial armies almost always used them in tandem with infantry. Cavalry served primarily as scouts and flank guards and only rarely as a shock arm, but occasionally proved useful for pursuit of an enemy force driven off by infantry drawn up in line or square, as at Ulundi, the final engagement of the Zulu War of 1879 in South Africa, or Omdurman, the battle in 1898 that avenged the death of 'Chinese' Gordon and destroyed the Mahdist theocratic state in the Sudan.

PART I

Motivation

From the early nineteenth century up until the Civil War and arguably well beyond, the US Army officer corps was greatly imbued with Napoleonic ideas of war. The main characteristics of this style of warfare were the primacy of the offensive and the quest for decisive battle. The obvious corollary to these concepts was the belief that only by carrying the war to the enemy could officers win the glory Bonaparte and the French had taught them to covet. US Army officers imbibed these Napoleonic ideas of war at West Point, where Professor Dennis Hart Mahan, for example, taught the principles of military strategy from his own translation of a French text.

The best example of how all of this might bear fruit when translated into the American context was General Philip Kearny, sometimes called 'the Murat of the American Army', a reference to Bonaparte's chief of cavalry, the archetype of the *beau sabreur*. As a schoolboy, Kearny slept 'under an old but very fine engraving of Napoleon Bonaparte, tri-color in hand, at the bridge of Lodi, perhaps for the purpose of deriving inspiration from the picture in his dreams'.[83] If such a stratagem was intended, it appears to have worked. After serving briefly in the Far West as a lieutenant of dragoons under his uncle, General Stephen Watts Kearny, the Mexican–American War hero of later years, 'Phil' Kearny decided 'that much was needed to fill the gaps in [his] and the dragoons' military education; and [he] was determined to go abroad to study and report on the subject; and to practice war with foreign armies, if that were possible'. Scion of a wealthy family, well-connected in government, Kearny got himself named to an *ad hoc* 'Commission to Study Cavalry Tactics in Europe' by the Secretary of War, Stephen Poinsett, a family friend, and in 1839 embarked for France, where he enrolled at the Royal Cavalry School at Saumur.[84]

But Kearny was less interested in learning the fundamentals of cavalry tactics than 'practicing war'. 1840 found the twenty-six-year-old 'practicing' in Algeria, in the ranks of the First Regiment of the Chasseurs d'Afrique. Kearny took part in a campaign to take the Mitidja, an agricultural area near Algiers, from the Arabs. It was here that he became a devotee of 'glory' in the Napoleonic vein, a kind of recklessness that would cost him an arm in Mexico in 1847 and his life in Virginia during the Civil War. A French companion recalled 'often' seeing him 'charging the Arabs with his sword in one hand, his pistol in the other, and his reins in his teeth'.[85]

It might be profitable to pause here for a moment to contemplate the career and legend of the Napoleonic officer who inspired Kearny and so many other cavalrymen of his day, in the US and other armies. Joachim Murat, born the twelfth child of an innkeeper in 1767, ended his career as a Marshal of France and Prince and King of Naples. En route, he established a reputation for himself as the 'archetypal cavalryman', the 'supreme personification of the beau sabreur', a soldier of 'enormous courage and penetrating tactical eye, but no strategic or common sense at all'.[86]

Murat was also famous for devising fantastic uniforms for himself and for a towering vanity that, to his credit, did not desert him in his final, harrowing hours. Sentenced to death by firing squad, he declined the traditional blindfold and instructed the soldiers to 'Spare my face, aim at the heart'.[87]

Kearny's death in battle near Chantilly, Virginia, in 1862, typically as a result of a headlong charge that carried him into Confederate lines, did not spell the end of Murat emulation in the US Army. Indeed, the mantle would pass with a flourish to an officer on his very staff, and a great admirer of his, one Lieutenant George Armstrong Custer. Paul Hutton has written that

> Custer made his debut at Gettysburg sporting a floppy, broad-brimmed hat, crimson scarf, and a black velvet jacket trimmed with gold braid onto which flowed his shoulder-length hair. He had studied the life of Napoleon's flamboyant cavalry leader Murat and understood the usefulness of flair to impress soldiers and civilians.[88]

Well before this, however, Custer had given clear evidence of his embrace of the Murat ethos. It was probably no accident that his first real service in the Civil War was, as we have seen, on the staff of 'Phil' Kearny. He would later express his admiration for Kearny in terms that bear quoting at some length.

> Kearny was a man of violent passions, quick and determined impulses, haughty demeanor . . . brave as the bravest of men can be, possessed of unusually great activity, both mental and physical, patriotic as well as ambitious, impatient under all delay. . . . He constantly chafed under the restraint and inactivity of camp life and was never so happy and contented as when moving to the attack. . . . Brave in battle, impetuous in command, and at times domineering toward those beneath him, no one could wear a more courtly manner than Kearny unless he willed otherwise.[89]

Remarkably, after Kearny's death, Custer was assigned to the staff of another equally famous but very different soldier, General George McClellan. There, like his hero, Murat, Custer showed his contempt for staff work – and military discipline – by abandoning his post to gallop to where the action was hottest on the battlefield. McClellan does not seem to have minded terribly. He called Custer 'simply a reckless, gallant boy', albeit one with a keen eye for what was happening on the battlefield and a talent for crafting 'clear and intelligible reports'. 'I became much attached to him', the 'Little Napoleon' confessed. The feeling was mutual. Custer became a McClellan fanatic, a commitment which would have a negative effect on the young man's military career once his benefactor's star waned.[90]

Custer outlived the stigma of having been a 'McClellan man', however, and emerged from the Civil War a brevet major general and one of the great heroes

PART I

of the Union army. Once a byword in army and public alike for gallantry, dash, and – yes – recklessness, his name seemed destined to disappear from view as peace descended upon the nation. In 1866, however, opportunity briefly beckoned. In Mexico, the republican movement of Benito Juárez was gearing up for a final confrontation with the armies of the French-imposed Emperor Maximilian, and Custer was offered command of the *Juarista* cavalry. The 'boy general' had wanted to accept, but President Andrew Johnson scuttled the offer by naming Custer to his bodyguard.[91] So Custer, the new 'American Murat', demoted to colonel, became a man of the plains, an Indian fighter, as commander of the newly formed Seventh Cavalry in 1867.

The American military's affinity for things French in the first three-quarters of the nineteenth century, as exemplified in the careers of 'Phil' Kearny and George Armstrong Custer, received a boost from the considerable interest of military professionals and public alike in the French conquest of Algeria. American soldiers came to see the Indians of the western plains as analogous to the Bedouin tribes they understood the French to have been fighting in Algeria and believed that the methods used to subdue them could be employed effectively against the Indians of the Far West. We have already noted Captain Randolph Marcy's interest in the French conquest of Algeria and his belief that, given 'the remarkable similarity between the habits of the Arabs and those of the wandering tribes that inhabit our Western prairies', the methods used by the French to subdue the Algerians could be successfully adapted to the Indian campaigns in the American West.[92]

Despite his claims to the contrary, this analogy very likely had not come to Marcy like a bolt out of the blue Texas sky. It was an idea that had been implanted in the American military mind much earlier and by Marcy's time had come to inhabit the highest reaches of the US military establishment. Since early in the nineteenth century the nomadic tribes that inhabited the Western plains had been comprehended by educated Anglo-American society as New World versions of 'the Bedouins of the Arabian desert, the Tartars of Asiatic steppes'.[93] In the 1840s, Senator Thomas Hart Benton, once again, did not risk being misunderstood in describing the Indians of the southern Plains – the Comanches Marcy had set out to impress – as 'Arabs of the New World'.[94]

On his return to the United States, Kearny had handed the Secretary of War a report on his experiences abroad in which he extolled the French strategy for subduing the indigenous population of Algeria and called for adoption of some of its principles on the plains of the American West. Kearny also provided a translation of the official French manual on cavalry tactics, which was adopted almost verbatim by the War Department in 1841 and became the 'bible' of the dragoon regiments of the US Army.[95]

There are a number of superficial resemblances between the French Army's conquest of Algeria in the 1830s and '40s and the US Army's more gradual winning of the West. As Colonel Callwell observed, both armies faced mobile, elusive foes who could only be beaten if they could be lured into set-piece battles in which the armies' disciplined firepower could be brought to bear or, most often, if caught immobilised in their villages and encumbered with women, children and old people. Both armies eventually adopted a strategy of 'total war' to vanquish their 'native' enemies, the French well before the Americans. The French general Comte Pierre de Castellane described the French approach in the 1840s in terms that would have been perfectly understood by his American counterparts twenty years later. 'In Europe', he wrote,

> Once [you are] master of two or three large cities, the entire country is yours. But, in Africa, how do you act against a population whose only link with the land is the pegs of their tents? . . . The only way is to take the grain which feeds them, the flocks which clothe them. For this reason, we make war on silos, war on cattle, [we make] the *razzia*.[96]

American 'exceptionalists' will likely take issue with the suggestion here that not only the way the antebellum US cavalry arm was organised and behaved, but also the way it fought, was derived from a French model. They will argue that US soldiers did not need to turn to Marshal Bugeaud and his Algerian *razzias* for examples of how to bring marauding Indians to heel. And indeed there are plentiful examples in American history of frontiersmen and soldiers carrying destruction into Indian country. From at least King Philip's War in colonial New England in the late 1600s through General John Sullivan's expedition into the lands of Britain's Iroquois allies during the American War of Independence to General Andrew Jackson's depredations in Creek country during the War of 1812, American armies had sought to bring Indian peoples to their knees by destroying their homes, possessions and means of livelihood. Presumably, these experiences, when taken together, should have comprised a fund of knowledge upon which succeeding generations of American soldiers could draw when confronted by Indian resistance. Given the well-known tendency of the military mind to 'reinvent the wheel' with each succeeding generation, however, it is doubtful that much of an 'institutional memory' of such measures ever existed. But even if it had, in a derivative army such as that of the USA in the pre-Civil War era, it would have been much more prestigious and authoritative to invoke methods of warfare employed by the acknowledged European 'masters of war' of the era, the French.

French influence on the US military establishment waned, however, after France's defeat by the Prussians in 1870–71. The main external influence now became German, as reflected in the writings of General Emory Upton (especially his *The Armies of Europe and Asia*). The German influence did not alter the traditional orientation toward offensive warfare, as the Prussians had been as offensive-minded as the French, but rather affected thinking on the logistics and the planning of war. Prussian victory in the 1870 war had been widely attributed to the fact that the Prussians had a General Staff to plan and oversee the execution of war strategy and their defeated opponents had not.

Now, everyone, including the USA, scrambled to establish general staffs of their own.

Canada

The Canadian armed forces, who did not have this Napoleonic baggage to contend with, proved content to adopt a generally defensive posture, in any case a necessity since the country's major military concern throughout the nineteenth century was invasion by the USA. But Canadian officers who yearned for the opportunity to go on the attack and win glory had an outlet that their American counterparts had forfeited in 1783: the British Empire. Canadian soldiers served in General Sir Garnet Wolseley's abortive attempt to rescue 'Chinese' Gordon in Khartoum in 1884, in the Second Boer War (1899–1902), and, of course, in both world wars in the twentieth century.

Until 1871, Canada's land defences remained the responsibility of the British Army, although there were provisions for local militia companies whose mission was to support the regulars in time of war. Before the War of 1812, British troops had occupied forts on both the American and Canadian shores of the Great Lakes and in the Old Northwest. Together with their Indian allies and the Canadian militia, British regulars had managed to ward off two American invasions of Canada during the 1812–15 war, and had been on the offensive in the upper Mississippi River valley when the conflict ended. Nonetheless, the Treaty of Ghent (1815), which brought the War of 1812 to an end, and the subsequent Bagot–Rush Agreement (1817) which more or less demilitarised the Great Lakes, ushered in a long period of British retrenchment in North America. London appears to have concluded that, in view of Britain's other imperial commitments and the perennial fear of invasion from a France never reconciled to the verdict of Waterloo, it would be impossible to defend Canada against a serious invasion by the USA. 'It is certainly a fine country,' Rear Admiral Sir David Milne wrote of Upper Canada (Ontario), 'but too distant for us to defend against so powerful a neighbour.'[97]

By the 1850s, British troops in Canada were largely confined to the Citadelle in Quebec City, home to the 60th Rifle Regiment, and the garrison supporting the large Royal Navy base at Halifax, Nova Scotia. There was a brief build-up of British forces in Canada during the American Civil War, when it appeared that Union anger at British support for the Confederacy might lead to a punitive invasion of Canada. But this was only a temporary measure. When the Liberals of William Ewart Gladstone came to power in Britain in 1868 on a platform of imperial retrenchment, the end of the British military presence in Canada was in sight. As Edward Cardwell, the reforming Secretary of War in the Gladstone cabinet, warned, Canada's defence 'would ever principally depend upon the spirit, the energy and the courage of her own people'.[98]

Troops from the 60th Rifles would take part in the 1870 Red River expedition to Western Canada, as we will see, but it was Britain's last hurrah.

On 11 November 1871, a troopship arrived to take the redcoats home and 'the 60th Rifles – the old Royal Americans – marched down the narrow streets from the Citadel for the last time'.[99]

Britain's post-1815 military presence in Canada had had little to do with the colony's Indian population. In eastern Canada, most Indians had been settled on reserves and, although there was Indian grumbling about government efforts to turn them into Christian yeoman farmers, there were no revolts. And though the Red River colony of Manitoba was situated on the edge of the Great Plains, home to the formidable Cree and Blackfoot buffalo hunters, the 1870 expedition to the Red River did not concern them but, rather, was intended to quash an uprising by the region's Métis or mixed-bloods, who believed (rightly) that their longstanding autonomy was threatened by the sale of western Canada to Ottawa by the Hudson's Bay Company. But more even than this lay behind the rapid dispatch of troops to the Red River. The overriding concern was that the USA might use the turmoil in Manitoba to justify an invasion of western Canada to 'restore order'.

The departure of British land forces a year later left a vacuum that was only slowly filled. From 1871 down to the First World War, Canada's armed forces consisted of a congeries of rural and urban militia companies, composed of three-year volunteers, whose training was entrusted to a small permanent cadre of professional soldiers, at first largely British but increasingly Canadian as the years wore on. It was this 'army' that would fight the only war in Canadian history in which both sides were Canadian, the North-West Rebellion of 1885.

The militia tradition was, if anything, even stronger in Canada than in the neighbouring USA. Many Canadians took the view that it was their militia, not British regulars, that repulsed the Americans during the War of 1812. As this outlook suggests, the militia mystique occupied a crucial place in the growth of national feeling in Canada. None of this would abate after Dominion status was granted in 1867. Most of the troops that took part in the suppression of the North-West Rebellion in 1885 were militia. Many of them came away from the conflict contemptuous of the British officers placed over them, whom they believed had tried to steal the limelight of victory.[100]

Mexico

Mexico's armed forces, especially after the loss of Texas in the 1830s, found themselves strictly on the defensive. Even after the peace treaty that concluded the Mexican–American War of 1846–8, which cost Mexico half of her national territory, the country's number one military priority remained defence against US invasion. But close behind this preoccupation came Mexico's Indian problems. Given the country's massive indigenous population, these were far more serious than the challenges faced by Canada or the USA. Recurrent Yaqui uprisings kept Sonora and its neighbouring state to the south, Sinaloa, in turmoil for most of the nineteenth century. Apache and Comanche raids into

Mexico from the USA virtually depopulated the frontier regions of the northern states of Sonora and Chihuahua. The Indian wars exhausted the already scant resources of the Mexican states where the fighting occurred, and on whose shoulders most of the burden of defence rested until the coming to power in 1876 of General Porfirio Díaz. The new president committed the resources of the federal government to the struggle against the Yaquis and it was only then that their rebellions could be contained. Putting a stop to the cross-border raids by the Apaches and Comanches quite logically required the cooperation of US forces. US Army campaigns in Texas in the 1870s defeated the Comanches and put them on reservations, thus ending some one hundred years of Comanche raids into Mexico. In the 1880s, with the surrender of Geronimo and his guerrilla band to the US Army, nearly two centuries of Mexican–Apache wars also came to an end, although the victory had been purchased by granting US troops in Arizona the right to cross the Mexican border at will in pursuit of Apache fugitives, a departure that some Mexican patriots regarded as an ominous abridgement of national sovereignty.

From independence on, Mexico's land forces comprised a national regular army (*permanentes*) and state militias, the latter intended to supplement the regulars during national emergencies. The Mexican regular army was unique among the armed forces under consideration here for its reliance upon conscription (the *leva*) to fill its ranks. This policy was highly unpopular. 'The mere rumor of an impending levy was sufficient to trigger a mass exodus of eligible males...'. Shortfalls in recruitment due to widespread hostility to conscription led the government to call upon the states to round up their 'undesirables' and send them off to the nearest military camp, 'some in chains, others incarcerated at each stop until [they reached] their destination'. We should not be surprised to learn that, apart from drunks and vagrants, the great majority of the 'undesirables' shipped off for military service were Indians, mestizos and *pardos* (Mexicans with some African blood).[101]

Bad conditions of army service were made even worse by low pay, erratic paydays and shortages of everything from food to weapons. Some of this can be blamed on Mexico's weak economy and consequent poor tax base, but waste also played a major role. While the military sometimes garnered up to 85 per cent of the country's annual federal budget, much of the largesse was directed to the regiments near the capital whose general officers used them as counters in the political gamesmanship that occupied so much of their time. Precious little found its way to the soldiers stationed in the presidios on the frontier, who 'were reduced to raiding the commissary, selling firewood, or hunting wild game to survive'.[102] By the 1840s, the number of regulars stationed on the frontier had dwindled to such an extent that almost all of the burden of defence against Indian incursions and uprisings had come to rest on the shoulders of the state militias of the region.

In 1846, national legislation decreed that all males between the ages of 18 and 50 in the frontier states were liable for service in the militia. The law stipulated, however, that those who could afford it could avoid service by paying an exemption tax. The upshot of this was flight over the border to the USA of significant numbers of citizens who could not afford to buy their way out of militia service. So bad did the situation become that, by 1856, state governments were once again rounding up 'undesirables' to fill the ranks.[103] It was in these circumstances that officials in the states of Chihuahua and Sonora began to turn to mercenaries for help, to scalp hunters who were paid so many pesos for Apache scalps, and to friendly Indians, like the Tarahumaras and Pimas, who had their own reasons for not liking the raiders from the north.[104]

3

WORLD VIEWS AND FIGHTING FAITHS

Introduction

It has become widely accepted in the Western world that, to quote the Prussian soldier–intellectual Carl von Clausewitz, 'War is simply a continuation of political intercourse, with the addition of other means'.[1] By this we understand that armies are formed and, when necessary, sent to war as instruments of the political will of the state (or, in the case of stateless peoples, of the community) they serve. But armies are more than the orders they receive from on high and the weapons, rations, officers, training and doctrine they are given in order to fulfill their mission. They inevitably reflect in large measure the particular culture, understood in its broadest sense, from which they emanate. And it is this cultural baggage that does so much to give armies their individual character, the attributes that distinguish them from one another and ultimately determine how faithfully they serve the state or community that has nurtured them.

Religion

Religion and the Indian way of war

Religion suffused every aspect of Indian life, war included. Most Indian peoples believed in some form of supreme being or giver of life, but also beseeched lesser gods associated with natural forces for fine weather, bountiful harvests or good hunting and triumph in war.

The peoples of the Creek confederation worshipped a supreme being they called the Maker of Breath, a spirit that 'extends above all things and . . . hath created them'.[2] The Shawnees also believed in a Great Spirit. Their creation story taught that 'A flood destroyed the world and its inhabitants, except for an old woman, who ascended to the clouds and whose grief induced the Creator . . . to repeople the earth'.[3]

Across the Mississippi River, amongst the Plains Indians, even the Comanches of Texas, sometimes called the 'sceptics' of the plains because they had no organised religion and no shamans, believed in a supreme being, a creator who had put the Comanches on earth and would call the upright and courageous among them to 'the land beyond the sun' after death.[4] The Pawnees of Kansas and Nebraska worshipped a supreme being known as Tirawa, a sort of Deist creator who had shaped the cosmos, set the world in motion, and then left its fate to a bevy of subordinate gods. Generally speaking, however, Plains tribes like the Sioux or Crees lacked any sort of established religion, but operated spiritually on the basis of individual revelation, either voluntary, through dreams, or induced, by way of sleep deprivation or self-torture, as in the Sun Dance.[5]

Both the Indian and white worlds in North America were traversed by a series of revivalist movements beginning in the late 1700s and continuing on into the twentieth century. The so-called Second Awakening which brought evangelical religion to the frontier communities of Kentucky and Tennessee at the dawn of the nineteenth century,[6] is perhaps better known, but the wave of what have been called 'revitalisation movements' that gripped the American Indian world during the same period was no less important. If the revivalism of the Second Awakening was in the first instance a reaction to the rationalism of the French Revolution (and of the Founding Fathers of the American Republic), the Indian revitalisation movements came into being as a response to the threatened extinction of Indian culture and identity by the remorseless spread of European civilisation across the New World. According to the American anthropologist Anthony F.C. Wallace, in its most basic sense, a revitalisation movement is

> A deliberate, organized, conscious effort by members of a society to construct a more satisfying culture. Revitalization is thus, from a cultural standpoint, a special kind of culture change phenomenon: the persons involved in the process . . . must perceive their culture, or some major areas of it, as a system (whether accurately or not); they must feel that this cultural system is unsatisfactory; and they must innovate not merely discrete items, but a new cultural system, specifying new relationships as well as, in some cases, new traits.[7]

Revitalisation movements have taken radically different paths. The 'cargo cults' of the Pacific Islands, for example, sought to revitalise Melanesian society by adapting select elements of Western culture. The several Indian revitalisation movements of North America, on the other hand, tended to follow a 'nativist' trajectory, placing a crucial emphasis on 'the elimination of alien persons, customs, values and/or material' from the life of the tribe and on the revival of 'the old life', the 'Golden Age' that existed before the coming of the white man.[8]

As we will see, this was not the path taken by the Indians of Mexico who concern us, the Yaquis and Mayas. While both of these peoples embraced dynamic and influential movements of revitalisation during the nineteenth century, these bore unmistakable elements of traditional Catholicism, which over the centuries of Spanish rule had sunk deep roots in most Mexican Indian communities.

Back in North America, it will become apparent as this book unfolds that almost every Indian people that found itself threatened by defeat at the hands of the whites experienced some variant of the 'nativist' brand of revitalisation. For our purposes, the first revitalisation movement of importance was that of the Delaware prophet Neolin, counsellor to Pontiac, the Ottawa leader who attempted to forge an Indian confederation against the British in the wake of French defeat in the Seven Years' War. Neolin would inspire the even more influential movement led during the first two decades of the nineteenth century by Tenskwatawa, the Shawnee Prophet and younger brother of the famed Tecumseh. The Prophet's Code, as Tenskwatawa called his new religion, borrowed some of its ideas from Christianity (like many Indians, the Prophet was much taken with the Christian notion of the Resurrection), but preached 'a return to Shawnee lifeways, a revival of communal ownership of property, an end to intertribal warfare, and the rejection of all things white'.[9]

The Prophet's teachings provided the spiritual basis for the Shawnee-inspired confederation's looming struggle with the 'Long Knives', the Americans. The Great Spirit acknowledged having been 'the father of the English, of the French, of the Spaniards and of the Indians', he said. But,

> The Americans I did not make. They are not my children, but the children of the Evil Spirit. They grew from the scum of the great water, when it was troubled by the Evil Spirit, and the froth was driven into the woods by a strong east wind.[10]

Religion and the European–American way of war

Although, as we have just seen, religion was integral to the 'war systems' of the Indian peoples of the Americas, this was not the case with their white opponents. Whilst religious enthusiasms of various sorts gripped the general populace of Canada, Mexico and the USA during the nineteenth century, these stirred only faint echoes in their military establishments. This may have been, as V.G. Kiernan has observed, because 'A European army marched on its stomach, not its soul, and looked to alcohol for most of its higher flights'.[11]

In the USA, the army's enlisted ranks contained a high proportion of immigrants, many of whom were Roman Catholic. At the same time, the army officer corps was overwhelmingly (if nominally) Protestant. To avoid the explosion latent in a mixture of this sort, the military officially observed a policy on religious observance that was advertised as neutrality but, in fact, bordered on indifference. No chaplain corps existed in the US Army from 1818 to 1838 and even after its reconstitution many military posts lacked chaplains and had to avail themselves of religious services in the nearest town. There is some evidence that this situation was not entirely displeasing to the officer corps. Piety and the prudery often associated with it were traits little admired in the antebellum US Army, as the early career of General Oliver O. Howard demonstrates. Young Howard's evangelical Christianity and criticism of drinking and profanity among his fellow cadets at West Point made him many enemies. One of them, General Joseph Hooker, who had been his superior at one point during the Civil War, said of him in later years,

> If he [Howard] was not born in petticoats he ought to have been, and ought to wear them. He was always taken up with Sunday schools and the temperance cause. These things are all very good, you know, but have very little to do with commanding an army corps.[12]

But it also needs to be said that whereas religion served as a cohesive force in Indian society in both peace and war, it had a divisive effect when it intruded into the armies of the white invaders. In Canada and the USA governments struggled to insulate their armed forces from the religious currents that swirled through the general population. In Canada, mindful of the risk of further alienating the large French-speaking population of Quebec, government and military leaders worked to keep out of the militia the anti-Catholic feeling that was rife in much of the English-speaking population, particularly the Ontario communities where the Orange lodges had influence. These divisive sentiments boiled to the surface in both the 1870 and 1885 campaigns in Western Canada against the French-speaking Métis.[13]

The great test of the US Army's policy of religious tolerance came during the war with Mexico in 1846–8. Religious zealots on both sides were eager to portray the war as a religious conflict. The US Army, aware of the large number of Catholics amongst its enlisted men, bent over backwards to discourage Protestant crusading in the ranks, even appointing Jesuits to serve as chaplains at one point. This should not be taken to mean that the nineteenth-century US Army lacked deeply religious soldiers. General Oliver O. Howard, whose difficult West Point years were alluded to above, went on to become an Indian fighter, a Civil War hero, and a champion of black emancipation, all the while being known throughout the service as the 'praying' or 'Christian' general for his devout Methodism.[14]

In Mexico, meanwhile, where Roman Catholicism was the only faith tolerated, the problems attendant upon religious diversity in military ranks were absent. As well, the Mexican army's indigenous Indian foes also professed the faith of Rome. Nevertheless, there was a religious dimension to the Mexican–Indian wars. Both the Yaqui and Maya peoples were deemed to practise a barbarous and impure form of Catholicism, and one of the professed goals of the federal and provincial forces who fought these Indians was to impose more orthodox practices upon them.

PART I

Comparative Indian policies

Although they frequently found themselves at odds with the Indian policies of their governments, the officers and men of the Indian fighting armies of North America had little choice but to accept them as the parameters within which they operated in the field. In both Canada and the United States, civilian control of the military was never seriously contested during the nineteenth century, which meant that military conduct toward Indians was ultimately determined by lawmakers and administrators in the national capitals, not by the men on the spot. This relationship differed considerably from that which obtained between soldiers and their civilian masters in the European colonial wars, particularly those of France in West Africa. There, it was often the 'man on the spot', the colonial officer, who had the upper hand, employing a mixture of provocation and appeals to national pride to initiate wars of conquest. This should not be taken to mean that there were no great issues of disagreement between US army officers, for example, and officials in Washington. One such issue was the incessant demand of the soldiers for authority over the reservations on which they had placed the various Indian tribes. Officers such as generals Nelson Miles and George Crook – who could agree on nothing else – repeatedly complained that the Indian Bureau officials of the Department of the Interior were either too inept or corrupt to manage reservation Indians.

The situation was different in Mexico. Whilst the governments of the Mexican Republic laid down elaborate and often very sophisticated policies with respect to the country's Indian population, they lacked the power to force military compliance with them. Even more important, until the 1880s the states on the northern frontier, such as Sonora and Chihuahua, where most of the Indian fighting took place, paid little attention to directives from Mexico City.

The new Mexican republic thought it could solve its 'Indian problem' by making all Indians, even nomadic Apaches and Comanches Mexican citizens, 'an effort to implement the ideals of liberty and equality, for which the young Mexican nation stood'.[15] But frontier soldiers found it hard to believe that the nomadic tribes could qualify for citizenship since they understood nothing and cared nothing about their 'rights'. In 1835, the *comandante general* of Chihuahua asked the secretary of war: 'Should [the Apaches and other rebellious tribes] be considered as children of the great Mexican family, or as enemies to be driven beyond the boundaries of the state?' The reply came from no less a personage than the then President of the Republic, António López de Santa Anna, who said that the raiders 'were Mexicans, because they were born and live in the Republic . . . The state of barbarity in which they are raised prevents them from knowing their universal obligations, and those that belong to them as Mexicans'. The President recommended that 'kindness and consideration' be used to bring the Indians to civilisation, with force being used only as a last resort. Mexico's frontier soldiers must have smiled at this idealistic approach and state governments in the region chose to treat roving Indians not as fellow citizens but as sovereign powers, much as their North American counterparts did.[16]

In Canada, the Indian policy of the new Dominion government after 1867 mirrored that of the British colonial regime. Its aim was assimilation of the country's Indian peoples, by placing them on reserves and gradually 'de-Indianising' them by exposing them to Christianity, giving them the vote and inculcating the spirit of private enterprise by dividing up tribal lands into individual lots. In the West, it was recognised that this process would be somewhat more difficult and prolonged than had been the case in Eastern Canada, since the nomadic peoples of the Plains had had little exposure to settled white society and its values. All the same, the government in Ottawa moved quickly to impose its authority over the Plains tribes, since it was eager to have them safely on reserves and out of the way of the Canadian Pacific railway then under construction and of the wave of white settlers expected to move into Western Canada in its wake. Negotiated treaties with the affected Indian peoples, securing their agreement to move to reserves, were coupled with the creation of a frontier police force, the North-West Mounted Police, whose main job was to make sure the Indians remained peaceful. When these measures proved insufficient in 1885, and mixed-bloods and some of the reserve-bound Indians rose up in revolt, the government was obliged to send militia west to put out the fire.[17]

One of the major differences between Canadian and American policies towards Indians and those of Mexico was that relations of the former with Indian peoples were based on treaties which recognised the 'distinct legal character' of Indian tribes and nations. This Anglo-Saxon tradition drew upon British precedents. The Mexicans, however, whose inspiration was Spanish colonial practice, worked from much different premises. The Spaniards had from the beginning of their penetration of the Americas

> branded the *indios* as *gente sin razón*, that is, primitives apparently impervious to European rationales. They stubbornly held, into the twentieth century in Mexico and other places, that Indians were incapable of managing their own affairs, even with the evidence of the Aztecs and Incas lying all about them.[18]

As a result, the Spanish never entered into treaties with the Indian tribes they encountered, and never allowed them much in the way of 'residual legal independence'. On the other hand, it bears noting that, 'even when they reduced the Indian population to a state of practical dependency or oppressive servitude', the Spanish and other Latin powers who established empires in other parts of the globe were prepared to promote intermarriage and to facilitate assimilation with indigenous peoples, wherever they set foot, to a much greater extent than the Anglo-Saxon powers.[19]

PART I

Doctrine

It is notorious that none of the New World armies under scrutiny here developed anything like a doctrinal approach to irregular warfare, including Indian fighting, during the nineteenth century.[20] Only in the United States, however, has this doctrinal vacuum been deemed a subject of pressing historical importance. This may have something to do with the current obsession with 'doctrine' among US military reformers, which stems largely from the widely held belief that the setting out of a rational and effective 'warfighting doctrine' was key to the restructuring of the US Army in the aftermath of US defeat in the Vietnam War.

For Russell Weigley, reflecting back on the phenomenon from the vantage point of that US defeat in Vietnam, the problem was not so much the US Army's indifference to 'doctrine' per se as its refusal to

> Contemplate seriously the prospect of any kind of war except conventional warfare in the European style. When the Army has nevertheless had to participate in unconventional, insurrectionary, or guerrilla war, the experiences soon have been dismissed as aberrant. Indeed, throughout a long history of warfare against the North American Indians, the Army never bothered to develop a doctrine fitted to the particular problems of Indian war as such conflict differed from European war; even in the wake of George Armstrong Custer's disaster on the Little Bighorn, the preoccupation of the Army's nascent professional school system was with Europe.[21]

In other words, the culture of professionalism regnant in the nineteenth century US Army demanded a focus on fighting 'real wars', i.e. European wars. Earlier, Weigley had argued that the Army's bias against small wars doctrine was rooted in the culture of American society. '[G]uerrilla warfare is so incongruous to the natural methods and habits of a stable and well-to-do society', he wrote, 'that the American Army has tended to regard it as abnormal and to forget about it whenever possible. Each new experience with irregular warfare has required, then, that appropriate techniques be learned all over again.'[22]

Other participants in the debate over doctrine have eschewed the 'cultural' perspective of Weigley for less abstract explanations. Clyde R. Simmons accepts that the Army consciously refused to devise a doctrine for fighting Indians, but puts the refusal down to an instinct for self-preservation. The Army, he writes, realised that in the eyes of the American public 'Indians posed only a minor regional threat', a 'modest . . . threat' that, in fact, would soon disappear. Because of this, most Americans, including members of Congress, were largely indifferent to the Army's western campaigns and provided only enough support and money to keep the military effort in the West alive. If the Army wanted to grow and thrive as the kind of professional force its staff officers in particular believed it to be, then, it was imperative that it shed its timeworn image as 'a largely constabulary force and [begin] to see its future as [one] oriented on external threats'. But what threats? Since there were no obvious foreign threats on the horizon, Simmons suggests, they had to be imagined, and the only possible imagined threats would be those coming from European powers.[23] But, writes Jerry Cooper, despite the exertions of reformers like General Emory Upton, who argued that American national security required a large professional army on the Prussian model, most Americans continued to believe 'that the nation was secure for the immediate future from any outside threat' and so were not prepared to expand or alter the mission of the US military establishment.[24]

There has always been a school of thought that argues that Indians posed no real military challenge to the US Army and therefore that it was unnecessary to formulate any special doctrine for fighting them. Over thirty years ago, John M. Gates, in an influential piece called 'Indians and Insurrectos: The US Army's Experience with Insurgency', argued that while Indians were superb scouts and gatherers of intelligence and were 'widely known for their stealth and ferocity', they possessed only a rudimentary knowledge of tactics and no strategic sense at all. 'They fought as they did because it was the only way they knew how to fight, and their success in keeping in the field as long as they did resulted as much from the Army's meager size as from the Indians' prowess as warriors'.[25]

Thirty years on, American colonial historian Guy Chet is even more dismissive of Indian military capabilities and even more certain that conventional Western ways of war were sufficient to defeat Indians. Although Chet's critique of Indian military 'prowess' refers to the period of the colonial wars in America, it has broader application and merits being quoted at length.

> When Indian societies are analyzed on their own terms, [rather than as a means to critique European society] a more realistic image emerges . . . [which] reveals epidemic-ridden, impoverished peoples devoid of any of the advantages enjoyed by European armies ['stable bureaucracies', 'political unity', 'heavy investments in martial education', 'extensive and disciplined training in large formations', 'standardized weaponry', 'professional literature'].[26]

In other words, conventional warfare was quite sufficient to defeat Indians and thus no special doctrinal provisions were necessary.

Five years before Chet's book appeared, Andrew Birtle suggested that the debate over why the US Army failed to develop an Indian fighting doctrine might actually be a bit of a tempest in a teapot. Although the Army did not have 'an extensive, formal, written doctrine for the conduct of small wars', Birtle admitted, it had evolved an 'informal' doctrine composed of

> custom, tradition, and accumulated experience that was transmitted from one generation of soldiers to the next through a combination of

official and unofficial writings, curricular materials, conversations, and individual memories.

This 'informal' doctrine, Birtle maintains, worked well enough and, in any case, was probably the most that could be expected in the circumstances, since the Army lacked a 'formal system for generating doctrine' in the nineteenth century.[27] Just how effective this 'informal' dissemination of doctrine was, however, is open to question. We have seen Major 'Sandy' Forsyth avail himself of just such 'informal' advice on how to fight Indians before heading off to his rendezvous with the Cheyennes at Beecher Island, and then promptly ignore it, choosing instead to believe in the innate superiority of white men over red and his all-purpose genius as a West Pointer and veteran of the Civil War.

Military ethos

In a general comment on Western armies in the nineteenth century, Marcus Cunliffe observed that

> the spirit of the armies . . . was, within the officer corps, aristocratic (the French army was a partial exception), unreflective and deeply conservative. Stultifying years in garrison or on parade were interrupted by occasional popular disturbances or – for the British and French – by experience in small wars overseas, against militarily inferior opponents.[28]

Like their counterparts in the colonial armies of the European powers, soldiers of the New World armies who went off to the nineteenth-century Indian wars carried with them into the field certain perceptions of themselves, of the citizenry they fought to defend and of their adversaries, that had been imbibed at an early age, but that nonetheless deeply influenced their conduct in both peace and war. As soldiers, however, the Indian fighters of Canada, Mexico and the USA also acquired attitudes about themselves and their enemies from the specific cultures of the military institutions into which they had inserted themselves. In some cases, particularly with respect to officers, those attitudes, as we shall see, might be considerably at odds with prevailing sentiment in the society at large.

As the nineteenth century unfolded, white society in Mexico and North America adopted increasingly racialistic attitudes toward the Indian populations in their midst and across their frontiers. Among the Anglos of Canada and the USA, a bible-derived notion of the common ancestry and ultimate equality of all peoples had held sway in the early years of the century and had helped to shape the Indian policies of their respective governments.[29] In the 1820s and '30s, but especially in the 1840s, however, the white inhabitants of North

America increasingly came to subscribe to a belief in what was known as *polygenesis*, the notion of the separate and unequal creation of the various races. This theory, promoted by, among others, the so-called American School of ethnology, posited a hierarchy of races, with whites at the pinnacle and, unsurprisingly, 'redskins' at the bottom. A melding of this theory with the even more widespread idea that the 'character' of the races into which humankind was divided was not environmentally, but genetically, determined and that some peoples were therefore innately inferior and incapable of being 'civilised', seriously undermined any popular consensus that might have existed for government policies aimed at the 'improvement' of the Indian peoples and their eventual absorption into the general population. And, it heightened speculation that, without substantial adulteration by white 'blood', an unlikely prospect in view of the growing Anglo-Saxon aversion to racial 'mixing', the Indian peoples were doomed to extinction. As Dr. Josiah C. Nott of Mobile, Alabama, one of the leading genetical determinists, put it, with regard to the Cherokees and Chickasaws, so-called 'Civilised Tribes' of the Eastern woodlands lately removed to Indian Territory,

> Whatever improvement exists in their condition is attributable to a mixture of races. Their Chiefs and Rulers are whites and mixed bloods, and the full blood Indian is now what he always has [been] and always will be.[30]

'Scientific racism' so-called also gained ground in Canada during the early 1800s and provided a justification for the seizure of Indian lands in the Maritime Provinces and Upper Canada (Ontario). Here, however, the ideas that served as a basis for the new outlook tended not to be homegrown, as in the USA, but imported from Britain. For example, the Empire Loyalists and British immigrants who were beginning to take up land across the non-French-speaking areas of eastern Canada were much attracted to the new pseudo-science of phrenology, which sought to discriminate among the races on the basis of cranium size. Not surprisingly, phrenologists like the Englishman Charles White found the Caucasian race to have the most spacious crania and thus to be destined to rule over the other less fortunate races.[31]

Later in the nineteenth century, Social Darwinism, the notion that certain races of humankind, like certain animal species, were biologically incapable of keeping up with the pace of progress and thus destined for extinction, gained an audience among certain elements of European and New World society. Popular among imperialists as an explanation of Western hegemony over 'lesser breeds without the law', Social Darwinism achieved a certain vogue in those circles in the USA, for example, that sought 'scientific' proof for the long-held view that the Indian was incapable of 'civilisation' and thus doomed to become the 'vanishing American'.

Such racialist ideas probably had a greater impact on civilian society in North

America than on its armed forces, however. Isolation on the frontier no doubt had something to do with this, but so did soldiers' constant exposure to 'Indian-hating' frontiersmen, whose crudity and avarice hardly seemed to qualify them as a 'superior race'. In any case, alongside a few unrepentant bigots or self-professed Social Darwinists like 'Sandy' Forsyth, there were many officers whose attitudes toward the Indians they fought were, to say the least, ambiguous. William Skelton, in his seminal study of the officer corps of the US antebellum army, found that 'When they commented on the sources of Indian–white violence, regulars universally blamed frontier whites, whose dishonesty and greed for land subjected the Indians to intolerable stresses'. On the other hand, 'officers' unfavourable assessment of Indian nature also led many to regard the bloodthirstiness of the Indian as a factor precipitating violence'. Such 'contradictory themes often appeared in the same writings', Skelton found.[32]

Officers' attitudes toward Indians did not change much in the post-Civil War era, according to Sherry L. Smith's exhaustive account of the subject. '[N]either unconscionable exterminationists nor civilization's heroic saviors', army officers emerge from her study as 'complex, contradictory, and ambiguous human beings, caught in a morally difficult and often terribly bloody struggle for control of a continent'. Though there was 'no monolithic military mind' with respect to treatment of Indians, and, in fact, much criticism of the rapacity of settlers and the corruption and ineptitude of the US government, soldiers seldom 'took issue with the ultimate goals of policy or seriously challenged the assumptions about civilization and savagery that served as the intellectual underpinning of that policy'.[33]

One of the 'assumptions' that no US Army officer (or his counterparts elsewhere in the New World) seems ever to have questioned is that exposure to the principles of free enterprise and private property was the essential step in bringing Indian peoples to 'civilisation'. Most officers appear to have been oblivious or indifferent to the fact that whereas Indian peoples encouraged the accumulation of private wealth, they only respected those wealthy persons who made a virtue out of sharing their possessions and looking after the indigent. Officers also never came to grips with the fact that Indians as a rule had no concept of private property in land. The idea that their hunting grounds might be divided up among private individuals was entirely alien to the buffalo-hunting tribes of the plains. But settled agricultural peoples like the Yaquis and Mayas of Mexico also rejected the notion of private landholding. One of the main issues in the long struggle between these peoples and the white population of Mexico and Yucatán was Indian insistence on communal land ownership. Even George Crook, otherwise so sensitive to Indian ways of thinking, failed to take note of the fundamental differences between white and Indian economics. He believed that paying Indian scouts a regular salary would simultaneously ensure their loyalty and place them firmly on the path to civilisation. Farming, with its end-of-season economic rewards, he thought, would win over Apaches to reservation life, even such an inveterate opponent of the white man as Geronimo.

In 1884 he wrote that 'No sermon that was ever preached on the "Dignity of Labor" could print upon the savage mind the impression received when he sees that *work* means *money*, and that the exact measure of his industry is to be found in his pocket book'. What he apparently failed to realise – and this was a considerable oversight for someone as close to the Apaches as Crook – was the primordial importance to Apache males of opportunities to achieve and maintain warrior status. Proving oneself as a warrior, as he must have known, was the sole way to achieve distinction in Apache society. It was this, not the money, that made scouting for the white man desirable; growing hay and watermelons on the reservation, even if it made you rich, was no substitute.[34]

It was almost an article of faith amongst soldiers of the imperial age that 'savage' peoples would never live at peace or follow the path to 'civilisation' until they had been taught a lesson on the battlefield, given 'a good dusting', as General Horatio Herbert Kitchener, scourge of 'Fuzzy-Wuzzy' and the Boers of South Africa, put it so colourfully. In the same vein, US Army Captain Thomas Williams believed that only strong measures would lead to peace with the Sioux and Cheyennes. 'I'm not sure that good policy would not decide they should receive a sound thrashing first, and peace afterwards', he wrote to his wife on 11 July 1858. 'The Indians of the Plains are all alike, in that they have to be flogged into decency and flogged out of their predatory and murderous habits. . .'.[35] These views did not disappear as the century wore on. Lieutenant Walter S. Schuyler, one of General Crook's inner circle during the Apache wars in Arizona, wrote to his father on 6 July 1873 that 'The [Tonto Apaches on the reservation he had been put in charge of] act well enough as they have been well whipped, but the Yumas and Mojaves have not been thoroughly punished and . . . are the very worst bands in the country. . . . They can be ruled . . . only with a hand of iron'.[36]

How did enlisted men in the Old Army of the USA view their Indian opponents? Common soldiers tended to write less about their experiences than their officers – many, in fact, were illiterate – but we do have some memoirs of enlisted men in which they talk about their attitudes toward Indians. Prussian-born Eugene Bandel, who began his service in the US Army on the High Plains and ended up in the Southwest, took a generally dim view of the Indian foe. Commenting on the Mojave Indians of the California–Arizona border region, once again, Bandel said that their attacks on whites passing through the area had to be punished. 'The Indians in due course must either become civilized or be shot', he said.[37] Don Rickey, Jr., devotes thirteen pages of his indispensable account of the other ranks in the post-1865 US Indian wars, *Forty Miles a Day on Beans and Hay*, to an analysis of enlisted men's attitudes toward Indians. He concludes that, while private soldiers tended to agree with their officers that greedy white settlers were largely responsible for the outbreak of frontier warfare, they did not view Indian fighting as 'civilised' and therefore were loath to give much quarter to the enemy. A compound of fear for their own lives and experience of the torture or mutilation of fellow soldiers by Indians, their

PART I

attitude towards their foe tended to be harsher and less forgiving than that of their officers. Some no doubt subscribed to the frontiersman's dictum that 'The only good Indian is a dead one'. This view did not extend to all Indian peoples without exception. The Nez Percé Indians of the Pacific Northwest, for example, who were nearly all Christians and who had never killed a white person before war broke out with the US Army in 1877, were much admired by the enlisted men who fought them.[38]

Mexico

The *criollo* or American-born middle-class rebels who succeeded in overthrowing Spanish colonial rule and securing the independence of Mexico in 1821 were much imbued with Enlightenment principles, as transmitted through the filter of Spanish liberalism, and had enshrined those principles in the charter of the revolution, the Plan of Iguala (1821), and in the constitution of the new Mexican republic, adopted in 1824.[39] Thus, the corporate identities and hierarchical distinctions that had characterised Spanish colonial society were swept aside in favour of a mass society comprised of autonomous individuals. 'Racial, caste, and class distinctions were legally abolished, and all peoples were to enjoy equally the rights and responsibilities of citizens'.[40] The Plan of Iguala conferred citizenship upon 'all the inhabitants of New Spain [as Mexico had been called under Spanish rule], without any distinction between Europeans, Africans, or Indians'. The various state charters emulated the federal constitution of 1824 in extending citizenship to all inhabitants, regardless of race or social class. The constitution of the state of Sonora, enacted in 1825, for instance, defined as citizens 'all those born and resident in the state who have reached the age of 21 years or 18 years if married'.[41] These provisions were intended to extinguish, among other vestiges of the 'old regime', the communitarian identities enjoyed by the various Indian peoples of Mexico, which the liberal leadership of republican Mexico believed had 'kept the Indians segregated from Europeans, inhibited their learning Spanish, and prevented them from entering the "rational world"'.[42]

The revolutionaries also sought to extend the blessings of private property to all of the republic's citizens. This included the Indian peoples who up to then had held their land in common with the agreement of the Spanish colonial power. The great post-independence liberal intellectual and politician Lorenzo de Zavala believed that this had been one of the most retrograde policies of the Spanish crown, since it had prevented the Indians from acquiring 'the sense of personal independence which came from the "sentiment of property"'.

In the wake of uprisings by the Yaqui Indians of Sonora in defence of their tribal identity and common lands in the 1820s and '30s, Zavala argued that the 'nation must compel the barbarous Indians to settle down in regular communities, or, [in a reference to the contemporary clearance of Indian peoples from the eastern United States] like the North Americans, [force them] to leave the territory of the republic'.[43] Mexico's new constitution stipulated that the Indians' communal lands were to be divided up among the individuals tilling them. The state would guarantee these individual land titles in return for the payment of property taxes. Under Spanish rule, Indians had been exempted from taxes, instead paying tribute directly into the royal coffers.[44]

4

CHIEFS AND WARRIORS

Introduction

Warfare between Indians and whites in the Americas demanded certain qualities of the combatants, chiefs and warriors alike.[1] Indian leaders had to be brave but at the same time sparing of the blood of their warriors. They also had to be, as Napoleon liked his generals to be, 'lucky'. But luck among Indian peoples had less to do with the chance blessing of Fortuna than with powers bestowed by the spirit world: imperviousness to bullets, the ability to 'see' enemies across great distances. The chiefs of the white armies, the generals and colonels, also believed that leaders should lead from the front, but they knew as well that their civilian masters cared more about results than glory. Generals had to be good managers of resources and men, and if they were, the absence of dash and pluck might easily be overlooked.

The distance between leaders and led among the Indians they fought was much less great than white soldiers tended to believe. Paramount chiefs with authoritarian powers were few and far between among Indians in spite of white beliefs (and wishes) that it were otherwise, and the direct democracy that characterised Indian society was not left behind when war bands hit the trail. A leader who failed to devise an effective plan for a raid or who needlessly put his band at risk might be abandoned by his men in mid-campaign. And every warrior knew that if he performed brave deeds and could demonstrate that he possessed strong 'medicine', he could become a war leader and men would follow him. Thus, Napoleon's quip that each of his private soldiers carried a marshal's baton in his knapsack had far greater application to the typical Indian war band than to the white armies whose commanders so idolised the great Bonaparte. The distance between officers and men in the white armies, including that of the democratic United States, was a yawning gulf and few of the other ranks could hope for promotion to officer status. Nor did European American troops in the field ever experience anything like the every-man-for-himself democracy of the Indian war band. Officers, no matter how incompetent or foolhardy, had to be obeyed, and discipline could be severe. The prestige accorded to Indian warriors by their admiring people also eluded these unfortunates. For the most part driven into military service by personal misfortune or economic downturn, poorly paid, indecently housed and badly fed, common soldiers in the US Army often found themselves despised by both their officers and the public at large. That they fought as well as they did in such circumstances is remarkable. The other ranks in the Mexican armed forces, regulars and militia alike, were, if anything, even worse off than their US counterparts.

Indian leadership

Indian war leaders were not trained or otherwise specially prepared for their role. They tended to be men, although women war leaders were not unknown. Until fairly recently, little was written about the role of women in Indian warmaking. A prominent exception would have been Lozen, the sister and companion-in-arms of the great Warm Springs Apache chief, Victorio, and, after her brother's death at the hands of the Mexicans in 1882, of Geronimo. 'Her prowess as a warrior and her extraordinary ability to locate the enemy [even at great distances] earned her a legendary status among her people'. And, one might add, among whites of her time as well.[2] Although women warriors would appear to have been more common among the Apaches than other Indian peoples (or at least better studied), other examples of Indian women fighters can be cited. One of them, Yellow Haired Woman, took part in the battle of Beecher Island, charging the dug-in scouts four times along with fellow Cheyenne warriors, in a bid to kill herself out of grief for the loss of her husband in war the previous year. But, even though 'Each time she came back with more holes in her dress from the near misses of their bullets . . . there was no blood upon the garment'. Yellow Haired Woman went on to become a regular participant in Cheyenne war parties and a respected member of her husband's warrior society.[3]

Other Magpie, a Crow woman warrior, rode with the scouts from her tribe engaged by General George Crook during the Great Sioux War of 1876 (see Chapter 7). In the running fight between Crook's Crow and Shoshoni scouts and the Sioux and Cheyenne attackers who opened the battle of the Rosebud on 17 June, Other Magpie, 'armed only with a short belt knife and willow coup stick, broke the [Sioux] charge and counted coup on a [Sioux] warrior'. When the warrior subsequently was killed, Other Magpie scalped him. But, unlike Yellow Haired Woman, Other Magpie found her exploits acclaimed only by a female audience – which continues to recount her deeds in Crow circles – since male warriors refused to acknowledge what she had done.[4] This points up the fact that, despite the remarkable exploits of some women warriors, Indian warfare was very much a male world.

To be a warrior was a lifetime occupation for Plains Indian men, but most women who went to war did not pursue a warrior's life permanently. . . . The prestige system of the Plains cultures was clearly male-dominated, centering on warlike activities and personality traits considered masculine [and] the masculine prestige system was the measure for both sexes.[5]

The typical Indian chief, then, tended to be a man who had established a reputation for leading successful raids that also proved to be light on casualties. Drawing upon his own experiences, an Apache informant told the anthropologist Grenville Goodwin that war chiefs first had to prove themselves as raiders and then as leaders of raids to steal horses or weapons. The chief of a war party 'was always a man who knew about war, had gone many times and who was brave'. He didn't have to be anyone special in the tribe, a clan chief, for instance. 'He was just a common man.'[6] The Plains tribes were a bit more exacting in their requirements for leadership. Among the Crow people of Wyoming and western Montana, only warriors who had accomplished four prescribed battle feats could hope to become leaders of war parties. In order of importance these feats were: counting coup, i.e. striking an enemy with a weapon or a whip; cutting out an enemy's horse tied outside the door of his tipi; recovery of an enemy's weapon in battle; and riding down a foe.[7] The Sioux warrior's code said that although as many as four men could count coup on an enemy, the first one to do so got to wear an upright golden eagle's feather, while the last one to touch the enemy had to make do with a vulture feather hanging down. Killing an adversary in hand-to-hand combat counted as a coup and merited painting a red hand on one's shirt or horse. Saving a fellow warrior in battle and successfully scouting the enemy also ranked as meritorious actions among the Sioux.[8] It should be clear from the above that 'Nearly everywhere [counting] coup definitely outranked the killing of a man'. And even in those few tribes that did assign merit to killing a foe, doing it with a firearm was not considered valorous. Among the Plains Cree, for example, 'to use a club in slaying a man was worthier than to lay him low with firearms'.[9] But counting coup on a live enemy was, necessarily, a risky business. At the Battle of Platte Bridge in eastern Colorado in July 1865, a Southern Cheyenne warrior named High-Backed Wolf was killed when he turned back from a retiring war party 'and charged the soldiers near the post [at the bridge] in order to count coup'.[10]

But even if a warrior had passed tests of valour, it was unlikely that he would be accepted as a war leader unless he could demonstrate that he also possessed potent spiritual 'power' or 'medicine'. For there was a spiritual dimension to Indian leadership which was largely absent amongst its white counterpart. Most of the great Indian war chiefs were deemed to enjoy the blessings of the gods. Some great leaders, like the Sioux Sitting Bull, Roman Nose of the Northern Cheyennes, as we have seen, Big Bear of the Plains Crees or Geronimo among the Apaches, enjoyed as much or more esteem for their spiritual qualities as for their martial attributes. Indeed, Geronimo and Sitting Bull were not war chiefs in the traditional sense but shamans.

War 'medicine' derived from visions the warrior experienced as a result of prolonged fasts or, sometimes, simple dreams. These visions gave signs of impending success in battle or on a raid. They often involved creatures from the natural world who possessed qualities that would be advantageous in war. Such visions enabled a warrior to create a 'medicine bundle' containing items that reflected the contents of his vision and thus would bring him and his war band good luck, should he win approval as a war leader.[11] The Crow war chief Two Leggings carried a medicine bundle with him on raids which contained: a piece of blue cloth to bring luck; a herb bag to give his horse a second wind; an eagle's head to impart great powers of vision, flight and stealth; a swallow for power to evade the enemy; an otter-skin and eagle-claw sash to aid in pouncing on the enemy; and a bear's hair and claws to keep his horse fat and healthy.[12]

Some Indian peoples made sharp distinctions between civil and military leadership. The Comanches of the southern Great Plains, for example, recognised two sets of leaders, peace chiefs and war chiefs. Neither were elected or chosen but instead rose to eminence over time because of acquired reputations for wisdom and good sense in the first case and personal bravery and martial skill in the second. Wallace and Hoebel are right in observing that 'For [such] a warlike people this separation was quite remarkable'.[13] It was not, however, unique. The Creeks probably carried this distinction farther than any other Indian tribe. All Creek towns, some of which boasted as many as 1,000 residents, were designated as either 'war' or 'peace' towns, or in Creek parlance, 'red' or 'white' towns. 'Among all the southeastern tribes, the colour white symbolised peace and purity; red – the color of blood – represented war'.[14] But within each Creek town, even the 'white' towns given over to the arts of diplomacy and negotiation, a *Tustunnuggee* or 'Great Warrior' was selected by the paramount chief (*mico*) and the tribal council to prepare its young men for the eventuality of war.[15]

According to the Frenchman Louis Milfort, quoted earlier, what distinguished the Creeks from most other woodland tribes (and certainly from their counterparts on the western plains) was their willingness to fight as a collective unit, rather than a collection of individuals. Milfort's comments in this regard are worth quoting at some length. When the Creeks go to war, he said,

> they observe a very rigorous discipline. When they draw near the enemy, they walk in single file, the chief of the party at their head, and all manage to step in the footprints of the leader. . . . When they stop for a while or when they camp, they form a circle, and leave only one opening large enough for one man to pass through. . . . The chief is opposite the opening in the circle, which no soldier can leave without his permission. When it is time to sleep, he gives the signal and no one budges.[16]

The Shawnee people of the Old Northwest, who enjoyed close relations with the Creeks and, indeed, lived among them from time to time, also observed strict discipline on campaign. On the march out to enemy country, the war chief kept a tight rein on his men. War parties seem to have been divided into two groups on the basis of age and experience, with the younger, untried warriors doing the mundane jobs in the field, like keeping fires going and cooking. Conduct was governed by strict rules: warriors were forbidden to talk about women or home. Unlike the Creeks, however, the Shawnees ceased operating as a collective body once the arrows or lead began to fly. War chiefs could exhort their followers to fight as a unit, but had few means of compulsion at their disposal. Basically, war among the Shawnees was a matter of every warrior for himself once an ambush, the tribe's favourite battle tactic, had been sprung.[17]

Amongst the Plains Indians, the ability of war chiefs to exert control over their fighting men varied somewhat from tribe to tribe, but, generally speaking, discipline weakened considerably the closer a war party got to its goal. This was very much the case among the Comanches, the most powerful tribe on the South Plains. Any Comanche male theoretically could lead a war party, but unless he had established a record for bravery and leadership, he was unlikely to win a following. It was also important to have 'power', what we might call 'moral authority', which might derive from a vision or just a conviction that he could lead a successful expedition. All of the other men in the band would weigh the would-be leader's 'power' and decide as individuals whether to follow him or not.[18]

Once a Comanche war party had hit the trail, however, its leader was an 'absolute dictator': it was he who decided the goal of the raid, the route to be taken, where to camp and how long to rest, the tactics to be followed in the attack, and how the hoped-for booty was to be divided up. Only the leader could order a retreat or negotiate a truce. The men followed their leader without question: 'Each knew that a brave leader never asked of his men what he himself would not readily do'. Warriors also realised that dissension could put the war party in danger.[19] This harmony began to dissipate, however, as the war party approached the enemy. Whilst 'the leader planned the attack, when the battle began each man was free to fight according to the dictates of his own medicine and his personal inclinations'. This freedom of action could be counter-productive. There would be times when Comanche ambushes or surprise attacks failed because overeager warriors jumped the gun.[20]

The Yaquis

Of all the Indian peoples treated in this book, the Yaquis probably came closest to producing what might be called leaders of 'national stature'. Juan Banderas in the 1820s and '30s and Cajeme in the 1880s exercised effective control over Yaqui war bands and dictated military strategy. Their powers were far from unlimited, however. Councils of elders in the eight 'sacred pueblos' of the

Yaquis could – and did – veto leadership initiatives that were deemed too authoritarian. Banderas was reined in when he began to take on regal airs and Cajeme when he tried to interfere with the administration of justice.[21]

The Mayas

Although the generals who commanded Mayan troops ostensibly were chosen by popular election, they most often came from the ranks of the upper classes, the *batabs* or *caciques* who served as village or regional chiefs. The two leaders of the Mayan armies at the outset of the Caste War, Cecilio Chi and Jacinto Pat, for example, came from this sort of background. The table of ranks in the Mayan army closely followed that of the ladino armed forces. Thus, below the rank of general in the hierarchy of Mayan officers came that of *comandante* or major, then captain and lieutenant. Non-coms included sergeants and corporals.[22]

The Mayan military leadership seems to have gone in for more careful planning and organisation of its campaigns than that of most other Indian peoples. 'When [the Mayas] plan to carry out a raid, the main chief communicates his orders several days beforehand to the area whose warriors should form the section of operations.' The troops chosen are told when and where to assemble and given an estimate of how long the campaign will take. 'On the determined day they gather at the orders of their leaders, and these place themselves under the chief designated to assume command'.[23]

Military societies

Military societies were an integral component of the social structure of most of the Indian tribes covered in this book. Most of them performed police functions along with what appears to have been their main task, promoting what one specialist in the subject has called a 'martial ethos'.[24] Among some Plains tribes, the military societies enforced the rules of the buffalo hunt, for example, that everyone had to start hunting at the same time, and were charged with punishing those who infringed them.[25] Military societies sometimes had close religious associations. The Yaqui society, for example, was connected to the Catholic Church and its patroness was the Virgin of Guadalupe.[26] The army of the Mayan rebels in Yucatán in the 1880s was simply an outgrowth of the body formed to protect the priests of the Cult of the Speaking Cross.[27]

The best-known Indian military societies were those of the Plains tribes, whose characteristics were adoption of distinctive group names (such as the Crooked Lance Society to which Roman Nose belonged), going to war as a collective unit and celebrating warfare and individual martial deeds.[28] Of all the Plains Indian military societies, probably the most famous was the Cheyenne Dog Soldiers. Originally just an ordinary pan-tribal sodality or volunteer society, the Dog Soldiers acquired 'outlaw' status within the tribe in 1837, when one of their leaders, Porcupine Bear, murdered another Cheyenne in a brawl. As punishment, Porcupine Bear and those who chose to follow him were forced to camp apart from the rest of the tribe; eventually, the group became a separate band of the tribe and played a major role in the alliance which took shape in the mid-1800s with the Sioux. Intermarriage was common between members of the band and the Sioux; it will be recalled that Bad Heart, who counted coup on the Forsyth Scouts at Beecher Island, was a product of such a match.[29] Gradually, the Dog Soldiers' military prowess earned them a special position within the Cheyenne tribe, as unofficial defender of the tribe against the encroaching whites.[30] In fact, it might be argued that, as conflict with the US Army intensified in the 1860s, the Cheyenne tribe experienced the equivalent of a military takeover, as the Dog Soldiers increasingly dominated tribal councils.[31] What had earned them this special position was a reputation for extraordinary bravery. Symbolic of this was the practice of Dog Soldier warriors 'staking themselves out', anchored in one spot by a rope tied to a picket pin, and vowing never to leave unless dead or victorious. This kind of reputation meant, however, that the society would become a special target of the US military. On 11 July 1869, US cavalry, guided by Pawnee scouts, attacked the main camp of the society at Summit Springs, Colorado Territory, and killed 52 Dog Soldiers, including their leader, Tall Bull. The battle of Summit Springs proved to be the last time a Dog Soldier, one Wolf with Plenty of Hair, 'staked himself out'. The battle finished the society as a fighting force on the plains.[32]

The Indian fighters

Officer Corps

Military leadership in Mexico, Canada and the USA increasingly devolved upon men who had been specially educated and trained for the job, in the face of considerable public and even official opposition. By 1850, most ranking officers in the US Army were graduates of West Point, the national military academy. In spite of this, there were still strong currents of opinion in the United States that branded West Pointers as elitists and held that the best leaders were those who sprang forth from the people in times of need. Andrew Jackson, the 'border captain', was the *beau idéal* for Americans who held this view.

The transition from confidence in the spontaneity of popular militias to defend the United States to reliance upon a regular army, small to be sure but officered by professionals trained in a national military academy, was a slow and frequently contested process. As Timothy D. Johnson, biographer of General Winfield Scott, perhaps the antebellum era's supreme military elitist, has pointed out,

> Increased emulation of elitist European officers and a greater emphasis on specialised training reinforced the opinion that such developments

constituted a dangerous trend away from democratic principles. As Scott's own elitism and arrogance became widely known, average Americans increasingly viewed him as the embodiment of these evil tendencies.[33]

The struggle waged from within the army to make the force more professional faced its greatest challenge during the presidential administration of the epitome of the American self-made leader of men, Andrew Jackson. Many of Jackson's closest supporters wanted to do away with West Point, the fount of the evil they saw assailing the American military spirit. 'Pot-house soldiers and school-house officers' was the deprecating phrase used by the Jacksonian tribune, Senator Thomas Hart Benton, to portray the American regular army of his day.[34] Those Americans who subscribed to this view sought to place the militia at the centre of the United States strategy for defence and to rely upon heroic figures in the Jacksonian mould to spring forth from the people to lead the nation to victory when crisis loomed. Their allies within the military itself may have harboured reservations about the reliability of the militia, but they were not in two minds about the unsuitability of the West Pointers who increasingly held a monopoly on the leadership of the army.

We should be careful, however, not to follow the Jacksonians too far in equating elitism with a West Point education. Winfield Scott, perhaps the supreme egoist in an army historically renowned for its egomaniacs, had never darkened the doors of West Point. Nor should we assume that all of the US Army's prominent nineteenth-century general officers had graduated from the Point. 'Mad Bear' Harney, the most notorious if not the most famous of the antebellum army's Indian fighters, did not attend the Academy. A friend and protégé of Andrew Jackson, Harney was perhaps the last of the rough-and-tumble 'border captains'.[35] Robert Utley's candidate for the best of the post-1865 generation of Indian fighters, Nelson Miles, went straight from clerking in a Boston china shop to service in the Union Army in 1861. He rose rapidly through the ranks and came out of the war a major general of volunteers. His appointment as commander-in-chief of the Army in 1895 capped a brilliant career in the Indian wars but one marred by incessant feuds with West Pointers he believed were being unfairly promoted above him, particularly George Crook.[36]

What spoiled the professionals for their task, the critics said, was their slavish emulation of European military models, particularly the French. This struggle over the soul of the new American army assumed its starkest form in the long public row between generals Winfield Scott and Edmund Pendleton Gaines in the 1830s and '40s. Scott, translator of French military texts, friend of the Marquis de Lafayette and husband of a wife who spent as much of her life as possible in Paris, was belaboured by Gaines, an Indian fighter in the Jacksonian tradition, as one of the army officers

PART I

Who have acquired distinction only in the mazes of French Books, with only that imperfect knowledge of the French language which is better adapted to the Quackery of Charlatans, than the common sense science of war.[37]

Canada

In Canada, meanwhile, military leadership remained in the hands of British professionals until 1867, when the country became a self-governing dominion and Britain began pulling out its troops. Even afterward, the country's key military positions continued to be held by British officers, for example Major General Sir Frederick Middleton, commander of the Canadian force that suppressed the Métis–Cree uprising in Saskatchewan in 1885. Nationalist resistance to British command had been growing for some time, however, and, starting in the 1880s, a Canadian officer corps began to take shape. A Royal Military College was established at Kingston, Ontario, in order to supply officers to militia units and the 'permanent force', a small cadre of regulars set up to train the militia. But, as in the USA, the notion persisted that military leaders ought to come from the population at large rather than some military caste graduated from special schools.

Mexico

Mexico, too, had its national military academy, the *Colegio Militar,* located at Chapultepec near Mexico City and modelled, like the US Military Academy at West Point, on France's École Polytechnique. Schooling at the academy remained under the influence of the French long after this had waned in the USA. 'The uniforms of the cadets, as well as [those of] the rest of the personnel of the army, were patterned on French styles, and the list of textbooks used in 1886 showed an overwhelming French influence'.[38] But the French system did not go unchallenged in Mexican military circles. Victoriano Huerta, an 1877 graduate of the Colegio Militar and a future general and provisional president of the republic during the Mexican Revolution, argued in the 1880s that Mexican history showed that 'guerrilla warfare was the natural method of fighting in Mexico', and that, as a consequence, tactics and strategy 'based upon European textbooks might not always be suitable for a Mexican field commander'.[39] Another advocate of 'Mexicanisation' of the armed forces was the dictator Porfirio Díaz's nephew, Colonel Felix Díaz. Although a graduate of the Colegio Militar and an engineer, Colonel Díaz wanted to reduce the importance of artillery and fortifications in Mexican military thinking, on the grounds that Mexican armies had won their victories because of 'their fighting spirit and physical hardiness, and these advantages, combined with the understanding and intelligent use of the unique Mexican terrain, would win battles'.[40] In the end, however, this populist outlook, so similar to that voiced in Jacksonian America half a century earlier, failed to make much of a mark on Mexican military education. As in the USA once again, an element also surfaced in the Mexican army which favoured adopting the doctrine and way of war of the army of imperial Germany. This tendency, which was able to displace French influence in Chilean military circles at this time, did not prosper in Mexico, since its leading proponent, the head of the Colegio Militar, General Bernardo Reyes, came to be viewed as a potential rival by President Díaz and was sacked in 1906. In any case, the Germans were at a serious linguistic disadvantage in Mexico and, despite carving out a market for Mauser rifles and Krupp cannon in the country, were never entirely successful in unseating France as its major source of armaments.[41]

The Colegio Militar had been established to produce officers for Mexico's national army, but until the 1880s these were few in number and almost none commanded troops in the country's Indian wars.[42] Frontier military leaders were drawn largely from the *hacendado* class, big landowners like the Terrazas family of Chihuahua or the Pesqueira clan of Sonora. The troops these *caudillos* commanded were almost always state National Guard and local militia units, since for most of the nineteenth century the national army found itself too distracted by the constant struggles for power in Mexico City and threats of foreign invasion to take part in the Indian wars. In Mexico, as in the USA and Canada, the regular army had its detractors and the militia its champions, although the debate in Mexico was even more politically charged. Those who feared the army as a threat to popular rule, not a fantastic notion after all, tended to see the militia as a locally controlled, more democratic alternative.[43] Something of the same view adhered to the National Guard, which came into being during the 1850s and '60s, the years of the *Reforma* struggle. Recent scholars have been divided over the extent to which the Guard was a benevolent influence at regional and local level. Some see it as a guardian of local autonomy and popular sovereignty, while others contend that the Guard was created to 'ensure the dominance of "hispano–mestizo power"' over the Indians in the countryside.[44]

Yucatán

The general officers who exercised command over the Yucatán armed forces were, like their counterparts on the northern Mexican frontier, drawn from the state's great landholding families. The Acereto and Cantón families of the Vallodolíd region were typical examples. Both produced generals who led troops during the Caste War, although without a great deal of success.[45] Below the rank of general in the Yucatecan military hierarchy came the *comandante* (major), captain, lieutenant and subaltern. The comandante commanded the equivalent of a regiment, while the captain served as company commander.

PART I

Physiognomy of the US Army officer corps

The physiognomy of the officer corps of the nineteenth-century US Army – the Old Army – was more varied than the movies and popular histories would have us believe. While native-born graduates of West Point increasingly dominated the officer corps after 1815, foreign-born adventurers still accounted for a significant part of it, even in the declining decades of the nineteenth century. Most of these men had fought in the US Civil War (with few exceptions in the Union army), but they had also taken part in various European and colonial wars and thus possessed the broadest range of experience amongst US Army officers. The elements of the Seventh Cavalry that followed Custer to the Little Bighorn provide a particularly vivid example of this. The Irish-born Captain Myles W. Keogh, who commanded the right-wing companies of Custer's force at the 'Last Stand', not only fought in 34 battles in the US Civil War, but was before that a highly decorated soldier in the Papal Guard in Rome and a veteran of service in Algeria in the French Foreign Legion.[46] A fellow Irishman and close friend of Keogh's in the Seventh, Second Lieutenant Henry J. Nowlan, came from a family of soldiers. A graduate of the Royal Military Academy, Sandhurst, Nowlan served with distinction in the British Army in the Crimean War before emigrating to the United States and enlisting in the Union Army. He would not be at the Little Bighorn with his friend Keogh, however, as he was serving on detached duty some miles away with the campaign commander General Alfred Terry at the time.[47] The adjutant of the Seventh Cavalry and a close friend of Custer, Lieutenant William W. Cooke, was born into a family of Empire Loyalists in Canada. Because of his erect military bearing and long, Lord Dundreary-style side whiskers, Cooke became known as 'The Queen's Own' to his messmates.[48]

Lieutenant Charles C. DeRudio, born Carlo Camilio di Rudio near Venice, was the most colourful of them all. A former officer in the Austrian army turned Italian nationalist revolutionary, DeRudio had taken part in the abortive Orsini plot to assassinate the French Emperor Louis Napoleon in 1858. Saved from the guillotine by a plea to the French Empress Eugénie from his wife, DeRudio's sentence was commuted to life imprisonment on Devil's Island, the notorious French prison off the coast of South America, from which he promptly escaped, eventually coming to the United States. At the Little Bighorn, he took part in Major Reno's failed attack on the Indian village and was caught behind enemy lines. After a night in hiding, DeRudio managed to make it back to safety.[49] Truly one of history's great survivors.

Although some 400 US Army officers were killed or wounded fighting Indians during the nineteenth century, they were not the only officer casualties of the Indian wars. In his biography of General Ranald Mackenzie, Charles M. Robinson concludes that 'A review of the persona of the Indian Wars reveals a disproportionately large number of Union Army veterans with personality problems when compared with those who entered the service after the Civil

War'. Robinson goes on to argue that these personality disorders stemmed largely from the 'differences in military life' experienced by the Civil War veterans, especially 'having to face an enemy – the Indian – which many judged to be less than legitimate. . .'.[50] While there is no doubt a great deal of truth to this, it is probably not a good idea to exaggerate the extent to which the Civil War served as a kind of watershed in terms of officers' attitudes towards and reactions to service on the frontier. The frustrations of antebellum officers, in fact, seem remarkably similar to those felt by the Civil War veterans. Taught at West Point and elsewhere to covet glory in the Napoleonic style, they found fighting Indians a considerable comedown and in the course of the Second Seminole War, the nineteenth century's longest and most difficult Indian war, resigned their commissions in droves.[51] The responses of the antebellum officer corps to the indignity of being obliged to fight an enemy they considered much inferior to themselves were also very similar to those of their post-Civil War brethren. In some cases, they may have been even more extreme. For example, drowning one's sorrows in whisky was probably more common among frontier officers before the Civil War than it was after.

While there may have been more individual officers with personality problems in frontier garrisons after 1865 than there were before, it is doubtful that any exhibited greater mental instability than General William S. Harney (except, of course, for the subject of Robinson's biography, Ranald Mackenzie, who actually ended up in a lunatic asylum). Harney, who was obliged to quit the Army in 1861 (probably wrongly) because of alleged Southern sympathies, suffered from what looks very much like acute schizophrenia. (The great British historian of empire, James Morris, on the other hand suggests 'Perhaps he was a psychotic'.[52]) Known for his love of flowers and animals (he once burst into tears at the sight of a mistreated mule), the general's name was also a byword in certain quarters for vengefulness and cruelty. He came close to losing his commission in the early 1830s when he was brought before a civilian court for bludgeoning a female slave to death. One of his favourite pastimes while serving in Florida during the Second Seminole War was getting slaves and enlisted men to fight each other while he looked on.[53] During the Mexican–American War, knowing superiors handed Harney the job of executing the last 30 of a group of some 70 soldiers, members of the Saint Patrick's Battalion (many were Irish-born), who had deserted to the enemy, which he proceeded to carry out in his usual brutal fashion.

> [H]e arranged them in a line across the backs of wagons pulled side by side under a long gallows. With their arms and legs bound and nooses looped around their necks, the condemned men stood for two hours while their captors observed the battle [of Chapultepec] in the distance. . . . Harney had declared that as soon as the American flag appeared over Chapultepec they "will have seen the last of earth".

PART I

> When the Stars and Stripes appeared, he gave the order and the teamsters moved the wagons forward, leaving the prisoners choking to death.[54]

Later, Harney would transfer his talents to the Northern Plains, where he bullied a peaceful Brulé Sioux village into a near massacre,[55] and then to the Pacific Northwest, where in 1859 he did his best to turn a dispute between an American farmer and the Hudson's Bay Company over a wandering pig into a war with the British.[56] Admiring contemporaries may have called Harney 'Prince of Dragoons', but the Plains Indians he fought knew him as 'Squaw Killer' and 'Mad Bear'. General Ethan Allen Hitchcock left the Army after fifty years' service rather than serve under him.[57]

The nineteenth-century US Army was not alone amongst the armies of its day in producing officers who were loose cannons. Sir Garnet Wolseley, who led an Anglo–Canadian force across the Laurentian Shield to the Red River in Manitoba in 1870 (see Chapter 9), was a great colonial soldier, perhaps *the greatest* colonial soldier of the last half of the nineteenth century, but he was not a nice man. A snob despite his own modest antecedents, an inveterate racist and a closet praetorian, Wolseley also practised a rampant cronyism, which helped to divide the British officer corps of his time into competing 'rings' and thus discounted the value of attendance at Britain's nascent officer training schools.

Other ranks

United States

The common soldiers of the Old Army of the United States would be much more familiar to modern-day Americans than would its officer corps. Like their counterparts in today's US Army, they were all volunteers, generally came from the poorer reaches of society, and were frequently recent arrivals on American soil. In some years, in fact, the majority of US private soldiers came from immigrant backgrounds. This was particularly true before the Civil War. Whereas just after the War of 1812, around 80 per cent of recruits were native-born, by 1840 the figure had slipped to 54 per cent and, a decade later, to 40 per cent. Official data in 1859 showed that foreign-born recruits accounted for about 9,000 out of a total strength of some 16,000 men in the US Army.

> The Irish element . . . predominates, and next to it, the Germans. It is estimated that we have over two thousand ex-English soldiers in the army and marine corps, besides a large number of Prussians, French, Austrians, Poles and natives of every other European state.[58]

After the Civil War, the proportion of immigrant to native-born recruits declined somewhat. Over half of the enlistees in the Army from 1865 into the 1890s appear to have been born in the United States. Still, 'So many Irishmen were included in the ranks of the Regular Army that General Charles King, the most popular contemporary writer on the subject, repeatedly used the old-line Irish soldier as a stock character'.[59]

Living conditions for common soldiers in the frontier forts were never very good and were sometimes deplorable. During a tour of Western army posts in 1866, General William Tecumseh Sherman, the new commander-in-chief of the US Army, said, "Surely, had the southern planters put their Negroes in such hovels, a sample would, ere this, have been carried to Boston and exhibited as illustrative of the cruelty of the man-masters'.[60]

Service in the Old Army was hard for common soldiers at the best of times. Pay remained low during the whole of the period under review here. Accommodation, as we have just seen, was often shockingly bad. So was the food. The discipline to which the infantry soldier or cavalry trooper was subjected was often arbitrary and frequently cruel. It is perhaps understandable that civilians who knew about conditions in the army might wonder what manner of men would be prepared to put up with them and draw unflattering conclusions.[61] The following lament from the pages of the *Army and Navy Journal* makes clear how great was the lack of public esteem for soldiering in the years after the Civil War, the so-called Gilded Age.

> The people at large seem to think the Army composed of fugitives from justice, and whenever they hear that a neighbor's son has enlisted, break out into ejaculations of pious horror. The name soldier, as they use it, seems to be a synonym for all that is degrading and low, and whenever they meet a person bearing it they cannot forbear showing their contempt.[62]

Charles King wrote that when in retirement during the same period in his native Milwaukee, Wisconsin, he had often been asked by army veterans for help in finding civilian jobs. But he had very little success and a businessman finally told him why. 'You see, it's this way', the man said. 'We naturally reason that a man couldn't have been of any account if the best he could get for himself all these years was a job at soldiering'.[63]

Training

None of the New World armies of the 1800s provided much in the way of training for their troops until relatively late in the century.

Canada

The militia who made up the bulk of Canada's land forces after the departure of most of the British garrison in 1871 enlisted for three years' service and were expected to attend a twelve-day training camp each summer. In practice, only the smart city militia battalions attended annual summer camps. Rural battalions only gathered every other year for training. 'Training', wrote Desmond Morton, 'was simple and repetitious'. Drilling occupied much of the men's time, although there was also usually a trip to the shooting range to fire 30 rounds or so from their cast-off British rifles, and sometimes a mock battle or ceremonial review to wind things up.[64]

Mexico

The conscripts who made up most of the Mexican national army received little training in the fundamentals of their trade, but since many of them were serving under duress, as we have seen, morale was very low and it is doubtful that training would have had much impact on performance in any case. This began to change somewhat with the greater professionalisation of the army in the time of President Díaz in the last quarter of the century.

The state militias, who bore most of the burden of frontier defence from the 1830s to the 1880s, were supposed to receive training from local cadres of the regular army, but this was cursory at best. Most militiamen probably acquired most of the military skills they possessed from what they learned on the job, pursuing Indian raiders or participating in the revolutionary upheavals of the first half of the century, in the armies of the regional caudillos who dominated Mexican provincial politics.[65]

United States

The US volunteer army, meanwhile, provided thorough training for those of its officers who passed through the national military academy at West Point, but the training of its other ranks, in the artillery, cavalry and infantry, was rudimentary at best. The general practice until late in the century seems to have been to assume that recruits would learn their trade on the job. The recruit depots to which volunteers reported were often nothing more than way stations on the road to active duty. Recruits might be issued uniforms there, learn the manual of arms or receive some instruction in how and when to salute, but there was no guarantee of even this sort of slapdash training. The amount of time recruits spent at the depots depended entirely on how quickly their services were needed on the frontier. And, given the small size of the army throughout the Indian wars and its high rates of wastage due to illness and desertion, the need for fresh troops was often acute. The result was, wrote the Secretary of War John B. Floyd in 1858, that units frequently received new men who 'have no earthly idea of the duties they will be called on to perform or of the discipline they will be required to undergo'.[66] It might have been expected that with the Civil War experience under their belts, the US government would have taken steps to improve recruit training after 1865. This was not the case. As late as the Great Sioux War of 1876–7, it was not unusual for cavalry recruits who had never been on a horse to show up for duty at Western army posts.

> [Jacob] Horner and 77 other Seventh Cavalry replacements went out on campaign with the regiment about one month after enlistment, including one week of waiting at Fort Snelling, Minnesota. None of these men had been trained in horsemanship, and none had received any instruction in the use of their arms. Several died with Custer, June 25, 1876.[67]

Recruits, as we have just seen, often went into the field to fight Indians without ever having fired a shot, in anger or otherwise. Even when there was time for some training in marksmanship, it might be passed over in favour of other duties. To start with, the various forms of instruction – drill, marksmanship, horsemanship – required officers to dispense them, and there were never enough officers in the US frontier army. Also, some officers dismissed target practice as a waste of scarce ammunition. The officers were right: ammunition was scarce, thanks to Congressional parsimony. When weapons were issued to the troops, even new items like Gatling guns and breech-loading rifles, there was never enough ammunition to train the soldiers in how to use them. Of course, this penny-pinching backfired when untrained troops were sent into combat. Unschooled in marksmanship and unnerved by being in close proximity to an actual enemy, they tended to fire at will and indiscriminately. On the second day of the battle of the Little Bighorn, the besieged Seventh Cavalry troops under Major Reno's command had to be ordered to fire only when their officers told them to, 'because most of them were unable to hit a hostile and merely wasted their ammunition'.[68]

This lack of training and proper preparation of troops for combat can only be taken as a further indication of the indifference of the US government and the army leadership toward Indian fighting. The recruits who went West with so little preparation were fortunate that the Indians were few in number and therefore tended to avoid combat whenever it was not to their advantage. And, if they often had too little ammunition to practise marksmanship, their Indian opponents had even less and, with a few exceptions, were just as poor shots as they were. The American regular who fought Indians in the nineteenth century was also fortunate that hand-to-hand combat occurred as seldom as it did. The cases of close combat between US Army troops and Indians do not reflect well on the bluecoats. Percival Lowe, who served as an enlisted man with the Army in the West in the antebellum years, wrote that Indians 'had learned enough to convince them that the superiority of the soldier was in his arms, not in his horsemanship . . . nor in his strength and prowess as a warrior'.[69]

PART I

Fear

New World soldiers would have understood implicitly and fully agreed with the sentiments expressed in this often-repeated verse from the bard of British imperialism, Rudyard Kipling.

> When you're wounded and left on Afghanistan's plains,
> An' the women come out to cut up what remains,
> Jest roll to your rifle and blow out your brains,
> An' go to your Gawd like a soldier.[70]

Although it was a crucial factor in the nineteenth-century wars waged across the globe against so-called 'savage' opponents, the word 'fear' doesn't appear in the index to Callwell's primer for the colonial soldier, *Small Wars*. Nor is it often the subject of close analysis by historians of, for example, the wars fought in Africa against tribesmen such as the Hadendowa of the Sudan (Kipling's 'Fuzzy-Wuzzy') or the Zulus, or in the American West against foes such as the Apaches, Comanches or Sioux.[71] And yet fear was often palpable in confrontations between Indians and the Indian-fighting armies in the New World (not to mention settlers on the frontier) and in some cases spelled the difference between defeat and victory. What made Indians so frightening to whites was the belief that as 'savages' they did not respond to the finer sentiments of civilised society such as honour, fair play, kindness to the less fortunate (such as prisoners or the wounded), and protectiveness towards women and children.

Although not all Indian peoples indulged in torture or scalped or otherwise mutilated their victims, Americans (and to a somewhat lesser extent Canadians and Mexicans) routinely assumed that they did and seem to have imbibed with their mothers' milk a certainty that death was a blessing compared to being taken alive by Indians. Like Kipling's young soldier in Afghanistan, they were prepared to commit suicide rather than fall alive into Indian hands. 'Save the last bullet for yourself', was standard advice to new recruits in American Indian-fighting armies going all the way back to the colonial era. Frontier women received the same advice; some carried poison in amulets or pouches around their necks, which they were urged to take in the last extremity in order to spare themselves 'a fate worse than death'.[72] Indian raiders were almost routinely accused of raping settler women, despite strong taboos against it among many tribes, including the much-feared Apaches. Warriors in most tribes underwent purification rituals before going to war or on raids, in order to acquire the kind of 'medicine' they believed would bring them success in the field. For most of them, sexual intercourse or even thinking about it whilst on the warpath was one of the surest ways to dilute the power of one's 'medicine'. The Comanches, legendary raiders on the Texas frontier and deep into Mexico, were one of the most noteworthy exceptions to this rule.[73]

It wasn't only 'tenderfeet' like eighteen-year-old Sigmund Shlesinger, one year away from the sidewalks of New York City and suddenly confronted at

Beecher Island in the wide open spaces of Colorado by several hundred painted, whooping warriors, who were 'terrified' by Indians. Andrew Jackson's Tennessee militia, another of those bands of 'hardy frontiersmen', broke and ran at the battle of Enotachopco Creek in Alabama in 1813 at the sight of nearly naked, black-and-vermilion painted Creek warriors, 'the monster too hideous to be withstood', boiling out of the brush after them.[74] The successful stampeding of their horses by Sioux warriors so terrified the troopers of Lieutenant James Calhoun's L Company of the Seventh Cavalry, holding the line south of Battle Ridge at the Little Bighorn, that 'The soldiers behaved just like a herd of buffalo shattered into panicked bunches by a force of yipping, shooting Indian hunters. Like buffalo, the soldiers fell by the dozen and then by the score.'[75]

Of all the Indian peoples of North America, however, it was probably the Apaches of the Southwestern borderlands who inspired the greatest dread among white opponents. The following example of the kind of terror the Apaches evoked merits recounting at some length. First Lieutenant David N. McDonald of the US Fourth Cavalry recalled that in the course of pursuing Apache raiders in 1882 his troop came upon two prospectors in the New Mexico mountains. Apparently, the two men mistook McDonald's Apache scouts for 'hostiles'. 'To say that they were frightened out of their wits would not convey any idea of their condition', McDonald later told a reporter.

> These two men ran in circles, with their hands, jaws and apparently the very skin of their bodies shaking and quivering, the guns in their hands oscillating like the hands of a palsied person. Perspiration in huge drops ran down their faces, hair and beard[s], and they were utterly incapable of making the slightest defense. Although I stood before them in my blue uniform and spoke to them, telling them who we were, it was several moments before they seemed to realize they were not to be massacred.[76]

Fear of Indians often provoked collective hysteria as well. One of the most striking examples occurred in the new state of Wisconsin in the aftermath of the Sioux uprising in neighbouring Minnesota in August 1862. In the eastern part of Wisconsin, hundreds of miles away from the fighting, 'At the cry "The Indians are coming!" farmers left their harvesting, loaded their families into wagons and took to the roads in search of security'. Some 4,000 flooded over the single drawbridge into the town of Sheboygan, on the shores of Lake Michigan, 'but later arrivals found the bridge up, it having been raised to keep the Indians out'. By 14 September the terror had reached Milwaukee in the extreme southeastern corner of the state and 'all that day and night an unbroken string of teams and wagons passed through [the suburb of] Wauwatosa, seeking refuge in the city'.[77]

Indians, too, had a horror of what might happen to them at the hands of their white captors. Their greatest fears were of execution by hanging and being

PART I

locked up in prison. Many Indian peoples believed that the bodies of the fallen were reborn in the spirit world in the condition they were found in after death. Thus, a warrior who died on the scaffold would travel through eternity with the broken neck and ghastly countenance of the hanged man. Being put in prison also inspired dread. The two Cree leaders locked away for their alleged role in the North-West Rebellion in Canada in 1885, Big Bear and Poundmaker, had to be freed early due to illness and died not long after.[78] The Kiowa war chief Satanta jumped to his death from a top-story prison window in 1878 rather than endure a second stint in a Texas penitentiary.[79]

Weaponry

The slow pace of innovation in the armament of its frontier troops once again reflected the general lack of interest of the US government and army leadership in the Indian wars. Compared to the European imperial powers, for example, the US was slow to adopt such modern weapons as magazine rifles, machine guns, smokeless powder and quick-firing artillery. The French armed forces were the first to adopt a magazine rifle for standard use, the 11 mm Gras-Kropatschek, in 1885.[80] On the insistence of their commander, Colonel Joseph Gallieni, marines fighting in West Africa were the first French troops to receive the new rifle.[81] The US Army, meanwhile, would not choose a magazine rifle for use by its troops, the Danish-designed .30 calibre Krag-Jorgensen, until 1893, when the Indian wars were over and the army was beginning to gear up for European-type war.[82] A similar lag operated with respect to automatic weapons. Although the Gatling gun was invented by an American, European troops made much more use of it in their colonial campaigns than did the US Indian-fighting army.[83] The US Army was particularly slow to introduce the kind of innovations in artillery that European colonial armies were taking advantage of in Africa and Asia by the 1880s, for example quick-firing guns.[84] Although smokeless powder had been in general use among European artillerists since the 1880s, the big guns fielded by the US in the Spanish–American War in 1898 were still using black-powder ammunition, which might have been all right for fighting Indians, but was a major liability in combat against European armies capable of counter-battery fire.[85]

Infantry armament in the US Army changed little from the time of the American War of Independence down to the 1840s. Although efforts were made to introduce rifles into more general use in the army – skirmishers and ranger units had been carrying them since the eighteenth century – the smooth-bore .69 calibre flintlock musket remained the standard infantry shoulder weapon until the introduction of a percussion cap fired smooth-bore in 1842. This innovation, however, was quickly superseded by the advent of a small revolution in infantry weaponry, inspired by the invention of a French infantry captain named Claude-Étienne Minié. In 1849 the captain patented a new shoulder arm whose ammunition would overcome the big obstacle to introducing rifling into the barrels of muzzleloaders: up to this point, unless soldiers held the weapon upright, the ball was likely to roll out of a rifled barrel. But Minié's rifle fired a bullet with 'greased grooves running horizontally around its base, which facilitated its loading into a rifled barrel. When fired, the skirts of the bullet expanded to fit the rifling, resulting in improved accuracy and range'.[86] Captain Minié's bullet ('minnie ball' to the Anglo-Saxons who adopted it) was made the standard ammunition for infantry shoulder arms in Britain in 1851 and in the USA in 1855; in the latter case, the 1842 model muskets were simply rebored to take the new round at .58 calibre.[87]

The shoulder arm most often carried by the militiamen who made up the bulk of the Canadian force in the North-West Rebellion of 1885 was the Snider-Enfield Mark III single-shot breech-loader. The Snider had first been issued to British troops in the late 1860s and had seen extensive use in imperial warfare. By 1885, however, only troops in the colonies like Canada's militia were still using it. (Canadian military historian Desmond Morton refers to the Sniders carried by the militia as 'worn out, obsolete'.)[88] The British army had moved on to a new shoulder weapon, the Martini-Henry breechloader used in the Zulu War of 1879. Some of the Canadian militiamen, however, had been equipped with the American-made Winchester Model 1873 rifle, one of the most popular shoulder arms of the era. The fast-firing lever-action Winchester was a favourite of both Indian and white combatants in North and South America. The North West Mounted Police who marched alongside the militia were carrying an even more impressive weapon, the magazine-fed Model 1876 Winchester carbine. The carbine's magazine held nine rounds and it could fire a round every two seconds.[89]

Over the first three-quarters of the nineteenth century, Mexico's armed forces were equipped with the cast-off weapons of European armies, mainly the British and French. The 'Brown Bess' flintlock musket, the standard British shoulder arm from the mid-eighteenth century until the Napoleonic wars, found its way into Mexico in large quantities after independence. These would have gone primarily to units of the regular army. Army reservists and state militiamen were often required to provide their own weapons and many of these would have been shotguns or ancient blunderbusses.[90] The 'Brown Bess' also featured prominently in the Caste War in Yucatán, given the brisk trade in guns and ammunition with both sides in the war by merchants in British Honduras.[91]

The weaponry of the Mexican armed forces began to improve during the tenure of the dictator who ruled Mexico from 1876 to 1910, Porfirio Díaz, a former army general. During the 1880s the United States became the main purveyor of armaments to the Mexican army. The infantry were equipped with .43-calibre Remington rifles, the cavalry and artillerymen with .50-calibre Remington carbines.[92] Just a decade later, however, the government decided to diversify its sources of military weaponry. The Remington gave way to the 7 mm Spanish-pattern German Mauser as Mexico's standard infantry shoulder

PART I

weapon. The bolt-action repeater version of this rifle began to be imported in large numbers in 1895, and the Remingtons would subsequently be fobbed off on militia and reserve troops.[93] But there was also an effort at import substitution, by trying to manufacture weapons at the *Fabríca de Armas*, the national armoury near Chapultepec, which had been producing much of the nation's supply of gunpowder since earlier in the century.[94]

Mounted warfare in the New World was given something of a fillip by the appearance in the 1850s of the Colt revolver, the 'six-shooter' of Wild West fame, as 'Rip' Ford, the old Texas Ranger, told the artist Frederic Remington in 1896. Had he ever been charged by a Mexican lancer, Remington asked Ford. Ford admitted that he had been, 'many times', but it had never worried him too much, because 'I reckoned to be able to hit a man every time with a six-shooter at one hundred and twenty-five yards'.[95] This was a Texas 'tall tale', which may or may not have taken in Remington, the Eastern 'tenderfoot'. Ford would have been hard-pressed to see clearly, much less hit, a target with a revolver at such a distance. What the Rangers and, soon, their Indian foes actually used pistols for was close-in shooting, what the Texans called 'powder-burning', since it was very difficult to hit foes with a revolver from a moving horse unless you were right on top of them.[96] Despite these limitations, the Colt and the other types of revolvers that quickly came on the market proved to be useful additions to the arsenal of weapons available for mounted warfare, and pistol duels among horsemen soon became a feature of Plains warfare.

While all three armies under study here fielded artillery in the Indian wars, the big guns for the most part played a decisive role only in those rare instances when Indians decided to sit still in one place or shut themselves up in fortified positions. The latter seems to have happened most often in Mexico. The decision of the Yaqui leader Cajeme in the 1880s to defend the newly declared 'Yaqui Republic' from behind a network of forts played into the hands of the Mexican army, whose academy-trained officers were skilled in the use of artillery.[97] In the 1890s, the drystone barricades which Mayan insurgents had used so effectively for so long to thwart attacks by the Yucatecan National Guard proved no match for the new Krupp cannon of the Mexican army.[98] Mexican artillery prowess came to the fore only towards the end of the 1800s, however, when President Díaz, once again, saw to it that his country's army was equipped with modern guns, German Krupp and French Saint-Chamond and Schneider breech-loading cannon.[99] Elsewhere, artillery only occasionally had a decisive impact in battles between whites and Indians. One such occasion was the battle of Apache Pass in July 1862, when an advance party of General James Carleton's California Volunteers used artillery to foil a Chiricahua Apache ambush. This seems to have been these Apaches' first exposure to artillery.[100] The big guns also proved crucial at the first battle of Adobe Walls in the Texas Panhandle in November 1864, where two mountain howitzers held off a large band of Comanche and Kiowa attackers long enough for Colonel

Christopher 'Kit' Carson to extricate his hard-pressed California and New Mexico militia and beat a retreat back to Santa Fe.[101]

Canadians carted along a lot of artillery in their campaign against the Métis and Indians in 1885. Two batteries of horse-drawn nine-pounder howitzers, nine pieces in all, from the Dominion's 'permanent force', accompanied the militia units west to the prairies. Some of these units also boasted artillery of their own, usually seven-pounder muzzle-loading mountain guns, designed to be disassembled and carried on packhorses. Though the big guns seem to have served some purpose in frightening Métis and Indians, they had only a limited role in securing ultimate victory for the Canadians. At the battle of Cut Knife Hill in May 1885, in which Cree Indians drove off Colonel William Otter's largely Toronto militia, both of Otter's cannons were put out of action when their wooden carriages collapsed.[102]

The colonial wars of the late nineteenth century coincided with the advent of machine guns, beginning with manual varieties like the Gatling gun and culminating in the fully automatic machine guns – Gardner, Hotchkiss, Maxim and Nordenfelt, to name only a few models – that began to appear in the 1880s. The hand-cranked, multi-barrelled Gatling gun made its debut toward the end of the US Civil War. It fired 350 rounds of .50 calibre rifle ammunition a minute through a bank of ten barrels fed by gravity from a drum or vertical clip.[103] Although it did see some service in the American Indian wars, many officers elected to give the weapon a wide berth. General Nelson Miles, for example, thought the Gatling was 'worthless for Indian fighting' because 'the range is no longer than [that of] a rifle and the bullets are so small that you cannot tell where they strike'.[104] Other commanders baulked at fielding the Gatling gun because of its penchant for jamming. Its black powder ammunition tended to foul the barrels, which affected accuracy and eventually shut down the gun altogether. Stoppages also occurred because of overheating, since there was no provision for cooling the weapon.[105] Finally, some officers complained that the Gatling gun was too heavy and cumbersome for use in fighting Indians, where mobility was a prime consideration. This concern lay behind Custer's much-debated decision to leave his four Gatlings behind when he set off for the Little Bighorn.[106] Historians can still be found who believe that this was 'Long Hair's' fatal mistake.[107] The Canadian militia took along two Gatling guns in their 1885 expedition to the prairies. The guns, recently purchased in the United States and served by an American volunteer (Captain Arthur L. Howard of the Connecticut National Guard, known affectionately to the troops as 'Gatling Howard'), saw some use in the fighting, for example by Colonel Otter's column in the Cut Knife Hill battle, but had little discernible effect.[108]

PART II

INTRODUCTION

Flux

The first six decades of the nineteenth century were a time of considerable flux in many parts of the world, as we saw in Chapter 1. Looking more closely at the New World, our attention is quickly drawn to the instability which gripped the three European American states at the centre of this study. The United States, of course, was troubled by sectional strife throughout the first half of the century, culminating in a great civil war between North and South. Mexico, meanwhile, suffered almost incessant upheaval, as Liberals and Conservatives, centralists and federalists, competed for power, with the military playing the role of arbiter. This chronic instability opened the door to predators near and far. In the Mexican–American War of 1846–8, the USA seized one-half of the territory of its sister republic, and in the 1860s the French were able to impose a foreign monarch upon the hapless nation for a time. British Canada, finally, experienced almost constant tension between its Anglophone and French-speaking populations. Unrequited demands for home rule sparked rebellions in Lower (Quebec) and Upper (Ontario) Canada in 1837. Although unsuccessful, the uprisings had much to do with Britain's decision to grant dominion status to the colony thirty years later.

But even these momentous events do not begin to describe the fluidity of the era. The United States experienced prodigious demographic movements during the period, by no means limited to its European American population. Although the bulk of attention in this regard has been lavished on the white pioneers who began traversing the Great Plains during this time, it should not be forgotten that almost the entire Indian population of the Eastern USA either moved voluntarily or was forced beyond the Mississippi River in the 1820s and '30s.

Consolidation

The flux that had characterised the history of the Americas in the first half of the 1800s abated considerably in the second part of the century, ushering in a period of relative consolidation. In Canada, the boundaries of the new Dominion were extended all the way to the Rocky Mountains in the stroke of a pen, through the purchase from the Hudson's Bay Company in 1869 of all the territory from Manitoba to British Columbia. In 1870 and again in 1885, the Canadian state defended its new acquisition against Métis and Indians for whom the takeover meant a definitive end to self-rule and their traditional wandering life on the plains. Canadian territorial consolidation, it also needs to be said, put paid to any plans the United States might have harboured to redirect the thrust of Manifest Destiny northward.

The USA embarked upon an era of prodigious national consolidation of its own after mid-century, preserving the nation's territorial integrity and dream of sovereignty 'from sea to shining sea' by stifling Southern separatism in a bloody civil war and then moving to effectively occupy the Western half of the country, much of it up to this point still populated by indigenous peoples. It needs to be borne in mind, however, that when the decisive decade of Plains wars began in the late 1860s a large proportion of the Indian peoples involved were resident on reservations under the terms of treaties signed with supposedly representative leaders. The image we come away with from films and TV programmes about the era, of Indian peoples roaming the plains at will, is only partially true. A fair number of the Sioux warriors who fought Custer at the Little Bighorn in 1876 were actually living on reservations in South Dakota and had come out for a few weeks to hunt the buffalo, as they were allowed to do under the terms of the treaties that confined them – as long as the buffalo still roamed the plains. The same was true on the South Plains. The Comanches sought by the army in the Red River War of 1874–5 represented a remnant of the tribe, the greater part of which was confined on a reservation in the Indian Territory. The census of 1890, which announced the closing of the frontier and prompted Frederick Jackson Turner to write his seminal essay, 'The Significance of the Frontier in American History', taken together with the suppression of the Sioux Ghost Dance movement at Wounded Knee, South Dakota, in the same year, marks the terminal point of this process of consolidation.

In Mexico, the coming to power in 1876 of the dictator General Porfirio Díaz opened an era of unprecedented stability and economic development, albeit purchased at a high cost to the country's lower classes and indigenous peoples. For the first time, political power was effectively centralised in Mexico City. The regional bosses, the *caudillos*, were effectively reined in and deprived of control over local militia and National Guard units, which they had employed as virtual private armies. The national army, too, was brought under central control and its energies directed away from meddling in politics to quelling the Yaqui and Mayan revolts whose distant origins were traced in the preceding chapter. The army, aided by a new national rural police force, was largely successful in this endeavour, although in the case of the Yaquis it was found necessary to engage in a campaign of virtual extermination in order to bring guerrilla warfare to an end.

5

THE 'GREAT CLEARANCE', 1815–42

Introduction

The North American theatre of the Napoleonic Wars, the conflict known to Americans and Canadians as the War of 1812, may have ended in a narrow military victory for the British, but for their Indian allies the war was an unmitigated disaster. Not only did the fighting cost the life of the Shawnee chief Tecumseh, architect with his brother Tenskwatawa of a great Indian confederation in the Old Northwest, an alliance against white encroachment that fell to pieces with his death, but it also brought ruin to the Indian tribe that was intended to serve as the southern anchor of Tecumseh's confederation, the Creeks.

Defeated in the bloody First Creek War (1813–14), this formidable people lost nearly two-thirds of their ancestral lands in what are now the states of Georgia and Alabama. Although some diehards would take refuge among their Seminole cousins in the forests and swamps of Florida, the power of the Creek people was definitively broken, and once Andrew Jackson, the man who had beaten them, acceded to the US presidency in 1828, their days in occupation of even a shrunken portion of their old homeland were numbered. A Second Creek War, a last-ditch effort to avert dispossession and emigration, was drowned in blood in 1836. Along with their ancient enemies to the north and east, the Cherokees, and to the west, the Choctaws and Chickasaws, they would be herded along a 'Trail of Tears' across the Mississippi River to the prairies of Indian Territory, in what is today the state of Oklahoma.

Farther to the north, Tecumseh's Shawnees also found themselves pushed across the Mississippi, along with the other tribes in their wartime confederation: Delawares, Kickapoos, Potawatomies. Among the last to go would be the so-called 'British Band' of the Sauk and Fox people, who, under the leadership of Black Hawk, would go to war in 1832 to retain possession of their lands in Illinois.[1] Their fighting retreat northward across Wisconsin Territory would end in disaster on the banks of the Mississippi. These various peoples of the Old Northwest would also make their way to Indian Territory, from whence some of their number would wander into Mexico, where we will find them at mid-century collecting pesos from the Chihuahua authorities for bringing in Apache scalps.

Of all the Indian peoples of the Eastern USA, the ones who fought longest and most successfully were the Seminoles of Florida. The Second Seminole War (1835–42) proved to be the longest of the North American Indian wars and the most costly to the US government in blood and treasure. At its conclusion, most of the Seminoles had been removed to the Indian Territory as the government had sought, but a small band remained at large and unconquered in the depths of the Everglades, where its descendants still live.

Death blow

Cavalrymen usually avoided fighting in wooded areas. Dense foliage hampered vision and low-hanging limbs could sweep riders off their horses. Tight spaces made it hard to wield a sabre or bring a gun to bear. Because of these obstacles, horsemen were largely absent from the European or American orders of battle in the Indian wars of woodland North America. There were some significant exceptions to this pattern, however. The frontiersmen of Kentucky and Tennessee made a special effort to adapt mounted units for use in Indian fighting. With some success, too, as General William Henry Harrison, who used them to good effect during the War of 1812, could attest. 'The American backwoodsmen ride better in the woods than any other people,' he claimed. 'A musket or rifle is no impediment to them, being accustomed to carry them on horseback from their earliest youth.'[2]

And so it was that anomaly of woodland Indian fighting, an attack by mounted men, that would bring death to Tecumseh, the greatest Indian strategist of the age, and in so doing destroy whatever chance remained to forge a broad pan-Indian movement to stem the westward flow of American settlement. The Shawnee leader had travelled widely through what was left of Indian country east of the Mississippi, and even beyond, in 1811–12, in a bid to convince tribes ranging from the Creeks of the Southeast to the Osages of the prairies that it was imperative to make a stand against the Long Knives, that only by acting together could they hold on to what remained of their tribal lands.[3] Tecumseh had thrown in his lot with the British in the War of 1812, trusting in their word that they were committed to the creation of a great Indian homeland in the Old Northwest once the Americans had been defeated, and had led an army of Western Indians to their aid in resisting the American invasion of Upper Canada in 1813. Until recently, the common wisdom has held that Tecumseh was mistaken to come to the aid of the British, that London was unwilling to make Indian demands for the establishment of a 'Native State' in the Old Northwest a priority in the 1812 war.[4] This view lately has been challenged by Canadian historian Sandor Antal, who has shown that successive British commanders pledged 'that there would be no peace [with the Americans] until

Native lands were restored'. That the British Crown eventually went back on this pledge, in the Peace of Ghent which brought the War of 1812 to a close, does not mean, Antal argues, that the soldiers' promise was false.[5]

Now, as an American army under General Harrison brought the British to bay on 5 October 1813 at a place in the Ontario wilderness known as Moraviantown, the warriors of Tecumseh would be the mainstay of the redcoat army. General Henry Procter's small British force, cold, wet, hungry and short of ammunition, broke its retreat on open terrain amid deep woods just outside the Delaware Indian mission at Moraviantown, and deployed for action. Procter had only 877 British troops, mostly infantry of the 41st Foot, to pit against an American army of some 3,500. But he could also count on around 500 Indian warriors on his right flank, led by Tecumseh and positioned in a tangled wood between two swamps and sufficiently forward that they would be able to rake both the left flank and the front of the oncoming Americans. Procter, meanwhile, posted his British infantry in extended order in two thin lines stretched across the open space in the woods, with its left flank resting on the Thames River.[6] It was their extended order that would be the undoing of the British infantry. For, unbeknownst to them, Kentucky horsemen had scouted their position and, having noted how they were deployed and how thin their lines were, had reported to General Harrison that the British would be especially vulnerable to mounted attack.[7]

The general had not wanted to attack, having so few regulars at his disposal, but under pressure from the Kentuckians, had finally agreed to launch an assault. As it turned out, this was a fortuitous decision. For its time, launching a mounted attack without infantry and artillery 'softening-up' may have been an unorthodox way to proceed, but it was the right tactic in the circumstances. In the age of the musket, the traditional way for foot soldiers to 'receive' horsemen was formed up in a square, as British infantry shortly would do at the battle of Waterloo. But Procter's men were unaware of the composition of Harrison's army and thus deployed in anticipation of what they had every reason to expect: an infantry assault. (To be sure, Harrison did have infantry, but they were mostly raw Kentucky militia and he might have been uncertain of their steadiness in the face of British regulars.)[8]

It was all over on the British part of the field in a matter of minutes. With visibility only about twenty feet because of the wooded terrain, most of the men of the 41st Foot never saw the Kentucky mounted infantry until the horsemen were on top of them. Over 600 of them surrendered; 43 were killed or wounded. General Procter and his entourage fled the field.[9] The most serious fighting of the day took place on the right flank of the British position, where the Indians of Tecumseh's party were posted. They were assailed first by a wave of Kentucky mounted riflemen under the command of Colonel Richard Mentor Johnson. The dilemma Johnson and his men now found themselves in serves to remind us of the limitations on the use of mounted troops in wooded areas. 'To their chagrin the Kentuckians found their horses floundering in impenetrable and swampy ground. Many of the riders dismounted to fight on foot, closing face-to-face with their opponents over logs and [brush]'.

Colonel Johnson himself, already badly wounded, was forced to dismount when his horse got entangled in the branches of a tree. On foot, he found himself face to face with 'a large but likely looking Indian' whom he subsequently claimed to have shot and killed. Although he was almost immediately evacuated to have his wounds tended and never saw the Indian's body again, Johnson would swear that the warrior he had shot was Tecumseh, a claim that would later help propel the Kentuckian into the vice-presidency of the United States (1837–41). Johnson was not the only person to claim to have killed the great Shawnee chief, however, and even today the Tecumseh biographer John Sugden, who has probably devoted more serious research to this question than any other historian, finds it impossible to say who the slayer was. All that is certain, says Sugden, is that Tecumseh was killed on the battlefield and that his death, when it was learned, completely demoralised the warriors of his multi-tribal party and led to their retreat, thus bringing the battle of Moraviantown to a close.[10]

Tecumseh's death, taken together with events unfolding in the war zone to the southeast, where the Shawnee leader's allies among the Creek people were engaged in a bloody war with another of the era's great American 'border captains', Andrew Jackson, would put paid to efforts to create a pan-Indian confederacy to forestall the expansion of the Americans and would ultimately make inevitable the enforced migration across the Mississippi of most of the Eastern Indian peoples. The first death blow to Tecumseh's dream of Indian solidarity was administered on the battlefield of Moraviantown in the beech forests of eastern Canada, as we have seen. The second and final blow fell on a spit of land caught in the loop of the Tallapoosa River in the pine woods of east central Alabama, where on 27 March 1814 Jackson and his army of Tennesseans, with crucial help from a contingent of Cherokee and allied Creek warriors, smashed the Creek confederacy in the bloodiest battle of the North American Indian wars.

The First Creek War, 1813–14

The Creek war against the United States in 1813–14 is best seen as a delayed reaction to white abridgement of Creek political autonomy, encroachment on Creek lands and undermining of the Creek system of collective land ownership, in which ways it resembled the Yaqui Indian upheaval in Mexico a little over a decade later (see next chapter). On the eve of the War of 1812, in which many of them would join forces with the British, the Creeks found themselves surrounded by white settlers on three sides. The Creek homeland in what is today northern and central Alabama and southern Georgia, a well-watered mixture of forest and grassland, had long been coveted by whites in the present-day states of Mississippi, Tennessee and Georgia.[11] White land hunger had intensified over the 1790s and into the early 1800s as a combination of the newly invented cotton gin and soaring international prices for cotton made cotton-growing a much more attractive business. The Creeks just happened to occupy a large portion of some of the best agricultural land in the South.[12]

Differing reactions to the growing American presence in the region had led to a bitter civil war amongst the Creek towns two years before the conflict with the US broke out. Although the Creek confederacy traditionally had been divided socially among clans and kinship groups, politically between Lower (eastern Alabama and southern Georgia) and Upper (northern and central Alabama) towns and militarily between White (peace) and Red (war) towns, the split which opened up in 1811–12 went even deeper.[13] At what seems to have been its most important level, the civil war represented a boiling to the surface of long-simmering discontent among the inhabitants of the Creek towns, especially those in the Upper Creek region, over the 'plan for civilisation' being pushed by the US government agent for the Creeks (1797–1815), Benjamin Hawkins. This 'plan' did not originate with Hawkins, having been articulated as official government policy towards the Indian population of the new United States as far back as George Washington's first administration, and was provoking similar divisions among the Indian peoples of the Old Northwest and among the Creeks' Cherokee, Chickasaw and Choctaw neighbours. Hawkins subscribed to the 'plan' with almost evangelical fervour and worked assiduously to implement it in Creek country.[14] The Indian agent, wrote Robert S. Cotterill, was 'outraged' by

> the Creek working combination of political anarchy and economic communism. With the typical American inability to tolerate noncomformity, he had set to work to refashion the Creeks in the American image by promoting a stronger governing authority and by encouraging the hitherto undeveloped idea of private property.[15]

The 'civilisation' programme aimed at putting in place a strong Creek tribal 'executive', composed of leaders who supported the 'plan for civilisation', and deepening and making permanent socio-economic changes already at work in the Creek country, particularly the Lower Creek towns, as a result of decades of trade and intermarriage with the whites of neighbouring Georgia and Mississippi Territory. What Hawkins sought to promote in the Upper Creek towns, up to this point less affected by interaction with white settlers than the Lower Creek area, amounted to a transformation of male hunters and warriors into yeoman farmers, growing corn and maize and raising cattle, chickens and hogs, and of female farmers into spinners and weavers of cotton cloth. In addition to rescuing the Creek economy from collectivism and awkward gender roles, these sweeping changes would, of course, considerably reduce the amount of land required to support the Indian population and thus open the way to white settlement of a large chunk of the Creek homeland.[16]

PART II

The Red Sticks

Resistance to white settler pressure on Creek lands and the plan being promoted by Hawkins took the form of what one writer has termed a 'sacred revolt', the sudden emergence and rapid growth of a nativist spiritual movement that urged rejection of American culture in all its manifestations and a return to the 'Golden Age' that presumably existed before the arrival of the white man.[17] This classic 'revitalisation' movement appears to have had its origins in contact between Creek shamans and the Shawnee Prophet and his followers. The impressions carried away from Prophetstown and propagated in the Alabama and Georgia towns by Creek pilgrims were reinforced by a visit by Tecumseh to the Creek homeland during his tour of Indian country in 1811. The Shawnee leader and his entourage introduced a new war dance to their Creek hosts, known as the 'Dance of the Lakes', which would enjoy great popularity, but, more importantly, Tecumseh seems to have left behind a powerful prophecy, that the anger of the Great Spirit with the corruption of his Indian peoples by contact with the Americans would shortly manifest itself in a great shaking of the earth.

Not long after his departure from the Creek country, on 16 December 1811, the massive New Madrid earthquake occurred in northeastern Arkansas. This most devastating earthquake in US history altered the course of the Mississippi River and produced tremors and aftershocks that terrified people as far away as the Cherokee towns in North Carolina. This seeming fulfilment of Tecumseh's prophecy greatly strengthened the nativist cause among the Creeks. 'If the earth shook', its leaders contended,

> It was because the Maker of Breath [Great Spirit] could no longer stand the evils that the Anglo–Americans forced on creation and on the people of the land. The Maker of Breath, the land, the cosmos, and the ancestors demanded that the Muskogee [Creek] people repel the invaders – and their native collaborators as well.[18]

The nativist movement would provide not only the spiritual leavening but also much of the political and military leadership of the growing opposition to the Americans and their numerous sympathisers within the Creek confederacy. This, in turn, would do much to shape the way the insurgents fought, first against their internal enemies and ultimately against the Americans. The important role of these holy men in the First Creek War is far from unique in American Indian military history. Sitting Bull, not a war chief but a shaman or holy man, was the soul of Lakota resistance during the Great Sioux War of 1876–7.[19] Geronimo, the famous leader of the last Apache war band to surrender to US troops, in 1886, was first and foremost a medicine man.[20] North of the US border, the Plains Cree chief Big Bear owed his authority at the time of the war with Canadian troops in 1885 to his reputed spiritual powers.[21] But it was south of the border, in the ranks of the Mayan resistance in Yucatán, that nativist religion played its greatest military role, as we shall see. The priests of the Cult of the Speaking Cross organised and led the Indian armies in a largely successful effort to preserve Mayan autonomy in the declining decades of the nineteenth century.

The new group of Creek spiritual leaders or shamans included men who would stand out both as prophets and warriors. Three of them were chosen for special comment in George Stiggins's memoir of the First Creek War, one of the most useful contemporary primary sources available to us.[22] Perhaps the best known of these shamans was Josiah Francis, the son of a Creek woman and a white trader–blacksmith of French origin. Francis gained fame for his skills as a diviner, which he passed along to another Red Stick prophet, his protégé Cussetaw Haujo, alias High-Head Jim, described by Stiggins as 'one of [the rebel faction's] greatest warriors and prophets'.[23] In the wake of defeat in the war with the Americans, Francis would lead Red Stick survivors to Spanish Florida, where they took refuge among their Seminole brethren.[24] In April 1818, following his return to Florida from a trip to London to seek British aid, he was lured onto an American man-of-war flying British colours, from which he was subsequently removed in irons and hanged, on orders from his old nemesis, Andrew Jackson, then in the process of invading the Spanish colony.[25]

The third Creek holy man singled out for comment by Stiggins was the shaman and linguist Paddy Walch (or Walsh), who had taken the family name of his adopted father, James Walch, a white Tory who had fled to Creek country from South Carolina during the American War for Independence. Master of several Indian languages, Walch served as an interpreter for the Creek rebels, but also aspired to military command amongst them by virtue of his alleged ability to render his followers impervious to bullets. He would be one of the leaders of the war party that massacred the inhabitants of Fort Mims in August 1813, about which more will be said below.[26] In 1814, the prophet was captured by US troops, but escaped. Not long after, some of his own people, fearing retribution if they failed to do so, turned Walch over to the soldiers, and he was hanged at Fort Claiborne, Alabama. As Stiggins said: 'tho he was small ugly and a diminutive man in his personal appearance, he was the greatest prophetic warrior the Ispocoga or [C]reek tribe ever had. . .'.[27]

Although the shamans and their revitalisation movement were crucial elements in the Creek war against white encroachment, their role should not be allowed to obscure the part played by what might be called the secular military leadership. The most famous of the traditional war chiefs was William Weatherford (1780–1824), known amongst his people as Red Eagle. Weatherford, although a reluctant adherent to the Red Stick faction, would share command at the Fort Mims massacre with Peter McQueen and the shaman Paddy Walch. He would acquire his greatest fame, however, for riding in alone to surrender himself to Andrew Jackson after the Horseshoe Bend debacle, offering his life in exchange for sustenance for his starving people.[28]

PART II

Peter McQueen (1780?–1820) was a second important secular leader of the Red Sticks. In addition to his role in the attack on Fort Mims, he would lead the repulse of Andrew Jackson's first invasion of the Creek homeland at the battles of Emuckfaw Creek and Enotachopco Creek. Following the Creek defeat at Horseshoe Bend, McQueen fled south to Seminole country, where he would take part in the First Seminole War. In 1820, after years of fighting the Long Knives, he died of an unknown illness on an island off the Florida coast. McQueen left behind, however, a great nephew named Asi-Yaholo (Osceola to the whites) to carry on the fight. Osceola would become the most famous war chief of the Seminoles in their 1835–42 war against the whites in Florida.[29]

Finally, there was Menawa, who served as secular war chief of the Creeks at Horseshoe Bend

> and fought with his warriors to the last. Wounded seven times, one of them a serious wound to the face, he fell near sundown and lay unconscious until dark, when he awoke to find himself under a pile of dead warriors. Under the cover of night, he dragged himself to the river, managed to find a canoe, climbed in, and floated downriver to safety.

Following the war, Menawa, having recovered from his wounds, once again became a leader of the Upper Creeks and a fierce opponent of US government efforts to get the Creeks to cede their remaining lands in Alabama and Georgia and move to Indian Territory. When, in February 1825, a coterie of pliant chiefs led by the Lower Creek notable, William McIntosh, signed the Treaty of Indian Springs, selling Creek lands to the US government, Menawa vowed to take revenge. In April 1825, a band of warriors under his leadership killed McIntosh and sacked and burned his plantation.[30]

The Creek insurgents who followed the shamans, Weatherford, McQueen and Menawa, were called Red Sticks, after the red-painted clubs whose circulation traditionally served among the Creeks as a call to war. The Red Stick credo was summarised, if in somewhat polemical fashion, by Alexander Cornells, one of the more prominent Creek mixed-bloods and a loyal ally of the Americans:

> Kill the old chiefs, friends to peace; kill the cattle, the hogs, and fowls; do not work, destroy the [spinning] wheels and looms, throw away your plows, and everything used by Americans. Sing the song of the Indians of the northern lakes, and dance their dance. Shake your war clubs, shake yourselves; you will frighten the Americans; their arms will drop from their hands.[31]

While most historians today would reject the once-popular notion that the division between the Red Sticks and their opponents in the Creek civil war was simply a split between the 'less advanced' Upper and more 'modernist' Lower Creek towns, they remain at odds over who exactly among the Creeks joined the Red Stick movement and who did not, about the motivations of the insurgents and the relative breadth of the uprising they promoted. Until fairly recently, US historians of the Creek civil conflict found it convenient to ascribe its outbreak to those early 'outside agitators', Tecumseh and his brother, the Prophet. The Shawnee leader's 'fervent oratory and impassioned opposition to the white man's civilization' during his visit to Creek country in 1811 'provided the spark' which 'kindled the fire of nationalism – even fanaticism' among the Creeks, while the religious mystics who led the Red Sticks formed an order 'clearly patterned after the activity of Tecumseh's brother, Tenskwatawa', according to one writer.[32] Wealth has also been seen as a source of division, with the less well off rallying to the Red Sticks. Recently the historian Claudio Saunt has argued that the Creeks separated along class lines, with the 'market-oriented Creeks, many of whom were wealthy métis [mixed-bloods]', backing the Americans and their Creek allies, whilst the Red Sticks tended to represent less well-off dissidents. Saunt argues that the civil conflict was largely a reaction to the Americans' 'plan for civilisation'.[33] Perhaps the most interesting perspective on this subject is the argument by the anthropologist Ross Hassig that one of the most meaningful cleavages in the Creek population during the civil war was generational, with youth tending to back the Red Sticks and older Creeks rallying in their majority to the agent Hawkins and the traditional chiefs.[34]

The opening shots in the First Creek War were fired in July 1813 in a skirmish known to history as the Burnt Corn Fight. It was not an auspicious beginning for the Americans. Burnt Corn Creek, where the incident took place, is in southern Alabama and on the day of the engagement was the campground of a party of Creeks on their way home from Pensacola in Spanish Florida, where they had acquired a supply of firearms and ammunition. The Creeks were surprised in camp by a force of local white and mixed-blood militia, who seized most of their guns and ammunition before being attacked themselves and driven off. The Americans appear to have been distracted by counting their booty. According to one account, 'The battle of Burnt Corn, on the whole, was damaging to the prestige of American prowess. For many years its participants had to endure the ridicule of their neighbours and friends; for it was not considered creditable to any one to claim that he had been a soldier in the Burnt Corn battle'.[35] The unprovoked attack sparked calls for revenge from the Red Sticks and brought into the fray large numbers of Creeks who had remained neutral up to this point. It should be emphasised that, as was the case with most of the Indian peoples we will be covering in this book, revenge was one of the key motives for war among the Creeks. In this particular instance, the main target of the Red Stick attackers was the mixed-bloods among their assailants at Burnt Corn Creek, fellow Creeks who had taken up the gun on the side of the Americans, and who now took refuge in nearby Fort Mims.[36] The

PART II

upshot was an assault on the fort on 30 August 1813, which took the lives of some 250 people gathered there, one of the bloodiest days for Americans in the whole of the nineteenth-century Indian wars.[37]

Fort Mims Massacre

Fort Mims was a new structure, built expressly to offer refuge to settlers in southern Alabama in case war broke out with the Creeks. On the day of the Creek attack, the modest fort was home to around 300 people: white settlers, blacks, mixed-blood Creeks, and a few deserters from the Spanish garrisons in Florida. Soldiers, mostly Mississippi militia, mixed-bloods and whites, accounted for just under half of Fort Mims's population; the rest unfortunately included a large number of women and children. The fort's senior officer was Major Daniel Beasley, who commanded the Mississippi militia.[38] He would be largely responsible for its fall to the Red Sticks.

The seizure of Fort Mims by Creek warriors is one of the very few examples of a successful Indian assault on a fortified place in North American history. However, it has to be said that the Creek victory was a fortuitous one, made possible by mind-boggling negligence on the part of the fort's commander and garrison. Despite repeated warnings from the regional military commander, General Ferdinand L. Claiborne, that a hostile Creek force was operating nearby, only dilatory efforts were made to scout the surrounding area, and when sightings of Indians in war paint were reported, they were discounted by the fort's commander. Thus, a large body of Creeks was able to approach the fort and lie in wait undetected until the time was ripe for an attack. The Creeks, meantime, had scouted the fort thoroughly and gathered further useful information from black slaves in the neighbourhood. They had learned from spies that the fort's inhabitants had spent Sunday, the day prior to the attack, drinking and otherwise enjoying themselves and that for reasons best known to himself, the fort's commander, Major Beasley, had ordered the celebrations carried over into the following day. Thus, much of the fort's population was either drunk or hung-over when the assault took place.

The Creeks also found out that the best time to attack the fort was at midday, when the garrison stacked arms before taking their noon meal. Finally, they discovered that gaining entrance to the fort would be remarkably easy – if they were able to get close enough to rush the place. To begin with, the stockade's firing loopholes were so close to the ground that attackers could fire through them into the fort and, if need be, even crawl through them. But, most astounding of all, they could see from their hiding places that one of the fort's gates had been left wide open. Incredibly, Major Beasley seems to have purposely left the gate open to show his contempt for his Indian enemies. In any case, when the luncheon gun sounded at midday inside Fort Mims, on Monday 30 August 1813, Creek warriors burst whooping from their places of

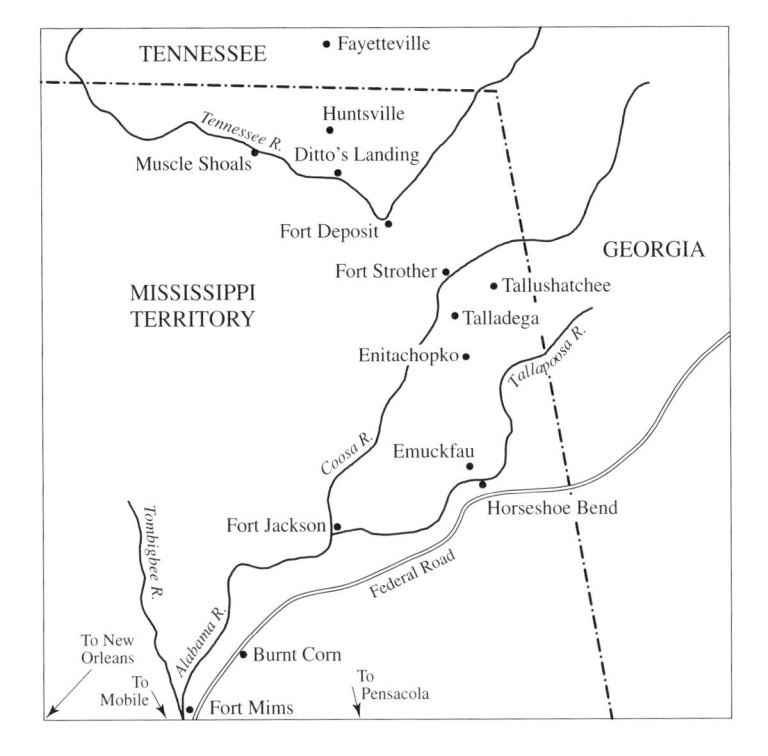

Map 5.1 First Creek War, 1813–14.

concealment and were almost at the fort walls before the fort's lone sentry could give the alarm. Stirred from his drunken stupor, Major Beasley frantically tried to close the gate ahead of the attackers, but it had been standing open so long that sand had built up against it and it could not be budged. Beasley was shot in the process of trying to shut the gate and died shortly thereafter.

The interior of the stockade now became a butcher's yard. Many of its occupants were killed early in the fighting by warriors shooting through the firing loopholes. Others were cut down by Red Sticks who burst through the open gate. Most of the remainder, including the mixed-blood militiamen most sought by the attackers, took shelter in the Mims family buildings around which the fort had been constructed. Entry of Red Stick reinforcements by a second gate sealed their doom.[39] The fort's buildings were set alight and the defenders were killed as they tried to escape. Only some twenty whites and mixed-bloods are thought to have escaped the massacre. Most of the black slaves in the fort, however, were spared and many departed with the Red Sticks. Indeed, one author points to collusion between the blacks and the Indians before and during the struggle for Fort Mims, claiming that not only did slaves in the area provide

PART II

crucial intelligence about the fort to the attackers, but that slaves within the fort joined in the slaughter of the defenders by the Indians.[40] The threat of a 'red–black' alliance became an ingredient in the hysteria that now gripped the white settlements on the Indian frontier and prompted the invasion of Creek country in 1813 by Andrew Jackson and his army of Tennesseans.

Horseshoe Bend

Andrew Jackson's 1813–14 war against the Creeks has all the hallmarks of a classic 'war against nature', but it would be a mistake to see it as only that. It is certainly true that throughout the war in Alabama logistics proved to be a worrying problem. Jackson's soldiers were forced to build wagon roads as they made their way through the wilderness. Rivers sometimes proved too shallow for his supply boats. But Jackson's campaigns also suffered mightily from the indiscipline of his largely militia army. At Enotachopco Creek, during his first foray into Indian country, in 1813, most of his militia turned and ran ('broke like Bullocks' was how Jackson put it).[41] In camp and on the march the other ranks of the militia – and sometimes their officers as well – refused to obey orders; turning a deaf ear to their commander's entreaties, whole units returned home at the end of their term of service or even before. On the eve of the Horseshoe Bend battle, *'pour encourager les autres'* Jackson felt compelled to court-martial and execute a young militiaman who had refused to obey a direct order.[42]

In his first, abortive expedition into the Creek heartland, Jackson's Indian scouts had informed him of a new and imposing Creek village on a peninsula in a bend of the Tallapoosa River known to the Indians as *tohopick* (meaning 'a fortified place'; later corrupted by whites to 'Tohopeka') and to the Americans as Horseshoe Bend. Hard-pressed by the Creeks, short on supplies, Jackson had been forced to retreat before he could approach this new fortified sanctuary of the Red Sticks. But, now, in the spring of 1814, the 'border captain' was back in Creek country at the head of a force of some 3,300 soldiers. Most of them were Tennessee militia, some 2,100 of the total, but this time there was also a stiffening core of professional soldiers, 600 regulars of the 39th US Infantry.[43] Jackson also had brought along two artillery pieces, but they were light guns – a six- and a three-pounder – and would have a negligible impact on the fighting. The Tennesseans were joined on the eve of their march against the Creek stronghold by some 600 Cherokee and Lower Creek allies. Jackson was not entirely happy to see these new arrivals. He found them 'a very serious tax on my provision-stores', he wrote, and intended to get rid of all of them except for a few guides as soon as possible.[44] But, as John Buchanan has remarked, Jackson's 'judgment . . . was premature, and he would soon have reason to be grateful for their attachment to the army'.[45]

Jackson's army would find arrayed against it around 1,000 Creek warriors and their some 350 dependents, gathered in a newly thrown together village on a roughly one-hundred acre peninsula in a sweeping curve of the Tallapoosa River. Across the narrow neck of the peninsula the Indians had built a five- and in some places eight-foot-high barricade of logs and earth with loopholes cut into it through which the defenders could subject attackers to flanking fire. The 350-yard-long Creek defensive work presented the American attackers with a formidable obstacle, as Jackson reported to his commander-in-chief, General Pinckney:

> It is impossible to conceive a situation more eligible for defence than the one they had chosen; and the skill which they manifested in their breast-work was really astonishing. It extended across the point in such a direction that a force approaching it would be exposed to a double fire, while they lay entirely safe behind it.[46]

So formidable was the barricade that at least two historians have questioned whether Indians could have built it without outside help. Some years ago, the late John Mahon suggested that the wall had been built 'with some white help, probably Spanish'.[47] More recently, Sean Michael O'Brien opined that 'this was no ordinary Native American work' and might have been constructed with 'the direct aid of Spanish agents'. Failing that, O'Brien guesses that it might have been designed by the Red Stick secular military leader, William Weatherford, who 'was familiar with the Spanish defenses at Pensacola'.[48] A charitable view would be to say that these theories of how the Horseshoe Bend barricade got built betray an ignorance of or lack of faith in Indian engineering capabilities. Numerous examples of Indian-built fortifications in the region can be attested, for example fortified towns among the Cherokees of Georgia and North Carolina, close neighbours and enemies of the Creeks. This tradition *precedes* contact with white settlers, as do similar 'forting-up' techniques among the Tuscarora people of northeastern North Carolina. To take the point a step further, anthropologists and archaeologists have produced considerable evidence to show that the Cherokees derived their fortification techniques from the earlier Mississippian Period or Mound Builder culture to their west.[49] Archaeological data demonstrate fairly conclusively that the immediate ancestors of the Creeks were a mound-building people who disappeared from history some two centuries before whites came to the region. In comparison to the sorts of fortifications built by their forebears, the rude log and earth barrier thrown up by the Red Sticks at Horseshoe Bend, effective as it was, seems quite primitive.[50]

The American and allied Indian army now set about investing the Creek stronghold, preparatory to storming the log barricade. Jackson sent his second-in-command, General John Coffee, with a mixed force of Tennessee mounted infantry and rangers and Cherokee and allied Creek Indians across the Tallapoosa and into position on the bank opposite the rear of the Red Sticks' village. The aim of this manoeuvre was two-fold, to block a Creek retreat and to forestall any attempts by other Creek forces to come to the aid of the now surrounded camp at Horseshoe Bend. An eventual attack on the rear of the Creek position by the Cherokees and allied Creeks under Coffee's command would be the decisive move of the engagement.

The Americans opened the battle by cannonading the Creek breastworks for two hours. The pounding was without effect on the log barricade, although it did kill some defenders within the enclosure. 'The balls passed thro the works without shaking the wall', Jackson wrote to his wife, 'but carrying destruction to the enemy behind it'.[51]

Meanwhile, the Americans' Indian allies had begun to swim across the river in the rear of the Creek position in order to carry off the large number of dugout canoes left there for use in case of retreat. This operation quickly turned into a full-blown Cherokee and allied Creek assault on the Red Stick village, occupied mainly by women and children and defended by a handful of warriors. Jackson's Indian allies drove the Creek defenders out of the village and set it on fire, then proceeded to attack the Creeks manning the barricade from the rear. This manoeuvre, however, engendered a fierce resistance and the Cherokees and allied Creeks were pushed back. Seeing that the attack on the rear of the defenders was 'wholly insufficient' to overcome the Creeks, Jackson ordered a frontal assault on the barricade by his regulars and militia. This was not only a diversion to take the heat off his Indian allies, of course, but an opportunity to catch the enemy between two fires. The American advance was right out of the Napoleonic drill book: drums beating, troops formed up in lines, firing a volley and then charging with fixed bayonets. Jackson had foreseen it all as unfolding in this way. 'The enemy calculate', he had warned his men earlier in the campaign,

> [to throw] you into a panick by their hideous yells . . . but brave men will laugh at this subterfuge by which they calculate to alarm you, and meet their hallooing and approach, by a firm and steady charge, and what Indians ever stood a charge with the bayonet?[52]

The Americans, led by the regular infantry, managed to breach the barricade, despite fierce fighting. Lieutenant Sam Houston, of later Texas fame, was wounded three times, once in surmounting the barricade and twice in the mêlée which now took place within the perimeter where the encircled Creeks were obliged to make their stand.[53] Some of the warriors managed to break through the cordon and reach the river, only to be gunned down by the men of Coffee's command. The fighting, increasingly the flushing out and killing of Indians who tried to hide in the brush or in crannies along the riverbank, lasted until nightfall, Jackson wrote, and 'The carnage was dreadfull'.[54] This was not Jacksonian hyperbole. The Red Sticks had given no quarter and received none. Of the 1,000 or so Creek warriors at Horseshoe Bend, 557 were killed on the battlefield and its margins. The 'border captain' could be sure of the tally: his soldiers had cut off the ends of the noses of the dead Indians and counted them. Only four wounded warriors eventually were taken prisoner. The rest appear to have perished in the river, shot down or drowned while trying to escape. The remaining women and children, their exact number unknown, were given into the care of the allied Indians; most probably ended up as slaves.[55] Jackson's army, meanwhile, suffered casualties of 32 dead and 99 wounded among the American contingent, 18 killed and 36 wounded among the Cherokees and five dead and 11 wounded among the allied Creeks.[56]

Although Creek war bands remained in the field, there was not much fight left in them. The First Creek War came to an end with the slaughter at Horseshoe Bend. Over 1,800 Creek warriors had died, along with untold numbers of women and children. Some fifty Creek towns and villages had been destroyed by the white armies and the fields around them ravaged. Many of the survivors of the war were starving. At Fort Jackson, 'Old Hickory' waited for the defeated leaders of the Creeks to come in to surrender. If they agreed to accept his terms, they would be allowed to return to their people. One of these leaders, however, was to receive no mercy. This was Red Eagle, William Weatherford, the secular military chief of the Red Sticks, whom Jackson threatened to hang.

The story of Weatherford's dramatic entry, alone, into the American camp, his eloquent speech of surrender and Jackson's surprising decision, sealed in a round of drinks, not only to spare his life but to accept him as an ally and friend, has been told too often to be repeated here.[57] What does need to be underlined here, however, is that Jackson's generosity to Red Eagle did not extend to his people, even those among them who had fought alongside the Americans at Horseshoe Bend. The Treaty of Fort Jackson imposed on the assembled Creek chiefs by 'Sharp Knife', as Creeks called Jackson, on 9 August, was punitive in the extreme. Half of the Creek lands, some 23 million acres, were to be ceded to the US government.[58] Not only the Upper Creeks who had been the backbone of the Red Stick movement, but the Lower Creeks who had fought for the Americans against them, were forced to give up territory. Pleas by leaders of the Lower Creeks failed to move Jackson. The war just over had been the fault of the Creek nation as a whole, Jackson said. It had failed as a nation to reject the overtures of Tecumseh and the British intriguers who stood behind him and now the nation must pay the price.[59]

The First Seminole War, 1818[60]

The Treaty of Ghent bringing the War of 1812 to a close did nothing to ease American pressure on Florida and its Seminole inhabitants. Americans 'felt that Florida belonged to the United States as a foot belongs to a leg', wrote John Mahon.[61] But the 1818 invasion of Florida by US troops was sparked by more than mere greed for land on the part of neighbouring Georgians and Alabamians, powerful though that might have been. Large numbers of blacks, both slave and free, had come to live in Florida in the late 1700s, often in large villages in Seminole country. The existence of these large 'Maroon' communities in Florida was deemed an encouragement to slaves elsewhere to escape. In addition, slave owners had been clamouring for some time for the return of slaves they had reason to believe had gone to Florida. Toward this end, they invoked the 1796 Treaty of Colerain in which the Creeks had promised to return fugitive slaves who had come into their lands — and those of the Seminoles. This white insistence that Seminoles were simply Creeks who had run away to Florida flew in the face of reality: Seminoles, to begin with, had long since stopped thinking of themselves as Creeks and, in any case, the Creek writ did not run across the border into Spanish Florida.

In January 1818 Andrew Jackson was given command of an American invasion of Florida and in March US troops crossed the border. Jackson's army of 3,500 men, which included no less than 2,000 Creek warriors, had been dispatched, or so Washington said, on a mission of self-defence against what its commander called 'a savage foe', who, in conjunction with 'a band of Negro brigands', had been 'carrying on a cruel and unprovoked war against the citizens of the United States'.[62] The First Seminole War, now launched, may be the one war engaged in by the USA in the previous millennium which, by Washington's definition at least, fits Colonel Callwell's third category of 'small wars': a foreign campaign to avenge wrongs or eliminate a dangerous enemy.[63]

It wasn't much of a war. The Seminoles and their black allies lacked guns and ammunition, and the Spanish were too few and too demoralised to resist. Though there were few battles worthy of the name, Seminole towns were burned and the Indians and black refugees driven deeper into Florida. American forces seized the main Spanish strongholds of St. Augustine and Pensacola. In the end, President James Monroe's administration in Washington somewhat facetiously repudiated the bumptious 'border captain' and apologised to the Spanish for his 'excesses'. Their main purpose apparently was to avoid putting obstacles in the way of negotiations with the Spanish aimed at securing an American takeover of Florida. This was duly achieved in the Adams–Onís Treaty of 1819. In July 1821 the Spanish flag came down for the last time in Florida. Its replacement by the Stars and Stripes would set the stage for a much more serious conflict with the Seminoles, in the Second Seminole War of 1835–42. But that war is best seen in the context of the removal in the 1830s of most of the Indians of the Eastern USA to a new and very different home across the Mississippi River.

Removal

Between 1831 and 1838, some 70,000 American Indians moved of their own free will or under duress from their homelands in the Eastern USA to new homes in what was then part of the state of Arkansas,[64] an area that would soon be known as Indian Territory and subsequently as the state of Oklahoma.[65] Their removal had been long anticipated. President Thomas Jefferson was the original advocate of the removal policy, arguing at the time of the Louisiana Purchase in 1803 that removal would give willing Indian peoples the time and space they needed to develop, with help from the federal government, the institutions and skills required to effectively assimilate into white society. But it would seem that the Sage of Monticello also saw the West as a kind of dumping ground for Indian peoples who did not wish to assimilate or who waged war on the United States and that, while he may have hoped that the Indians would leave willingly for their new homes, he was not averse to using force to compel them to go.[66] Jefferson's fellow Virginian, President James Monroe, believed removal was imperative. 'The hunter or savage state requires a greater extent of territory to sustain it', he wrote to General Andrew Jackson in 1816, 'than is compatible with the progress and just claims of civilised life, and must yield to it'.[67]

But despite the urging of Monroe and his Secretary of War, John C. Calhoun, no Indian removal policy was forthcoming during the 1820s, largely due to the insistence of John Quincy Adams, first as Secretary of State and then as president, that in traditional practice the Indian peoples had been treated as sovereign nations and thus could not be removed unless treaties of land cession were negotiated with them. This stand, however, seemed 'absurd' to Adams's successor in the White House in 1829, Andrew Jackson. He held that Indians were subjects of the US, not citizens of sovereign states, and that the fate of their tribal lands could be decided by a simple act of Congress, on the basis of the right of eminent domain. Such an act was duly passed by the Congress and signed into law on 28 May 1830.[68]

Most of the Indian emigrants came from the 'Five Civilised Tribes' in the southeast.[69] The first ones to depart were the Choctaws of central and southern Mississippi, who crossed the Mississippi River in three stages from 1831 to 1833. One of the USA's most distinguished foreign visitors observed the Choctaw removal in progress and left some perceptive comments on it. Aléxis de Tocqueville, French author of the classic study, *Democracy in America*, happened to be in Memphis, Tennessee, when a procession of Choctaws passed through on their way to the Indian Territory. It was bitterly cold and the Choctaws were all on foot, a whole people on the move, from 'children newly born' to 'old men on the verge of death'. Tocqueville watched them embark on boats that were to take them across the Mississippi.

> And never will that solemn spectacle fade from my remembrance. No cry, no sob, was heard among the assembled crowd; all was silent. Their calamities were of ancient date, and they knew them to be irremediable.

PART II

Map 5.2 Woodland Indian tribes of the eastern USA prior to removal.

The Frenchman did not believe that Indian removal to the West would enable the tribes to shore up their threatened cultures or recover their lost economic well-being, as some proponents of the removal policy had claimed. Their new Indian neighbours would 'receive them with jealous hostility', Tocqueville contended, and 'the importunate whites will not let them remain ten years in peace'. It was the whites, and only they, who stood to benefit from the policy of removal. 'In this manner do the Americans obtain, at a very low price, whole provinces, which the richest sovereign of Europe could not purchase'.

But although 'hunger is in the rear, war awaits them, and misery besets them on all sides', Tocqueville believed that the greatest disaster awaiting the Southern Indians in their new home was the disintegration of their societies, the loss of their sense of community, as they descended into that possessive individualism that he saw as the besetting sin of the American way of life.

> To escape from so many enemies, they separate, and each individual endeavors to procure secretly the means of supporting his existence .... The social tie which distress had long since weakened is then dissolved; they have no longer a country; and soon they will not be a people; their very families are obliterated. . . .[70]

While Tocqueville underestimated the resiliency of the Indian peoples removed to the West, his sense of the enormity of the tragedy that had engulfed them and his estimate of the challenges awaiting them in their new home were not misplaced.

The task of overseeing the transfer of the Eastern Indians to their new home was confided to the US Army. It was soldiers who led the last batch of Choctaws to Indian Territory in 1833, who fought a nasty little war against the Creeks in 1836 before herding them and their Chickasaw neighbours into the West,[71] and who, in the most ignoble undertaking of all, led the Cherokees of Alabama, the Carolinas, Georgia and Tennessee over the 'Trail of Tears' to their new home on the prairies in 1838. 'Of all the eastern tribes', wrote Allan Peskin, the most recent biographer of General Winfield Scott, who oversaw the final phase of their removal, 'the Cherokees were the most thoroughly acculturated [Indians], having adopted agriculture, representative government, a written language, Negro slavery and other aspects of civilization'.[72] Removing them was a job about as distant from the Napoleonic pursuit of glory so dear to America's antebellum army as one could imagine, and most of the soldiers involved, officers and other ranks alike, loathed it. Regulars have always disliked being deployed to contain domestic disorder – strikes, riots, looting – but the mission of shepherding 17,000 or so Cherokees from their ancestral homes in the Eastern US to the Indian Territory may well rank as the most onerous task ever assigned to the US Army. Brigadier General John E. Wool, who was put in charge of organising the Cherokee exodus in 1836, informed his superiors in Washington that 'The whole scene since I have been in this country has been nothing but a heart-rending one' and declared that 'humanity revolts' at the behaviour of the Georgia militia over whom he had no control but who were looting Cherokee homes and driving their occupants onto the roads west without food or clothing. Complaints from the Georgia state government led to Wool's dismissal by President Jackson in July 1837.[73] But some enlisted men also protested at what one of them called 'the blackest chapter on the pages of American History'. Private John G. Burnett, of the Mounted Infantry, 'made the long journey to the west with the Cherokees and did all that a Private soldier could to alleviate their sufferings'. At one point, he faced a court martial for splitting open the head of a teamster who had used a bullwhip on an elderly Cherokee man.[74]

Following Wool's dismissal, command of the 7,000 US troops assigned to effect the removal of the Cherokees was turned over to the Army commander-in-chief, General Winfield Scott. The general directed that 'Every possible kindness' should be shown by the troops.[75] Scott no doubt was sincere, but the soldiers could do little to counter the ravages of disease, hunger and heartbreak which took such a heavy toll on the emigrants. By the time they reached the end of the 'Trail of Tears', over 20 per cent of the Cherokees who had set out from their homes in the east were dead, the majority from disease and exposure.[76] No less an observer than William Tecumseh Sherman later wrote: "If ever a curse could fall upon a people or nation for pure and unalloyed villainy towards a part of God's creatures, we deserve it for not protecting the Cherokees that lately lived and hunted in peace and plenty through the hills and valleys of western Georgia'.[77]

The Second Seminole War, 1835–42

The Jackson administration also tried to force the removal of the Seminoles from Florida. Although the close of the First Seminole War in 1818 had eventually led to a treaty (Moultrie Creek, September 1823) setting aside most of central Florida for use as a Seminole reservation, many Seminoles refused to live there and the white settlers now beginning to flood in, especially from neighbouring Georgia, ignored its boundaries.[78] Washington began to be bombarded with complaints from the settler population, demanding the expulsion of the Seminoles and the return of the large number of fugitive slaves presumed to be living amongst them.

In May 1832, a treaty was signed at Payne's Landing, Florida, between agents of the US government and fifteen Seminole chiefs providing for the dispatch of a delegation of Seminole leaders to Indian Territory to ascertain if land set aside there by Washington would be suitable as a new home for the tribe. Upon the leaders' return, their verdict would be submitted to the whole of the Seminole 'nation' for its approval. If the leaders opted for emigration and the 'nation' gave its consent, the Seminoles were to be gone from Florida in three years' time. They would be paid some two cents an acre for the just over four million acres presumed to belong to them. A final clause in the agreement, and one which was highly controversial, stipulated that the Seminoles were expected to make their home in the West among the Creek 'nation', to which most whites insisted they belonged. This despite the century-long separation between the two peoples and the enmity that smouldered between the Seminoles and the pro-American faction that had taken control of what was left of the Creek confederation after 1814.

Seven Seminole chiefs, deemed by their white interlocutors to be the leading figures of the 'nation', ultimately made the trip to Indian Territory. In March 1833, after a brief 'reconnaissance' of the land the government proposed to set aside for them, the chiefs signed a document indicating their approval of the site and stating that the Seminole people would be willing to settle down near, if not among, the Creek confederation. It would appear that the chiefs were not aware that under the terms of this Treaty of Fort Gibson[79] their word was binding on the whole Seminole 'nation'; the idea of a subsequent poll of the Seminole people on the matter, a prominent feature of the Payne's Landing treaty, had been quietly dropped by the author of the Fort Gibson accord, the Seminole agent John Phagan. There is also evidence to suggest that the Seminole leaders were coerced into signing the treaty, it having been insinuated that if they failed to do so, they would have to make their own way back to Florida.[80]

Back in Florida, a stalemate now ensued between the Seminoles, most of whom refused to accept the terms of the Treaty of Fort Gibson, and territorial and federal officials and Florida settlers, who insisted that the terms be honoured. As positions hardened, a new leader emerged at the head of the Seminole faction most opposed to removal. He was Asi-Yaholo (called 'Osceola' by whites), a Creek emigré and great-nephew of the arch-Red Stick, Peter McQueen. He and his mother had come to Florida as part of McQueen's entourage in the wake of the slaughter at Tohopeka in 1814, and, true to his heritage, Osceola had taken part in the First Seminole War four years later.[81] He opposed emigration both in principle and because he believed removal would provide whites with a pretext to seize the large number of black slaves and freemen who lived among the Seminoles. Blacks were numerous amongst his constituency within the tribe; at the time it was also said that Osceola's favourite wife was black, but this appears not to have been true.[82] In any case, Osceola began to denounce Seminole leaders who either had accepted removal at the time of the Fort Gibson treaty or who had acquiesced under white pressure later. One of these was Charley Emathla. Although he had signed the Fort Gibson agreement, Emathla later claimed that he had not known what he was doing. Nonetheless, by 1835 he was ready to sell up and emigrate to Indian Territory. Having sold his livestock, the old chief was making his way home when he was accosted on the road by Osceola and a band of his followers. Osceola, who never left killing to others, personally shot Emathla and scattered his money across the countryside.[83] Not long afterwards, fighting erupted between the Seminoles and soldiers from the small regular army contingent stationed in Florida, some 550 officers and men spread across the territory from Pensacola to Key West and Miami to St. Augustine.

The war which now broke out occupies a special place in the history of the North American Indian wars. On the American side, it was the only Indian war in which the US Navy and Marine Corps were involved. Navy vessels plied up and down the coasts of the Florida peninsula, ferrying troops and supplies for the army. The Navy's West India Squadron cruised between Florida and Spanish Cuba and the British-owned Bahamas, seeking to intercept (largely imaginary) shipments of arms and ammunition intended for the Seminoles. Meanwhile, other Navy ships put landing parties ashore to attack Seminole camps or to search for arms in Cuban fishing settlements on the Florida coast. But, most important, the Navy detached officers and men to join marines and soldiers in waging 'riverine warfare' deep in the Everglades. Moving along waterways through the jungle-like terrain in dugout canoes, the sailors and their comrades located and burned Seminole villages and maize fields. These 'search-and-destroy' expeditions rank among the most innovative tactics employed by US armed forces during the nineteenth century. But the successes they gained, and they were not overwhelming, came at a high cost, as we will see.[84]

The Seminoles also were 'rather daring military innovators'. They often carried out night attacks, 'something very rare in the annals of Indian warfare'. In one night-time operation, Seminole warriors launched an amphibious assault, supported by cannon fire, on a naval base at Indian Key in South Florida, a truly unique event in the North American Indian wars.[85] The Seminoles also proved to be more dogged at conducting sieges than most Indian peoples, at one point investing an army blockhouse for 48 days before relief arrived. And, once they decided to fight a pitched battle, Seminole war bands emulated their white opponents in taking steps to prepare the battlefield. On the eve of the battle of Okeechobee in December 1837, warriors cleared brush and trees from in front of their positions in order to create a field of fire.[86]

A main feature of the Second Seminole War was a continuation of the 'red–black' alliance originally encountered at the time of Jackson's incursion into Florida in 1818. Blacks, both free and slave, once again fought in significant numbers alongside the Seminoles. The nature of the black–Seminole partnership lately has become a topic of some controversy, however. A Seminole historian, Susan A. Miller, has argued that what she sees as the tendency of recent historians to 'play up' the black role in the Indian resistance 'was framed by concepts of the [US] Civil Rights Movement' and that the resulting accounts bear little resemblance to what actually transpired. Worse, Miller writes, these modern interpreters have built much of their argument on what she calls 'American military propaganda' of the 1835–42 war, according to which blacks were the real leaders of the Seminole resistance, or as one US Army commander, General Thomas Jesup, put it, 'the negroes rule the Indians'. This 'propaganda' was rooted in the belief of some soldiers that because the blacks 'had a better knowledge of the white man and of his customs ... and were indispensable as go-betweens and interpreters', they in time became counsellors to the Seminole leaders and ultimately the power behind the throne. This claim also had utilitarian value, Miller charges, since it fed the fears of Southern slaveholders, still at panic level just five years after the Nat Turner slave revolt in Virginia, and thus made it easier to get Congress to authorise additional troops and funds for the Florida war.[87]

Another interesting facet of the Seminole struggle was the Indians' alleged links to 'foreign powers' in offshore waters, another fear that provoked near hysteria among their American enemies. Although naval vessels under the command of Commodore Alexander J. Dallas regularly stopped and searched

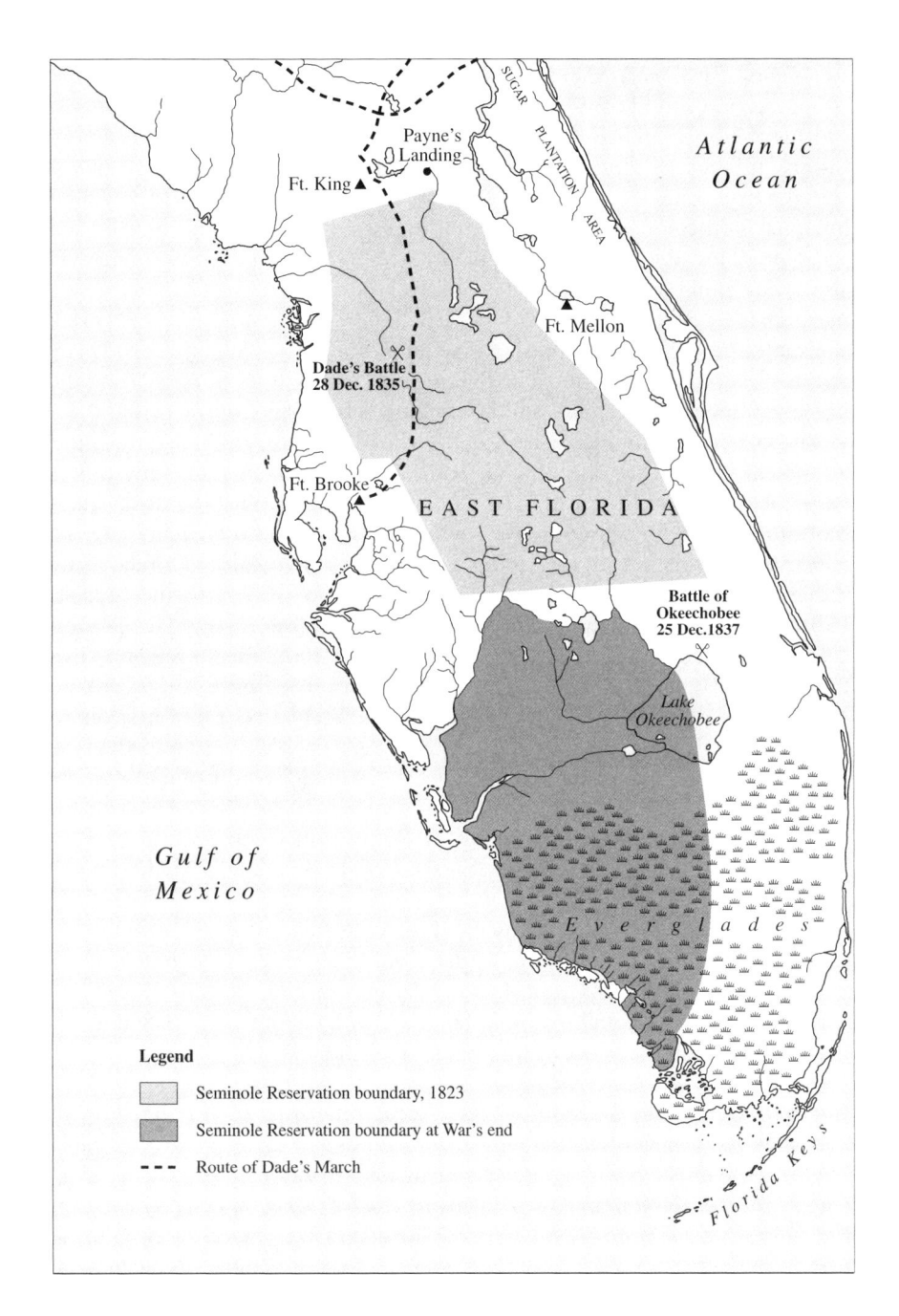

Map 5.3 Second Seminole War, 1835–42.

PART II

shipping in the waters between Cuba and the Bahamas and Florida, suspected shipments of arms and other matériel to the Seminoles failed to materialise.[88]

The second round of warfare between the United States and the Seminole Indians of Florida proved to be the longest continuous Indian war in American history. It lasted just under seven years, from December 1835 to June 1842. It was also one of the US Army's costliest Indian wars: 1,466 regulars lost their lives, 328 of them to enemy fire, the rest to disease, the heat, wild animals, and accidents. This added up to a casualty rate of 14 per cent. Fifty-five militiamen also died, along with some 100 civilians, mostly settlers. The Seminoles, meanwhile, suffered casualties of 'several hundred or more' and their black allies at least 40. By 1842, some 4,000 Seminoles and Black Seminoles had been removed to Indian Territory. The fighting cost the territory of Florida and the US government between $30 and $40 million, a huge sum for the period.[89]

The Second Seminole War also has the distinction of being the most unpopular US conflict until the Vietnam War of 1965–75. The army officer corps seems to have been particularly unhappy with the war. '[V]irtually all of those [officers] who wrote on the conflict questioned its desirability and the effectiveness of the means used to fight it'. The southern half of Florida, many thought, was not habitable by whites and ought to be left to the Indians. Florida, wrote the medical officer Jacob Rhett Motte, was 'The poorest country two people ever quarreled over. . . . It is a most hideous region to live in, a perfect paradise for Indians, alligators, serpents, frogs, and every other kind of loathsome reptile'.[90] Not a few regulars found themselves more attracted to the Seminole enemy than to the white settlers they were supposed to be protecting.[91] The settlers, they came to believe, were unworthy of the sacrifices being made on their behalf by the nation's soldiers. When he left Florida for duty elsewhere in May 1838, Lieutenant Henry Prince expressed no regrets. 'Waked at one o'clock to see the last end of Florida' he wrote in his diary.

> Vile country! I have risked my life three years for you! As the worst – most unwelcome – occurrence that could happen to your heartless population, I wish that your Indian War may speedily terminate! And you left to work your bread out of the soils with neither Uncle Sam nor the Indians in the way of your plundering hand![92]

But there were other dissenting views as well: some army officers agreed with the Seminole leader Osceola that a main purpose of the war was to enable Southern slaveholders to 'reclaim' the many black slaves who had taken refuge among the Seminoles, and who in many cases had become acculturated as Indians. General Thomas Jesup, who commanded US troops in Florida during part of the war, warned Southerners in 1836 that the conflict 'you may be assured is a negro and not an Indian war, and if it is not speedily put down, the South will feel the effects of it before the end of next season'.[93] General Ethan Allen Hitchcock in later years contended that 'The invasion of the peninsula by sheriffs [after runaway slaves] and the consequent concealment of the fugitives by their brown friends marked the beginning of the hostilities that became known as the "Florida War".'[94] Most officers, however, were unhappy with the war because 'Jungle skirmishes did not fit the conventional image of Napoleonic battle that permeated officers' socialization and civilian ideas of warfare; patrols and convoy escorts were unlikely scenes for winning reputation and fame. . . .'[95]

As 'A Subaltern' wrote in the *Army and Navy Chronicle*, 'In a regular war, there is something noble, something inspiring. . . . It makes me sick to read the accounts. . . . No wonder the army should have become disgusted with this thankless . . . unholy war'.[96] Army commanding general Winfield Scott, who led troops in the 1836 campaign against the Seminoles, said, 'The war against the Seminole Indians is one of unmitigated privation and suffering, without the least possible expectation of fame or glory to individuals'.[97]

Winfield Scott knew whereof he spoke. The Second Seminole War did little to enhance the reputations of the nation's military leaders. Scott, a hero of the War of 1812 and the future conqueror of Mexico, floundered about in the Florida swamps through most of 1836, trying in vain to apply Napoleonic *grande guerre* tactics to jungle warfare.[98] But Scott was only one of a number of prominent US generals whose reputations suffered as a result of their failure to defeat the Seminoles. General Zachary Taylor, another future Mexican–American War hero, managed to give the Seminoles a bloody nose at the battle of Okeechobee, when they opted to fight a pitched battle, but when the Indians reverted to their usual hit-and-run tactics, Taylor got no better results than the other commanders.[99] The general whose reputation suffered most from the Florida war, however, was Thomas Sidney Jesup. It was Jesup who, in October 1837, ordered the seizure under a flag of truce of the Seminole leader Osceola. Although the general would defend his action on the grounds that it was an extreme measure intended to bring a bloody war to an early close, US public opinion considered it dishonourable and Jesup would spend the rest of his career trying to live it down. And 130 years later, John K. Mahon, the dean of Seminole War historians, could still write: 'General Jesup may finally have convinced himself of the honourableness of his conduct, but he was still writing justifications of it 21 years later. Viewed from the distance of more than a century, it hardly seems worthwhile to grace the capture with any other label than treachery'.[100]

The upshot of this inglorious war was an unprecedented wave of resignations of army officers, over 200 between 1835 and 1837 (117 in 1836 alone) or about eighteen per cent of the entire army officer corps.[101] And when the haemorrhage eventually subsided in 1839 it was not because officers had changed their minds about the nature and objectives of the war but because the government in Washington had made it clear that it would not terminate the war short of victory. The government would reverse course again by 1842 but, in the meantime, the soldiers on the spot would take desperate initiatives in a last-gasp effort to break the will of the Seminoles. These measures would include

PART II

campaigning in the ferocious summer heat and undertaking canoe expeditions into the swamps where those Seminoles still in the field had taken refuge.

The 'Dade Massacre'[102]

The first major engagement of the Second Seminole War is also its best known. This battle, the 'Dade Massacre' of 28 December 1835, not long after the war began, probably ranks as the second most famous white battlefield catastrophe of the US Indian wars, after the 'Custer Massacre' in Montana some forty years later. It was the result of an attack on 108 regular Army soldiers under the command of Major Francis L. Dade en route from Fort Brooke on Tampa Bay to a beleaguered Fort King in the Florida interior. Dade's column consisted of eight officers and 100 other ranks, the latter of whom were mostly artillerymen converted to infantry. They had brought a six-pounder artillery piece along with them. The column's guide was a mulatto named Louis Pacheco, who has been charged with telling the Indians beforehand of the strength of the force and its destination. Pacheco would strenuously deny this. The only proof offered of his treachery was that he left the battle site with the enemy after the massacre was over.[103]

Since the route taken by the soldiers in their sky-blue uniforms was 'a perfectly plain gash in the otherwise heavy wilderness where there was no other road and few trails', the Indians shadowing them had little difficulty following their progress. Dade and his men seem never to have known that they were being scouted, although almost down to the last day the major had put out flankers on both sides of the road. Now, on 28 December, as the column set out on what it had reason to believe would be the last leg of its march to Fort King, these precautions were relaxed. Dade seems to have concluded that any danger there might have been was past; if the Seminoles had intended to attack, they would have made their move earlier, in the course of one of the two river crossings made by the column. So, on the fatal day, no flankers were out and there was no way the soldiers could have known that some 180 Seminole and black warriors were waiting in the tall grass alongside the track. Private Ransom Clark, who survived the massacre, later told officers at Fort King that the first shot was fired just as Major Dade, sitting his horse at the head of the column, was winding up telling the men they could celebrate a belated Christmas when their march was over. The major fell dead from his horse and the ensuing volley killed about half of the men.

Remarkably, given the surprise nature of the attack, the fifty or so men who survived the first volley did not panic but took cover where they could and began to return fire. The lone artillery piece was wheeled about and brought into action and, some sources suggest, was instrumental in bringing on the 45 minute hiatus in the attack which now took place. 'The fire so chastened the attackers that they drew off for three-quarters of an hour', according to John

Mahon.[104] This was not the way Alligator, the Seminole leader present at the massacre, recalled it. 'The cannon was discharged several times, but the men who loaded it were shot down as soon as the smoke cleared away; the balls passed over our heads', the chief recalled, adding 'we avoided [the cannon fire] by dodging behind the trees just as they applied the fire [to the touch-hole]'.[105]

Alligator's observations are hauntingly reminiscent of those made by witnesses to another massacre, one we have already noted, over a generation later and a continent away. Three Zulu veterans of the slaughter of some 1,400 British soldiers and their African allies at Isandlwana in Zululand, South Africa, on 22 January 1879, recalled that they had felt less fear of the shells from the redcoats' seven-pounders than of their rifle volleys. The British writer who gathered their story rendered the Zulu warriors' testimony as follows:

> When they saw the gunners stand clear, they either fell down or parted ranks, allowing the shots to pass as harmlessly as wind. . . . They took this evasive action with no hurry or confusion, as if they had been drilled to it.[106]

At issue here is the seemingly automatic assumption by all too many military historians that artillery, a weapon which few indigenous armies possessed and even fewer knew how to use, became by its very presence on the battlefield a decisive – or potentially decisive – factor in small wars such as those against the Seminoles or Zulus. That, as we shall see, this does sometimes appear to have been the case, as for example at the battle of Apache Pass in Arizona in 1862 or the first battle of Adobe Walls in Texas in 1864, only demonstrates the need to examine this question on a case-by-case basis.

Close analysis will show that what held up the Zulu onslaught at Isandlwana was not artillery fire, but a conscious decision to let the central segment of their attacking force stand and take the brunt of devastating British rifle fire while its left- and right-flank wings surrounded the defenders and choked off retreat. This was how Zulu *impis* had fought since the time of Shaka Zulu in the 1820s.[107] Similarly, the Seminoles, who, like most Indian peoples, were chary of accepting the kind of heavy casualties that come with frontal assaults, would have been content to remain in the cover of the pine and palmetto scrub and dodge the sporadic artillery fire, while they continued to pick off the gunners and riflemen across the way. This was the Seminole 'way of war' and we do not need to invoke the presence of a cannon on the battlefield to explain why Alligator and his companions failed to follow up their opening volley with a charge.

In the face of the continuing enemy fusillade, the Americans managed to cobble together a triangular log breastwork behind which they now took cover. But it was only a breastwork and could not adequately protect them from the aimed fire that continued to pour from the bush across the road. The six-pounder fell silent as its powder was exhausted and one by one the bluecoats fell. When shots stopped coming from the breastwork, Seminole warriors emerged from cover. They seem to have paid little attention to the bodies behind the fortification, being concerned mainly with carrying off food, weapons and ammunition. The dead were not stripped and no scalps were taken. It was the black contingent in the war party who saw to dispatching the wounded and took scalps, according to Alligator.[108] The battle had lasted some three hours. Three white men would survive the ambush and two would make it to Fort King alive; the Seminoles lost three dead and five wounded.[109]

Riverine warfare

What followed was a punishing war for foot soldiers and, as the newly formed Second Dragoons learned at the very outset, for horsemen and their mounts as well. An unidentified officer of the unit recalled that their first exposure to Florida, on a 'march from Fort Mellon [south of St Augustine] to the southern portion of Florida was marked by much suffering and fatigue to officers and soldiers and great destruction of the finest horses I have ever seen'.[110] It was the first war for the Second and they spent most of it dismounted. As the conflict dragged on, more and more of the fighting was concentrated in the Everglades, that great swampland which stretches across southern Florida just to the west of the present-day city of Miami. Much of it was knee-deep in water or mud and overgrown with seven-foot-high 'saw-grass'. In the 'Glades,

> The vegetation was so dense in most parts that the sun's rays seldom penetrated to the earth's surface. Water stood year round with little movement, and a thick layer of green slime covered most of the area. When this surface was disturbed, foul toxic vapors arose which caused the men to retch.[111]

The only exceptions to this dismal prospect were the wooded islands, called 'hammocks' (not 'hummocks', for some reason), which rose out of the swamp at intervals. Some of these 'hammocks' were as much as twenty miles long and ten miles wide and provided not only hideouts for the Seminole warriors and their families but also land on which to grow maize and other crops during the long, hot summers when fighting came to a halt. 'In many hammocks no troops can operate', our anonymous Second Dragoon informant explained, 'but the enemy have small, beaten trails, with which they are familiar, and pass out of our reach'.[112]

The American military commanders took unprecedented and remarkably innovative steps in order to penetrate the inhospitable landscape in which the Seminoles had taken refuge. Already in October 1836, the US Navy lieutenant Levin M. Powell had been ordered to lead a waterborne detachment of sailors and marines into the Everglades in search of Indian encampments. Powell, subsequently hailed as the founder of riverine warfare in the USA, quickly learned that the navy whaleboats he had requisitioned for the mission were useless for navigating the streams that crisscrossed the great swamp. What was needed were flat-bottomed dugout canoes like those used by the Indians.[113] Although Powell's 1836 foray accomplished little, later waterborne forays by US marines, sailors and soldiers proved more successful.

In December 1840, for example, a canoe-borne force of soldiers under the command of the redoubtable Lt. Colonel William S. Harney managed to surprise a village of so-called 'Spanish Indians' deep in the Everglades and took captive what remained of its population after a firefight. This had been what Colonel Callwell would have called a 'revenge' expedition, intended in this case to get even with the 'Spanish Indians' for an earlier nocturnal raid on Harney's camp, in which a number of soldiers had been killed and Harney had barely managed to escape in his underwear. As we have noted, Harney's was not the sort of temperament that took such indignities lightly. Thus we will not be surprised to learn that he ordered all the male captives in the Everglades camp to be hanged save one, who was 'convinced' to guide the soldiers on their return journey.[114]

A February–April 1842 canoe expedition into the 'Glades under the command of US Navy Lieutenant John Rodgers, perhaps the best documented of the riverine operations during the Second Seminole War, clearly shows the high price paid by the men who carried them out. The Passed Midshipman George Henry Preble, who commanded a four-boat 'division' of the 16-canoe expedition, kept a diary of the 60-day foray and noted that some two weeks into the mission, he celebrated his birthday (25 February) by 'punishing one of my men, John Bath, with eighteen lashes for drunkenness and insubordination, and for endangering the whole command with his noise'. On the night of 10 March, two sailors deserted, disappearing into the swamps with a musket, twelve cartridges, and some food and clothing. They were never seen again. A week later, Preble ordered two more of his sailors to be flogged, this time for 'quarreling and laziness'. The young midshipman himself would be placed on the sick list on his return to base, with both legs ulcerated due to sawgrass cuts that had become infected. The doctors had wanted to amputate, but Preble had refused. It took two years for the sores to heal, 'and for years I felt the effects of these sixty days in a dug-out canoe in Florida', he wrote.[115]

In order to bring this distasteful and increasingly costly war to a close, the army in 1841 had undertaken the unprecedented step of campaigning in the summer. Under the personal command of General William Jenkins Worth, the commander of the Florida operation, some 600 men had set forth in boats and canoes for the heart of the Everglades. In the course of the operation, the soldiers found few Seminole warriors, but they did destroy a number of villages and burn the fields around them. Many Seminole families now faced the prospect of starvation over the coming year. In a sense, however, the physical damage done by Worth's troopers was less important than the psychological impact their mass penetration of the wilderness had upon the Seminoles. It warned warriors that the white soldiers would no longer suspend operations in the summer, that there would be no relief from their pressure, that the Everglades refuges were no longer safe for them and their families. Seminole bands now came forth from the swamps to surrender and offer themselves up for removal to Indian Territory.[116]

But the summer campaign had been costly for the bluecoats as well. Of the 600 men who went into the Everglades in June 1841, '220 of them were from time to time reported sick', and 130 were sent to general hospital, unfit for duty.[117] There would be no repeat of the 1841 summer excursion and, a year later, although a sizeable body of Seminoles was still roaming the swamps, the government in Washington, at army urging, had decided it was not worth continuing the Florida war, and brought the troops home.

Because it lasted as long as it did, the Second Seminole War inevitably sucked into its vortex almost the entire US Army officer corps and a good number of its enlisted men as well. Many of the younger army officers – the future general Oliver O. Howard is only one example – got their first taste of combat in the swamps of Florida.[118] And, as we have seen, the army's new Second Dragoon Regiment received its baptism of fire in Florida, although horseless for the most part. The Second Seminole War was the US military's first extensive experience of warfare in semi-tropical conditions, but it cannot be said that the army learned much from it. When the next American war in the tropics erupted, during the 'pacification' of the Philippine Islands from 1899 to 1902, the lessons that might have been taken away from Florida would have had to be learned all over again – if the army had deigned to employ them. As the leading historian of the Navy's Everglades expeditions has written, 'The practice of riverine warfare was almost forgotten after the Civil War. Not until the Vietnam conflict was the necessary geographical setting again provided, and striking similarities may be observed between the naval operations of the [Second] Seminole War and those of the Vietnam War'.[119]

George Rollie Adams, General Harney's latest biographer, has tried to make the case that the combined arms operations carried out in south Florida by Harney and others in the last years of the conflict imparted general lessons in counter-insurgency warfare that the Indian-fighting army would avail itself of in future campaigns in far different milieux. 'In its thoroughness, relentlessness, and design to wear down the enemy', he wrote, the tactics employed in Florida '. . . anticipated campaigns that Brigadier General George F. Crook and Brigadier General Nelson A. Miles waged against the Apaches in the Southwest nearly thirty years later'.[120] Here again we encounter the assumption that there must have been some sort of institutional memory that would store up these lessons for future use by the army. The most that safely can be said is that if there was such an institutional memory, it did not function very well. Certainly, lessons that might have been learned from the Second Seminole War would seem to have had little or nothing to do with the campaigns of Crook and Miles in the Southwest. As we will see, Crook's success in fighting the Apaches came by way of the application of tactics he had derived from campaigns against Indians in similar mountainous terrain in the Pacific Northwest before the Civil War and perfected later. Miles's campaigns against the Apaches (and, earlier, against the Plains tribes), meanwhile, were inspired by directives from his commander, General Philip Sheridan, whose knowledge of how to harry enemies into submission had been acquired in the Shenandoah Valley of Virginia during the Civil War.

6

INDIAN WARS IN MEXICO, 1821–76

Introduction

It is one of the sad ironies of modern history that the European Enlightenment, generally thought to be one of the great progressive movements in Western civilisation, should have served as handmaiden to the destruction of so many of the world's non-Western cultures. Nowhere was this more evident than in the Americas, where two of the Enlightenment's fundamental tenets, individualism and the right of private property, provided the philosophical underpinning for a white settler onslaught on the lands and way of life of a succession of Indian peoples.

The *criollo* or American-born middle-class rebels who succeeded in overthrowing Spanish colonial rule and securing the independence of Mexico in 1821 were much imbued with Enlightenment principles, as transmitted through the filter of Spanish liberalism, and had enshrined those principles in the charter of the revolution, the Plan of Iguala (1821), and in the constitution of the new Mexican republic, adopted in 1824.[1] Thus, the corporate identities and hierarchical distinctions that had characterised Spanish colonial society were swept aside in favour of a mass society comprised of autonomous individuals. 'Racial, caste, and class distinctions were legally abolished, and all peoples were to enjoy equally the rights and responsibilities of citizens'.[2] The Plan of Iguala conferred citizenship upon 'all the inhabitants of New Spain [as Mexico had been called under Spanish rule], without any distinction between Europeans, Africans, or Indians'. The various state charters emulated the federal constitution of 1824 in extending citizenship to all inhabitants, regardless of race or social class. The constitution of the state of Sonora, enacted in 1825, for instance, defined as citizens 'all those born and resident in the state who have reached the age of 21 years or 18 years if married'.[3] These provisions were intended to extinguish, among other vestiges of the 'old regime', the communitarian identities enjoyed by the various Indian peoples of Mexico, which the liberal leadership of republican Mexico believed had 'kept the Indians segregated from Europeans, inhibited their learning Spanish, and prevented them from entering the "rational world"'.[4]

The revolutionaries also sought to extend the blessings of private property to all of the republic's citizens. This included the Indian peoples who up to then had held their land in common with the agreement of the Spanish colonial power. The great post-independence liberal intellectual and politician Lorenzo de Zavala believed that this had been one of the most retrograde policies of the Spanish crown, since it had prevented the Indians from acquiring 'the sense of personal independence which came from the "sentiment of property"'.

In the wake of uprisings by the Yaqui Indians of Sonora in defence of their tribal identity and common lands in the 1820s and '30s, Zavala argued that the 'nation must compel the barbarous Indians to settle down in regular communities, or, [in a reference to the contemporary clearance of Indian peoples from the eastern United States] like the North Americans, [force them] to leave the territory of the republic'.[5] Mexico's new constitution stipulated that the Indians' communal lands were to be divided up among the individuals tilling them. The state would guarantee these individual land titles in return for the payment of property taxes. Under Spanish rule, Indians had been exempted from taxes, instead paying tribute directly into the royal coffers.[6]

The Yaqui resistance

Two substantial components of the population of the new Mexican republic, however – the Yaqui Indians who inhabited the fertile valley of the river of the same name in the northwestern state of Sonora and the Maya Indians of the Yucatán peninsula in southeastern Mexico – did not share the enthusiasm of Mexico's new rulers for either republican citizenship or private property. The Yaquis, in particular, had made it clear that they wanted no part of Mexican independence or of the new regime which had replaced the old royal government. They had raised 'one or two companies' of their feared bowmen to support the royal cause during the independence struggle.[7] Now, they demanded that Mexicans 'stay out of their affairs'. They were particularly adamant that 'Yaqui territory belong communally, as one piece, to all the Yaqui people'. They had not sought, and 'hence did not acknowledge, the status of citizenship' which the constitution of 1824 had bestowed upon them. 'When pressed to express their allegiance to Mexico by serving in its military or paying taxes, they baulked. When pressed harder, they took up arms to defend their autonomy.'[8]

These were not new, utopian positions, but positions which sought confirmation of the longstanding Yaqui status quo. During the eighteenth century, the reforming Bourbon monarchy of Spain had entered into a "colonial pact" with the Indians on its northern borders which guaranteed their control of ancestral lands and granted them significant local political autonomy, including the right to choose their own *captain-general* or political and military interlocutor with the Spanish authorities, in return for Indian agreement to provide labour for the mines of the region and warriors for defence of the frontier against Apache raiders.[9]

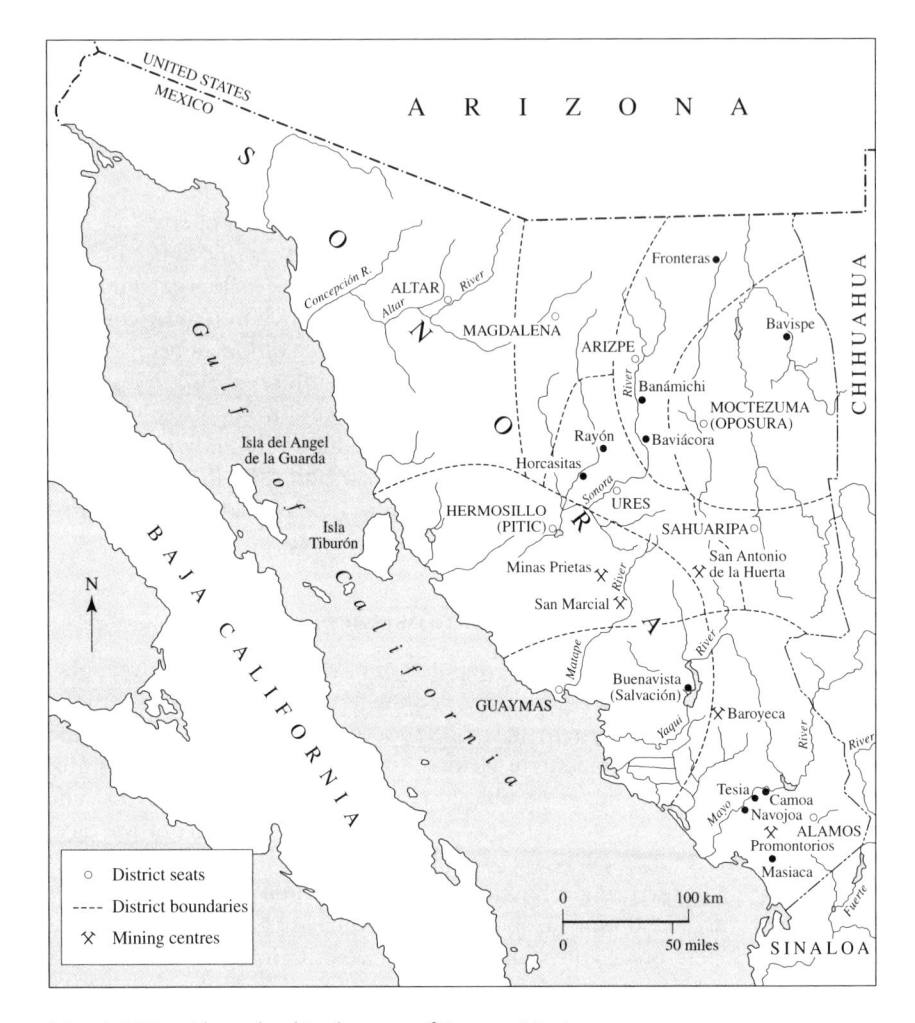

Map 6.1 Yaqui homeland in the state of Sonora, Mexico.

As far as the Yaquis were concerned, this royal pact merely confirmed the status they had occupied in the society of New Spain since the seventeenth century, when they first came under the influence of the Society of Jesus. The Jesuits had brought Christianity to the Yaquis and had seen to it that the Indians were protected against white slaving expeditions and land grabbers, but also made sure that the Yaquis were kept away from the white man's liquor and guns.[10] The friars had convinced them to abandon their isolated settlements or *rancherías* to form towns, where they engaged in intensive agriculture and developed artisanal skills that would remain in high demand in northwestern Mexico down into the twentieth century.

Yaqui revolt against Mexico's republican government, which would continue almost without let-up into the early years of the twentieth century, began in 1825, when government officials initiated twin campaigns to undermine Yaqui autonomy. One effort involved dispatching Sonora officials, backed by troops, to the Yaqui towns to divide up the communal lands and evaluate them for tax purposes. The second attempt involved federal authorities and concerned a bid by the new regional army commander, General José Figueroa, to reinstate a captain-general sacked by the Yaquis for agreeing to send Yaqui soldiers north to help fight the Apaches on the Colorado River. Figueroa led troops into the Yaqui towns and a battle took place on 25 October 1825 which sparked off a decade of intermittent fighting between the whites and Yaquis, the latter under the command of one Juan de la Cruz Banderas or Juan Banderas for short.

The rise and fall of Juan Banderas

Banderas had begun life as Juan Ignacio Jusacamea, and on the eve of the outbreak of fighting had been the flag-bearer in the military fraternity of Rahum, one of the traditional 'Eight Towns' of the Yaqui Valley. He had led local opposition to the division of Yaqui communal lands and had gone to jail for his pains. While in jail, Jusacamea began having visions. Upon gaining his freedom, he issued a proclamation identifying himself as Juan Banderas and declaring himself to be the bearer of the standards of 'Our King Moctezuma' and 'Our Lady of Guadalupe'. (His new name means 'flags' in Spanish.) Banderas invited all the Indian peoples of the region, Mayos, Opatas, and Pimas, to join his own Yaqui people in a great confederation to drive out the whites and mestizos and restore the 'crown' of Moctezuma, which he claimed had been stolen by the *gachupines* (peninsular Spaniards).[11]

Some historians have suggested that Banderas was influenced in his beliefs by the revolutionary rhetoric of Father Miguel Hidalgo y Costilla, the 'priest with a gun in his cassock' who had been largely responsible for the onset of the Mexican War of Independence in 1810.[12] Hidalgo had appropriated the banner of the Indian Virgin of Guadalupe as the flag of his revolution; so would Banderas.[13] Hidalgo charged that the people of Mexico had been despoiled by the arrogant peninsular Spaniards, the gachupines, who must now be held accountable for their crimes; as we have seen, Banderas echoed this sentiment. But if the Yaqui leader drew on what he knew of the ideas of Father Hidalgo – and it seems indisputable that he did – he also went beyond them to link the legend of the Virgin of Guadalupe with that of the martyred king of the Aztecs, Moctezuma, murdered by the conquering gachupines. Banderas declared that he had been sent by the Virgin 'to restore the sovereignty of Emperor Moctezuma' and bring back the Golden Age of the Aztec Empire. 'To enhance the validity of his messianic message, Banderas often represented himself as the designated heir of Moctezuma with the high sounding title of "King and Emperor"'.

Banderas appealed to neighbouring Indian peoples as well as his own to rally urgently to his banners in order to vanquish the whites. 'Those who join my banner would be lords of their lands and victors over the gachupines', he proclaimed, 'for I need your help in destroying the gachupines. They are responsible for our lost lands and so I wait for all of you to come with me as soon as possible.'[14]

By 1826, Banderas could claim that he had 2,000 fighters in his ranks and that he had expelled the *yoris* (a Yaqui word for 'whites' which soon came into general use by both sides in the struggle) from the Yaqui Valley. It was not superior weaponry that gave Banderas's armies the upper hand, but a raiding strategy that wreaked havoc on the local economy and struck fear into the hearts of the yoris. It would constitute the Yaqui 'way of war' for most of the nineteenth century. When fighting began, Yaqui war bands would descend upon the farms and ranches of the whites, killing the owners and driving off the stock. Threats of attack and the disappearance of their Yaqui workers would force mines to close. Whites and mestizos who had settled in the Yaqui towns would flee for their lives. Pitched battles were avoided. Robert Hardy, the English traveller, encountered Yaqui rebels in the field during his jaunts around Sonora in the 1820s. '[S]ome [were] armed with bows and arrows, but the greater part with sticks, slings and stones', he recalled. Hardy remembered the Yaqui insurgents as less a fighting force than an army of locusts, 'roving over the countryside, looting *blanco* haciendas and mines, holding up travellers and calling upon Yaquis working outside the pueblos to support them'. Hardy, who took a great interest in Juan Banderas but only seems to have known him by reputation, believed that this penchant for plundering was, in fact, a key part of Banderas's war strategy, for it enabled him not only to buy recruits for his armies and allies for his putative Indian confederation but also helped to reassure 'the old men of the different towns which had elected him their Generalissimo'.[15] Hardy's observation about the 'old men' seems to indicate that Yaqui democracy, represented through the pueblo councils, continued to function in the midst of war and in spite of the charisma of Juan Banderas.

An understandably paranoid Sonora government, meanwhile, suspected that Yaqui success owed much to Banderas's strategy of recruiting spies among the many Yaquis who had left the Eight Towns to work on the ranches and in the mines of the yoris. They were not mistaken. 'This system of intelligence gathering,' writes Evelyn Hu-DeHart, 'would become a permanent feature of the Yaqui rebellion of the nineteenth century'.[16]

Most observers, both contemporary and later, friendly and hostile, have seen Juan Banderas's leadership as crucial to the success of the Yaqui uprising. Robert Hardy praised his intelligence and skill as a military strategist and diplomat. A more recent and considerably less friendly Mexican commentator, the historian Claudio Dabdoub, ascribed Banderas's ascendancy to a darker genius, to his ability to stir up the ancient resentments of the Indian peoples, to his fanatical determination to 'exterminate' the whites and restore the 'kingdom of Moctezuma'. The Yaqui uprising was nothing less than a *guerra de castas* or race war, Dabdoub asserted.[17]

Two years after the uprising began, however, both sides were prepared for a truce. The Sonora authorities, who had received little help from the central government in Mexico City, feared the impact of continued warfare on the state's already fragile economy. Banderas, meanwhile, had heard that the local yoris were about to be reinforced by militia units from neighbouring Chihuahua. The result was a peace agreement, which, while appearing to meet some of the demands of the Yaquis and their allies, actually left the door open for continued intervention by the state government in Indian affairs. Thus, while the Indian population of the region was exempted from paying the property tax and the *alcabala*, or sales tax, and would continue to enjoy local political autonomy (Banderas was even made governor [*alcalde mayor*] of the Yaqui Valley), the Sonora state legislature decreed that whereas the Indians' control of their lands would be guaranteed, title would be issued only to individuals, not to the community. Furthermore, the legislature ruled that all Indian lands not in use by individuals would revert to the state, which could then sell them. The Sonora legislators' argument on this score would have resonated strongly with contemporaries in the Yankee republic to the north. Like James Monroe and Andrew Jackson, the Sonora politicians argued that if Indians could not make their lands productive, then the law of progress demanded that others should have the right to occupy and use them. The state also moved to abolish Yaqui military fraternities and to oblige Indian children to be educated in public schools employing the Spanish language, something which traditionally had been strongly resisted by the Yaquis. Then, in 1830, the federal government in Mexico City suddenly departed from its usual inattention to provincial affairs and overruled the Sonora legislature, declaring an end even to the trappings of Yaqui self-government and exemption from taxation. The upshot was a second Yaqui–Mexican war, with Banderas again at the head of the Indian armies.[18]

Over the next two years, profiting from the perennial lack of cooperation between Sonora and the federal authorities, and the panic aroused by renewed Apache raids on the frontier, Banderas's mobile Yaqui army carried the war to the enemy in hard-hitting raids against towns, ranches and mines in Sonora. And, although it still fought mainly with bows and arrows, the Yaqui army was now beginning to acquire more modern weapons, as Banderas saw to the purchase of muskets from traders and Yaqui artisans learned from yori deserters how to repair weapons and make bullets.[19] But Banderas knew that the ultimate key to Yaqui success was the revival of the Indian confederation he had managed to put together in the 1820s. He was less successful this time, succeeding only in bringing over the neighbouring Mayo people. Failure to secure mass support among the Opatas would contribute substantially to his downfall.[20]

The Yaqui leader also faced growing opposition within his own ranks as the war raged on. The Sonora government may have lacked the resources to crush the Yaqui revolt by force, but they seem to have been able to compensate for this by fomenting disunity within the Yaqui towns. A faction opposing Banderas began to take shape around one Juan María Jusacamea, a relative of the Yaqui leader who had been promised Mexican support in obtaining the captain-generalship of the tribe once peace was restored.[21] On this score, Banderas appears to have hurt his own cause among the councillors of the Eight Towns by his lapses into demagoguery, as in his depictions of himself as an 'emperor' and the reincarnation of Moctezuma.

As it turned out, however, the issue would be decided not in tribal council but on the battlefield. In the second year of the renewed war, Banderas seems to have come to believe that he had won over the Opatas to the north to his cause. This belief appears to have been rooted in promises made to him by the two main Opata leaders, the brothers Virgen and Dolores Gutiérrez. It was in expectation of being reinforced by a large contingent of Opatas that Banderas led his army of Yaquis and Mayos in a bold attack against the Sonora stronghold of Arizpe in December 1832. The new state governor, Manuel Escalante, called out the militia and launched a two-pronged riposte to the Indian offensive. One militia force headed off to attack the Mayo and Yaqui towns, while a second, comprised of 400 men led by the governor's brother, Leonardo Escalante, moved to intercept Banderas's troops. On 6 December, the two armies collided outside Soyopa, a mining town in the central Yaqui Valley, where the Yaqui leader waited for his Opata allies to join him. Only a few Opatas showed up, however, led by their chief Dolores Gutiérrez, and the Indian army was routed. Banderas and Gutiérrez were captured and taken to Arizpe, where, on 7 January 1833, along with eleven other Yaqui, Mayo and Opata 'leaders' of the rebellion, they were executed.[22]

Before his execution by firing squad, Juan Banderas made a public confession in which he attempted to take upon himself full blame for the Yaqui rebellion. According to his confessor, Father José Joaquín García Herreros, who took down his words, Banderas told the crowd that he had set a 'bad example' for his people and 'exhorted them to work hard as good Christians should, to respect the authorities, and to coexist peacefully with their yori neighbours'. Although it no doubt is true that, as Evelyn Hu-DeHart has suggested, Banderas's confession was motivated by a desire to 'divert military action against his people'[23], his exhortation also offers us a glimpse into an ideology of resistance only partially emancipated from the Yaqui past and, particularly, from the long Yaqui tutelage under the Jesuits. For all its novelty, in linking messianic Catholicism with the redemption of Moctezuma, Banderas's appeal to his Yaqui constituents and potential allies represents only a partial step toward the forging of a movement of resistance capable of coming to grips with the realities of post-independence Mexico. Banderas's most prominent successor as leader of the Yaqui people in revolt, Cajeme, would couch his call to arms in a very different language. Placed at the head of the Yaqui towns in the 1870s and '80s, he would position himself not as heir to the mantle of Moctezuma or the standard bearer for an Indian saint but as a soldier, a former officer in the yori armies with experience in modern warfare, and would call not for a return to the 'colonial pact' of yesteryear but for the establishment of an autonomous Yaqui republic.

Yaquis and Hacendados

With the collapse in 1833 of the rebellion led by Banderas, the Yaquis were obliged to adopt a new strategy for survival, what Evelyn Hu-DeHart has described as 'alliance with a major outside party or faction, putting themselves in a subordinate, essentially combatant, capacity'. In practice, this meant taking sides in the civil war between Conservatives and Liberals which dominated Mexican public life almost from the first years of the Republic and culminated in the War of *La Reforma* in 1858–60. The Yaquis backed the Conservatives, who had promised not to touch their communal landholding system or to infringe upon their political autonomy. The Liberals, meanwhile, took measures to divide up Indian lands into individual plots and to subordinate Indian communities to rule by the central government.[24] The Lerdo Law of 1856, best known for its impact on Church landholding in Mexico, also demanded the breaking up of collectively held Indian lands, in order to fulfill the Liberal dream of transforming the Indians into 'money-conscious freeholders'.[25] In Sonora, the Conservatives were led by the Gándara family, one of the state's most powerful hacendado clans. Yaqui warriors served as one of the mainstays of the Gándara coalition, which at different times also included Mayos, Opatas and Pimas. In 1857, the Yaquis administered two stinging defeats to Liberal forces, at El Redito and Pitahaya, and went on to attack the Sonora port of Guaymas, although they ended up being driven off by the local National Guard.

But the tide now began to turn in Sonora, with the ascent of a rival hacendado clan, the Pesquieras, adherents to the Liberal cause. Colonel Ignacio Pesquiera, the head of the clan and soon to be governor of the state of Sonora, invaded Yaqui country in 1858. Determined to punish the Indians for their support of his rivals, Pesquiera proposed to colonise the Yaqui and Mayo river valleys with white and mestizo settlers, especially *californios*, people from Sonora who had taken part in the California Gold Rush and returned empty-handed.[26] To clear the way for the new settlers, Pesquiera adopted a policy toward the Yaquis that Edward Spicer called 'wholesale and apparently indiscriminate killing'. Troops stationed in the Yaqui country took advantage of reports of Yaqui violence to descend on their towns, shooting some people and taking others prisoner.[27] Pesquiera believed that the preaching of racial hatred by Yaqui women was a major factor behind the Indians' truculence, and saw to it that, whenever possible, Yaqui males and females were separated, with the latter being deported or taken into urban households as servants.[28] In the circumstances, it is not surprising that the Yaquis flocked to the banner of the imperial government imposed on Mexico by the French in the 1860s.

PART II

The French interlude

Paris had sent an expeditionary force to Mexico in 1864 for the ostensible purpose of forcibly collecting debts owed to France by the Mexican government. It soon became clear, however, that the French had a much more ambitious agenda than this. France's ruler at the time, Emperor Louis Napoleon, saw himself as a champion of Latin civilisation, which he believed to be threatened in the Americas by the remorseless expansion of the Anglo-Saxons of the USA. He believed that as the cultural heir of Rome and the Eldest Daughter of the Catholic Church, France had a duty to help create a bulwark against Yankee expansionism in Mexico. The Emperor had other, less noble aims in mind in sending his troops to Mexico, however. High up on the list were the silver mines of Sonora, whose great wealth had been extolled to Louis Napoleon in 1863 by the former California senator William M. Gwin, a Confederate sympathiser. Gwin urged the Emperor to make Sonora a French colony and open it up to settlement by Confederate refugees.[29] The Yaquis were cast by the French as a key element in this scheme.

In March 1865, French troops under the command of Colonel Isidore-Théodule Garnier leapfrogged up the Mexican coast from Sinaloa and seized the Sonoran port of Guaymas.[30] Although some historians have assumed that the aim of the invaders was to deny the Liberal forces of Benito Juárez a port that could be used to bring in war supplies, Garnier seems to have been pursuing grander ambitions.[31] One of the civilian passengers with the invasion fleet was the former Conservative governor of Sonora, Manuel María Gándara. Colonel Garnier's baggage also contained orders from the French military commander in Mexico, General François-Achille Bazaine, 'to use all convenient and necessary expenditures to attract and use the Yaqui tribe'. Thus, soon after landing at Guaymas, Garnier made contact with the Yaqui leader, José María Marquín, and promised him the rank of general and 'an honorarium' of 100 pesos if he would form a Yaqui force to march alongside the French. Adding his voice, Manuel María Gándara wrote to Marquín exhorting him to 'obey the "*jefe francès*" in all matters'.[32]

Garnier now advanced into the interior and twelve miles inland at a place called La Pasión, with the support of Yaquis and local forces, met and soundly defeated a Sonora Republican army led by Ignacio Pesquiera. The French victory was a signal for a general revolt by the Yaquis, under the leadership of José María Marquín, soon to be followed by the Mayos and finally the Opatas and Pimas.

The Franco–Indian alliance went from strength to strength, taking the capital, Hermosillo, without firing a shot. In August 1865 the city of Ures welcomed Garnier's army with open arms, and Ignacio Pesquiera was obliged to flee across the border to Arizona. Gwin's Confederate settlement scheme, and plans under consideration in Paris to make Sonora a French colony, soon went by the board, however, as pressure from Washington obliged the French to move back from the border with the United States. General Bazaine ordered his troops to concentrate in the centre of the country, which left France's Indian and Conservative allies in Sonora and Chihuahua to deal alone with resurgent Republican forces.[33]

In 1866, Napoleon III called the French troops home, thus condemning to an early death the Mexican Empire he had created and placed under the stewardship of the Austrian prince, Maximilian. Without Bazaine's regulars, the Conservative–Church alliance was not strong enough to sustain the imperial regime. Even so, its death might have been avoided or at least postponed, some critics have argued, had the Emperor followed the French lead and forged a nationwide alliance with Indian peoples like the Yaquis. During his first year as emperor, argued Jack Autry Dabbs, Maximilian owed nothing to the Mexican conservatives and 'could have founded his empire on Indian support and drained the Juarist armies of their manpower'. As events in Sonora had demonstrated, there was good potential for Indian–Conservative cooperation, so long as Indian demands for political autonomy and collective land ownership were met. But the French had taken the process a step further. In 1863, Louis Napoleon had ordered General Bazaine to create a unit in the Foreign Legion 'in which Indians were favoured'. The new regiment was to be composed of volunteers serving under French officers and was to receive 'the same training, equipment and treatment as the Foreign Legion'. In addition, the Indians 'were to be allowed to work their way up through the ranks as in the [West] African regiments. In effect, the French policy in Africa was to be applied in Mexico.'[34] Time, however, proved to be too short, and by the time the French left Mexico three years later only two Indian companies, some 175 men, had been incorporated into the Foreign Legion.[35]

Maximilian failed to follow up on this initiative, in Dabbs's view, because his ministers 'soon fell into the slough of Mexican custom' and turned their backs on the Indians.[36] A better explanation would be that the Emperor's conservative supporters had no wish to be beholden to Indian allies for victory in the civil war with the Juáristas and, in any case, seem to have believed that they could obtain victory without them. This, of course, proved illusory. Within a year after the French departure, the Emperor's Mexican army was overwhelmed in battle and he was captured by the Juaristas, tried and convicted of treason, and shot.

Incident at Bacúm

As might have been expected, Ignacio Pesquiera, back from exile in Arizona to lead the Republicans to victory in Sonora, adopted a fiercely punitive policy against the Yaquis. A large militia force under General Jesus García Morales was turned loose in Yaqui and Mayo country, with orders to employ a scorched earth policy if necessary to bring the Indians back to obedience. In February 1868 'an atrocity so terrible that it got a permanent place in the history of

Sonora, not only as told by Yaquis but even as written by Mexicans, was committed by troops under García Morales' command'.[37] Major Prospero S. Bustamante was given a large force of infantry and cavalry (and 250 Yaqui auxiliaries), and ordered to comb the Yaqui towns for weapons. When too few guns were found, the major took 450 Yaqui men, women and children prisoner and, having locked them in a church in the town of Bacúm, announced that he would release one prisoner for every firearm turned in. Ten Yaqui 'leaders' were held hostage on the understanding that they would be shot if the prisoners tried to escape. Two artillery pieces were trained on the church door. Major Bustamante later reported to his superiors that at around 9.30 in the evening of 24 February prisoners broke down a wall of the church and tried to escape, hurling bricks at the soldiers on guard and shouting that they would rather die than remain locked up. Confusion ensued, the Major said, and soldiers opened fire on the church with artillery, setting the building ablaze. When this Mexican Oradour-sur-Glâne was over, 120 bodies were recovered from the ashes; 59 Yaquis survived, though all were badly burned; and the remainder escaped into the night. The ten hostages were shot.[38]

Coming of Cajeme

Though the massacre at Bacúm would never be forgotten by the Yaquis, General García Morales's relentless campaigning, plus catastrophic floods in the Yaqui river valley in late 1868, 'finally weakened the Yaquis' strength and spirit. For close to another decade, they did not take up arms again'. When the Yaquis did return to the fray in 1875, having concluded that their old nemesis, the Liberal caudillo Ignacio Pesquiera, was finally losing his grip, the political and military situation in Sonora and, indeed, in Mexico generally, was on the verge of monumental change. The arrival in power a year later of General Porfirio Díaz, hero of the war against the French and later rival of Benito Juárez for leadership of the Liberal faction in Mexican politics, would give Mexico its first effective central government since the country became independent from Spain in 1821. For the first time, the authority of Mexico City was extended throughout the length and breadth of the land, penetrating even into the remote northern border states. In Sonora, for example, the Pesquiera family would be pushed aside in the 1870s in favour of the clan of General Luis Torres, who, along with his cronies Ramón Corral and Rafael Izábal, would manage state politics on behalf of the Díaz government down to its demise. The arrival in power of the Torres clique would effectively nullify the Yaqui strategy of maintaining the status quo by playing off the great hacendado families against each other.

A new Yaqui strategy of resistance was clearly called for, and was not slow in coming. Coincidental with the decline of the old order in Sonora, a new leader emerged in Yaqui country with a new vision of Yaqui independence. He was a former soldier, in the armies of Ignacio Pesquiera no less, named José María

Leyva, better known to his people as Cajeme ('He who does not drink'). In 1875, with the approval of the municipal councils of the Eight Towns, Cajeme declared the Yaqui lands an independent republic and turned the skills he had acquired in service with the yoris to forging a more modern Yaqui army and to building a network of fortifications to defend the new republic against invasion. The wars that would come in the 1880s would be the bloodiest yet waged between Yaquis and Mexicans.

The 'Caste War' in Yucatán

Introduction

The uprising in Yucatán that would become known as the 'Caste War', pitting as it did the Mayan Indian masses of the southern and eastern part of the region (who called themselves 'the people' or *masewalob*) against the white ruling class or *ladinos*, began on 30 July 1847 with an Indian assault on the provincial town of Tepich. The long struggle which ensued proved to be the bloodiest American Indian war since the conquest of Mexico by Cortez. As many as a third to a half of Yucatán's six hundred thousand inhabitants may have died in the struggle.[39]

Given its savagery and long duration – the last group of rebels made peace only in the 1930s – it is probably not surprising that historians continue to argue about the causes of the Caste War. Until fairly recently, the accepted wisdom held that the 'War of the Castes flared up from the smouldering embers of racial hatred, kept alive in the Indians by their long mistreatment by the Whites'.[40] This view began to change with the generation of historians of the war whose work appeared from roughly the end of the Second World War to the 1990s. They tended to see Mayan 'mistreatment' more in economic than in racial terms. The conflict was brought on in the first place, they argued, by the greed for land and power of Yucatán's new post-revolutionary creole ruling class, symbolized most dramatically in the rise of the henequen plantation with its notorious recourse to debt peonage and slave labour. Another key stimulant to 'caste war' in the view of these historians was the ladinos' failure to abide by a promise to abolish Indian property taxes in return for their involvement in the successful struggle for independence from Mexico in 1839–40.[41]

This so-called 'materialist' explanation for the Maya uprising has been challenged in recent years by writers who see political factors playing a more important role, particularly the alienation of Mayan elites and the frustration of Indian expectations of a 'partnership' with whites in running the country after independence.[42] Historians who have taken an interest in the more strictly military aspects of the Caste War, meanwhile, have underlined the importance of Mayan militia service in the Yucatán independence struggle of 1839–40, an unprecedented event in the history of the region and one made possible only by the desperate need of the ladino rebels for troops. 'Fighting . . . under their own

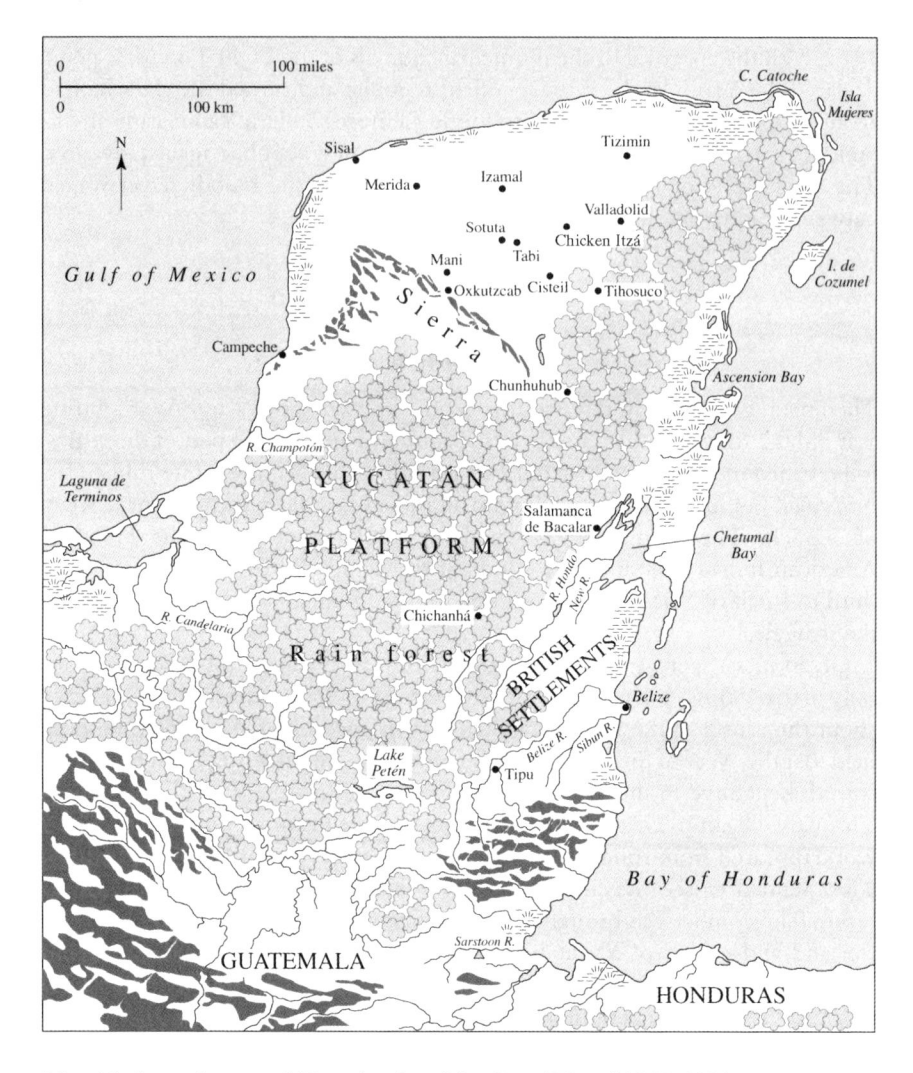

Map 6.2 A terrain map of Yucatán, site of the Caste War of 1847–1900.

leaders and for their own objectives . . . they learned to like the sound of the bugle and drum, the excitement of battle, the pride of victory won.'[43] Perhaps. What seems more likely is that, having gained military experience and having been allowed to bear arms in combat for the first time in the course of their stint in the independence movement, the Indians sensibly had come to believe that this would considerably improve their chances of victory should a showdown come with the ladinos.[44]

The Mayan army

Clearly, the way the Mayans organised their military owed much to their experience fighting alongside the whites during the war of independence. As in the ladino militia, the core unit of the masewalob army was the battalion, comprised of 800–1,200 men divided into eight companies. *Comandantes* (majors) commanded at battalion level, while captains served as company commanders. One interesting adaptation of ladino military practice concerned the transformation of traditional *ligero* or skirmisher formations into multi-purpose field service units. In the Mayan armies, ligeros were responsible for bringing up ammunition, evacuating their own wounded and, unhappily, dispatching those of the enemy with their machetes, the only weapon they carried.[45]

But the Mayan military differed from its white counterpart in one important way. Like indigenous armies all over the world, the Mayan army was a family affair. Wives and children accompanied soldiers into battle, not only to help carry the tools of war and cook meals, but also because in 'the method of war adopted as soon as the rebellion began . . . anyone, male or female, armed or not, could add to the shouts and constant noise that were the hallmarks of rebel battle'.[46]

The Ladinos face defeat

For the first year, the fighting went very badly for the whites. To begin with, they were heavily outnumbered. The ladino population was placed on a virtual total war footing: All men between the ages of 16 and 60 were ordered to report for military duty and, if they owned guns, to bring them with them. The army that took the field would be largely middle and upper class in composition, since the bulk of the Yucatecan lower classes, the Indians, were on the other side. Before assistance began to arrive in the 1890s from the Mexican regular army, the ladinos fought the war almost exclusively with militia, the state National Guard. The only regular unit available for service was a Light [Infantry] Battalion.[47] Before the Caste War ended, 'approximately 17% of the Ladino population would be under arms . . . compared with about 2% of Americans in the American Revolution, and 10% in the Second World War'.[48]

Nor could the ladino army expect much aid from outside. The opening phase of the Caste War coincided with the US–Mexican War, but, even without this distraction, little help could be expected from the Mexican state, since Yucatán had fought for and managed to win its independence from Mexico in 1840. For the duration of the US–Mexican War, the US Navy maintained a blockade of the Yucatán coast, which for a short while kept out supplies from a sympathetic Spanish colonial regime in Cuba. Finally, the efforts of British authorities in Jamaica to curb arms sales to the Mayan rebels by merchants in British Honduras (Belize) enjoyed little success.[49]

PART II

The white armies also suffered from a lack of experience of the kind of bush warfare they were obliged to fight. Since most of the peasantry was on the other side, the ladino forces were composed largely of urban dwellers. Nelson Reed gives a graphic description of the hurdles they had to overcome in order to fight effectively against the Mayas.

> They had to learn how to march ten or twenty miles, down rocky, winding, jungle paths, with shoes or sandals that could take the wear, with feet that didn't blister. They had to conserve water; not to drink when thirst was strong and sweat it all away, but to rest a time in the shade and then rinse the dust from the mouth. They had to learn to cook and eat miserable food, to sleep on the ground wrapped in a blanket and still be able to move the next day.[50]

Whatever technological edge the ladinos might have enjoyed was of little use to them in the bush. The jungle fighting weapon par excellence was the machete, whose use 'couldn't be taught; it was simply a matter of slashing before you were slashed, with no nonsense about cut and thrust'. The Mayas also possessed superior means of communication. While ladino columns tried to signal with bugles, usually without much success, the Mayas used a hollow log drum called a *tunkul*, 'whose voice could be heard for miles'.[51]

The hard-pressed ladinos tried to take comfort in the notion that the inferior *indios* would eventually lose ground because they were incapable of generating leadership of their own, and would be forced to rely for generalship upon mestizos or whites who came over to their side. This consolation quickly evaporated, however, as the masewalob were seen to employ 'tactics entirely new to the country, unknown by the whites'. They shunned pitched battles in the open, choosing instead to dig in behind parapets scattered here and there throughout the deep woods they knew so well. The rebels waged a 'war of pure surprises', of 'ambushes skillfully disposed and devised'. In this kind of fighting, the Mayas 'held an immense superiority' over their town-bred enemies. As they blundered through the forest, Yucatecan soldiers would suddenly find themselves confronted by 'barricades of boulders or tangled logs and branches thrown across the road, and in the instant of recognition would come a withering fire from the barricade and either roadside'.[52]

The Mayan way of war

The Mayas soon demonstrated that their uprising was no simple peasant *jacquerie*. Although the rebels did sack many of the great plantations and burn the *nohoch cuenta*, documents held by the landlords that were used to justify Indian debt peonage, they also laid siege to a number of towns and cities, with a surprising degree of success. Throughout history, peasant armies like those of the masewalob have repeatedly courted defeat by entering into sieges, which require a certain amount of technical skill and, most importantly, the capacity to feed, clothe, shelter and keep motivated large numbers of besiegers for months on end. Most irregular armies have done poorly at this; the Mayan rebels of the Yucatán Caste War may be the great exception to the rule. For they not only successfully besieged the garrison town of Ichmúl for a month at the end of 1847, but in March 1848 forced the evacuation of the city of Valladolíd and repeatedly interdicted the refugee column, killing large numbers of soldiers and civilians.[53] By the time the first phase of the war came to an end in mid-1848, rebel troops were at the gates of the Yucatán capital, Mérida, and US

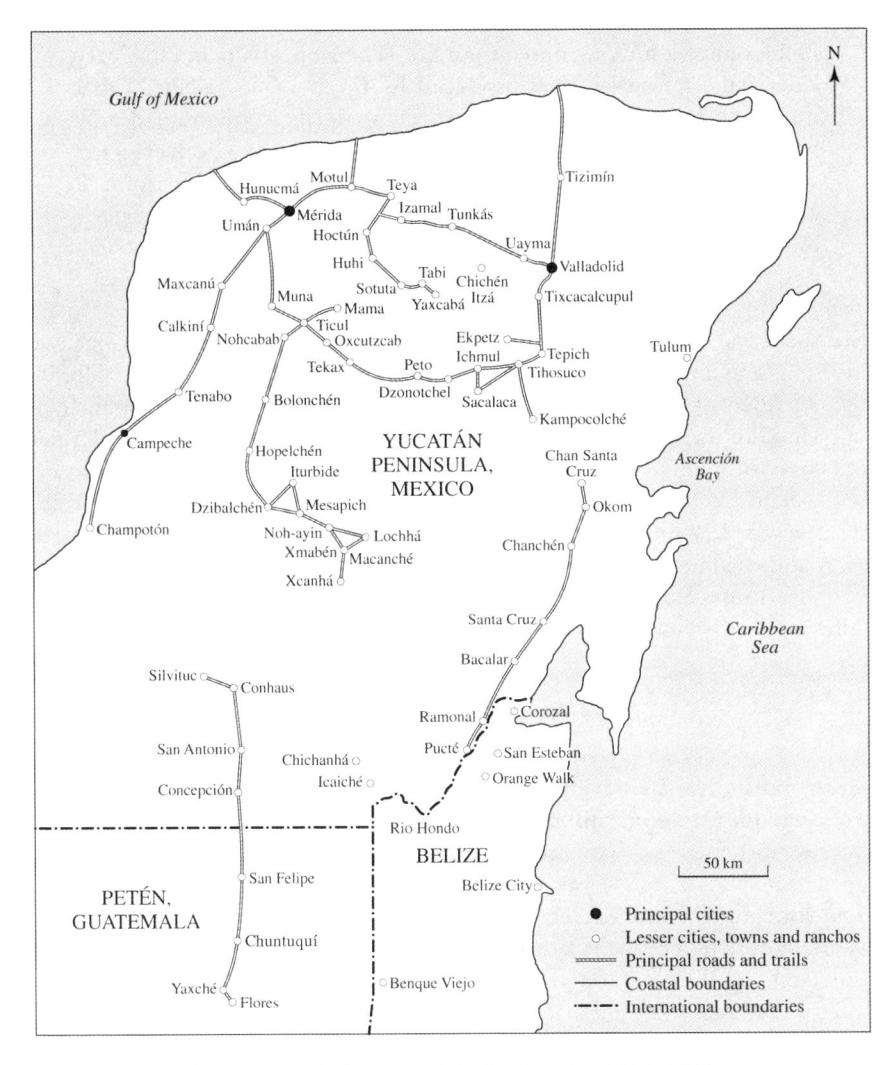

Map 6.3 Sites of importance in the Caste War in Yucatán, 1847–1900.

Marines had been landed to protect the foreign community in the port city of Ciudad Carmen against encircling Indian armies.[54]

Mayan success in the war so far owed something to the terror *indios* inspired in the ladino population. One element in this was the knowledge that 'all the wounded who remain on the field of battle are invariably killed' by the rebels, usually by chopping them up with the ubiquitous machete. '[T]his fact has been the main cause of the state National Guard's demoralization'.[55] But the Mayas also excelled in terrorizing the Yucatecan civilian population. A veteran general officer described in harrowing terms the psychological warfare employed by the Mayas to capture besieged towns.

> [T]he din of a heavy, constant gunfire (albeit uncertain and not very lethal); the infernal uproar produced by the horrible yelling of that multitude of unarmed people who accompanied . . . [the rebels] only with the aim of instilling fear by their yells; and among whom even the women and children mingled; the fires; and the isolation from all communication, came to prey on the defender's mind . . . so they ended by trying to flee from it even when they had the power to resist, preferring to find death outside rather than in that frightful . . . enclosure.[56]

But there was also method in the rebels' siege technique. Before a target was invested, buildings for several kilometres around were burned down, to deprive the defenders of cover. Then a unique system of barricades would be thrown up. Much of the open country of Yucatán is littered with loose rocks. Under the cover of smoke from huge fires, the rebels would roll these rocks forward with their feet until they got within musket range of the enemy walls, whereupon they piled them up into drystone barricades from which to blaze away at the ladino defenders. In the siege of Ichmúl, the Mayas ringed the town with drystone barriers, defended them against successive sorties by the defenders, and eventually starved the inhabitants into flight.[57]

Yucatán seeks help from the USA

A desperate Yucatán government now turned to foreign powers – to Britain, Spain and the USA – for help, even offering to accept protectorate status in exchange for economic and military assistance. The US government signalled interest and Yucatán's governor, Santiago Mendez, sent his son-in-law, the liberal intellectual Justo Sierra O'Reilly, to Washington to negotiate a treaty. The young envoy saw Secretary of State James Buchanan, was invited to the White House by President James K. Polk, and watched from the gallery as the President called upon Congress to authorise the dispatch of an expeditionary force to Yucatán, warning that if the USA did not go to the aid of the embattled country, the whole region would fall under the sway of the British. The President's address touched off a storm of fiery rhetoric among members of his

Democratic party in Congress. Senator Jefferson Davis of Mississippi was particularly strident. Cuba and Yucatán were 'the salient points on the Gulf of Mexico', the future president of the Confederacy explained, 'which I hold to be a basin of water belonging to the United States. . . . I am ready for one, to declare that my step will be forward, and that the cape of Yucatán and the island of Cuba must be ours'.[58]

But Sierra O'Reilly's mission came to naught. The opposition party in Congress, the Whigs, made a determined stand against US intervention, while public interest in a Yucatán venture, which had been high when the Yucatecan envoy first arrived in Washington, faded quickly once the US–Mexican War ended in February 1848. The American retreat into indifference forced the Yucatecans to rethink their relationship with Mexico, and on 17 August 1848, a treaty was signed reintegrating Yucatán into the Mexican Republic.[59] But expectations of aid from Mexico proved groundless. Some money and a few rifles were forthcoming, but substantial Mexican assistance against the Mayan rebels would come only in the 1890s. Thus, although, as we will see, some mercenaries would come to its aid, for the most part the white population of Yucatán would be left to struggle on alone against its Mayan foes.[60]

The tide of war turns

But the Mayan armies had serious weaknesses, too, and these were already evident in the headiest days of the uprising's success. To begin with, as was so often the case in Indian warfare, disunity in the ranks of the insurgents threatened to nullify battlefield victory. The western Maya, 'long adjusted to the status quo of white rule', not only failed to support their eastern and southern brethren but actually provided foot soldiers for the ladino cause. And, among those Mayas who did take the field, triumphs too often brought dispute over who should take the credit and carry off the spoils. Factions emerged around the two main leaders of the insurrection, generals Jacinto Pat and Cecilio Chi, who fell to fighting among themselves in mid-1848; both protagonists were murdered by rivals in the course of the next year.[61]

The greatest weakness of the masewalob army, however, was its very peasant composition. Simultaneously farmers and soldiers, the Mayan insurgents could only wage war seasonally. When it was time to plant corn, the Indian trooper 'rolled up his blanket and put it in his food pouch, tightened the thongs of his sandals and started for his home and his cornfield'. Thus, the Mayan army that had won numerous pitched battles, successfully besieged cities, and had the ladino enemy at its mercy in the spring of 1848, melted away on the eve of a great victory. 'They had beaten the [whites], taken thousands of rifles and loot beyond counting, and that was good; but now it was time to plant corn'. But Nelson Reed, who is our best English-language source on the military side of the Caste War, fails to see that, however unfortunate this exodus from the battlefield might have been for the Mayan cause, it was almost certainly unavoidable. Without corn, the peasant army could not stay in the field, much less feed the families who remained at home. Besides, the planting of corn had a religious significance for the Mayas that transcended even this practical consideration. Failure to plant corn would not only leave empty the bellies of the insurgents' children but cost them the grace of God as well.[62]

The return of the Mayas to their fields gave the hard-pressed Yucatecans a breathing space which they quickly put to good use. Incompetent officers were sacked and new troops recruited. And experience appears to have taught ladino soldiers much-needed bush fighting skills. A rebel told a captive priest that the Yucatecan troops he faced in late 1848 were made of sterner stuff than the soldiers he had fought earlier.

> These are not, Señor Vicario, those who abandoned Vallodolíd [in January 1847]. . . . When we besiege these people, they counter-besiege us quickly; when we think to surprise them with our ambushes, we ourselves are surprised from the rear.[63]

Also, the rebels' supply of weapons and ammunition was interrupted for a time by Yucatecan seizure of the town of Bacalar, on the border with British Honduras. This supply lifeline would change hands again in the course of the fighting, and would only cease to be a factor in the contest in the 1890s when the British finally signed an agreement with the Mexican government in which they promised to enforce a moratorium on the arms traffic with the Mayas. In 1849, the white army went on the offensive for the first time, and, as the year wore on, the Mayas were pushed back, in the direction of the nearly impenetrable rainforests of the southeast.

The Yucatecan army campaigned now for the first time as an army of occupation. Large garrisons were established in towns big enough to support them and satellite outposts or *cantones* radiated out over the surrounding countryside. These cantones served as surveillance posts but also as bases for foraging operations, since the ladino troops now lived off the land, as the masewalob army had always done.[64]

The invading army included a small North American contingent, veterans of the US–Mexican War recruited by the Yucatecans with a promise of $8 a month and 320 acres of land once the fighting was over. These were the first of a long series of Yankee filibusters who sought to expand the dream of Manifest Destiny to encompass the Caribbean and Central America.[65]

The 1,000-man North American force, under the command of one Joseph A. White, a former captain in the Louisiana Volunteers and now a self-promoted 'colonel', went into action in December 1849. The Yucatecans had divided White's 'regiment' into battalions and separated these from each other by several days' march. This may have been done to discourage the development of a proprietary feeling about the country among the North Americans. Or it may have been to keep them from ruining the Yucatecan army's battle plan. 'The noise of [the North Americans'] heavy boots as they marched, the constant loud talking in the ranks, the pipe smoking and flower picking', inspired little confidence. But White insisted that his men be given a chance to show their stuff and the regional commander, Colonel Juan de Dios Novelo, finally relented.

> And when they met their first barricade, they laughed at Novelo's suggestion of the usual flanking [manoeuvre], fixing bayonets to make a frontal assault, knowing that no Mexican, much less an Indian, could face cold steel. They were wrong. The first volley caught them point blank, and Novelo had his hands full bringing out the forty casualties, one slung on either side of a mule.

Years later, a Mayan veteran of the Caste Wars, Leandro Poot, told a North American interviewer that

> It was easy to kill the strange white men, for they were big and fought in a line, as if they were marching, while the white men of Mérida and Valladolíd fought as we do, lying down and from behind trees and rocks.[66]

Despite the setback suffered by their North American allies, the ladino armies continued to recapture lost territory. The Mayas were gradually pushed eastward into the region where the rebellion had begun. By 1853, nearly half of the insurgents had surrendered or simply gone home. Many of them retreated into the wastelands in southern Yucatán, where they enjoyed de facto separation from the central government. Known as *pacíficos*, they found themselves under attack from time to time by their diehard former comrades-in-arms, the so-called *bravos* who occupied the dense rainforests near the border with British Honduras. The proximity of the bravos to the British colony gave them continued access to arms and by the mid-1850s the fortunes of the Mayan rebellion began to revive.[67]

The cult of the Speaking Cross

The stiffening of Mayan resistance, however, was due less to military supplies from British Honduras than to a religious revival that had begun deep in the southeastern forests. There, toward the end of 1850, a Speaking Cross had appeared, carved on a mahogany tree in the village of Chan Santa Cruz. The cross told the Indians who began to gather in the village that it was the Holy Trinity come to earth to aid the Mayas in their struggle and to protect them against the white man's bullets. The cult of the Speaking Cross, which would eventually become the mainstay of both the political and military wings of the Mayan rebellion, was from the outset described by the ladinos as an 'invention' of a mestizo ally of the masewalob named José María Barrera, although the 'voice' of the cross was presumed to have been a Mayan ventriloquist called Manuel Nahuat. It seems worth pausing here to note, once again, the reluctance of whites to ascribe the origins of anything momentous, even a religious cult they despised, to mere Indians. A Maya could, of course, be the voice of the Speaking Cross, but the *idea* of the Cross and the content of the messages it conveyed had to emanate if not from a white man, at least from a mestizo. Some at least of the ladinos who propagated this tale of mestizo 'invention' of the Speaking Cross should have known better. The notion of talking crosses had a long history among the Maya, going back to the early days of their conversion to Catholicism. The anthropologist Alfonso Villa Rojas concludes that 'It is not surprising, therefore, that the Cult of the Cross, reviving as it did practices already deeply rooted in religious tradition, was so readily accepted by the Maya. . .'.[68]

The Cult of the Speaking Cross must be seen as another of the 'revitalisation movements' by which sorely pressed Indian peoples sought to preserve their way of life from white encroachment by making 'a deliberate, organized, conscious effort . . . to construct a more satisfying culture'.[69] To some extent, the Mayan cult, whose members referred to themselves as the *Cruzob* or 'People of the Cross', resembled the 'nativistic' brand of revitalisation practised by the Shawnee Prophet Tenskwatawa and the Creek Red Sticks and described by anthropologist Ralph Linton, in that it preached total isolation of the faithful from the surrounding white society and implacable hostility toward it. 'The whole society emphasized group solidarity and a hostility toward all outsiders', wrote Villa Rojas.[70] But in other important ways the cult fell short of being nativist. It did not, for example, preach a return to an earlier, purer existence, shorn of alien cultural accretions, as did Tenskwatawa or the Creek Red Stick prophets. The leaders of the Cult of the Speaking Cross continued to organise their military along the lines of the ladino militia units and were as assiduous in acquiring firearms from the traders in British Honduras as their predecessors had been. As we have seen, they even contemplated amalgamation into the neighbouring colony of British Honduras. The culture of Chan Santa Cruz thus can best be described as a blend of older elements dating from colonial times with new ones deriving from the struggle for independence. Villa Rojas was of the view that 'the Catholic forms of ceremonial, submission to the priests and to the Church, [the] authority of the *caciques* [regional strongmen] and village chiefs [and] religious fiestas' could be categorised as holdovers from the colonial era. The Caste War and the struggle to create a new, independent form of government, meanwhile, had produced 'the politico-religious systems of social control with the Cult of the [Speaking] Cross at [their] center, [and, as we will shortly see] division into military companies, the Guard of the Saint, strong sentiments of group solidarity reinforced by hostility to outsiders, [and] the use of the death penalty. . .'.[71]

The cult survived a raid by ladino soldiers against Chan Santa Cruz on 23

March 1851, in which the Speaking Cross, now ensconced in a church, was carried off by the invaders and the ventriloquist Nahuat killed. The village was quickly reoccupied by the Mayas and 'three new wooden crosses, said to have descended from heaven' came to take the place of the one carted off by the enemy. The new crosses were described as being the 'daughters' of the original one and, like it, possessed the power of speech. They were placed in a sanctuary within the church in Chan Santa Cruz to which only the priests of the cult of the Speaking Cross were admitted. At this point, the messages of the crosses ceased to be exclusively oral, as 'written letters containing instructions, exhortations and commands' began to emerge from the sanctuary. These written directives were conveyed to the faithful of Chan Santa Cruz and surrounding villages by the priests of the Speaking Cross, principally Juan de la Cruz Puc, 'who claimed to be its minister through his power of entering heaven and conferring with God, angels, and cherubim'. Puc's communications were variously signed 'Son of God', 'Creator of the Christians' or 'Our Lord Jesus of the Holy Cross'.[72]

Gradually the priesthood of the Cross assumed control over all official business in Chan Santa Cruz, which now became the capital of the maselawob rebellion. In time its power spread to encompass the whole of the rebel zone in southeastern Yucatán.

> It not only determined general policies but transacted foreign affairs, and specified many details of internal life in the [rebel territory], stating the amounts and kinds of labor and tribute needed, disposition of prisoners of war, material improvements which were to be made, and which Yucatecan towns were to be attacked.

Eventually all of this became too much for the priests to handle and they were obliged to create a triumvirate of officials to manage day-to-day affairs. The triumvirs bore religious titles – Patron of the Cross, Interpreter of the Cross, and Organ of the Word – but their duties were overwhelmingly secular, including oversight of the rebel armies. For a new-style armed force had grown up in the shadow of the Speaking Cross. Its nucleus was the Guard of the Saint or simply *Guardia* that had been formed around 1850 to protect the sanctuary of the Speaking Cross. The Guardia gave rise to a new militia, composed of 150-man companies grouping all males over the age of 16. Each of these companies was commanded by a hierarchy of officers, ranging from corporal (*cabo*) through major (*comandante*). When the cabos died or were promoted, their replacements were elected by an assembly of all company personnel; vacancies at the top were filled by promotion. Officers of the militia wore no insignia of rank; the only way one could identify a comandante was 'a better quality of earring in the left ear'.[73]

During the 1860s the bravos and their new military formation went on the offensive, taking advantage of the financially strapped ladino government's inability to keep a large army in the field. These were the great years of the Cult of the Cross, with government forces in retreat and a return to the rebel fold of about half of the pacíficos who had opted out of the struggle in the early 1850s. In time, however, the bravos camp found itself in the throes of a religious schism as dissidents stormed the sanctuary at Chan Santa Cruz and forced the priests and their followers to take refuge in the neighbouring town of Tulum. The two factions of the Cult remained at odds through the 1870s and into the succeeding decade.[74] By then, however, the Mayan separatist movement faced an even greater threat, the arrival in power in Mexico City of the regime of Porfirio Díaz.

Conclusion

In the years to come, both the Yaqui and Mayan rebellions would find themselves confronted with a new and potent challenge: a centralised and interventionist Mexican state which viewed Indian demands for political autonomy and collective ownership of land as insidious barriers to economic development. This new era was ushered in by the coming to power in 1876 of General Porfirio Díaz, who would rule Mexico as a virtual dictator until his ousting by the Revolution of 1910. Díaz would bring to an end the political division which had gripped his country since independence and which had offered so much room for manoeuvre to Yaqui and Mayan dissidents. Under Díaz's iron hand, the great caudillos of the North, whose jostling for power had allowed the Yaquis to play them off against each other, were now stripped of their power, the local National Guard units which had functioned as their private armies were reduced to obedience to Mexico City. Although part-Indian himself, Don Porfirio had no sympathy for the Indian insurgents who chose to defy the authority of his regime. Indeed, he saw them as a major impediment to economic development, whose promotion was the main preoccupation of his government. The '*paz octaviana*' he had imposed upon Mexico's rebellious generals and great landlords was seen as a necessary first step in encouraging an influx of foreign capital to finance national economic development. An equally vital second step would be the suppression of Indian dissidence. North American investors, for example, could not be expected to sink capital into a country where wild Indians were allowed to disturb the public peace and flout the authority of the state. They had to be brought to heel, by seduction where possible, by force where necessary. Díaz's government would deploy the Mexican army in the Indian wars to a much greater extent than its predecessors had done, and in both the Yaqui and Mayan conflicts its intervention would be decisive. And when the Indians proved unwilling to accept the verdict of battlefield defeat, as was the case with the Yaquis, Díaz was prepared to employ even sterner measures. In the early years of the twentieth century, hundreds of Yaquis would be rounded up by Díaz's troops and his new rural police force and deported to faraway Yucatán, where they would toil alongside captured Mayan insurgents as virtual slaves in the henequen fields.[75]

7

WAR ON THE PLAINS, 1848–77

The 'Mexico Moon'

A profound fatalism about cross-border Indian raids seems to have gripped the population of the Mexican states bordering on Texas, as reported, if with some exaggeration, by a North American traveller, George F. Ruxton, in the 1840s. Describing the reaction of the people of the state of Chihuahua to Comanche raids, Ruxton found it 'unbelievable' that so little effort was made to resist the incursions, 'since Comanche invasions were seasonal and along known routes and should not have caught the people unprepared'. Part of the problem, Ruxton believed, was that most Chihuahuans were not allowed to own weapons and therefore did not know how to use them. Knowing this, he said, the Comanches 'never hesitate to attack superior numbers'. The usual outcome, as he reported it, was pitiful.

> When in small parties the Mexicans never resist, even if armed, but fall upon their knees and beg for mercy. Sometimes, however, goaded by the murder of their families and friends, the *rancheros* collect together, and, armed with bows and arrows and slings and stones, go out to meet the Indians (as occurred when I was passing), and are slaughtered like sheep.[1]

The Comanche raids usually came in the autumn, beginning in the month of September, which was marked out as 'the Mexico Moon' on the Comanche calendar. The war parties, meeting little opposition, ventured further and further afield as time passed, sometimes raiding as far south as Zacatecas or even San Luis Potosí, halfway to Mexico City.[2] The 'staging area' for these raids was at the Big Springs of the Colorado River, in western Texas close to the New Mexico border. From there the Comanches moved south over war trails so large and well-known 'that they appeared on period maps of the region'. A Texas scout described them as 'Twenty-five deep worn and much used trails [which] made a great road . . . a highway by which each year the Comanche of the North desolate Durango and Chihuahua.'[3] The lament of the Chihuahua legislature in 1846 betrays the despair and sense of helplessness of residents of the state faced with constant Indian raids.

> [W]e travel the roads ... at their whim; we cultivate the land where they wish and in the amount that they wish; we use sparingly the things they have left us until the moment that it strikes their appetites to take them for themselves.[4]

But help was on the way, from the very same US Army that invaded Mexico and relieved it of half of its national territory in the 1846–8 war. This help did not arrive by way of the terms of the Treaty of Guadalupe–Hidalgo which had brought the war to an end, as Mexicans had hoped. Article XI of the treaty had stipulated that the US would be responsible for the Indians in its new territories (including Texas) and that Mexican citizens could sue the US government for damages caused by those Indians as a result of cross-border raids. The US government, however, had had second thoughts about this pledge and managed to get the Mexicans to agree to abrogate the article during negotiations in 1853 on the so-called Gadsden Purchase, a 29,640 square mile strip of land in what is today southern Arizona and New Mexico acquired from Mexico for $10 million.[5] The relief from the raids of the Comanches (and the Apaches) would come only later and as a by-product of campaigns by the US Army to make Texas and the Southwest safe for Anglo settlers.

Texas frontier wars

Although the relationship did not begin that way, the inhabitants of Texas soon took their place alongside the Mexicans as hereditary enemies of the Comanches and their Indian allies. The Comanches had made a distinction between Mexicans and the North Americans who had come to Texas as colonists when the territory was part of Mexico. In 1822, a band of Comanches had surprised Stephen Austin, the leader of the North American emigrants, and two companions and robbed them of their belongings. When they learned that the men were North Americans and not Mexicans, the Indians restored the stolen goods. But the influx of American settlers after the independence of Texas in 1836 began to change this attitude. Relative peace continued during the administration of the first president of the Texas Republic (1836–8), Sam Houston, companion-at-arms to Andrew Jackson at the battle of Horseshoe Bend, as we have seen, but also a lifelong friend of the Cherokees. Houston's conciliatory policy was rejected by his successor, President Mirabeau Buonaparte Lamar, who called for 'an exterminating war ... which will admit of no compromise and have no termination except in their [the Comanches] total extinction or expulsion'.[6]

The point of no return was reached in what is known as the 'Council House Fight' at San Antonio on 19 March 1840. A delegation of Comanches had

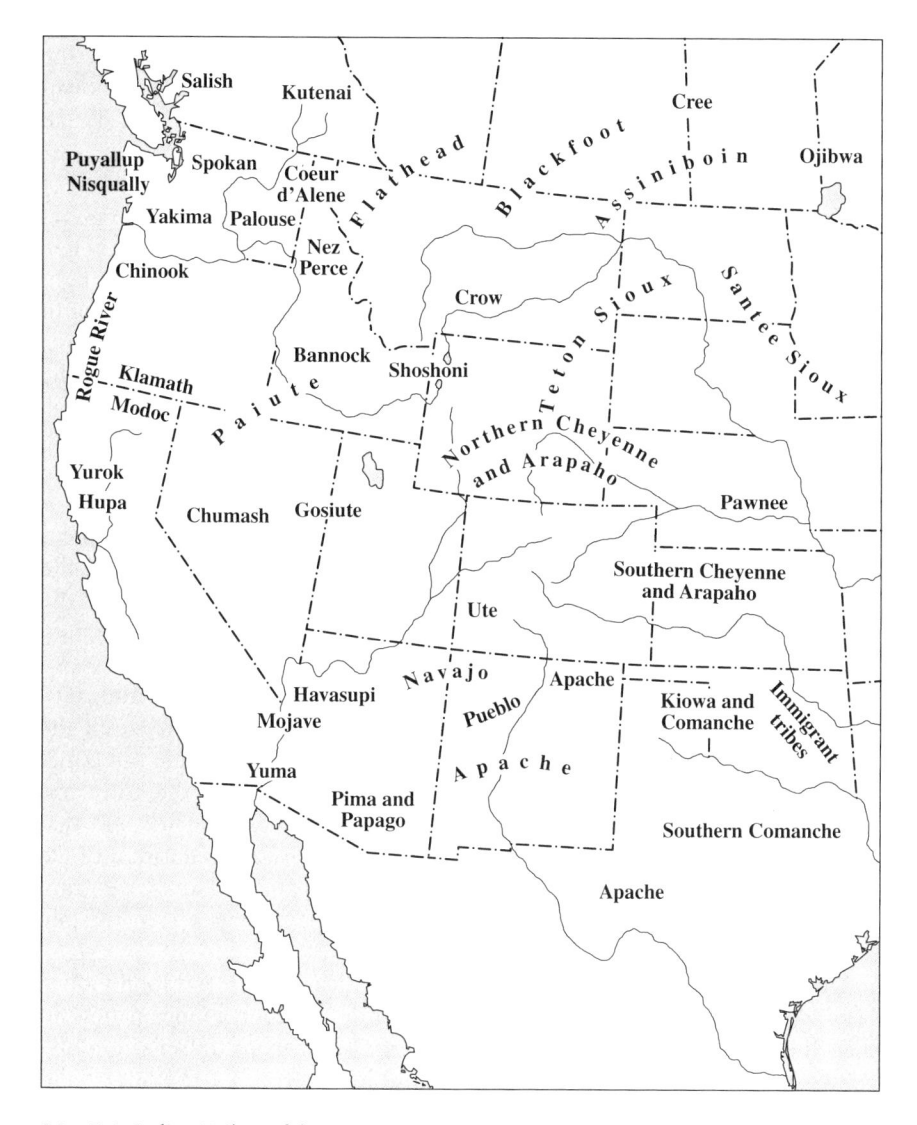

Map 7.1 Indian Tribes of the western USA in 1850.

come to the town to negotiate a treaty of peace with commissioners of the Texas Republic. The Indians had been told that peace would only be possible if they surrendered all of the white captives and property they had accumulated in the previous years of frontier warfare. When it turned out that the Comanches had only brought some of their captives with them, their chiefs were informed that they would be held as hostages until all of the captives had been brought in. A scuffle ensued in the Council House, leading to a general mêlée in the streets of San Antonio in which 35 Comanches were killed and the rest taken prisoner. Over the next two years, the Texans carried out an offensive which drove the Comanches further to the north and west of the Republic. But, 'the Indians neither forgot nor forgave their losses at San Antonio. Thereafter a Texan received no more consideration than a Mexican or a Spaniard'.[7]

Until Texas became part of the United States in 1845 the main burden of defence against the Indians rested upon the shoulders of the Texas Rangers, yet another of those bodies of 'hardy frontiersmen' recruited to fight Indians in lieu of the regular army. The Rangers had come into being in 1835 to fight Mexicans, not Indians, however, and their first service was in the liberation of Texas from the army of Mexican President Antonio López de Santa Anna. Once independence had been won, they received the mandate of guarding the borders of the new Republic of Texas against Mexican and Indian marauders. The Texas Rangers cannot be easily defined. As one source says: 'The Rangers were an irregular body, mounted but furnishing their own horses and arms; they had no surgeon, no flag, nor any of the paraphernalia of a regular army or state militia'.[8] While they became 'commissioned state law enforcement officers' in 1874 when Reconstruction began winding down in Texas, the Rangers clearly played a quasi-military role in the state – indeed served as the state's de facto army – prior to that time, even after the primary responsibility for frontier defence had been handed over to the US Army following Texas's entry into the Union. Down to the War Between the States, they continued to mount campaigns against Indians, in some cases with the knowledge of the regulars, in other cases not. Relations between the two forces were not good. Texas luminaries such as Sam Houston were convinced that the army was incapable of defending settlers against the fast-moving Comanches and that only frontier fighters like the Rangers could do the job. The regulars' attitude toward the Texas Rangers, meanwhile, was probably summed up by the army surgeon Albert J. Meyer's description of the typical Ranger as a 'lazy ruffianly scoundrel'.[9]

Under the command of officers like Benjamin McCulloch and John Coffee Hays, the Texas Rangers fought a number of battles against the Comanches and their Indian allies, usually in tandem with large numbers of Indian scouts and combatants. In 1858, for example, 'Rip' Ford led a force of 102 Rangers and 113 Indians from a number of tribes into Indian Territory in search of Comanche raiders.[10] In the course of establishing their sprawling secondary empire on the southern plains, the Comanche confederation, like that of the Sioux to the north, had accumulated a wide array of Indian enemies, peoples such as the Lipan Apaches, Osages, Tonkawas and Wichitas. These victims of the 'Lords of the South Plains' proved eager to supply the Texas Rangers with scouts and spies. When the task of defending the Texas frontier fell to the regular army after Texas joined the Union in 1845, the Comanches' Indian foes turned to serving the bluecoats, along with Eastern Indians from Indian Territory: Delawares, Shawnees and Black Seminoles.[11]

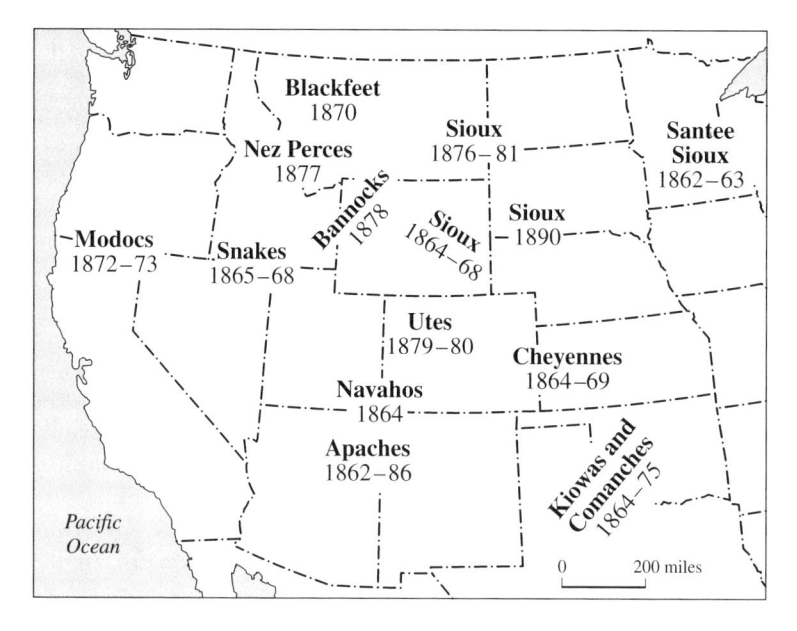

Map 7.2 Sites of the US Indian wars, 1862–90.

The defeat of the Southern Cheyennes

The years just after the Civil War brought vigorous efforts by the US Army and the government in Washington to bring the Plains Indian wars to a close. While General Sherman, commander of the troops in the West, argued for an aggressive forward policy, particularly in the wake of the Fetterman Massacre of 1866, the government found itself under considerable pressure to give peace a chance from humanitarian interests in the East, who took the Sand Creek Massacre of 1865 as *their* point of reference. The result was a compromise, at least as far as the South Plains were concerned, whereby General Winfield Scott Hancock, the Union hero of Gettysburg, would lead a large armed force into the region to, as Sherman reported to army headquarters, 'confer with [the Comanches, Kiowas and Southern Cheyenne and Arapaho] to ascertain if they want to fight, in which case he [Hancock] would oblige them'.[12] The record seems to indicate that Sherman held out little hope for a peaceful settlement, indeed thought that fighting not only would be necessary but preferable. Hancock left for the plains with a warning from Sherman ringing in his ears: 'This [state of affairs] cannot be tolerated for a moment. If not a state of war, it is the next thing to it, and will result in war unless checked'. Indian agents on the South Plains got an even sterner briefing from Hancock. He was going into the field, they were told, 'prepared for war and will make it if a proper occasion presents. . . . No insolence will be tolerated'.[13]

PART II

The force Hancock led onto the plains was one of the largest yet mustered for a Western Indian campaign, some 1,400 men. There were eleven troops of the new Seventh Cavalry, led by Colonel George Armstrong Custer, making his debut as an Indian fighter, seven companies of infantry and a battery of artillery. For scouts, the general had the services of fifteen Delaware warriors. His courier was no less a Western icon than James Butler 'Wild Bill' Hickok, the frontier gunfighter and lawman who would later serve as chief of scouts for General Philip Sheridan. And, to round off the cast, the reporters covering the campaign included Henry Morton Stanley, soon to earn undying international fame as the intrepid newspaperman who 'found' Dr. Livingstone.[14]

Hancock's little army, however, was less formidable than it appeared on paper. Raw recruits filled the ranks and the units they served in had only been in existence for a few weeks. The cavalrymen scarcely knew how to ride while the infantry had never been on an extended outing before. The troops also had only the slightest acquaintance with their weapons, single-shot, muzzle-loading rifled muskets.[15]

On 12 April, Hancock met with a small group of Brulé Sioux and Cheyenne chiefs at Pawnee Fork, Kansas, among them Tall Bull, the leader of the Cheyenne Dog Soldiers. If the Pawnee Fork conclave was intended to be the carrot of Sherman's policy, it failed entirely in its aim. To give Hancock his due, he did try to strike a conciliatory note. He and his men had fought great battles during the Civil War, he said, whilst the Indians had only fought in small skirmishes. 'There was, therefore, no renown to be gained in fighting Indians, and [he and his troops] did not desire to do so.'[16] Reports of the Pawnee Fork conference do not tell us what Tall Bull and his Dog Soldiers thought of that line of reasoning. They do, however, tell us that when the Cheyenne leader complained that all the railroad building on the plains was scaring off the game, Hancock broke in to say, 'If you should ever stop one of our trains, and kill the people on it, you would be exterminated'.[17]

Not surprisingly, when Hancock announced his intention to continue the dialogue at the Cheyenne–Sioux camp further up the Pawnee Fork, the chiefs expressed some reluctance. When Hancock nonetheless marched on the village on 14 April, he encountered an Indian skirmish line under the command of that redoubtable Cheyenne warrior, Roman Nose. Its purpose, however, was not to fight Hancock's host, but to gain time for the women and children in the village to flee.[18] Thus, when Hancock entered the camp the next day, it was empty. The general's subsequent decision to burn down the Pawnee Fork encampment and to unleash Custer and the Seventh Cavalry in pursuit of the 'hostiles' meant that the war many in the government back in Washington were hoping to avoid was now inevitable. General Hancock's attempt 'to bully the Southern Plains tribes', wrote Robert Utley, 'touched off a bloody and perhaps needless war'.[19]

General Sheridan now devised a strategy for putting an end to the Cheyenne threat. In a winter campaign, when the Indians were most vulnerable, three columns would converge on their villages in the region of the Texas Panhandle. One column would march from Fort Lyon in Colorado, a second from Fort Bascom in New Mexico, and a third from Fort Dodge in Kansas. The major engagement of the campaign turned out to be Colonel Custer's 29 November 1868 surprise attack on a camp of Cheyennes on the Washita River in Kansas. Custer's Seventh Cavalry troopers descended on the camp at dawn from four directions, killing more than 100 Cheyennes, taking 53 women and children prisoner, and slaughtering some 900 Indian ponies. But the village was only one of a series of Indian encampments in the area and Custer was obliged to leave in a hurry to avoid reprisals. In his haste, he left behind a detachment of fifteen troopers under the command of Major Joel Elliott, last seen galloping down the river valley in pursuit of fleeing Indians. Their bodies later were found along the Washita. Some officers took the view that Custer had knowingly abandoned Elliott and his men to their fate; this was the beginning of the bitter feud within the Army between Custer loyalists and detractors.[20] There were also charges from Eastern peace advocates that the Washita raid was another Sand Creek, but Custer managed to convince his superiors that the Cheyenne village was in fact a war camp, containing plentiful evidence of raids on white settlements, along with four white captives, two of whom died in the attack.[21]

The final blow for the Southern Cheyennes in this round of fighting came on 11 July 1869 at Summit Springs, Colorado Territory, where Major Eugene Carr and his Fifth Cavalry troopers, guided by Pawnee scouts, surprised a camp of Cheyenne Dog Soldiers and put them to flight, killing 50 warriors and their leader, Tall Bull, in the process.[22] The Southern Cheyennes and Arapahoes now all repaired to the Indian Territory reservation set aside for them, but hopes that this would remove the Indian nomads from the South Plains proved to be premature. Rather than leaving the reservation in Indian Territory during the summer season to hunt buffalo on the Staked Plain of Texas and then returning once the hunt was over, as provided for under the terms of the Treaty of Medicine Lodge of 1867, significant numbers of Comanches, Kiowas and Cheyennes seemed determined to remain permanently on the plains. In fact, some of the Comanches, the fierce Qahadi band led by Quanah Parker, had never gone onto the reservation at all.

The Red River War, 1874–5

In 1874, General Sherman decided to put an end to the Southern Plains Indian problem. In late June 1874, a force of perhaps 700 of these Indians had descended upon Adobe Walls, the former trading post in the Texas Panhandle where their people had fought 'Kit' Carson ten years before. This time, they had come to wipe out a party of buffalo hunters who were using the site as a camp. This was a large war party, and its size gives an indication of the hatred the Indians felt for the hunters, who were in the process of killing off what remained of the Southern buffalo herd, the Indians' traditional source of

PART II

sustenance. Urged on by a Comanche shaman, Isatai, who had promised them victory, the allied Indian force, under the leadership of Quanah Parker, launched what they expected would be a surprise early morning attack on the camp. Unfortunately for them, the hunters were already up and about, in the process of repairing a beam in a saloon on the post that had broken in the night. Although there were only 29 of them, the white men (and one white woman) had long-range buffalo guns, plenty of ammunition and thick adobe walls to shelter behind. As was so often the case, the Indian attackers proved unwilling to undertake a sustained frontal assault on a dug-in enemy, despite a big advantage in numbers. After losing 13 of their warriors to the hunters' rifles, and

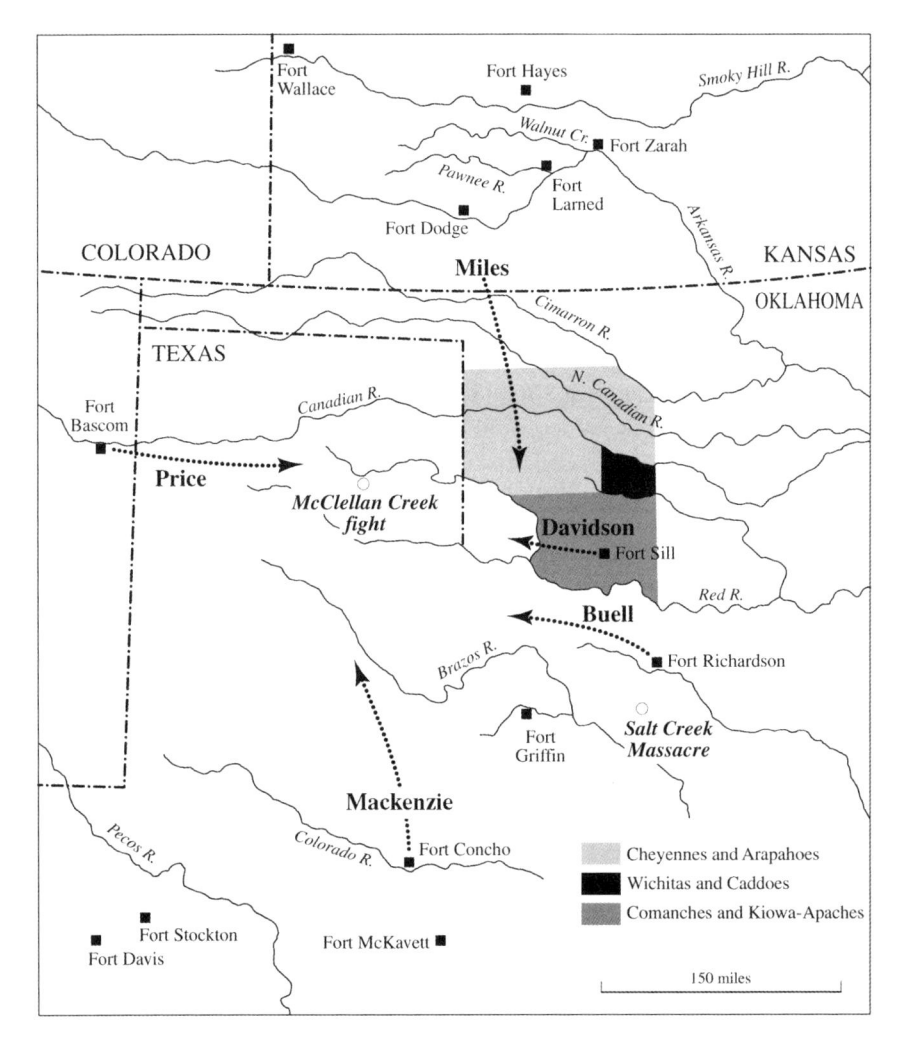

Map 7.3 South Plains War against the Comanches and Kiowas, 1874-75.

with Quanah Parker wounded, the war party withdrew in the course of the afternoon. It was an embarrassing repulse and a hapless Isatai, the medicine man who had promised them success, was made to bear the brunt of the blame.[23]

A large force under General Nelson Miles now converged in six columns on the western portion of Indian Territory and the Texas Panhandle, where scouts said the itinerant Comanches, Kiowas, Cheyennes and Arapahos could be found. The bluecoat army comprised 46 companies, amounting to over 3,000 men. The war it waged proved to be much more of a 'war against nature' – against 'blue northers', the fierce storms that struck suddenly on the Texas plains; thirst; dysentery from a surfeit of fresh buffalo meat – than the battle against a resolute and fearsome foe that many of the troopers may have anticipated. The Comanches and their Kiowa, Cheyenne and Arapaho allies had deteriorated considerably as a fighting force since their heyday in the pre-Civil War years. The destruction of the Southern buffalo herd had taken a heavy toll, but so had incessant warfare and disease. By 1874, there may have been no more than 2,500 Comanches left – men, women, and children – on the reservation and off.[24] The numbers of Kiowas and Cheyennes had also declined considerably (the Southern Arapahoes, never numerous in any case, were a negligible factor).

It was the 450 men of a Fourth Cavalry column, led by the hard-driving Colonel Ranald Mackenzie, who struck the fatal blow of the Red River War, at the battle of Palo Duro Canyon on the edge of the Staked Plain. The canyon, a gash cut some 800 feet deep and an average of six miles wide in the prairie, had long been a favoured winter hideout of the Qahadis. Well-watered, with plenty of forage for the Indians' large pony herd, the canyon in late September 1874 sheltered 'a literal forest of Cheyenne, Kiowa and Comanche tipis'.[25] It was Mackenzie's Tonkawa Indian scouts who found the camp and brought his cavalry to the canyon brink to peer down into the gulf below, just after dawn on 28 September.[26] After a lengthy search, the troops finally found a narrow path leading down into the canyon and the men began to descend. En route, they were spotted by a Comanche sentry, who fired off a warning shot. Although the sound echoed off the canyon walls, the vast camp below did not stir. '[O]nce again the lie-abed habits of the Indians, and their lack of organization, played them false', surmised Wilbur S. Nye.[27] Another way to put it might be that the Comanches and their allies had allowed themselves to be lulled into a false sense of security. In any case, by the time Mackenzie's soldiers reached the canyon floor, most of the Indians were fleeing down the 40-mile-long valley. In the ensuing exchange of fire, only four Indians were killed and one soldier wounded. Nonetheless, the battle was a devastating defeat for the Comanches and their allies. The troops burned the Indians' tents and belongings and slaughtered over 1,000 of their horses. With winter upon them, the destitute Comanches and Kiowas had little choice but to head for the reservation at Fort Sill. Quanah Parker and his Qahadi band held out in their old home on the Staked Plain for as long as they could, but, in the end, they, too, came in to the fort to surrender.[28] They were followed the next year by the last of the Southern Cheyennes, defeated at the Battle of Sappa Creek, Kansas, by the US Sixth Cavalry in April 1875. Indian resistance on the South Plains was over.[29] And, the Mexico Moon was no more.

Warfare on the Northern Plains

At mid-century it may have seemed remarkable that there had been no significant trouble between the expansionist Sioux confederation and the Americans since Lewis and Clark had denounced them at the turn of the century as the most potent threat to US interests on the High Plains. This informal truce was about to be shattered, however. The breakdown came because of the great flood of emigrants that accompanied the Gold Rush in California. The wagon roads across the plains drove a wedge into the great North American buffalo herd – and, by consequence, split the Cheyenne and Arapaho peoples – into northern and southern branches. The dispersal of the buffalo and the growing scarcity of other game and forage along the wagon routes brought attacks on emigrants by neighbouring Indian tribes and forced the government in Washington to undertake the building of military posts along its course. Amongst these were Fort Kearny in Nebraska and Fort Laramie in Wyoming. Neither this nor the negotiating of the Treaty of Fort Laramie with the Plains tribes in 1851, promising them $50,000 a year in trade goods, would stave off the coming of war between the Sioux confederation and the US Army, however.

The first outbreak of violence between the Sioux and the army took place, as we have seen, in August 1854, when an infantry unit from Fort Laramie under the command of a recent West Point graduate, Lieutenant John L. Grattan, tried to arrest a Miniconjou warrior who had slaughtered a stray cow from a passing wagon train. When the warrior refused to surrender, the soldiers provoked a confrontation in which the entire 29-man command perished; one trooper managed to crawl back to the fort and give the alarm before dying.[30] As Colonel Callwell had emphasised, it was an iron rule of colonial warfare that outrages such as this must not go unpunished.[31] Revenge for the massacre of Grattan's command was a year in coming, but when it came it was thorough. Punishment of the Sioux was administered by a soldier who by this time was known throughout the Old Army as a specialist in matters of this sort: General William S. Harney, last seen in these pages hanging Irish deserters from the US Army during the Mexican War. As recounted in Chapter 4 above, on 3 September 1855, at Ash Hollow in Nebraska, Harney provoked a fight with a band of Brulé Sioux he later claimed were party to the Grattan massacre; in the ensuing battle 85 warriors perished and 70 women and children were taken prisoner.[32]

The Civil War period, rather than offering a hiatus to Indians in the West, actually greatly increased their vulnerability. The image of North and South ignoring the West while they fought each other east of the Mississippi is highly misleading. The West's growing supplies of gold and silver were crucial to the Union war effort and the government in Washington saw to it that the shipments of precious metals got through. Troops also were detailed to guard the country's new transcontinental telegraph network, completed in 1861, and to protect the emigrants who continued to make their way west in spite of the war. Indeed, two of the most notorious incidents of the US western Indian wars occurred while the nation's attention presumably was directed eastward.

Uprising in Minnesota

The first of these incidents, however, an uprising of the Santee Sioux in 1862, took place in the woodlands of eastern Minnesota, closer to the Mississippi River than to the Great Plains. (A scene from this uprising graces the cover of this book.) The sources of the discontent which led to the outburst of violence in Minnesota will be familiar by now to readers of this book. While some members of the Santee Sioux had managed to adjust to a settled reservation life, becoming farmers and even intermarrying with nearby white families,[33] others became restive as the contours of their old life progressively faded. Prominent among the discontented were the members of the tribe's warrior societies, who saw the prospects for valorisation through war diminishing. The spark that lit the fire, however, was government failure to keep promises of food and other supplies for the Indians, as guaranteed by treaty. On 15 August 1862, Sioux who went to the Indian Agency in search of food were told by a trader called Andrew Myrick, in a New World version of the Marie Antoinette story, that if they were hungry they could eat grass. The next day warriors attacked the Indian Agency, killing 20 whites and leaving Myrick dead with his mouth stuffed with grass. In all, some 400 whites, many of them recent emigrants from Germany and Scandinavia, died that day as Indian raiders struck across the region. Leadership of the rising devolved upon Little Crow, descendant of a prominent Santee chief of the same name and a man previously distinguished by his pliability in the face of white demands. He had been, for example, largely responsible for acceptance of an agreement in 1858 which divided up what was left of the Santee lands into individual plots. All the evidence indicates that Little Crow did not believe that an uprising could succeed and that he counselled against it when it was being planned. But like William Weatherford, secular military leader of the Creeks during the 1813–14 war, Little Crow bowed to the popular will and even took a leadership role in the rebellion. He subsequently showed a firmer grasp of the tactical and strategic necessities of the struggle than most of his cohorts.

It appears clear in retrospect that the Santee revolt would have achieved greater success if Little Crow's strategic proposals had been followed. He argued that the major target of the insurgents should be the only big army post in the state, Fort Ridgely, whose capture would have left the frontier defenceless. The warrior society members on the war council, however, managed to win support for a strategy which focused instead on killing settlers and plundering their communities. Much time and energy were subsequently expended on futile attacks on the town of New Ulm. Large numbers of federal troops were eventually drafted into Minnesota under the command of General Henry L. Sibley, many of them recruits intended for service with the Union Army in the East. On 23 September 1862, Sibley's force defeated the Santees at the battle of Wood Lake and forced the surrender of most of those in the field. Three months later, on 26 December 1862, 38 Santees convicted of murder and rape were hung at Mankato, Minnesota. Little Crow, meanwhile, met a more mundane fate. He was shot and killed by two white settlers while picking berries in a remote part of Minnesota.[34]

Little Crow's revolt stirred reverberations further west, as Santee survivors of the fighting who were resettled on Sioux reservations in Dakota Territory aired their grievances to their brethren. This led to a further burst of campaigning against the Sioux by General Sibley, in the Dakotas this time, in tandem with a force under the command of General Alfred Sully. Although General Sully managed to defeat the Sioux at the Battle of Killdeer Mountain in South Dakota, the victory did nothing to restore peace to the region.[35] Instead, it set the stage for even more serious fighting between the Sioux and the bluecoats after the conclusion of the Civil War.

The Minnesota uprising also set the stage for possible complications in US relations with British Canada. The Santee Sioux had fought alongside the British in the War of 1812 and had continued to entertain hopes that should they enter into conflict with the Americans, they could expect help from the British in Canada. This hope appears to have been an ingredient in the war planning of the Santees. After the Wood Lake defeat, Little Crow and a delegation of Santees went to the Red River Colony in Manitoba to seek help. None was given, but the American authorities remained wary of British activities in the region. The suspicion that Britain was prepared to aid Indian dissidents in areas of the USA adjacent to Canada appears to have led to renewed discussions in Washington about the feasibility of annexing Manitoba and western Canada in general.[36]

Sand Creek

People called them the 'Bloodless Third'. It rankled. The Third Colorado Volunteer Cavalry had enlisted in the summer of 1864 for 100 days of campaigning against hostile Cheyennes. Now it was November; their time was almost up and they had yet to kill a single Indian. Their commander, however, was not 'bloodless'. Colonel John M. Chivington had led a Colorado volunteer regiment into New Mexico in the summer of 1861 and had won plaudits for his role in the defeat of a Confederate army at the battle of Glorieta Pass. But this triumph was not enough for the ambitious Chivington. He had political aspirations. Earlier, he had failed in a bid for a US Congress seat and appears to have concluded that a successful campaign against the Cheyennes and Arapahos said to be periodically on the warpath in the eastern part of Colorado Territory would help repair his political fortunes. But Chivington was not only a colonel of volunteers and a political hopeful, he was also a man of God. In fact, he had made his reputation as a Methodist preacher, bringing the gospel to the rough mining camps of Colorado. They called him the 'Fighting Parson'.

On 29 November Chivington led a force of some 725 men of the 'Bloodless Third' in a dawn attack against a camp of Cheyennes and Arapahos near Sand Creek, Colorado. There were about 500 people in the camp. Since many of the men were away hunting, almost all of them were women, children and old people. The residents of the camp believed themselves to be under the protection of federal troops at nearby Fort Lyon. Their chief, Black Kettle, was flying an American flag from his tipi.

The Coloradans opened their assault with a barrage of howitzer fire, then galloped into the camp from two sides with guns blazing. The Indians fled, many of them to the nearby stream bed, where they frantically tried to dig holes for shelter. Chivington's troopers bombarded the cowering mass with howitzer and rifle fire, killing about 150 of them. The rest, a surprising number in the circumstances, escaped onto the prairie. The soldiers spent the remainder of the day burning the camp, rounding up Indian ponies, and scalping and mutilating the dead. On 22 December they rode back down the streets of Denver, displaying the scalps and severed genitalia of their Cheyenne and Arapaho victims to cheering crowds.

The Sand Creek massacre led to almost immediate retaliatory attacks by Indian war bands, not just Cheyenne and Arapaho but also sympathetic Sioux. The town of Julesburg, Colorado, was sacked twice and transportation across the plains was virtually halted. The massacre was condemned by public opinion back East as well and gave a strong boost to the movement for a peaceful resolution of differences with the Indians. A special commission was formed to investigate the massacre and congressional and military inquiries were launched. Though Chivington and the ex-'Bloodless Third' were condemned by the investigators for their unprovoked attack on the Sand Creek camp, no one was ever prosecuted for the deed. Chivington resigned his military commission before he could be court-martialed.[37]

In 1865 the army found itself occupied with Indian efforts to avenge the Sand Creek massacre. These included an engagement at Platte Bridge Station in central Wyoming on 25 July, in which a cavalry unit led by Second Lieutenant Caspar Collins was nearly wiped out by a large force of Cheyennes, Arapahos, and Sioux. The army fought back by mounting a retaliatory expedition into the Powder River country of Wyoming under the command of General Patrick Connor. The expedition was a three-pronged affair reminiscent of the later, ill-fated campaign of General Albert Terry against the Sioux, in which Custer's Seventh Cavalry was destroyed. The main column, led by Connor, was to

PART II

move northwest from Fort Laramie along the eastern flank of the Big Horn Mountains; a second column under the command of Colonel Nelson Cole had the mission of skirting the east and north sides of the Black Hills; and a third column led by Lt. Colonel Samuel Walker was to march directly north from Fort Laramie, making contact with Cole's force in the vicinity of the Cheyenne River headwaters, after which the combined force would join up with General Connor along the Tongue River. The expedition was not a success. Although Connor's column managed to destroy an Arapaho village on the Tongue River in late August 1865, the Cole and Walker columns found themselves beset by perhaps the largest Indian army ever to take the field during the Indian wars, some 3,000 Cheyenne, Arapaho, and Sioux warriors led by the famous war leader Roman Nose. The man with the powerful medicine rode straight at the bluecoat ranks.

> But not a bullet touched him, although the soldiers had shot at him from only twenty yards away down the entire line of defense. Three times Roman Nose rode up and down the soldier line until they shot his horse out from under him. Roman Nose catapulted to the ground but quickly picked himself up and calmly walked away . . . his back arrogantly turned to the soldiers, the power of his war bonnet still protecting him from the soldier bullets.[38]

The battle came to be known in Cheyenne history as simply 'Roman Nose's fight'. Only skillful use of artillery enabled the beleaguered columns to extricate themselves from Indian encirclement. The 8 September engagement was followed by a storm of freezing rain, which killed 414 horses and pack animals. Cole's and Walker's force was finally located by Pawnee scouts from Connor's column and directed back to Fort Connor, completely exhausted and useless for further service.[39]

Sheridan's master plan

But the Army's travail on the high Plains did not end with the failure of the Connor expedition. Its continuation was assured by the increase in emigrant traffic on the wagon roads west that followed the discovery of gold in Montana. Attempts by government negotiators to win approval from chiefs from the Sioux confederation for use of a new road to Montana fell through when one of the principal Sioux leaders, Red Cloud, baulked at the simultaneous construction of new forts along the route. Throughout 1866 the Sioux confederation held these forts under virtual siege, in the process killing 96 officers and men and 58 civilians. Most of the soldiers perished in the Fetterman Massacre on 21 December 1866, when Brevet Lieutenant William Judd Fetterman ignored explicit orders to the contrary and led 80 troopers away from the fort in pursuit of Indian raiders. In an ensuing ambush by some 1500 Sioux and Cheyennes,

Fetterman's force perished to a man.[40] The defenders of the forts did better in two engagements the following year – the Hayfield and Wagon Box fights of 1–2 August – but when in renewed negotiations at Fort Laramie Red Cloud demanded abandonment of the forts, the army quickly agreed.[41]

The army's willingness to abandon the forts was the result of a decision to focus protection on the last lap of construction of the transcontinental railroad. The Union Pacific Railroad was moving through southern Wyoming at the time, destined for link-up with its western counterpart, the Central Pacific Railroad, at Promontory Point, Utah, on 10 May 1869. The Treaty of Fort Laramie, signed in the autumn of 1868, created a Great Sioux Reservation comprising the western half of what is today the state of South Dakota, and set aside an 'unceded' region between the Black Hills of South Dakota and the Bighorn Mountains of Montana as an exclusive Indian hunting ground and a 'no-go' area for whites. The terms of the treaty held, further, that no change in these arrangements could be made without the agreement of three-quarters of the Indians involved.

Five years later the Treaty was defunct, done to death by violations of its letter and spirit by settlers and railroad surveyors. The mass invasion by whites of the Black Hills in Dakota Territory, sacred to the Sioux and promised to them in perpetuity by the Laramie treaty, following rumours of a gold strike in 1875, was the final blow to peace. When government efforts to buy the region from the Sioux for six million dollars were rebuffed, it was decided at a high-level conference in Washington, involving President Grant and his cabinet and generals Sheridan and Crook, that the Indian problem on the High Plains would have to be resolved for once and all. The Sioux and allied bands that continued to roam the once-inviolate unceded area between the Bighorn Mountains and the Black Hills would be placed on reservations set aside for them, by force if necessary. Messengers informed the Indians in the unceded region that they had until the last day of January 1876 to report to their reservations. When they gave no sign of complying, General Sheridan launched a major expedition to surround the Indians and force them to accede to government orders.

Sheridan's master plan for achieving this aim combined the two by now classic strategies evolved by the US Army for fighting Plains Indians, i.e. it called for a winter offensive against the Sioux and Cheyennes, employing the converging columns strategy that had worked so well on the South Plains the year before. Columns of troops coming from the west, south and east were to surround the Indians and oblige them to fight or surrender. A considerable flaw in this strategy quickly came to light, however. As we will shortly see, Sheridan's subordinate General George Crook would learn in an abortive foray into Montana's Powder River region in March 1876 that campaigning in winter on the South Plains, 'blue northers' or no, was like a spring outing compared to what troops could expect to put up with in winter on the High Plains. As Sheridan's biographer Paul Hutton has observed, '[Sheridan's]

Map 7.4 Great Sioux War, 1876–77.

logistical problems – enormous on the southern plains – were insurmountable in the north'. There was, however, a much more serious, and ominous, flaw to the general's strategic plan than its unrealistic timetable: the gross underestimation of the Indian enemy that informed it. In Paul Hutton's words,

> Sheridan's most grievous error . . . was his refusal to recognize the ability of the hostiles to muster large numbers of warriors or to comprehend their willingness to stand and fight. No amount of evidence could dissuade him from his conviction that large numbers of Indians could not stand against his troops.

Sheridan's view held – and it was an outlook widely shared among his subordinates – that no matter how many Indians were wandering around loose on the High Plains, the force being sent against them was more than adequate to prevail. The big challenge, Sheridan assured his commanders, would not be to defeat the Sioux and their confederates, but to catch them before they ran away. '[Sheridan's] worry was that the troops might not find the Indians, not that they could not be defeated if they did find them'.[42]

Even after an early spring setback to General Crook's column on the Powder River had demonstrated Sioux and Cheyenne resolve, Sheridan continued to scoff at the Indian threat. On 19 May 1876, as he was preparing to launch his summer campaign, he to wrote his commander-in-chief, General Sherman, that reports of large numbers of Indians on the move were irrelevant: a big Indian force, he said, 'cannot keep the field as a body for [more than] at most ten days'. Not that it would pose that much of a threat to his troops if it did. Sheridan told his superior that he was abandoning the part of his grand strategy that had called for concerted operations against the 'hostiles'. The mountainous terrain precluded such close co-ordination in any case, Sheridan said. An even more important factor in Sheridan's decision, however, was his abiding belief in the impotency of the Indian enemy in the face of his bluecoats. He told Sherman that each of the three columns he was sending forth 'will be able to take care of itself, and of chastising the Indians should it have the opportunity'.[43]

Overall command of Sheridan's campaign was given to General Alfred H. Terry, a lawyerly, self-effacing Civil War hero and, off and on since 1866, commander of the Army's Department of Dakota. Terry would also exercise direct command over the eastern column of the converging forces, a post that was to have gone to Colonel George Armstrong Custer, the Seventh Cavalry leader. Custer, however, had incurred the wrath of President Ulysses S. Grant by testifying for the prosecution in a corruption case involving Grant's administration and had been ordered to remain behind when the column set out. An appeal to the president by his wartime cavalry chief, General Sheridan, had managed to get Custer back in harness at the last minute, but not as commander of the eastern column. General Terry was at its head when the column marched west out of Fort Abraham Lincoln in Dakota Territory on 17 May 1876, while General Custer rode at the head of the Seventh Cavalry. Terry's was the largest of the three columns, over 1,000 men, with Custer's Seventh, its 'strike force', making up about two-thirds of the total.

A second column, meanwhile, was to come in upon the Indians from the west under the command of another Civil War hero, Colonel John Gibbon, head of the Army's District of Montana. Unlike Terry's column, Gibbon's 500 or so troops were mostly infantry. Lastly, a third force, led by General George Crook, was to close the gap from the south by moving up from Fort Fetterman in Wyoming. Crook, the renowned Apache fighter, was at the time the commander of the Army's Department of the Platte. He would field the second largest column, a mix of cavalry and infantry just under 900 strong. Typical of Crook, his force was accompanied by a large body of Indian scouts, in this case Crows and Shoshonis.

Weather, however, had proved a stumbling block, as we have seen, and the plans for concerted winter operations had to be shelved. As Charles M. Robinson has put it, 'Sheridan's own experience was in the southern plains, and he had no grasp of the severity of winter in Montana'.[44] General Crook's column did try to launch a winter campaign, moving north from their Wyoming base into the Powder River country of Montana on 1 March 1876. The 'Big Horn Expedition', as it was called, was not a big success. One of Crook's officers, Brevet Major General Joseph J. Reynolds, attacked and destroyed a Cheyenne and Sioux village on 17 March, only to be driven off by a fierce counterattack in which the Indians managed to retrieve their pony herd. Worse, it turned out that Reynolds had attacked the wrong village. The Indians he had despoiled had been peaceful. Crook was furious at Reynolds's bungling and the hapless officer would later end up before a court martial. The general may not have realised it at the time, but Reynolds's attack had been more than a botched military operation; Indians in the unceded territory took it as an unprovoked assault on innocent people, a veritable declaration of war, a view reinforced by the appearance in their camps of the destitute victims of the raid.[45]

In the meantime, the temperature fell precipitously, reaching −39 degrees F. at one point. As Crook's aide-de-camp, Lieutenant John Gregory Bourke, wrote: 'Mustaches and beards coated with pendant icicles several inches long and bodies swathed in raiment of furs and hides made this expedition of cavalry resemble a long column of Santa Clauses'.[46] The 'Big Horn Expedition' struggled back to Wyoming. It would not return to the fray until the following June. As it turned out, it was a bad winter everywhere on the Northern Plains and none of the columns were able to set out for Indian country until well into the spring.

When commanders began to sit down to put the final touches to the summer campaign plan, it became clear that Sheridan's convergence strategy lacked a precise target. This was for the very good reason that the only commander who knew where the Sioux and Cheyennes were to be found, Colonel John Gibbon in Montana, had neglected to share his information with any of his colleagues. Gibbon's Crow scouts had found the 'hostiles' encamped on the Rosebud River in southeastern Montana, in the heart of the unceded territory. It was here that an unsuspecting General Crook would encounter them when he moved north once again in early June.

From the Rosebud to the Little Bighorn

Sometime between 21 and 24 May, while the non-treaty Sioux and their Northern Cheyenne allies were camped on the Rosebud River in eastern Montana, they were called together by the great Hunkpapa shaman, Sitting Bull, who told them that he had dreamed of a great clash that had taken place between his people and the white soldiers. It had been like a collision of powerful natural forces, he told them, and the Indians had won. A few days later, on 8 June, Sitting Bull took part in a Sun Dance in the Rosebud Valley village and issued a second, more famous prophecy. After having sacrificed 100 pieces of flesh from his arms to Watantanka, the Great Spirit, and danced for a long time with his face turned to the sun, the holy man had fainted, but remained standing. Later, he told of a vision that had come to him as he stared into the sun. A voice had ordered him to look just below the sun, he said, and there he had beheld 'numerous as grasshoppers, soldiers and horses bearing down on an Indian village below. They came, men and animals both, upside down, their feet in the sky, their heads to the earth with hats falling off'. Sitting Bull had told the listening crowd what the dream meant, but that probably had been unnecessary. Crook's winter campaign had warned them that the horse soldiers were coming, now Sitting Bull's Sun Dance vision told them there was to be a great battle, that the Indians would triumph and that all the whites would die. The vision instilled in the warriors who heard about it a sense that war was inevitable but also brought them a confidence in victory, even a feeling of invincibility.[47]

George Crook's would be the first of the converging bluecoat columns to experience the new combativeness of their Indian foes. When the general took the field again, reinforced up to some 1,000 infantry and cavalry, matters did not go much better than in March. On 17 June, Crook's troops fought an all-day engagement on the Rosebud River in Montana against a much smaller Sioux and Cheyenne force, and once again ended up in retreat. Indeed, had it not been for the alertness of his Crow and Shoshone scouts, Crook might have taken a real beating. The column had stopped for an early morning break along the Rosebud. 'The men unsaddled and no one, even though in Sioux country, thought to take the usual precautions against surprise. The general played whist with some of his officers, while his soldiers made coffee'. Fortunately, Crook's Indian scouts sensed trouble and rode out to have a look. It was the scouts' subsequent fighting withdrawal from the surrounding hills, pursued by Cheyenne and Sioux warriors, that saved Crook and his men from disaster.[48] Although Crook would later claim that 'My troops beat these Indians on a field of their own choosing and drove them in utter rout from it, as far as the proper care of my wounded and prudence would justify,' some of his officers concluded at the time that the column had suffered a strategic defeat, a verdict generally confirmed by later historical research.[49] Crook was unable to advance and link up with the other two columns and this may well have sealed Custer's fate later at the Little Bighorn.

Meanwhile, Terry and Custer had finally joined forces with Colonel Gibbon's column on 9 June and had laid their plans for winding up the campaign. A 'hammer and anvil' strategy was agreed upon, with Custer, in command of the expedition's 'strike force' playing the role of 'hammer', while Gibbon's infantry-heavy and thus slower-moving column would serve as the 'anvil'. Custer was to proceed up Rosebud Creek and head east and south of the Little Bighorn Valley, where it was believed the main Indian camp lay. Then he was to turn and move toward the camp heading north. Gibbon, meanwhile, was to go up the Bighorn River and enter the valley from the north. Custer and

Gibbon were expected to link up on 26 June, at which point the Indians would be surrounded and obliged to give up. What Terry and his subordinates had sketched out was, in essence, a constabulary operation. As Colonel Gibbon would later recall, the aim of the plan was 'to prevent the escape of the Indians', not to attack them. This was probably what Terry hoped, perhaps even believed, would happen: the Indians would be surrounded and give up. Nonetheless, he gave Custer, the 'hammer' of the operation, a relatively free hand. He could go on the attack if conditions seemed to warrant it. 'It is of course impossible to give you any definite instructions with regard to this movement', Terry's orders read, 'and were it not impossible to do so, the Department commander places too much confidence in your zeal, energy, and ability to wish to impose upon you precise orders, which might hamper your action when nearly in contact with the enemy'.[50]

In retrospect, it can be seen that giving Custer a free hand was an unfortunate deviation from the overall plan. If this was to be a constabulary operation, Custer was the wrong man to lead its 'strike force'. Custer was no policeman. He was the Murat of the Wild West, the '*beau sabreur*' of the US Army. Prior to leaving Fort Abraham Lincoln for Montana, he had told Captain William Ludlow, the chief engineer with the Terry column, that he intended to 'cut loose' from General Terry at the first opportunity.[51] Further, Custer held the same low estimate of Indian fighting ability as his superior, General Sheridan. Early in his career on the Plains, in 1868, he had told a fellow officer that 'There are not Indians enough in the country to whip the Seventh Cavalry'. On 24 June 1876, the eve of his last day on earth, he had not changed his mind. When told by a scout that there were enough Sioux in the camp in the valley of the Little Bighorn below 'to keep them [Seventh Cavalry] fighting two or three days', Custer smiled and replied, 'I guess we'll get through them in one day'.[52]

The Little Bighorn

The battle of the Little Bighorn is the most celebrated engagement of the North American Indian wars and one of the best-known battles of the age of imperial conquest. For this reason alone, any account of the New World Indian wars that ignores the battle or gives it short shrift would be considered woefully incomplete. In what follows, however, the narrative of the engagement has been reduced to the essentials, leaving scope for more extensive analysis, not so much of what transpired in those two fearful hours on 25 June 1876 atop the bluffs above the Little Bighorn River in southeastern Montana, but why.

First, a general observation. Campaigns relying on mounted troops alone, like the one that Custer was about to embark upon, which by 1876 had become a standard feature of warfare against the Plains Indians, were an anomaly in the small wars of the nineteenth century. Elsewhere in the New World, the Mexicans generally used infantry supported by artillery against the Yaquis, whilst the Canadian campaign against mixed-bloods and Indians on the western prairies in 1885 proved to be too light on cavalry, not the other way round. As the historian of imperial warfare, Douglas Porch, has observed, in colonial wars 'cavalry was most effective when it cooperated with artillery and infantry'.[53] American commanders like General Sheridan, however, had no compunction about sending unsupported cavalry against Indians because, first, this strategy had worked well in, for example, Colonel Custer's 1868 victory on the Washita and again in the South Plains war just concluded. There was no reason to assume that it would not work again. Second, and here it is necessary to underscore a point made earlier, recent experience seemed to have shown that mobility, the ability to escape capture, was the only real advantage held by the Indians and that the only effective way of dealing with this was to use the US army's most mobile arm, mounted troops.

It needs to be borne in mind, however, that cavalry attacks like the one Custer would launch on 25 June relied heavily on surprise for success. The Washita and Palo Duro Canyon attacks had been part of campaigns conducted in the winter, when the Indians were largely immobilised, and had come at dawn. As we will see, neither of these conditions would obtain on the Little Bighorn, but Custer would attack anyway, employing convergence tactics similar to those that had brought him victory on the Washita.[54] Again, we have to assume that Custer proceeded to attack because he believed that the biggest challenge he faced would be stopping the Indians from running away. He did not believe they would stand and fight.

What was so important about surprise attacks was that they allowed the cavalry to hold the initiative, to operate offensively. For, whenever the tide of battle went against mounted troops like Custer's Seventh Cavalry and forced them on the defensive, they found themselves operating at a considerable disadvantage. To begin with, cavalry firepower was limited. US cavalrymen – indeed, mounted troops everywhere – carried carbines and revolvers, short-range weapons with little hitting power. A determined and numerous enemy, like the Sioux and Cheyenne warriors who brought Custer to bay on the Little Bighorn, would not be held up for long by such weapons. A second problem was the horses. When US cavalrymen had to dismount to take up defensive positions, every fourth man was pulled off the line to hold the horses, reducing firepower still further. Even more damaging, the horses frequently became terrified by the smoke and noise of battle – plus Indian attempts to spook them – and bolted, sowing panic and confusion. Such an event was the beginning of the end for Custer's troopers on Battle Ridge. 'One man held the horses while the others shot the guns', Hunkpapa Sioux chief Gall said. 'We tried to kill the holders, and then by waving blankets and shooting we scared the horses down that coulee, where the Cheyenne women caught them.'[55]

After leaving Terry, Custer put his troopers through a long, rigorous march, which brought them to a point some 25 miles east of the Little Bighorn Valley late in the day on 24 June 1876.[56] About nine o'clock that evening, scouts told Custer that the Indian trail they had been following led down into the valley.

PART II

Custer allowed his troops a few hours' rest and then resumed following the trail through the night. Terry's plan for an extended scout was now abandoned. At dawn, Arikara scouts ascended the Crow's Nest, a high hill overlooking the Little Bighorn Valley, and reported sighting a very large Indian camp. How large this camp was has remained a matter of some dispute. Until fairly recently historians tended to believe that the Sioux and Cheyenne camp stretched between three and four miles along the Little Bighorn River and held anywhere from 4,000 to 10,000 people and 1,000 to 3,000 warriors. But according to Gregory Michno in his groundbreaking book, *Lakota Noon*, the Indian village 'was enormous only in the imagination of the participants and chroniclers who, consciously or subconsciously, wanted to or had to see it that way'. Michno's spatial analysis has demonstrated conclusively that the camp was no more than a mile and a half long and some 300 yards wide and that it was probably host to no more than 800 to 1,200 warriors.[57]

The scouts also told Custer that parties of Sioux had been seen moving through the area, which convinced him that his force had been discovered, and that he had no choice but to attack if he was to keep the Indians from escaping. An earlier plan to hole up the next day and attack the Indians at dawn on 26 June was now scuttled. Viewed in retrospect, this can be seen as a risky decision. As noted earlier, dawn attacks had become standard practice in the Plains wars, since they usually caught the Indians unawares and gave the cavalry the advantage of surprise.

It was around 2.00 p.m. that Custer's command came within sight of the Indian village in the Little Bighorn valley. His lead Crow scout, Half Yellow Face, observing movement in the camp below, told Custer that the Indians 'must be running away'. This was enough to convince the colonel that the Indians were alarmed and fleeing and that 'It was a case of attack now or never'.[58]

Custer now split his command into four parts. Major Marcus A. Reno was to take A, G and M Companies, 95 men in all plus Indian scouts, and assault the camp, while Custer, with C, E, F, I and L Companies kept to the high ground to the right of the valley, searching for a place to ford the river and come up behind the Indian camp, thus cutting off retreat. Captain Benteen, meanwhile, was ordered off to the left with D, H and K Companies, presumably to see if there were other Indian camps further along the Little Bighorn valley. The remaining troops of Custer's command were left behind to guard the pack train, under Captain James McDougall.

Major Reno's attack on the camp went badly. Although he initially had the element of surprise on his side, Reno encountered far more Indians – and far more aggressive ones – than anyone had expected and was forced to order his men to dismount to fight. When Indian numbers seemed to have become overwhelming and a flanking movement appeared to be underway, the Major ordered a retreat back to the woods from which his troopers had launched their attack. When that position appeared to be in danger of being overrun, Reno, by now seized by terror, ordered his men to mount up once again and head for the

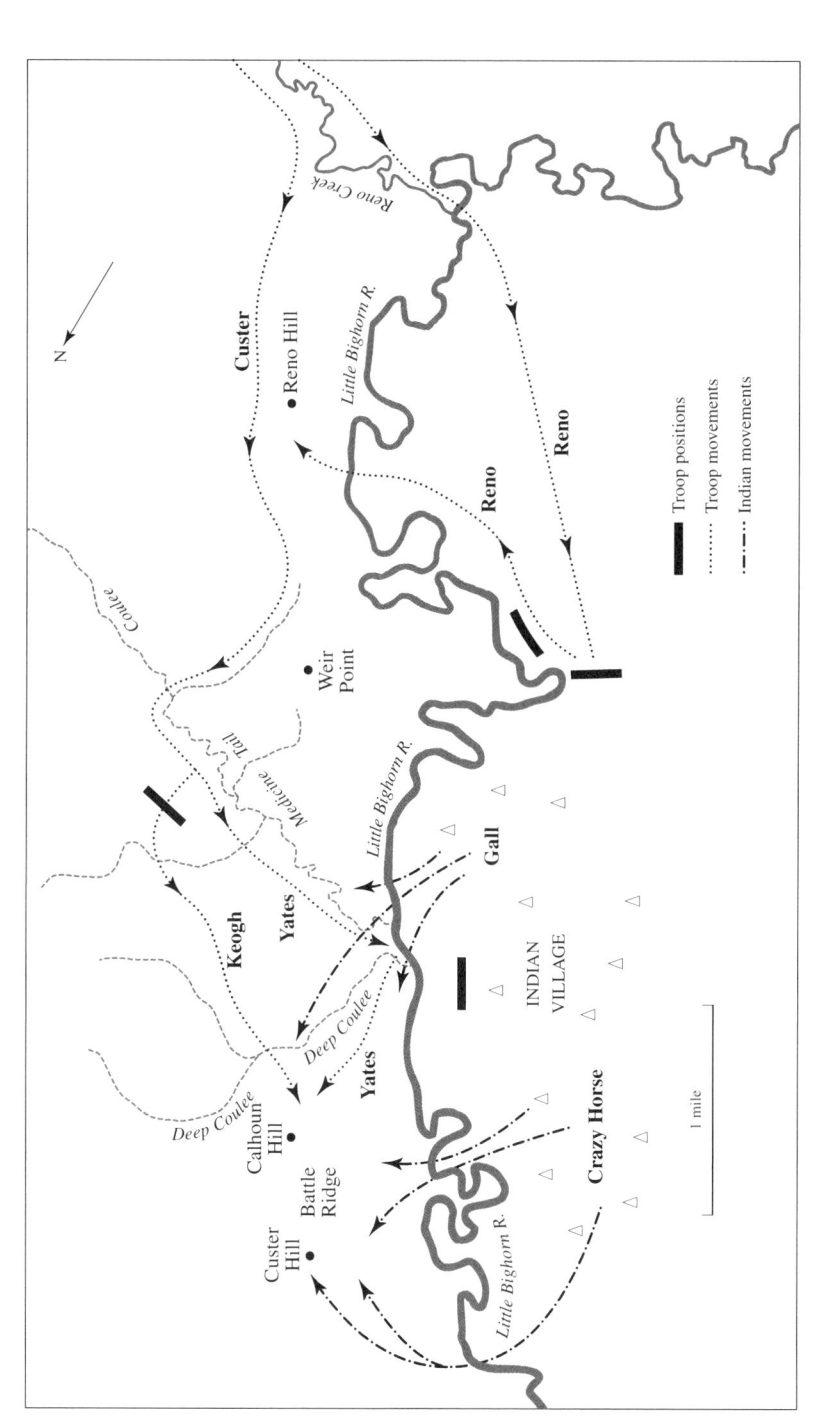

Map 7.5 Battle of Little Bighorn, 25 June 1876.

PART II

bluffs across the river. This was where he had left Custer and he apparently assumed that the main force was still there. In the headlong retreat that ensued, Reno's command managed to cross the river and entrench in makeshift fashion on the bluffs. Some forty troopers were killed in the process, however, and Reno was so distraught at the end of it that Benteen, who by now had given up scouting and returned to the bluffs with his men, had to take over command. Captain McDougall soon appeared with the pack train, but Custer was nowhere to be seen.

What did happen to Custer? We know from John Gray's careful reconstruction of the battle that the Colonel's remaining companies moved along the bluffs parallel to the valley and were able, at least at intervals, to follow the course of Reno's attack. Thus, Custer and his men were able to observe the Major's force halt, dismount and form a skirmish line. This does not appear to have caused a great deal of anxiety, however. John Gray believes that 'Long Hair' assumed that Reno could hold off the attackers, at least long enough for him to launch a converging attack of his own. But Custer's command could find no way down into the valley and was forced to continue its march along the bluffs in search of one. The situation had become worrying enough for Custer to send off a courier to urge Captain McDougall to bring up his pack train, with its precious ammunition, as quickly as possible. At about 3.30 p.m., the command halted again to take stock of events down in the valley. By this time, Reno's men could be seen holed up in the timber and under attack by a large force of Indians. Again, Custer seems to have believed that Reno, provided his ammunition held out, could stave off the Indians for a time, time he now desperately needed, because no near route down from the bluffs had yet been found.[59]

The moment of truth, if indeed there was one at the Little Bighorn, would have come at around 4.00 p.m., according to John Gray's calculations. It was at this juncture that Custer's chief of scouts, Mitch Boyer, and the Crow scout Curly, observing the fighting in the valley below, intercepted Custer's command to announce that Reno was in headlong retreat and that the great mass of warriors who had driven him off were now free to attack elsewhere. Reno's flight placed Custer's 211-man force in danger for the first time, 'more in need of help than able to help'.[60] The trumpeter John Martin (born Giovanni Martini and a former drummer boy in Garibaldi's army) was now sent galloping off to Benteen with his famous cryptic message, penned in haste by the adjutant William W. Cooke: 'Come on. Big village. Be quick. Bring packs. W.W. Cooke. P.S. Bring pacs (sic)'.[61] Custer now also sent two companies of his command down Medicine Tail Coulee toward the river, in what John Gray believes was a feint, a threat to attack the village, now occupied largely by women and children, which would draw off warriors to their defence and relieve the pressure on Reno. The rest of the command waited on the bluff top for the arrival of Benteen's troopers and McDougall's pack train. There is every indication, according to Gray, that had these reinforcements arrived, Custer, with the companies in Medicine Tail Coulee back under his command, would have attacked the village. But Benteen and McDougall did not arrive and by 4.40 p.m. or thereabouts, Custer's force was beginning to come under fire. Mitch Boyer, the chief of scouts, who had spurned Custer's offer to let the scouts depart and stayed to fight alongside the soldiers, 'knew they were doomed', says Gray, 'and it would be surprising indeed if Custer was not reading the same handwriting on the wall'.[62]

Thanks to a fortuitous natural disaster, we are better equipped today to understand what transpired on Battle Ridge, as the position Custer and his embattled force now occupied has become known. In 1983 a grass fire laid bare the battlefield site, and archaeological digs and sweeps of the area by metal detectors in 1984–5 revealed artefacts and other indicators of the flow of battle unknown to earlier observers. We now have a much better idea than previously of who was where at the different stages of the fight.[63] But that knowledge has also been aided greatly by the work of the independent historian John S. Gray, whose painstaking time and motion studies of the movements of Custer's battalion at the Little Bighorn have given us a much improved notion of what happened where and when on the battlefield, at least from the cavalry side.[64] Subsequently, the National Parks historian Gregory F. Michno has performed a similar task with respect to the Indian participants in the battle. Using oral testimony gathered over the years from Indian veterans of the battle, he has been able to plot the movements of warriors in the engagement from beginning to conclusion.[65] As a result of the work of Gray and Michno, we now have a much better idea of the sequencing of the battle.

When he got to the area that would become the Custer Battlefield, Custer formed up his troops into two wings. C, I and L Companies, under the command of Captain James Calhoun, made up the right wing. It remained in position, waiting for the left wing, composed of E and F Companies, to find a place to ford the Bighorn River. Having found a suitable spot down Medicine Tail Coulee, as we have seen, the latter two companies returned to the main body, but the attack on the village which appears to have been the object of Custer's manoeuvring would never take place.

The battle opened with the appearance of Indians to the southeast of the position held by Captain Calhoun's three companies. Some of the approaching Sioux and Cheyennes were armed with Henry repeating rifles and, when they poured a withering fire on an unwitting C Company, caught out in the open skirmishing, and subsequently chased off many of their horses, the soldiers broke and ran. The rout spread to the rest of Capt. Calhoun's command, who fled in disorder. Now the attackers turned their attention to Captain Miles Keogh's three-company command. It was a 'daring' Bad Heart-type run through the ranks of Keogh's companies by the great Sioux war chief Crazy Horse and White Bull, Sitting Bull's nephew, which brought death to the Irishman and his troops. When watching warriors saw that every soldier in Keogh's command had fired at the two riders without hitting them, they thought the troopers' guns must be empty and launched an attack. Keogh and his men went down in fierce hand-to-hand fighting. This left some 40 survivors on Custer Hill, where the famous 'Last Stand' would now take place. Chief Gall, once again, described how the end came for Custer and the remnants of his command. 'The dust and smoke was black as evening. Once in a while we could see the soldiers through the dust, and finally we charged through them with our ponies. When we had done this . . . the fight was over.'[66] The battle had lasted perhaps an hour.[67]

The Custer massacre has excited controversy from the day it occurred and it shows no sign of abating in our own time. Probably the major reason for this is the obvious fact that no troopers under Custer's command survived to tell the tale. There has always been Indian witness, at least since the time, fairly recently, when Indians were convinced that they would not be punished for saying what happened to 'Long Hair' and his men. Until quite recently, however, no serious researchers were willing to take Indian witnesses seriously. In addition to suspicions of bias, the Indian accounts were thought to be too impressionistic, a bit too limited to individual perspectives, to be reliable. This has changed in recent years and more sensitive efforts to recapture Indian insights on the battle, like those of Gregory Michno, have borne much valuable fruit.

Controversy still rages, however, over how it was that Custer, the great Civil War hero and Indian fighter, and his 215 men came to grief on a lonely hill in Montana. Was it because there were just too many Indians? Because they outgunned the horse soldiers (those Henry repeaters)? Or was the fault Custer's, because he allowed that overweening pride and ambition, that thirst for glory we documented above, to cloud his judgement? Our conclusion, already hinted at, is that the Seventh Cavalry troopers who died on the Little Bighorn were both victims of others' mistakes and of the hubris and hunger for glory of their commander. The campaign strategy set out by Sheridan and implemented by Terry was seriously flawed. Neither officer knew or, more importantly, cared what the mood of the Indian enemy was. Both were convinced that no body of Indians could or would stand up to the soldiers they were sending against them. Nothing scouts or newspapermen could report would change this view. Custer shared this outlook. For this reason, it seems to us pointless to consider the argument that had Custer known how many Indians were in the camp in the Little Bighorn valley and how angry they were about the invasion of the Black Hills and the summons to go back to the Dakota reservations, he might not have put his command at risk by launching an attack. While it is true that Custer never ordered a proper reconnaissance of the Sioux camp in the valley, and thus was in the dark about the numbers and intentions of the Indians until almost the last moment, it is also irrelevant. There may have been a moment of hesitation, when he saw Reno's troops fall back in disarray. But it was a moment of hesitation only, never one of indecision. No retreat was ordered, no avenue of escape located. The column waited on the bluffs above the river, poised to attack, waiting for the reinforcements and ammunition train that never came.[68] But even when the battle was upon him and his men, when masses of Indians began to appear in front of and behind his embattled companies, one has to believe that Custer's faith in his Seventh Cavalry as an instrument of white American cultural and racial superiority and his belief in the battle-deciding value of the Western way of war would have held firm.

Later that day and the next, while the stripped and mutilated bodies of Custer's men lay baking in the sun, the Sioux and Cheyennes turned their attention to Major Reno's men dug in on the bluffs above the river. Although the soldiers were desperately short of water and food, they managed to repel the Indian attacks, even counterattacking to save themselves from being overrun. On the evening of 26 June the Indians withdrew and firing ceased. Next morning, it was discovered that the whole huge camp, with its great pony herd, was gone, heading north.

Shortly before noon on 27 June, scouts from Gibbon's column found the bodies of Custer and his men on Custer Hill. They were buried where they fell, in makeshift graves. Reno's force was now relieved and it was discovered that it had lost 47 men and had large numbers of wounded. These last would be removed by the river steamer, the *Far West*, to Fort Abraham Lincoln for treatment. The news of the 'Custer Massacre' now spread to an incredulous nation, in the midst of preparations for the 100th anniversary of American independence.

Public demands for retribution were not long in being answered. On 5 September, Crook's army, now on the move once again but out of supplies and reduced to walking because of the weakness of their horses, stumbled onto a Sioux camp at Slim Buttes. In a two-day battle, the soldiers succeeded in driving off the Indians and gorged themselves on captured dried meat and the flesh of Indian ponies. Crook's 'Starvation March' then proceeded to the Black Hills, where he and his command rested until November, when they left for Wyoming and a resumption of the war against the Sioux and their allies.[69]

The ensuing winter campaign against the Northern Cheyennes went some way towards restoring Crook's plummeting reputation, although he personally had little to do with it. It was his subordinate, the aggressive General Ranald Mackenzie, commanding 600 troops of the Fourth Cavalry accompanied by over 400 Indian scouts, who discovered the camp of the Cheyenne leader, Dull Knife, on the Powder River and destroyed it. The Cheyennes were now thrust out onto the prairie, their shelter burned and food supplies gone, with winter coming on. This was the end of Northern Cheyenne resistance.[70]

Meanwhile, General Nelson A. Miles and the Fifth Cavalry had found Crazy Horse's village on the Tongue River in the Wolf Mountains. On 8 January, Miles routed some 500 Sioux and Northern Cheyenne. He kept after the fleeing Indians, and in April 1877, some 300 Sioux and Cheyennes surrendered to Miles on the Tongue River, while the remainder of the Cheyennes were turning themselves in at Red Cloud Agency in Nebraska. A month later, Crazy Horse and his band of just under 900 Sioux men, women and children surrendered at Fort Robinson in Nebraska.[71] Sitting Bull, meanwhile, had led

PART II

his band of Sioux across the northern border into the Land of the Great Mother, where they remained until 1881.[72] The Great Sioux War of 1876–77 was over.

Epilogue: to the Golden Gate

The war against the Sioux confederation was bracketed by two conflicts with Indian peoples which seemed sufficiently instructive to be included here as an epilogue to the events of 1874–7, when the Plains tribes were beaten and driven on to reservations.

The Modoc War, 1872–3[73]

The war which pitted the Modoc Indians against the United States army was over land, specifically the Lost River Valley in extreme southern Oregon, part of the tribe's ancestral homeland. In 1864 the Modocs had signed a treaty with the federal government giving up the river valley and agreeing to move to the reservation of their Klamath brethren further east in Oregon. This arrangement did not prosper. Although the Modocs had once been part of the Klamath tribe and spoke a similar language, they did not get along with their relatives very well. Government officials had to maintain a kind of 'no-man's-land' between the two groups on the reservation to keep them from feuding. Also, the officials, in a typical quest to find a single 'leader' they could hold responsible for tribal behaviour, chose the more tractable Old Schonchin over Keintpoos, known to whites as Captain Jack, with the result that the latter fled from the reservation along with a band of followers and returned to the Lost River Valley in 1865. White settlers, who had moved into the area after the 1864 treaty, protested against their presence and in 1869 the separatists were persuaded to go back to the reservation. But relations with the Klamaths did not improve and the following spring, Captain Jack and his followers fled the reservation once again and reverted to their old hunter-gatherer existence in the Lost River Valley.

Settler disquiet at the return of Captain Jack led to an attempt to forcibly remove the Indians in the winter of 1872. The subsequent fracas was the result of yet another breakdown in state and federal cooperation. The state of Oregon's new Indian superintendent, T.B. Odeneal, decided to use US troops to disarm Captain Jack's Modocs without securing the approval of their commander, General Edward R.S. Canby. A fight broke out in the Modoc camp in which several white soldiers were killed. Captain Jack and his band took refuge in the Lava Beds around Lake Tule in northern California, a formidable natural stronghold, as US troops sent to evict them would soon learn.

The original band were soon joined by two other groups of Modoc dissidents, warriors who proved to be even more intransigent than Captain Jack. One band was led by 'a power-seeking shaman' known as Curly-Headed Doctor and his son-in-law, Hooker Jim. This group had been responsible for the deaths of 14 settlers en route to the Lava Beds and knew that they would receive no mercy from the whites if they gave up. The other band of new arrivals were known as the Hot Creek Modocs. They had just barely escaped being lynched by angry whites and thus were in no hurry to surrender. These two groups would combine to block any attempts by Captain Jack to open negotiations with the white soldiers who now descended on the Lava Beds.

From December 1872 to June 1873, the Modocs, although they numbered only some fifty warriors, managed to hold on in their stronghold, using the terrain and superior marksmanship to keep the American soldiers at bay. The troops sent to quell the Modoc revolt were admittedly a scratch force – the best units in the army were on Reconstruction duty in the South – but, even so, they performed badly, stumbling about the Lake Tule basin, letting themselves get ambushed, getting spooked by noises in the night. At one point (17 January 1873), the tiny Modoc band administered a stinging defeat to an army force of 309 men under Lt. Colonel Frank Wheaton. This prompted Washington to undertake a peace initiative under the direction of General Canby, the ex-Indian superintendent of Oregon, Alfred Meacham, and a Methodist minister, Eleasar Thomas. On 11 April 1873 these three men met with a delegation of Modoc warriors led by Captain Jack. What the federal negotiators did not know was that the pro-war faction back in the Lava Beds, led by Curly-Headed Doctor and Hooker Jim, had forced Captain Jack to agree to kill Canby and the other white officials. They had argued that the death of General Canby would demoralise the troops and bring the campaign to an end. And so, under a flag of truce, Captain Jack drew a concealed gun and shot the general. The Reverend Thomas was also killed. Rather than disrupting the military campaign against them, the death of General Canby provoked national outrage and demands for revenge. Canby was a Civil War hero and the only US general to be killed in the Indian wars.

For a time, the forbidding terrain and Indian fighting skills continued to stymie the troops, but in late May a first defeat was inflicted on the Modocs at a place called Dry Lake. This appears to have demoralised the war party in the Lava Beds, who now surrendered to the army and, in order to save their own skins, agreed to lead the soldiers to the hideouts of the Modocs who were still at large. On 1 June 1873, Captain Jack was captured. The war was over. The Modoc insurgents were moved to Fort Klamath, Oregon, where a military tribunal met to try those Modocs deemed responsible for the deaths of Canby and Thomas. Captain Jack and five others were found guilty and sentenced to death by hanging. Two of the convicted men had their sentences commuted to life imprisonment on Alcatraz Island. On 3 October 1873, Captain Jack, Schonchin John, Black Jim and Bogus Charley were executed. The rest of the Modocs were now transferred to the Quapaw reservation in Oklahoma, fast becoming the US dumping ground for unwanted Indians. They would remain there until 1909, when they were allowed to return to the Klamath reservation in Oregon.

PART II

The Modoc War lasted seven months and cost the US government some $500,000, a large sum for the time. But its importance was greater than its impact on the federal budget. The murder of General Canby under a flag of truce practically put paid to the Grant administration's peace policy toward the Indian peoples of the West. At the same time, however, the repeated examples of ineptitude by Army officers and men in the Modoc campaign also cast doubt on the ability of the regulars to bring the Indian wars to a successful conclusion. The 1877 war with the Nez Percé tribe a bit further north would do nothing to dispel the image of army ineptitude.

The Nez Percé War, 1877[74]

The war against the Nez Percé Indians of the Pacific Northwest probably garnered the highest public disapproval rating of any of the United States's many Indian wars. Even before the 1877 conflict, the Nez Percé had enjoyed much acclaim among the US population. Early on, they had shown a singular eagerness to embrace Christianity, even though a subsequent Protestant–Catholic split disrupted tribal cohesion, and had demonstrated an unfailing friendship for the white man, despite repeated provocations by white miners and settlers over the course of the nineteenth century. The Nez Percés were probably the only Indian people in North America in the 1870s who could boast that they had never killed a white settler.

This honeymoon would come to an end in 1877 in a dispute between the US government and a part of the tribe that had never taken up residence on the reservation set aside for the Nez Percés in Idaho. Following the Custer massacre, Washington had decided that all Indians in the USA had to be placed on reservations. Pressure was put on the non-reservation Nez Percés to give up their hunting and grazing lands – in addition to their herds of the famous Appaloosa horses, they had begun to raise cattle – in eastern Oregon and repair to the reservation in Idaho. Resistance led to an incident in which Americans were killed by young warriors.

The war which now began would last from June to October 1877 and spread over 1,500 miles, across the states of Oregon, Idaho, Wyoming and Montana, as the Nez Percé dissidents fought their way toward sanctuary in Canada. Though there were never more than 145 warriors in their band, and their flight was hampered by the presence of some 500 women, children, and old people, the Nez Percés managed to give better than they got in their encounters with the American armies that pursued them. On 17 June they soundly defeated troops at White Bird Canyon. Although surprised on the Clearwater River on 11 July by soldiers led by the 'Christian general', Oliver O. Howard, the Nez Percés managed to break free and continue their trek toward Canada. On 9 August, Colonel John Gibbon again surprised their camp at the Big Hole River, but again the Nez Percés escaped, though this time with heavy losses. They fought their way across Yellowstone National Park, disrupting the holiday there of

General William T. Sherman, and then moved north through Montana. But here, the vigorous pursuit of troops under the command of General Nelson Miles and the ravages of hunger and disease among the families of the warriors combined to bring the flight to an end, just 40 miles from the 'Medicine Line'. It was here that the chief that Americans chose to believe had been the leader of the exodus, Joseph, made his famous statement to Miles, 'From where the sun now stands I will fight no more forever'. The Nez Percé War had reached its climax just 40 miles from sanctuary in Canada.

Wounded Knee

The US Indian wars are traditionally thought to have reached their dénouement in a bloody massacre of Sioux men, women and children by troopers of the Seventh Cavalry in South Dakota in the winter of 1890. The Sioux, in flight from their reservation following the killing of the great shaman, Sitting Bull, by Indian police in the employ of the government on 15 December 1890, were cornered by the soldiers in open country at a place called Wounded Knee. In an ensuing fusillade, including fire from the army's new Hotchkiss artillery and Gatling guns, from 200 to 350 Sioux were killed. The remainder of the band were rounded up and herded back to their reservation.[75] Traditionally, historians have attributed the ferociousness of the army repression to fear of a revival of Indian militancy as a result of the Ghost Dance 'craze' then sweeping the West. This ultimate 'revitalisation' movement among Indians whose way of life was in peril preached that participation in Ghost Dance rites would lead to the disappearance of the white invaders and restoration of the old free life on the plains. Ghost dancers also wore Ghost Shirts which presumably rendered them invulnerable to the white man's bullets.[76] More recently, some historians have concluded that the military's use of 'overwhelming force' was motivated less by fear of a new Indian war than a desire to show that only the army could maintain order on the Indian reservations. The Army and the Department of the Interior, whose Indian Bureau personnel ran the reservations, had been at odds for decades over this issue and it has been argued that the army commander in the region, the ambitious General Nelson Miles, saw the flight of the Sioux as an opportunity to demonstrate the ineffectiveness of the Indian Bureau in administering the reservations.[77] Whatever the case, Wounded Knee would be the last important violent encounter between the soldiers of the Great Father and the Indians of the Plains.

8

CONQUEST OF APACHERÍA, 1860–86

Introduction

A number of factors made the Apaches the most difficult to defeat of the Indian peoples discussed in this book. Most historians have tried to explain their ability to remain unconquered for so long by pointing to the unforgiving climate and terrain in which the Apache wars were fought, and there is no doubt that this was a factor favouring the Apaches, who were much more at home in these surroundings than the Americans or even the Mexicans were. Lieutenant Leonard Wood, who participated in the capture of Geronimo in Mexico in 1886, has left a striking portrayal of the conditions which he and his fellow soldiers had to endure in pursuing Apache war bands. Wood's testimony is the more valuable for the fact that he was a surgeon by training.

> One who does not know [the mountains and deserts of northern Sonora] cannot realize what this kind of service means – marching every day in the intense heat, the rocks and earth being so torrid that the feet are blistered and rifle-barrels and everything metallic being so hot that the hand cannot touch them without getting burnt. It is a country rough beyond description, covered everywhere with cactus and full of rattlesnakes and other undesirable companions of that sort. The rain, when it does come, comes as a tropical tempest, transforming dry canyons into raging torrents in an instant.[1]

It would be a mistake, however, to lean too heavily on the 'wars against nature' thesis here. Attention also needs to be paid to the Apache decision, apparently after the setback at the battle of Apache Pass in 1862, to eschew pitched battles and concentrate exclusively on hit-and-run warfare of the kind their Yaqui neighbours to the south had employed to such good advantage earlier in the century. What happened, actually, was that the Apaches fused into one the two kinds of armed activity they had traditionally engaged in, raiding and warfare. And, of course, raiding was something the Apaches had always been very good at. Apache raiders possessed extraordinary mobility, an ability to get from A to B quickly that US cavalrymen were never able to match. One of the main

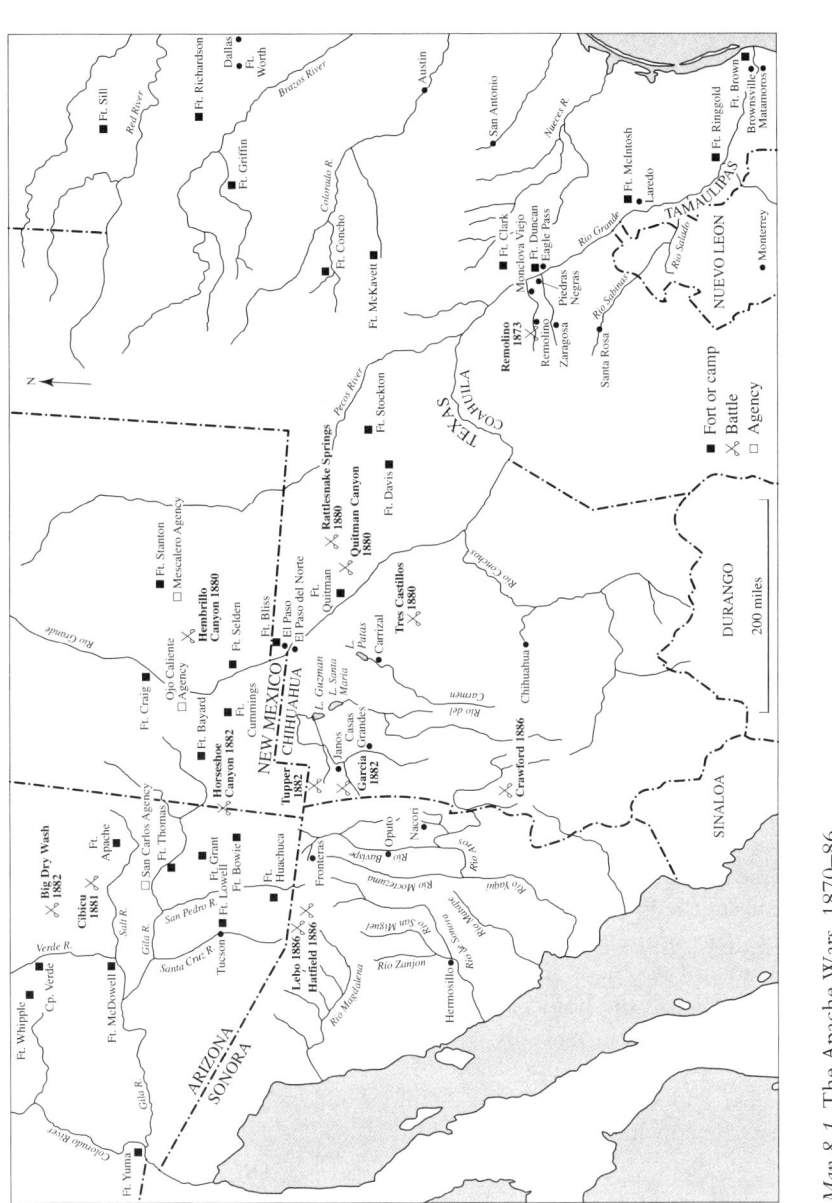

Map 8.1 The Apache Wars, 1870–86.

PART II

reasons for this was the Apaches' total lack of Anglo-Saxon sentimentality about horses. They rode their mounts until they dropped dead, then carved them up for meat and replaced them with stolen stock.

The Apaches also proved to be quick about adapting the white man's military gear, including weapons, to their use. Although they were formidable bowmen, and never entirely gave up the bow as a weapon, they probably boasted a greater arsenal of modern small arms than any other of the US Army's Indian foes. They took a special liking to the Winchester lever-action repeater and the Colt .45 pistol, both of which they seem to have possessed in large quantities. They also found field glasses useful, and adopted the cavalry's McClellan saddle.

Apache raids into Mexico

Apache attacks on the Hispanic borderlands did not abate with the coming of Mexican independence or the transfer of control over the Apache homeland from Mexico to the USA as a consequence of the 1846–8 war. In fact, the tempo of violence accelerated in the 1820s as the new Mexican government abandoned the Spanish policy of issuing the Apaches rations in return for their agreement to stop raiding and form communities around the missions and presidios. Although the Mexican government apparently believed that making the Apaches citizens of the new republic would more than compensate for the lost rations, the measure did not have its desired effect. The Apaches returned to raiding on an even more massive scale than before, and as the government in Mexico City gradually abandoned the presidio system that had defended the frontier districts, there was little to stop them. Mexican state and local governments possessed few resources to resist the Apache attacks. Both Sonora and Chihuahua, the main targets of the raiders, suffered from a 'chronic dearth of weapons, ammunition, and adequate horses' and could find only 'ill-trained and ill-fed, poorly dressed and poorly armed' local irregulars to fill in for the professional soldiers who had once manned the frontier defences.[2]

By the mid-nineteenth century, Apache raiding, which was more or less constant, not seasonal as in the case of the Comanches, had rendered the northern part of the state of Sonora 'practically uninhabitable'. Settlers abandoned ranches and mines, even whole towns, to move to the southern part of the state or across the border into the new US states and territories. The US consul in the Sonoran port city of Guaymas, Alexander Willard, reported in 1870 that over the previous decade some 8,500 Sonorans had migrated to California, and 7,500 to Arizona, while around 4,000 had been killed by Apaches. He concluded that the depredations had become so severe that deaths had begun to outstrip births in Sonora.[3] For all practical purposes, northern Sonora had become part of Apachería. 'Some Apaches, who had learned Mexican ways from years of close contact, even collected taxes on occasion from persons traveling between New Mexico and Sonora, and they kept abreast of events by reading mail that they appropriated from couriers'.[4] As late as 1883,

Map 8.2 The Mexico–US borderlands.

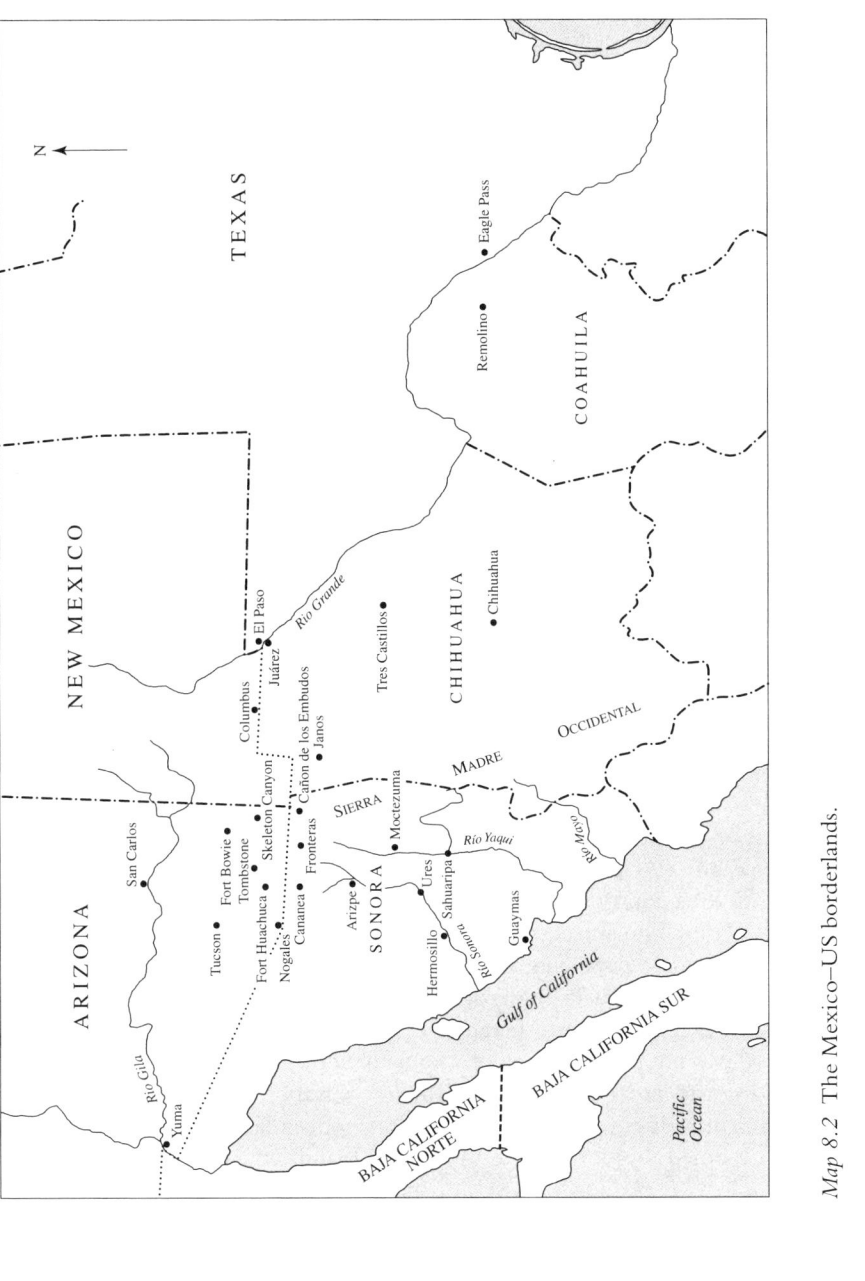

the US general George Crook, on the trail of Apache raiders in Mexico's Sierra Madre Mountains, found Sonoran villagers completely at the mercy of the Apaches.

> The condition of these little Mexican communities was deplorable. Apache attacks were to be looked for at any moment. No man could venture far away from the vicinity of his hamlet. All the available force of the settlement was constantly on the alert for an enemy as cunning, as stealthy and bloodthirsty as so many Bengal tigers.[5]

The sense of virtual helplessness against these fast-moving, hard-hitting raiders bred a hatred toward Apaches among Sonorans that exceeded any animosity they might have felt towards even the Yaquis, despite a century of nearly ceaseless hostilities. Hatred of the Apaches was also fuelled by the widespread belief among Sonorans that the raiders were opening the way for a North American takeover of the state. Sonoran leaders from Colonel García to the veteran politician and historian Ramón Corral contended that the Yankees were arming the Apaches in the hope that they would empty the state of Mexican inhabitants so they could move in.[6] These fears were fed by ominous statements by prominent North Americans. A well-known Arizona mining entrepreneur and real estate speculator, Sylvester Mowry, wrote in 1864 that the 'Apache Indian [is] preparing Sonora for the rule of a higher civilization than the Mexican'.[7] General John B. Frisbee, veteran of the Mexican–American War and a frontier soldier, hoped that the Apaches would drive out the Mexicans in Sonora, so that it could be acquired by the US 'without the racial issue that would result with the annexation of a "mongrelized race"'.[8]

The governments of Chihuahua and Sonora took extreme measures to cope with the Apache raids. The first of these was the hiring of mercenaries to 'exterminate' the raiders. Beginning in 1835, the Sonora government paid bounties of 100 pesos (c. $100) on the scalps of Apache males, and efforts were made to capture Apache women and children, so that they could be shipped off to parts of the country away from the frontier or taken into Mexican homes as servants. The Chihuahua government went even further. Its scalp bounty law of 1837 authorised payments of 100 pesos for Apache warriors' scalps, 50 pesos for women's scalps and 25 pesos for children's scalps. 'The policy frankly sought extermination', wrote Dan Thrapp, 'evidence that genocide has widespread roots and was not the invention of a single nation'.[9]

Perhaps the most notorious of the mercenary gangs employed by the Mexican authorities was that of the North American James Kirker, whose scalp hunters roamed the borderlands in the 1850s and '60s. But the Chihuahuans also hired gangs of North American Indians to collect Apache scalps. These were usually transplanted Shawnee, Delaware and Creek warriors from Indian Territory, referred to collectively as 'Sahuanos' by Mexicans. This campaign had to be discontinued in the 1860s, in part because of adverse publicity on both sides of the border but also because Kirker and other bounty hunters began taking the scalps of peaceful Indians and Mexicans as well as those of bronco Apaches.[10] It is unclear how many Apaches were killed by the scalp hunters. Kirker claimed that his gang killed 487 Apaches for the loss of only three men.[11]

In the end, the most successful strategy for defence against Apache raiders proved to be the one that the Spanish authorities had employed long before: large-scale use of Indian auxiliaries. The governments of both Sonora and Chihuahua had for some time been using Tarahumara scouts to help track down Apache raiding parties. Now, they also began employing Opatas, Papagos and Pimas as irregular cavalry and infantry to repel the Apaches and hunt them down. These peoples had themselves been victimised for decades by the Apaches and had no compunction about aiding the Mexicans by killing raiders and bringing in their scalps for pay.[12] Ramón Corral described one fierce battle in 1871 between Papagos and Apaches which left some one hundred Apaches dead.[13] It was generally conceded by most observers that Sonora's Indian allies in the end constituted 'the main brake on Apache incursions'.[14]

The Apache raids in Mexico continued on into the 1880s, when a combined effort by the US and Mexican regular troops, heavily assisted by Indian scouts and fighters, put a stop to the depredations through a series of cross-border operations. Until this happened, however, Apache raiding proved to be a serious, even destabilising, problem for the new nation. Along with the massive toll in lives and property caused by the Apache raids into Mexico, there was the further dilemma that fighting the Apaches was a serious diversion for the Mexican governments and armed forces which were trying, at the same time, to contain the rebellions of the Yaquis and Mayas. Indeed, there were Mexican soldiers and statesmen who believed that a gigantic Indian plot had been hatched against the security of Mexico and that the periodic uprisings by Yaquis in Sonora were fomented by the Apaches from their lairs across the border and in the Sonora mountains. The contemporary writer José Francisco Velasco voiced perhaps the ultimate nightmare of Sonorans, in observing that 'if ever the Apaches in the north and the Yaquis in the south formed an alliance, Mexican Sonora would be lost'.[15]

Mangas Coloradas

It took the Apaches some time to discover that they didn't like the Americans, who began entering their territory in large numbers around the time of the Mexican–American War. In 1846 the great Chiricahua leader, Mangas Coloradas (1795?–1863), and his Eastern Chiricahuas[16] had extended a warm welcome to General Stephen Watts Kearny's US troops in transit to California, offering to join them in the fight against the detested Mexicans. It was only in the early 1860s, some fifteen years later, that relations between the Apaches and Americans deteriorated to the point of war. Many historians of the Apache wars have found it convenient to date the commencement of hostilities precisely from February 1860, in the wake of one of the most notorious 'incidents' in the historiography of the North American Indian wars, the alleged whipping by American miners of Mangas Coloradas.

The story holds that the chief had come to the miners' camp to try to convince them to leave his people's lands alone and try their luck in Mexico, and that the miners had tied him to a tree and beaten him with an ox whip. 'It was the greatest insult that could be inflicted even on an ordinary Indian and Mangas Coloradas was a great Chief', wrote the novelist and popular historian Paul Wellman.[17] It now appears, however, that this event may never have taken place. A careful examination by Edwin Sweeney, Mangas Coloradas's biographer, of the sources on which accounts of the whipping are based has demonstrated convincingly that the story that so many scholars have relayed over the years as fact was a product of rumour, misconstrued evidence, or perhaps even outright 'fabrication'.[18]

Whether or not they ever took the lash to Mangas Coloradas, it is nonetheless true that miners bore a heavy responsibility for the outbreak of the Apache wars. It was the arrival of large numbers of gold miners in the new Arizona Territory over the 1850s that more than anything turned the Apaches against the Americans. D.C. Cole writes that the Apaches had a 'phobia' about gold that caused them to take special exception to miners.[19] This no doubt refers to their dislike for the way mining operations violated the earth, the creation and gift of the creator god Ussen to the Apache people. There were other, less spiritual considerations as well. The miners came in large numbers and built shanty towns which, along with their digging, drove away the game. And it soon appeared that, unlike the traders and trappers who had visited Apachería in earlier days, the miners intended to stay at least as long as the gold held out and looked upon the Apaches as territorial rivals. Inevitably, the presence of miners in the Apache lands would encourage other whites to come: farmers, ranchers and storekeepers to service the mining towns, and ultimately, soldiers to 'protect' the newcomers from Indian attack. Dan Thrapp puts it succinctly: 'It was gold that finally defeated the Apaches and wild Indians in much of the West, for it was gold that brought in population. . .'.[20]

Cochise

It was a constellation of events in the early 1860s that brought on the war between the Chiricahuas and Americans that would continue, with the occasional breathing spell, for the next 25 years. Edwin Sweeney dates the beginning of the long struggle to an assault by miners on the band of Mangas Coloradas on the Mimbres River in New Mexico Territory in December 1860 and the notorious Bascom Affair involving the chief's even more famous son-in-law, Cochise, which took place two months later.

Cochise would become the greatest Apache war chief after Mangas Coloradas, and the Apache leader best known to posterity with the possible exception of

Geronimo. Born in 1823 or 1824, he was known to American travellers before the Civil War as a friend to whites. This would change dramatically in February 1861, as a result of the Bascom Affair.[21] On 4 February a US Army detachment of some 60 men approached Apache Pass in search of some stolen livestock and a white boy named Felix Ward who had been carried off in October 1860 by Apaches. The detachment, largely composed of infantrymen mounted on mules, was under the command of Second Lieutenant George N. Bascom, a young officer just out of West Point. Bascom had been convinced by Ward's foster father, who accompanied the detachment, that Cochise and his band had taken the stock and the boy. This does not appear to have been the case. Having lured the Chiricahua leader and his five companions to a tent in his detachment's camp near the pass, Bascom demanded the return of the boy, and when Cochise denied responsibility for the abduction soldiers surrounded the tent. Cochise was informed that he and his companions would be held as hostages until young Felix Ward was brought in.[22]

> According to the generally accepted story, Cochise whipped out his knife, slashed the rear wall of the tent, and burst through the cordon of surprised soldiers, gaining the safety of the surrounding hills despite the 50 or more shots fired at him.[23]

Lieutenant Bascom was able, however, to seize the five Apaches who had accompanied Cochise and hold them as hostages. The chief swiftly replied in kind, taking hostages of his own. When Bascom and Cochise failed to agree on an exchange of prisoners and army reinforcements began to appear in the area, Cochise killed his hostages. The next day, Bascom hanged six Apache prisoners in retaliation.[24] Unfortunately for the young lieutenant and for the population of Arizona Territory, the executed Apaches included Cochise's brother and two nephews. Revenge, as we have seen, was the prime motive for war among the Apaches, and Cochise was perhaps more quick to seek vengeance than most of his people. In any case, he now led his Chiricahua band on a rampage that ultimately spiralled into a general conflict that raged on, with one brief hiatus in the mid-1870s, until 1886, and may have cost 5,000 American and Mexican lives and hundreds of thousands of dollars worth of property.[25] The Americans' good friend was transformed into one of their most deadly enemies. In a final irony, the abducted boy turned out not to have been killed by the Apaches, as many whites had suspected, and was eventually freed. A few years later, he would surface as a scout for General George Crook, under the name of Mickey Free.

Battle of Apache Pass

The Bascom Affair probably made it inevitable that when Union troops of the California Column passed through Arizona on their way to take New Mexico Territory from the Confederates in 1862, they would come under attack by

Apaches. According to Thrapp, the ambush of an advance party of the column at Apache Pass on 14 July 'was the greatest massing of Apache warriors for a fight in written history'.[26] It certainly brought together a most remarkable array of Apache luminaries; every great Apache war leader, then and in the future, seems to have been there: Mangas Coloradas, Cochise, Victorio, Nana, Juh, perhaps even Geronimo.[27] The California Volunteers who fell into the trap were under the command of Captain Thomas L. Roberts and their objective was to secure the springs in the pass for the use of the column. Roberts's 150 soldiers[28] and 30 civilian teamsters were desperately in need of water themselves, as were the 22 teams of horses and 242 head of cattle they had in tow. The battle which followed can best be characterised as a contest for the springs between an exceptionally large force of Apache warriors and a heavily outnumbered, thirst-maddened column of soldiers. Although the more numerous Apaches also had the advantage of surprise and the tactical edge of operating from concealed positions in the rocks above the pass, it was the bluecoats who prevailed.[29] As we already saw in Chapter 4, it was the detachment's mountain howitzers, a weapon hitherto unknown to the Apaches, that tipped the balance in its favour. Over 60 Apaches were killed in the battle, almost all by artillery shells. Thrapp believes that the Apache leaders who were present at the Battle of Apache Pass took away from it 'the dictum to avoid pitched battle with regular troops unless the soldiers were at a disadvantage, and then to make it short, sharp, and decisive'.[30] There is, of course, no real way of verifying this but it is clear that this was the last large-scale pitched battle between Apaches and their American and Mexican enemies.

Murder of Mangas Coloradas

Whatever chance might have remained for restoring peace was wrecked for years to come by the murder of Mangas Coloradas by US soldiers in January 1863. Accounts vary as to how the Chiricahua leader fell into army hands. The official report claimed he was 'captured', but Private Daniel E. Conner, a former prospector, who was present when Mangas Coloradas was taken prisoner and throughout his detention, later wrote that he had been lured into an army camp by a flag of truce. In any case, the army column which made him prisoner had been on patrol near the new Pinos Altos mining complex, which the regional commander, General James Carleton, believed was being threatened by Mangas Coloradas and his 'band of murderers and robbers'. The chief was taken to nearby Fort McLane and held under guard. Robert Utley has written that the fort's commander, Brigadier General Joseph R. West, 'had no intention of letting Mangas go'.[31] During the night of 18 January, Mangas Coloradas was killed trying to escape from detention, according to the official report. Private Conner, however, wrote that he saw army guards apply heated bayonets to the soles of the chief's feet, and then shoot him when he jumped up to protest. But, in the eyes of the Apaches at least, worse was yet to come.

Mangas Coloradas's body was dumped in a gully outside the fort, where it was later found by a party of soldiers under the command of the post surgeon, a man with the unlikely name of Sturgeon. The soldiers scalped the corpse, then the doctor cut off the head, boiled it and sent it off to a New York museum, where it seems to have caught the interest of local phrenologists.[32]

The Apaches considered the mutilation of Mangas Coloradas's body after death a worse affront than his murder. 'The killing of an unarmed man who has gone to an enemy under truce was an incomprehensible act, but infinitely worse was the mutilation of his body', the one-time Apache warrior, James Kaywaykla, told the oral historian Eve Ball.[33] 'To an Apache', Asa Daklugie, a nephew of Geronimo, explained to Ball, 'the mutilation of the body is much worse than death, because the body must go through eternity in the mutilated condition'.[34]

Already enraged by the killing of his relatives in the Bascom Affair, the murder of his father-in-law, Mangas Coloradas, by US troops launched Cochise on a nine-year blood-letting spree in Arizona and Sonora. This was only brought to an end in 1872 when the Chiricahua leader's growing weariness with the bloody cycle of violence he was engaged in coincided with a peace initiative from a government in Washington desirous of finding ways to make peace with its Indian adversaries.[35] The Grant administration sent General Oliver O. Howard, accompanied by his aide, Captain Joseph A. Sladen, to Arizona to try to negotiate a peace settlement with Cochise and his Chiricahuas. Howard was a natural choice for the job. Known throughout the army as the 'praying' or 'Christian' general, he was on excellent terms with the church groups who dominated the Peace Policy circle that more or less dictated the Grant administration's Indian policy at this point. Howard's most difficult task, as it turned out, was finding Cochise. Earlier peace feelers to the Chiricahua leader had failed because negotiators had insisted that he come down from his mountain lair to one of the Arizona forts for talks. Understandably wary of white envoys since the Bascom Affair, Cochise had refused. Howard knew that he had to go to Cochise but discovered that no one – at least in the white community – knew where the chief's ranchería was. One local civilian, however, knew Cochise well enough to get a message to him. This was Thomas J. 'Tom' Jeffords, who had traded with the Chiricahuas over the years and enjoyed their confidence. Jeffords sent out two Apache scouts as emissaries and they were able to arrange a meeting with Cochise at his camp in the Dragoon Mountains in southeastern Arizona in October 1872. The talks, attended by Howard, Sladen, Jeffords and two Apache scouts on the government side, ended in acceptance of a peace agreement by Cochise in return for the offer of a large reservation for his people, encompassing most of southeastern Arizona. Although other Apache bands launched raids from time to time, and raids into Mexico continued unabated, Arizona came closer to peaceful coexistence with the Apaches during the subsequent five-year period than at any time between the early 1860s and 1886, when Geronimo and his band finally surrendered.[36]

PART II

George Crook's way of war

Not everyone was happy with Howard's peace agreement with Cochise. The commander of the Arizona military district, General George Crook, was one of the dissenters. He believed that the agreement encouraged Apaches to think that the Americans were afraid of them and thus undermined his efforts to impose a military solution on the 'Apache problem'. Crook was also upset that he had no authority over the large reservation set aside for Cochise and his Southern Chiricahuas. He thought that the 'Bible-thumping' Howard had been hoodwinked by Cochise, who would now simply use the reservation as a base for continuing raids in Arizona and down into Mexico. But the general did have authority to proceed militarily against raiders from the Western Apache bands further north in Arizona and in November 1872 he launched a 'grand offensive' against them. This was the first of two classic Crook campaigns against the Apaches. All of the elements of his famous counter-insurgency strategy can be discerned in this 1872 campaign. Before departing for the field, the general spent weeks carefully planning operations and issuing strict orders to his subordinates, gathering resources and assembling transport, picking scouts and officers to lead them.[37] In his attention to detail and meticulous planning, as well as in his care for the welfare of his soldiers and scouts, Crook very much resembles Britain's pre-eminent colonial soldier, whom we shall meet in the next chapter: Sir Garnet Wolseley.[38]

Two aspects of his preparations became hallmarks of his campaigns and merit special attention. First, there was the matter of how best to transport supplies on the expedition. General Crook became well known throughout the US Army for what Emmett Essin calls his 'concept of pack transportation'. In mountainous country like Arizona, the wagon trains the army generally used to transport supplies were out of the question. This meant using mule transport. The keys to Crook's system were his personal involvement in the selection of packers and mules and his hands-on approach to the packing process. Crook personally observed the packing to make sure that each mule had enough padding so that its back would not be rubbed raw and to see that its load was evenly distributed.[39] The general saw to it that packers were well paid and that the mules were well fed and cared for. He spent a lot of time with his packers and often ate with them on campaign (to the disgust of some of his more status-conscious fellow officers).[40] Indeed, Crook's common touch probably had a great deal to do with the success of his transport arrangements. He was anything but a martinet and he cared little for the pomp and flummery of military dress and tradition. He rode a mule on campaign against the Apaches and can be seen in photographs on his favourite mount, Apache, togged out in a canvas suit and a Japanese straw hat, with a double-barrelled shotgun across his knees. This helps to explain why he managed to get the kind of good service out of his civilian employees that so many of his fellow officers could not.

The second element in his campaign preparations that merits being emphasised was Crook's talent in picking subordinates. Although he was notoriously partial to his coterie of aides – John Gregory Bourke, Charles King and Azor Nickerson – it needs to be pointed out that these were highly competent officers and not the kind of drones who too often hold staff positions. Where Crook particularly shone, however, was in choosing officers to command the large numbers of Indian scouts he took into the field with him. Captains Emmet Crawford, Britton Davis and Charles Gatewood would be superb in this role, winning the confidence not only of their scouts but also of the Apache 'hostiles' they fought because of their faithfulness to commitments. This was a principle that Crook drummed into his officers: Never promise anything you can't deliver, but when you do make a promise, you must keep it no matter what.

The campaign that followed succeeded in breaking the resistance of the Western Apaches and forcing them to go onto the reservations set aside for them. It was Crook's ability to stay in the field, thanks to his pack-mule transport system, and to maintain unrelenting pressure on the enemy, to hunt him out in even the most inaccessible places, thanks to his Apache scouts, that brought success. One of the Western Apache leaders who came in to surrender, Cha-lipun, conceded as much to Crook. 'You see', he said, 'we are nearly dead from want of food and exposure – the copper cartridge has done the business for us. I am glad of the opportunity to surrender, but I do it not because I love you, but because I am afraid of General'.[41] The 1872–3 campaign waged by Crook, taken together with Howard's accord with Cochise, brought relative peace to Arizona for most of the remainder of the 1870s.[42] It was a signal achievement and won Crook much acclaim both in Arizona and Washington.[43]

The breakdown in 1879 of the peace agreement struck with Cochise owed much to the US government's decision to abrogate earlier pacts with the Apaches and concentrate all of the diverse and often hostile bands of the Apache people 'on the furnace-like patch of rocky desert at San Carlos, on the upper Gila River'.[44] The concentration policy took its inspiration from Washington bureaucrats who believed they could bring peace to the Southwest by confining all the Apaches in one place, 'in part to educate them and make them into the white definition of "productive citizens", and in part so that the government could keep an eye on them'.[45] The government's concentration strategy may have possessed the virtue of bureaucratic symmetry, but it was not very successful on the ground. To begin with, it brought together, cheek by jowl, feuding Apache bands that the government would have been better off trying to keep apart. Many of the Apaches confined there, the Warm Springs and Chiricahua bands in particular, believed themselves to have been betrayed by the US, never were reconciled to the move and constantly sought opportunities to break out. They were also attracted by the example of the bands who had never given in to the white man's pressure and had continued to roam free in the fastnesses of the Sierra Madre Mountains in Sonora.[46]

PART II

Victorio

The struggle which now took place between the Apaches and the Americans and Mexicans has been called the Victorio War after the war chief of the Warm Springs band who became the principal Apache leader in the conflict. 'A worthy successor of the great Mangas Coloradas', wrote Robert Utley, 'Victorio was a dynamic, aggressive leader, impatient of any form of restraint, highly skilled in the methods of Apache warfare'.[47] From their base in the Candelaría Mountains of northern Chihuahua, Victorio's band raided across the border into the USA, particularly western Texas and New Mexico, but also as far west as Arizona, where they tried to lure other Apaches off the San Carlos Reservation and onto the warpath.

The task of catching the fast-moving Apache raiders fell to the 'Buffalo Soldiers' of General Edward Hatch's New Mexico-based Ninth Cavalry and General Benjamin H. Grierson's West Texas-based Tenth Cavalry. In April and again in May 1879, Hatch's troopers got close enough to Victorio and his raiders to engage them in battle in the New Mexico mountains, but proved unable to stop them from returning to their Mexican lair.[48] General Grierson, who correctly surmised that Victorio's next entry into the USA would come by way of West Texas, now moved to thwart it by guarding all the watering holes the Apache warriors were likely to use. The scheme worked admirably, forcing the Apaches to abandon their invasion of Texas and return to Mexico. Victorio and his band now became the objects of a massive international manhunt, involving two large US forces under the command of Colonels George P. Buell (New Mexico) and Eugene A. Carr (Arizona) and 1,000 Mexican troops led by Colonel Joaquin Terrazas.[49]

The failure of Hatch and Grierson's 'Buffalo Soldiers' to catch the Apaches came in for severe criticism by the frontier population at the time and, in the view of Robert Utley, their campaigns have been given short shrift by historians ever since.[50] William F. Leckie, a leading historian of the black regiments in the West, has put this down to racism. 'Hatch and Grierson,' he wrote, 'were objects of bitter criticism, and the latter has sometimes been pictured as little more than a buffoon.' Meanwhile, 'the men in the ranks more often than not were and have been tailored to fit the stereotype of grinning, fumbling misfits incapable of independent thought or action.'[51] A further reason for contemporary criticism of the efforts of the Buffalo Soldiers may well have been the fact that when Victorio and his raiders were finally cornered and destroyed, it was the despised Mexicans who did it.

The campaign to wipe out Victorio and his band was to have been a cooperative effort by the US and Mexican forces, with the explicit blessing of the Mexican President, Porfirio Díaz. Thus, several American columns crossed the border into Mexico on 10 September 1880, intending to join up with Terrazas's Mexican army for a massive sweep across the Candelaría Mountains. This plan came unstuck, however, when Victorio and his warriors burrowed deeper into Chihuahua rather than staying put or moving west into Sonora as expected. Not happy with the prospect of an army of Americans so far inside his country, Colonel Terrazas asked the American commanders to return to the US. The general cited as his reason for the request the perennial Mexican claim that the Apache scouts accompanying the American force could not be trusted. Utley, however, has suggested that the real motive may have been that Terrazas, 'a prominent political figure, felt confident of destroying Victorio without foreign help and did not intend to share any credit with Americans'.[52]

In any case, it was the Mexicans who finally brought Victorio to bay. Five days later, Terrazas's Tarahumara scouts trailed the Apaches to a canyon in the Tres Castillos Mountains in Chihuahua. An attack the following morning, 15 October 1880, ended in the death of 60 Apache warriors and eighteen women and children. Victorio also died in the fray, apparently shot by a Tarahumara sharpshooter, Mauricio Corredor, who, upon presentation of the chief's scalp to the authorities in Chihuahua City, was given 3,000 pesos and a nickel-plated rifle as a reward. Although a handful of warriors escaped, the battle of Tres Castillos effectively brought an end to the Victorio War.[53] The death of Victorio and the destruction of his band did not bring the Apache wars to a close, however. On the troubled San Carlos Reservation, a new and even more fearsome war leader was emerging to direct the energies of those who refused to accept the white man's road. He was a Chiricahua and his name was Geronimo.

The Cibicu Creek incident

The rise of Geronimo, however, was only one side of the Apache response to confinement on the San Carlos Reservation. Not long after the destruction of Victorio's band, a movement of spiritual regeneration was launched on the reservation by a medicine man and prophet named Nakai'-dokli'ni. By mid-1881, the prophet's message of 'Apache renaissance' had attracted enough of a following on the reservation to become worrying to the military authorities who had charge of its administration. On 30 August 1881, Nakai'-dokli'ni was taken into custody by Sixth Cavalry troopers and Apache scouts from nearby Fort Apache under the command of Colonel Eugene Carr. The detachment's camp at Cibicu Creek, near where the arrest had taken place, came under attack that evening by followers of the prophet. Some of the Apache scouts, apparently swayed by Nakai'-dokli'ni's teachings, joined the attackers. The prophet died in the ensuing firefight, along with eight soldiers. Subsequently, three of the Apache scouts who had turned their rifles on their employers – Sergeants Dandy Jim and Dead Shot, and Corporal Skippy – were convicted of mutiny by a court martial and hanged, while two others were sentenced to long terms on Alcatraz Island off San Francisco, California, then a prison for Indians.[54]

The Cibicu Creek Incident, as it came to be known, would have an impact on the North American Indian wars that went far beyond the turmoil that gripped Arizona Territory in its wake, as furious Apaches lashed out at white settlers and even briefly laid siege to Fort Apache. Although theirs was the only example to date of 'treachery' in the long history of the employment of Indian scouts by the US Army, the revolt of the Apache scouts at Cibicu Creek was proof enough in the minds of many army officers to justify doing away with Indian auxiliaries altogether. This view, interestingly, would be strongest in the upper echelons of the army, where, for example, it enjoyed the support of, among others, General Philip Sheridan, commander of the army in the West. Officers in the field felt differently. They knew from long experience that all the Buffalo Bill Codys and Wild Bill Hickoks in the West could never replace their Indian scouts. They simply lacked the wilderness skills, stamina and trustworthiness of their Indian counterparts. But, as we will see, as far as the Apache scouts were concerned, it would be the doubters who would have the last word, five years after Cibicu Creek, when the Apache wars finally came to an end.

Crook vs. Geronimo

This, however, was all in the future, as the turmoil which set in following the incident on Cibicu Creek provoked demands by both settlers and soldiers for a return to the theatre of General George Crook. It is interesting that in trying to restore order the first item of business on Crook's agenda was to reaffirm his faith in the Apache scouts. In fact, he increased their numbers to 250. Having listened to the complaints of Apaches, Crook became convinced that bad conditions on the reservation were at the root of the current troubles and that the Cibicu Creek confrontation was an accident. If the Apaches had planned an attack, as some had charged, he said, 'not one of our soldiers would have gotten away from there alive'.[55] A central credo in Crook's programme for dealing with Indians was General Order No. 43, issued on 5 October 1882. In it, he directed officers and soldiers in the Arizona Department to behave equitably toward Apaches and whites; 'to make no promises not in their power to carry out'; to redress grievances within their jurisdiction; to apply force only when absolutely convinced of its necessity, 'that they may not . . . allow the troops under them to become instruments of oppression'.[56]

Crook further concluded that the presence of the bronco Apache bands in the Sierra Madre Mountains in Mexico was a grave threat to the peace of the Arizona Territory, since their freewheeling existence offered a vivid contrast to the 'farmer-Indian' life being crafted for reservation Apaches by the whites, and the exploits of the raiders were enormously attractive to bored young (and not so young) males on the reservation. Thus, when the Sonora bands crossed the border into Arizona and New Mexico in March 1883, in search of ammunition and recruits from the reservations, Crook decided it was necessary to lay plans for dealing with the 'renegades' once and for all. His first step was to co-ordinate his campaign as closely as possible with his Mexican counterparts. To that end, he travelled by train to Guaymas and Hermosillo in Sonora where he conferred with the state governor, Major General Luis Torres, and the two federal military commanders in the state, Major Generals Bonifacio Topete and Guillermo Carbo (the former was in charge of Apache operations in Sonora). Crook received a green light to pursue the Apaches into Sonora, but was warned that unless some way could be found to identify his Apache scouts, they could well be taken for hostiles by Mexican troops. Crook promised that the scouts would henceforth wear red headbands. On the return trip to Arizona, Crook went by way of Chihuahua, where he held similar talks with the governor, Luis Terrazas, and other officials and was again assured of cooperation.[57]

The expedition that Crook now led into Sonora stands out sharply in the history of the North American Indian wars. By far the largest component of the force were 193 Apache scouts under the command of Captain Emmett Crawford. The only white regulars were a company of the Sixth Cavalry: just two officers, 42 other ranks, a surgeon and hospital orderly, under the command of Captain Adna R. Chaffee.[58] Crook's meticulously prepared and equipped pack-train consisted of 350 mules, 'the maximum which could be supplied by the use of every available pack animal in the Department [of Arizona] and the minimum with which I could hope to be successful. . .'. The mules carried into Mexico enough supplies for 60 days' operations, including 150 rounds of ammunition per man. As it turned out, this proved to be only barely sufficient, for reasons that Crook could not realistically have foreseen.[59]

Following an engagement in the Sierra Madre between Crawford's scouts and 'hostiles' on 15 May, Crook came to believe himself in a sufficiently advantageous position to open negotiations with the Apache leadership in the Sonora mountains. In subsequent days he was proved correct. Most of the Apache leaders, including Geronimo and Naiche, Cochise's son, came in to parley and ultimately to surrender. On 12 June 1883 Crook's column crossed the frontier into Arizona to a tumultuous welcome. He had brought with him 348 Apache prisoners, all of whom had pledged to return to the San Carlos Reservation. Only a tiny handful of Apache warriors remained on the loose in Mexico, under the war chief Juh. The welcome home accorded to Crook was all the warmer because many Arizonans had feared that he was dead, since he and his force had been incommunicado for over a month. A warm welcome awaited him in the East as well. These were Crook's salad days. His disappointing performance during the Sioux War of 1876 appeared to have been forgotten, including by General Sheridan, recently one of his severest critics (and soon to be once again), who invited him to address the graduating class at West Point on 16 June 1884.

Disaster followed quickly on the heels of success. In May 1885 Geronimo escaped from the reservation once again and headed into Mexico, killing and plundering as he went. And once again, in March 1886, Crook and his Apache scouts tracked him down in the Sierra Madre Mountains and convinced him to give up and return to Arizona, on the understanding that he would be exiled to a detention camp in the eastern United States for two years. This time, however, the Chiricahua leader did not keep his word. In the wake of a drinking spree just short of the Arizona border, Geronimo and a small band of followers fled into the mountains and eluded pursuit by Crook's troops. This proved to be the last straw for General Sheridan. Already upset by what he saw as Crook's leniency toward Geronimo (he had wanted the old raider exiled from Arizona indefinitely), and suspicious of his penchant for employing 'wild' Chiricahua Apache scouts, Sheridan relieved Crook of his duties and appointed General Nelson Miles to replace him.[60]

Nelson Miles and the white cocks

The longstanding and virulent rivalry between Crook and Miles by itself assured that the new broom in Arizona would sweep cleanly. But Miles also brought to his task a strong distaste for Crook's 'way of war', especially his reliance upon friendly Apache scouts and combatants to carry the main burden of the fighting. Miles wrote in his memoirs that he had 'no confidence' in the 'integrity' of the Apache scouts and 'did not believe they could be trusted'. He subsequently 'took measures to have nearly all of them discharged'.[61] But his desire to get rid of the Apache scouts stemmed from more than his belief that 'they were naturally more friendly to their own blood relatives than they could be to our service'. Miles contended that Crook and the soldiers who served with him had lost faith in themselves and their civilisation and had come to believe that the Apaches could only be beaten by other Apaches. He had listened to this kind of talk when he first arrived in Arizona, he said, and had countered that 'with our superior intelligence and modern appliances we ought and would be able to counteract, equal or surpass all of the advantages possessed by the savages'.[62] Miles had come to Arizona, wrote Dan Thrapp, 'imbued with Sheridan's notion that the proper way to fight the Apache was with white troops, and he labored to put this into practice'.[63]

Miles's choice of officers to lead the renewed campaign against Geronimo sheds further light on the general's thinking. To command the expedition, he chose Captain Henry W. Lawton, at 6'5" 'perhaps as fine a specimen of a man as could be found', but also one who 'was of that class who believed the Indians could be overcome'.[64] His choice of Lawton's second in command is even more revealing. The nod went to 'another splendid type of American manhood', Captain Leonard Wood, at the time a contract surgeon with the Army but keen for more robust service. The 24-year-old Wood was, wrote Miles, 'A native of Massachusetts, a graduate of Harvard, a fair-haired, blue-eyed young man of great intelligence, sterling, manly qualities and resolute spirit.'[65]

General Miles's obvious concern that whites not only triumph in the Indian wars but *be seen to triumph* was widely shared among imperial soldiers of the time. A little more than a decade before Miles's campaign against Geronimo, Sir Garnet Wolseley, Britain's greatest colonial soldier, had gone to war against the Kingdom of Ashanti on Africa's Gold Coast convinced that national honour and the future of the white race in Africa demanded that the campaign be waged by white soldiers, not 'native' levies. And, Wolseley was, if anything, even more convinced than Miles of the superiority of white soldiers over 'savages'. In a pamphlet destined for distribution to British troops on the eve of the 1873–4 war, he wrote that

> Providence has implanted in the heart of every native of Africa a superstitious awe and dread of the white man that prevents the negro from daring to meet us face to face in combat. A steady advance or charge, no matter how partial, if made with determination always means the retreat of the enemy.[66]

A little less than a decade after Lawton and Wood set out to find Geronimo, the governor of the Portuguese colony of Mozambique in East Africa, António Enes, preparing to wage war against the Gaza Nguni people, cousins of the Zulus, told his cabinet that this time Portugal must not rely upon African troops to fight its battles. Victory against the Nguni would not be seen as victory unless it was won by Portuguese soldiers, by the 'white cocks' as he called them.[67]

Miles's two paragons, Lawton and Wood, set forth to bring in Geronimo and his elusive Apache band with an impressive array of power behind them. Before the 'Geronimo campaign' was over, Miles put some 5,000 soldiers in the field, about a quarter of the total strength of the US Army of the day. He set up thirty heliograph stations along the border – including in Sonora – enabling him to communicate on a regular basis with troops in the field from his base at Fort Bowie, Arizona.[68] But it would take more than Nelson Miles's 'modern appliances', even when combined with the powerful physique of Henry Lawton, to round up Geronimo. Miles 'ran his men literally ragged in the mountains of Mexico', wrote Dan Thrapp, 'and had little to show for it'.[69] Although their troops and subordinate officers had been handpicked for the expedition, Lawton and Leonard Wood were the only two white men who managed to stay in the field until the end. And, as Robert Utley has observed, although the expedition was able, albeit with great difficulty, to stay on Geronimo's trail, without Apache scouts to lead the way, they were unable 'to close with them'. In the end, Miles was forced to call out of retirement Charles Gatewood, one of Crook's chiefs of scouts, and send him along with two veteran Apache scouts into the hills to secure Geronimo's surrender. The Apache fugitives simply did not trust Miles's men; Gatewood was at the time probably the only white man in Arizona who held the trust of Geronimo and his band and could negotiate a surrender with them. And so it was Gatewood who brought Geronimo out of the hills and face-to-face with Miles at Skeleton Canyon in Arizona to hear the terms of his surrender.[70]

The terms, dictated by the highest echelons of the US government, determined to put an end once and for all to the Chiricahua menace, were harsh. Geronimo and his followers were to be exiled to Florida for an indefinite period of time; the intimation was that they would never return to Arizona. Moreover, it was determined that not only the Apaches who had been taken prisoner but also the Apache scouts who had been instrumental in hunting them down, were to be incarcerated in Florida. What was intended was the permanent relocation of the Chiricahua Apache people, an undertaking only slightly less drastic in intent, and certainly in its consequences, than the policy adopted two decades later by the Mexican government to relocate the Yaquis of Sonora to forced labour in the henequen fields of Yucatán. The betrayal of the Apache scouts was followed by a violation of the terms of Geronimo's surrender whereby he and the warriors of his band were placed in a separate location from their families. The exiled Chiricahuas did not prosper in their new home. Many died of disease, others from an inability to reconcile themselves to permanent deportation. The treatment of the Apache prisoners of war remains a subject of passionate controversy down to the present day.[71]

9

WAR ON THE CANADIAN PRAIRIES, 1870–85

Introduction

At the time of the US Civil War, the nucleus of the nation we today call Canada was known as British North America and was ruled directly by the British Crown. It consisted of a congeries of colonies in the eastern part of the country, principally Quebec, Ontario, Nova Scotia and New Brunswick.[1] Meanwhile, the vast western portion of the future nation, some one-third of its total land area, was, as it had been for almost 200 years, the exclusive fief of the great trading monopoly, the Hudson's Bay Company. Called Rupert's Land, in homage to its first governor, Prince Rupert of the Rhine (the warrior cousin of Charles II, who had granted the company its charter in 1670), the Company's domain stretched from just beyond the western end of Lake Superior to the Rocky Mountains and from the US border to the Arctic Circle. In 1867, however, all of this would change. As a result of the happy confluence of a Canadian yearning for greater self-government and a British desire for imperial retrenchment, extension by the Crown of dominion status to its North American colonies brought into being a Canadian confederation exercising virtual self-government from its capital in Ottawa.[2]

This government wasted no time in negotiating the incorporation of Rupert's Land into the new confederation, in the process extending its sovereign sway from the Atlantic to the Pacific.[3] For the sum of £300,000 sterling, the Hudson's Bay Company was persuaded to cede its political and territorial rights over the Canadian West to Ottawa.[4] James Morris, in volume one of *Heaven's Command*, his masterful narrative history of the British Empire, puts into perspective the high stakes behind the creation of this vast new Canada and the sense of urgency felt by its creators.

> All at once Canada became a nation, coast to coast, and the politicians, the financiers, the engineers and the surveyors began planning a railroad which, by linking the Atlantic and Pacific shores, would make the whole enormous territory an exploitable British whole, proof against the expansionist tendencies of the Americans to the south.[5]

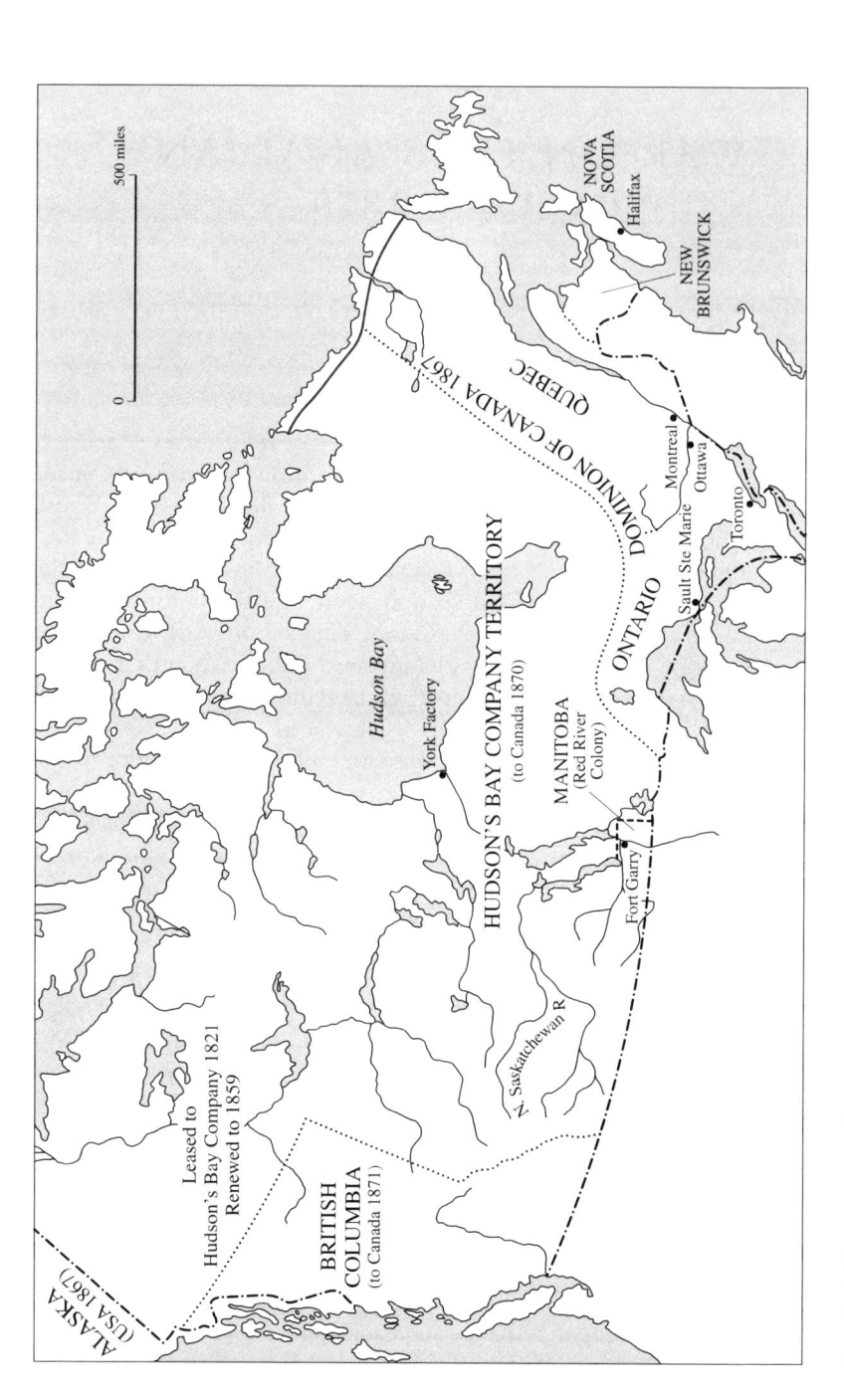

Map 9.1 The creation of the Dominion of Canada, 1869–70.

But the cession of Rupert's Land to the Confederation did not go as smoothly as planned. The Métis people of Manitoba's Red River Colony, who had not been consulted about the transfer of power and who rightly suspected that it would bring an end to their autonomous existence, began holding meetings in the summer of 1869 to mount a campaign of resistance. There were, however, strong local cultural, ethnic and religious overtones to the emerging struggle and two factions quickly surfaced in the Colony: the more moderate one was composed of English-speaking Protestant mixed-bloods, supported by Canadian migrants, largely from Ontario; the other faction, made up of the more numerous French-speaking Catholic mixed-bloods, proved to be much more radical in its demands. Led by Louis Riel, a one-time candidate for the priesthood turned articulate lawyer, they were more adamant about resistance, fearing that a takeover by Ottawa would not only put an end to their autonomous political status but might also abrogate the land titles in Manitoba granted them by the Hudson's Bay Company. Equally important, they suspected that Canadian rule would privilege English-speakers in Manitoba and curtail free exercise of their language and religion.

In December 1869, having won an ensuing power struggle against their English-speaking opponents, Riel and his supporters proclaimed a Métis Republic at Fort Garry. For a time, it looked as if a compromise might be worked out with the Canadian government, but this hope went a-glimmering when Riel's Provisional Government tried and executed by firing squad one Thomas Scott, an 'Irish Protestant with a long record of enmity to the Métis', on charges of taking up arms against the Republic. This action infuriated Protestants in Ontario province, Scott's place of origin, and six months later, the Canadian authorities decided to dispatch an armed force to the Red River. Although Ottawa billed the Red River Expedition as a 'benevolent constabulary', it was in actual fact 'a punitive expedition, and much relished the prospect of an affray in Manitoba'.[6]

The Red River Expedition

Of all the military undertakings covered in this book, none more closely fits the description of a 'war against nature' than the Anglo–Canadian Red River Expedition of 1870. From conception to conclusion, the risks of failure were always associated with terrain and weather, and a race against time, not human foes. And, in the end, what made the expedition a success was not victory in the field: no battles were fought and there were no casualties on either side during the whole of the campaign. Rather, it was the expedition's demonstration that, contrary to American claims (and hopes), it was possible for Canadian armed forces to traverse the inhospitable lands that lay between Eastern Canada and the prairie West and thus help to draw together a vast but disparate country.

The expedition's commander, Colonel Garnet Wolseley, was 'perhaps the most promising young officer of the British Empire' (he was 37) and 'probably the most cocksure'. He was deputy quartermaster general of the British Army in Canada and a much decorated veteran of campaigns in Burma, the Crimea, India and China. This was, however, Wolseley's first command and he was determined to make it a success. Promotion came slowly in the peacetime army.[7] The main body of the colonel's force consisted of 373 officers and men from the 60th Rifle Regiment of the British Army, 382 militiamen from Ontario and 389 from Quebec.[8]

In sheer logistical terms, the challenge facing Wolseley and his troops was enormous. Since an unfriendly US government would not allow his little army to take the easy route to Manitoba by train through the Upper Middle West, the colonel was obliged to take it overland 660 miles through the mosquito-infested forests, swamps and muskeg of the Laurentian Shield, from Thunder Bay on the western edge of Lake Superior to the Red River and Fort Garry in Manitoba. There was a rough road for the first 45 miles of the journey, but after that Wolseley planned to take his force by water, through a maze of rivers, many uncharted, across the vast Lake of the Woods, and on to Lake Winnipeg and the Red River. The trip would 'entail an infinity of laborious portages'.

In what would become a hallmark of his campaigns, Wolseley, soon to be hailed as Britain's greatest colonial soldier, planned meticulously, selected his soldiers and boat crews with skill and saw to it that the care and well-being of his men was assured as far as possible. Since no supplies were to be had en route, everything required for the 60-day journey had to be carried by large canoes of the sort used by the fur traders of the Hudson's Bay Company. Wolseley had the boats specially designed, each to carry eight to nine soldiers and two to three *voyageurs*, together with all manner of rations, tents, ammunition, cooking gear, blankets, axes, nets to catch fish and six-pounder cannon to chastise the Métis. The colonel himself, 'dapper and undaunted', travelled in 'a light birch-bark canoe with a crew of sinewy Iroquois. . .'.[9] The journey to the west began on 12 May.

It was an epic journey. The men, regulars and militia alike, emerged from the forests and lakes and onto the Red River ragged and mosquito-bitten, but sunburned, healthy and remarkably fit. And spoiling for a fight. But there was to be no fight. The expedition arrived at Fort Garry in a downpour on 23 August to find the fort empty and the birds flown. But only just. Believing that the Wolseley expedition was the 'benevolent constabulary' it was advertised to be, Louis Riel and the government of the Métis Republic had remained in place until the last moment. Then, word was received that the executioners of Scott were to be arrested. Riel took his leave with an uneaten meal still on the table and purportedly disappeared around one corner of his house just as Wolseley's soldiers came around the other. He fled south to the USA, where he would remain until 1884.[10] Close call or not, for Wolseley and his troops, 'The anticlimax was pathetic'.[11]

It was just as well that Riel and his Métis government had decamped before Wolseley's little army occupied the Red River settlement. The colonel's

Protestant Ontario militiamen were burning to avenge Thomas Scott and he himself was not too well-disposed to Riel and Co., as he told his wife. 'Hope Riel will have bolted', he wrote to her, 'for although I should like to hang him to the highest tree in the place, I have such a horror of rebels and vermin of his kidney, that my treatment of him might not be approved by the civil powers'.[12]

Wolseley and his regulars returned to eastern Canada as soon as the British flag was run up the Fort Garry flagpole. The 60th Royal Rifles were due to leave Canada for home as part of the British government's retrenchment of overseas garrisons. Colonel Wolseley, meanwhile, would go on to more and more elaborate colonial adventures. His defeat of the West African Kingdom of Ashanti in 1873–4 won him the accolade of 'Britain's only soldier' from Benjamin Disraeli, the prime minister. But an even higher tribute was in store in 1879, when Gilbert and Sullivan feted him as 'the very model of a model major general' in *Pirates of Penzance*.[13]

Prairie Fire, 1885

The Indian peoples of the North-West Territories had not taken part in the 1870 dispute between the Métis and the Canadian government. In fact, relations between the two groups had been strained at this juncture. The Crees had long resented Métis intrusion into what they considered their tribal hunting grounds in pursuit of the diminishing buffalo. Still, the Crees had familial ties with some of the French-speaking mixed-bloods and these would open the way to a partial alliance between the two peoples at the time of the North-West Rebellion of 1885. Such an alliance might never have been formed, however, had it not been for the growing dissatisfaction of Cree bands with life on the reserves to which most of them had repaired as a result of a series of land cession treaties with the Canadian government in the 1870s. These treaties had been negotiated in great haste, as Ottawa was keen to have relations with the western Indians sorted out before white settlement began in earnest on the prairies and construction started on the Canadian Pacific Railway. The Canadian authorities were eager to avoid what they saw as one of the major problems in white–Indian relations in the USA: that the US government had only moved to deal with its western Indians *after* white settlers had flooded onto Indian lands, setting the stage for a bloody confrontation. Seven numbered treaties were signed with the prairie tribes – Plains Ojibwas, Assiniboines, Plains Crees and the Blackfoot Confederation – from 1871 to 1877. Treaty No. 6 covered most of the Crees in Saskatchewan, who occupied reserves near the seat of rebellion in 1885. A few would respond positively to Métis calls for an alliance against the Canadians; most of the Crees who went to war, however, did so for reasons that had little to do with the Métis cause, but a great deal to do with Indian feelings of having been forgotten by the Canadian authorities once the numbered treaties were signed.

The treaties with the prairie tribes, such as No. 6, obliged the Indians affected to move permanently onto assigned reserves, usually not in proximity to each other, where they would be provided with the seed, implements and technical assistance that would enable them to make the transition to a settled agricultural existence. Until this process ran its course, the government agreed to provide the Indians with food, as hunting would only be allowed during the seasons prescribed for white hunters. Some Crees delayed going to the reserves as long as possible, such as the bands of the prominent chiefs Big Bear and Poundmaker.[14] Others who did go willingly to the reserves grew discontented with the sedentary life there and with the federal government's cavalier fulfilment of its obligation to help the Indians make a go of farming and to feed them until they could feed themselves. Starvation stalked some reserves. This assured the existence of elements amongst the Crees which would rally to calls for resistance to the Canadian authorities.

Perhaps fearing that an explosion of this sort was building on the Saskatchewan reserves, the chiefs Big Bear and Poundmaker undertook measures to ameliorate their people's conditions short of armed resistance. During the hungry '80s, Poundmaker called on Ottawa to honour its treaty obligations, whilst Big Bear laboured to organise a pan-Indian confederation on the prairies that would have the strength to force the state to renegotiate the numbered treaties in order to provide more secure benefits for the Indian peoples. These initiatives rang alarm bells in Eastern Canada. Big Bear's prairie diplomacy had envisaged bringing the Blackfoot confederacy, quiescent up to this point, into an alliance with the Crees to force Ottawa's hand. The Blackfeet were even more feared by Canadian whites than the Crees, and the prospect of a pact between the two hitherto deadly enemies was profoundly troubling. The Canadian authorities also saw a symmetry between Indian and Métis restiveness and were prepared to believe in the likelihood of a league between the two camps in the event that the mixed-bloods should cease protesting and take up the gun. These fears would produce a mood of near-hysteria across Canada when the 1885 rebellion broke out and would lead to a disproportionate wave of repression once the fighting had ceased.

Whilst the Cree reserves festered, discontent mounted in the Métis settlements established on the South Saskatchewan River, in the west central part of the province, following the collapse of the Red River Republic in 1870. Once again, the main issues were mixed-blood fears of losing title to their lands, suffering from religious discrimination, and seeing their cultural and linguistic identity eroded. In June 1884, a delegation of Métis travelled south to Montana, where Louis Riel, now a US citizen, was living. They successfully prevailed upon the former head of the Red River Republic to come to Saskatchewan to lead the Métis community there in the second of its confrontations with the Canadian authorities. But the Riel who now returned north of the border was a much changed man from the Riel who had fled Fort Garry in 1870. He had suffered a severe mental depression and had spent some time in an asylum. Much like the jailed Yaqui leader Juan Banderas, Riel had experienced religious revelations while locked away, as a result of which he began to style himself a prophet who had been called to establish a new social order.

On 19 March 1885, Riel announced the formation of a provisional government with its capital in the central Saskatchewan village of Batoche. It was not the kind of secular government he had presided over in Manitoba, but an uneasy combination of political republic and spiritual utopia. Whatever the exact flavour of the Métis republic might have been, the Canadian government in Ottawa showed no intention of negotiating with it. In short order, another Canadian army was moving west to chastise the mixed-bloods. This was a much larger force than the one Wolseley had taken to the Red River and, unlike its predecessor, the army of 1885 went west prepared to fight not only dissident Métis but also the Cree Indians who lived in close proximity to them and who appeared to be about to take to the warpath in large numbers as well. In fact, it was fear of Indian massacres on the frontier that more than anything determined the speedy dispatch of Canadian troops to Saskatchewan.

The fear of massacre hung over the North-West Rebellion like a shroud. The terror that often accompanied it had little to do with Canada then or in the past, but was inspired by events that had taken place elsewhere, often far away. Montana was just over the border from Saskatchewan, and the Custer massacre on the Little Bighorn less than a decade earlier weighed on the Canadian popular mind in these years, especially on the western prairies.[15] But Canada also was part of the far-flung British Empire. Thus, Canadian militiamen went off to war in the spring of 1885 with news of the death of the greatest of all Victorian heroes, General Charles 'Chinese' Gordon, and the massacre of his troops at the hands of 'savages' in Khartoum the previous January still fresh in their minds. After all, Canadians had taken part in an abortive effort by an army under the command of Sir Garnet Wolseley to rescue Gordon.[16] The passions aroused by the killing of a handful of white settlers by dissident Crees at a place called Frog Lake just over the Saskatchewan border in Alberta must be seen in this international context of fear of massacre by savages to be properly understood.

The Frog Lake massacre was the result of the collapse of Big Bear's authority over the young warriors in his band. Angry at the Canadian government's apparent indifference to the starvation that gripped the reserve they had been consigned to, the young men had refused to listen to Big Bear's pleas for caution and had opted instead to follow the band's war chief, Wandering Spirit, 'who made no secret of his undying hatred of whites'.[17] Big Bear had foreseen this turn of events, he later told Bill Cameron, a Hudson's Bay Company factor at Frog Lake.

> When I was in the Long Knives' [Americans'] country [visiting Louis Riel in Montana in 1880] I had a dream, an ugly dream. I saw a spring shooting up out of the ground. I covered it with my hand, trying to smother it, but it spurted up between my fingers and ran over the back of my hand. It was a spring of blood.[18]

PART II

On 2 April 1885 Wandering Spirit and a band of Cree warriors took over the frontier village of Frog Lake, killed nine inhabitants in cold blood, and carried off into captivity the widows of two of the dead. The targets of the warriors' wrath provide a clear demonstration of why some Crees had decided to take up the gun. The Canadian Indian Department agent assigned to Big Bear's reserve, Thomas Quinn, was one of the first to be shot. Quinn may have been a special case. Though his mother was part Cree and he had a Cree wife, Quinn disliked Indians and his behaviour toward them had earned him the nickname 'The Bully'.[19] Another victim of Cree vengeance was the farm instructor for the reserve, John Delaney. '[T]he Indians particularly disliked the luckless men who were assigned to teach them agriculture'.[20] But also marked for death were two Catholic priests in the village, Fathers Léon-Adélard Fafard and Félix Marchand. The priests' bodies were thrown into the basement of the local church and the building was burned.[21] A few days before this, the Cree chief Poundmaker had told another Canadian farm instructor that the Crees had 'returned to the God we know. The buffalo will come back, and the Indian will live the life that God intended him to live'.[22] The killings at Frog Lake, plus a simultaneous 'siege' of the nearby town of Battleford by Poundmaker's Cree band, seem to have convinced Eastern Canadian public opinion that an Indian massacre was in the offing and lent wings to the dispatch of a Canadian army to Saskatchewan.[23]

The North-West Field Force that went west to fight the Métis and their ostensible Indian allies numbered around 6,000 officers and other ranks, only 363 of whom were regulars. The remainder were militia and North-West Mounted Police. Some 3,000 of the militia came from eastern Canada and, so as to counter the impression that the expedition was an Anglo–Canadian war party bent on settling an ethnic feud, it included French-speaking artillery and light infantry units from Quebec province.[24] The militia units from eastern Canada were very much a mixed bag. Toronto sent its two smartest militia battalions, the Queen's Own Rifles and the 10th Royal Grenadiers. 'One company of the Queen's Own, made up entirely of undergraduates from the University of Toronto, celebrated their departure by . . . singing songs in Latin'. The departure of the Midland Battalion, made up of militiamen from a number of largely untrained units in rural Ontario, was a bit less genteel. 'Some of the men had never drilled or soldiered before, and knew nothing of order or discipline,' Private Joseph Crowe later recalled. 'Most of us had been "smelling the cork" and as a result there were quite a few that had to be put in the guard room for the night'.[25]

Private Crowe's morning-after hangover did not deter Joseph Kinsey Howard from depicting the North-West Field Force as 'the most righteous army to take the field in modern times and the most ingenuous'. Heavily middle-class in origin, 'reared in the strictest nineteenth-century Protestant tradition', the young militiamen who predominated in its ranks 'were punctilious about church attendance, even while on the march on the prairie', he wrote. Unlike the 'hard-bitten United States cavalry . . . just to the south of them', the North-West Field Force 'had virtually no liquor and no women; of five thousand men only one required hospital treatment for alcoholism and there were no recorded hospital cases of venereal disease'.[26]

There was also a Far West wing to the expeditionary force, mounted in Alberta and at the outset employing strictly local talent, militia and volunteers, including cowboys from the ranches around Calgary. Command of the Alberta Field Force was given to an ex-British Army artillery officer, Major General Thomas Bland Strange, better known as 'Gunner Jingo'. Strange had served for a time as commanding officer of the regular artillery battery in Quebec but had recently retired to Alberta, where he raised remounts for the British cavalry on his Military Colonisation Ranch. His wing of the campaign, whose overriding purpose was to make sure that the Blackfeet in Alberta remained neutral, would eventually include the few men of the NWMP left in Alberta plus the two French–Canadian militia units sent west to achieve 'racial balance' in the force.[27] High command distrusted the Quebec troops 'on both military and political grounds' and packed them off to Alberta to avert the possibility of collusion between them and the French-speaking Métis. Strange was glad to have the *Canadiens*. He spoke fluent French and had developed a good rapport with the French Canadians during his years of service in Quebec.[28]

Overall command of the expeditionary force went to Major General Sir Frederick Dobson Middleton, a 'stout white-whiskered veteran' whose military pedigree could be traced back to the Indian Mutiny of 1857, where he had been nominated twice for the Victoria Cross. Although Sir Fred's career had started off in promising fashion – he had commanded British forces in New Zealand during the Maori wars of the 1860s and served for a decade as commandant of the Royal Military Academy at Sandhurst – prospects had dimmed in later years and he had found himself threatened with early retirement on half pay in the 1880s, when Canadian connections saved him. Sir Fred had once served in Canada and, in addition to acquiring a Canadian wife, had made some important contacts in military and political circles. These now came to the rescue in securing him an appointment to command of the Canadian militia, which carried the local rank of Major General. This was a gift from heaven for the 55-year-old officer, an Anglo-Irishman like his predecessor on the trail of the Métis, Garnet Wolseley.[29] Sir Fred's strategy for the coming war was simplicity itself: the centre of gravity of the rebellion was the Métis' capital, Batoche; seize it and the rebellion would be over.[30]

But first the army had to get there. This, as it turned out, was more of a challenge for the raw militia than the actual fighting. It was hoped that the troops coming from the east would be able to breeze all the way to the war on the new Canadian Pacific Railway and thus avoid the arduous marching and canoeing Colonel Wolseley's force had struggled with in 1870. The railway was still unfinished, however, and the militia were forced to cross part of the soggy, desolate Laurentian Shield of western Ontario in sleighs and in some cases on foot, dragging their cannon with them. Once out of the bog, the troops mounted the trains again but the weather was still cold and, while their officers toasted themselves in heated cabooses, the other ranks rode bundled up as best they could on open flatcars. In Saskatchewan, the railway disappeared once again and General Middleton was obliged to make do by hiring teamsters and hundreds of horses and oxen to haul men and supplies and commandeering the steamboats plying the rivers of the province. Although this makeshift transportation system worked to the advantage of the army in the end, there was a considerable hiatus between the time the troops arrived in the field and the moment when the logistical apparatus caught up with them. Getting supplies to a railhead or river port was one thing, getting them out to the men on the march was another. Spring had arrived on the prairie but there was no grass yet, which rendered the wagoneers (and cavalry) nearly immobile until forage could be brought in from the east. 'When you get to be 200 miles from your base, the team horses nearly eat what they carry', an exasperated General Middleton complained to his superiors back in Ottawa.[31]

Meanwhile, command of the Métis army had been vested in 48-year-old Gabriel Dumont, scion of one of the mixed-blood community's most prominent families. Although Dumont enjoyed the confidence and friendship of the leader of the Métis republic, Louis Riel, who called him 'Uncle', he could not have been more unlike the cosmopolitan Riel, product of a classical education in eastern Canada. 'As long as the buffalo lasted,' wrote Dumont's biographer, George Woodcock, 'he was the greatest of the Métis hunters, and few Indians of any nation knew more than he did of the lore of the wilderness.' Gabriel Dumont, 'the natural man par excellence, adapted perfectly to the life of the wilderness', may be one of the few genuine examples of the 'hardy frontiersman' to emerge in this book.[32] But did being a skilled hunter, a crack shot and master of Indian languages qualify the illiterate Dumont for command of an army in a modern war? The military historian Jack Granatstein, in his recent history of Canada's army, describes Dumont as a 'skilled tactician and natural commander' who understood his people's strengths – their hardiness, mobility and marksmanship – and weaknesses – lack of discipline – and framed his strategy for the coming conflict accordingly.[33] Dumont is said to have brought another important strength to the Métis war effort: his family's longstanding ties to various Indian peoples. The few Crees and Sioux who fought alongside the Métis at the battles of Fish Creek and Batoche did so because they were 'faithful to old treaties with the Dumont clan'.[34]

But some of the praise accorded Dumont verges on the hyperbolic. His admiring biographer, George Woodcock, portrays him as a sort of prairie Napoleon, a rustic military genius who had devised a strategy for confronting the oncoming Canadians that would have forced them on the defensive, perhaps even obliged the government in Ottawa to negotiate to avoid a long stalemate – but was unable to implement it because of interference from the impractical, otherworldly Riel.[35] This view was helped along by Dumont's own postmortem on the war, given in 1888 to a Quebec journalist, Benjamin A.T. de Montigny.[36] The Métis general said that he had proposed to fight a guerrilla war against the Canadians, featuring destruction of the railways and bridges over which their crucial supplies had to come, raids on their camps to unnerve the green militia, capture of their stock and seizure of their much-needed guns and ammunition. Woodcock believes that if this strategy had been implemented it would not only have halted the Canadian advance but would have encouraged the Indians and Métis still on the sidelines to join the fray. In the end, he contends, the prime minister, John A. Macdonald, would have had to negotiate some kind of favourable settlement with the Métis and Indians to avoid a long military stalemate. But, the argument continues, Riel vetoed this sensible strategy, voicing multiple objections. To begin with, the sort of campaign Dumont was proposing was 'Indian warfare', and the Métis were not savages; the violence and bloodshed it was certain to provoke would only further alienate the Canadians. Second, going off on long-range raids against the enemy line of communications would deprive the capital of the Métis, the holy city of Batoche, of protection. Finally, Riel feared that some of the French Canadians he mistakenly believed were marching with Middleton might be killed in Dumont's raids.[37]

Bob Beal and Rod Macleod, in their book, *Prairie Fire*, now the standard work on the North-West Rebellion, take issue with the thesis of a Métis guerrilla army held in check by the saintly Riel. They argue that carrying the war to the enemy, even in the form of a guerrilla raiding strategy, was never part of the Métis military culture.

> The identity of the Métis as a separate people had been forged to an important degree by successful battles which were celebrated in their songs and folk memory. These battles shared a common feature: they were all defensive.[38]

Digging in, firing on the enemy from prepared positions in rifle pits, was the Métis paradigm of war, originated and perfected in battles against Indian peoples over buffalo hunting grounds earlier in the century, particularly the Sioux.[39] The Métis had learned in these struggles that they fought most successfully on the defensive and they saw no reason to abandon these tactics when they confronted the Canadians. 'In the crisis of 1885 the natural reaction of the Métis was to do what had worked in the past: dig in and wait'.[40]

Beal and Macleod may be right about the decisive weight of Métis military culture at the end of the day, but this did not deter Dumont from carrying out in late April exactly the kind of ambush Riel had decried, as his scouts reported the ponderous but steady approach of Middleton's 400-man force from the south. On 23 April, having convinced a still hesitant Riel that action was required, Dumont led 200 men south from Batoche to intercept the Canadian line of march at a place called Fish Creek. The creek meandered through a small

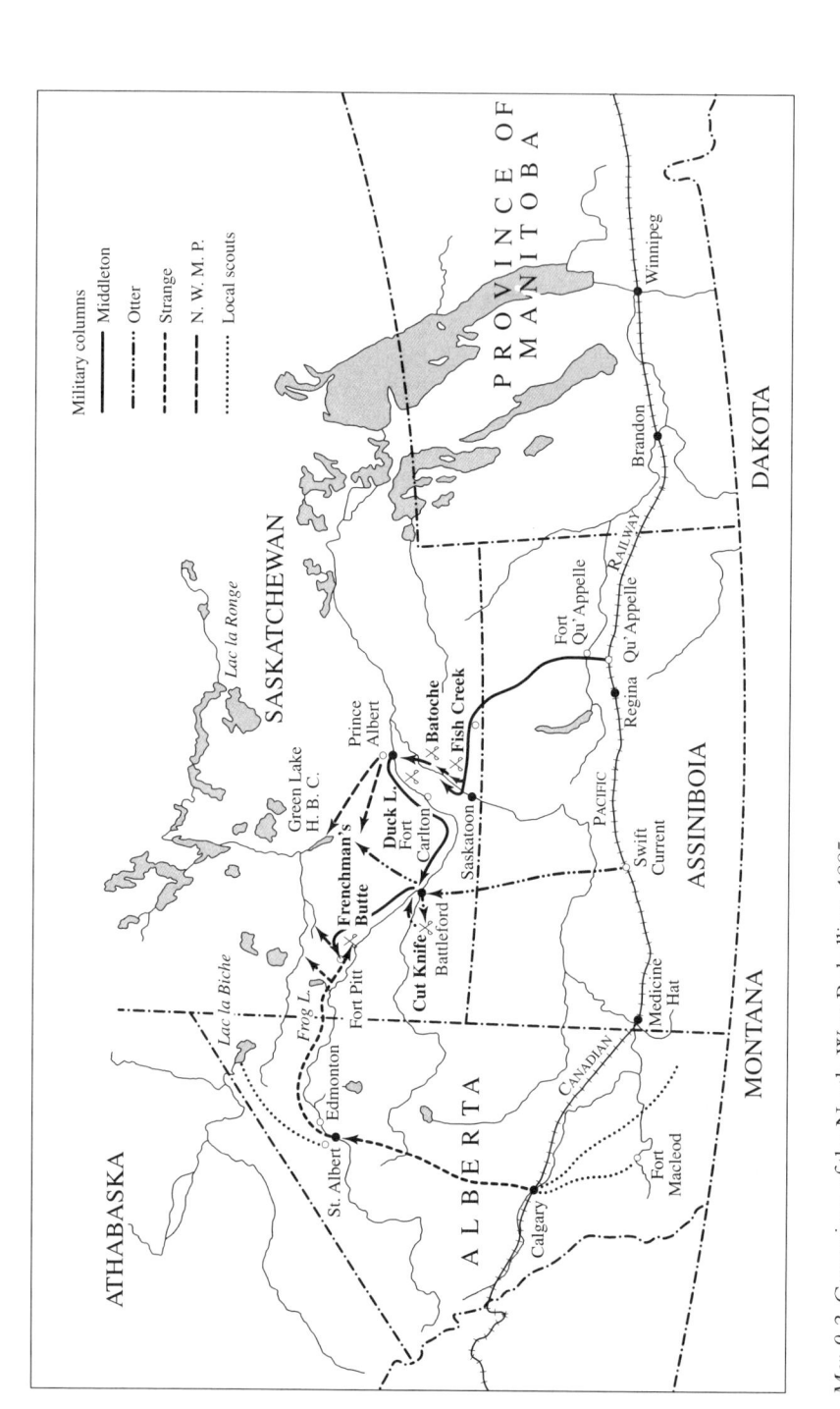

Map 9.2 Campaigns of the North-West Rebellion, 1885.

ravine, or what the Métis called a *coulée*, and it was here that Dumont staged his ambush, positioning 130 men in the deep brush on the valley floor. He would later compare his trap to a buffalo 'pound'; 'I wanted to treat them [the Canadians] like buffalo', he said.[41]

But Métis indiscipline would ruin Dumont's buffalo trap. Middleton had by this time been joined by a body of light cavalry, Boulton's Scouts from Manitoba, and he had sent them out in advance of his infantry to reconnoitre. Unable to restrain themselves, some of Dumont's men had fired upon the scouts, giving away their position and alerting the cautious Middleton to the threat of an ambush. In the all-day fight that followed, the Canadian infantry formed up in a European-style line of battle and pushed into the coulee, only to be driven back by deadly gunfire from the well-concealed Métis. Middleton's artillery was no help. The gunners were unable to site their guns on the lip of the ravine in order to fire down into it for fear of being picked off. Shells sailed harmlessly over the heads of the enemy. Even so, some of Dumont's troops, never having faced artillery fire before, panicked and fled. By evening, the Métis chief was down to 54 men. Middleton had more than six times as many fit to fight, but he had had enough and it was the Canadians who broke off the engagement. The North-West Field Force had suffered heavy casualties. Fifty of Middleton's men, one in eight, had been wounded or killed; ten had been killed outright or would die later of their wounds.[42] Fish Creek was the general's first brush with the Métis and he 'was badly shaken by it'. In a report to the Duke of Cambridge, Queen Victoria's cousin and commander-in-chief of the British Army, he wrote, 'I could not help feeling sorry to see these poor citizen soldiers laying dead and wounded. Most of them being well-to-do tradesmen's sons or in business who thought they were going out for a picnic.'[43]

The Canadian militia received another bloody nose a few days after the Fish Creek battle, this time from Cree Indians, at Cut Knife Hill, between Battleford and the Alberta border.[44] The militia force had been dispatched by General Middleton to lift the 'siege' of Battleford, which they had accomplished without incident on 23 April. This was supposed to have been the limit of their mission, but the detachment's ambitious commander, Lt. Colonel William Dillon Otter, decided otherwise.[45] Having learned that Poundmaker's Cree band, which had sacked Battleford and terrified its inhabitants back in late March, had returned to their reserve some forty miles to the west, Otter set out after them with 300 men in some 50 horse-drawn wagons, along with two cannon and one of the Field Force's two Gatling guns. Since he had no orders to undertake such a mission, Otter passed it off to General Middleton as a 'reconnaissance in force'.[46] In the early morning of 2 May, Otter's wagon-borne troops forded Cut Knife Creek and pulled up in a meadow on the adjacent Cut Knife Hill to have breakfast. As Beal and Macleod comment, 'the most accident-prone commander could not have picked a worse place to have breakfast'. For the large Cree camp they had been looking for was just on the other side of the hill, 'undetected by Otter's scouts'. But even so, despite the racket his troops had made crossing the stream, the Indians might not have been aware of Otter's presence if it had not been for an old man who rose early, heard the commotion and gave the alarm.[47] Cree camp security, like that of most Indians everywhere, left something to be desired.

The battle which now took place lasted some seven hours and ended in the retreat of the militia force Otter had brought from Battleford. The Cree warriors, supported by some 40 Métis and a few members of an Assiniboine warrior society, managed to keep Otter's men on the defensive by adroit use of rifle pits hidden in the furrowed terrain and heavy brush at the top and sides of the hill and, by the time the Canadians withdrew just before midday, had nearly surrounded them. The Canadians' artillery had not helped much, since the carriages of their two pieces – leftovers from the Red River Expedition of 1870 – collapsed early on in the battle, and the Gatling gun, served by the American 'Gatling' Howard himself, 'with its rattle and spray of bullets, at first alarmed the Indians but they rapidly realized that the bullets were passing harmlessly over their heads'.[48]

Although Otter would later receive high marks for his skill in withdrawing his troops, the battle of Cut Knife Hill was the second defeat for the North-West Field Force in two outings. The retreating troops 'laagered-up'[49] their wagons on the other side of the stream, which may have prevented pursuit and heavy casualties[50], although a host of historians have argued down through the years that what saved the Otter's militia from being destroyed in detail was Poundmaker's forceful dissuasion of the Cree warriors.[51] Evidence for this view appears to come from the testimony of two white prisoners in the Cree camp, Robert Jefferson, the farm instructor we took note of before, and a Catholic priest, Father Louis Cochin. Jefferson, who was highly critical of both what he saw as Otter's reckless provocation of a peacefully inclined Indian camp and his conduct of the subsequent battle, concluded that 'But for the Grace of God and the complaisance of Otter's Indian opponent . . . there would have been no survivors'.[52] Cochin, meanwhile, reported that the Assiniboine and Cree warriors had wanted to mount up and go after the retreating Canadians but 'Poundmaker prevented them' since 'It was his intention not to leave the reserve but only to keep himself on the defensive. . .'.[53]

Dénoument at Batoche

The prairie war ended, as General Middleton had said all along it would, with the taking of the Métis capital at Batoche. When the militia force finally moved into position to attack the town, they found the Métis dug in on its outskirts. The target of their campaign over the prairies, Batoche, was not the grand capital on the European model that the conquering soldiers from the East might have desired. The village straggled along both sides of the South Saskatchewan River and consisted of a church, some shops, a few substantial homes and a collection of shacks.

Middleton came on slowly, with 850 men, four cannon, Howard and his Gatling gun and a train of 150 wagons. The lumbering column, George Woodcock wrote, must have had 'some of the unwieldiness of the vast, straggling armies of pre-Mutiny India that Middleton had known in his youth'. It was also vulnerable to guerrilla attack, strung out across the prairie as it was, but Riel had insisted on a static defence of the Métis citadel and so Dumont and his 300 men set about digging in. They built 'lines of defences consisting of carefully spaced rifle pits and trenches, disguised by loopholed logs and parapets of turf, that would make the defenders of Batoche invisible and invincible as long as their ammunition lasted'. But that was the problem. Ammunition was in short supply and some of the defenders were without guns. A Sioux in Dumont's force who knew something about gunsmithing spent his days before the battle began putting old muskets in working order.[54]

But Middleton could not know how poorly armed the defenders of Batoche were. He did know that he had faced Métis gunmen gone to ground before, at Fish Creek, and had been forced to give way. He knew that, 'reconnaissance in force' or no, Otter's fight with the Crees at Cut Knife Hill had been a disaster for Canadian arms. His troops were equally disconcerted. They were fighting an enemy that could fire upon them with impunity and yet could not be seen, much less grappled with. The following description of the militiamen's dilemma by Staff Sergeant Walter Stewart of the Midland (Ontario) Battalion is eerily prophetic of what British soldiers would experience during the disastrous opening days – 'Black Week' – of the Second Boer War. 'We got no sight of the enemy', Stewart wrote in his diary,

> they were well hidden in their rifle pits. This was a rather different way of fighting from what we expected. We calculated on seeing the enemy anyway, we were all fully under the impression that in aiming our rifles we would have something to aim at in the shape of a human form.[55]

Compare Sergeant Stewart's comment with the remarks of Major General Neville Lyttleton, commander of the British 4th (Light) Brigade, contrasting his experience of the 1898 battle of Omdurman against a Sudanese jihad army with that of the battle of Colenso in South Africa a year later: 'In the first 50,000 fanatics streamed across the open regardless of cover to certain death, while at Colenso I never saw a Boer all day till the battle was over, and it was our men who were the victims'.[56]

It was George F.G. Stanley, the first major historian of the North-West Rebellion, writing in 1936, when memories of the South African War were still relatively fresh, who first remarked upon the similarities between the fighting styles of the Boers and the Métis. His analysis is worth quoting at some length.

> In many respects the half-breed tactics were similar to those used by the Boers. The rolling prairie, like the South African veldt, offered

PART II

extensive cover to the defending force which invariably appeared to be much stronger than it really was. Like the Boers, the métis kept to the valleys, coulees and hollows, thus placing their adversaries against the skyline whenever they attempted to advance down the slopes. Silhouetted against the sky the troops were admirable targets for the métis marksmen, many of whom were old buffalo hunters and all of whom were familiar with every foot of the ground upon which they fought. The wonder is, not that the small numbers of half-breeds and Indians were able to check Middleton and Otter, but that the casualties of the civilian militia were not more numerous.[57]

Some of the same thoughts may have been going through the mind of General Middleton. For four days he poked at the Métis defences, unwilling to launch a full-scale assault. His correspondence with superiors during this period indicates that he was seriously considering withdrawal, rather than suffer the heavy casualties he was sure would occur if his militiamen stormed the enemy positions. Preparations were begun for a siege.[58] But the Midland Battalion, those country boys who had spent the night in the guardhouse before departing for the West, 'tired of what they believed to be General Middleton's dithering', disobeyed his orders and attacked. As Sergeant Stewart recorded:

> Firing as we went in rushes . . . the whole line with a rush advanced across the plowed field right through and around the houses and for half a mile. . . . The village was ours.[59]

Though enterprising, the militia attack still might have come to grief if the dug-in Métis had not been desperately short of ammunition. As it was, some of the men in the trenches were reduced to firing scrap metal or stones out of the muskets or shotguns they were using. The younger men among the Métis decamped when they saw the Midland Battalion rushing toward them, but the older fighters stayed to fight to the end, perhaps not wanting to live on in the new world that defeat would bring them and their people. Prisoners were taken, but Riel and Dumont were not among them.[60]

On 15 May Louis Riel gave himself up to Middleton's troops and on 26 May Poundmaker and a number of other Plains Cree chiefs came in to surrender to the general. This left only Big Bear and his band still at large. A manhunt was now launched, involving the Middleton and Strange columns as well as the NWMP. Strange's Alberta Field Force, having en route comforted the populace of Edmonton, who had not only the Crees to be terrified of but also the Blackfeet, ran into some of Big Bear's warriors on 28 May at a place in northwestern Saskatchewan known to history as Frenchman or Frenchman's Butte. Strange later reported that the enemy had occupied 'an impregnable position', so, after a frontal attack supported by cannon that went nowhere, and a failed flanking manoeuvre, 'Gunner Jingo' ordered a retreat. The Indians withdrew as well, heading north, but Strange did not pursue them. As he often said, he had no intention of 'committing Custer'.[61] On 2 July, alone except for his youngest son, Horse Child, Big Bear surrendered to the four-man Mounted Police garrison at Fort Carlton just to the northwest of Batoche.[62] 'As one of his pursuers remarked rather sourly, Big Bear surrendered to the only four men in the North-West Territories who weren't looking for him'.[63] The North-West Rebellion was over. By the end of July, all of the Canadian militia who had taken part in the campaign had returned home.

Conclusion

It had not been a great war. The Canadian force had suffered 23 dead and 103 wounded. Although no reliable figures exist with respect to the losses of the Métis and those Indians who went to war at the same time, the numbers of their dead and wounded could not have been high. But outcomes in colonial wars such as this one cannot be measured in terms of the butcher's bill alone. The North-West Field Force and its Alberta counterpart suffered precious little in terms of dead and wounded, but few armies have gained so much for so small a sacrifice. The destruction of the Métis republic confirmed for once and all the transfer of power in western Canada from the Hudson's Bay Company to Ottawa. With Riel in prison and Gabriel Dumont in exile in the USA, with its rank and file scattered across the Canadian West and over the border in Montana and North Dakota, the Métis movement was finished. Riel would be convicted of treason in a trial before an English-speaking jury in Regina, Saskatchewan, and hanged on 16 November 1885. His death caused a national uproar at the time and opened a rift between Francophone and English-speaking Canadians that has not closed to this day.

But for all their suffering, the Métis suffered less than their alleged Cree allies. Although they had never in any real sense rallied to the Métis, although their leaders had made a determined effort to curb their young warriors and to remain true to their pledge of loyalty to the Queen, the Crees were subjected to a formidable wave of postwar persecution. Despite clear evidence that they had more than once taken action to save white lives, the two principal Cree chiefs, Big Bear and Poundmaker, were placed on trial for treason and sentenced to prison terms. Wandering Spirit, the war chief of Big Bear's band, meanwhile, went to the gallows for ordering the murder of white settlers, principally in the Frog Lake killings. He was joined on the scaffold by eight warriors from his band who had been sentenced to death for their part in the massacre.

The aftermath of the 1885 rebellion resulted in what has accurately been described as the 'subjugation' of the Plains Crees. Deprived of their freedom, destitute and now totally dependent upon the Canadian government for their survival, the Crees now found themselves with no choice but to follow the white man's road, to put on the white man's clothes, embrace his religion, and transform themselves into homemakers and tillers of the soil. Their children

PART II

were sent to Canadian schools, even in some cases taken away from their parents and placed in foster homes. They were forbidden to dress in the Indian way or to celebrate their ancient ceremonies. The Sun Dance was outlawed and tribal gatherings strictly regulated. In prison, Chief Big Bear, although old and sick, was made to cut off his braids; his fellow chief, Poundmaker, was spared this indignity because Crowfoot, the Blackfoot chief who had done so much to keep the feared warriors of his confederacy out of the prairie war, had intervened on his behalf.[64]

10

INDIAN WARS OF THE PORFIRIATO, 1876–1900

Introduction

The character of Mexico's Indian wars changed abruptly with the rise to power in 1876 of General Porfirio Díaz. For all practical purposes president for life and only driven from office by the Revolution of 1910, Díaz gave Mexico its first effective central government since independence from Spain in 1821. Dominated by technocrats (the so-called *Científicos*) whose first objective for Mexico was rapid capitalist development, the government of Don Porfirio believed that the recalcitrance to central authority of the country's Indian peoples and their refusal to embrace the institution of private property would serve to discourage the flow of foreign investment needed to fuel Mexico's economic 'take-off'. Thus, for the first time, the central government deployed large numbers of federal troops to aid in the suppression of the Yaqui and Mayan revolts and by the early years of the new century had largely succeeded in stamping them out. As we have seen, the Díaz regime also managed to strike an accord with the USA which made possible international cooperation in eliminating the Apache menace from the northern border regions, while keeping Mexican sovereignty largely intact.

The Mexican army which suppressed the Mayas and Yaquis and helped bring the Apaches to heel was better equipped and led than its predecessors had been and, perhaps most important, it proved unswervingly loyal to the central government. President Diaz, an old soldier himself, saw to it that the army got weaponry roughly the equivalent of that in use in the best European armies. And, although he had no formal military training himself, the President mandated a sharp increase in the enrolment at Mexico's federal military academy, the Colegio Militar, with the result that by the beginning of the twentieth century, a majority of the country's field grade officers were graduates of the school.

A final innovation of the Diaz years that would have an impact on the Indian wars was the expansion of the rural constabulary founded by Díaz's predecessor and popularly known as the *Rurales*.[1] This was no Mexican equivalent of the Royal Canadian Mounted Police, but a sort of combination of the Texas

Rangers and Spain's *Guardia Civil*. Heavily armed and furnished with a 'shoot-first-and-ask-questions-later' philosophy of law enforcement, the Rurales had as a mission not only the suppression of banditry and smuggling, but also assisting the army in enforcing the will of the state upon dissident elements among the nation's Indian population.

There has been a tendency of late to downplay the importance and impact of the Rurales. Paul Vanderwood, for example, sees them as a perfect reflection of Porfirian Mexico: 'a nicely polished skin but rotten at the core'. Though they looked formidable on parade, in the splendid uniforms Diaz himself had designed for them, they were in fact thin on the ground and the few of them who did find their way into the field were poor horsemen and even worse shots, Vanderwood contends. A 'sham', in other words.[2] It no doubt is true that the Rurales never achieved much of a presence in Mexico as a whole, but in the border state of Sonora, where, quite naturally, one of their largest contingents was stationed, they were a force to be reckoned with. It was the Rurales who were given the job of tracking down and rounding up dissident Yaquis and shipping them off to the henequen fields of Yucatán. And, as Yaquis would have been quick to agree, they proved to be quite good at their job.[3]

Building and defending a Yaqui republic

In 1875, even before General Díaz assumed power, the Yaquis threw down the gauntlet to the central government, taking 'the boldest step yet in their historical struggle against Mexico: they declared the independence of the Yaqui nation'. A Yaqui republic was eventually proclaimed, under the stewardship of 'the most extraordinary leader in Yaqui history', José María Leyva, better known to history as 'Cajeme'.[4]

Unlike his great predecessor, Juan Banderas, Cajeme spent most of his adult life in the world of the yoris and knew it well. As a boy, he went to California with his father to pan for gold, and was apparently involved in a gun battle between Mexicans and Yankees over the precious metal. Interestingly, his sojourn in California meant that Cajeme learned to speak English before Spanish. It was only upon his return to Sonora that he attended school long enough to learn to read and write in Spanish. His trilingualism would stand Cajeme in good stead during his subsequent military career. This began almost immediately upon leaving school, when he joined the Guaymas militia and took part in a successful defence of the port in 1854 against a force of French filibusters from California led by the colourful adventurer, Count Gaston Raousset-Boulbon.

Subsequently drafted by force into the San Blas Battalion, a unit of the regular army, he deserted at his first opportunity. This does not appear to have hurt Cajeme's prospects as a soldier, however, for not long afterwards, he would surface as a trooper in the army of General Ramón Corona, whose forces took part in the successful campaign to drive the old dictator, Antonio López de

Santa Anna, from power and into exile in 1854. Because of his language skills, Cajeme was made aide-de-camp to General Corona, who would go on to serve as a division commander in the War of Reform and in the Liberal opposition to the French-imposed Empire of Prince Maximilian.[5] Thus began a most unusual preparation for eventual leadership of the Yaqui people in their struggle for independence.

Unlike the great majority of his fellow Yaquis, Cajeme would enlist in the Liberal cause in the War of Reform and, even more remarkably, go on to spend over a decade in the employ of Ignacio Pesquiera, the Yaquis' great enemy, rising to the rank of captain in the caudillo's cavalry. It is even alleged that Cajeme was present at the infamous massacre of Yaqui prisoners by Pesquiera's troops in Bacúm in 1868.[6] For his role in the crushing of an uprising against the Pesquiera clan in Guaymas in 1873 Cajeme was made the *alcade mayor* or governor of the Yaqui pueblos. His long years of service had convinced Don Ignacio that he could be counted upon to implement the Pesquieras' scheme for colonisation of the Yaqui valley and to rally the Yaquis to their side in the looming power struggle in Sonora with the Torres family, supporters of the new Mexican strongman, Porfirio Díaz.[7]

The Yaquis first showed their hand at the end of 1875, as the Pesquieras faced a challenge from a local rival, José Serna. Their revolt against the government so incensed José J. Pesquiera, who had been chosen by his father Ignacio to succeed him as governor, that he ignored his yori opponents for the moment and made crushing the Yaquis his first priority. He led a force from Guaymas into the Yaqui country in November 1875 consisting of three battalions of infantry, a battery of artillery and a squadron of cavalry. This invasion led to a battle near the Yaqui pueblo of Torím between a detachment of the Sonora troops and 1500 Yaquis under the command of Cajeme. The day was saved for the Sonorans by their artillery, as the Yaquis charged the guns in a bid for victory, only to be driven off with 60 dead and numerous wounded. However the governor, Pesquiera, proved unable to bring the Yaquis to bay again and was forced to abandon his campaign in Indian territory, as the troops of his rival Serna were beginning to mobilise. Because Pesquiera withdrew, the outcome of the episode was touted as a Yaqui victory, which gave Cajeme the opening he had apparently been seeking to distance himself from his yori benefactors. From this point on, he gradually assumed leadership of the traditional Yaqui autonomist movement and transformed it into a movement for fully fledged independence. It remains unclear to this day why the one-time protégé of the Pesquieras chose to alter his course so radically. Ramón Corral, in his biographical sketch of the Yaqui leader, suggested that once back in his homeland for good, he had been 'conquered by the Yaquis' imperishable tendency to maintain themselves independent'. This view was echoed by the Mexican historian Claudio Dabdoub, who has Cajeme 'succumbing' to the Yaquis' longstanding desire for freedom.[8]

Having gained some breathing space, Cajeme now moved to take over the traditional post of captain-general and restructure the Yaqui political system, investing his supporters as *gobernadores* or governors of the Eight Towns. Under them came the 'captains of war', who saw to it that each pueblo had a certain number of men under arms who could be mobilised quickly if needed. Cajeme also promoted the cultural and spiritual welfare of the people by reviving the post of *temastian* or sacristan. These people replaced the regular priests, who had fled the Yaqui country when fighting broke out and, despite later efforts by local and national authorities on their behalf, never really managed to reestablish themselves. Finally, although Cajeme was for the most part recognised as the supreme war leader of the Yaquis, he was astute enough to recognise that this power did not necessarily translate into *political* authority. Thus he moved to make the popular councils in the various pueblos, in which every Yaqui adult had a voice, the chief decision-making bodies.[9]

Although independence was the watchword of the new order in Yaqui territory, Cajeme didn't entirely close off the republic to outsiders. He allowed trade to continue, with salt mined by Yaquis along the coast a major commodity. He set up a tax system to siphon off revenue from trade, the first in Yaqui history.[10] To promote Yaqui self-sufficiency, Cajeme revived an idea from mission days: community plots. 'Each pueblo in the Yaqui [valley] had to plant a field of a certain size and maintain a rotation of workers to cultivate [it]. Some of the harvest might have been traded, but most of it was stored.'[11]

Despite what appears to have been a considerable political acumen, Cajeme was at bottom a soldier and it was as a soldier that he made his greatest contribution to the nascent Yaqui republic. Before he came upon the scene, the Yaquis had basically employed a raiding strategy in their wars with the yoris, as described in Chapter 4. Cajeme taught the Yaquis new ways to wage war, ways he had imbibed in his long years of service in the armies of the enemy. The raids on the yori population would continue, but on a reduced scale, since the main preoccupation of the Yaquis under Cajeme would be defence of the republic. To this end, regular cavalry and infantry units were formed and provided with as many modern weapons as could be obtained. Ship captains on the Yaqui River were ordered to deliver a set amount of guns and ammunition into Yaqui hands or give up trading; travellers in the area were also obliged to surrender their guns to the Yaqui cause, as were deserters from the state and federal armies who hid out in Yaqui territory. The revival under Cajeme convinced people in the Yaqui diaspora to return, and they were a further source of weapons for the cause.[12] Efforts were made to obtain artillery as well, but met with little success.[13]

Cajeme's most important innovation, however, was the building of a system of fortifications to defend the Yaqui republic against invaders, who would now include regulars of the Mexican army. The result was one of the largest and most complex networks of forts constructed by an indigenous resistance movement in the nineteenth century, on a par with the famous *pa* of the Maoris in New Zealand or the less well-known but equally formidable strongholds of the Barue kingdom in the Zambezi highlands of Mozambique.[14] But, as we will see, Cajeme's decision to abandon the traditional Yaqui war of movement for a strategy of static defence would prove as disastrous for his people as the decision to shut themselves behind barricades at Horseshoe Bend had been for the Creeks in 1814.

Nonetheless, the new round of warfare with the yoris started off in promising fashion for Cajeme and his 'new model' army. With the Pesquieras out of the picture, the victorious Torres clan appealed for federal help against the Yaquis. Mexico City was not overly enthusiastic but finally agreed to send troops if the Sonora governor, the Torres stand-in Carlos Ortiz, would agree to launch a programme of military colonisation in the Yaqui lands. An attempt to start up such a programme was repulsed in 1881 at the battle of Capetamaya, in which Cajeme with his whole army surprised a small Sonoran force (150 infantry, 130 cavalry) led by the Governor's brother, Colonel Augustín Ortiz. Although it was the Yaquis who quit the field at the end of the day, the battle was regarded as a tactical victory for Cajeme and his troops, as Ortiz's force was obliged to withdraw from Yaqui territory.[15]

Ortiz's poor showing at Capetamaya appears to have convinced the federal government that the Sonora state militia was incapable of defeating the Yaquis, or the Apaches for that matter, and prompted the sending of a large federal army into the state for the first time since independence. The Mexican army which now began operating in Sonora – some 1,200 strong and under the command of no less than five generals – would be instrumental in the defeat of both the Yaquis and, later, the Apaches.[16]

The campaign did not go well at the outset for the combined federal and Sonora National Guard force, however. Cajeme's system of fortifications seemed insuperable. A siege of the major fort at El Añil at the end of June 1885 failed ignominiously. Cornelius C. Smith, Jr., has provided a graphic portrait of the formidable structure in his biography of the Rurales chief Emilio Kosterlitzky, who fought at El Añil as an officer in the Sonora National Guard.

> In essence, Añil was a fortress, a great pit dug into the side of a mountain and surrounded by a strong palisade of great trees, whose butt ends were buried deep in the earth. Apertures and firing ports enabled its defenders to pour [a] withering fire onto attackers approaching from any quarter. Outside, the forest was so thick that maneuver in force upon the fortress was impossible. . . . Inside the fortress and well-stocked with food, water, and ammunition, the Yaquis might hold out indefinitely.

The combination of the great fortress and its heavily forested surroundings proved too much for the invading army. On the approach march, some of its flankers got lost in the dense woods and never took part in the fighting. The forest also proved too thick for Captain Kosterlitzky and his National Guard cavalrymen, who ended up fighting on foot. The Mexican commander, General Fausto Topete, somehow managed to bring up artillery – two old-style mountain guns and two new quick-firing pieces – and to place it at point-blank range, some 140 feet from the El Añil bastion. But to no avail. '[T]he balls did little damage to the huge logs' of the fortress. Topete and his men were obliged to withdraw, and the defensive strategy of Cajeme seemed to have been vindicated.[17]

A little less than a year later, however, the federal and state forces were back outside El Añil, under a new commander and possessed of a new battle plan. The new man in charge was one of the federal army's more effective – and ruthless – commanders, General Angel Martínez.[18] In the months since the failed first siege, Mexican forces had received detailed information about the strongpoints of the Añil fort from a Yaqui boy whose mother had deserted to the enemy. A 30-foot-wide road was cut through the forest in order to bring up troops and artillery and a field of fire was cleared before the walls of the fortress. General Martínez ordered seizure of high ground around the fort, which required desperate fighting in some cases, in order to place his artillery in elevated positions above it.

The subsequent artillery barrage caused 'terrible damage' to the 4,000 or so Yaquis, warriors and non-combatants, crowded into the fort, but when the federal army and Sonora National Guard troops stormed its walls, the defenders

> resisted the attack of our column with true courage, never vacillating for a moment. When it became necessary to retire, they did it without flight, but step by step, with heroic calmness, stopping from time to time to fire at us. . . .[19]

Most of the Yaqui warriors managed to escape, along with Cajeme, but they left behind some 1,000 non-combatants, many of whom were 'little more than skin and bones', evidence that food and water had run out long before the bombardment had begun. Others were dying from smallpox.[20] It was a great defeat for the Yaquis but worse was still to come.

Cracks now started to appear in popular support for the Yaqui republic. The unity of the Yaqui population behind Cajeme began to weaken as his 'regime came under constant Mexican attack. After each military setback, less resolved Yaquis could be seen leaving' the river valley. But Cajeme's position was also undermined by an increase in factionalism, promoted by 'deliberate Mexican attempts to foment dissension'. Some of this dissent, however, seems to have been smouldering under the surface since the Yaqui republic's early days. While most Yaquis were willing to accept Cajeme's military and, within limits, political authority, opposition arose when he tried to assume judicial powers, 'making decisions in regard to land use and interfamily disputes'. This had led to an attempt on his life in 1885, apparently with the connivance of the Mexican authorities.[21] What these developments seem to indicate is that, as the case of

Juan Banderas had already demonstrated, even the most charismatic leaders were unable to override the democratic instincts of the Yaqui people, who, even in times of great crisis, refused to grant powers to them that would abridge the traditional liberties of the 'Eight Pueblos'.

The final blow to Cajeme's scheme of static defence was the taking of the huge fortress of Buatachive in the Bacatete Mountains to the north of the Yaqui river valley. 'Enclosed by natural protective barriers, Buatachive was thought to be impregnable. Cajeme ordered his men, their families, and all available food and cattle behind its walls'. The Mexican commander, General Martínez, saw matters differently. He believed that Cajeme had 'entrapped himself with all his people and resources' in the mountain fortress, and ordered the entire federal and state invasion force to concentrate around Buatachive. The siege began on 8 May 1886 and four days later, 'the soldiers attacked from all sides. Although the Yaquis defended themselves with their usual valor, there was really no contest'. While Cajeme and most of his fighters, minus some 200 dead, escaped into the mountains, taking their weapons with them, almost all their women and children were left behind. Martínez's men found some 2,000 Yaquis, mostly non-combatants, inside the fort, many stricken from yellow fever, 'the result of unsanitary and crowded conditions, insufficient food, and lack of fresh water'.[22]

Although many Yaquis now surrendered to General Martínez, Cajeme remained at large with a band of some 800–1,000 men, who reverted to the old raiding strategy. Frustrated by the ensuing guerrilla warfare, Martínez 'sent his men like hunters into the forests and the sierra, killing any moving person on sight, confiscating all cattle and [foodstuffs]'. While this campaign produced still more Yaqui prisoners, Cajeme was not among them, so 'the persecution intensified, with troops relentlessly chasing after the rebels in their circular flight from the [Yaqui] river to the sierra, from the sierra to the [Guaymas] valley and from the valley back to the river. . .'.[23]

Betrayed by one of his own people, Cajeme was finally taken prisoner near Guaymas on 12 April 1887 by a squad of soldiers under the personal command of General Martínez. In a remarkable gesture of respect for the fallen leader, the general put him up in his own quarters, where he was allowed to receive visitors. These included the veteran Sonora politician and future vice-president of Mexico, Ramón Corral, whose long interview with Cajeme in General Martínez's quarters remains our main source of biographical information about the Yaqui leader. But, while Cajeme was fielding Corral's questions, he was being secretly tried by court martial and sentenced to death. On 21 April, he was taken by ship to the Yaqui River. When a guard told him he was going home, Cajeme is reported to have said, 'Do not waste your jokes on a man who is about to die'.[24] He was taken to a place called Tres Cruces, on the north boundary of the Yaqui lands, where at 11.05 in the morning of 23 April 1887, he was shot by firing squad. His body was returned by muleback to the nearby Yaqui town of Cocorít for burial. The corpse bore seven bullet wounds and a sabre slash across the face, according to a reporter from the *Tucson Daily Citizen*, who was present. 'On the site of the execution Cajeme's bloody hat was nailed to a tree', along with a paper on which was written, '"Con cinco balas, pago sus males" (With five bullets, he paid for the evil he did)'.[25]

Guerrilla warfare

From the execution of Cajeme down to the revolution that ousted the Díaz regime in 1910, the state of Sonora was the theatre of one of the longest-running and most bitterly contested guerrilla wars in history. Except for a two-year hiatus in 1897–9, the so-called Peace of Ortiz, the insurgents and the Mexican regulars and National Guardsmen who hunted them remained in the field for 23 years. And in terms of the strategy and tactics employed by both sides, it was a war of striking modernity.

The Yaqui rebels, led until his death in battle in 1900 by Juan Maldonado, better known under his tribal name of Tetabiete, practised a kind of guerrilla war that would become increasingly familiar in the twentieth century. Operating out of the rugged Bacatete Mountains, they waged a continuous war of raids and sabotage against the Torres clique who managed Sonora politics on behalf of the Díaz regime in Mexico City. Swooping down from their rancherías in the most isolated parts of the Bacatete, the guerrillas interdicted government patrols and raided haciendas in the lowlands, then either fled quickly back into the mountains or disappeared into the mass of Yaqui labourers employed on the land or down the mines of the region. These workers and their families were, in fact, the key element in the Yaqui guerrilla strategy, the 'sea' in which the insurgent 'fish' were able to swim, to use the later, well-known phrase of Mao Zedong. In addition to providing them with places to hide, the Yaqui mass also supplied the guerrillas with food, money, and guns and ammunition. Interestingly, this surreptitious activity often was carried on with the knowledge of the employers of the Yaqui collaborators. Desperate for the diligent – and relatively cheap – labour provided by Yaqui workers, these employers, especially farmers and ranchers, either looked the other way or, in some cases, even helped their workers hide guerrillas, to the consternation of the Sonora authorities.

The Yaqui insurgents and their collaborators also made use of another familiar weapon in the modern guerrilla arsenal, the cross-border 'sanctuary'. The border between Sonora and Arizona Territory in the USA was porous and Yaquis on the run had little difficulty crossing it to safety. They would find refuge among the growing communities of Yaquis around towns such as Tucson, comprised of workers who had either fled repression in Sonora or been lured across the border by the higher wages paid by American employers. Arizona also proved to be a major source of arms for the rebels. When troops in Sonora did manage to run down Yaqui guerrillas, they often found them carrying Springfield or Winchester rifles 'Made in the USA'. Efforts by the Mexican authorities to secure American cooperation in stifling the cross-border arms trade or repatriating guerrilla refugees were never very successful. As in Sonora, Yaqui workers were prized by Arizona employers for their hard work and modest wage demands.

Over the course of the 1890s, the Mexican army gradually took charge of the anti-guerrilla campaign and developed a multi-faceted strategy for coping with the elusive rebels, the so-called *broncos* (wild ones).[26] It would incorporate a number of counter-insurgency measures that have become standard in combating guerrillas in the twentieth century. Some of these were administrative in nature and involved the police rather than the military.

All Yaquis had to register with local authorities, who issued them with identification papers they would be required to produce upon demand. Employers now had to submit rolls containing the names of their Yaqui employees for regular checks by the police and were required to notify authorities of the their comings and goings. Outlets for firearms were more tightly regulated to assure that weapons were not sold to Yaquis. A closer watch was maintained on the Arizona frontier in order to thwart border crossings by refugees and to stop the importation of arms.

Meanwhile, the Mexican army took measures to, first of all, confine the guerrillas to their Bacatete lair and then move in and wipe them out. The mountain region was meticulously mapped, to identify the exits used by the guerrillas in their descents to the valley below and to locate the wells and waterholes available to them on their travels. Troops were designated to watch these areas, while others combed the mountains looking for rebel rancherías. In the course of these operations, it became obvious that cavalry could not negotiate the rough terrain and would have to be replaced with infantry. It also became clear that Mexican troops would never be able to flush out the broncos without help from Indian scouts. The Pima and Opata peoples to the north provided some of these, but the most effective force in this regard was a unit of Yaqui irregulars under the command of one Loreto Villa, a former lieutenant of the guerrilla chief Tetabiate. As had been the case with George Crook's famous Apache scouts, the presence of Yaqui scouts in the Mexican army not only heightened the chances of finding the elusive guerrillas, but also produced a negative psychological effect upon them.

But the Mexicans did not simply limit their counter-insurgency strategy to police work and military operations. There was a 'hearts-and-minds' component as well. The Yaquis who remained in the river valley were offered multiple inducements to accept the extension of state authority over them and the division of their lands into individual plots. Seed and farm implements were distributed gratis by the government, canals were dug to promote irrigation and construction was begun on a railway to facilitate trade in agricultural produce. The Mexican government also showed concern for the souls of their Yaqui charges. The North American Josephite order of priests was brought in to introduce a more 'civilised' brand of Catholic worship.[27]

In spite of this array of measures, the guerrillas were never entirely subdued.

Despite its careful mapping and patrolling on a year-round basis, even in the ferocious heat of summertime, the army was never able to shut off all of the exits from the Bacatete and so the guerrilla raids continued. Then, in January 1900, Loreto Villa's Yaqui scouts discovered that, for some reason, the broncos had taken the fatal step of shutting themselves up on a fortified plateau in the mountains called Mazocoba. On 18 January, troops led by General Lorenzo Torres attacked from three directions. In a battle that raged from the morning until sunset, often waged hand-to-hand, the Yaquis were finally beaten. Some 3,000 rebels, including women and children, had taken refuge in the supposedly impregnable fortress; at day's end, 400 Yaqui fighters were dead and 1,000 prisoners were led off to captivity. But, even so, the government's victory was incomplete. Some of the guerrillas had escaped the slaughter, including, most prominently, their leader, Tetabiate, and so the struggle would continue. Even the death of the bronco leader, ambushed by Villa's scouts in July 1901, did not bring a halt to the rebel attacks. In August 1901 the Mexican army decided to bring its increasingly expensive counterinsurgency operations to a close.[28] The government in Mexico City had decided upon a new course to bring the revolt to an end, a strategy Evelyn Hu-DeHart has called the 'final solution'.[29]

Deportation

Solving the Yaqui 'problem' through extermination or en masse deportation had been considered periodically from the 1860s on, but humanitarian concerns and, especially, the opposition of Sonora employers had always forced the authorities to seek other alternatives. Now, in 1902, the state government of Sonora, supported by the Díaz regime in Mexico City, began implementing a programme of deportation that, by its cessation in 1910, would see several thousand Yaqui men, women and children shipped as virtual slave labourers to the cane fields of Oaxaca or, most often, to the henequen plantations of Yucatán.[30] Meanwhile, thousands of others would flee into exile in other parts of Mexico or across the border to the USA.[31]

Edward Spicer has provided an account of how the deportation programme worked.

> Yaquis, along with Mayos, Opatas, and Pimas were regularly rounded up on the haciendas, placed temporarily in jails in Hermosillo and Guaymas and then shipped by boat to San Blas in Nayarit. From there they were herded on foot across Mexico, either to be dropped off in northern Oaxaca or pushed on to Vera Cruz for final shipment to Yucatán.[32]

By 1910, two-thirds of the 15,000 or so Yaquis in Sonora at the turn of the century were scattered over an area of some 3,500 miles, from Los Angeles, California, to Yucatán. 'They had become the most widely scattered native people of North America. . . . Not even the Cherokees, whose deportation in 1835 from Georgia to Oklahoma had inititated a scattering over the United States, were so widely dispersed'.[33]

'Yaquis regarded deportation as the harshest punishment they ever had to suffer in their long history of rebellion', wrote Hu-DeHart. Many died en route to the cane and henequen fields. Some killed themselves in jail before departure; others jumped into the sea from the steamers taking them to Yucatán. And, many of those who did make it to their destination did not survive. 'Direct and often brutal punishment, chiefly whipping, was relied upon to break men's spirit and reduce them to acceptance of the rigid work regime and the very low standard of living'.[34]

Even worse in the long term than the terrible suffering of the Yaquis in deportation was the 'atomisation' of Yaqui society that deportation produced. 'The type of Yaqui community which had been the wellspring and focus of Yaqui life during the 19th century no longer existed.' So devastating was deportation, argued Edward Spicer, that had it continued for another 25 to 30 years, 'there would have been total disintegration of Yaquis as a people'.[35]

In January 1909, the majority of the rebels still hiding out in the Bacatete Mountains surrendered to the authorities, who promised to allow some to occupy vacant land in the Yaqui river valley and to find work for the rest elsewhere in Sonora. In return, the head of the broncos who had surrendered, Luis Buli, agreed to help the army bring in the handful of rebels who remained at large under the leadership of Luis Espinosa. But neither the carrot of promises of state assistance nor the stick of punitive patrols made much of an impression on the fugitives, who were still raiding the lowlands of Sonora when the Revolution of 1910 broke out.[36]

Buli's surrender, then, did not bring the guerrilla war to an end, nor did it halt deportations. What saved the Yaqui people was the outbreak of revolution against the Díaz regime in 1910. It put a stop to deportation, as the Torres clique was driven from power in Sonora, to be replaced by representatives of the hacendados who had opposed the policy in the first place.[37] And the revolution set free the slave labourers in the cane and henequen fields, enabling those Yaquis fortunate enough to survive to make their way back to Sonora, some as soldiers in the revolutionary armies.[38]

The end of the Caste Wars in Yucatán

In 1886, when it became clear that the renewed insurrection by the Mayas could not be contained by state forces, the Yucatán government turned to Mexico City for help. It found out, however, that the government of Porfirio Díaz was in no hurry to come to its aid. It still had the Yaquis to contend with and, aside from the few politicians who fretted about foreign schemes to take over Yucatán, no one in Mexico City felt pressed to come to the aid of a state with such a reputation for going its own way. Only when foreign and national forest-extraction companies, previously based in Veracruz and Tabasco and driven by the chewing gum craze in the United States, expressed an interest in exploiting the rich stands of [chicle], cedar and mahogany in the forest did the [Díaz] government take steps to deal with the rebel Maya.[39]

Federal troops entered the fray with a considerable technological edge. There had been a time, back in the 1850s, when the ladino and Indian armies had operated at virtual parity as far as weaponry was concerned. True, the Yucatecans had had artillery and a cavalry force and the masewalob had not, but the jungle terrain in which most of the fighting occurred had nullified this advantage. In the crucial category of shoulder weapons, there had been little difference between the two armies. Both carried the longtime standard British infantry musket, the Brown Bess, purchased from the large stocks put on sale when the Napoleonic Wars ended and, later, as the British army shifted over to a new breechloading rifle. Arms parity had come to an end in Yucatan in the 1870s, as it did for indigenous resistance forces all across the non-European world. What now happened to the Mayan bravos would happen as well to the Muslim warriors who resisted French imperialism in West Africa during these years, and to Mahdist armies who fought the British in the Sudan. In Yucatán,

> when breechloading arms with their specialized ammunition came into wide use, the rebels fell behind. Dependence on such sophisticated arms was impractical for them, and they stopped with the muzzle-loading single-shot rifled weapon [whose] ball-and-powder technology was more appropriate to their condition.[40]

By the 1890s the gap in military technology between the two sides had become a yawning divide. The Mexican army now came into the field against the Mayan bravos equipped with the latest weaponry: Mauser magazine rifles, Maxim guns, Le Creusot cannon. They were also under the command of one of President Díaz's most celebrated generals, General Ignacio Bravo, who had just come from fighting the Yaquis. In a letter to President Díaz, the general explained the philosophy that would guide his campaign. The Mayas, he said, 'are a race that for humanity's sake must be extinguished, because they will never amount to anything good. . . . I am convinced that the only way to guarantee the interests of the Zone (southeastern Yucatán) is to finish off the race, if that would be possible'.[41]

However, the general's exterminationist philosophy and the firepower of his regulars proved less crucial to the outcome of the struggle than might have been thought, since Yucatecan national guardsmen, still carrying single-shot Remington breechloaders of 1870s vintage, ended up doing much of the fighting. Over 2,000 of them lost their lives in the campaign, many from disease and privation. Besides, the enemy they were fighting were no longer at the top of their form. A visiting German geographer, Karl Sapper, reported that by the 1890s the ranks of the bravos had been thinned considerably by 'rum, pestilence, and war'. Smallpox and whooping-cough epidemics in 1892 may have cut masewalob numbers in half.[42]

Federal troops spent most of their time guarding the road and railway building projects launched by the Díaz government to tap the wealth of southeastern Yucatán.[43] General Bravo, more an engineer than a fighting general, waged war through building. Slowly and methodically, he drove a railway across the southeast, protected by armoured trains, four battalions of infantry and breechloading cannon, and directed at the rebel shrine of Chan Santa Cruz. And, in keeping with the economic spirit that animated federal involvement in the Yucatán campaign, the general's railway had the added virtue that it opened up the southeastern region to exploitation. The remaining cruzob sought to fight back in the old way, but their drystone barricades were blown apart by cannon fire and their attacks choked off by fire from magazine rifles. Still, it was not the enemy's firepower that so disheartened the cruzob, but rather the 'slow, deliberate movement, the cleared road pointing at the shrine city, straight and wide through forest untouched for forty years'.[44] The fate of the Mayan rebels was sealed by the arrival of General Bravo's 'navy', four armed vessels loaded with infantry, at the mouth of the Rio Hondo, on the border with British Honduras, and the subsequent seizure of Bacalar, the border town that had so long served as a conduit for arms shipments to the rebels. The occupation gave needed teeth to an international pact signed between Mexico and Britain back in 1893, depriving the Mayas of arms from British Honduras.[45]

The symbolic conclusion of the Caste War came on 5 May 1901, the festival of 'Cinco Mayo', when General Bravo entered Chan Santa Cruz at the head of his troops. The general now modestly had the city rechristened Santa Cruz de Bravo and made it the capital of the new federal district of Quintana Roo, carved out of the southeastern rainforests by order of President Díaz, to the great fury of the Yucatán government. General Bravo became the first governor of Quintana Roo and remained at his post, filling his pockets with the proceeds from various commercial concessions, until removed by the Revolution of 1910. The revolution sent the octogenarian general off into ignominious exile and returned his capital to the Mayas, who made it once again Chan Santa Cruz. 'Stunned by this sudden and fantastic turnabout', says Nelson Reed, the Mayas 'ventured uneasily into the Dzul [white man's] town that had once been their shrine, and fell on their knees to give thanks for this final victory of the Speaking Cross'.[46]

But Chan Santa Cruz could never be redeemed, so defiled had it been by the long presence of the conqueror within its walls. And so the returning Mayas

> stared for a time at [the white man's] transformations, then set to work with the purifying torch, ax, and dynamite. The locomotives, coaches, and platform were burned, the railroad tracks torn up in several places

and thrown into the jungle, telegraph lines cut; the new market, the pump, and the reservoir were dynamited, and the former school buildings flanking the temple, which had been used as barracks, were burned. . . . [Then] the Cruzob returned to their villages.[47]

The Speaking Cross never returned to Chan Santa Cruz and, in time, the town lost the name that had been restored to it. Today it bears the entirely secular name of Felipe Carillo Puerto. But, although the southeastern region and its spiritual centre had fallen under the sway of the Mexican government in 1901, an inhospitable portion deep in the jungle stayed in rebel hands until the 1930s when the last of the bravos gave up their arms to President Lázaro Cárdenas, whose willingness to countenance a tribal identity for Indian peoples would also bring an end to the long Yaqui struggle against the Mexican state.

CONCLUSION: LONG SHADOWS

The Indians

Canada

The legacy of Canada's nineteenth-century wars against the Métis and, to a lesser extent, the Plains Crees, has been twofold. The execution of the Métis leader Louis Riel and the scattering of his people in the wake of the 1885 war caused reverberations of discontent among French-speaking Canadians which have still not died out. The harsh treatment of Canada's Western Indian population, not just the few Crees who rose up in 1885 but those tribes, like the Blackfeet, who remained neutral, has also left a bitter residue in Canadian public life. The government's post-1885 policy foresaw the rapid transformation of the former plains nomads into farmers by the introduction of 'the Bible and the plough' onto the reserves. 'Savage' practices such as the Sun Dance, potlatch, and wearing feather headdresses were made illegal.[1]

It was hoped that this rigid pursuit of assimilation might be relaxed after the First World War, when 35 per cent of eligible Canadian Indians volunteered for military service, but this proved illusory. A similar level of Indian participation in the Second World War again raised expectations of a change in government Indian policy. A government white paper on the subject in 1969, however, recommended intensive measures aiming at assimilation as a solution to what it recognised as an enormous disparity in the living standards of Indian and white Canadians. Indian mobilisation in recent years to convince Ottawa to change course, including embarrassing petitions to the United Nations Human Rights Commission, seems to have brought at least some policy makers around to the notion that assimilation has not worked and will not work. There is now much talk of a white–Indian political 'partnership' to find a better way, but so far concrete results have not been forthcoming.[2]

Mexico

The Yaquis who survived the henequen fields of Yucatán returned to a homeland largely in the hands of others and much changed by the 'development' programme launched during the Díaz years. Foreign capital, mostly American, had been secured to fund the large-scale irrigation projects and rail and road links necessary to support intensive cash-crop farming over a wide area. The eight 'sacred pueblos' were now home to more Mexican newcomers than to Yaquis. In these circumstances, it is understandable that the Yaqui diaspora would continue to grow, not only in other parts of northern Mexico, but in the USA as well. Yaqui discontent over the situation in the tribal homeland led to a revival of armed resistance in the 1920s.[3]

In 1937 Mexico's reformist president, Lázaro Cárdenas, a former general who had actually fought the Yaquis in the 1920s, emerged as their benefactor. He issued a decree to establish a *Zona Indígena*, a sort of reservation, for the Yaquis on one half of their ancestral homeland. It was the only Indian reservation ever authorised in Mexico. In the Zona, the Yaquis would be able to reconstitute their 'sacred pueblos' and exercise a degree of self-government. Collective agriculture once again became a going concern, under the *ejido* system brought into being as a result of the 1910 Revolution.[4]

The new Yaqui homeland made possible by the Cárdenas reforms has not been the great success many Yaquis thought it would be. Until the 1950s all seemed to be going well. What has undone the Yaquis' attempt to recapture their past is the economic revolution which has come to Sonora, and especially to the rich farmlands of the Yaqui Valley, in recent decades. The building of dams on the Yaqui River and the so-called 'Green Revolution' of the 1950s have given a tremendous boost to agricultural production without adding to the agricultural labour force. 'For the first time in their history Yaquis were not in demand and valued as a source of good, cheap labour; thus, they became socially dispensable'. The inability to earn wages as farm labourers seems to have definitively put paid to the ancient trade-off, going back to the Jesuits in the eighteenth century, whereby providing cheap and diligent labour for the yoris won the Yaquis the right to exercise a meaningful degree of political autonomy and to practise a system of collective subsistence agriculture. It was this trade-off which more than anything else enabled the Yaquis to survive as a people through over a century of repression. Now, there is a widespread fear that what neither the Sonora caudillos nor the Mexican state could achieve by armed force or even a campaign of extermination will be accomplished by market economics: 'the erosion of Yaqui identity and community, of ethnic cohesion and the extraordinary historical ability to unite and mobilize for self-preservation when seriously challenged by an outside force'.[5]

Yucatán

The Caste War was the bloodiest Indian war in the modern history of the New World and one of the bloodiest of the many wars waged against indigenous peoples in the long era of Western expansion. When it was over, Yucatán's total population had declined by one-third from its prewar level of just over 500,000.[6] Some of the loss can be attributed to emigration: ladinos tired of the endless fighting left for Mexico, Cuba or the USA; Mayas sought exile in communities of their people abroad, in the state of Chiapas in Mexico, in Guatemala and British Honduras. But many of the departed had set off on a longer journey. Untold thousands had died on both sides, many in the long years of warfare, but more perhaps from those deadly companions to war, disease and starvation.

For the Mayan population, rebel or otherwise, there were concrete gains from the upheaval, in spite of the heavy loss of life. There was a degree of political and territorial autonomy for those Mayas who had refused to submit to ladino rule, as the state of Quintana Roo was partitioned from Yucatán and set aside for them. Although there had been de facto recognition of the area as an autonomous Mayan enclave after the 1910 Revolution, the status was confirmed in the 1930s by President Cárdenas, a benefactor for the Mayas as he had been for the Yaquis. In addition, taxes on the Mayan population, one of the major causes of the Caste War, were reduced, while the most blatant forms of racial discrimination disappeared from the law code. The communal landholding patterns that the creole liberals had found so retrograde in the nineteenth century were reaffirmed in the new *ejido* system of collective agriculture introduced as a result of the Revolution of 1910. The Caste War had brought into being a new religious order, the Cult of the Speaking Cross, served by an indigenous priesthood and providing the structure for an organ of self-defence, the *Guardia*.[7] That cult not only survived the repression brought down upon it during and after the Caste War but continues to be followed in those areas that constituted the heartland of the revolt of 1847.[8]

What remains to be seen is how the legacy of the Caste War and the Mayan separatism it promoted will fare in the face of the unprecedented opening up of Yucatán to the wider world in recent years. Rail and road links now tie Yucatán to the rest of Mexico. Tourism, both to enjoy the sea and sand of Cancún and other resorts and to visit ancient Mayan historical sites such as Chichen Itza, has already fostered an unprecedented economic boom in the peninsula, even greater than the henequen boom of the late nineteenth century or the chicle boom of the early twentieth. Mayas are leaving their villages to find work in the cities and resort areas; tourists are coming in busloads to the Mayan ruins deep in the hinterland, many of them close to those remote places in the southeast where the Cult of the Speaking Cross is still practised. There are even signs that a campaign may be underway to make the centres of cult worship and the sites associated with the Caste War tourist destinations. If and when that happens, the Cruzob will find themselves confronting a challenge to their traditional way of life and their unique form of religious practice even more formidable than that faced by their ancestors in the dimly remembered Caste War of 1847–1901.[9]

United States

American Indian population numbers fell like a stone in the years after the cessation of the Indian wars. This despite an ambitious programme of assimilation, including the opening of a number of boarding schools to 'civilise' Indians and teach them trades;[10] the Dawes Severalty Act of 1887, which divided up reservation lands into individual plots; and efforts to introduce on the reservations what were deemed 'responsible'– i.e. representative democratic as opposed to direct democratic – forms of government.[11]

In spite of these programmes and the culture shock sustained by Indians in the USA since their confinement on reservations, some older traditions have persisted. For example, 'Plains Indians . . . continue to hold the warrior in great esteem; as in the old days, a young male can find special recognition . . . among his people through wartime military service'.[12] Indians have served in numbers out of all proportion to their share of the population in the United States' many twentieth-century wars.[13] Despite being the most unpopular US war since the Second Seminole War of 1835–42, the Vietnam War of 1965–75 attracted a large number of Indian volunteers. Of the Indians who served there, only some 20 per cent were conscripted. Indian soldiers in Vietnam also saw a lot of combat: 84 per cent of them served in combat units, and 31 per cent were killed or wounded.[14]

The European Americans

Canada

The only recent confrontation between soldiers and Indians in Canada took place, not on the prairies of the West, but in the forests of Quebec Province, where in July 1990 Mohawk tribesmen barricaded roads in an attempt to reclaim land allegedly stolen from them by way of an early nineteenth-century treaty. Local French Canadian troops employed 'overwhelming force' to subdue the Indians and the incident was brought to a close without bloodshed. There was much praise for the army's handling of the situation. 'It had been rare in the twentieth century that soldiers were popular heroes in French Canada, and the pleasure, however short-lived, was savoured'.[15]

Mexico

In 1994, fighting broke out between Mexican soldiers and Indians in Chiapas, Mexico's southernmost state. The struggle that ensued, between government troops and militants of the Zapatista National Liberation Army (EZLN), had obvious overtones not only of the Mexican Revolution of 1910 but also of Mexico's nineteenth-century Indian wars. The movement led by the EZLN was comprised largely of Mayas, and its demands, for regional autonomy and freedom from the encroachment on communal lands by agribusiness, were reminiscent of those made to Mexican authorities in the 1800s by the Mayas of neighbouring Yucatán and the Yaquis of Sonora. The tactics of the government forces also would have been familiar to students of those earlier struggles. Villages were looted and burned, crops destroyed, hostages taken. The fighting came to an end in 2000, with the victory in national elections of the opposition PAN party. The new Mexican president, Vicente Fox, withdrew the troops and opened a dialogue with the Chiapas dissidents. An uneasy peace prevails in the region at the time of writing.[16]

United States

The Indian-fighting army that had served the United States since the early days of the new American republic did not fade away with the end of the Indian wars. The US military historian Russell Weigley found it still lingering on as late as the eve of the Second World War, most quixotically in the resistance of General George Patton to the disbandment of the Army's horse cavalry in 1940. Nothing that had happened in the interim, Weigley would argue – not the Spanish–American War, the Philippine Insurrection, the Root reforms or the First World War – had changed the basic profile of the army. The reason for this was that the army never found a 'mission' to replace the constabulary function it had performed from the end of the American Revolution until 1890. The Spanish–American War and the Philippine Insurrection 'brought campaigning not unlike the army's historic campaigning against the North American Indians'. The reforms spearheaded by the war secretary Elihu Root, aimed at creating a European-style professional army to complement the new US role as a world power, foundered on the failure to find a 'plausible rival' on land against which to mobilise. This lack of a 'plausible' enemy also made it difficult for the army to formulate a doctrine or conception of war. (The US Navy, Weigley argued, did not have these problems because it had found a 'plausible rival' in Japan against which to formulate doctrine and make war plans.) Thus, Weigley concludes, since the army 'could not readily find a new raison d'être to replace the police mission that had sustained it for so long . . . in its psychology, attitudes, and organization, it long continued to be the Indian-fighting army'.[17]

Longer even than the late, lamented Professor Weigley had surmised. At least in terms of the rhetoric and vocabulary of the twentieth and twenty-first century 'American way of war', it is with us still. Since at least the American phase (1965–75) of the Thirty Years' War in Indochina (1945–75), the 'dark and evil' lands and 'treacherous and hostile' terrains of the Third World into which American soldiers have repeatedly inserted themselves have become routinely referred to as 'Indian Country'.[18]

Observers have been quick to point out that whereas this terminology appears to have been absent from the American rhetoric of war during the two world wars, it surfaced rather abruptly once the enemy was no longer European and 'advanced'. Frances Fitzgerald, in her study of the background to the Vietnam War, *Fire in the Lake*, cautioned that the term 'Indian Country' was no mere figure of speech: 'It put the Vietnam War into a definite mythological and historical perspective: the Americans were once again embarked upon a heroic . . . conquest of an inferior race'.[19] Whereas the great historian of American frontier mythology, Richard Slotkin, considered that the Vietnam War was 'our last great Indian war', this does not seem to have been the case.[20] In a story filed from 'Camp Scorpion, Iraq' in late summer 2003, the United Press International correspondent Pamela Hess found the Indian-fighting analogy alive and well among US Marines engaged in 'pacifying' the Fertile Crescent. 'Northern Babil province is what the Marines call, in their typically politically incorrect way, 'Indian country', she wrote.[21] More recently, however, the term 'Indian country' has been borrowed from the soldiers and given a whole new geopolitical relevance by advocates of a more aggressive posture in the 'global war on terror' being waged by the United States. In a *Wall Street Journal* editorial, the neoconservative pundit Robert D. Kaplan made the case in terms that bear repeating at some length.

> An overlooked truth about the war on terrorism, and the war in Iraq in particular, is that they both arrived too soon for the American military: before it had adequately transformed itself from a dinosauric, Industrial Age beast to a light and lethal instrument skilled in guerrilla warfare, attuned to the local environment in the way of the 19th century Apaches. My mention of the Apaches is deliberate. For in a world in which mass infantry invasions are becoming politically and diplomatically prohibitive – even as dirty little struggles proliferate, featuring small clusters of combatants hiding out in Third World slums – the American military is back to the days of fighting Indians.
>
> The red Indian metaphor is one with which a liberal policy nomenklatura may be uncomfortable, but Army and Marine field officers have embraced it because it captures perfectly the combat challenge of the early 21st century'.[22]

The shadow of the United States Indian-fighting army would seem to be long indeed.

NOTES

PREFACE

1 Vandervort, *Wars of Imperial Conquest in Africa, 1830–1914*, Bloomington, Ind., Indiana University Press, 1998, p. xvi.
2 Yucatán broke away from Mexico in 1839 and remained independent until 1843. Even afterwards, separatist tendencies continued to be strong in the peninsula.
3 R.E. May, *Manifest Destiny's Underworld: Filibustering in Antebellum America*, Chapel Hill, N.C., University of North Carolina Press, 2002, p. 14.
4 G. Nash, 'Whither Indian History: Review Essay', *Journal of Ethnic Studies*, 1976, vol. 3, pp. 69–70, 73.
5 Robinson and Gallagher with A. Denny, *Africa and the Victorians: The Official Mind of Imperialism*, 2nd edn, London, Macmillan, 1981 [1961].
6 For the Ethiopian case, see J. Dunn, 'For God, Emperor, Country: The Evolution of Ethiopia's Nineteenth Century Army', *War in History*, 1994, vol. 1, p. 284. In certain cases, however, dependency was not very great; the Zulus, for example, imported thousands of firearms, but used them only sporadically, since to have done otherwise would have wrecked their finely tuned military system and, with it, their society. Vandervort, *Wars of Imperial Conquest*, pp. 8–9.
7 Another source gives 932 Army personnel killed and 1,061 wounded from 1866 to 1891 and says that Indian casualties are unknown. [Oliver Knight], 'Indian Wars', in H. Lamar (ed.), *New Encyclopedia of the American West*, New Haven, Conn., Yale University Press, 1998, p. 545.
8 J.K. Howard, *Strange Empire: A Narrative of the Northwest*, New York, William Morrow and Co., 1952, p. 500.
9 A. Wells and G.M. Joseph, *Summer of Discontent, Seasons of Upheaval: Elite Politics and Rural Insurgency in Yucatán, 1876–1915*, Stanford, Calif., Stanford University Press, 1996, p. 27. D.E. Dumond, *The Machete and the Cross: Campesino Rebellion in Yucatán*, Lincoln, Neb., University of Nebraska Press, 1997, p. 412, believes that flight to neighbouring regions to escape the violence by people from both sides may account for some of this population loss.
10 A vivid account of the battle of Isandlwana is given in R.B. Edgerton, *Like Lions They Fought: The Zulu War and the Last Black Empire in Africa*, New York, Ballantine Books, 1989 [1988], pp. 78–91.
11 About 50 per cent of the total Italian force died on the battlefield at Adowa, the greatest level of loss sustained in combat by any Western army in the nineteenth century. The Ethiopian dead, although some 7,000, accounted for less than ten per cent of the Ethiopian army committed to the battle. N. Labanca, *In Marcia verso Adua*, Turin, Einaudi, 1993, pp. 356, 359.

NOTES

INTRODUCTION

1 J.H. Monnett, *The Battle of Beecher Island and the Indian War of 1867–69*, Niwot, Colo., University Press of Colorado, 1992, pp. 143–4.
2 The most complete modern treatment of this encounter is contained in Chapters 6 to 9 of Monnett's *Battle of Beecher Island*. I am much indebted to this account for the battle narrative which follows.
3 Quoted in T. Goodrich, *Scalp Dance: Indian Warfare on the High Plains, 1865–1879*, Mechanicsburg, Pa., Stackpole Books, 1997, p. 94.
4 Patented in 1860, the Spencer .50 calibre carbine was the first repeating rifle to be issued in large numbers to US troops, in this case Union cavalry in the Civil War. The Spencer featured a tube in the stock from which rounds were fed into the chamber. J. Walter (ed.), *Dictionary of Guns and Gunmakers*, London, Greenhill, 2001, p. 492.
5 Monnett, *Battle of Beecher Island*, pp. 119, 124.
6 D. Dixon, *Hero of Beecher Island: The Life and Military Career of George A. Forsyth*, Lincoln, Neb., University of Nebraska Press, 1994, p. 76.
7 Although our main inspiration for this synopsis of the battle of Beecher Island, John Monnett, writes (*Battle of Beecher Island*, p. 127) that the Sioux present at the battle were members of the Brulé branch of the tribe, other authors identify them as Oglalas. See, for example, R.M. Utley, *Frontier Regulars: The United States Army and the Indian, 1866–1891*, New York, Macmillan, 1973, p. 148. Dixon, *Hero of Beecher Island*, has solved the problem by placing both Brulés and Oglalas on the Arickaree (p. 76).
8 Hurst, 'The Beecher Island Fight', *Kansas Historical Collections (1919–1922)*, vol. 15, pp. 540–1. Quoted in Goodrich, *Scalp Dance*, p. 98.
9 Forsyth, *The Soldier*, vol. 2, New York, The Brampton Society, 1908 [1900], p. 217.
10 E. A. Brininstool, *Fighting Red Cloud's Warriors: True Tales of Indian Days When the West was Young*, Columbus, Ohio, Hunter-Trader-Trapper Co., 1926, pp. 88, 90. Quoted in Monnett, *Battle of Beecher Island*, p. 132.
11 Forsyth, *The Soldier*, vol. 2, p. 218.
12 Monnett, *Battle of Beecher Island*, p. 132, gives Murphy and Stillwell credit for the idea of taking up a defensive position on the island. Dixon, Forsyth's biographer, in *Hero of Beecher Island*, p. 76, says it was Stillwell who pointed the way.
13 Hurst, 'The Beecher Island Fight', p. 532. Quoted in Monnett, *Battle of Beecher Island*, p. 133.
14 Hurst, 'The Beecher Island Fight', p. 534. Quoted in Monnett, *Battle of Beecher Island*, p. 137.
15 In his memoir, *Thrilling Days in Army Life*, New York, Harper and Bros, 1902, p. 73, Forsyth wrote that when the commander of the rescue column, Captain Louis H. Carpenter, approached him, 'I affected to be reading an old novel that one of the men had found in a saddle pocket. It was only affectation, though, for I had all I could do to keep from breaking down . . .'. Quoted in Monnett, *Battle of Beecher Island*, p. 171.
16 Dixon, *Hero of Beecher Island*, pp. 87–8.
17 Monnett, *Battle of Beecher Island*, pp. 4–5.
18 Dixon, *Hero of Beecher Island*, p. 167. Beecher also claimed that the Cheyenne chiefs had field glasses.
19 S.E. Ambrose, *Crazy Horse and Custer – The Parallel Lives of Two American Warriors*, New York, New American Library, 1975, p. 247.
20 R.K. Andrist, *The Long Death: The Last Days of the Plains Indian*, New York, Macmillan, 1964 [1933], p. 148.
21 Nor was Sigmund Shlesinger the only greenhorn among the scouts. Dr. Mooers told

NOTES

friends he was joining up in hopes of seeing 'a real, live, wild Indian'. Dixon, *Hero of Beecher Island*, p. 71.

22 Crook, *General George Crook: His Autobiography*, ed. and annot. M.F. Schmitt, Norman, Okla., University of Oklahoma Press, 1946, p. 213.

23 A detailed account of the rivalry of these two generals and their coteries is given in R.A. Johnson, '"Russians at the Gates of India"? Planning the Defence of India, 1885–1900', *Journal of Military History*, 2003, vol. 67, pp. 697–745.

24 Forsyth, *Thrilling Days*, p. 7. Later in life, Forsyth would adopt an unvarnished Social Darwinist view of the people he had fought. War on the plains, he wrote, represented 'the advance of civilization against barbarism, with the assurance in the end of the "survival of the fittest", a harsh, cruel, but seemingly inexorable law, that has obtained since the dawn of creation'. Ibid. Quoted in Dixon, *Hero of Beecher Island*, p. 65.

25 Andrist, *Long Death*, p. 149.

26 Dixon, *Hero of Beecher Island*, p. 71.

27 Monteil, *De Saint-Louis* [Senegal] *à Tripoli, par le lac Tchad, voyage à travers du Soudan et du Sahara accompli pendant les années 1890–91–92*, Paris, Alcan, 1895.

28 The post surgeon Charles Page, quoted in P. Hedren, *The Massacre of Lieutenant Grattan and his Command by Indians*, Glendale, Calif., Arthur H. Clark, 1983, p. 50. To be more precise, one trooper did manage to escape with his life, but died from his wounds a few days later. R.M. Utley, *Frontiersmen in Blue: The United States Army and the Indian, 1848–1865*, New York, Macmillan, 1967, pp. 113–15.

29 The scout Louis McLoughlin, in interview with Denver, Colo., *Rocky Mountain News*, 22 April 1900. Quoted in Monnett, *Battle of Beecher Island*, p. 120.

30 Dixon, *Hero of Beecher Island*, p. 72.

31 Hurst, 'The Beecher Island Fight', p. 531. Quoted in Goodrich, *Scalp Dance*, p. 97.

32 Miles, *Personal Recollections and Observations of General Nelson A. Miles*, New York, Werner, 1897, p. 481.

33 Belich, *The Victorian Interpretation of Racial Conflict: The Maori, the British, and the New Zealand Wars*, Montreal and Kingston, McGill-Queen's University Press, 1989 [1986], p. 316.

34 Hurst, 'The Beecher Island Fight', p. 153. Quoted in Monnett, *Battle of Beecher Island*, p. 136.

35 Leckie, *The Military Conquest of the South Plains*, Norman, Okla., University of Oklahoma Press, 1963, p. 76.

36 Utley, *Frontier Regulars*, p. 148.

37 Hoig, *Tribal Wars of the Southern Plains*, Norman, Okla., University of Oklahoma Press, 1993, p. 252.

38 Monnett, *Battle of Beecher Island*, p. 135.

39 Ibid., p. 144.

40 Andrist, *Long Death*, pp. 152–3.

41 Monnett, *Battle of Beecher Island*, p. 131.

42 A. Mills, *My Story*, Mechanicsburg, Pa., Stackpole Books, 2003 [1918], p. 409. Mills commanded a troop of the Third Cavalry during the battle, which ended in defeat for Crook's force and a retreat that may have contributed to the isolation and subsequent slaughter of Custer's Seventh Cavalry at the Little Bighorn a week later.

43 McLoughlin, 'The Forsyth Scouts at Beecher Island', *Beecher Island Annual: Sixty-Second Anniversary of the Battle of Beecher Island, September 17–18, 1868*, Wray, Colo., Beecher Island Battle Memorial Association, 1930, p. 88. Quoted in Monnett, *Battle of Beecher Island*, pp. 139–40.

44 J. Laband, *Kingdom in Crisis: The Zulu Response to the British Invasion of 1879*, Manchester, Manchester University Press, 1992, p. 57, estimates the size of Cetshwayo's

NOTES

army at 41,900 men, of whom only about 29,000 might have been available for service at any one time. Even so, this was a considerably larger force than any New World indigenous people could mass for war, except the Mayas of Yucatán.

45 J.H. Moore, 'Cheyennes', *Encyclopedia of the Great Plains*, ed. D.J. Wishart, Lincoln, Neb., University of Nebraska Press, 2004, p. 569.
46 His name in Cheyenne, *Woqini*, meant 'hook nose', which whites rendered as Roman Nose.
47 A. McGinnis, 'Strike and Retreat: Intertribal Warfare and the Powder River War, 1865–1868', *Montana: the Magazine of Western History*, 1980, vol. 30, p. 33.
48 Monnett, *Battle of Beecher Island*, p. 47.
49 G.B. Grinnell, *The Cheyenne Indians*, vol. 2, New Haven, Conn., Yale University Press, 1923, pp. 119–21.
50 Monnett, *Battle of Beecher Island*, pp. 147–9.
51 Utley, *Frontier Regulars*, pp. 104–7. For more details, see D. Brown, *The Fetterman Massacre*, Lincoln, Neb., University of Nebraska Press, 1984 [1962].

1 WORLDS IN MOTION

1 R.F. Betts, 'Immense Dimensions: The Impact of the American West on Late Nineteenth-Century European Thought about Expansion', *Western Historical Quarterly*, 1979, vol. 10, p. 149. Lord Bryce's comment can be found on p. 130 of vol. 2 of his *The American Commonwealth*, New York, Macmillan, 1889.
2 Curzon, *Frontiers: The Romanes Lecture of 1907*, Oxford, Clarendon Press, 1907, p. 8. Quoted in Betts, 'Immense Dimensions', p. 150.
3 M.J. Simonin, 'De Washington à San Francisco: À travers le continent américain', *Le Tour du Monde*, 1874, vol. 27, p. 221. Quoted in Betts, 'Immense Dimensions', p. 152.
4 *Congressional Record*, 56th Congress, 1st session, 7 March 1900. Quoted in W.L. Williams, 'United States Indian Policy and the Debate over Philippine Annexation: Implications for the Origins of American Imperialism', *Journal of American History*, 1980, vol. 66, p. 817. Lodge was a Republican senator from Massachusetts.
5 Callwell, *Small Wars: Their Principles and Practice*, Lincoln, Neb., University of Nebraska Press, 1996 [1896], pp. 40, 75, 135–7, 188.
6 Marcy, *Thirty Years of Army Life on the Border*, Philadelphia, J.B. Lippincott, 1963 [1866], p. 49. Marcy was the father-in-law of the prominent Civil War general, George B. McClellan, and served as his chief of staff during the 1861–5 conflict. He ended his career as Inspector-General of the US Army.
7 Report, 1 December, US Secretary of War, Annual Reports, 1856, pp. 5–6.
8 T. Dunlay, *Wolves for the Blue Soldiers: Indian Scouts and Auxiliaries with the United States Army, 1860–90*, Lincoln, Neb., University of Nebraska Press, 1982, p. 24.
9 O. Faulk's exhaustive account of this abortive undertaking, *The US Camel Corps: An Army Experiment*, New York, Oxford University Press, 1976, fails, however, to mention the influence of the news from Algeria on Davis's decision to authorise the importation of camels. For this, see Jefferson Davis, 'Report of the Secretary of War', 1 December 1853, *House Exec. Doc. No. 1*, 33rd Cong., 1st Sess., in D. Rowland (ed.), *Jefferson Davis, Constitutionalist: His Letters, Papers and Speeches*, Jackson, Mississippi Department of Archives and History, 1923, p. 321.
10 United States War Department, Adjutant General's Office, Military Information Division, J.S. Herron (compiler), *Colonial Army Systems of the Netherlands, Great Britain, France, Germany, Portugal, Italy, and Belgium*, Washington, DC, Government Printing Office, 1901.
11 J. Frémeaux, *L'Afrique à l'ombre des épées, 1830–1930*, Vincennes, Service Historique de l'Armée de Terre, 1993, pp. 19–22.

NOTES

12 Gump, *The Dust Rose Like Smoke: The Subjugation of the Zulu and the Sioux*, Lincoln, University of Nebraska Press, 1996 [1994], pp. 138–9.
13 J. Connor, *The Australian Frontier Wars, 1788–1838*, Sydney, University of New South Wales Press, 2001, p. xii.
14 R. Hughes, *The Fatal Shore*, New York, Vintage, 1988 [1986], p. 277.
15 J. Belich, *The Victorian Interpretation of Racial Conflict: The Maori, the British, and the New Zealand Wars*, Montreal and Kingston, McGill-Queen's University Press, 1989 [1986], pp. 22–3.
16 J.K. Howard, *Strange Empire: A Narrative of the Northwest*, New York, William Morrow, 1952, pp. 27–8. Dakota Territory was formed in 1861. In 1889 it was divided up into the present-day states of North and South Dakota.
17 Beaujour, *Sketch of the United States of North America, at the Commencement of the Nineteenth Century, from 1800 to 1810*, trans. W. Walton, London, J. Booth, 1814. Quoted in G.E. Stearn (ed.), *Broken Image: Foreign Critiques of America*, New York, Random House, 1972, p. 19.
18 P.H. Carlson, *The Plains Indians*, College Station, Tex., Texas A and M University Press, 1998, p. 142.
19 H.R. Trevor-Roper, 'The Rise of Christian Europe', *The Listener*, 28 November 1963, pp. 871–5. Quote is from p. 871. This article is a printed version of the first in a series of five BBC television lectures by Trevor-Roper, who was at the time Regius Professor of Modern History at Oxford University.
20 R.B. Ferguson and N.L. Whitehead (eds), *War in the Tribal Zone: Expanding States and Indigenous Warfare*, Santa Fe, N.Mex., School of American Research Press, 1992, p. 6.
21 Curtin *et al.*, *African History: From Earliest Times to Independence*, 2nd edn, Harlow, Longman, 1995, p. 398.
22 B. Vandervort, *Wars of Imperial Conquest in Africa, 1830–1914*, Bloomington, Ind., Indiana University Press, 1998, p. 2.
23 For more on this massive upheaval, see R.J. Smith, *Mercenaries and Mandarins: the Ever-Victorious Army in Nineteenth Century China*, Millwood, N.Y., KTO Press, 1978; J.D. Spence, *God's Chinese Son: The Taiping Heavenly Kingdom of Hong Xiuquan*, New York, W.W. Norton, 1996; and S.Y. Teng, *The Taiping Rebellion and the Western Powers: A Comprehensive Survey*, Oxford, Clarendon Press, 1971.
24 Parkman's view, which dominated US historiography on the period for over a century, was set forth in his magisterial *The Conspiracy of Pontiac and the Indian War after the Conquest of Canada*, 3rd edn, 2 vols., Lincoln, Neb., University of Nebraska Press, 1994 [1870; 1851].
25 The scholars who have led the way in underscoring the importance of nativist religion to Indian resistance in the Old Northwest are Gregory Evans Dowd and Anthony F.C. Wallace. Dowd's thesis is most conveniently packaged in 'Thinking and Believing: Nativism and Unity in the Ages of Pontiac and Tecumseh', *American Indian Quarterly*, Summer 1992, vol. 16, pp. 309–35, but is developed in greater detail in his books, *A Spirited Resistance: The North American Indian Struggle for Unity, 1745–1815*, Baltimore, Md., Johns Hopkins University Press, 1991, and *War Under Heaven: Pontiac, the Indian Nations and the British Empire*, Baltimore, Md., Johns Hopkins University Press, 2002. For a more broadly theoretical treatment which compares the North American phenomena to similar movements elsewhere, see A.F.C. Wallace, 'Revitalization Movements: Some Theoretical Considerations for Their Comparative Study', *American Anthropologist*, 1956, vol. 58, pp. 264–81.
26 A.F.C. Wallace, 'New Religions among the Delaware Indians', *Southwestern Journal of Anthropology*, 1956, vol. 12, pp. 1–21.
27 Also known as 'The Open Door', Tenskwatawa has been accorded much more attention by scholars than his Delaware predecessor and inspiration, Neolin. There is

a biography by R.D. Edmunds, *The Shawnee Prophet*, Lincoln, Neb., University of Nebraska Press, 1983, plus a substantial periodical literature, among which see especially, Edmunds, 'Tecumseh, the Shawnee Prophet, and American History: A Reassessment', *Western Historical Quarterly*, 1983, vol. 14, pp. 261–76, and T. Willig, 'Prophetstown on the Wabash: The Native Spiritual Defense of the Old Northwest', *Michigan Historical Review*, 1997, vol. 23, pp. 130–5.

28 The role of Pontiac in the 1763–5 war is explored at great length in Dowd, *War under Heaven*. The best source for Tecumseh's influence on the early nineteenth-century confederation movement is the work of John Sugden. See his powerful biography, *Tecumseh: A Life*, New York, Henry Holt, 1997, and 'Early Pan-Indianism: Tecumseh's Tour of the Indian Country, 1811–1812', *American Indian Quarterly*, 1986, vol. 10, pp. 273–304.

29 The lengthy process of Seminole tribal formation in Florida was first described in detail in an article by W. C. Sturtevant, 'Creek into Seminole', in E.B. Leacock and N. O. Lurie (eds), *North American Indians in Historical Perspective*, New York, Random House, 1971, pp. 92–128, that anthropologists consider the seminal exposition of the concept of ethnogenesis. But also see J.W. Covington, 'Migration of the Seminoles into Florida: 1700–1825', *Florida Historical Quarterly*, 1968, vol. 46, pp. 340–57.

30 R. Law, 'Horses, Firearms, and Political Power in Pre-Colonial West Africa', *Past and Present*, 1976, vol. 72, pp. 112–32.

31 Although the topic lies outside the scope of this study, mention should be made of the early nineteenth century expansion of the Araucanian Indian people of Chile, the fearsome Mapuches, across the Andes and onto the pampas of Argentina, where they established a grassland empire whose horsemen held the armies and gauchos of that white settler state at bay for more than six decades. On the Chilean Mapuches, see J. Bengoa, *Historia de pueblo Mapuche (siglo XIX e XX)*, Santiago, Ediciones Sur, 1985. For the so-called 'Desert War' of 1879–80 which brought Araucanian hegemony on the pampas to an end, see D. Schoo Lastra, *El Indio del desierto* [de Argentina], *1535–1879*, Buenos Aires, Agencia General de Librería y Publicaciones, 1928, and J. C. Walther, *La Conquista del desierto* [de Argentina], 2nd edn, Buenos Aires, Circulo Militar, 1964.

32 E. Wallace and E.A. Hoebel, *The Comanches, Lords of the South Plains*, Norman, Okla., University of Oklahoma Press, 1958 [1952], p. 12. The Kiowa-Apaches spoke an Athapascan language similar to that of the Apache peoples of Arizona and New Mexico but they were not, as some writers have assumed, a remnant of the Apaches who had been driven from the plains by the Comanches in the eighteenth century.

33 The other bands were the Kotsotekas (Buffalo Eaters), Nokonis (Wanderers) and Penatekas (Wasps). The latter, the southernmost of the Comanche bands, were the one most friendly to whites, having been longest in contact with them. J.L. Haley, *The Buffalo War: The History of the Red River Indian Uprising of 1874*, New York, Doubleday, 1976, pp. 14–16.

34 J.S. Ford, *Rip Ford's Texas*, ed. S.B. Oates, Austin, Tex., University of Texas Press, 1963, p. 130.

35 Data on the Comanche population are difficult to locate and may vary considerably from source to source. Wallace and Hoebel, *The Comanches*, pp. 31–2, put Comanche numbers at the end of the 1700s at around 20,000. In 1837, they report, US Army sources estimated the number of Comanche warriors at around 4,500. By 1866, it was thought that the whole tribe probably numbered no more than 4,700 people. Haley, *The Buffalo War*, p. 14, estimates that the Comanche people probably numbered less than 2,500 individuals on the eve of the 1874–5 war which forced the

last of the free-ranging bands to take up residence on the reservation in Indian Territory set aside for them.
36 R.H. Lowie, *Indians of the Plains*, New York, McGraw-Hill, 1954, pp. 10–11.
37 F.R. Secoy, *Changing Military Patterns on the Great Plains (17th Century through Early 19th Century)*, Seattle, Wash., University of Washington Press, 1966 [1953], pp. 41–2.
38 C.G. Calloway, *One Vast Winter Count: The Native American West before Lewis and Clark*, Lincoln, Neb., University of Nebraska Press, 2003, p. 309; G.C. Anderson, 'Early Dakota Migration and Intertribal War: A Revision', *Western Historical Quarterly*, 1980, vol. 11, pp. 17–36.
39 The Santee Sioux were in turn comprised of the Mdewakanton, Wahpekute, Wahpeton and Sisseton bands.
40 The other branches of the Teton Sioux are the Blackfoot Sioux, the Brulés, the Miniconjous, the Sans-Arcs and the Two Kettles.
41 R.B. Hassrick, *The Sioux: Life and Customs of a Warrior Society*, Norman, Okla., University of Oklahoma Press, 1956, p. 57.
42 Gump, *The Dust Rose Like Smoke*, pp. 41–4.
43 For a concise account of Sioux 'secondary imperialism', see R. White, 'The Winning of the West: The Expansion of the Western Sioux in the Eighteenth and Nineteenth Centuries', *Journal of American History*, 1978, vol. 65, pp. 319–43.
44 R.G. Thwaites (ed.), *Original Journals of the Lewis and Clark Expedition, 1804–1806*, 8 vols., New York, Dodd, Mead and Co., 1904–5, vol. 6, p. 98. Quoted in White, 'The Winning of the West', p. 547.
45 J.S. Milloy, *The Plains Cree: Trade, Diplomacy and War, 1790 to 1870*, Winnipeg, University of Manitoba Press, 1988, p. xiv.
46 J.R. Miller, *Skyscrapers Hide the Heavens: A History of Indian–White Relations in Canada*, 3rd edn, Toronto, University of Toronto Press, 2000 [1989], pp. 157–8.
47 By the mid-nineteenth century, long-term collaboration and intermarriage had made the Plains Crees, Assiniboines and Plains Ojibwas virtually indistinguishable as peoples. It was at the insistence of white officials who negotiated treaties with them in the 1870s that the notion that they constituted separate ethnic groups was revived. P. Albers, 'Changing Patterns of Ethnicity in the Northeastern [Canadian] Plains', in J.D. Hill (ed.), *History, Power, and Identity: Ethnogenesis in the Americas, 1492–1992*, Iowa City, Iowa, University of Iowa Press, 1996, p. 91.
48 Stanley, *The Birth of Western Canada: A History of the Riel Rebellions*, Toronto, University of Toronto Press, 1960 [1936], p. 196.
49 Milloy, *The Plains Cree*, pp. xv–xvi.
50 For a lyrical evocation of this period of Canadian Plains Indian history, see D. Jenish, *Indian Fall: The Last Great Days of the Plains Cree and the Blackfoot Confederacy*, Toronto, Penguin Viking, 1999.
51 In 1870, the Crees made a bid to drive their Blackfoot enemies permanently from the Cypress Hills country of extreme southern Alberta, where the last big concentration of Canadian buffalo was located. In an October battle on the Belly (or Oldman) River near present-day Lethbridge, Alberta, a large Cree force was decisively defeated by the Blackfeet, losing between 200 and 400 warriors. G.E. Friesen, *The Canadian Prairies: A History*, Toronto, University of Toronto Press, 1984, p. 133.
52 William A. Dobak, 'Killing the Canadian Buffalo, 1821–1881', *Western Historical Quarterly*, 1996, vol. 27, pp. 33–52, ascribes the disappearance of the Canadian buffalo to the pressure of hunting by a growing Indian population in the first half of the 1800s. The main reason for overkill was to supply the Hudson's Bay Company with buffalo robes and pemmican (chipped buffalo meat in melted fat) for their trade convoys on the rivers of the Northwest. Dobak thinks that Indians took one third

more buffalo than they needed for subsistence in order to meet the commercial demand for buffalo products. Ibid., pp. 51–2. Jenish, *Indian Fall*, pp. 9–10, chooses to blame the decimation of Canada's buffalo herds on 'the American repeating rifle and American demand for buffalo hides'.
53 Friesen, *Canadian Prairies*, p. 130.
54 Ibid., p. 137.
55 Morton, *The Last War Drum: The North West Campaign of 1885*, Toronto, Hakkert, 1972, p. 16.
56 Geronimo, once feared and hated not only by Americans and Mexicans but by many of his own Chiricahua people, is today seen by many Americans as a wise and benevolent father of his people. See C.L. Sonnichsen, 'From Savage to Saint: A New Image for Geronimo', in Sonnichsen (ed.), *Geronimo and the End of the Apache Wars*, Lincoln, Neb., University of Nebraska Press, 1990 [1986], pp. 5–34.
57 Cocker, *Rivers of Blood, Rivers of Gold: Europe's Conquest of Indigenous Peoples*, New York, Grove Press, 2000, p. 189.
58 Crook, 'The Apache Problem', *Journal of the Military Service Institution of the United States*, 1886, vol. 7, p. 268. Crook's essay has been conveniently reprinted in P. Cozzens (ed.), *Eyewitnesses to the Indian Wars, 1865–1890*, vol. 1: *The Struggle for Apachería*, Mechanicsburg, Pa., Stackpole Books, 2001, pp. 593–603. The quote from Crook is on p. 602.
59 The Opatas, who inhabited northern Sonora, were known as the 'spoiled children of the Spanish crown' because of their eagerness to embrace the Spanish language and Spanish ways. 'Of all the tribes the Spaniards encountered in North America none adopted the Spanish way of life more readily or more successfully than the Opatas.' Although, as we will see, they proved to be less pliable to Mexican wishes than they had been to those of the Spanish, by the middle of the nineteenth century the Opatas had virtually disappeared as a people because of acculturation and intermarriage with their white neighbours. D.E. Worcester, *The Apaches: Eagles of the Southwest*, Norman, Okla., University of Oklahoma Press, 1979, p. 13.
60 Quoted in D. Roberts, *Once They Moved Like the Wind: Cochise, Geronimo, and the Apache Wars*, New York, Simon and Schuster, 1993, p. 14.
61 Angie Debo, in her *Geronimo: The Man, His Time, His Place*, Norman, Okla., University of Oklahoma Press, 1976, pp. 27–8, contends that fighting between the Apaches and the Spanish originated in Spanish slaving forays into Apachería. In this, she follows Jack D. Forbes's argument that the Apaches were an essentially peaceable people until the Spanish came along. Forbes's main contention is that by disrupting their extensive trading relations with other Indian peoples, the Spaniards forced the Apaches to take up raiding as a supplement to their basic hunter-gatherer economy. Forbes, *Apache, Navaho and Spaniard*, Norman, Okla., University of Oklahoma Press, 1960, p. 24.
62 García, *Apuntes sobre la campaña contra los salvajes en el estado de Sonora*, Hermosillo, Sonora, Imprenta de Roberto Bernal, 1883, p. 6. Own translation.
63 Faulk, *The Geronimo Campaign*, New York, Oxford University Press, 1969, p. 6.
64 L. Lejeune, *La guerra Apache en Sonora*, trans. M. Antochiw, Hermosillo, Sonora, Gobierno del Estado de Sonora, 1984 [1887], p. 17. Own translation.
65 Lejeune, *La guerra Apache*, pp. 14–16.
66 R.F. Acuña, *Sonoran Strongman: Ignacio Pesquiera and His Times*, Tucson, Ariz., University of Arizona Press, 1974, p. 7.
67 S.F. Voss, *On the Periphery of Nineteenth-Century Mexico: Sonora and Sinaloa, 1810–1877*, Tucson, Ariz., University of Arizona Press, 1982, pp. 48–9.
68 D.L. Thrapp, *The Conquest of Apachería*, Norman, Okla., University of Oklahoma Press, 1967, p. viii.

NOTES

69 E.H. Spicer, *The Yaquis: A Cultural History*, Tucson, Ariz., University of Arizona Press, 1980, p. 64.
70 T.E. Sheridan, 'The Yeomem (Yaquis): An Enduring People', in Sheridan and N.J. Parezo (eds), *Paths of Life: American Indians of the Southwest and Northern Mexico*, Tucson, Ariz., University of Arizona Press, 1996, pp. 37–8, 40.
71 E. Hu-DeHart, *Yaqui Resistance and Survival: The Struggle for Land and Autonomy*, Madison, University of Wisconsin Press, 1984, p. 19.
72 Spicer, *The Yaquis*, p. 128; and Spicer, 'Yaqui Militarism', *The Arizona Quarterly*, 1947, vol. 3, p. 40.
73 R.W.H. Hardy, *Travels in the Interior of Mexico in 1825, 1826, 1827 and 1828*, London, Henry Colborn and Richard Bentley, 1829, pp. 438–9. Quoted in Hu-DeHart, *Yaqui Resistance*, p. 20. Hardy was a commercial traveller for the British General Pearl and Coral Company.
74 Acuña, *Sonoran Strongman*, pp. 5–6. Hernández's remarks first appeared in P. Nicoli, *El Estado de Sonora: Yaquis y Mayos*, Mexico, Imprenta de Francisco Díaz de Leon, 1885, p. 93.
75 Hu-DeHart, *Yaqui Resistance*, pp. 81, 181–2.
76 Ibid., pp. 66, 80, 122, 162–3.
77 For more on this, see N.M. Fariss, *Maya Society under Colonial Rule: The Collective Enterprise of Survival*, Princeton, N.J., Princeton University Press, 1984.
78 A convenient, up-to-date summary of the ongoing debate about the origins of the Caste War is given in R.T. Alexander, *Yaxcaba and the Caste War of Yucatán: An Archaeological Perspective*, Albuquerque, N.Mex., University of New Mexico Press, 2004, pp. 16–21.
79 These figures come from the Yucatán census of 1846. N. Reed, *The Caste War of Yucatán*, Stanford, Calif., Stanford University Press, 1964, p. 127.

2 THE NEW WORLD IN A CENTURY OF SMALL WARS

1 R.B. Ferguson and N.L. Whitehead (eds), *War in the Tribal Zone: Expanding States and Indigenous Warfare*, Santa Fe, N.Mex., School of American Research Press, 1992, p. 3.
2 D.C. Cole, *The Chiricahua Apache, 1846–1876: From War to Reservation*, Albuquerque, N.Mex., University of New Mexico Press, 1988, pp. 48–9, 56. Not all Apaches were forced off the plains. The Lipan Apaches of western Texas continued to hunt buffalo well into the nineteenth century, as did the Jicarilla Apaches of northeastern New Mexico. Even the Warm Springs Apache band of western New Mexico appears to have hunted buffalo from time to time. In his remarkable book, *I Fought with Geronimo*, written with W.S. Nye, Harrisburg, Pa., Stackpole Books, 1953, pp. 33–4, Warm Springs Apache Jason Betzinez recalled such a buffalo hunt on the plains in his early youth.
3 Cole, *Chiricahua Apache*, p. 24.
4 E.A.H. John, 'Nurturing the Peace: Spanish–Comanche Cooperation in the Early Nineteenth Century', *New Mexico Historical Review*, 1984, vol. 59, pp. 345–69. The Mexicans, however, were only periodically successful in fomenting war between the Comanches and Apaches because their frontier defences enjoyed less respect than those of the Spanish and because, after all, it was the weaker Mexicans 'who had the resources both Indian groups wanted'. W.B. Griffen, *Utmost Good Faith: Patterns of Apache–Mexican Hostilities in Northern Chihuahua Warfare, 1821–1848*, Albuquerque, N.Mex., University of New Mexico Press, 1988, p. 128.
5 Cole, *Chiricahua Apache*, p. 55.
6 Ferguson and Whitehead (eds), *War in the Tribal Zone*, p. 3.

NOTES

7 L.L. Milfort, *Memoirs or a Quick Glance at My Various Travels and My Sojourn in the Creek Nation*, ed. and tr. B. McCary, Savannah, Ga., Beehive Press, 1979 [1959; 1802], p. 98.
8 R.V. Remini, *Andrew Jackson and the Course of American Empire, 1767–1821*, New York, Harper and Row, 1977, vol. 1, p. 208.
9 J.S. Bassett (ed.), *Correspondence of Andrew Jackson*, Washington, D.C., Carnegie Institution, 1926, vol. 1, p. 451.
10 F.R. Secoy, *Changing Military Patterns on the Great Plains (17th century through Early 19th century)*, Monographs of the American Ethnological Society, Seattle, Wash., University of Washington Press, 1966 [1953], pp. 1–2.
11 B. Mishkin, *Rank and Warfare among the Plains Indians*, Monographs of the American Ethnological Society, Seattle, Wash., University of Washington Press, 1940, p. 9.
12 R.N. Richardson, *The Comanche Barrier to South Plains Settlement*, Glendale, Calif., Arthur H. Clark Co., 1933, p. 26.
13 Mishkin, *Rank and Warfare*, pp. 18–20.
14 Secoy, *Changing Military Patterns*, p. 18.
15 Cole, *Chiricahua Apache*, p. 60.
16 T.W. Kavanagh, *Comanche Political History: An Ethnohistorical Perspective, 1706–1875*, Lincoln, Neb., University of Nebraska Press, 1996, pp. 61–2.
17 While presumably useful in keeping Indians less mobile and thus less dangerous to their European masters, the prohibition on Indian use of horses actually stemmed from a feudal social practice imported from Spain, whereby the 'noblest of beasts' could only be ridden by nobles and noble-led cavalrymen. D.E. Worcester, *The Apaches: Eagles of the Southwest*, Norman, Okla., University of Oklahoma Press, 1979, p. 10.
18 The Choctaw Indians of what would become the state of Mississippi appear to have acquired horses toward the end of the seventeenth century and used them in warfare before their removal to Indian Territory in the 1830s. J.T. Carson, 'Horses and the Economy and Culture of the Choctaw Indians, 1690–1840', *Ethnohistory*, 1995, vol. 42, pp. 495–513. Many of the Sauk and Fox insurgents during the Black Hawk War in Illinois and Wisconsin in 1832 were mounted. In his memoirs, Black Hawk, the Sauk war chief who lent his name to the war, recalled how already at the time of the American War of Independence, 'several hundred horses' were pastured outside his native village on the Rock River in northern Illinois. R.L. Nichols, *Black Hawk and the Warrior's Path*, Arlington Heights, Ill., Harlan Davidson, 1992, p. 7.
19 For information on these and other Indian peoples who served as scouts, guides and auxiliaries for the US Army during the wars on the plains, see T.W. Dunlay's indispensable *Wolves for the Blue Soldiers: Indian Scouts and Auxiliaries with the United States Army, 1860–1890*, Lincoln, Neb., University of Nebraska Press, 1982. Among the Eastern Indian peoples who provided similar services for Mexican military units were the so-called Black Seminoles, descendants of black slaves and freedmen who had settled among the Seminole Indians of Florida and had been removed along with them to Oklahoma in the 1830s and '40s, from whence some of them moved to Mexico to escape being re-enslaved. On this topic, see K.W. Porter, *The Black Seminoles: History of a Freedom-Seeking People*, rev. edn, A.A. Amos and T.P. Senter, Gainesville, Fla., University Press of Florida, 1996, pp. 124–71. For the view that the praise for the Black Seminole scouts stems more from US Civil Rights era hyperbole than from an honest assessment of their achievements, see S.A. Miller, *Coacoochee's Bones: A Seminole Saga*, Lawrence, Kans., University Press of Kansas, 2003, pp. 60–1.
20 P. Nabokov, *Two Leggings: The Making of a Crow Warrior*, New York, Thomas Crowell Co., p. 162.
21 Finerty, *Warpath and Bivouac: The Big Horn and Yellowstone Expedition*, ed. M.M.

Quaife, Lincoln, Neb., University of Nebraska Press, 1955 [1890], p. 106. The Chasseurs d'Afrique, a French light cavalry division permanently stationed in North Africa, enjoyed considerable prestige in US military circles during much of the nineteenth century because of their high-profile role in the conquest of Algeria, a conquest thought to be pregnant with 'lessons' US cavalrymen could use in their battle for the Great Plains, and because of their valour in the Crimean War and the Italian War of Independence. As will be related below, their reputation in the US owed much to service of one of the US Army's leading cavalry officers, General Philip Kearny, with the Chasseurs in Algeria in the 1840s and in Italy in 1859. The 'Macmahon' referred to by Finerty was Marshal Marie-Edmé-Patrice MacMahon, a former commander of the Chasseurs and the Foreign Legion, and, at the time of Finerty's ramblings on the plains, President of the French Third Republic.

22. Hämäläinen, 'The Rise and Fall of Plains Indian Horse Cultures', *Journal of American History*, 2003, vol. 90, pp. 846–8.
23. Ibid., pp. 841, 844–5. Texas Ranger 'Rip' Ford noted a sharp fall in the size of Comanche horse herds as early as the 1850s because the animals were being consumed for food. Ford, however, thought that the Indians could have replenished their declining stocks if they had still had access to wild horse herds in south Texas, by this time part of white territory. J.S. Ford, *Rip Ford's Texas*, ed. S.B. Oates, Austin, Tex., University of Texas Press, 1963, p. 132.
24. Hämäläinen, 'Rise and Fall', pp. 860–1.
25. Hassrick, *The Sioux: Life and Customs of a Warrior Society*, Norman, Okla., University of Oklahoma Press, 1956, p. 70.
26. T.E. Mails, *The Mystic Warriors of the Plains*, Garden City, N.Y., Doubleday, 1972, pp. 477–8.
27. J.C. Ewers, *The Horse in Blackfoot Indian Culture, with Comparative Material from Other Western Tribes*, Bureau of American Ethnology, Washington, D.C., Smithsonian Institution, GPO, 1955, p. 13.
28. Secoy, *Changing Military Patterns*, p. 2.
29. Ibid., p. 90.
30. D.J. Weber, *The Mexican Frontier, 1821–1846: The American Southwest under Mexico*, Albuquerque, N.Mex., University of New Mexico Press, 1982, pp. 95–102, provides extensive information on the supply of weapons to Indians in the Mexican Southwest by American traders and the impact this had on Hispanic settlers in the area. The view that this trade was part of a plot by the USA to take over northern Mexico, operative both before and after the Mexican–American War of 1846–48, continues to be held by some Mexican historians. For a discussion of the historiography of the issue in Mexico, see J.A. Stout, '"Filibusteros" and Indians on the North Mexican Frontier, 1848–1921: Mexican Sources and Interpretations', in V. Guedea and J.E. Rodriguez O. (eds), *Five Centuries of Mexican History/Cinco Siglos de historia de Mexico*, San Juan Mixtoac and Irvine, Calif., Instituto Mora and University of California Irvine Press, 1992, pp. 431–2. This problem was exacerbated by the Mexican government's attempt to restrict gun ownership by individuals. R.A. Smith, in 'Indians in American–Mexican Relations before the War of 1846', *Hispanic–American Historical Review*, 1963, vol. 43, p. 34, lays the blame for this policy on the 'dictatorship' imposed in Mexico in 1835.
31. E. Hu-DeHart, *Yaqui Resistance and Survival: The Struggle for Land and Autonomy, 1821–1910*, Madison, Wisc., University of Wisconsin Press, 1984, p. 208.
32. N. Reed, *The Caste War of Yucatán*, Stanford, Calif., Stanford University Press, 1964, p. 46.
33. E.S. Connell, *Son of the Morning Star: Custer and the Little Bighorn*, New York, North Point Press, 1997 [1984], p. 310.
34. Reed, *Caste War of Yucatán*, pp. 61–2.

NOTES

35 S. Vestal, *New Sources of Indian History, 1850–1891*, Norman, Okla., University of Oklahoma Press, 1934, p. 140. Quoted in J.D. McDermott, *A Guide to the Indian Wars of the West*, Lincoln, Neb., University of Nebraska Press, 1998, p. xviii. Although Benteen was a highly decorated veteran of both the US Civil War and the Indian wars, his main claim to fame was his very public dislike of George Armstrong Custer, the commander of the Seventh Cavalry in which he served. Benteen made no bones about his belief that the Custer massacre was the direct result of the general's faulty leadership. For a lengthy and colourful account of Benteen's career, see Connell, *Son of the Morning Star*, pp. 30–40.

36 Mails, *Mystic Warriors of the Plains*, p. 477. On the facing page, Mails provides an illustration of an Indian warrior reloading a musket in this fashion.

37 Crook comment in *Army and Navy Journal*, 29 June 1878, vol. 15, p. 758. Quoted in R.M. Utley, *Frontier Regulars: The United States Army and the Indian, 1866–1891*, New York, Macmillan, 1973, pp. 71–2. The Winchester lever-action rifle proved especially popular with the kinds of warriors Crook faced, especially the Apaches, because it was so easy to reload on horseback.

38 Mails, *Mystic Warriors of the Plains*, p. 477.

39 R.B. Edgerton, *The Fall of the Asante Empire: The Hundred-year War for Africa's Gold Coast*, New York, Free Press, 1995, pp. 55–6; B. Vandervort, *Wars of Imperial Conquest in Africa, 1830–1914*, Bloomington, Ind., Indiana University Press, 1998, p. 174.

40 D.E. Dumond, *The Machete and the Cross: Campesino Rebellion in Yucatán*, Lincoln, Neb., University of Nebraska Press, 1997, p. 110.

41 Wallace and Hoebel, *The Comanches*, pp. 257–8.

42 Ibid., pp. 258–9.

43 Ibid., pp. 264–5. The dodge of splitting up into smaller and smaller bands to elude pursuers was a classic horse Indian manoeuvre. The Apaches were especially well known for it.

44 Ibid., pp. 265–6. Comanches and Apaches were among the few western Indians with a taste for horseflesh. Some commentators have argued that Apaches were always more interested in eating horses than in riding them.

45 J.K. Mahon, *History of the Second Seminole War, 1835–1842*, Gainesville, Fla., University of Florida Press, 1967, p. 16.

46 Reed, *Caste War of Yucatán*, pp. 36–8.

47 J.R. Swanton, *The Indians of the Southeastern United States*, New York, Greenwood Press, 1969 [1946], p. 694.

48 Wallace and Hoebel, *The Comanches*, p. 253.

49 'An Anonymous Report on Rebel Military Capacity', in T. Ruggeley (ed.), *Maya Wars: Ethnographic Accounts from Nineteenth Century Yucatán*, Norman, Okla., University of Oklahoma Press, 2001, p. 91.

50 P.H. Carlson, *The Plains Indians*, College Station, Tex., Texas A and M University Press, 1998, p. 56.

51 G. Goodwin, *Western Apache Raiding and Warfare*, ed. K.H. Basso, Tucson, Ariz., University of Arizona Press, 1971, pp. 256–7.

52 Callwell, *Small Wars: Their Principles and Practice*, Lincoln, Neb., University of Nebraska Press, 1996 [1896], p. 21. Callwell adds that the term 'small wars' has nothing to do with the scope of the conflicts in question, but rather, for lack of a better term, is used 'to denote . . . operations of regular armies against irregular, or comparatively speaking irregular, forces'. Ibid.

53 Ibid., p. 25.

54 Along these lines, J.G. Dawson, III, in a book review in *The Journal of Military History*, 2004, vol. 68, p. 576, draws an obviously unfavourable distinction between

NOTES

what he calls the 'distant overseas subordinate colonies of the British Empire' in the 1800s and 'the contiguous lands that became co-equal states of the Union' of the USA during the same period. Nonetheless, the kind of defensiveness that prompts rationales of this sort, which confuse end results and process, seems to have faded with the end of the Cold War. Today, Americans seem much less reluctant to use the term 'empire' to describe their nineteenth-century acquisitions or, indeed, to characterise the USA's current relationship with other parts of the world.

55 Callwell, *Small Wars*, pp. 32–3. The 'Kaffirs' the colonel refers to were the Xhosa, Nelson Mandela's people, who lost their lands in South Africa, roughly between the Bushman's and Great Kei rivers, to British troops in a series of wars over the first eight decades of the nineteenth century. The Boers he lists as British opponents were those who took up arms in the First Boer War of 1881.

56 The standard biography of this contentious soldier now is G.R. Adams, *General William S. Harney: Prince of Dragoons*, Lincoln, Neb., University of Nebraska Press, 2001.

57 Surprisingly, it has taken until the new millennium for Crook to find his biographer, in C.M. Robinson, III, *General Crook and the Western Frontier*, Norman, Okla., University of Oklahoma Press, 2001.

58 Callwell, *Small Wars*, p. 72. Or as General Mikhail Skobolev, one of the Russian conquerors of Central Asia in the mid-1800s, put it, in a phrase cited admiringly by Callwell, 'Do not forget that in Asia he is the master who seizes the people pitilessly by the throat and imposes upon their imagination'. Ibid.

59 A thorough but concise summary of the debate over and constraints upon US antebellum Indian-fighting strategy and tactics can be found in Chapter 3 of R.M. Utley's *Frontiersmen in Blue: The United States Army and the Indian, 1848–1865*, New York, Macmillan, 1967.

60 Again, Utley provides the most convenient discussion of the problem, in Chapters 3 and 4 of his *Frontier Regulars*.

61 W.A. DePalo, Jr., *The Mexican National Army, 1822–1852*, College Station, Tex., Texas A and M University Press, 1996, pp. 32–4.

62 Callwell, *Small Wars*, p. 57.

63 Black, *America as Military Power from the American Revolution to the Civil War*, Westport, Conn., Praeger, 2002, p. 75.

64 R.L. Clow, 'Mad Bear: William S. Harney and the Sioux Expedition of 1855–1856', *Nebraska History*, 1980, vol. 61, pp. 143–5.

65 F.P. Prucha, *The Sword of the Republic: the United States Army on the Frontier, 1783–1846*, New York, Macmillan, 1969, pp. 365–8.

66 The US cultural historian Michael Adas, for example, seems breathtakingly oblivious to the French impact on the pre-Civil War US. Ever since the wars with French Canada in the colonial period, he writes, 'the French have been represented in elite discourse and popular culture [in the US] as languid, emotional, politically inept, and incurably sentimental'. Recent US antipathy toward France, as in President Franklin Delano Roosevelt's virulent opposition to French colonial rule in Indochina, he concludes, stems from 'deeply-rooted sentiments and a long history of summary dismissals'. Adas, 'A Colonial War in a Postcolonial Era: The United States' Occupation of Vietnam', in A.W. Daum, L.C. Gardner and W. Mausbacher (eds), *America, the Vietnam War, and the World: Comparative and International Perspectives*, Cambridge, Cambridge University Press, 2003, p. 34.

67 Weigley, *Towards an American Army: Military Thought from Washington to Marshall*, New York, Columbia University Press, 1962, p. 42.

68 Fort McHenry, from whose ramparts the 'Star-Spangled Banner' author Francis Scott Key watched 'the rockets' red glare' and 'bombs bursting in air' during the

NOTES

British assault on Baltimore, Maryland, in 1814, was built by the French military engineer Jean Fontin. The 'damned' torpedoes were launched from Fort Mobile, Alabama, in a vain attempt to stop the Union navy, under the command of Admiral David Farragut, from seizing that key Gulf Coast port in August 1864. Kennedy, *Orders from France: The Americans and the French in a Revolutionary World, 1780–1820*, New York, Knopf, 1989, pp. 10, 458.

69 Weigley, *Towards an American Army*, p. 44.
70 S.T. Ross, *From Flintlock to Rifle: Infantry Tactics, 1740–1866*, London, Frank Cass, 1996 [1979], p. 179.
71 36th Congress, Senate, Ex. Doc. No. 60, *Military Commission to Europe in 1855 and 1856. Report of Major Alfred Mordecai of the Ordnance Department*, Washington, D.C., George Bowman, Printer, 1860, pp. 162, 135.
72 *Military Commission to Europe in 1855 and 1856*, p. 54.
73 Colonel Robert E. Lee was a member of the Napoleon Club while Superintendent at West Point from September 1852 to March 1855, while his future Civil War adversary, General George McClellan, attended meetings of the Club while a West Point cadet in the 1840s. Ross, *From Flintlock to Rifle*, pp. 179–81.
74 Scott to Secretary of War Charles M. Conrad, 30 November 1850, *Annual Report of the Secretary of War, House Executive Document 1*, serial 595, pp. 114–15. Quoted in D. Ball, *Army Regulars on the Western Frontier, 1848–1861*, Norman, Okla., University of Oklahoma Press, 2001, p. xx. Emphasis in original.
75 Wormser, *The Yellowlegs: The Story of the United States Cavalry*, Garden City, N.Y., Doubleday and Co., 1966, p. x.
76 Mahan, *An Elementary Treatise on Advanced-Guard, Out-Post, and Detachment Service of Troops, and the Manner of Posting and Handling Them in Presence of an Enemy. With a Historical Sketch of the Rise and Progress of Tactics, &c., &c.*, New York, John Wiley, 1864 [1847], pp. 43–6. Quoted in R. Weigley, *Towards an American Army*, p. 48.
77 J.S. Hutchins, 'Mounted Riflemen: Real Role of Cavalry in [the North American] Indian Wars', in K.R. Toole *et al.* (eds), *Probing the American West: Papers from the Santa Fe Conference*, Santa Fe, N.Mex., Museum of New Mexico Press, 1962.
78 P. Kearny, *Service with the French Troops in Africa*, New York, n.p., 1844, p. 32.
79 Worcester, *The Apaches*, p. 62.
80 Kip, *Indian War in the Pacific Northwest: The Journal of Lieutenant Lawrence Kip*, Lincoln, Neb., University of Nebraska Press, 1999 [1859], pp. 57–8. To be fair, the infantry didn't do any better when they passed the halted dragoons to take up the pursuit. '[T]he men were so totally exhausted', wrote Kip, 'that many had fallen out of the ranks, and Captain [Erasmus D.] Keyes was obliged to order a short halt to let them come up.' By this time, of course, the Indians were long gone. Ibid., p. 58.
81 Utley, *Frontiersmen in Blue*, p. 332. Starvation also stalked the men of the lost columns. As horses dropped dead, observed one of their commanders, 'if they happened to be in good flesh 20 men would pounce on them and in less time than I can tell it [their] bones would be stripped and devoured raw'. Ibid., p. 330.
82 Callwell, *Small Wars*, p. 404.
83 J.W. De Peyster, *Personal and Military History of Philip Kearny, Major-General United States Volunteers*, Elizabeth, N.J., Palmer and Co., 1870, p. 45.
84 T. Kearny, *General Philip Kearny, Battle Soldier of Five Wars*, New York, G.P. Putnam's Sons, 1937, pp. 47–9.
85 Ibid., pp. 56, 63–6.
86 R. Holmes, 'Murat, Marshal Prince Joachim, King of Naples (1767–1815)', in Holmes (ed.), *The Oxford Companion to Military History*, Oxford, Oxford University Press, 2001, p. 607. The authoritative summary of Murat's life and career is in the *Dictionary of the Napoleonic Wars*, New York, Simon and Schuster, 1993 [1979], pp. 294–5, by the great Napoleonic scholar, D.G. Chandler.

NOTES

87 'Murat, Prince Joachim', in J. Keegan and A. Wheatcroft (eds), *Who's Who in Military History from 1453 to the Present Day*, London, Routledge, 1996 [1976], p. 213.
88 Hutton, 'From Little Big Horn to Little Big Man: The Changing Image of a Western Hero in Popular Culture', in Hutton (ed.), *The Custer Reader*, Lincoln, Neb., University of Nebraska Press, 1992, p. 396.
89 C.J. Brill, *Custer, Black Kettle, and the Fight on the Washita*, Norman, Okla., University of Oklahoma Press, 2001 [1938], p. 35. Brill believed (ibid., p. 36) that Custer was really describing himself in his eulogy to Kearny. Unfortunately, Brill does not cite the source of Custer's remarks and I have been unable to locate it.
90 R.M. Utley, *Cavalier in Buckskin: George Armstrong Custer and the Western Military Frontier*, rev. edn, Norman, Okla., University of Oklahoma Press, 2001 [1998], pp. 18–19.
91 Brill, *Custer, Black Kettle, and the Fight on the Washita*, p. 40.
92 Marcy, *Thirty Years of Army Life on the Border*, Philadelphia, J.B. Lippincott, 1963 [1866], p. 49.
93 E. Bryant, *What I Saw in California: Being the Journal of a Tour of the Emigrant Route and South Pass of the Rocky Mountains, across the Continent of North America*, New York, D. Appleton, 1848, p. 98. Quoted in H.N. Smith, *Virgin Land: The American West as Symbol and Myth*, Cambridge, Mass., Harvard University Press, 1950, p. 177n.
94 Benton, *Thirty Years View; or, A History of the Working of the American Government for Thirty Years, from 1820 to 1850*, 2 vols., New York, D. Appleton, 1854–6, vol. 1, p. 4. Quoted in Smith, *Virgin Land*, p. 177n.
95 Kearny, *General Philip Kearny*, p. 66.
96 Quoted in D. Porch, 'Bugeaud, Gallieni, Lyautey', in P. Paret (ed.), *Makers of Modern Strategy: from Machiavelli to the Nuclear Age*, Princeton, N.J., Princeton University Press, 1986, p. 380.
97 D. Morton, *A Military History of Canada: From Champlain to Kosovo*, 4th edn, Toronto, McClelland and Stewart, 1999 [1985], p. 71.
98 Ibid., p. 85.
99 Ibid., p. 93.
100 On the slow growth of military professionalism in Canada and the corresponding long life of the militia tradition, see S.J. Harris, *Canadian Brass: The Making of a Professional Army, 1860–1939*, Toronto, University of Toronto Press, 1988.
101 DePalo, *The Mexican National Army, 1822–1852*, pp. 30–1.
102 Ibid., p. 32.
103 M. Tinker Salas, *In the Shadow of the Eagles: Sonora and the Transformation of the Border during the Porfiriato*, Berkeley, Calif., University of California Press, 1997, pp. 72, 74–5.
104 These Indian allies often operated in conjunction with local Mexican militia units and, on occasion, managed to mount large expeditions against enemy raiders. D.J. Weber, *The Mexican Frontier, 1821–1846: The American Southwest under Mexico*, Albuquerque, N.Mex., University of New Mexico Press, 1982, pp. 117–20.

3 WORLD VIEWS AND FIGHTING FAITHS

1 Clausewitz, *On War*, ed. and trans. M. Howard and P. Paret, Princeton, N.J., Princeton University Press, 1976, p. 605.
2 J.W. Martin, *Sacred Revolt: The Muskogees' Struggle for a New World*, Boston, Mass., Beacon Press, 1991, p. 127. Ethnohistorians and anthropologists call the Creeks

NOTES

'Muskogees' or 'Muscogulge', a reference to the language group to which most members of the Creek confederation belonged.

3 J. Sugden, *The Shawnee in Tecumseh's Time*, Nortorf, Germany, Abhandlungen der Voelkerkundlichen Arbeitsgemeinschaft, 1990, p. 13.

4 E. Wallace and E.A. Hoebel, *The Comanches, Lords of the South Plains*, Norman, Okla., University of Oklahoma Press, 1958 [1952], pp. 185–6, 188.

5 R.H. Lowie, *Indians of the Plains*, New York, McGraw-Hill, 1954, p. 160.

6 W.G. McLoughlin, *Revivals, Awakenings, and Reform: An Essay on Religion and Social Change in America, 1607–1977*, Chicago, Ill., University of Chicago Press, 1978.

7 Wallace, 'Revitalization Movements: Some Theoretical Considerations for their Comparative Study', *American Anthropologist*, 1956, vol. 58, p. 265.

8 Ibid., p. 267.

9 [P.R. Metcalf], 'Tenskwatawa ("the Shawnee Prophet")', in H.R. Lamar (ed.), *The New Encyclopedia of the American West*, New Haven, Conn., Yale University Press, 1998, p. 1100.

10 Sugden, *The Shawnee in Tecumseh's Time*, p. 17.

11 Kiernan, *Colonial Empires and Armies, 1815–1960*, Montreal and Kingston, McGill-Queen's University Press, 1998 [1982], p. 152.

12 J.A. Carpenter, *Sword and Olive Branch: Oliver Otis Howard*, New York, Fordham University Press, 1999, pp. 24–5. While this kind of virulence is no more than one would expect from the notoriously dissolute Hooker, Carpenter is probably right in saying that Howard's 'associates found it difficult to believe that a man who was so religious could possibly be a soldier' and that 'In that day, as this, the army was not the place where one normally sought or found opponents of liquor and intemperate language'. Ibid., p. 25.

13 J. Morris, *Heaven's Command: An Imperial Progress*, New York, Harcourt Brace Jovanovich, 1980 [1973], p. 352, notes the presence of large numbers of Ontario Orangemen under Anglo-Irish command in the 1870 expedition to the Red River Colony: 'congenitally anti-French and pro-Empire'. Anti-French and anti-Catholic sentiment again burst to the surface during the North-West Rebellion in 1885, again mainly in Ontario Province. Within the army itself, Orangism had much less of a purchase in the ranks than in 1870, but there was suspicion amongst the officers of the reliability of French Canadian troops. D. Morton, *The Last War Drum: The North West Campaign of 1885*, Toronto, Hakkert, 1972, pp. 112, 136–7, 158–9.

14 Carpenter, *Sword and Olive Branch*, pp. 24–5.

15 C.J. Sierra, *Los Indios de la frontera (Mexico–Estados Unidos)*, Mexico, Ediciones de la Muralla, 1980, p. 9.

16 D. J Weber, *The Mexican Frontier, 1821–1846: The American Southwest under Mexico*, Albuquerque, N.Mex., University of New Mexico Press, 1982, pp. 103–5.

17 R.J. Surtees, 'Canadian Indian Policies', in W.C. Sturtevant (ed.), *Handbook of North American Indians*, Washington, D.C., Smithsonian Institution, 1978–86, pp. 90–1.

18 T.R. Fehrenbach, *Comanches: The Destruction of a People*, New York, Knopf, 1974, p. 11.

19 W.E. Washburn, 'Introduction', *History of Indian–White Relations*, Washington, D.C., Smithsonian Institution Press, 1988, pp. 2–3.

20 The definition of 'doctrine' used here has been borrowed from Andrew Birtle. In his important book, *US Army Counterinsurgency and Contingency Operations Doctrine, 1860–1941*, Washington, D.C., US Army, Center of Military History, 1998, p. 5, Birtle writes that doctrine 'is that body of knowledge disseminated through officially approved publications, school curriculums, and textbooks that represents an army's approach to war and the conduct of military operations'.

NOTES

21 Weigley, 'Reflections on "Lessons" from Vietnam', in P. Braestrup (ed.), *Vietnam as History: Ten Years after the Paris Peace Accords*, Washington, D.C., University Press of America and Woodrow Wilson International Center for Scholars, 1984, p. 116.
22 Weigley, *History of the United States Army*, New York, Macmillan, 1967, p. 161.
23 Simmons, 'The Indian Wars and US Military Thought, 1865–1890', *Parameters*, 1992, vol. 22, pp. 60–1, 66–7.
24 Cooper, 'The [US] Army's Search for a Mission, 1865–1900', in K.J. Hagan and W.R. Roberts (eds), *Against All Enemies: Interpretations of American Military History from Colonial Times to the Present*, New York, Greenwood Press, 1986, pp. 173, 188.
25 *Parameters*, 1983, vol. 13, pp. 59–68. Quote comes from p. 62.
26 Chet, *Conquering the American Wilderness: The Triumph of European Warfare in the Colonial Northeast*, Amherst, Mass., University of Massachusetts Press, 2003, p. 143.
27 Birtle, *US Army Counterinsurgency and Contingency Operations Doctrine*, pp. 5–6.
28 M. Cunliffe, *The Age of Expansion, 1848–1917*, Springfield, Mass., G. and C. Merriam, 1974, p. 283.
29 R. Horsman, 'Scientific Racism and the American Indian in the Mid-Nineteenth Century', *American Quarterly* (1975), vol. 27, pp. 152–68.
30 Ibid., pp. 159–60, 162. A leading proponent of the thesis of genetic determinism in US government circles was Joel R. Poinsett, the South Carolinian who became Secretary of War in the cabinet of President Martin Van Buren (1837–41). Poinsett believed that 'only racial interbreeding could change the nature of the Indian'. Ibid., p. 155, n. 14.
31 J.R. Miller, *Skyscrapers Hide the Heavens: A History of Indian–White Relations in Canada*, 3rd edn, Toronto, University of Toronto Press, 2000 [1989], p. 122.
32 Skelton, *An American Profession of Arms: The Army Officer Corps, 1784–1861*, Lawrence, Kans., University Press of Kansas, 1992, p. 318. See also Skelton, 'Army Officers' Attitudes Toward Indians, 1830–1860', *Pacific Northwest Quarterly*, 1976, vol. 67, pp. 113–24.
33 Smith, *The View from Officers' Row: Army Perceptions of Western Indians*, Tucson, Ariz., University of Arizona Press, 1990, pp. 182–4.
34 C.M. Robinson, III, *General Crook and the Western Frontier*, Norman, Okla., University of Oklahoma Press, 2001, p. 270.
35 Skelton, 'Army Officers' Attitudes Toward Indians', p. 122.
36 D. Thrapp, *The Conquest of Apachería*, Norman, Okla., University of Oklahoma Press, 1967, p. 155. Schuyler was known as one of 'Crook's bloodhounds' for his relentless pursuit of Apache 'hostiles'. Robinson, *General Crook and the Western Frontier*, p. 124. Schuyler ended his career in relative comfort, as a colonel in the 'Pineapple Army' in Hawaii. E.M. Coffman, *The Regulars: The American Army, 1898–1941*, Cambridge, Mass., Harvard University Press, 2004, pp. 33–4.
37 Bandel, *Frontier Life in the [US] Army, 1854–1861*, trans. O. Bandel and R. Jente, Glendale, Calif., Arthur H. Clark, 1932, p. 252. Diary entry for 15 January 1859. Bandel participated as an infantryman in the battle of Ash Hollow against the Brulé Sioux and approved highly of General Harney's brutal treatment of them. In a diary entry for 3 September 1857, he wrote: 'Today two years ago we had the fight with the Sioux near Ash Hollow. I shall remember that day as long as I live'. Ibid., p. 185.
38 Rickey, *Forty Miles a Day on Beans and Hay: The Enlisted Soldier Fighting the Indian Wars*, Norman, Okla., University of Oklahoma Press, 1963, pp. 225–38. According to Rickey, the troopers of the Seventh Cavalry, half of whose number had perished with Custer at the battle of the Little Bighorn, were the most entrenched 'Indian haters' in the frontier army. Ibid., pp. 230–1.
39 The principles on which the new Mexican constitution was based were drawn from the abortive Spanish liberal constitution of 1812.

NOTES

40 C.A. Hale, *Mexican Liberalism in the Age of Mora, 1821–1853*, New Haven, Conn., Yale University Press, 1968, p. 217.
41 P.H. Ezell, 'Indians under the Law: Mexico, 1821–1847', *America Indígena*, 1953, vol. 15, p. 211.
42 Hale, *Mexican Liberalism*, p. 221. This view was particularly clearly articulated by Hale's exemplar of Mexican liberal thought, the influential ideologue José María Luis Mora.
43 Zavala, *Ensayo historico de las revoluciones de Megico desde 1808 hasta 1830*, 2 vols, Paris, Imprimerie de P. Dupont et G. Laguionie, 1831–32, vol. 1, p. 387; pp. 335–36. Quoted in Hale, *Mexican Liberalism*, pp. 221, 234. Zavala, who had served as a Mexican government land agent in Texas in the 1820s, was perhaps the most prominent member of the small group of Mexican liberals who believed that the USA was the great hope of liberalism in the Western Hemisphere. He supported the *norteamericano* revolt of 1835–6 in Texas against his own countrymen but presumably 'died in despair' while serving as vice-president of the new Texas Republic. T.R. Fehrenbach, *Fire and Blood: A History of Mexico*, New York, DaCapo, 1995 [1983], p. 382.
44 E. Hu-DeHart, *Yaqui Resistance and Survival: the Struggle for Land and Autonomy, 1821–1910*, Madison, University of Wisconsin Press, 1984, p. 19.

4 CHIEFS AND WARRIORS

1 Using the term 'warrior' to describe modern-day soldiers, as seems to be the fashion these days in military circles, has an anachronistic ring to it, since not many of today's troopers are ever likely to close with an enemy in hand-to-hand combat, but the word still retained some meaning in the nineteenth century, when the chances of being done to death by a knife, tomahawk, lance, machete or bayonet were still very real.
2 K.M. Buchanan, *Apache Women Warriors*, El Paso, Tex., Texas Western Press, 1986, p. 1.
3 Yellow Haired Woman's story was collected by the great anthropologist and historian of the Cheyennes, George Bird Grinnell, in a 1908 interview. R.G. Thomas, 'Daughters of the Lance: Native American Women Warriors', *Journal of the Indian Wars*, 2000, vol. 1, p. 147.
4 Other Magpie's exploits were recounted to anthropologist Frank Linderman by Crow chief Pretty Shield, who also drew attention to her gendered audience. Thomas, 'Daughters of the Lance', pp. 150–1.
5 S. Lang, '[Indian] Women Warriors', in D.J. Wishart (ed.), *Encyclopedia of the Great Plains*, Lincoln, Neb., University of Nebraska Press, 2004, pp. 341–2.
6 Goodwin, *Western Apache Raiding and Warfare*, ed. K.H. Basso, Tucson, Ariz., University of Arizona Press, 1971, p. 235.
7 P. Nabokov, *Two Leggings: the Making of a Crow Warrior*, New York, Thomas Crowell and Co., 1967, p. 34.
8 R.B. Hassrick, *The Sioux: Life and Customs of a Warrior Society*, Norman, Okla., University of Oklahoma Press, 1956, pp. 90–1.
9 R.H. Lowie, *Indians of the Plains*, New York, McGraw-Hill, 1954, p. 108.
10 A. McGinnis, 'Strike and Retreat: Intertribal Warfare and the Powder River War, 1865–1868', *Montana: the Magazine of Western History*, 1980, vol. 30, p. 35.
11 Nabokov, *Two Leggings*, pp. 25–6.
12 Ibid., photo and caption between pp. 98 and 99.
13 E. Wallace and E.A. Hoebel, *The Comanches: Lords of the South Plains*, Norman, Okla., University of Oklahoma Press, 1958, pp. 210–11, 216.

NOTES

14 K.E.H. Braund, *Deerskins and Duffels: the Creek Indian Trade with Colonial America, 1685–1815*, Lincoln, Neb., University of Nebraska Press, 1993, pp. 7–8.
15 Braund, *Deerskins and Duffels*, p. 21.
16 L.L. Milfort, *Memoirs or a Quick Glance at My Various Travels and My Sojourn in the Creek Nation*, Savannah, Ga., Beehive Press, 1979, p. 81.
17 J. Sugden, *The Shawnee in Tecumseh's Time*, Nortorf, Germany, Abhandlungen der Voelkerundlichen Arbeitsgemeinschaft, 1990, pp. 56–8. The Shawnees also liked to launch dawn attacks on enemy camps or settlements, accompanied by unnerving yells.
18 Wallace and Hoebel, *The Comanches*, p. 250.
19 Ibid., p. 255.
20 Ibid., pp. 257–8.
21 E. Hu-DeHart, *Yaqui Resistance and Survival: The Struggle for Land and Autonomy, 1821–1910*, Madison, Wis., University of Wisconsin Press, 1984, pp. 47, 116–17.
22 'A Second Anonymous Report on Rebel Military Capacity', in T. Rugeley (ed.), *Maya Wars: Ethnographic Accounts from Nineteenth Century Yucatán*, Norman, Okla., University of Oklahoma Press, 2001, p. 96.
23 'An Anonymous Report on Rebel Military Capacity', in Rugeley (ed.), *Maya Wars*, p. 92.
24 W.C. Meadows, *Kiowa, Apache, and Comanche Military Societies: Enduring Veterans, 1800 to the Present*, Austin, Tex., University of Texas Press, 1999, pp. 8–9. A main function of Meadows's book is to demonstrate how participation of tribesmen in the United States's recent wars has enabled the Plains Indian military societies to 'endure'.
25 Ibid., pp. 4–5.
26 E.H. Spicer, *Cycles of Conquest: The Impact of Spain, Mexico, and the United States on the Indians of the Southwest, 1533–1960*, Tucson, Ariz., University of Arizona Press, 1970 [1962], p. 511.
27 A. Villa Rojas, *The Maya of East Central Quintana Roo*, Washington, D.C., Carnegie Institution, 1945, pp. 23–4.
28 Meadows, *Enduring Veterans*, p. 9.
29 J.H. Monnett, *The Battle of Beecher Island and the Indian War of 1867–1869*, Niwot, Colo., University Press of Colorado, 1992, pp. 40–1. See also J. Afton, D.F. Halaas and A.E. Masich, *Cheyenne Dog Soldiers: A Ledgerbook History of Coups and Combat*, Boulder and Denver, Colo., University Press of Colorado and Historical Society of Colorado, 1997, p. xvii.
30 D.J. Berthrong, *The Southern Cheyennes*, Norman, Okla., University of Oklahoma Press, 1963, pp. 68–9.
31 J.A. Greene, *Washita: The US Army and the Southern Cheyennes, 1867–1869*, Norman, Okla., University of Oklahoma Press, 2004, pp. 26–7.
32 J.H. Monnett, 'Summit Springs, Battle of', in D.J. Wishart (ed.), *Encyclopedia of the Great Plains*, Lincoln, Neb., University of Nebraska Press, 2004, p. 838.
33 Johnson, *Winfield Scott: The Quest for Military Glory*, Lawrence, Kans., University Press of Kansas, 1998, p. 71. Scott's reputation would have sunk even lower in the public estimation had it been widely known that he spent part of his time in Paris on a fact-finding mission in 1815–16 studying 'the techniques of military tailoring and French gourmet cooking'. Ibid.
34 This is not far from Tony Simpson's characterisation of the nineteenth-century British army as 'scum led by fools'. Simpson, *Te riri pakeha. The White Man's Anger*, Auckland, N.Z., Hodder and Stoughton, 1986 [1979], p. 75. Senator Benton's quip was made on the floor of Congress on 27 February 1855, in the course of a debate in which he went on to assert that 'the Indian wars will have to be ended, as others have

been, by citizen rangers and volunteers'. Quoted in R.M. Utley, *Frontiersmen in Blue: The United States Army and the Indian, 1848–1865*, New York, Macmillan, 1967, p. 14.
35 G.R. Adams, *General William S. Harney: Prince of Dragoons*, Lincoln, Neb., University of Nebraska Press, 2001, p. 74.
36 R. Utley, 'Crook and Miles: Feuding and Fighting on the Indian Frontier', in R. Cowley (ed.), *Experience of War: An Anthology of Articles from MHQ: The Quarterly Journal of Military History*, New York, W.W. Norton, 1992, pp. 42–52. The late great US military historian T. Harry Williams detected a historical dichotomy in the US Army officer corps between the egomaniacs and those with the 'common touch'. Williams thought Generals Dwight Eisenhower ('folksy') and Douglas MacArthur ('majestic') epitomised this division. 'The Macs and the Ikes: America's Two Military Traditions', *American Mercury*, 1952, vol. 75, pp. 32–9.
37 Gaines's letter of 6 May 1836 to Secretary of War Joel Poinsett. Quoted in Johnson, *Winfield Scott*, p. 97.
38 J.R. Kelley, 'The Education and Training of Porfirian Officers: Success or Failure?', *Military Affairs*, 1975, vol. 34, p. 126.
39 G.J. Rauch, Jr., 'The Early Career of Victoriano Huerta', *Americas*, 1964, vol. 21, p. 138. Probably the most capable general to surface during the Mexican Revolution of 1910, Huerta showed that he knew a thing or two about guerrilla warfare by putting down the rebellion of Emiliano Zapata in 1911. In 1913, he overthrew the liberal regime of President Francisco Madero, and made himself provisional president of the republic but failed to hang onto power in part because he antagonised the pro-Madero Wilson government in the United States.
40 Kelley, 'The Education and Training of Porfirian Officers', p. 127.
41 Ibid., p. 126.
42 Prior to the 1870s Mexico's military academies never graduated more than twenty or so officers per year. By 1887, however, thanks to encouragement from President Díaz, the Colegio Militar was graduating all the technical officers needed by the army and most of the line officers it required as well. Kelley, ibid., pp. 124–5.
43 For a clear explication of the ideological overtones of the militia vs. regular army debate in Mexico, see P. Santoni's fine essay, 'A Fear of the People: The Civic Militia of Mexico', *Hispanic American Historical Review*, vol. 68, 1988, pp. 269–88.
44 For the more positive view of the role of the National Guard, see P. Garner, *Porfirio Díaz*, London, Longman, 2001; and G. Thomson, 'Popular Aspects of Liberalism in Mexico, 1848–88', *Bulletin of Latin American Research*, 1991, vol. 10, p. 280. M. Carmagnani, *El regreso de los dioses. El proceso de reconstitución de la identitad etníca en Oaxaca siglos XVII y XVIII*, Mexico, Fondo del Cultura Economica, 1988, p. 234, on the other hand, sees the Guard's main function as repression of the Indian population at local level.
45 Don Pedro Acereto managed to lead an expedition into an ambush in 1860 which cost the lives of most of its 2,000 men. In 1865, a 500-man force led by Colonel Francisco Canton extricated itself from an ambush only by leaving behind all its artillery, baggage and wounded. 'An Anonymous Report on Rebel Military Capacity', in Rugeley (ed.), *Maya Wars*, pp. 93, n. 5 and 94, n. 6.
46 Some writers believe Keogh was the last man to die on the Little Bighorn battlefield and thus the soldier Indian warriors later remembered as 'The Bravest Man the Sioux Ever Fought'. Some of the enlisted men who served under the hard-drinking Keogh, however, chose to remember him as the 'insolent, drunken brute' who lashed out at them with his silver-headed swagger stick when he was in his cups. T. Hatch, *A Custer Companion: A Comprehensive Guide to the Life of George Armstrong Custer and the Plains Indian Wars*, Mechanicsburg, Pa., Stackpole Books, 2002, pp. 205–7.

NOTES

47 Nowlan came upon the site of the massacre with Terry's column the day after the battle occurred and recognised his friend Keogh's horse, Comanche, the only living thing found on the battlefield. Nowlan was responsible for saving the life of the badly wounded horse, which would later become a famous symbol of the 'Last Stand'. Hatch, *The Custer Companion*, pp. 251–2.

48 It was Cooke who scrawled the well-known note to Custer's subordinate Captain Frederick Benteen, imploring him to 'Come on. Big Village. Be Quick. Bring Packs'. This plea to get Benteen to speed much-needed ammunition to Custer's column was carried to the captain by his trumpeter, Private John Martin, born Giovanni Martini in Italy, who was the last person to see Custer and his men alive. Hatch, *The Custer Companion*, pp. 40–2. Lord Dundreary was a character in the popular English play, 'Our American Cousin', that President Abraham Lincoln was watching on the night of his assassination.

49 Hatch, *The Custer Companion*, pp. 232–5.

50 Robinson, *Bad Hand: A Biography of General Ranald S. Mackenzie*, Austin, Tex., State House Press, 1993, p. 337.

51 S. Watson, '"This Thankless . . . Unholy War": Army Officers and Civil–Military Relations in the Second Seminole War', in P.D. Dillard and R.L. Hall (eds), *The Southern Albatross: Race and Ethnicity in the American South*, Macon, Ga., Mercer University Press, 1999, p. 13.

52 J. Morris, *Heaven's Command: An Imperial Progress*, New York, Harcourt Brace Jovanovich, 1980 [1973], p. 371.

53 S. Watson, '"This Thankless . . . Unholy War"', p. 37.

54 G.R. Adams, *General William S. Harney: Prince of Dragoons*, Lincoln, Neb., University of Nebraska Press, 2001, pp. 102–3.

55 The battle of Ash Hollow or Bluewater Creek in Nebraska was fought in September 1855 to punish the Sioux for the massacre a year earlier of Lieutenant John L. Grattan and 30 US soldiers near Ft. Laramie, Wyoming. The Indians had tried to surrender, but Harney had refused and in the ensuing engagement killed over 100 of them. He was later censured by the army commander-in-chief Winfield Scott for 'the killing of women and children that had occurred at Ash Hollow'. J.P. Dunn, Jr., *Massacres of the Mountains: A History of the Indian Wars of the Far West*, Mechanicsburg, Pa., Stackpole Books, 2002 [1886], p. 236.

56 S. Kaufman, *The Pig War: The United States, Britain, and the Balance of Power in the Pacific Northwest, 1846–72*, Lanham, Md., Lexington Books, 2003.

57 In his memoirs Hitchcock characterised Harney as 'ignorant and brutal', a man lacking in 'education, intelligence or humanity'. He was, Hitchcock wrote, the man he held 'in least respect of all the men in the army'. W.A. Croffut (ed.), *Fifty Years in Camp and Field: The Diary of Major-General Ethan Allen Hitchcock, USA*, New York, G.P. Putnam's Sons, 1909, pp. 414, 418.

58 M. Cunliffe, *Soldiers and Civilians: The Martial Spirit in America, 1775–1865*, Boston, Little, Brown and Co., 1986, pp. 119–20. Official figures for 1859 come from 'Statistics of the Army of the United States', *New York Military Gazette*, 15 May 1859, vol. II, p. 151. As Cunliffe suggests in *Soldiers and Civilians*, p. 451, n. 18, many of the so-called 'ex-English soldiers' alluded to in the data were probably actually Irish, given the large number of Hibernians in the British Army at any given time.

59 D. Rickey, Jr., *Forty Miles a Day on Beans and Hay: The Enlisted Soldier Fighting the Indian Wars*, Norman, Okla., University of Oklahoma Press, 1963, pp. 17–18. King, who has been called 'America's Kipling', wrote some 70 novels about the Old Army in the West. His fiction, widely read in its day both in military circles and out, was rooted in personal experience, King having served thirteen years in the frontier army. He retired as a captain in 1879 and was later promoted up the ladder to general

NOTES

in the Wisconsin National Guard. O. Knight, *Life and Manners in the Frontier Army*, Norman, Okla., University of Oklahoma Press, 1978, pp. 8–18.

60 Utley, *Frontiersmen in Blue*, p. xii. No source given.
61 European visitors to the United States took a generally dim view of the 'quality' of the other ranks of the antebellum US Army. F.P. Prucha, 'The United States Army as Viewed by British Travelers, 1825–1860', *Military Affairs*, 1953, vol. 17, pp. 113–24.
62 13 January 1883, p. 526.
63 Knight, *Life and Manners*, p. 222. We have very few detailed portraits of the kinds of soldiers who served in the ranks of the US Army during the Indian wars. One of the exceptions is J.A. Greene, 'Faces of War: Five Soldiers of General Crook's Big Horn and Yellowstone Expedition, 1876', *Nebraska History*, 2002, vol. 83, pp. 198–202.
64 D. Morton, *A Military History of Canada: From Champlain to Kosovo*, 4th edn, Toronto, McClelland and Stewart, 1999 [1985], pp. 94–6.
65 M. Tinker Salas, *In the Shadow of the Eagles: Sonora and the Transformation of the Border during the Porfiriato*, Berkeley, Calif., University of California Press, 1997, p. 70.
66 E.M. Coffman, *The Old Army: A Portrait of the American Army in Peacetime, 1784–1898*, New York, Oxford University Press, 1986, p. 156. Prior to the Civil War, infantry recruits reported to Fort Columbus in Ohio, or Governor's Island in New York, while their cavalry counterparts went to Carlisle Barracks in Pennsylvania and apprentice artillerymen passed through Newport Barracks in Kentucky. After 1865, infantry recruits began to be processed at David's Island near New Rochelle, New York, while cavalry training was shifted west, to Jefferson Barracks near St. Louis, Missouri. Artillery recruits, however, continued to report to Newport Barracks. Ibid., pp. 156–7, 336.
67 Based on 'Jacob Horner of the 7th Cavalry', *North Dakota History*, 1949, vol. 16, pp. 77–9. In Rickey, *Forty Miles a Day*, p. 86, n. 15.
68 Rickey, *Forty Miles a Day*, pp. 99, 101.
69 Lowe, *Five Years a Dragoon ('49 to '54) and Other Adventures on the Great Plains*, 2nd edn, Norman, Okla., University of Oklahoma Press, 1965 [1906], p. 112.
70 Kipling, 'The Young British Soldier', *Barrack-Room Ballads* and *Other Ditties*, London, Methuen, 1973 [1892].
71 One notable exception to this is D. Rickey, who devotes a chapter (pp. 301–36) of his book *Forty Miles a Day*, to the subject of 'Cowardice, Heroism, and the Aftermath of Combat' during the post-1865 Indian wars. Rickey, however, makes no real distinction between the reactions of his Indian-war troopers to 'savage' enemies and those of soldiers then or in more recent times to 'conventional' foes.
72 T. Abler, 'Scalping, Torture, Cannibalism and Rape: An Ethnohistorical Analysis of Conflicting Cultural Values in War', *Anthropologica*, 1992, vol. 34, pp. 3–20.
73 E. Wallace and E.A. Hoebel, *The Comanches: Lords of the South Plains*, Norman, Okla., University of Oklahoma Press, 1958 [1952], p. 253.
74 J. Buchanan, *Jackson's Way: Andrew Jackson and the People of the Western Waters*, New York, John Wiley and Son, 2001, p. 272.
75 R.M. Utley, *The Lance and the Shield: The Life and Times of Sitting Bull*, New York, Henry Holt and Co., 1993, p. 156. The 'driving buffalo' metaphor, 'apt' in Utley's opinion, derives from an interview given in 1909 by Julia Face, an Oglala Sioux woman who had been present at the battle. Ibid., pp. 156 and 363, n. 27.
76 Interview with Lieutenant McDonald in Tucson *Arizona Star*, 2 May 1882, quoted in D. Thrapp, *The Conquest of Apachería*, Norman, Okla., University of Oklahoma Press, 1967, p. 242.
77 M.M. Quaife, 'The Panic of 1862 in Wisconsin', *Wisconsin Magazine of History*, 1920, vol. 4, pp. 166–95. Quoted in R.N. Current, *The History of Wisconsin*, vol. 2,

NOTES

The Civil War Era, 1848–1873, Madison, Wis., State Historical Society of Wisconsin, 1976, pp. 319–20.

78 B. Beal and R. Macleod, *Prairie Fire: The 1885 North-West Rebellion*, Edmonton, Alta., Hurtig, 1984, p. 339.

79 W.H. Leckie, *The Military Conquest of the South Plains*, Norman, Okla., University of Oklahoma Press, 1963, pp. 220–1, n. 21.

80 H.L. Peterson (ed.), *Encyclopedia of Firearms*, 3rd edn, New York, E.P. Dutton, 1967, p. 187. The Kropatschek, as it was known to French soldiers, gave rise to the 8 mm Lebel magazine rifle, the first shoulder weapon in the world to use smokeless powder. The Lebel, which was the standard French infantry rifle in the First World War, began to be issued to troops in 1887. Ibid., p. 302.

81 B. Vandervort, *Wars of Imperial Conquest in Africa, 1830–1914*, Bloomington, Ind., Indiana University Press, 1998, p. 48.

82 R.F. Weigley, *History of the United States Army*, New York, Macmillan, 1967, p. 290.

83 The Maxim gun, which became the standard automatic weapon in European imperial armies, was invented by an American, Hiram Maxim of Maine, but developed and patented in Britain. It was never used to any extent by the US army and, in any case, came along too late for employment in the Indian wars.

84 The term 'quick-firing' refers to the development of recoil-absorbing devices that removed the need to re-aim an artillery piece after each firing.

85 Weigley, *History of the United States Army*, p. 291.

86 Utley, *Frontiersmen in Blue*, p. 27.

87 Ibid., p. 27. The British Army actually developed their own version of the Minié rifled musket, while, as indicated here, the US Army only adopted the Minié ammunition. S.C. Wood, 'Minié Rifle', in R. Holmes (ed.), *The Oxford Companion to Military History*, Oxford, Oxford University Press, 2001, p. 590.

88 Morton, *The Last War Drum: The North West Campaign of 1885*, Toronto, Hakkert, 1972, p. 48.

89 R.H. Caldwell, 'We're making history, eh? An Inquiry into the Events that Occurred near Cut Knife Hill, North West Territories, 1–2 May 1885', in D.E. Graves (ed.), *More Fighting for Canada: Five Battles, 1760–1944*, Toronto, Robin Brass Studio, 2004, pp. 106–7. Drawings of all the weapons described above can be found on p. 107.

90 W.A. DePalo, Jr., *The Mexican National Army, 1822–1852*, College Station, Tex., Texas A and M University Press, 1996, p. 34.

91 D.E. Dumond, *The Machete and the Cross: Campesino Rebellion in Yucatán*, Lincoln, Neb., University of Nebraska Press, 1997, p. 393. For a brief history of use of the 'Brown Bess' in the armed forces of Britain and its colonies, see R. Holmes, *Redcoat: The British Soldier in the Age of Horse and Musket*, New York, W.W. Norton, 2002, p. 12.

92 G. Fuentes, *El ejercito mexicano*, Mexico, Grijalbo, 1983, pp. 210–11; T.A. Janvier, 'The Mexican Army', in Anon., *The Armies of Today: A Description of the Armies of the Leading Nations at the Present Time*, New York, Harper and Bros., 1893, p. 369.

93 Fuentes, *El ejercito Mexicano*, p. 211; D. Gutierrez Santos, *Historia militar de Mexico*, 3 vols., Mexico, Ediciones Ateneo, 1955–61, vol. 3, p. 21.

94 Janvier, 'The Mexican Army', pp. 369–70.

95 J.S. Ford, *Rip Ford's Texas*, ed. S.B. Oates, Austin, Tex., University of Texas Press, 1963, p. xiv.

96 T.W. Kavanagh, *Comanche Political History: An Ethnohistorical Perspective, 1706–1875*, Lincoln, Neb., University of Nebraska Press, 1996, pp. 268–9.

NOTES

97 C. Dabdoub, *Historia de el valle del Yaqui*, Mexico, Libreria Manuel Porrúa, 1904, pp. 130–8, provides detailed coverage of the Mexican reduction of the Yaqui forts.

98 N. Reed, *The Caste War of Yucatán*, Stanford, Calif., Stanford University Press, 1964, p. 240.

99 Gutierrez Santos, *Historia militar de Mexico*, vol. 3, p. 21.

100 There is an extensive account of this encounter in J. C. Cremony, *Life Among the Apaches*, San Francisco, A. Roman and Co., 1868, pp. 157–67. Cremony, who commanded the cavalry at Apache Pass, wrote that an Apache warrior later told him that 66 of his comrades had been killed in the battle, all but three by artillery. 'We would have done well enough', the Apache said, 'if you had not fired wagons at us' (p. 164). Cremony's account is conveniently summarised in Utley, *Frontiersmen in Blue*, p. 250.

101 R.M. Utley, 'Kit Carson and the Adobe Walls Campaign', *The American West*, 1965, vol. 2, pp. 4–11, 73–5.

102 D. Morton, *A Military History of Canada: From Champlain to Kosovo*, 4th edn, Toronto, McClelland and Stewart, 1999, p. 104.

103 For useful brief descriptions of the Gatling gun and its performance, see T.R. Brereton, 'Gatling Gun', in J.W. Chambers, III, (ed.), *Oxford Companion to Military History*, New York, Oxford University Press, 1999, p. 286, and Wood, 'Gatling gun', p. 346.

104 Letter from Miles to General Sherman, 8 July 1876, Sherman Papers, vol. 44, Library of Congress. Quoted in R.M. Utley, *Frontier Regulars: The United States Army and the Indian, 1866–1891*, New York, Macmillan, 1973, p. 73.

105 Rickey, *Forty Miles a Day*, p. 219.

106 Utley, *Frontier Regulars*, p. 73.

107 Roger Ford, a historian of the development of automatic weapons, argues that, had Gatling guns been used more widely in the Indian wars, 'the lives of many American soldiers might have been saved, notably those of General Custer's Seventh Cavalry at the Battle of the Little Big Horn in 1876 . . .'. Ford, *The Grim Reaper: The Machine Gun and Machine Gunners*, New York, Sarpedon, 1996, p. 23.

108 Beal and Macleod, *Prairie Fire*, pp. 238, 243, 247–8. Otter's Gatling was parked alongside the artillery and was almost lost when the Indians launched a sudden attack on the Canadian guns. Ibid., p. 248.

5 THE 'GREAT CLEARANCE', 1815–42

1 Black Hawk and his followers were known as the 'British Band' because many of them had fought alongside the British in the War of 1812. Black Hawk continued to make periodic visits to British Indian Department headquarters in Malden, Ontario during the 1820s in search of support against the 'Long Knives'. R.D. Hurt, *The Indian Frontier, 1763–1846*, Albuquerque, N.Mex., University of New Mexico Press, 2002, p. 179.

2 J. Brannan, *Official Letters of the Military and Naval Officers of the United States during the War with Britain in the Years 1812, 13, 14, 15*, Washington, D.C., Gideon and Way, 1823, p. 236. Quoted in A. Starkey, *European and Native American Warfare, 1675–1815*, Norman, Okla., University of Oklahoma Press, 1998, p. 163.

3 For more on Tecumseh's journey, see J. Sugden, 'Early Pan-Indianism: Tecumseh's Tour of the Indian Country, 1811–1812', *American Indian Quarterly*, 1986, vol. 10, pp. 273–304.

4 See, among others, C.G. Calloway, 'The End of an Era: British–Indian Relations in the Great Lakes Region after the War of 1812', *Michigan Historical Review*, 1986, vol. 12, pp. 1–20. Calloway sees Britain's abandonment of her Indian allies as a result of

preoccupation with the Napoleonic wars in Europe and the pull of more profitable and less troublesome imperial ventures elsewhere.
5 Antal, *A Wampum Denied: Procter's War of 1812*, Ottawa, Carleton University Press, 1997, p. xi.
6 Because the battle was fought on the banks of this river, Americans know it as the battle of the Thames.
7 G.J.W. Urwin, *The United States Cavalry: An Illustrated History, 1776–1944*, 2nd edn, Norman, Okla., University of Oklahoma Press, 2003 [1983], p. 46.
8 Procter's disposition of his troops and Harrison's response are discussed in J.R. Elting, *Amateurs to Arms! A Military History of the War of 1812*, New York, DaCapo, 1995 [1991], pp. 112–13, and D. Morton, *A Military History of Canada: From Champlain to Kosovo*, 4th edn, Toronto, McClelland and Stewart, 1999 [1985], p. 62. For the role of Tecumseh and his Indian contingent in the battle, see J. Sugden, *Tecumseh: A Life*, New York, Henry Holt, 1999 [1997], pp. 369–70.
9 Elting, *Amateurs to Arms*, p. 113; Morton, *Military History of Canada*, p. 62; Sugden, *Tecumseh*, p. 373.
10 J. Sugden, *Tecumseh's Last Stand*, Norman, Okla., University of Oklahoma Press, 1985, pp. 137, 139, 142.
11 At the time of the First Creek War, the region now comprising the state of Alabama was part of Mississippi Territory. Alabama would be organised as a separate territory in 1817 and admitted to the Union as a state two years later.
12 R. Ethridge, *Creek Country: The Creek Indians and Their World*, Chapel Hill, N.C., University of North Carolina Press, 2003, pp. 12–13. For more on the burgeoning 'cotton revolution' in the early nineteenth-century South, see the old but still serviceable U. Phillips, *Life and Labor in the Old South*, New York, Little, Brown, 1929, pp. 21–9.
13 A convenient brief introduction to Creek socio-economic and political structures can be found in K.E.H. Braund, *Deerskins and Duffels: The Creek Indian Trade with Anglo–America, 1685–1815*, Lincoln, Neb., University of Nebraska Press, 1993, pp. 6–21. For a more detailed discussion, see Ethridge, *Creek Country*, pp. 92–119.
14 For a summary of the 'plan for civilisation' and the thinking behind it, see Ethridge, *Creek Country*, pp. 13–15. On Hawkins and the 'plan', see F. Henri, *The Southern Indians and Benjamin Hawkins, 1796–1816*, Norman, Okla., University of Oklahoma Press, 1986.
15 Cotterill, *The Southern Indians: The Story of the Civilized Tribes before Removal*, Norman, Okla., University of Oklahoma Press, 1954, pp. 124–5.
16 Scholarly opinion continues to be divided over the extent to which Hawkins was sincere in his desire to bring 'civilisation' to the Creeks. Some writers have seen his project as largely cynical and a front for a land grab by white settlers. Others have pointed to Hawkins's Enlightenment-inspired outlook and close relationship with Thomas Jefferson as evidence that the Indian agent believed that 'civilisation' would promote assimilation and thus save the Creeks from extinction. These varying points of view are neatly summarised in Ethridge, *Creek Country*, pp. 16–20.
17 J.W. Martin, *Sacred Revolt: The Muskogees' Struggle for a New World*, Boston, Beacon Press, 1991.
18 Ibid., p. 128. Tecumseh's diplomacy *vis-à-vis* the Creeks and his prediction of a powerful earthquake are dealt with in detail in Sugden, 'Early Pan-Indianism', pp. 283–91.
19 Sitting Bull's great prestige amongst his people stemmed from his ability to prophesy. See R.M. Utley, *The Lance and the Shield: The Life and Times of Sitting Bull*, New York, Henry Holt and Co., chapter 3, 'Wichasa Wakan' (holy man).
20 Like many famous Indian prophets and medicine men, Geronimo was said to possess the power to render bullets harmless, but his greatest claims to fame as a spiritual

NOTES

leader were his reputed ability to hold back daylight and to 'see' enemies at great distances. A. Debo, *Geronimo: The Man, His Time, His Place*, Norman, Okla., University of Oklahoma Press, 1976, pp. 38, 145, 170–1.

21 S. Carter, *Aboriginal People and Colonizers of Western Canada to 1900*, Toronto, University of Toronto Press, 1999, p. 141, observes that Big Bear was respected by his people 'for his religious and medical wisdom', as well as his political acumen.

22 Although Stiggins's memoir has since been published in book form, I have used the version, then known simply as the 'Stiggins Narrative', printed in the journal *Ethnohistory* as a tail-wagging-the-dog appendix to T.H. Nunez, Jr.'s piece, 'Creek Nativism and the Creek War of 1813–1814', 1958, vol. 5, nos. 1–3, pp. 1–44; 131–75; 292–301. The book version is entitled *Creek Indian History: A Historical Narrative of the Genealogy, Traditions and Downfall of the Ispocoga or Creek Tribe of Indians*, Birmingham, Ala., Birmingham Public Library, 1989. Although the mixed-blood Stiggins fought on the other side in the First Creek War, as a volunteer in the Mississippi militia, he later married the daughter of William Weatherford, the wartime secular military leader of the Red Sticks. His account of the war was composed in 1836 'through the solicitation of many of my friends', Stiggins wrote (Nunez, 'Creek Nativism', p. 17).

23 High-Head Jim died in January 1813 in battle against Georgia militia at Calabree Creek in eastern Alabama. S.M. O'Brien, *In Bitterness and in Tears: Andrew Jackson's Destruction of the Creeks and Seminoles*, Westport, Conn., Praeger, 2003, p. 127.

24 Nunez, 'Creek Nativism', p. 297. On Francis, see F.L. Owsley, Jr., 'Prophet of War: Josiah Francis and the Creek War', *American Indian Quarterly*, 1985, vol. 9, pp. 273–93.

25 O'Brien, *In Bitterness and in Tears*, pp. 109, 111; D.S. Heidler and J.T. Heidler, *Old Hickory's War: Andrew Jackson and the Quest for Empire*, Mechanicsburg, Pa., Stackpole Books, 1996, pp. 144–5.

26 Nunez, 'Creek Nativism', p. 299.

27 Ibid., pp. 300–1.

28 On Weatherford's life, see B.W. Griffith's comparative study, *McIntosh and Weatherford: Creek Indian Leaders*, Tuscaloosa, Ala., University of Alabama Press, 1988. William McIntosh, a Lower Creek and like Weatherford a mixed-blood, was the key leader of the pro-American Creeks and fought alongside Jackson at Horseshoe Bend.

29 J.M. Keefe, 'McQueen, Peter', in D.S Heidler and J.T. Heidler (eds), *Encyclopedia of the War of 1812*, Annapolis, Md., Naval Institute Press, 2004 [1997], pp. 335–6.

30 O'Brien, *In Bitterness and in Tears*, pp. 149, 228–9.

31 Cornells's insight into Red Stick ideology appears to have been passed on to the US Indian agent Benjamin Hawkins, with whom he was closely associated in implementing the 'plan for civilisation'; in any case, his account formed the basis of a belated warning by Hawkins to Creek chiefs against the seductions of Tecumseh, since become a British ally. Letter of 16 June 1814, in *American State Papers, Indian Affairs*, vol. 1, p. 845. Quoted in Nunez, 'Creek Nativism', p. 14.

32 J.W. Holland, 'Andrew Jackson and the Creek War: Victory at the Horseshoe', *The Alabama Review*, 1968, vol. 21, p. 244.

33 Saunt, *A New Order of Things: Property, Power, and the Transformation of the Creek Indians, 1733–1816*, Cambridge, Cambridge University Press, 1999, pp. 249–59.

34 Hassig, 'Internal Conflict in the Creek War of 1813–1814', *Ethnohistory*, 1974, vol. 21, pp. 251–71.

35 H.S. Halbert and T.H. Ball, *The Creek War of 1813 and 1814*, University, Ala., University of Alabama Press, 1969 [1885], p. 141.

36 It should be noted, however, that civil war had already broken out among the

NOTES

Creeks over the hunting down and killing of eleven warriors charged with the murder in February 1813 of white settlers on the Ohio River and in Tennessee. Hawkins, the Indian agent, had demanded that the pan-tribal Creek executive he had put in place take action against the malefactors. The killing of these warriors in April 1813 brought Red Stick militants into the field and led to the deaths of a number of chiefs thought to be too friendly to the Americans, as well as the destruction of symbols of white 'civilisation' such as cattle, pigs, fowl and looms. J. Buchanan, *Jackson's Way: Andrew Jackson and the People of the Western Waters*, Hoboken, N.J., John Wiley, 2001, pp. 210–12.

37 Ibid., p. 224. The exact number of dead in the massacre will never be known, both because it has never been established exactly how many people were present in the fort at the time of the attack and because the bodies of the victims were frequently so badly dismembered by the Red Sticks that it was impossible for the troops who eventually reached the fort several days after the massacre to make an accurate count. Thus, while Halbert and Hall, *Creek War of 1813 and 1814*, believe 583 persons were in the fort, Buchanan, *Jackson's Way*, puts the figure at 300. I have accepted the lower figure. The account of the Fort Mims massacre which follows is based on Halbert and Hall, *Creek War of 1813 and 1814*, pp. 149–76; Buchanan, *Jackson's Way*, pp. 220–5; and O'Brien, *In Bitterness and in Tears*, pp. 43–8. Also see F.L Owsley, Jr., 'The Fort Mims Massacre', *Alabama Review*, 1971, vol. 24, pp. 192–204.

38 Halbert and Hall, *Creek War of 1813 and 1814*, p. 148.

39 O'Brien, *In Bitterness and in Tears*, p. 46.

40 Martin, *Sacred Revolt*, pp. 156–7.

41 Buchanan, *Jackson's Way*, p. 272. Also see J.A. Reid, 'Prelude to Horseshoe Bend: The Battles of Emuckfaw and Enotochopco (January 1814)', *Journal of the Indian Wars*, 1999, vol. 1, pp. 1–20.

42 The condemned militiaman, 17-year-old John Woods, had been in service one month when the incident occurred. He was charged with mutiny. Woods was the first US serviceman to be executed for violation of the code of military justice since the War for Independence. J. Reid and J.H. Eaton, *The Life of Andrew Jackson*, University, Ala., University of Alabama Press, 1974 [1817], pp. 142–3.

43 These soldiers were not, however, battle-hardened veterans, but recruits from the eastern Tennessee region with less than a year's service under their belts when they marched on the Red Sticks at Horseshoe Bend. As late as January 1814, only about a third of the regiment was armed. Compared to the militia, though, the men of the 39th were well-officered and disciplined. Elting, *Amateurs to Arms*, p. 171.

44 Letter of 23 March 1814 to General Thomas Pinckney, in A. Jackson, *Papers of Andrew Jackson*, vol. 3, ed. H.D. Moser *et al.*, Knoxville, Tenn., University of Tennessee Press, 1980, p. 50. Pinckney, based in Charleston, S.C., was the commander of US troops in the Southeast.

45 Buchanan, *Jackson's Way*, p. 284.

46 J.S. Bassett, (ed.), *Correspondence of Andrew Jackson*, vol. 1: *To April 30, 1814*, Washington, D.C., Carnegie Institution, 1926, pp. 488–9. Jackson's report to Pinckney was contained in a letter written on 28 March 1814, the day after the battle of Horseshoe Bend.

47 Mahon, *The War of 1812*, Gainesville, Fla., University of Florida Press, 1972, p. 243.

48 O'Brien, *In Bitterness and in Tears*, p. 137.

49 W.E. Lee, 'Fortify, Fight, or Flee: Tuscarora and Cherokee Defensive Warfare and Military Culture Adaptation', *Journal of Military History*, 2004, vol. 68, pp. 727, 748–9.

50 S.C. Hahn, *The Invention of the Creek Nation, 1670–1763*, Lincoln, Neb., University of Nebraska Press, 2004, pp. 13–15. For the history of pre- and post-contact

NOTES

fortification techniques among the Indian peoples of the Southeast, see pp. 125–35 of D.E. Jones, *Native North American Armor, Shields, and Fortifications*, Austin, Tex., University of Texas Press, 2004.

51 Letter of 1 April 1814, in Bassett (ed.), *Correspondence of Andrew Jackson*, vol. 1, p. 492.
52 From Jackson's General Order to troops on departure from Fort Williams (24 March 1814), in Bassett (ed.), *Correspondence of Andrew Jackson*, vol. 1, p. 486.
53 Buchanan, *Jackson's Way*, p. 289.
54 Letter to wife Rachel, 5 August 1814, in *Papers of Andrew Jackson*, vol. 3, p. 105.
55 O'Brien, *In Bitterness and in Tears*, p. 152.
56 Buchanan, *Jackson's Way*, p. 291. Two fine recent articles on the Horseshoe Bend battle are T. Kanon, '"A slow, laborious slaughter": The Battle of Horseshoe Bend', *Tennessee Historical Quarterly*, 1999, vol. 58, pp. 2–15; and J.A. Reid, 'The Battle of Horseshoe Bend (March 27, 1814)', *Journal of the Indian Wars*, 1999, vol. 1, pp. 21–9.
57 There is a rather romantic account of this famous encounter on pp. 156–7 of O'Brien's *In Bitterness and in Tears*.
58 This amounted to one-fifth of the territory of the state of Georgia and three-fifths of the future state of Alabama. Buchanan, *Jackson's Way*, p. 300. The slice of Alabama left to the Creeks was described in the treaty as autonomous, but, in practice, it was anything but that as the US was given the right to build roads, trading posts and forts on this 'sovereign' territory. O'Brien, *In Bitterness and in Tears*, p. 162.
59 O'Brien, *In Bitterness and in Tears*, p. 163. For the terms of the Treaty of Fort Jackson, see P. Faber, 'Fort Jackson, Treaty of', in Heidler and Heidler, *Encyclopedia of the War of 1812*, pp. 191–2.
60 Except where indicated otherwise, the information on which this section is based comes from J.D. Heidler and J.T. Heidler, *Old Hickory's War: Andrew Jackson and the Quest for Empire*, Mechanicsburg, Pa., Stackpole Books, 1996, esp. chapters 2–6.
61 J.K. Mahon, *History of the Second Seminole War, 1835–1842*, Gainesville, Fla., University of Florida Press, 1967, p. 19. The imperial component in US policy with respect to Spanish Florida and other European holdings in North America is spelled out in D.S. Heidler, 'The Politics of National Agression: Congress and the First Seminole War', *Journal of the Early Republic*, 1993, vol. 13, pp. 501–30; and R. Horsman, 'The Dimension of an "empire for liberty": Expansionism and Republicanism, 1775–1825', *Journal of the Early Republic*, 1989, vol. 9, pp. 1–20.
62 Mahon, *History of the Second Seminole War*, p. 26.
63 C. Callwell, *Small Wars: Their Principles and Practice*, Lincoln, Neb., University of Nebraska Press, 1996 [1896], p. 25.
64 Arkansas actually became a state during the process of Indian removal, in 1836.
65 The literature on the removal of the Eastern Indians is substantial. Among monographs, an older but still useful account is G. Foreman, *Indian Removal: The Emigration of the Five Civilized Tribes of Indians*, Norman, Okla., University of Oklahoma Press, 1953. The thought and policy decisions behind the removal measures are traced in general but concise terms in R. Horsman, *The Origins of Indian Removal, 1815–1824*, East Lansing, Mich., Michigan State University Press, 1970, and more narrowly in M.D. Green, *The Politics of Indian Removal: Creek Government and Society in Crisis*, Lincoln, Neb., University of Nebraska Press, 1982. T. Perdue has described the process of removal in 'The Trail of Tears: Removal of the Southern Indians', in P. Weeks (ed.), *The American Indian Experience: A Profile, 1524 to the Present*, Arlington Heights, Ill., Forum Press, 1988, pp. 96–117. R.V. Remini explores the less exploitative dimensions to Jackson's removal policy in 'Indian Removal', in Remini, *The Legacy of Andrew Jackson: Essays on Democracy, Indian Removal, and Slavery*, Baton Rouge, La., Louisiana State University Press, 1988, pp.

45–82. An alternative to the 'Trail of Tears' is discussed in J.W. Silver, 'A Counter Proposal to the Indian Removal Policy of Andrew Jackson', *Journal of Mississippi History*, 1942, vol. 4, pp. 207–15.
66 A.F.C. Wallace, *Jefferson and the Indians: The Tragic Fate of the First Americans*, Cambridge, Mass., Harvard University Press, 1999, p. 275.
67 Bassett (ed.), *Correspondence of Andrew Jackson*, vol. 2, pp. 331–2.
68 Hurt, *Indian Frontier*, pp. 138, 140.
69 The Cherokees, Chickasaws, Choctaws, Creeks and Seminoles.
70 Tocqueville, *Democracy in America*, New York, A.A. Knopf, 1945, pp. 339–41.
71 There is a brief account of this hopeless, bloody conflict in the Epilogue, 'An Indiscriminate Slaughter', to O'Brien, *In Bitterness and in Tears*, pp. 235–40. For more, see J.A. Campbell, 'The Creek War of 1836', *Transactions of the Alabama Historical Society*, 1899, vol. 3, pp. 162–6; P.A. Brannon, 'Creek Indian War, 1836–37', *Alabama Historical Quarterly*, 1951, vol. 13, pp. 156–8; and K.L. Valliere, 'The Creek War of 1836, A Military History', *Chronicles of Oklahoma*, 1979–80, vol. 57, pp. 463–85.
72 Peskin, *Winfield Scott and the Profession of Arms*, Kent, Ohio, Kent State University Press, 2003, p. 106.
73 Wool was subsequently court-martialed in September 1837 on charges of 'trampling on the rights of the citizens' of Georgia but was resoundingly exonerated. J.F. Corn, 'Conscience of Duty: General John E. Wool's Dilemma with Cherokee Removal', *Journal of Cherokee Studies*, 1978, vol. 3, pp. 37, 39.
74 Young Burnett was never brought to trial because his superior officer, one Captain George McClellan, came to his defence. J.G. Burnett, 'The Cherokee Removal Through the Eyes of a Private Soldier', *Journal of Cherokee Studies*, 1978, vol. 3, pp. 51–3.
75 Peskin, *Winfield Scott and the Profession of Arms*, p. 106.
76 T.D. Johnson, *Winfield Scott: The Quest for Military Glory*, Lawrence, Kans., University Press of Kansas, 1998, p. 133.
77 Letter of 10 March 1844 to Hugh B. Ewing. Quoted in W.B. Skelton, 'Army Officers' Attitudes Toward Indians, 1830–1860', *Pacific Northwest Quarterly*, 1976, vol. 67, p. 119.
78 J.K. Mahon, 'The Treaty of Moultrie Creek, 1823', *Florida Historical Quarterly*, 1962, vol. 40, pp. 350–72.
79 Fort Gibson, then in Arkansas Territory, was the terminus of the 'Trail of Tears' and the staging area from which Indian emigrants were dispatched to the parcels of land set aside for them in Indian Territory. For more, see G. Foreman, *Fort Gibson: A Brief History*, Norman, Okla., University of Oklahoma Press, 1936, and B. Agnew, *Fort Gibson, Terminal on the Trail of Tears*, Norman, Okla., University of Oklahoma Press, 1980.
80 The background to and terms of the treaties of Payne's Landing and Fort Gibson are dealt with authoritatively in chapter 5 of what remains the standard history of the Seminole–American conflict, Mahon's *History of the Second Seminole War*.
81 Perhaps surprisingly, Osceola seems to have been less favoured by biographers than any major Indian leader of the nineteenth century. There is only one substantial biography, P.R. Wickman's 1991 study, *Osceola's Legacy* (Tuscaloosa, Ala., University of Alabama Press). The *Florida Historical Quarterly* devoted two issues of its volume 33 (January and April 1955) to Osceola; see especially M.F. Boyd, 'Asi-Yaholo or Osceola', pp. 249–305.
82 K.W. Porter, 'The Episode of Osceola's Wife: Fact or Fiction?' *Florida Historical Quarterly*, 1947, vol. 26, pp. 92–8.
83 Mahon, *History of the Second Seminole War*, p. 101.

84 G.E. Buker, *Swamp Sailors: Riverine Warfare in the Everglades, 1835–1842*, Gainesville, Fla., University Presses of Florida, 1975, pp. 4–6.
85 Buker, *Swamp Sailors*, pp. 11, 108. On another occasion, Seminole warriors 'repelled a small [US] naval detachment by turning the white man's cannons on the approaching boats . . .'. Ibid., p. 12.
86 Ibid., p. 12.
87 S.A. Miller, *Coacoochee's Bones: A Seminole Saga*, Lawrence, Kans., University Press of Kansas, 2003, pp. 64–6. Whether or not it was inspired by the Civil Rights movement, as Miller believes, there has been considerable interest in the Black Seminoles of late. Book-length treatments include R. Howard, *Black Seminoles in the Bahamas*, Gainesville, Fla., University Press of Florida, 2002; B.E. Twyman, *The Black Seminole Legacy and North American Politics, 1693–1845*, Washington, D.C., Howard University Press, 1999; P. de Moral, *Tribus olvidadas de Coahuila* [Forgotten tribes of Coahuila], Mexico, Consejo Nacional para la Cultura y las Artes, 1999; D.F. Littlefield, *Africans and Seminoles: From Removal to Emancipation*, Jackson, Miss., University Press of Mississippi, 2001; J.F. Lancaster, *Removal Aftershock: The Seminoles' Struggle to Survive in the West, 1836–1866*, Knoxville, University of Tennessee Press, 1994; K. Mulroy, *Freedom on the Border: The Seminole Maroons in Florida: The Indian Territory – Coahuila and Texas*, Lubbock, Tex., Texas Tech University Press, 1993. Articles on the subject include J.D. Milligan, 'Slave Rebelliousness and the Florida Maroon', *Prologue*, 1974, vol. 6, pp. 4–18; K. Mulroy, 'Ethnogenesis and Ethnohistory of the Seminole Maroons', *Journal of World History*, 1993, vol. 4, pp. 287–305.
88 Buker, *Swamp Sailors*, pp. 35–6.
89 J.W. Covington, *The Seminoles of Florida*, Gainesville, University Press of Florida, 1993, p. 72. In addition, 69 US sailors died during the war, most from disease. Mahon, *Second Seminole War*, p. 325. Finally, 61 of the some 300 US Marines who served in Florida died in the war. E.H. Simmons, *The United States Marines: A History*, 4th edn, Annapolis, Md., Naval Institute Press, 2003 [1974], pp. 38–9.
90 J.R. Motte, *Journey into Wilderness; An Army Surgeon's Account of Life in Camp and Field during the Creek and Seminole Wars, 1836–1838*, ed. J.F. Sunderman, Gainesville, Fla., University of Florida Press, 1953, p. 199. This useful source remained in manuscript until it was edited for publication in 1953.
91 See J.M. Denham, '"Some prefer the Seminoles": Violence and Disorder among Soldiers and Settlers in the Second Seminole War, 1835–1842', *Florida Historical Quarterly*, 1991, vol. 70, pp. 38–54.
92 Prince, *Amidst a Storm of Bullets: The Diary of Lt. Henry Prince in Florida, 1836–1842*, ed. F. Laumer, Tampa, Fla., Tampa University Press, 1998, pp. 121–2. All scholars of the Seminole wars will want to express their gratitude to Frank Laumer for carrying out the painstaking task of transcribing this recently discovered, invaluable primary source and to the University of Tampa Press for publishing it.
93 Quoted in Miller, *Coacoochee's Bones*, p. 65.
94 W.A. Croffut (ed.), *Fifty Years in Camp and Field: Diary of Major General Ethan Allen Hitchcock, U.S.A.*, New York, G.P. Putnam's Sons, 1909, p. 76.
95 S. Watson, '"This Thankless . . . Unholy War": Army Officers and Civil–Military Relations in the Second Seminole War', in P.D. Dillard and R.L. Hall (eds), *The Southern Albatross: Race and Ethnicity in the American South*, Macon, Ga., Mercer University Press, 1999, p. 16.
96 'Florida War, No. 4', 1839, vol. 8, p. 220. Quoted in Watson, '"This Thankless . . . Unholy War"', p. 33.
97 Letter of 14 June 1836 to Secretary of War Lewis Cass. Quoted in Johnson, *Winfield Scott*, p. 121.

NOTES

98 Johnson, *Winfield Scott*, pp. 115–16.
99 J. Missall and M.L. Missall, *The Seminole Wars: America's Longest Indian Conflict*, Gainesville, Fla., University Press of Florida, 2004, pp. 159–60.
100 Mahon, *Second Seminole War*, pp. 214–17. Quote is on p. 217. C.L. Kieffer's *Maligned General: The Biography of Thomas Sidney Jesup*, New York, Presidio Press, 1979, attempts to salvage the general's reputation.
101 Watson, "'This Thankless . . . Unholy War'", p. 10.
102 The authoritative source for this major episode of the Second Seminole War is F. Laumer, *Dade's Last Command*, Gainesville, Fla., University Press of Florida, 1995. Unless otherwise indicated, the account of the massacre which follows is derived from pp. 176–218 of Laumer's book.
103 The accusation against Pacheco seems to have originated with the only soldier survivor of the massacre to leave an account of what happened, Private Ransom Clark. In a 13 March 1836 interview with the *Portland Daily Advertiser* in his native Maine, Clark called Pacheco 'a great scoundrel' and said he was untrustworthy. Quoted in Laumer, *Dade's Last Command*, p. 152. In a statement made some years after the Seminole War ended, Pacheco claimed that as a scout he was operating on the flank of the army column and thus had been closer to where the Seminoles were lying hidden than to the column when the fighting began. He hid behind a tree, he said, but was quickly captured by the Indians. Pacheco claimed that his life was spared by a Seminole chief, Jumper, because he was a slave and thus not responsible for his actions. Pacheco's statement, first recorded in vol. 2 of D.B. McKay's *Pioneer Florida*, Tampa, Fla., Southern Publishing Company, 1959, pp. 480–1, is reproduced in an appendix to Laumer, *Dade's Last Command*, pp. 241–3.
104 Mahon, *Second Seminole War*, p. 106.
105 J.T. Sprague, *The Origins, Progress, and Conclusion of the Florida War*, Tampa, Fla., Tampa University Press, 2000 [1848], pp. 90–1.
106 The Zulu warriors' reminiscences were collected and published by Bertram Mitford in *Through the Zulu Country: Its Battlefields and People*, London, Kegan Paul, 1883, p. 160.
107 On the Zulu 'cow horns' formation, which aimed at achieving envelopment of the enemy, see B. Vandervort, *Wars of Imperial Conquest in Africa, 1830–1914*, Bloomington, Ind., Indiana University Press, 1998, p. 12.
108 Sprague, *Florida War*, p. 91.
109 In addition to Private Ransom Clark, already mentioned, Private John Sprague, although wounded, had managed to hide in a swamp next to the battlefield and straggled into Fort Brooke on New Year's Day. According to Private Clark, the third man to come out of the battle alive, Private Edwin DeCourcy, the son of a British officer in Canada, was later killed on the road to Fort Brooke by a Seminole on horseback. A fourth survivor from Dade's column, although not present at the battle, was Private John Thomas, who had been injured on 25 December and left to make his own way back to the fort. He arrived there four days later. Laumer, *Dade's Last Command*, pp. 99–100; 211–13.
110 T.F. Rodenbough, *From Everglade to Canyon with the Second United States Cavalry*, Norman, Okla., University of Oklahoma Press, 2000 [1875], p. 31.
111 Buker, *Swamp Sailors*, p. 104.
112 Rodenbough, *From Everglade to Canyon*, p. 31.
113 Buker, *Swamp Sailors*, p. 55.
114 Buker, *Swamp Sailors*, p. 110. Also see G.R. Adams, *General William S. Harney, Prince of Dragoons*, Lincoln, Neb., University of Nebraska Press, 2001, pp. 71–2, 75–7.

115 G.H. Preble, 'A Canoe Expedition into the Everglades in 1842', *Tequesta*, 1945, vol. 5, pp. 30–51.
116 Rodenbough, *From Everglade to Canyon*, pp. 58–63.
117 Ibid., p. 63.
118 It is interesting that the first assignment of the intensely devout Howard, fresh out of West Point, was as ordnance officer to our old friend Lt. Colonel Harney, one of the most volatile and profane men in the US Army. Adams, *Prince of Dragoons*, p. 152.
119 Buker, *Swamp Sailors*, p. 139.
120 Adams, *Prince of Dragoons*, p. 153. Adams is wrong about the date of Miles's campaign against the Apaches. It took place in the mid-1880s, some *40 years* after the conclusion of the Second Seminole War.

6 INDIAN WARS IN MEXICO, 1821–76

1 The principles on which the new Mexican constitution was based were drawn from the abortive Spanish liberal constitution of 1812.
2 C.A. Hale, *Mexican Liberalism in the Age of Mora, 1821–1853*, New Haven, Conn., Yale University Press, 1968, p. 217.
3 P.H. Ezell, 'Indians under the Law: Mexico, 1821–1847', *America Indígena*, 1953, vol. 15, p. 211.
4 Hale, *Mexican Liberalism*, p. 221. This view was particularly clearly articulated by Hale's exemplar of Mexican liberal thought, the influential ideologue José María Luis Mora.
5 Zavala, *Ensayo histórico de las revoluciones de Megico desde 1808 hasta 1830*, 2 vols, Paris, Imprimerie de P. Dupont et G. Laguionie, 1831–2, vol. 1, p. 387; pp. 335–6. Quoted in Hale, *Mexican Liberalism*, pp. 221, 234. Zavala, who had served as a Mexican government land agent in Texas in the 1820s, was perhaps the most prominent member of the small group of Mexican liberals who believed that the USA was the great hope of liberalism in the Western Hemisphere. He supported the *norteamericano* revolt of 1835–6 in Texas against his own countrymen but presumably 'died in despair' while serving as vice-president of the new Texas Republic. T.R. Fehrenbach, *Fire and Blood: A History of Mexico*, New York, DaCapo, 1995 [1983], p. 382. For more on Zavala and the other *Tejanos* who supported the Anglo uprising in Texas, see G.O. Coalson, 'Texas Mexicans in the Texas Revolution', in *The American West: Essays in Honor of W. Eugene Hollon*, ed. R. Lora, Toledo, Ohio, University of Toledo Press, 1980, pp. 209–30.
6 E. Hu-DeHart, *Yaqui Resistance and Survival: The Struggle for Land and Autonomy, 1821–1910*, Madison, Wis., University of Wisconsin Press, 1984, p. 19.
7 E.H. Spicer, *The Yaquis: A Cultural History*, Tucson, Ariz., University of Arizona Press, 1980, p. 129.
8 Hu-DeHart, *Yaqui Resistance*, p. 19.
9 C. Radding, 'The Colonial Pact and Changing Ethnic Frontiers in Highland Sonora, 1740–1840', in D.J. Guy and T.E. Sheridan (eds), *Contested Ground: Comparative Frontiers on the Northern and Southern Edges of the Spanish Empire*, Tucson, Ariz., University of Arizona Press, 1998, pp. 52–3.
10 The crucial Jesuit interlude in Yaqui history is treated in great detail in Spicer, *The Yaquis*, pp. 5–59. The isolation imposed by the Jesuits meant that, unlike their counterparts in the new United States, where most Indian warriors had long been familiar with guns, the Yaquis of the new state of Mexico entered the nineteenth century and began their wars of resistance against white encroachment largely

NOTES

innocent of the use of firearms. C. Dabdoub, *Historia de el valle del Yaqui*, Mexico, Librería Manuel Porrúa, 1964, p. 111. As Dabdoub points out, however, the taboo against guns in the Yaqui lands was not a peculiarity of the Jesuit fathers, but rather enforcement of a Spanish policy for the whole of New Spain aimed at keeping guns out of the hands of Indians.

11 Hu-DeHart, *Yaqui Resistance*, p. 24.
12 Fehrenbach, *Fire and Blood*, pp. 319–20.
13 Actually, Banderas need not have appropriated the symbol of the Virgin of Guadalupe from Father Hidalgo. The Virgin was coincidentally the patroness of the military society of the Yaquis. E.H. Spicer, *Cycles of Conquest: The Impact of Spain, Mexico, and the United States on the Indians of the Southwest, 1533–1960*, Tucson, Ariz., University of Arizona Press, 1970 [1962], p. 511.
14 Hu-DeHart, *Yaqui Resistance*, pp. 24–6.
15 R.W.H. Hardy, *Travels in the Interior of Mexico in 1825, 1826, 1827 and 1828*, London, Henry Colborn and Richard Bentley, 1829, pp. 391, 393–4, 395. Quoted in Hu-DeHart, *Yaqui Resistance*, p. 27.
16 Hu-DeHart, *Yaqui Resistance*, p. 28. Of the some 50,000 Yaquis living in Sonora at the time, more than half probably lived outside the Eight Towns.
17 Dabdoub, *Historia de el valle de Yaqui*, pp. 108–9.
18 S. F. Voss, *On the Periphery of Nineteenth Century Mexico: Sonora and Sinaloa, 1810–1877*, Tucson, Ariz., University of Arizona Press, 1982, pp. 52–4, 66.
19 Spicer, *The Yaquis*, p. 130; Dabdoub, *Historia de el valle del Yaqui*, p. 109.
20 Voss, *On the Periphery*, pp. 66–7.
21 Hu-DeHart, *Yaqui Resistance*, pp. 36, 43–4.
22 Voss, *On the Periphery*, pp. 66–7.
23 Hu-DeHart, *Yaqui Resistance*, p. 47.
24 Ibid., pp. 8–10.
25 Some 60 per cent of Indian communally held land in Mexico was divided up as a result of this law. M. Mörner, *Race Mixture in the History of Latin America*, Boston, Mass., Little, Brown, 1967, p. 104.
26 Dabdoub, *Historia de el valle del Yaqui*, pp. 111, 113.
27 Spicer, *The Yaquis*, p. 145.
28 M. Tinker Salas, *In the Shadow of the Eagles: Sonora and the Transformation of the Border during the Porfiriato*, Berkeley, Calif., University of California Press, 1997, p. 61.
29 J. Ridley, *Maximilian and Juárez*, New York, Ticknor and Fields, 1992, p. 187. Ridley erroneously makes Gwin a senator from Mississippi. It would appear that the conduit between Gwin and the Emperor was the latter's illegitimate half-brother and close adviser, the Duc de Morny.
30 J. A. Dabbs, *The French Army in Mexico, 1861–1867: A Study in Military Government*, The Hague, Mouton, 1963, p. 100.
31 For example, Ridley, *Maximilian and Juárez*, p. 187.
32 Hu-DeHart, *Yaqui Resistance*, p. 85.
33 Dabbs, *French Army in Mexico*, p. 100.
34 Dabbs's reference is to the *Tirailleurs sénégalais*, the black light infantry regiments formed in West Africa by the French in the 1850s, elements of which were actually serving in Mexico at the time of the Emperor's decree. At this point in the history of these units, Africans could 'work their way up through the ranks' to NCO rank, but no higher, as all officers were French. B. Vandervort, *Wars of Imperial Conquest in Africa, 1830–1914*, Bloomington, Ind., Indiana University Press, 1998, pp. 82–3.
35 Dabbs, *French Army in Mexico*, pp. 70–1.
36 Ibid., p. 283.
37 Spicer, *The Yaquis*, p. 144.

NOTES

38 Hu-DeHart, *Yaqui Resistance*, p. 89. For a Mexican account of the Bacúm massacre, see F.P. Troncoso, *Las guerras con los tribus Yaqui y Mayo del Estado de Sonora*, Mexico, Tipografía del Departamento del Estado Mayor, 1905, p. 58.
39 A. Wells and G.M. Joseph, *Summer of Discontent, Seasons of Upheaval: Elite Politics and Rural Insurgency in Yucatán, 1876–1915*, Stanford, Calif.: Stanford University Press, 1996, p. 27.
40 R. Redfield and A. Villa Rojas, *Chan Kom: A Maya Village*, Chicago, Ill., University of Chicago Press, 1962, p. 23.
41 This view is generally associated with the work of the US historian Howard F. Cline, in, for example, 'Regionalism and society in Yucatán, 1825–1847: a study of "progressivism" and the origins of the Caste War', *Related Studies in Early Nineteenth Century Yucatecan Social History*, Chicago, Ill., University of Chicago Library, 1950, pt. 5; and the Mexican historians Moíses González Navarro, *Raza y tierra: La guerra de castas y el henequen*, Mexico, El Colegio de Mexico, 1970, and Victor Suárez Molina, 'La Guerra de Castas y el problema de la tierra', *Revista de la Universidad de Yucatán*, 1977, vol.19, pp. 49–55. A definite exception to this trend was Victoria Bricker's *The Indian Christ, the Indian King: The Historic Substrate of Maya Myth and Ritual*, Austin, Tex., University of Texas Press, 1981, which saw the 1847 revolt as just the latest in a number of Mayan attempts to recover the kingdom destroyed by the Spanish conquerors three centuries before.
42 Perhaps the most outspoken advocates of this interpretation have been the US historians Terry Rugeley, *Yucatán's Maya Peasantry and the Origins of Caste War*, Austin, Tex., University of Texas Press, 1996; and Don E. Dumond, *The Machete and the Cross: Campesino Rebellion in Yucatán*, Lincoln, Neb., University of Nebraska Press, 1997. Both historians tend to see the Caste War as a peasant rebellion rather than the 'race war' described by earlier writers.
43 N. Reed, *The Caste War of Yucatán*, Stanford, Calif., Stanford University Press, 1964, p. 46.
44 Dumond, *The Machete and the Cross*, p. 37. As we have seen in the case of the Yaquis, the Mexican authorities tried to continue the Spanish policy of forbidding Indians to own firearms. This policy was never strictly enforced in Yucatán, where it was possible for Mayans to purchase firearms for use in hunting in colonial times. There had been a prohibition against Indian possession of military weapons, but that had lapsed with the 1839–40 war. Reed, *The Caste War*, pp. 45, 46.
45 'An Anonymous Report on Rebel Military Capacity', in T. Rugeley (ed.), *Maya Wars: Ethnographic Accounts from Nineteenth-Century Yucatán*, Norman, Okla., University of Oklahoma Press, 2001, p. 91. The original model for the *ligeros* was the *voltigeur* units of the French revolutionary and Napoleonic armies, lightly armed, mobile skirmishers operating out ahead of the regular infantry to screen its movements or to blunt the advance of enemy troops. The idea for such formations came to the Yucatecans from the Mexican army of the early 1800s. Ibid., p. 91, n. 4.
46 Dumond, *The Machete and the Cross*, pp. 107–8.
47 Reed, *The Caste War*, p. 76.
48 Ibid., p. 61.
49 Ibid., p. 85.
50 Ibid., p. 62.
51 Ibid., p. 73.
52 These comments on the Mayan 'way of war', taken from pp. 145–7 of an anonymous manuscript entitled 'Guerra de Castas en Yucatán: Su origen, sus consecuencías, y su estado actual', have been reliably attributed to General José Severo del Castillo, who commanded Yucatecan troops against the Mayas in the 1860s. See Dumond, *The Machete and the Cross*, p. 109.

NOTES

53 In 1866, a rebel army besieged the garrison town of Tihosuco for 54 days before launching a frontal assault upon it. The attackers were repulsed with the loss of 500 men. 'An Anonymous Report on Rebel Military Capacity', pp. 89–90.
54 Reed, *The Caste War*, pp. 67–8, 83–4, 97.
55 'An Anonymous Report on Rebel Military Capacity', p. 92.
56 The source of these remarks is once again the anonymous manuscript, 'Guerra de Castas en Yucatán: su origen, sus consecuencías, y su estado actual' (pp. 149–51), attributed to General Severo de Castillo. Quoted in Dumond, *The Machete and the Cross*, p. 110.
57 S. Baqueiro, *Ensayo historíco sobre las revoluciones de Yucatán desde el ano de 1840 hasta 1864*, 2 vols, Mérida, Yucatán, Imprenta de Manuel Heredía Arguëlles, 1878–9, vol. 1, pp. 338–9, 341, 349, 430.
58 For Davis's speech, see *Congressional Globe*, 30th Congress, session 1, part 2, app., p. 596. Quoted in R.W. Van Alstyne, *The Rising American Empire*, Chicago, Ill., Quandrangle Books, 1965 [1960], p. 149.
59 Reed, *The Caste War*, pp. 103–4.
60 Ibid., pp. 85–7.
61 Ibid., pp. 89, 287.
62 Ibid., pp. 98–100.
63 Baqueiro, *Ensayo historíco*, vol. 2, p. 4, quoted in Dumond, *The Machete and the Cross*, p. 145.
64 Dumond, *The Machete and the Cross*, p. 158.
65 R. E. May, *Manifest Destiny's Underworld: Filibustering in Antebellum America*, Chapel Hill, N.C., University of North Carolina Press, 2002, p. 14.
66 Reed, *The Caste War*, pp. 110–12.
67 The bravos apparently tried to negotiate absorption into the British colony during these years, but without success. Dumond, *The Machete and the Cross*, pp. 3–4. Yucatecan politicians at the time and Mexican nationalist historians since have seen these overtures as proof that the British were pulling the strings of the rebellion from behind the scenes. In fact, the less than 20,000 inhabitants of British Honduras were terrified of their Mayan neighbours and appear to have sold them guns and ammunition more out of fear than of sympathy with their cause. Ibid., p. 423. This fear was not entirely groundless. In August 1872, a rogue Mayan contingent crossed the frontier and attacked the town of Orange Walk, killing and wounding soldiers of a unit of the West Indian Regiment stationed there to protect local woodcutters. See 'The Battle of Orange Walk, Belize, 1872', in I. Hernon, *Britain's Forgotten Wars: Colonial Campaigns of the 19th Century*, Stroud, Sutton, 2003 [1998], pp. 695–706.
68 A. Villa Rojas, *The Maya of East Central Quintana Roo*, Washington, D.C., Carnegie Institution, 1945, p. 21.
69 A.F.C. Wallace, 'Revitalization Movements', *American Anthropologist*, 1956, vol. 58, p. 265.
70 Linton, 'Nativistic Movements', *American Anthropologist*, 1943, vol. 45, pp. 230–40; Villa Rojas, *Maya of East Central Quintana Roo*, p. 25.
71 Villa Rojas, *Maya of East Central Quintana Roo*, p. 25.
72 Ibid., pp. 21–2.
73 Ibid., pp. 23–4.
74 Dumond, *The Machete and the Cross*, p. 5.
75 The classic account of this controversial policy, a New World equivalent of the contemporary "Red Rubber" scandal that did so much to bring an end to the personal rule of King Leopold of the Belgians in the Congo Free State, is *Barbarous Mexico* by the American muckraker John Kenneth Turner, 2nd edn, Austin, Tex., University of Texas Press, 1969 [1910]. Turner's book, based on an on-the-spot

inquiry into the enslavement of the Yaquis (pp. 1–53), helped undermine once-widespread US public support for Díaz and thus contributed to his overthrow in 1910.

7 WAR ON THE PLAINS, 1848–77

1. Ruxton, *Adventures in Mexico and the Rocky Mountains*, Glorieta, N.Mex., Rio Grande Press, 1973 [1847], pp. 101–2.
2. W.B. Griffen, *Utmost Good Faith: Patterns of Apache–Mexican Hostilities in Northern Chihuahua Border Warfare, 1821–1848*, Albuquerque, N.Mex., University of New Mexico Press, 1988, pp. 137, 140.
3. J.R. Arnold, *Jeff Davis's Own: Cavalry, Comanches, and the Battle for the Texas Frontier*, New York, John Wiley and Sons, 2000, p. 15.
4. D.J. Weber, *The Mexican Frontier, 1821–1846: The American Southwest under Mexico*, Albuquerque, N.Mex., University of New Mexico Press, 1982, p. 87.
5. Washington apparently came to see Article XI as a licence to empty the US Treasury, particularly as it almost totally lacked the means to put a stop to Indian raids into Mexico at this point. A commission set up in 1868 to consider compensation for claims made by Mexican citizens in the 1848–53 period (366 in all) ruled in 1874 that none would be paid. C.H. Harris, III, *A Mexican Family Empire: The Latifundio of the Sanchez Navarros, 1765–1867*, Austin, Tex., University of Texas Press, 1975, pp. 198–9.
6. W.H. Leckie, *The Military Conquest of the Southern Plains*, Norman, Okla., University of Oklahoma Press, 1963, pp. 12–13. The quotation from President Lamar comes from *The Papers of Mirabeau Buonaparte Lamar*, ed. C. Gulick, Jr. and K. Elliott, 6 vols., Austin, Tex., Texas State Library, 1921, vol. 1, pp. 352–3.
7. Leckie, *Military Conquest of the Southern Plains*, p. 14.
8. J.B. Frantz, 'Texas Rangers', in H.R. Lamar (ed.), *The New Encyclopedia of the American West*, New Haven, Conn., Yale University Press, 1998, p. 1106.
9. Quoted in D. Ball, *Army Regulars on the Western Frontier, 1848–1861*, Norman, Okla., University of Oklahoma Press, 2001, p. 18.
10. T.W. Dunlay, *Wolves for the Blue Soldiers: Indian Scouts and Auxiliaries with the United States Army, 1860–90*, Lincoln, Neb., University of Nebraska Press, 1982, p. 21.
11. Dunlay, *Wolves for the Blue Soldiers*, pp. 20–2.
12. R.M. Utley, *Frontier Regulars: The United States Army and the Indian, 1866–1891*, New York, Macmillan, 1973, p. 114.
13. House Executive Documents, 41st Congress, 2nd session, no. 240, pp. 12–13, 98–9. Quoted in Utley, *Frontier Regulars*, pp. 15–16.
14. D.J. Berthrong, *The Southern Cheyennes*, Norman, Okla., University of Oklahoma Press, 1963, p. 272. Stanley would later write of his adventures with Hancock's force in *My Early Travels in America and Asia*, vol. 1, Lincoln, Neb., University of Nebraska Press, 1982 [1895], pp. 3ff.
15. W.S. Nye, *Plains Indian Raiders: The Final Phase of Warfare from the Arkansas to the Red River*, Norman, Okla., University of Oklahoma Press, 1968, p. 68.
16. Nye, *Plains Indian Raiders*, p. 70.
17. Berthrong, *The Southern Cheyennes*, p. 274.
18. Ibid., pp. 274–5.
19. Utley, *Frontier Regulars*, p. 14. Hancock's disposition during this phase of the campaign probably was not helped by the fact that Roman Nose had 'counted coup' on the general by lightly slapping his face with a quirt during the face-off on Pawnee Fork. J.H. Monnett, *The Battle of Beecher Island and the Indian War of 1867–1869*, Niwot, Colo., University Press of Colorado, 1992, p. 39.

NOTES

20 At the head of the detractors was Seventh Cavalry Captain Frederick H. Benteen. Benteen published a letter in a newspaper charging that Custer had abandoned Elliott in order to save his own skin, and refused to withdraw the accusation when Custer challenged him about it. This was the beginning of a feud between the two men that would enliven the small world of the US frontier army up to and beyond the debacle at the Little Bighorn. E.S. Connell, *Son of the Morning Star: Custer and the Little Bighorn*, New York, North Point Press, 1997 [1984], pp. 197–8.

21 The authoritative account of Custer's raid is now J.A. Greene, *Washita: The US Army and the Southern Cheyennes, 1867–1869*, Norman, Okla., University of Oklahoma Press, 2004. Older accounts include C.J. Brill's now dated *Custer, Black Kettle, and the Fight on the Washita*, Norman, Okla., University of Oklahoma Press, 2001 [1938]; L. Kraft's popular *Custer and the Cheyenne: George Armstrong Custer's Winter Campaign on the Southern Plains*, El Segundo, Calif., Upton and Sons, 1995; and S. Hoig's *The Battle of the Washita: The Sheridan–Custer Campaign of 1867–1869*, Garden City, N.Y., Doubleday, 1976.

22 For more on this engagement, see F.H. Werner, *The Summit Springs Battle: July 11, 1869*, Greeley, Colo., Werner Publications, 1991; and J.D. Filipiak, 'The Battle of Summit Springs', *The Colorado Magazine*, 1964, vol. 41, pp. 343–54.

23 The second battle of Adobe Walls has given rise to a respectable body of historical literature. The fullest account is T.B. Baker and B.R. Harrison, *Adobe Walls: The History and Archaeology of the 1874 Trading Post*, College Station, Texas A and M University Press, 2003 [1986]. But, also see G.D. West, 'The Battle of Adobe Walls (1874)', *Panhandle–Plains Historical Review*, 1960, vol. 36, pp. 1–36, and L.J. White, 'New Sources Relating to the Battle of Adobe Walls, 1874', *Texas Military History*, 1970, vol. 8, pp. 1–12. Figures on the size of the Indian war party which attacked the hunters vary greatly, from a low of 200 to a high of 700. J.L. Rodgers, 'Flint and Steel: Background of the Red River War of 1874–1875', *Texas Military History*, 1969, vol. 7, p. 174, n. 57, does not consider the high figure 'implausible'.

24 This is the estimate of J.L. Haley, *The Buffalo War: The History of the Red River Indian Uprising of 1874*, New York, Doubleday, 1976, p. 16.

25 Leckie, *Military Conquest of the Southern Plains*, p. 221.

26 For a particularly vivid account of the locating of the Palo Duro Canyon hideout, see C.M. Robinson, III, *Bad Hand: A Biography of General Ranald S. Mackenzie*, Austin, Tex., State House Press, 1993, pp. 170–2.

27 Nye, *Carbine and Lance: The Story of Old Fort Sill*, Norman, Okla., University of Oklahoma Press, 1937, p. 286.

28 Leckie, *Military Conquest of the Southern Plains*, pp. 220–2; Robinson, *Bad Hand*, pp. 170–8. Nye's account in *Carbine and Lance*, pp. 284–90, includes recollections by Indian participants, interviewed by the author many years afterward on the Fort Sill reservation.

29 The engagement at Sappa Creek, also known as Dark Water Creek, was labelled a massacre by Mari Sandoz in her best-selling book, *Cheyenne Autumn*, New York, Avon Books, 1964, on the grounds that more women and children were killed in the fight than warriors, a fact that Sandoz believed demonstrated genocidal intent on the part of the cavalry. Authors of more recent accounts of the encounter, while also sensitive to the plight of the Cheyennes, have been at some pains to disabuse readers of what they call 'presentism', a tendency to judge historical actors in the past, such as the cavalrymen at Sappa Creek, according to modern-day standards. See W.Y. Chalfant, *Cheyennes at Dark Water Creek: The Last Fight of the Red River War*, Norman, Okla., University of Oklahoma Press, 1997, and J.H. Monnett, *Massacre at Cheyenne Hole: Lieutenant Austin Henely and the Sappa Creek Controversy*, Niwot, Colo., University Press of Colorado, 1999. Henely commanded the Sixth Cavalry detachment at Sappa Creek.

NOTES

30 P. Hedren, *The Massacre of Lieutenant Grattan and his Command by Indians*, Glendale, Calif., Arthur H. Clark, 1983.

31 Callwell, *Small Wars: Their Principles and Practice*, Lincoln, Neb., University of Nebraska Press, 1996 [1896], pp. 27–8.

32 The most recent account of the Ash Hollow battle, R.E. Paul's *Blue Water Creek and the First Sioux War, 1854–1856*, Norman, Okla., University of Oklahoma Press, 2004, sees Harney's campaign of retribution as the opening episode in a drama which crested with Custer's defeat at the Little Bighorn and culminated in the Wounded Knee massacre of 1890. Blue Water Creek is a translation of the Sioux name for the Ash Hollow site.

33 The confused loyalties felt by some of the Santee Sioux are sensitively examined in G.C. Anderson, *Kinsmen of Another Kind: Dakota–White Relations in the Upper Mississippi Valley, 1650–1862*, Lincoln, Neb., University of Nebraska Press, 1984.

34 The Minnesota uprising struck fear into the hearts of white settlers far and wide at the time, as we saw above, and it has continued to attract the attention of historians ever since. A balanced history of the event is K. Carley, *The Sioux Uprising of 1862*, St. Paul, Minn., Minnesota Historical Society, 1976 [1961], but also see C.M. Oehler, *The Great Sioux Uprising*, New York, DaCapo Press, 1997 [1959], and D. Schultz, *Over the Earth I Come: The Great Sioux Uprising of 1862*, New York, St. Martin's Press, 1991. The most significant development in the historiography of the 1862 war in recent years has been the focus on the Indian view of what happened and why. On this, see G.C. Anderson and A.R. Woolworth (eds), *Through Dakota Eyes: Narrative Accounts of the Minnesota Indian War of 1862*, St. Paul, Minn., Minnesota Historical Society, 1988. G.C. Anderson has given us a biography of the Santee Sioux leader, *Little Crow, Spokesman for the Sioux*, St. Paul, Minn., Minnesota Historical Society, 1986.

35 M. Clodfelter, *The Dakota War: The United States Army versus the Sioux, 1862–1865*, Jefferson, N.C., McFarland and Co., 1998, covers these campaigns and much more from the military's point of view.

36 Politicians from the new state (1858) of Minnesota used claims of British support for the Santee Sioux uprising to pressurise the US government to annex the neighbouring province of Manitoba, by purchase if possible or by force if necessary. On this, see A. C. Gluek, *Minnesota and the Manifest Destiny of the Canadian Northwest: A Study in Canadian–American Relations*, Toronto, Toronto University Press, 1965.

37 There is a fine concise summary of the Sand Creek affair on pp. 3–25 of J.A. Greene and D.D. Scott, *Finding Sand Creek: History, Archaeology, and the 1864 Massacre Site*, Norman, Okla., University of Oklahoma Press, 2004, but also see B. Cutler, *The Massacre at Sand Creek*, Norman, Okla., University of Oklahoma Press, 1995; S. Hoig, *The Sand Creek Massacre*, Norman, Okla., University of Oklahoma Press, 1961; D. Schultz, *Month of the Freezing Moon: The Sand Creek Massacre, November 1864*, New York, St. Martin's Press, 1990; and L.J. White, 'From Bloodless to Bloody: The Third Colorado Cavalry and the Sand Creek Massacre', *Journal of the West*, 1967, vol. 6, pp. 535–81.

38 J.H. Monnett, *The Battle of Beecher Island*, pp. 48–9.

39 L.R. Hafen and A.W. Hafen, *Powder River Campaigns and Sawyer's Expedition of 1865*, Glendale, Calif., Arthur H. Clark Co., 1961, provides a detailed overview of this inglorious outing.

40 D. Brown, *The Fetterman Massacre*, Lincoln, Neb., University of Nebraska Press, 1984 [1962].

41 J. Keenan, *The Wagon Box Fight: An Episode of Red Cloud's War*, rev. edn, Conshohocken, Pa., Savas, 2000 [1988].

NOTES

42 Hutton, *Phil Sheridan and His Army*, Norman, Okla., University of Oklahoma Press, 1999 [1985], pp. 327–8.
43 Our dean of small wars theorists, Colonel Callwell, would not have agreed with General Sheridan. Indeed, the whole notion of launching individual columns to converge on an enemy seemed to him to risk being defeated in detail. Custer's defeat on the Little Bighorn, he wrote, 'illustrates the danger of tactical separation'. Callwell, *Small Wars*, 1996, p. 179.
44 Robinson, *General Crook and the Western Frontier*, Norman, Okla., University of Oklahoma Press, 2001, p. 164.
45 For more on this fiasco, see J.W. Vaughan, *The Reynolds Campaign on Powder River*, Norman, Okla., University of Oklahoma Press, 1961. The Indian reaction to Reynolds's attack is given in R.M. Utley, *The Lance and the Shield: The Life and Times of Sitting Bull*, New York, Henry Holt and Co., 1993, pp. 132–3.
46 Bourke, *On the Border With Crook*, Glorieta, N.Mex., Rio Grande Press, 1969 [1891], pp. 261–2.
47 Utley, *The Lance and the Shield*, pp. 136, 138.
48 Ibid., pp. 140–1.
49 C.M. Robinson, III, Crook's biographer, reports that after the battle, 'some of [Crook's] officers' recognized that, whatever Crook may have said, the army had been 'humiliatingly defeated'. Robinson, *General Crook and the Western Frontier*, 2001, p. 184. Andrist, *The Long Death*, p. 266, says that Crook knew in his heart of hearts that he had been defeated and lamented in later life that the Rosebud battle was the only defeat he had ever suffered at the hands of Indians.
50 R.M. Utley, *Cavalier in Buckskin: George Armstrong Custer and the Western Military Frontier*, rev. edn, Norman, Okla., University of Oklahoma Press, 2001 [1988], p. 176.
51 Ibid., p. 163.
52 T. Hatch, *The Custer Companion: A Comprehensive Guide to the Life of George Armstrong Custer and the Plains Indian Wars*, Mechanicsburg, Pa., Stackpole Books, 2002, pp. 85, 177.
53 Porch, *Wars of Empire*, London, Cassell, 2000, p. 103.
54 Indeed, the independent historian C. Lee Noyes has argued that his successful Washita campaign provided Custer with the template for the conduct of operations on the Little Bighorn. Noyes, 'A Tale of Two Battles: George Armstrong Custer and the Attacks at the Washita and the Little Bighorn', *Journal of the Indian Wars*, 1999, vol. 1, pp.5–31.
55 Quoted in Utley, *Cavalier in Buckskin*, p. 190.
56 The narrative which follows relies heavily on the accounts of the battle by Robert Utley in *Cavalier in Buckskin*, pp. 180–93, and the fine summaries of the Little Bighorn engagement in J.D. McDermott, *A Guide to the Indian Wars of the West*, Lincoln, Neb., University of Nebraska Press, 1998, pp. 159–62, and E.I. Stewart, 'Little Big Horn, battle of the (1876)', in H.R. Lamar (ed.), *The New Encyclopedia of the American West*, New Haven, Conn., Yale University Press, 1998, pp. 643–5.
57 Michno, *Lakota Noon: The Indian Narrative of Custer's Defeat*, Missoula, Mont., Montana Press Publishing Co., 1997, p. 18.
58 J.S. Gray, *Centennial Campaign: The Sioux War of 1876*, Ft. Collins, Colo., Old Army Press, 1976, pp. 173–4; Gray, *Custer's Last Campaign: Mitch Boyer and the Little Bighorn Reconstructed*, Lincoln, Neb., University of Nebraska Press, 1991, pp. 271, 275.
59 Gray, *Custer's Last Campaign*, pp. 343, 346.
60 Ibid., p. 357.
61 E.I. Stewart, *Custer's Luck*, Norman, Okla., University of Oklahoma Press, 1955, p. 341.

NOTES

62 Gray, *Custer's Last Campaign*, pp. 360–1, 383–4.
63 The archaeological team reported their findings in 1989. D.D. Scott, R.A. Fox, Jr. and M.A. Connor, *Archaeological Perspectives on the Battle of the Little Bighorn*, Norman, Okla., University of Oklahoma Press, 1989. Fox, who had been the lead archaeologist on the dig, offered a synthesis of the archaeological and historical evidence on the epic battle in *Archaeology, History, and Custer's Last Battle: The Little Bighorn Reexamined*, Norman, Okla., University of Oklahoma Press, 1993.
64 Gray began the process of reconstruction of the battle with his book *Centennial Campaign: The Sioux War of 1876*, Ft. Collins, Colo., Old Army Press, 1976, but brought it to full fruition in his *Custer's Last Campaign: Mitch Boyer and the Little Big Horn Reconstructed*, Lincoln, Neb., University of Nebraska Press, 1991. Boyer was a half-Sioux interpreter and scout who died with Custer's command at the Little Bighorn. Although Gray's book entertainingly reconstructs Boyer's fascinating life, its main value lies in its use of the hitherto disregarded testimony of another of Custer's scouts, the Crow Indian Curly, in verifying the events of the Last Stand. Curly had been told by Custer that he did not need to remain for the coming fight and, along with the other Crow scouts, had left the general's side just before the battle began. He had claimed to have watched it unfold from a nearby hill, however. His testimony generally had been considered suspect until Gray came along, perhaps because he was seen as a coward for not sticking with 'Long Hair'.
65 Michno, *Lakota Noon*, 1997.
66 Quoted in Utley, *Cavalier in Buckskin*, p. 191.
67 John Gray has calculated that the battle lasted exactly 67 minutes, from the first shots fired, on the detachment in Medicine Tail Coulee, until resistance was ended. *Custer's Last Campaign*, pp. 371–2. Robert Utley has given an estimate of two hours for the same sequence of events, *Cavalier in Buckskin*, p. 191. Chief Gall over time offered two different assessments of how long the fight lasted. On one occasion, he said it lasted 'as long as it takes a hungry man to eat his dinner'. Another time, he admitted the battle had taken a half hour. Stewart, *Custer's Luck*, p. 358.
68 According to the British military historian Hew Strachan, the extra ammunition may not have been needed. He claims, though without citing a reference, that Custer and his men 'discharged over 40,000 rounds for 60 Indians killed and 100 wounded'. Strachan, *European Armies and the Conduct of War*, London, George Allen and Unwin, 1983, p. 85.
69 B.A. Clements and A. Mills, 'The Starvation March and the Battle of Slim Buttes', in J.A. Greene (ed.), *Battles and Skirmishes of the Great Sioux War, 1876–1877: The Military View*, Norman, Okla., University of Oklahoma Press, 1993, pp. 96–115.
70 The authoritative account of this and other engagements in the closing phases of the Great Sioux War is J.A. Greene's *Morning Star Dawn: The Powder River Expedition and the Northern Cheyennes*, Norman, Okla., University of Oklahoma Press, 2003. But also see H.H. Bellas, 'The Crook–Mackenzie Campaign and the Dull Knife Battle, November 25, 1876', in Greene (ed.), *Battles and Skirmishes*, pp. 167–86.
71 H.R. Tilton and E. Butler, 'The Wolf Mountains Expedition and the Battle of Wolf Mountains, January 8, 1877', in Greene (ed.), *Battles and Skirmishes*, pp. 186–204.
72 Chapters 15 to 19 of R.M. Utley's biography of Sitting Bull, *The Lance and the Shield*, give copious details of the Sioux leader's years in Canada.
73 This account of the Modoc War has been drawn from the following sources: R. Dillon, *Burnt-out Fires: California's Modoc Indian War*, Englewood Cliffs, N.J., Prentice-Hall, 1973; K.A. Murray, *The Modocs and their War*, Norman, Okla., University of Oklahoma Press, 1959; and Arthur Quinn, *Hell With the Fire Out: A History of the Modoc War*, Boston, Mass., Faber and Faber, 1997.
74 Public sympathy for the Nez Percés, then and now, has assured an audience for a

steady flow of books on their war against the United States. Students will find the following volumes particularly useful: M.H. Brown, *The Flight of the Nez Percé: A History of the Nez Percé War*, New York, G.P. Putnam's Sons, 1967; J.A. Greene, *Nez Percé Summer: The US Army and the Nee-Me-Poo Crisis*, Helena, Mont., Montana Historical Society Press, 2000; B. Hampton, *Children of Grace: The Nez Percé War of 1877*, Lincoln, Neb., University of Nebraska Press, 2002 [1994]; and A. Josephy, Jr, *The Nez Percé Indians and the Opening of the Northwest*, New Haven, Conn., Yale University Press, 1965. (The Nez Percés called themselves the Nee-Me-Poo.)

75 The application of 'overwhelming force' by the army at Wounded Knee is put down to a desire by the troops to avenge the Custer massacre and to cow the Indians into final submission in Dee Brown, *Bury My Heart at Wounded Knee: An Indian History of the American West*, New York, Holt, Rinehart and Winston, 1971.

76 The classic account of the Ghost Dance phenomenon is J. Mooney, *The Ghost-Dance Religion and the Sioux Outbreak of 1890*, Washington, D.C., Smithsonian Institution, 1896, but also see J.W. Martin, 'Before and After the Sioux Ghost Dance: Native American Prophetic Movements and the Study of Religion', *Journal of the American Academy of Religion*, 1991, vol. 59, pp. 677–701.

77 The standard account of the Wounded Knee massacre is R.M. Utley, *The Last Days of the Sioux Nation*, New Haven, Conn., Yale University Press, 1963. The dissenting view, that the massacre was the result of an Army power play, is summed up in J. Ostler, 'Conquest and the State: Why the United States Employed Massive Military Force to Suppress the Lakota Ghost Dance', *Pacific Historical Review*, 1996, vol. 93, pp. 217–48.

8 CONQUEST OF APACHERÍA, 1860–86

1 N. Miles, *Personal Recollections and Observations of General Nelson A. Miles*, New York, Werner, 1897.

2 W.B. Griffen, *Utmost Good Faith: Patterns of Apache–Mexican Hostilities in Northern Chihuahua Border Warfare, 1821–1848*, Albuquerque, N.Mex., University of New Mexico Press, 1988, p. 173.

3 M. Tinker Salas, *In the Shadow of the Eagles: Sonora and the Transformation of the Border during the Porfiriato*, Berkeley, Calif., University of California Press, 1997, p. 62.

4 D.J. Weber, *The Mexican Frontier, 1821–1846: The American Southwest Under Mexico*, Albuquerque, N.Mex., University of New Mexico Press, 1982, p. 87.

5 Crook, *Annual Report of Brigadier General George Crook, US Army, Commanding, Department of Arizona, 1883*, n.d., n.p., pp. 27–8. Quoted in C.M. Robinson, III, *General Crook and the Western Frontier*, Norman, Okla., University of Oklahoma Press, 2001, pp. 262–3.

6 García, *Apuntes sobre la campaña contra los salvajes en el Estado de Sonora por el coronel del 6o batallón de infantería*, Hermosillo, Sonora, Imprenta de Roberto Bernal, 1883, p. 10; Corral, *Obras históricas, No. 1*, Hermosillo, Sonora, Biblioteca Sonorense de Geografía e Histórica, 1959, p. 107.

7 Mowry, *Arizona and Sonora: The Geography, History and Resources of the Silver Region of North America*, New York, Arno Press, 1973 [1864], p. 35. Mowry was an old Arizona hand, having served there as a soldier in 1858. A Confederate sympathiser during the Civil War, he had been allowed to return to the Territory only after the war ended. P. Cozzens (ed.), *Eyewitnesses to the Indian Wars, 1865–1890*, vol. 1, *The Struggle for Apachería*, Mechanicsburg, Pa., Stackpole Books, 2001, p. 653.

8 Quoted in Tinker Salas, *In the Shadow*, p. 64.

9 Thrapp, *The Conquest of Apachería*, Norman, University of Oklahoma Press, 1967, p. 9.

NOTES

10 Griffen, *Utmost Good Faith*, pp. 171–2. James Kirker's career receives surprisingly positive spin in R.A. Smith's *Borderlander: The Life of James Kirker, 1793–1852*, Norman, Okla., University of Oklahoma Press, 2000. The scalp-hunting strategy is treated more succinctly in Smith's 'Scalp Hunting; A Mexican Experiment in Warfare', *Great Plains Journal*, 1984, vol. 23, pp. 41–79.
11 Thrapp, *Conquest of Apachería*, p. 9, n. 9.
12 Tinker Salas, *In the Shadow*, p. 63.
13 Corral, *Obras históricas, No. 1*, p. 85.
14 L. Lejeune, *La guerra Apache en Sonora*, trad. M. Antochiw, Hermosillo, Sonora, Gobierno del Estado de Sonora, 1984, p. 21.
15 Velasco, *Noticias estadísticas del Estado de Sonora, 1850*, Hermosillo, Sonora, Gobierno del Estado, 1985, p. 96. Quoted in Tinker Salas, *In the Shadow*, p. 60, n. 15.
16 Mangas Coloradas's Red Paint People, or Eastern Chiricahua Apaches, are sometimes referred to as Mimbreños because their original homeland was along the Mimbres River in western New Mexico.
17 Wellman, *Death in the Desert*, Lincoln, Neb., University of Nebraska Press, 1987 [1938], p. 57.
18 Sweeney's meticulous survey of the evidence for this legend can be found on pp. 400–6 of his *Mangas Coloradas: Chief of the Chiricahua Apaches*, Norman, Okla., University of Oklahoma Press, 1998. Sweeney has concluded that the source for all subsequent accounts of the whipping is John C. Cremony's book, *Life Among the Apaches*, first published in 1868. A journalist, former soldier and veteran of some of the early engagements with the Chiricahuas, including the Apache Pass battle, Cremony's account had a powerful impact upon subsequent writing on the Apache wars. (His book was reprinted in 1969 by the Rio Grande Press of Glorieta, N.Mex.) Sweeney is nonetheless able to show that 'there is no other primary source material that would validate Cremony's version' of events and concludes that the story of Mangas Coloradas's whipping is 'probably apocryphal' (*Mangas Coloradas*, p. 400).
19 D.C. Cole, *The Chiricahua Apache, 1846–1876: From War to Reservation*, Albuquerque, N.Mex., University of New Mexico Press, 1988, p. 4.
20 Thrapp, *Conquest of Apachería*, p. 24.
21 The authoritative source for this event is R.M. Utley, 'The Bascom Affair: A Reconstruction', *Arizona and the West*, 1961, vol. 3, pp. 59–68.
22 Utley makes it clear that Cochise and his companions, a brother and two nephews and a woman and a small boy, approached the soldiers' camp out of curiosity and did not realise what Bascom wanted when they entered the tent 'for a talk'. A plan had already been laid to seize the group before they arrived; the rancher Ward was the person chosen to give the soldiers the signal to surround the tent. 'Bascom Affair', pp. 61–3.
23 Thrapp, *Conquest of Apachería*, p. 16.
24 The victims included the three men taken prisoner at the time of Cochise's escape and three Coyotero Apaches later caught stealing cattle. The woman and the small boy were freed. Utley, 'Bascom Affair', p. 68.
25 Thrapp, *Conquest of Apachería*, p. 18. The figures come from T.E. Farish, *History of Arizona*, 5 vols, San Francisco, Calif., Filmer Bros., 1915–18, vol. 2, pp. 22–3. Thrapp thinks the figures are too high. Utley, on the other hand, refers to a loss of 'millions of dollars and countless lives . . .'. 'Bascom Affair', p. 59.
26 Thrapp, *Conquest of Apachería*, p. 20.
27 Sweeney, *Mangas Coloradas*, p. 430. Sweeney doesn't include Geronimo among the Apache leaders at the battle, but Thrapp does. *Conquest of Apachería*, p. 23. Angie Debo, Geronimo's biographer, says that although his dictated memoirs give no account of the Apache Pass fight, 'Tradition says that [Geronimo] was there, and it is

NOTES

incredible that he would have failed to participate in an attack so carefully planned and involving his closest associates'. *Geronimo: The Man, His Time, His Place*, Norman, Okla., University of Oklahoma Press, 1976, p. 68.

28 Debo, *Geronimo*, p. 67, puts the number of soldiers at 122.
29 D.E. Worcester, *The Apaches: Eagles of the Southwest*, Norman, Okla., University of Oklahoma Press, 1979, p. 82; R.M. Utley, *Frontiersmen in Blue: The United States Army and the Indian, 1848–1866*, New York, Macmillan, 1967, pp. 250–1.
30 Thrapp, *Conquest of Apachería*, p. 23.
31 Utley, *Frontiersmen in Blue*, p. 251.
32 Sweeney, *Mangas Coloradas*, pp. 454–62. Prof. O.S. Fowler, a New York phrenologist who examined the dead chief's skull, reached the conclusion 'that it was larger than Daniel Webster's'. Thrapp, *Conquest of Apachería*, p. 23.
33 Ball, *In the Days of Victorio: Recollections of a Warm Springs Apache*, Tucson, Ariz., University of Arizona Press, 1970, p. 48.
34 Ball, with N. Henn and L. Sanchez, *Indeh: An Apache Odyssey*, Provo, Utah, Brigham Young University Press, 1980, p. 20.
35 The administration's initiative was prompted by fallout from the 'Camp Grant Massacre' which took place in southern Arizona the previous year. In the early morning of 30 April 1871, 54 members of the so-called Tucson Committee of Public Safety, supported by 94 Papago warriors, traditional enemies of the Apaches, descended upon a camp of Western Apaches living under the protection of the US Army and killed some 100 of them. All but two were women and children. The attackers appear to have blamed the inhabitants of the camp for recent attacks on settlers and travellers in the region. Pressure from Eastern public opinion, already sensitised by the Sand Creek Massacre seven years before, forced a trial of the perpetrators of the massacre in Tucson. All were acquitted, after nineteen minutes of jury deliberation. On the episode, see D. Schellie, *Vast Domain of Blood: The Story of the Camp Grant Massacre,* Los Angeles, Calif., Westernlore Press, 1968.
36 For a detailed account of the Howard–Cochise peace talks, see E.R. Sweeney (ed.), *Making Peace with Cochise: The 1872 Journal of Captain Joseph Alton Sladen*, Norman, Okla., University of Oklahoma Press, 1999. Sweeney's 'Introduction' to the book is particularly useful for background on white relations with Cochise and on the principals involved in the 1872 negotiations. The author of the journal edited by Sweeney, Captain Sladen, was born in England and held two medical degrees by the time he set out with Howard for Arizona. He had earlier served as an aide to Howard when the latter was head of the Freedmen's Bureau. Ibid., pp. 17–19.
37 Robinson, *General Crook and the Western Frontier*, pp. 118–23, 127–30. The term 'grand offensive' to describe Crook's 1872 campaign comes from Thrapp, *Conquest of Apachería*, pp. 119–20. On this campaign, also see J. Gates, 'General George Crook's First Apache Campaign (the use of mobile, self-contained units against the Apache in the Military Department of Arizona, 1871–1873)', *Journal of the West*, 1967, vol. 6, pp. 310–20; and G.E. Rothenberg, 'General George Crook and the Apaches, 1872–1873', *Westerner's Brand Book* (Chicago), 1955, vol. 13, pp. 49–56. A nuts and bolts view of Crook's campaign is provided in D.P. Maynard's 'Manpower, Weapons, and Tactics of the Apache Wars, 1871–1875', *Periodical: Journal of America's Military Past*, 1997, vol. 24, pp. 3–15.
38 Unfortunately, Crook also resembles Wolseley in his predilection for cronyism and for rowing with fellow officers.
39 E.M. Essin, *Shavetails and Bell Sharps: The History of the US Army Mule*, Lincoln, Neb., University of Nebraska Press, 2000 [1997], pp. 92–8.
40 The military intellectual Colonel Richard Irving Dodge was one of these officers. Listen to his complaint about Crook's social preferences. 'The cavalry and infantry

NOTES

are nobodies. The Indians [scouts] and pack mules have all the good places [in camp]. He scarcely treats [General Ranald Mackenzie and me] decently, but will spend hours chatting pleasantly with an Indian or a dirty scout . . .'. Dodge thought Crook's common touch was a fraud. W.R. Kime (ed.), *The Powder River Expedition Journals of Colonel Richard Irving Dodge*, Norman, Okla., University of Oklahoma Press, 1997, pp. 64–6. Quoted in Robinson, *General Crook and the Western Frontier*, p. 205.
41 Robinson, *General Crook and the Western Frontier*, p. 136.
42 For more than most people would ever want to know about the 1872–3 campaign, see C.M. Robinson, III (ed. and annot.), *The Diaries of John Gregory Bourke*, vol. 1, *November 20, 1872–July 28, 1876*, Denton, Tex., University of North Texas Press, 2003.
43 J. Gates, 'General George Crook's First Apache Campaign', pp. 310–20, is a modern appreciation.
44 Utley, *Frontier Regulars*, p. 357.
45 Robinson, *General Crook and the Western Frontier*, p. 253.
46 Utley, *Frontier Regulars*, pp. 357–8.
47 Ibid., p. 359.
48 Ibid., pp. 361–2.
49 Ibid., pp. 362–3.
50 Ibid., p. 364.
51 Leckie, *The Buffalo Soldiers: A Narrative of the Black Cavalry in the West*, rev. edn, Norman, Okla., University of Oklahoma Press, 2003, p. 232.
52 Utley, *Frontier Regulars*, p. 364.
53 For Terrazas's own account of the battle, see pp. 106–22 of his *Memorias; La guerra contra los Apaches*, Chihuahua, Centro Librero La Prensa, 1989 [1905]. Lejeune, *La Guerra Apache en Sonora*, p. 74, provides details of Corredor's exploit and subsequent reward. Lejeune goes on to argue that it was Corredor once again who shot and killed the US cavalry officer Emmett Crawford in an encounter between US troops and Mexican irregulars on 11 January 1885; the Mexican claim that they fired on Crawford and his soldiers because they thought they were Apaches – Apache scouts comprised the bulk of the American force – was hotly disputed by US authorities at the time and continues to be debated by historians today. Lejeune, ibid., p. 79, n. 7, identifies Corredor as Crawford's killer; the Tarahumara scout also died in the mêlée that followed.
54 Robinson, *General Crook and the Western Frontier*, pp. 253–4.
55 Utley, *Frontier Regulars*, p. 255.
56 Ibid., pp. 255–6.
57 Ibid., pp. 261–2.
58 Chaffee would later command the US Sixth Cavalry during the Boxer Rebellion in China (1900), and lead American troops in the 'pacification' of the Philippines just before the outbreak of the First World War. Following service in France during the 1914–18 war, Chaffee became one of the leading US advocates of armoured warfare. J.W. Chambers, II (ed.), *The Oxford Companion to American Military History*, New York, Oxford University Press, 1999, pp. 36, 57, 117, 548.
59 Utley, *Frontier Regulars*, p. 262.
60 Crook's second expedition to find Geronimo is covered in great detail in Chapters 4 and 5 of O.B. Faulk's *The Geronimo Campaign*, New York, Oxford University Press, 1969.
61 Miles, *Personal Recollections*, p. 495.
62 Ibid., pp. 495, 481.
63 Thrapp, *Conquest of Apachería*, p. 350.

64 Miles, *Personal Recollections*, p. 487. Frank Lockwood, *The Apache Indians*, New York, Macmillan, 1938, p. 296, concludes that Lawton was picked 'because of his extraordinary strength and toughness of physique and his confident belief that the Apaches could be outmanoeuvred, worn down, and subjugated by white soldiers'.
65 Miles, *Personal Recollections*, p. 487. Wood actually hailed from New Hampshire, not Miles's native Massachusetts. He also fell somewhat short of being the perfect Aryan specimen described by his commander, having grey eyes instead of blue.
66 Wolseley, *The Story of a Soldier's Life*, New York, Charles Scribner's Sons, 1903, vol. 2, p. 264; Wolseley, 'Memorandum of Guidance on Bush Fighting', 20 December 1873, p. 3.
67 Enes, *A guerra de Africa em 1895 (Memorias)*, 2nd edn, Lisbon, Ediçoes Gama, 1895, pp. 362–3.
68 Faulk, *Geronimo* Campaign, pp. 102–3; Thrapp, *Conquest of Apachería*, pp. 350–1.
69 Thrapp, *Conquest of Apachería*, p. 350.
70 Efforts were made by Miles and his entourage to discredit Gatewood's achievement, however, claiming that it was in fact Lawton who convinced Geronimo to give up. R.M. Utley, 'The Surrender of Geronimo', *Arizoniana: The Journal of Arizona History*, vol. 4, pp. 1–9.
71 The subject of the treatment of the Apache POWs has received considerable attention from historians in recent years. J.A. Turcheneske, Jr.'s 1979 Ph.D. dissertation on the subject at the University of New Mexico was published in 1997 by the University Press of Colorado at Niwot under the title, *The Chiricahua Apache Prisoners of War: Fort Sill, 1894–1914*. Also see Turcheneske, 'Arizonans and the Apache Prisoners of Mount Vernon Barracks, Alabama: "They do not die fast enough"', *Military History of Texas and the Southwest*, 1973, vol. 11, pp. 197–226. H.H. Stockel has published two recent books on the topic: *Survival of the Spirit: Chiricahua Apaches in Captivity*, Reno, Nev., University of Nevada Press, 1993; and *Shame and Endurance: The Untold Story of the Chiricahua Apache Prisoners of War*, Tucson, Ariz., University of Arizona Press, 2004.

9 WAR ON THE CANADIAN PRAIRIES, 1870–85

1 The remaining Maritime Provinces joined the Confederation later, Prince Edward Island in 1873 and Newfoundland only in 1949.
2 The instrument of confederation was the British North America Act, passed by the British Parliament in early 1867, to go into effect on 1 July of the same year.
3 Well, almost. British Columbia's accession to the Confederation in 1871 completed the process.
4 The Company did not, however, give up its own valuable real estate in the newly ceded territory. Subsequently, it would turn these holdings into the largest department store chain in Canada.
5 Morris, *Heaven's Command: An Imperial Progress*, New York, Harcourt, Brace, Jovanovich, 1980 [1973], p. 341.
6 There are powerful sectarian overtones to this whole affair, involving the Protestant Orange element in Ontario Province on one side and Fenian sympathisers on the other. Orangemen from Ontario bulked large in the Canadian emigrant community in the Red River Colony, whilst Irish Catholic Fenians backed Riel and his faction. The flag of the Métis Republic bore a fleur de lis and a shamrock on a white ground. Morris, *Heaven's Command*, pp. 348–50.
7 Ibid., p. 351.
8 Inclusion of the Quebec militia was intended to avoid giving the impression that the force was a sectarian undertaking. Many French Canadians sympathised with their

NOTES

fellow francophones and co-religionists in Manitoba, however, and in the end the Quebec contingent had to be filled by English-speakers. G.F.G. Stanley, *The Birth of Western Canada: A History of the Riel Rebellions*, Toronto, University of Toronto Press, 1960 [1936], p. 131.
9. Morris, *Heaven's Command*, pp. 352–4.
10. G. Friesen, *The Canadian Prairies: A History*, Lincoln, Neb., University of Nebraska Press, 1984, p. 127; J.K. Howard, *Strange Empire: A Narrative of the Northwest*, New York, William Morrow and Co., 1952, p. 207.
11. Morris, *Heaven's Command*, p. 355.
12. Friesen, *The Canadian Prairies*, p. 127.
13. For the career of Viscount, later Field Marshal, Sir Garnet Wolseley, see B. Vandervort, 'Wolseley, Garnet Joseph, 1853–1913', in C. Messenger (ed.), *Reader's Guide to Military History*, London, Fitzroy Dearborn Publishers, 2001, pp. 657–8.
14. Poundmaker's name derived from a skill he presumably inherited from his father, the ability to construct particularly deceptive 'pounds' or corral-like traps into which buffalo could be driven for mass slaughter. This method of 'hunting' buffalo, which had been common on the plains of North America prior to the coming of the horse and gun, persisted on the Canadian prairies until well into the nineteenth century because of the periodic decline of the horse population due to severe winter weather and shortages of grass.
15. D. Morton, *The Last War Drum: The North West Campaign of 1885*, Toronto, Hakkert, 1972, p. 24.
16. D. Morton, *A Military History of Canada: From Champlain to Kosovo*, 4th edn, Toronto, McClelland and Stewart, 1999 [1985], p. 109.
17. Howard, *Strange Empire*, p. 410.
18. W.B. Cameron, *Blood Red the Sun*, Edmonton, Alta., Hurtig, 1977 [1926], p. 36. Quoted in B. Beal and R. Macleod, *Prairie Fire: The 1885 North-West Rebellion*, Edmonton, Alta., Hurtig, 1984, p. 194.
19. It is thought that Quinn's attitude towards Indians stemmed from his childhood experience. In 1862 his father, a trader and interpreter for the US Army, had been killed in the Santee Sioux uprising in Minnesota and 'teenager Tom Quinn had barely escaped with his own life'. Another example, then, of how events elsewhere impinged upon the Canadian upheaval. Beal and Macleod, *Prairie Fire*, p. 191.
20. Howard, *Strange Empire*, p. 413.
21. Beal and Macleod, *Prairie Fire*, pp. 198–9. Father Marchand's death was a classic case of being in the wrong place at the wrong time. He was not a local priest, but visiting from nearby Onion Lake.
22. R. Jefferson, *Fifty Years on the Saskatchewan*, Battleford, Sask., Canadian North-West Historical Society, 1929, pp. 125–6. Jefferson had been taken prisoner by Poundmaker's band and became a valuable witness from inside the Cree camp of the battle of Cut Knife Hill. Quoted in Beal and Macleod, *Prairie Fire*, p. 185.
23. Poundmaker's band came into the town of Battleford on 30 March and looted a few shops and houses, but did not attempt to attack the North-West Mounted Police post to which the town's 400 or so frightened inhabitants had fled. Two whites were killed by the Indians before they left the area; one, predictably, was the farm instructor on the nearby reserve. What gave the impression of a 'siege' to the outside world was the flood of hysterical telegrams sent out by people cooped up in the NWMP fort. Beal and Macleod, *Prairie Fire*, pp. 180–9.
24. Around 1200 of the militiamen came from Manitoba and 800 from Saskatchewan and Alberta. Almost the entire North-West Mounted Police (the future Royal Canadian Mounted Police) was seconded to the expedition. J.L. Granatstein, *Canada's Army: Waging War and Keeping the Peace*, Toronto, University of Toronto Press, 2002, p. 29.

NOTES

25 Beal and Macleod, *Prairie Fire*, p. 174. Private Crowe's recollections come from 'Reminiscences of Joseph Crowe', Public Archives of Canada, Ottawa.
26 Howard, *Strange Empire*, pp. 446–7.
27 Morton, *The Last War Drum*, p. 36.
28 Beal and Macleod, *Prairie Fire*, p. 178.
29 Ibid., pp. 220–1.
30 Morton, *A Military History of Canada*, p. 102. Middleton's chief of staff for the campaign was Gilbert John Elliott, Lord Melgund, a former officer of the Scots Guards who had seen service with the Turks against the Russians in 1877, in Afghanistan in 1879, and with Wolseley in the invasion of Egypt in 1882. He was military secretary to the Governor-General of Canada, Lord Landsdowne, when the fighting began in the West, and would become Governor-General himself as Lord Minto in the 1890s. Morton, *The Last War Drum*, p. 38.
31 Granatstein, *Canada's Army*, pp. 29–30.
32 Woodcock, *Gabriel Dumont: The Métis Chief and his Lost World*, Edmonton, Hurtig, 1975, p. 11.
33 Granatstein, *Canada's Army*, p. 30.
34 Woodcock, *Gabriel Dumont*, p. 183. The Sioux who joined forces with the Métis were Lakotas who had remained behind in Canada when Sitting Bull returned to the USA to surrender. They had been given a reserve at Round Prairie south of Saskatoon. Ibid., p. 186.
35 Woodcock, *Gabriel Dumont*, p. 188; Granatstein, *Canada's Army*, p. 30.
36 Montigny, *La Vérité sur les questions métisses au Nord-Ouest: Biographie et récit de Gabriel Dumont sur les événements de 1885*, Montreal, n.p., 1889.
37 Woodcock, *Gabriel Dumont*, pp. 188, 192–3.
38 Beal and Macleod, *Prairie Fire*, p. 227.
39 The great defensive victory of the Métis had been the battle of Grand Coteau in the Dakotas in 1851 against the Sioux. Gabriel Dumont had participated in this battle as a young man. Woodcock gives a vivid account of the battle in *Gabriel Dumont*, pp. 55–62.
40 Beal and Macleod, *Prairie Fire*, p. 228.
41 Stanley, *Birth of Western Canada*, p. 358.
42 Beal and Macleod, *Prairie Fire*, p. 234.
43 Middleton to Duke of Cambridge, 6 May 1885, Cambridge Papers, Royal Archives, Windsor Castle. Quoted in Morton, *Last War Drum*, p. 70.
44 Historians now have at their disposal a painstakingly detailed analysis of the battle of Cut Knife Hill, R.H. Caldwell's '"We're making history, eh?": An Inquiry into the Events that Occurred near Cut Knife Hill, North West Territories, 1–2 May 1885', in D. Graves (ed.), *More Fighting for Canada: Five Battles, 1760–1944*, Toronto, Robin Brass Studio, 2004, pp. 75–146. I have relied heavily on Caldwell's narrative for my own account of the battle. The query about making history apparently was a quote from a North West Mounted Policeman involved in the struggle.
45 Otter was virtually the only Canadian professional soldier of his day who had never served outside the country. Most would have done a stint in the British Army. A store clerk in Toronto, Otter had developed an enthusiasm for the military life and had worked his way up through the ranks of the militia. His big break came in 1883, when he was made head of the permanent force's Infantry School in Toronto. Otter, who went on to command the Canadian expeditionary force in South Africa during the Second Boer War (1899–1902), ended his career as Sir William Otter and chief of staff of the Canadian Army with the rank of Major General. As can be ascertained from this biographical sketch, Otter's career was strikingly similar to that of his American contemporary, General Nelson Miles.
46 Beal and Macleod, *Prairie Fire*, p. 243.

NOTES

47 Ibid., p. 247.
48 Morton, *Last War Drum*, p. 105.
49 This term, frequently used by Canadian soldiers at the time and historians since, is, of course, the Boer expression for 'circling the wagons', something they did to protect themselves against attacks from Zulus and other indigenous enemies. Another 'imperial' term which found its way onto the prairies during the 1885 war was *zareba* (or *zariba*) an Arab word for a corral-like enclosure in the desert, originally constructed of thorn bushes, behind which men and animals could take shelter at night. The term was picked up by the British Army in the course of its wars in the Sudan. In western Canada, it referred to a constructed enclosure, rather than one made by circling wagons.
50 This is the opinion of Caldwell, our major source on this battle, in '"We're Making History, eh?"', pp. 130–1.
51 Stanley, *Birth of Western Canada*, p. 367; Howard, *Strange Empire*, p. 436; Beal and Macleod, pp. 232–3; Morton, *Last War Drum*, p. 108, are all agreed on the decisive role of Poundmaker in saving Otter's militia from, as Stanley put it, being 'cut to pieces'.
52 Jefferson, *Fifty Years on the Saskatchewan*, p. 143. Quoted in Caldwell, '"We're Making History, eh?"', p. 136.
53 Cochin, *The Reminiscences of Louis Cochin, OMI, a Veteran Missionary of the Cree Indians and a Prisoner in Poundmaker's Camp in 1885*, Battleford, Sask., Canadian North West Society, 1926, pp. 34–5. Quoted in Caldwell, '"We're Making History, eh?"', pp. 136–7. Father Cochin was a member of the Oblate Order, a prominent Catholic missionary group on the Canadian Plains.
54 Woodcock, *Gabriel Dumont*, pp. 208, 210–11.
55 Granatstein, *Canada's Army*, p. 30.
56 Lyttleton, *Eighty Years: Soldiering, Politics, Games*, London, Hodder and Stoughton, 1927, p. 212.
57 Stanley, *Birth of Western Canada*, pp. 358–9.
58 Beal and Macleod, *Prairie Fire*, pp. 268–71.
59 Granatstein, *Canada's Army*, pp. 30–1. The entries from Sergeant Stewart's diary are for 9 and 12 May, respectively.
60 Morton, *The Last War Drum*, p. 91.
61 Stanley, *Birth of Western Canada*, pp. 374–5. The battle did not take place where Strange thought it did. Frenchman's Butte actually lies a few miles to the south. This has not stopped subsequent historians (e.g. Stanley and Morton) from referring to the battle by the name Strange gave to it. Beal and Macleod, *Prairie Fire*, p. 286.
62 On 24 June the war chief of Big Bear's band, Wandering Spirit, gave himself up to the Mounties at Fort Pitt, just over the Saskatchewan border from Frog Lake where he had led the massacre that had so terrified eastern Canada. He later tried to kill himself with a knife, but failed, saving himself for the hangman. Howard, *Strange Empire*, p. 498.
63 Beal and Macleod, *Prairie Fire*, p. 286.
64 Poundmaker was the adopted son of the Blackfoot leader.

10 INDIAN WARS OF THE PORFIRIATO, 1876–1900

1 The official name of the force was *La Gendarmería Fiscal* (treasury police) because of their role in combating smuggling. Most Mexicans called them Rurales, however, because they operated largely in the countryside. C.C. Smith, Jr., *Emilio Kosterlitzky, Eagle of Sonora and the Southwest Border*, Glendale, Calif., Arthur H.

NOTES

Clark Co., 1970, p. 104. Colonel Kosterlitzky, born in Russia and widely known in Mexico as "the Cossack", was a Díaz loyalist and commander of the Rurales.

2 P. Vanderwood, *The Power of God Against the Guns of Government: Religious Upheaval in Mexico at the Turn of the Nineteenth Century*, Stanford, Calif., Stanford University Press, 1998, pp. 140, 144–6.

3 J.K. Turner, *Barbarous Mexico*, Austin, Tex., University of Texas Press, 1969 [1910], pp. xiii, 35.

4 E. Hu-DeHart, *Yaqui Resistance and Survival: the Struggle for Land and Autonomy, 1821–1910*, Madison, Wis., University of Wisconsin Press, 1984, pp. 93–4. The ultimate source of biographical information on Cajeme is the interview done with the Yaqui leader by the Sonora politician Ramón Corral shortly before the former's execution in 1887. 'Biografía de José María Leyva Cayeme', in Ramón Corral, *Obras históricas, No. 1*, Hermosillo, Sonora, Biblioteca Sonorense de Geografía e Historia, 1959 [1886], pp. 149–92. Corral's interview provides the material for the biographical sketches of Cajeme in Hu-DeHart, *Yaqui Resistance*, pp. 93–4, and in C. Dabdoub, *Historia de el valle del Yaqui*, Mexico City, Librería Manuel Porrúa, 1904, pp. 115–18. A helpful source which makes use of material other than that found in the Corral account is F.M. Hillary, 'Cajeme, and the Mexico of his Time', *Journal of Arizona History*, 1967, vol. 8, pp. 120–36.

5 Hillary, 'Cajeme', pp. 126–7. It was Corona who took the surrender of Emperor Maximilian's sword at Queretaro, where the armies of the Empire suffered their final defeat in May 1867.

6 Corral, *Obras históricas, No. 1*, p. 153; Hu De-Hart, *Yaqui Resistance*, p. 94. Hillary, 'Cajeme', pp. 130–1, claims that the 'Mexicanised' Cajeme led a unit of 'turncoat' Yaquis in Pesquiera's campaigns of repression. He says that Yaquis 'despised' the unit, but exhibited 'respect' for Cajeme's military prowess among the yoris.

7 Corral, *Obras históricas, No. 1*, pp. 153–4.

8 Ibid., p. 149; Dabdoub, *Historia de el valle del Yaqui*, pp. 117–18.

9 Hu-DeHart, *Yaqui Resistance*, p. 98.

10 Ibid, p. 97; Dabdoub, *Historia de el valle del Yaqui*, p. 119.

11 Hu-DeHart, *Yaqui Resistance*, pp. 97–8.

12 Ibid., p. 97.

13 Hillary, 'Cajeme', p. 134.

14 On the Maori *pa*, see J. Belich, *The Victorian Interpretation of Racial Conflict: The Maori, the British, and the New Zealand Wars*, Montreal, McGill-Queen's University Press, 1989 [1986], pp. 24–5. The formidable defence system of the Barue kingdom is described in some detail in A.F. Isaacman, *The Tradition of Resistance in Mozambique: The Zambezi Valley, 1850–1921*, Berkeley, Calif., University of California Press, 1976, pp. 49–74.

15 Dabdoub, *Historia de el valle del Yaqui*, p. 126.

16 R.F. Acuña, *Sonoran Strongman: Ignacio Pesquiera and his Times*, Tucson, Ariz., University of Arizona Press, 1974, p. 138.

17 Smith, *Emilio Kosterlitzky*, pp. 54–5.

18 Martínez had been one of the leading Liberal generals in the War of Reform and in the struggle against the Empire of Maximilian. On 14 August 1866 his army had recaptured Hermosillo, the capital of Sonora, and Martínez had ordered the execution of all Frenchmen in the city. J.A. Dabbs, *The French Army in Mexico, 1861–1867: A Study in Military Government*, The Hague, Mouton, 1963, p. 176. The general had been active in the suppression of the Yaquis in the late 1860s and had then transferred his energies to Europe, where he served with the German army during the Franco–Prussian War of 1870–1. Hillary, 'Cajeme', p. 130, n. 28.

19 Smith, *Emilio Kosterlitzky*, p. 62.

NOTES

20. Smith, *Emilio Kosterlitzky*, p. 63.
21. Hu-DeHart, *Yaqui Resistance*, pp. 116–17; E.H. Spicer, *Cycles of Conquest: The impact of Spain, Mexico, and the United States on the Indians of the Southwest, 1533–1960*, Tucson, Ariz., University of Arizona Press, 1970 [1962], p. 71.
22. F. Paso y Troncoso, *Las guerras con las tribus Yaqui y Mayo del Estado de Sonora*, Mexico, Tipografía Departamento de Estado Mayor, 1905, pp. 125–9; Corral, 'Cajeme', pp. 167–70; Hu-DeHart, *Yaqui Resistance*, pp. 110–11.
23. Hu-DeHart, *Yaqui Resistance*, p. 112.
24. Ibid., pp. 114–15.
25. Hillary, 'Cajeme', p. 136. Hillary's account of Cajeme's demise, based exclusively on the story filed by the *Tucson Daily Citizen* reporter and published on 25 May 1887, varies from that given in Corral, *Obras históricas, No. 1*, pp. 191–2. I have chosen to base my narrative on the newspaper story rather than Corral's remarks because the US reporter was on the spot and Corral was not. A final note: The difference between the 'cinco balas' of the epitaph pinned to the tree and the seven bullet holes in Cajeme's body noted by the Tucson reporter is explained by the *coup de grâce* administered by the captain of the firing squad.
26. Although, as we have seen, the distinction was quite artificial, the Mexican authorities tended to divide the Yaqui population into two groups, broncos and *pacíficos* (peaceful ones).
27. The most comprehensive English-language account of the Mexican government's counter-insurgency strategy I have found is in Hu-DeHart, *Yaqui Resistance*, pp. 119–33. For the period up to 1905, some of the same ground is covered from the perspective of the Mexican government in Paso y Troncoso, *Las guerras*, pp. 59–108.
28. Hu-DeHart, *Yaqui Resistance*, pp. 142–8.
29. This is the title of Chapter 6 of her book, *Yaqui Resistance*.
30. There was much debate at the time about the number of Yaqui deportees and that debate continues today. John Kenneth Turner, in his devastating muckraking account of the deportation programme, *Barbarous Mexico* [2nd edn, Austin, Tex., University of Texas Press, 1969 (1910)], wrote (p. 47) that 15,700 Sonora Indians, mostly Yaquis, were shipped off to the plantations. This figure has not been accepted, because it exceeds the likely total of Yaquis living in Sonora in 1900. Evelyn Hu-DeHart is prepared to accept a low figure of 8,000 (*Yaqui Resistance*, p. 188), while Edward Spicer says that 5,000 is a more reasonable 'conservative' estimate (*The Yaquis*, p. 160).
31. Spicer, *The Yaquis*, p. 236, estimated that 1,000 Yaquis took up residence in Arizona from 1900–10.
32. Ibid., p. 160. Because Yaquis during these difficult times frequently tried to pass themselves off as members of other Indian tribes, Sonora officials sometimes simply deported all the Indians in a given locality, on the assumption that most of them were probably Yaquis in disguise.
33. Ibid., p. 158.
34. Hu-DeHart, *Yaqui Resistance*, p. 182; Spicer, *The Yaquis*, p. 160.
35. Spicer, *The Yaquis*, pp. 158, 161.
36. Hu-DeHart, *Yaqui Resistance*, pp. 195–6.
37. Ibid., p. 207.
38. Spicer, *The Yaquis*, p. 161. The number of Yaquis who perished in Yucatán 'has not yet been determined', the author wrote in 1980. It has still not been 'determined' and probably never will be. We do know that some Yaquis escaped and made their way back to Sonora or to exile in Arizona. Other escapees may have formed a new Yaqui community in the southern jungles of Tabasco state. The majority of returnees, however, probably came back via service in the armies of the 1910 revolution.

NOTES

39 A. Wells and G.M. Joseph, *Summer of Discontent, Seasons of Upheaval: Elite Politics and Rural Insurgency in Yucatán, 1876–1915*, Stanford, Calif., Stanford University Press, 1996, pp. 44–5.
40 Dumond, *The Machete and the Cross*, p. 393. A major problem for indigenous armies was a lack of the skills and equipment necessary to repair the more sophisticated breechloading weapons and to reload the metallic cartridges they used. But, even in the few cases where resistance movements had developed these capacities, they found it increasingly difficult to purchase breechloading rifles, as the imperial powers pressured arms dealers to stop sales of such weapons to 'natives'. This ad hoc ban was formalised by an 1890 agreement among the European powers to prohibit the sale of breechloading weapons to Africans. Interestingly, no such ban ever took effect in the United States, where arms dealers not only supplied breechloaders to Indian tribes at war with the US cavalry, but also to the Yaqui insurgents in Mexico and to the Crees who joined in the Métis rebellion of 1885 in Canada. The upshot of this was that highly unusual phenomenon in the colonial wars, the situation in which white troops were outgunned by their opponents. The most famous example of this was the Custer massacre of 1876, as we have seen.
41 Wells and Joseph, *Summer of Discontent*, p. 45. General Bravo's letter, dated 15 June 1897, can be found in the Colección General Porfirio Díaz in the Mexican state archives.
42 'Karl Sapper on Late-Nineteenth Century Maya Settlements', in T. Rugeley (ed.), *Maya Wars: Ethnographic Accounts from Nineteenth-Century Yucatán*, Norman, Okla., University of Oklahoma Press, 2001, p. 164.
43 Dumond, *The Machete and the Cross*, p. 343; G. Fuentes, *El ejército mexicano*, Mexico City, Editorial Grijalba, 1983, pp. 210–11.
44 Reed, *The Caste War*, p. 240.
45 The Spencer–Mariscal Treaty of 8 July 1893, which also more clearly demarcated the boundary between British Honduras and Yucatán.
46 Reed, *The Caste War*, p. 249. The new federal district of Yucatán was named after Andrès Quintana Roo, a prominent Yucatecan who had served a number of Mexican governments as a diplomat and cabinet official. Dumond, *The Machete and the Cross*, p. 73, n. 30.
47 Reed, *The Caste War*, p. 250.

CONCLUSION: LONG SHADOWS

1 The post-1885 Indian assimilation programme in Canada is summarised in the concluding chapter (pp. 150–75) of S. Carter, *Aboriginal People and Colonizers of Western Canada to 1900*, Toronto, University of Toronto Press, 1999.
2 J.R. Miller, *Skyscrapers Hide the Heavens: A History of Indian–White Relations in Canada*, 3rd edn, Toronto, Toronto University Press, 2000 [1989], pp. 392–412.
3 E. Spicer, 'Potam: A Yaqui Village in Sonora', *American Anthropologist*, 1954, vol. 56, pp. 34–5, provides details of the 1926 rising of the Yaquis.
4 The Cárdenas decrees are discussed in A. Fabila, *Las tribus Yaquis de Sonora: Su cultura y anhelada autodeterminación*, Mexico, Departamento de Asunto Indigenes, 1940, pp. 295–313.
5 E. Hu-DeHart, *Yaqui Resistance and Survival: The Struggle for Land and Autonomy, 1821–1910*, Madison, Wis., University of Wisconsin Press, 1984, pp. 205–19. Quotes on pp. 213 and 217.
6 In some parts of Yucatán, the population fell by an astounding two-thirds as a result of the Caste War. R.T. Alexander, *Yaxcaba and the Caste War of Yucatán: An Archaeological Perspective*, Albuquerque, N.Mex., University of New Mexico Press, 2004, p. x.

NOTES

7. Alexander, *Yaxcaba*, p. x.
8. N. Reed, *The Caste War of Yucatán*, Stanford, Calif., Stanford University Press, 1963, pp. 275–6.
9. D. Dumond, *The Machete and the Cross: Campesino Rebellion in Yucatán*, Lincoln, Neb., University of Nebraska Press, 1997, p. 428.
10. Although some schools were set up on reservations in the nineteenth century, it was felt that for the best results, it was preferable to put as much distance as possible between Indians, especially Indian children, and their 'savage' environment. Thus large numbers of Indian children and a smaller number of Indian adults were shipped off to, for example, the Indian School at Carlisle, Pennsylvania, and the Hampton Industrial Institute in Hampton, Virginia, to be re-educated. Ironically, the Indian students at the Carlisle school were housed in the former army barracks where so many of the cavalrymen who had fought against their forebears were trained. For more, see D.W. Adams, *Education for Extinction: American Indians and the Boarding School Experience, 1875–1928*, Lawrence, Kans., University Press of Kansas, 1995; M. Archuleta et al. (eds), *Away from Home: American Indian Boarding School Experiences*, Phoenix, Ariz., Heard Museum, 2000; and C. Ellis, *To Change Them Forever: Indian Education at the Rainy Mountain Boarding School*, Norman, Okla., University of Oklahoma Press, 1996.
11. The best general treatment of the government's nineteenth-century assimilation programme is F. Hoxie, *A Final Promise: The Campaign to Assimilate the Indians, 1880–1920*, Lincoln, University of Nebraska Press, 1984.
12. S. Hoig, *Tribal Wars of the Southern Plains*, Norman, Okla., University of Oklahoma Press, 1993, p. 9.
13. See T.A. Britten, *American Indians in World War I: At War and At Home*, Albuquerque, N.Mex., University of New Mexico Press, 1997. Indian military service during the Second World War is chronicled in A.R. Bernstein, *American Indians in World War II: Toward a New Era in Indian Affairs*, Norman, Okla., University of Oklahoma Press, 1991; K.W. Townsend, *World War II and the American Indian*, Albuquerque, N.Mex., University of New Mexico Press, 2000; T. Holm, 'Fighting a White Man's War: The Extent and Legacy of American Indian Participation in World War II', *Journal of Ethnic Studies*, 1981, vol. 9, pp. 69–81, and B.W. White, 'The American Indian as Soldier, 1890–1919', *Canadian Review of American Studies*, 1976, vol. 7, pp. 15–25.
14. Hoig, *Tribal Wars*, p. 8. T. Holm, *Strong Hearts, Wounded Souls: Native American Veterans of the Vietnam War*, Austin, Tex., University of Texas Press, 1996, suggests that the Vietnam war may have been as traumatic for Indian veterans as it was for others who fought there.
15. D. Morton, *A Military History of Canada: From Champlain to Kosovo*, 4th edn, Toronto, McClelland Stewart, 1999 [1985], pp. 273–4.
16. There has been a flood of 'instant histories' of the Chiapas struggle. Notable among them are B. Weinberg, *Homage to Chiapas: The New Indigenous Struggles in Mexico*, London, Verso, 2000; T. Hayden (ed.), *The Zapatista Reader*, New York, Thunder Mouth Press, 2002; and N. Higgins, *Understanding the Chiapas Rebellion: Modernist Visions and the Invisible Indian*, Austin, Tex., University of Texas Press, 2004.
17. R.F. Weigley, 'The Long Death of the Indian-fighting Army', in G.D. Ryan and T.K. Nenninger (eds), *Soldiers and Civilians: The US Army and the American People*, Washington, D.C., National Archives and Records Administration, 1987, pp. 27, 29, 32, 34.
18. D. Espey, 'America and Vietnam: The Indian Subtext', http://www.english.upenn.edu/~despey/vietnam/htm. One of the more widely read novels produced by the 'Vietnam War generation' was the veteran Philip Caputo's *Indian Country*, New York, Bantam Press, 1987.

NOTES

19 Fitzgerald, *Fire in the Lake: The Vietnamese and Americans in Vietnam*, Boston, Mass., Little, Brown, 1972, pp. 367–8.
20 Slotkin, *Regeneration and Violence: The Mythology of the American Frontier, 1600–1800*, Middletown, Conn., Wesleyan University Press, 1973, p. 562.
21 Hess, 'Feature: Raid in Iraq's "Indian Country"', UPI, 8 June 2003.
22 Kaplan, 'War on Terrorism: Indian Country', *Wall Street Journal*, 21 September 2004.

BIBLIOGRAPHY

Note: In addition to the references cited in the endnotes above, this bibliography contains other sources that the author believes could be of assistance to students and readers who wish to know more about the New World Indian wars.

Primary sources

Bandel, E., *Frontier Life in the* [US] *Army, 1854–1861*, trans. O. Bandel and R. Jente, Glendale, Calif., Arthur H. Clark Co., 1932.

Bassett, J.S. (ed.), *Correspondence of Andrew Jackson*, vols 1 and 2, Washington, D.C., Carnegie Institution, 1926–7.

Cozzens, P. (ed.), *Eyewitnesses to the Indian Wars, 1865–1890*, vol. 1, *The Struggle for Apachería*, Mechanicsburg, Pa., Stackpole Books, 2001.

Cozzens, P. (ed.), *Eyewitnesses to the Indian Wars, 1865–1890*, vol. 2, *Wars for the Pacific Northwest*, Mechanicsburg, Pa., Stackpole Books, 2002.

Cozzens, P. (ed.), *Eyewitnesses to the Indian Wars, 1865–1890*, vol. 3, *Conquering the Southern Plains*, Mechanicsburg, Pa., Stackpole Books, 2003.

Cremony, J.C., *Life among the Apaches,* Glorieta, N.Mex., Rio Grande Press, 1969 [1868].

Croffutt, W.A. (ed.), *Fifty Years in Camp and Field: Diary of Major General Ethan Allen Hitchcock, USA*, New York, G.P. Putnam Sons, 1909.

Fay, G.E. (ed.), *Military Engagements between United States Troops and Plains Indians; Documentary Inquiry by the US Congress*, 5 vols, Greeley, Colo., Museum of Anthropology, University of Northern Colorado, 1972–80. Covers period 1854–1902; includes report of inquiry into Sand Creek Massacre (1864).

Ford, J.S., *Rip Ford's Texas*, ed. S.B. Oates, Austin, Tex., University of Texas Press, 1963.

Forsyth, G.A., *The Soldier*, 2 vols, New York, The Brampton Society, 1908 [1900].

Jackson, A., *The Papers of Andrew Jackson*, 6 vols, ed. S.B. Smith and H.C. Owsley, Knoxville, University of Tennessee Press, 1980–2002. Vol. 3 covers events of 1814–15.

Kip, L., *Indian War in the Pacific Northwest: The Journal of Lieutenant Lawrence Kip*, Lincoln, Neb., University of Nebraska Press, 1999 [1859].

Lowe, P., *Five Years a Dragoon ('49 to '54) and Other Adventures on the Great Plains*, 2nd edn, Norman, Okla., University of Oklahoma Press, 1965 [1906].

Macbeth, R.G., *Policing the Plains: Being the Real-life Record of the Famous North-West*

Mounted Police, Toronto, Musson, 1931 [1921]. Author recalls the early days on the plains of the NWMP.

Marcy, R., *Thirty Years of Army Life on the Border*, Philadelphia, Pa., J.B. Lippincott, 1963 [1866].

Miles, N., *Personal Recollections and Observations of General Nelson A. Miles*, New York, Werner, 1897.

Mills, A., *My Story*, Mechanicsburg, Pa., Stackpole Books, 2003 [1918]. Anson Mills commanded a cavalry unit in Crook's rebuff on the Rosebud in 1876.

Montigny, B.A.T., *La Vérité sur les questions métisses au Nord-Ouest: Biographie et récit de Gabriel Dumont sur les événements de 1885*, Montreal, n.p., 1889.

Motte, J.R., *Journey into Wilderness; An Army Surgeon's Account of Life in Camp and Field during the Creek and Seminole Wars, 1836–1838*, ed. J.F. Sunderman, Gainesville, Fla., University of Florida Press, 1953.

Prince, H., *Amidst a Storm of Bullets: The Diary of Lt. Henry Prince in Florida, 1836–1842*, ed. F. Laumer, Tampa, Fla., Tampa University Press, 1998.

Robinson, C.M., III (ed. and annot.), *The Diaries of John Gregory Bourke*, vol. 1, *November 20, 1872–July 28, 1876*, Denton, Tex., University of North Texas Press, 2003.

Rowland, D. (ed.), *Jefferson Davis, Constitutionalist: His Letters, Papers and Speeches*, Jackson, Miss., Mississippi Department of Archives and History, 1923.

Schmitt, M.F. (ed.), *General George Crook, his Autobiography*, Norman, Okla., University of Oklahoma Press, 1946. Crook's memoirs stop in 1876; the editor, Martin Schmitt, filled in the rest of the story on the basis of materials available to him in the 1940s.

Sweeney, E.R. (ed.), *Making Peace with Cochise: The 1872 Journal of Captain Joseph Alton Sladen*, Norman, Okla., University of Oklahoma Press, 1999.

Terrazas, J., *Memorías; la Guerra contra los Apaches*, Chihuahua, Centro Librero La Prensa, 1989 [1905]. Memoirs of the man whose troops defeated and killed the great Apache chieftain Victorio.

United States, Military Commission to Europe, 1855–6, *Report of the Secretary of War, Communicating the Report of Captain George B. McClellan (First Regiment, United States Cavalry), One of the Officers sent to the Seat of War in Europe, in 1855 and 1856*, Washington, D.C., A.O.P. Nicholson, 1857.

United States, Military Commission to Europe, 1855–6, *Report on the Art of War in Europe in 1854, 1855, and 1856*, Washington, D.C., George W. Bowman, Printer, 1860. Report of Major Richard Delafield.

United States, Military Commission to Europe, 1855–6, *The Armies of Europe*, Philadelphia, Pa., J.B. Lippincott, 1861. Report of Captain George B. McClellan.

United States, Military Commission to Europe in 1855 and 1856, *Report of Major Alfred Mordecai of the Ordnance Department*, Washington, George W. Bowman, Printer, 1860.

Utley, R.M. (ed.), *Life in Custer's Cavalry: Diaries and Letters of Albert and Jennie Barnitz, 1867–1868*, New Haven, Conn., Yale University Press, 1977.

Viola, H.J., *It is a Good Day to Die: Indian Eyewitnesses Tell the Story of the Battle of the Little Bighorn*, Lincoln, University of Nebraska Press, 2001.

Wolseley, G., *The Story of a Soldier's Life*, vol. 2, New York, Charles Scribner's Sons, 1903. Stops in 1874, although Wolseley's military career continued until 1902. Useful for his account of the 1870 Red River Expedition.

Reference works

Chambers, J.W., II (ed.), *The Oxford Companion to American Military History*, New York, Oxford University Press, 1999.

Dawson, J.G., III, *The Late 19th Century US Army, 1865–1898: A Research Guide*, Westport, Conn., Greenwood, 1990.

Hacker, B., *World Military History Bibliography: Premodern and Nonwestern Military Institutions and Warfare*, Leiden, Brill, 2003. Part 6 of this massive volume contains a list of works published on the Indian wars of the New World from 1962 to 1997.

Hatch, T., *A Custer Companion: A Comprehensive Guide to the Life of George Armstrong Custer and the Plains Indian Wars*, Mechanicsburg, Pa., Stackpole Books, 2002.

Heidler, D.S. and J.T. Heidler (eds), *Encyclopedia of the War of 1812*, Annapolis, Md., Naval Institute Press, 2004 [1997].

Lamar, H.R. (ed.), *The New Encyclopedia of the American West*, New Haven, Conn., Yale University Press, 1998 [1977].

Smith, T.T., *The Old Army in Texas: A Research Guide to the US Army in Nineteenth-Century Texas*, Austin, Tex., Texas State Historical Association, 2000.

Walter, J. (ed.), *Dictionary of Guns and Gunmakers*, London, Greenhill, 2001.

Wishart, D.J. (ed.), *Encyclopedia of the Great Plains*, Lincoln, Neb., University of Nebraska Press, 2004.

Secondary sources: general

Contemporary

Farrow, E.S., *A Handbook for Officers and Soldiers on the Frontiers*, Norman, Okla., University of Oklahoma Press, 2000 [1881]. Serves as an update of Marcy.

Lummis, C.F., *General Crook and the Apache wars*, ed. T.L. Fiske, Flagstaff, Ariz., Northland Press, 1966.

Lummis, C.F., *Dateline Fort Bowie: Charles Fletcher Lummis Reports on an Apache War*, D. Thrapp (ed. and annot.), Norman, Okla., University of Oklahoma Press, 1979 [1886]. Lummis was a Los Angeles journalist and travel writer who did much to capture the Southwest of his day in print.

Marcy, R., *The Prairie Traveler, a Hand-book for Overland Expeditions*, Williamstown, Mass., Corner House, 1978 [1859]. As close as the US Army came to providing its officers with a compendium of Indian-fighting doctrine.

Recent

Black, J., *America as a Military Power from the American Revolution to the Civil War*, Westport, Conn., Praeger, 2002.

Coffman, E.M., *The Old Army: A Portrait of the American Army in Peacetime, 1784–1898*, New York, Oxford University Press, 1986. Soldiers and soldiers' families on the frontier.

Coffman, E.M., *The Regulars: The American Army, 1898–1941*, Cambridge, Mass., Harvard University Press, 2004. Beyond our period, but suggestive for 'long shadow' of Indian-fighting army.

Cunliffe, M., *Soldiers and Civilians: The Martial Spirit in America, 1775–1865*, New York, Free Press, 1973 [1968]. Suggestive for whole history of US military.

Dunn, J.P., Jr., *Massacres of the Mountains: A History of the Indian Wars in the Far West*, Mechanicsburg, Pa., Stackpole Books, 2002 [1886].

Foner, J.D., *The United States Soldier between Two Wars, 1865–1898*, New York, Humanities Press, 1970.

Marshall, S.L.A., *Crimsoned Prairie: The Wars between the United States and the Plains Indians during the Winning of the West*, New York, Scribner's, 1972.

McDermott, J.D., *A Guide to the Indian Wars of the West*, Lincoln, Neb., University of Nebraska Press, 1998.

Paret, P. (ed.), *Makers of Modern Strategy from Machiavelli to the Nuclear Age*, Princeton, N.J., Princeton University Press, 1986. Sequel and update to E.M. Earle's *Makers of Modern Strategy*, also published by Princeton University Press (1943). Doug Porch's chapter on French colonial military strategy and tactics (pp. 376–408) is suggestive.

Perret, G., *A Country Made by War: From the Revolution to Vietnam – The Story of America's Rise to Power*, New York, Vintage, 1990 [1989].

Peterson, H.L. (ed.), *Encyclopedia of Firearms*, 3rd edn, New York, E.P. Dutton, 1967.

Rickey, D., Jr., *Forty Miles a Day on Beans and Hay: The Enlisted Soldier Fighting the Indian Wars*, Norman, Okla., University of Oklahoma Press, 1963. Indispensable.

Smith, H.N., *Virgin Land: The American West as Symbol and Myth*, Cambridge, Mass., Harvard University Press, 1950.

Utley, R.M., *Frontiersmen in Blue: The United States Army and the Indian, 1848–1865*, New York, Macmillan, 1967. Useful for all of the US Indian wars of the period with the exception of the Second Seminole War.

Utley, R.M., *Frontier Regulars: The United States Army and the Indian, 1866–1891*, New York, Macmillan, 1973. Covers all of the US Indian wars from Appomattox to Wounded Knee.

Utley, R.M., *The Indian Frontier of the American West, 1846–1890*, Albuquerque, N.Mex., University of New Mexico Press, 1984.

Weigley, R.F., *The American Way of War: A History of United States Military Strategy and Policy*, New York, Macmillan, 1973. Russell Weigley's death in 2004 was an enormous loss to the military history profession.

Weigley, R.F., *History of the United States Army*, New York, Macmillan, 1967. Still the standard.

Weigley, R.F., *Toward an American Army: [American] Military Thought from Washington to Marshall*, New York, Columbia University Press, 1962.

Wooster, R., *The Military and United States Indian Policy, 1865–1903*, New Haven, Conn., Yale University Press, 1988.

1 Worlds in motion

Books

Calloway, C.G., *One Vast Winter Count: The Native American West before Lewis and Clark*, Lincoln, Neb., University of Nebraska Press, 2003.

Carlson, P.H., *The Plains Indians*, College Station, Tex., Texas A and M University Press, 1998.
Cocker, M., *Rivers of Blood, Rivers of Gold: Europe's Conquest of the Indigenous Peoples*, New York, Grove Press, 2000.
Ferguson, R.B. and N.L. Whitehead (eds), *War in the Tribal Zone: Expanding States and Indigenous Warfare*, Santa Fe, N.Mex., School of American Research Press, 1992.
Lowie, R.H., *Indians of the Plains*, New York, McGraw-Hill, 1954.
Milloy, J.S., *The Plains Cree: Trade, Diplomacy and War, 1790 to 1870*, Winnipeg, University of Manitoba Press, 1988.

Articles and chapters

Albers, P., 'Changing Patterns of Ethnicity in the Northeastern [Canadian] Plains', in J.D. Hill (ed.), *History, Power, and Identity: Ethnogenesis in the Americas, 1492–1992*, Iowa City, University of Iowa Press, 1996.
Anderson, G.C., 'Early Dakota Migration and Intertribal War: A Revision', *Western Historical Quarterly*, 1980, vol. 11, pp. 17–36.
Betts, R.F., 'Immense Dimensions: The Impact of the American West on Late Nineteenth-Century European Thought about Expansion', *Western Historical Quarterly*, 1979, vol. 10, pp. 149–66.
Trevor-Roper, H.R., 'The Rise of Christian Europe', *The Listener*, 28 November 1963, pp. 871–5.
White, R., 'The Winning of the West: The Expansion of the Western Sioux in the Eighteenth and Nineteenth Centuries', *Journal of American History*, 1978, vol. 65, pp. 319–43.
Williams, W.L., 'United States Indian Policy and the Debate over Philippine Annexation: Implications for the Origins of American Imperialism', *Journal of American History*, 1980, vol. 66, pp. 810–31.

2 The New World in a century of small wars

Secondary sources

Books

Callwell, C.E., *Small Wars: Their Principles and Practice*, Lincoln, Neb., University of Nebraska Press, 1996 [1896]. The small wars 'bible'.
Ewers, J.C., *The Horse in Blackfoot Indian Culture, with Comparative Material from Other Western Tribes*, Bureau of American Ethnology, Washington, D.C., Smithsonian Institution, Government Printing Office (GPO), 1955.
Goodwin, G., *Western Apache Raiding and Warfare*, ed. K. Basso, Tucson, Ariz., University of Arizona Press, 1971.
Mails, T.E., *The Mystic Warriors of the Plains*, Garden City, N.Y., Doubleday, 1972.
Mishkin, B., *Rank and Warfare among the Plains Indians*, Monographs of the American Ethnological Society, Seattle, Wash., University of Washington Press, 1966 [1953].

Moten, M., *The Delafield Commission and the American Military Profession*, College Station, Tex., Texas A and M University Press, 2000.
Rowe, M.E., *Bulwark of the Republic: The American Militia in the Antebellum West*, Westport, Conn., Greenwood Press, 2003. An American institution in decline.
Secoy, F.R., *Changing Military Patterns on the Great Plains (17th Century through Early 19th Century)*, Seattle, Wash., University of Washington Press, 1966 [1953].
Wormser, R.E., *The Yellowlegs: The Story of the United States Cavalry*, Garden City, N.Y., Doubleday, 1966.

Articles and chapters

Carson, J.T, 'Horses and the Economy and Culture of the Choctaw Indians, 1690–1840', *Ethnohistory*, 1995, vol. 42, pp. 495–513.
Floyd, D.E., 'US Army Officers in Europe, 1815–1861', in D.H. White and J.W. Gordon (eds), *Proceedings of the Citadel Conference on War and Diplomacy, 1977*, Charleston, S.C., n.p., 1979, pp. 26–30.
Hämäläinen, P., 'The Rise and Fall of Plains Indian Horse Cultures', *Journal of American History*, 2003, vol. 90, pp. 833–62.
Hutchins, J.S., 'Mounted Riflemen: Real Role of Cavalry in [the North American] Indian Wars', in K.R. Toole *et al.* (eds), *Probing the American West: Papers from the Santa Fe Conference*, Santa Fe, N.Mex., Museum of New Mexico Press, 1962.

3 World views and fighting faiths

Secondary sources

Books

Birtle, A.J., *US Army Counterinsurgency and Contingency Operations Doctrine, 1860–1941*, Washington, D.C., Center of Military History, United States Army, 1998.
Bradford, J.C. (ed.), *The Military and the Conflict between Cultures: Soldiers at the Interface*, College Station, Tex., Texas A and M University Press, 1997.
Chet, G., *Conquering the American Wilderness: The Triumph of European Warfare in the Colonial Northeast*, Amherst, Mass., University of Massachusetts Press, 2003. Suggestive for later periods as well.
Smith, S.L., *The View from Officers' Row: Army Perceptions of Western Indians*, Tucson, Ariz., University of Arizona Press, 1990.

Articles and chapters

Abler, T., 'Scalping, Torture, Cannibalism and Rape: An Ethnohistorical Analysis of Conflicting Cultural Values in War', *Anthropologica*, 1992, vol. 34, pp. 3–20.
Cooper, J., 'The [US] Army's Search for a Mission, 1865–1900', in K.J. Hagan and W.R. Roberts (eds), *Against All Enemies: Interpretations of American Military History from Colonial Times to the Present*, New York, Greenwood Press, 1986, pp. 173–95.
Gates, J.M., 'Indians and Insurrectos: The US Army's Experience with Insurgency', *Parameters*, 1983, vol. 13, pp. 59–68.

Horsman, R., 'Scientific Racism and the American Indian in the Mid-Nineteenth Century', *American Quarterly*, 1975, vol. 27, pp. 152–68.
Simmons, C.R., 'The Indian Wars and US Military Thought, 1865–1890', *Parameters*, 1992, vol. 22, pp. 60–72.
Skelton, W.B., 'Army Officers' Attitudes Toward Indians, 1830–1860', *Pacific Northwest Quarterly*, vol. 67, pp. 113–24.
Weigley, R.F., 'Reflections on "Lessons" from Vietnam', in P. Braestrup (ed.), *Vietnam as History: Ten Years after the Paris Peace Accords*, Washington, D.C., University Press of America and Woodrow Wilson International Center for Scholars, 1984, pp. 115–24.

4 Chiefs and warriors

Secondary sources

Books

Dunlay, T.W., *Wolves for the Blue Soldiers: Indian Scouts and Auxiliaries with the United States Army, 1860–90*, Lincoln, Neb., University of Nebraska Press, 1982. Extremely useful.
Ford, R., *The Grim Reaper: The Machine Gun and Machine Gunners*, New York, Sarpedon, 1996.
Harris, S.J., *Canadian Brass: The Making of a Professional Army, 1860–1939*, Toronto, University of Toronto Press, 1988.
Jones, D.E., *Native American Armor, Shields, and Fortifications*, Austin, Tex., University of Texas Press, 2004.
Meadows, W.C., *Kiowa, Apache, and Comanche Military Societies: Enduring Veterans, 1800 to the Present*, Austin, Tex., University of Texas Press, 1999.
Nabokov, P., *Two Leggings: The Making of a Crow Warrior*, New York, Thomas Crowell and Co., 1967.

Articles and chapters

Brereton, T.R., 'Gatling Gun', in J.W. Chambers, III (ed.), *Oxford Companion to American Military History*, New York, Oxford University Press, 1999, p. 286.
Vargas, M.A., 'The Military Justice System and the Use of Illegal Punishments as Causes of Desertion in the US Army, 1821–1835', *Journal of Military History*, 1991, vol. 59, pp. 1–19.
Williams, T.H., 'The Macs and the Ikes', *American Mercury*, 1952, vol. 75, pp. 32–9.

5 The 'Great Clearance', 1815–42

Secondary sources

Books

Adams, G.R., *General William S. Harney: Prince of Dragoons*, Lincoln, Neb., University of Nebraska Press, 2001.

BIBLIOGRAPHY

Agnew, B., *Fort Gibson, Terminal on the Trail of Tears*, Norman, Okla., University of Oklahoma Press, 1980.

Antal, S., *A Wampum Denied: Procter's War of 1812*, Lansing, Mich., Michigan State University Press, 1997.

Ball, D., *Army Regulars on the Western Frontier, 1848–1861*, Norman, Okla., University of Oklahoma Press, 2001.

Black, J., *America as a Military Power: From the American Revolution to the Civil War*, Westport, Conn., Praeger, 2002.

Braund, K.E H., *Deerskins and Duffels: The Creek Indian Trade with Anglo-America, 1685–1815*, Lincoln, Neb., University of Nebraska Press, 1993.

Buchanan, J., *Jackson's Way: Andrew Jackson and the People of the Western Waters*, New York, John Wiley and Sons, 2001.

Buker, G.E., *Swamp Sailors in the Second Seminole War*, Gainesville, Fla., University of Florida Press, 1997 [1975].

Coles, H.L., *War of 1812*, Chicago, Ill., University of Chicago Press, 1965.

Cotterill, R.S., *The Southern Indians: The Story of the Civilized Tribes before Removal*, Norman, Okla., University of Oklahoma Press, 1954.

Covington, J.W., The *Seminoles of Florida*, Gainesville, Fla., University Press of Florida, 1993.

De Peyster, J.W., *Personal and Military History of Philip Kearny, Major-General United States Volunteers*, Elizabeth, N.J., Palmer and Co., 1870.

Dowd, G.E., *A Spirited Resistance: The North American Indian Struggle for Unity, 1745–1815*, Baltimore, Md., Johns Hopkins University Press, 1992.

Dowd, G.E., *War Under Heaven: Pontiac, the Indian Nations and the British Empire*, Baltimore, Md., Johns Hopkins University Press, 2002.

Downey, F., *Indian Wars of the US Army, 1776–1865*, Garden City, N.Y., Doubleday and Co., 1963.

Edmunds, R.D., *The Shawnee Prophet*, Lincoln, Neb., University of Nebraska Press, 1983.

Elting, J.R., *Amateurs to Arms! A Military History of the War of 1812*, New York, DaCapo Press, 1995 [1991].

Ethridge, R., *Creek Country: The Creek Indians and their World*, Chapel Hill, N.C., University of North Carolina Press, 2003.

Foreman, G., *Fort Gibson: A Brief History*, Norman, Okla., University of Oklahoma Press, 1936.

Foreman, G., *Indian Removal: The Emigration of the Five Civilized Tribes of Indians*, Norman, Okla., University of Oklahoma Press, 1953.

Goetzmann, W.H., *When the Eagle Screamed: The Romantic Horizon in American Expansionism, 1800–1860*, Norman, Okla., University of Oklahoma Press, 2000.

Green, M.D., *The Politics of Indian Removal: Creek Government and Society in Crisis*, Lincoln, Neb., University of Nebraska Press, 1982.

Griffith, B.W., *McIntosh and Weatherford: Creek Indian Leaders*, Tuscaloosa, Ala., University of Alabama Press, 1988.

Halbert, H.S. and T.H. Ball, *The Creek War of 1813 and 1814*, ed. F.L. Owsley, Jr., Southern Historical Publications No. 15, University, Ala., University of Alabama Press, 1969 [1895].

Hedren, P., *The Massacre of Lieutenant Grattan and His Command by Indians*, Glendale, Calif., A.H. Clark, 1983.

BIBLIOGRAPHY

Heidler, D.S. and J.T. Heidler, *Old Hickory's War: Andrew Jackson and the Quest for Empire*, Mechanicsburg, Pa., Stackpole Books, 1996.

Henri, F., *The Southern Indians and Benjamin Hawkins, 1796–1816*, Norman, Okla., University of Oklahoma Press, 1986.

Holmes, R., *Redcoat: The British Soldier in the Age of Horse and Musket*, New York, W.W. Norton, 2002.

Horsman, R., *The Origins of Indian Removal, 1815–1824*, East Lansing, Mich., Michigan State University Press, 1970. Lecture of 20 pp., but cogent.

Horsman, R., *The War of 1812*, New York, Knopf, 1969.

Hurt, R.D., *The Indian Frontier, 1763–1846*, Albuquerque, N.Mex., University of New Mexico Press, 2002.

Johnson, T.D., *Winfield Scott: The Quest for Military Glory*, Lawrence, Kans., University Press of Kansas, 1998.

Kaufman, S., *The Pig War: The United States, Britain, and the Balance of Power in the Pacific Northwest, 1846–72*, Lanham, Md., Lexington Books, 2003.

Kearny, T., *General Philip Kearny, Battle Soldier of Five Wars*, New York, G.P. Putnam's Sons, 1937.

Kieffer, C.L., *Maligned General: The Biography of Thomas Sidney Jesup*, New York, Presidio Press, 1979. Life of general who made Osceola prisoner under a flag of truce.

Lancaster, J.F., *Removal Aftershock: The Seminoles' Struggle to Survive in the West, 1836–1866*, Knoxville, Tenn., University of Tennessee Press, 1994.

Laumer, F., *Dade's Last Command*, Gainesville, Fla., University Press of Florida, 1995.

Laumer, F., *Massacre!*, Gainesville, Fla., University of Florida Press, 1968. Dade massacre; superseded by previous title.

Littlefield, D.F., *Africans and Seminoles: From Removal to Emancipation*, Jackson, Miss., University Press of Mississippi, 2001.

Mahon, J.K., *History of the Second Seminole War, 1835–1842*, rev. edn, Gainesville, University of Florida Press, 1967. Still the standard account.

Mahon, J.K., *The War of 1812*, Gainesville, University of Florida Press, 1972.

Martin, J.W., *Sacred Revolt: The Muscogees' Struggle for a New World*, Boston, Mass., Beacon, 1991.

Miller, S.A., *Coacoochee's Bones: A Seminole Saga*, Lawrence, Kans., University Press of Kansas, 2003.

Missall, J. and M.L. Missall, *The Seminole Wars: America's Longest Indian Conflict*, Gainesville, Fla., University Press of Florida, 2004. This popular history does not supplant Mahon's 1967 study.

Morton, D., *A Military History of Canada: From Champlain to Kosovo*, 4th edn, Toronto, McClelland and Stewart, 1999 [1985].

Nichols, R.L., *Black Hawk and the Warrior's Path,* Arlington Heights, Ill., Harlan Davidson, 1992.

O'Brien, S.M., *In Bitterness and in Tears: Andrew Jackson's Destruction of the Creeks and Seminoles*, Westport, Conn., Praeger, 2003.

Perdue, T., *"Mixed blood" Indians: Racial Construction in the Early South*, Athens, Ga., University of Georgia Press, 2003.

Peskin, A., *Winfield Scott and the Profession of Arms*, Kent, Ohio, Kent State University Press, 2003.

BIBLIOGRAPHY

Porter, K.W., *The Black Seminoles: History of a Freedom-Seeking People*, rev. edn, A.A. Amos and T.P. Senter, Gainesville, University Press of Florida, 1996.

Prucha, F.P., *American Indian Policy in the Formative Years: the Indian Trade and Intercourse Acts, 1790–1834*, Lincoln, Neb., University of Nebraska Press, 1970 [1962].

Prucha, F.P., *Broadax and Bayonet: The Role of the United States Army in the Development of the Northwest, 1815–1860*, Madison, Wis., State Historical Society of Wisconsin, 1953.

Prucha, F.P., *The Sword of the Republic: The United States Army on the Frontier, 1783–1846*, London, Macmillan, 1969. Utley's *Frontiersmen in Blue* picks up where this volume leaves off.

Reid, J. and J.H. Eaton, *Life of Andrew Jackson*, University, Ala., University of Alabama Press, 1971 [1817].

Remini, R.V., *Andrew Jackson and the Course of American Empire, 1767–1821*, vol. 1, New York, Harper and Row, 1977.

Richardson, R.N., *The Comanche Barrier to South Plains Settlement*, Austin, Tex., Eakin Press, 1996 [1933]. Dated, but still useful.

Rodenbough, T.F., *From Everglade to Canyon with the Second United States Cavalry*, Norman, Okla., University of Oklahoma Press, 2000 [1875].

Saunt, C., *A New Order of Things: Property, Power, and the Transformation of the Creek Indians, 1733–1816*, Cambridge, Cambridge University Press, 1999.

Skelton, W.B., *An American Profession of Arms: The Army Officer Corps, 1784–1861*, Lawrence, Kans., University Press of Kansas, 1992. Indispensable for understanding the rise of professionalism in the US antebellum army.

Sprague, J.T., *The Origin, Progress, and Conclusion of the Florida War*, repr. and intro. J.K. Mahon, Tampa, Fla., University of Tampa Press, 2000 [1964; 1848].

Starkey, A., *European and Native American Warfare, 1675–1815*, Norman, Okla., University of Oklahoma Press, 1998. The solid foundation on which my own book is built.

Sugden, J., *The Shawnees in Tecumseh's Time*, Nortorf, Germany, Abhandlungen der Voelkerkundlichen Arbeitsgemeinschaft, 1990.

Sugden, J., *Tecumseh: A Life*, New York, Henry Holt and Co., 1999 [1997].

Sugden, J., *Tecumseh's Last Stand*, Norman, Okla., University of Oklahoma Press, 1989 [1985].

Swanton, J.R., *The Indians of the Southeastern United States*, New York, Greenwood Press, 1969 [1946].

Van Alstyne, R.W., *The Rising American Empire*, New York, Oxford University Press, 1960.

Wallace, A.F.C., *Jefferson and the Indians: The Tragic Fate of the First Americans*, Cambridge, Mass., Harvard University Press, 1999.

Wallace, A.F.C., *The Long, Bitter Trail: Andrew Jackson and the Indians*, New York, Hill and Wang, 1993.

Wickman, P.R., *Osceola's Legacy*, Tuscaloosa, Ala., University of Alabama Press, 1991.

Wright, J.L., Jr., *Creeks and Seminoles: The Destruction and Regeneration of the Muscogulge People*, Lincoln, Neb., University of Nebraska Press, 1986. Muscogulge is the anthropologists' shorthand for 'Creek'.

Articles and chapters

Allen, R.S., 'His Majesty's Indian Allies: Native Peoples, the British Crown and the War of 1812', *Michigan Historical Review*, 1988, vol. 14, pp. 1–24.

Boyd, M.F., 'Asi-Yaholo or Osceola', *Florida Historical Quarterly*, 1955, vol. 33, pp. 249–305.

Boyd, M.F., 'Florida Aflame: Background and Onset of the Seminole War, 1835', *Florida Historical Quarterly*, 1951, pp. 1–115.

Brannon, P.A., 'Creek Indian War, 1836–37', *Alabama Historical Quarterly*, 1951, vol. 13, pp. 156–8.

Brauer, K.J., 'The United States and British Imperial Expansion, 1815–1860', *Diplomatic History*, 1988, vol. 12, pp. 19–37.

Burnett, J.G., 'The Cherokee Removal through the Eyes of a Private Soldier', *Journal of Cherokee Studies*, 1978, vol. 3, pp. 51–3.

Calloway, C.G., 'The End of an Era: British–Indian Relations in the Great Lakes Region after the War of 1812', *Michigan Historical Review*, 1986, vol. 12, pp. 1–20.

Campbell, J.A., 'The Creek War of 1836', *Transactions of the Alabama Historical Society*, 1899, vol. 3, pp. 162–6.

Clow, R.L., 'Mad Bear: William S. Harney and the Sioux Expedition of 1855–56', *Nebraska History*, 1980, vol. 61, pp. 133–51.

Corn, J.F., 'Conscience or Duty: General John E. Wool's Dilemma with Cherokee Removal', *Journal of Cherokee Studies*, 1978, vol. 2, pp. 35–9.

Covington, J.W., 'Migration of the Seminoles into Florida: 1700–1825', *Florida Historical Quarterly*, 1968, vol. 46, pp. 340–57.

Covington, J.W., 'White Control of Seminole Leadership', *Florida Anthropologist*, 1965, vol. 18, pp. 137–46.

Dean, L.S., 'Tecumseh's Prophecy: The Great New Madrid Earthquakes of 1811–1812 and 1841 in Alabama', *Alabama Review*, 1994, vol. 97, pp. 163–71.

Denham, J.M., '"Some prefer the Seminoles": Violence and Disorder among Soldiers and Settlers in the Second Seminole War, 1835–1842', *Florida Historical Quarterly*, 1991, vol. 70, pp. 38–54.

Dowd, G., 'Thinking and Believing: Nativism and Unity in the Ages of Pontiac and Tecumseh', *American Indian Quarterly*, 1992, vol. 16, pp. 309–35.

Edmunds, R.D., 'Tecumseh, the Shawnee Prophet, and American History: A Reassessment', *Western Historical Quarterly*, 1983, vol. 14, pp. 261–76.

Hassig, R., 'Internal Conflict in the Creek War of 1813–1814', *Ethnohistory*, 1974, vol. 21, pp. 252–71.

Heidler, D.S., 'The Politics of National Aggression: Congress and the First Seminole War', *Journal of the Early Republic*, 1993, vol. 13, pp. 501–30.

Holland, J.W., 'Andrew Jackson and the Creek War: Victory at the Horseshoe', *Alabama Review*, 1968, vol. 21, pp. 243–75.

Horsman, R., 'The Dimension of an "empire for liberty": Expansionism and Republicanism, 1775–1825', *Journal of the Early Republic*, 1989, vol. 9, pp.1–20.

Kanon, T., '"A slow, laborious slaughter": The Battle of Horseshoe Bend', *Tennessee Historical Quarterly*, 1999, vol. 58, pp. 2–15.

Lee, W.E., 'Fortify, Fight, or Flee: Tuscarora and Cherokee Defensive Warfare and Military Culture Adaptation', *Journal of Military History*, 2004, vol. 68, pp. 713–70. Welcome corrective to Eurocentric ideas about Indian fortification skills.

Mahon, J.K., 'The Treaty of Moultrie Creek, 1823', *Florida Historical Quarterly*, 1962, vol. 40, pp. 350–72.

[Metcalf, P.R.], 'Tenskwatawa ("the Shawnee Prophet")', in H.R. Lamar (ed.), *The New Encyclopedia of the American West*, New Haven, Conn., Yale University Press, 1998 [1977].

Milligan, J.D., 'Slave Rebelliousness and the Florida Maroon', *Prologue*, 1974, vol. 6, pp. 4–18.

Mulroy, K., 'Ethnogenesis and Ethnohistory of the Seminole Maroons', *Journal of World History*, 1993, vol. 4, pp. 287–305.

Nunez, T.A. (ed.), 'Creek Nativism and the Creek War of 1813–1814', *Ethnohistory*, 1958, vol. 5, pp. 1–47, 131–75, 292–301.

Owsley, F.L., Jr., 'The Fort Mims Massacre', *Alabama Review*, 1971, vol. 24, pp. 192–204.

Owsley, F.L., Jr., 'Prophet of War: Josiah Francis and the Creek War', *American Indian Quarterly*, 1985, vol. 9, pp. 273–93.

Perdue, T., 'The Trail of Tears: Removal of the Southern Indians', in P. Weeks (ed.), *The American Indian Experience: A Profile, 1524 to the Present*, Arlington Heights, Ill., Forum Press, 1988, pp. 96–117.

Porter, K.W., 'The Episode of Osceola's Wife: Fact or Fiction?', *Florida Historical Quarterly*, 1947, vol. 26, pp. 92–8.

Porter, K.W., 'Negroes and the Seminole War, 1817–1818', *Journal of Negro History*, 1951, vol. 36, pp. 249–80.

Preble, G.H., 'A Canoe Expedition into the Everglades in 1842', *Tequesta*, vol. 45, pp. 30–51.

Prucha, F.P., 'The United States Army as Viewed by British Travelers, 1825–1860', *Military Affairs*, 1953, vol. 17, pp. 113–24.

Reid, J.A., 'The Battle of Horseshoe Bend (March 27, 1814)', *Journal of the Indian Wars*, 1999, vol. 1, pp. 21–9.

Reid, J.A., 'Prelude to Horseshoe Bend: The Battles of Emuckfaw and Enotochopco (January 1814)', *Journal of the Indian Wars*, 1999, vol. 1, pp. 1–20.

Remini, R.V., 'Indian Removal', in Remini, *The Legacy of Andrew Jackson: Essays on Democracy, Indian Removal, and Slavery*, Baton Rouge, La., Louisiana State University Press, 1988, pp. 45–82. Puts best possible face on Jackson's Removal policy.

Silver, J.W., 'A Counter Proposal to the Indian Removal Policy of Andrew Jackson', *Journal of Mississippi History*, 1942, vol. 4, pp. 207–15.

Skelton, W.B., 'Army Officers' Attitudes toward Indians, 1830–1860', *Pacific Northwest Quarterly*, 1976, vol. 67, pp. 113–24.

Spiller, R.J., 'Calhoun's Expansible Army: The History of a Military Idea', *South Atlantic Quarterly*, 1980, vol. 79, pp. 189–203.

Stanley, G.F.G., 'The Indians in the War of 1812', *Canadian Historical Review*, 1950, vol. 31, pp. 145–65.

Sturtevant, W.C., 'Creek into Seminole', in E. Leacock and N.O. Lurie (eds), *North American Indians in Historical Perspective*, New York, Random House, 1971, pp. 91–128.

Sugden, J., 'Early Pan-Indianism: Tecumseh's Tour of the Indian Country, 1811–1812', *American Indian Quarterly*, 1986, vol. 10, pp. 273–304.

Sugden, J., 'Tecumseh's Travels Revisited', *Indiana Magazine of History*, 2000, vol. 96, pp. 151–68.

Thurman, M.D., 'The Shawnee Prophet's Movement and the Origins of the Prophet Dance', *Current Anthropology*, 1984, vol. 25, pp. 530–1.

Usner, D., Jr., 'American Indians and the Cotton Frontier: Changing Economic Relations with Citizens and Slaves in the Mississippi Territory', *Journal of American History*, 1985, vol. 72, pp. 297–317.

Valliere, K.L., 'The Creek War of 1836, A Military History', *Chronicles of Oklahoma*, 1979–80, vol. 57, pp. 463–85.

Wallace, A.F.C., 'New Religions among the Delaware Indians, 1600–1900', *Southwestern Journal of Anthropology*, 1956, vol. 12, pp. 1–21.

Wallace, A.F.C., 'Revitalization Movements: Some Theoretical Considerations for their Comparative Study', *American Anthropologist*, 1956, vol. 58, pp. 264–81.

Watson, S., '"This thankless . . . unholy war": Army Officers and Civil–Military Relations in the Second Seminole War', in P.D. Dillard and R.L. Hall (eds), *The Southern Albatross: Race and Ethnicity in the American South*, Macon, Ga., Mercer University Press, 1999, pp. 9–49.

Willig, T., 'Prophetstown on the Wabash: The Native Spiritual Defense of the Old Northwest', *Michigan Historical Review*, 1997, vol. 23, pp. 130–5.

Wooster, R., 'Military Strategy in the Southwest, 1848–1860', *Military History of Texas and the Southwest*, 1979, vol. 15, pp. 5–15.

6 Indian wars in Mexico, 1821–76

Secondary sources

Books

Acuña, R.F., *Sonora Strongman: Ignacio Pesqueira and his Time*, Tucson, Ariz., University of Arizona Press, 1974.

Baqueiro, S., *Ensayo histórico sobre las revoluciones de Yucatán desde el ano de 1840 hasta 1864*, Merída, Yucatán, Manuel Heredia Argulles, 1878–9 (vols 1 and 2); Tipografía de G. Canto (vol. 3). The establishment view, but important to know.

Dabbs, J.A., *The French Army in Mexico, 1861–1867: A Study in Military Government*, The Hague, Mouton, 1963.

DePalo, W.A., Jr., *The Mexican National Army, 1822–1852*, College Station, Tex., Texas A and M University Press, 1996.

Dumond, D.E., *The Machete and the Cross: Campesino Rebellion in Yucatan*, Lincoln, Neb., University of Nebraska Press, 1997. Fact-filled; author believes Caste War was in fact a peasant rebellion, not a race war.

Farriss, N.M., *Maya Society under Spanish Colonial Rule: The Collective Enterprise of Survival*, Princeton, N.J., Princeton University Press, 1984.

Guy, D.J. and T.E. Sheridan (eds), *Contested Ground: Comparative Frontiers on the Northern and Southern Edges of the Spanish Empire*, Tucson, Ariz., University of Arizona Press, 1998. Contains good essay on Yaqui religion and mythology.

Hale, C.A., *Mexican Liberalism in the Age of Mora, 1821–1853*, New Haven, Conn., Yale University Press, 1968.

Hu-DeHart, E., *Missionaries, Miners, and Indians: Spanish Contact with the Yaqui Nation of Northwestern New Spain, 1533–1820,* Tucson, Ariz., University of Arizona Press, 1981. The indispensable background book on the Yaqui wars.

Hu-DeHart, E., *Yaqui Resistance and Survival: The Struggle for Land and Autonomy, 1821–1910*, Madison, Wis., University of Wisconsin Press, 1984. Basic for understanding Yaqui wars.

Kessell, J.L., *Friars, Soldiers, and Reformers: Hispanic Arizona and the Sonora Mission Frontier, 1767–1856*, Tucson, Ariz., University of Arizona Press, 1976.

May, R.E., *Manifest Destiny's Underworld: Filibustering in Antebellum America*, Chapel Hill, N.C., University of North Carolina Press, 2002.

Olliff, D.C., *Reforma Mexico and the United States: A Search for Alternatives to Annexation, 1854–1861*, Tuscaloosa, Ala., University of Alabama Press, 1981.

Radding, C., *Wandering Peoples: Colonialism, Ethnic Spaces, and Ecological Frontiers in Northwestern Mexico, 1700–1850*, Durham, N.C., Duke University Press, 1997.

Reed, Nelson A., *The Caste War of Yucatán*, rev. edn, Stanford, Calif., Stanford University Press, 2001 [1964]. The classic account.

Rugeley, T., *Maya Wars: Ethnographic Accounts from Nineteenth-Century Yucatán*, Norman, Okla., University of Oklahoma Press, 2001. Collection of contemporary documents.

Rugeley, T., *Yucatán's Maya Peasantry and the Origins of Caste War*, Austin, Tex., University of Texas Press, 1996.

Salas, E., *Soldaderas in the Mexican Military: Myths and History*, Austin, Tex., University of Texas Press, 1990. Did women really play a big role in the Mexican military in the nineteenth century? What sort of role? What did they gain from it?

Serrano Ortega, J. A., *El contigente de sangre: Los gobiernos estatales y departmentales y los metodos de reclutamiento del ejercito permanente mexicano, 1824–1844*, Mexico, Instituto Nacional de Anthropologia e Historia, 1993.

Sierra, C.J., *Los indios de la frontera (Mexico–Estados Unidos)*, Mexico, Ediciones de la Muralla, 1980. Sierra reminds us that the Southwestern Indians – Apaches, Comanches, etc. – were citizens of Mexico before the Mexican–American War, after which they were something else again.

Voss, S.F., *On the Periphery of Nineteenth Century Mexico: Sonora and Sinaloa, 1810–1877*, Tucson, Ariz., University of Arizona Press, 1982.

Weber, D.J., *The Mexican Frontier, 1821–1846: The American Southwest under Mexico*, Albuquerque, N.Mex., University of New Mexico Press, 1982.

Zuñiga, I., *Rapida ojeada al estado de Sonora*, Hermosillo, Sonora, Gobierno del Estado de Sonora, 1985 [1835].

Articles and chapters

Ezell, P.H., 'Indians under the Law: Mexico, 1821–1847', *America Indígena*, 1955, vol. 15, pp. 199–214.

Forbes, J.D., 'Historical Survey of the Indians of Sonora, 1821–1910', *Ethnohistory*, 1957, vol. 4, pp. 335–68.

Frazer, D.J., 'La politica de desamortización en las communidades indígenas, 1856–1872', *Historia Mexicana*, 1972, vol. 21, pp. 615–52.

Griffen, W.B., 'Apache Indians and the North Mexican Peace Establishments', in C. Lange (ed.), *Southwestern Culture History: Collected Papers in Honor of Albert H. Schroeder*, Santa Fe, N.Mex., Ancient City Press, 1985, pp. 183–95.

Rippy, J.F., 'The Indians of the Southwest in the Diplomacy of the United States and Mexico, 1848–1853', *Hispanic–American Historical Review*, 1919, vol. 2, pp. 363–96.

Santoni, P., ' A Fear of the People: The Civic Militia of Mexico in 1845', *Hispanic American Historical Review*, 1988, vol. 6, pp. 268–88.

Spicer, E.H., 'Yaqui militarism', *The Arizona Quarterly*, 1947, vol. 3, pp. 40–8.

7 War on the plains, 1848–77

Secondary sources

Warfare on the South Plains

BOOKS

Arnold, J.R., *Jeff Davis's Own: Cavalry, Comanches, and the Battle for the Texas Frontier*, New York, John Wiley and Sons, 2000.

Baker, T.L. and B.R. Harrison, *Adobe Walls: The History and Archaeology of the 1874 Trading Post*, College Station, Tex., Texas A and M University Press, 2003 [1986].

Chalfant, W.Y., *Cheyennes at Dark Water Creek: The Last Fight of the Red River War*, Norman, Okla., University of Oklahoma Press, 1997. Complemented but not superseded by Monnett, *Massacre at Cheyenne Hole* (below).

Cutrer, T.W., *Ben McCulloch and the Frontier Military Tradition*, Chapel Hill, N.C., University of North Carolina Press, 1993. Officer of Texas Rangers who believed his aspirations for regular army command were thwarted because he was not a West Pointer.

Faulk, O., *The US Camel Corps: An Army Experiment*, New York, Oxford University Press, 1976.

Fehrenbach, T.R., *Comanches: The Destruction of a People*, New York, Knopf, 1974.

Goodrich, T., *Scalp Dance: Indian Warfare on the High Plains, 1865–1879*, Mechanicsburg, Pa., Stackpole Books, 1997.

Greene, J.A. and D.D. Scott, *Finding Sand Creek: History, Archaeology, and the 1864 Massacre Site*, Norman, Okla., University of Oklahoma Press, 2004.

Greene, J.A., *Washita: The US Army and the Southern Cheyennes, 1867–1869*, Norman, Okla., University of Oklahoma Press, 2004. Now the standard history.

Grinnell, G.B., *The Fighting Cheyennes*, Norman, Okla., University of Oklahoma Press, 1955.

Haley, J.L., *The Buffalo War: The History of the Red River Indian Uprising of 1874*, Garden City, N.Y., Doubleday, 1976.

Hoig, S., *The Battle of the Washita: The Sheridan–Custer Indian Campaign of 1867–69*, Lincoln, Neb., University of Nebraska Press, 1976.

Hoig, S., *Tribal Wars of the Southern Plains*, Norman, Okla., University of Oklahoma Press, 1993.

Kavanagh, T.W., *Comanche Political History: An Ethnohistorical Perspective, 1706–1875*, Lincoln, Neb., University of Nebraska Press, 1996.

Leckie, W.H., *The Military Conquest of the Southern Plains*, Norman, Okla., University of Oklahoma Press, 1963.

Monnett, J.H., *The Battle of Beecher Island and the Indian War of 1867–1869*, Niwot, Colo., University Press of Colorado, 1992. Now the authoritative account.

Monnett, J.H., *Massacre at Cheyenne Hole: Lieutenant Austin Henely and the Sappa*

BIBLIOGRAPHY

Creek Controversy, Niwot, Colo., University Press of Colorado, 1999. Useful, but also see Chalfant, *Cheyennes at Dark Water Creek* (above).

Nye, W.S., *Plains Indian Raiders: The Final Phases of Warfare from the Arkansas to the Red River*, Norman, Okla., University of Oklahoma Press, 1968.

Robinson, C.M., III, *Bad Hand: A Biography of General Ranald S. Mackenzie*, Austin, Tex., State House Press, 1993.

Utley, R.M., *Lone Star Justice: The First Century of the Texas Rangers*, Oxford, Oxford University Press, 2002. This is the book to read about the Texas Rangers.

Wallace, E. and E.A. Hoebel, *The Comanches, Lords of the South Plains*, Norman, Okla., University of Oklahoma Press, 1958 [1952].

Webb, W.P., *The Texas Rangers: A Century of Frontier Defense*, Austin, Tex., University of Texas Press, 1965 [1935]. Dated; celebratory.

ARTICLES AND CHAPTERS

Despain, S.M., 'Captain Albert Barnitz and the Battle of the Washita: New Documents, New Insights', *Journal of the Indian Wars*, 1999, vol. 1, pp. 135–44.

Leach, J.A., 'Search and Destroy: Counter Insurgency on the American Plains', *Military History of Texas and the Southwest*, 1971, vol. 9, pp. 55–60.

McCall, K.S., '"Vindictive earnestness" in Practice: The Campaign of Ranald S. Mackenzie as a Model of Post-Civil War Indian Policy', *Journal of the West*, 1995, vol. 35, pp. 67–81.

Rogers, J.L., 'The Flint and Steel: Background of the Red River War of 1874–1875', *Texas Military History*, 1969, vol. 7, pp. 153–75.

Smith, R.A., 'The Comanche Invasion of Mexico in the Fall of 1845', *Southwestern Historical Quarterly*, 1934–5, vol. 38, pp. 157–76.

Smith, R.A., 'The Comanche Invasion of Mexico in the Fall of 1859', *West Texas Historical Association Year Book*, 1959, vol. 35, pp. 3–28.

Smith, R.A., 'The Comanche Bridge between Oklahoma and Mexico, 1834–1844', *Chronicles of Oklahoma*, 1961, vol. 39, pp. 54–69.

Smith, R.A., 'The Comanche Sun over Mexico', *West Texas Historical Association Year Book*, 1970, vol. 46, pp. 25–62.

Smith, T.T., 'US Army Combat Operations in the Indian Wars of Texas, 1849–1881', *Southwestern Historical Quarterly*, 1996, vol. 99, pp. 500–31.

Taylor, J.F., 'The Indian Campaign on the Staked Plain, 1874–1875', *Panhandle–Plains Historical Review*, 1962, vol. 35, pp. 221–33.

Utley, R.M., 'Kit Carson and the Adobe Walls Campaign', *The American West*, 1965, vol. 2, pp. 4–11.

Wallace, E.S., 'General John Lapham Bullis: The Thunderbolt of the Texas Frontier', *Southwestern Historical Quarterly*, 1951, vol. 54, pp. 452–61 (April), 77–85 (July).

West, G.D., 'The Battle of Adobe Walls (1874)', *Panhandle–Plains Historical Review*, 1960, vol. 36, pp. 1–36.

White, L.J., 'New Sources Relating to the Battle of Adobe Walls, 1874', *Texas Military History*, 1970, vol. 8, pp. 1–12.

Wooster, R., 'The Army and the Politics of Expansion: Texas and the Southwest Borderlands, 1870–1886', *Southwestern Historical Quarterly*, 1989, vol. 93, pp. 151–67.

BIBLIOGRAPHY

Warfare on the High Plains

BOOKS

Ambrose, S.E., *Crazy Horse and Custer – The Parallel Lives of Two American Warriors*, New York, New American Library, 1975.

Andrist, R.K., *The Long Death: The Last Days of the Plains Indian*, New York, Collier, 1993 [1964].

Boye, A., *Holding Stone Hands: On the Trail of the Cheyenne Exodus*, Lincoln, Neb., University of Nebraska Press, 1999.

Brill, C.J., *Custer, Black Kettle, and the Fight on the Washita*, Norman, Okla., University of Oklahoma Press, 2001 [1938]. Dated, but the introductory matter is well worth a look.

Brown, D., *The Fetterman Massacre*, Lincoln, Neb., University of Nebraska Press, 1984 [1962].

Carpenter, J.A., *Sword and Olive Branch: Oliver Otis Howard*, Pittsburgh, Pa., University of Pittsburgh Press, 1964.

Dippie, B.W., *Custer's Last Stand: The Anatomy of an American Myth*, Lincoln, Neb., University of Nebraska Press, 1994 [1984; 1976].

Dixon, D., *Hero of Beecher Island: The Life and Military Career of George A. Forsyth*, Lincoln, Neb., University of Nebraska Press, 1994.

Finerty, J.F., *Warpath and Bivouac: The Big Horn and Yellowstone Expedition*, ed. M.M. Quaife, Lincoln, Neb., University of Nebraska Press, 1955 [1890].

Fox, R.A., Jr., *Archaeology, History and Custer's Last Battle: The Little Big Horn Reexamined*, Norman, Okla., University of Oklahoma Press, 1993.

Frost, L.A., *The Court-Martial of General George Armstrong Custer*, Norman, Okla., University of Oklahoma Press, 1968.

Goodrich, T., *Scalp Dance: Indian Warfare on the High Plains, 1865–1879*, Mechanicsburg, Pa., Stackpole Books, 1997. Popular, anecdotal, but offers a range of useful quotations from original sources.

Gray, J.S., *Centennial Campaign: The Sioux War of 1876*, Fort Collins, Colo., Old Army Press, 1976. The classic narrative.

Gray, J.S., *Custer's Last Campaign: Mitch Boyer and the Little Bighorn Reconstructed*, Lincoln, Neb., University of Nebraska Press, 1991. Meticulous, convincing reconstruction of the Custer debacle.

Greene, J.A. (ed.), *Battles and Skirmishes of the Great Sioux War, 1876–1877: The Military View*, Norman, Okla., University of Oklahoma Press, 1993.

Greene, J.A. (ed.), *Lakota and Cheyenne Indian Views of the Great Sioux War, 1876–1877*, Norman, Okla., University of Oklahoma Press, 1994.

Greene, J.A., *Morning Star Dawn: The Powder River Expedition and the Northern Cheyennes, 1876*, Norman, Okla., University of Oklahoma Press, 2003.

Greene, J.A., *Slim Buttes, 1876: An Episode of the Great Sioux War*, Norman, Okla., University of Oklahoma Press, 1982. The High Plains battle George Crook won.

Greene, J.A., *Yellowstone Command: Colonel Nelson A. Miles and the Great Sioux War, 1876–1877*, Lincoln, Neb., University of Nebraska Press, 1991.

Grinnell, G.B., *The Fighting Cheyennes*, Norman, Okla., University of Oklahoma Press, 1956 [1915]. Based on large chunks of valuable oral history.

BIBLIOGRAPHY

Hardorff, R.G., *Hokahey! A good day to die! The Indian Casualties of the Custer Fight*, Spokane, Wash., Arthur H. Clark, 1993.

Hassrick, R.B., *The Sioux: Life and Customs of a Warrior Society*, Norman, Okla., University of Oklahoma Press, 1956.

Hedren, P., *The Massacre of Lieutenant Grattan and his Command by Indians*, Glendale, Calif., Arthur H. Clark Co., 1983.

Heyman, M.L., *Prudent Soldier: A Biography of Major General E.R.S. Canby, 1817–1873*. Glendale, Calif., Arthur H. Clark Co., 1959. The only US general officer to be killed in the Indian wars.

Hoig, S., *Perilous Pursuit: The US Cavalry and the Northern Cheyennes*, Boulder, Colo., University Press of Colorado, 2002.

Hutton, P.A., *The Custer Reader*, Lincoln, Neb., University of Nebraska Press, 1992.

Hutton, P.A., *Phil Sheridan and his Army*, Lincoln, Neb., University of Nebraska Press, 1985.

Hutton, P.A. (ed.), *Soldiers West: Biographies from the Military Frontier*, Lincoln, Neb., University of Nebraska Press, 1987.

Isenberg, A.C., *The Destruction of the Bison: An Environmental History, 1750–1920*, Cambridge, Cambridge University Press, 2000.

Jensen, R.E., R.E. Paul and J.E. Carter (eds), *Eyewitness at Wounded Knee*, Lincoln, Neb., University of Nebraska Press, 1991.

Keenan, J., *The Wagon Box Fight: An Episode of Red Cloud's War*, rev. edn, Conshohocken, Pa., Savas, 2000 [1988].

Knight, O., *Life and Manners in the Frontier Army*, Norman, Okla., University of Oklahoma Press, 1978.

Larson, R.W., *Red Cloud: Warrior-Statesman of the Lakota Sioux*, Norman, Okla., University of Oklahoma Press, 1997.

Mangum, N.C., *Battle of the Rosebud: Prelude to the Little Bighorn*, El Segundo, Calif., Upton and Sons, 1987. Not George Crook's finest hour.

McEwan, G., *Sitting Bull: The Years in Canada*, Edmonton, Alta., Hurtig, 1973.

Michno, G.F., *Lakota Noon: The Indian Narrative of Custer's Defeat*, Missoula, Mont., Mountain Press Publishing Co., 1997. Invaluable reconstruction of Indian side of Little Bighorn battle from oral accounts of participants.

Mills, C.K., *Harvest of Barren Regrets: The Army Career of Frederick William Benteen, 1834–1898*, Glendale, Calif., Arthur H. Clark Co., 1985.

Ostler, J., *The Plains Sioux and US Colonialism from Lewis and Clark to Wounded Knee*, Cambridge, Cambridge University Press, 2004.

Paul, R.E., *Blue Water Creek and the First Sioux War, 1854–1856*, Norman, Okla., University of Oklahoma Press, 2004. Author sees a continuum from this battle (also known as battle of Ash Hollow) to Great Sioux War of 1876–7.

Rankin, C.E. (ed.), *Legacy: New Perspectives on the Battle of the Little Bighorn*, Helena, Mont., Montana Historical Society Press, 1996.

Rosenberg, B.A., *Custer and the Epic of Defeat*, University Park, Pa., Pennsylvania State University Press, 1974. An explanation of the endless fascination with a lost cause.

Sandoz, M., *Cheyenne Autumn*, Lincoln, Neb., University of Nebraska Press, 1992 [1942]. Much criticised for its inaccuracies and exaggerations, but a widely read and influential evocation of the trauma of the Plains Indians as they faced reservation life.

Scott, D.D. et al., *Archaeological Insights into the Custer Battle: An Assessment of the 1984 Field Season*, Norman, Okla., University of Oklahoma Press, 1987. First assessment of the results of the archaeological dig at the Little Bighorn in the wake of the 1984 fire.

Scott, D.D. et al., *Archaeological Perspectives on the Battle of the Little Bighorn,* Norman, Okla., University of Oklahoma Press, 1989. Further considerations of same.

Sklenar, L., *To Hell with Honor: Custer and the Little Bighorn*, Norman, Okla., University of Oklahoma Press, 2000.

Stewart, E.I., *Custer's Luck*, Norman, Okla., University of Oklahoma Press, 1955.

Utley, R.M., *Cavalier in Buckskin: George Armstrong Custer and the Western Military Frontier*, Norman, Okla., University of Oklahoma Press, 1988.

Utley, R.M., *Custer and the Great Controversy: The Origin and Development of a Legend*, Lincoln, Neb., University of Nebraska Press, 1998 [1992].

Utley, R.M., *The Lance and the Shield: The Life and Times of Sitting Bull*, New York, Henry Holt and Co., 1993.

Utley, R.M., *The Last Days of the Sioux Nation*, New Haven, Conn., Yale University Press, 1963. Best book on Wounded Knee.

Vaughn, J.W., *The Reynolds Campaign on Powder River*, Norman, Okla., University of Oklahoma Press, 1961. How Crook's first Great Sioux War offensive went wrong.

Werner, F.H., *The Summit Springs Battle: July 11, 1869*, Greeley, Colo., Werner Publications, 1991.

Wooster, R., *Nelson A. Miles and the Twilight of the Frontier Army*, Lincoln, Neb., University of Nebraska Press, 1993.

ARTICLES AND CHAPTERS

Athearn, R.G., 'War Paint against Brass: The Army and the Plains Indians', *Montana Magazine of History*, 1956, vol. 6, pp. 11–22.

Gillett, M.C., 'United States Army Surgeons and the Big Horn–Yellowstone Expedition of 1876', *Montana*, 1989, vol. 39, pp. 16–27.

Hutton, P., 'From Little Big Horn to Little Big Man: the Changing Image of a Western Hero in Popular Culture', *Western Historical Quarterly*, 1976, vol. 7, pp. 19–46.

Johnson, R.P., 'Jacob Horner of the Seventh Cavalry', *North Dakota History*, 1949, vol. 16, pp. 77–9.

McGinnis, A., 'Strike and Retreat: Intertribal Warfare and the Powder River War, 1865–1868', *Montana: The Magazine of Western History*, 1980, pp. 30–41.

Ostler, J., 'Conquest and the State: Why the United States Employed Massive Military Force to Suppress the Lakota Ghost Dance', *Pacific Historical Review*, 1996, vol. 65, pp. 217–48.

Ostler, J., '"They regard their passing as *Wakan*": Interpreting Western Sioux Explanations for the Bison's Decline', *Western Historical Quarterly*, 1999, vol. 30, pp. 475–97.

Quaife, M.M., 'The Panic of 1862 in Wisconsin', *Wisconsin Magazine of History*, 1920, vol. 4, pp. 169–95.

Utley, R.M., 'Crook and Miles Fighting and Feuding on the Indian Frontier', *Military History Quarterly*, 1975, vol. 78, pp. 271–91.

BIBLIOGRAPHY

8 Conquest of Apachería, 1860–86

Secondary sources

Books

Ball, E., *In the Days of Victorio: Recollections of a Warm Springs Apache*, Tucson, Ariz., University of Arizona Press, 1970.

Ball, E., with N. Henn and L. Sanchez, *Indeh: An Apache Odyssey*, Provo, Utah, Brigham Young University Press, 1980.

Betzinez, J., with W.S. Nye, *I Fought With Geronimo*, Harrisburg, Pa., Stackpole Books, 1959. Valuable eyewitness account from Apache side.

Bourke, J.G., *On the Border with Crook*, Glorieta, N.Mex., Rio Grande Press, 1969 [1872]. The beginning of the Crook legend.

Cole, D.C., *The Chiricahua Apache, 1846–1876: From War to Reservation*, Albuquerque, N.Mex., University of New Mexico Press, 1988. Useful anthropological perspective.

Collins, C., *Apache Nightmare: The Battle at Cibecue Creek*, Norman, Okla., University of Oklahoma Press, 1999.

Debo, A., *Geronimo: The Man, his Time, his Place*, Norman, Okla., University of Oklahoma Press, 1976. The old raider's side of the story.

Essin, E.M., *Shavetails and Bell Sharps: The History of the US Army Mule*, Lincoln, Neb., University of Nebraska Press, 2000 [1997]. Pp. 92–8 give the best account in print of the origins and development of George Crook's famous concept of pack transportation.

Faulk, O.B., *Crimson Desert: Indian Wars of the American Southwest*, New York, Oxford University Press, 1974.

Faulk, O.B., *The Geronimo Campaign*, New York, Oxford University Press, 1968.

García, L., *Apuntes sobre la campaña contra los salvajes en el Estado de Sonora por el coronel del 60 batallon de infantería*, Hermosillo, Sonora, Biblioteca Sonorense de Geografía e Historia, 1959 [1883].

Griffen, W.B., *The Apaches at War and Peace: The Janos Presidio, 1750–1858*, Albuquerque, N.Mex., University of New Mexico Press, 1988.

Griffen, W.B., *Utmost Good Faith: Patterns of Apache–Mexican Hostilities in Northern Chihuahua Border Warfare, 1821–1848*, Albuquerque, N.Mex., University of New Mexico Press, 1988.

Hatfield, S.B., *Chasing Shadows: Indians Along the United States–Mexico Border, 1876–1911*, Albuquerque, N.Mex., University of New Mexico Press, 1998. Apaches and Yaquis and how they complicated Mexican–US relations.

Kraft, L., *Gatewood and Geronimo*, Albuquerque, N.Mex., University of New Mexico Press, 1998. Interesting idea, but ends up apples and oranges.

Leckie, W.H., *The Buffalo Soldiers: A Narrative of the Black Cavalry in the West*, rev. edn, Norman, Okla., University of Oklahoma Press, 2003 [1967].

Lejeune, L., *La Guerra Apache en Sonora*, tr. M. Antochiw, Hermosillo, Sonora, Gobierno del Estado de Sonora, 1984 [1885].

Lockwood, F., *The Apache Indians*, New York, Macmillan, 1938.

Porter, J.C., *Paper Medicine Man: John Gregory Bourke and his American West*, Norman, Okla., University of Oklahoma Press, 1986. What the Apaches called Bourke, military intellectual and aide to George Crook.

Roberts, D., *Once They Moved like the Wind: Cochise, Geronimo, and the Apache Wars*, New York, Simon and Schuster, 1993. Elegantly written but tends to romanticise the subject.

Robinson, C.M., III, *General Crook and the Western Frontier*, Norman, Okla., University of Oklahoma Press, 2001. First genuine biography of Crook and a good one.

Robinson, S., *Apache Voices: Their Stories of Survival as told to Eve Ball*, Albuquerque, N.Mex., University of New Mexico Press, 2000.

Schellie, D., *Vast Domain of Blood: The Story of the Camp Grant Massacre*, Los Angeles, Calif., Westernlore Press, 1968. Vigilante murder of Indian women and children which did much to envenom the Apache wars.

Smith, R.A., *Borderlander: The Life of James Kirker, 1793–1852*, Norman, Okla., University of Oklahoma Press, 2000. Hunted Apache scalps for pesos.

Sonnichsen, C.L. (ed.), *Geronimo and the End of the Apache Wars*, Lincoln, Neb., University of Nebraska Press, 1990. Geronimo's legacy.

Stockel, H.H., *Shame and Endurance: The Untold Story of the Chiricahua Apache Prisoners of War*, Tucson, Ariz., University of Arizona Press, 2004.

Stockel, H.H., *Survival of the Spirit: Chiricahua Apaches in Captivity*, Reno, Nev., University of Nevada Press, 1993.

Stockel, H.H., *Women of the Apache Nation: Voices of Truth*, Reno, Nev., University of Nevada Press, 1991 [1974].

Sweeney, E.R., *Cochise: Chiricahua Apache Chief*, Norman, Okla., University of Oklahoma Press, 1991.

Sweeney, E.R., *Mangas Coloradas: Chief of the Chiricahua Apaches*, Norman, Okla., University of Oklahoma Press, 1998.

Thrapp, D., *Conquest of Apachería*, Norman, Okla., University of Oklahoma Press, 1967. Seminal.

Thrapp, D., *General Crook and the Sierra Madre Adventure*, Norman, Okla., University of Oklahoma Press, 1972.

Thrapp, D., *Victorio and the Mimbres Apaches*, Norman, Okla., University of Oklahoma Press, 2000 [1991; 1974].

Tinker Salas, M., *In the Shadow of Eagles: Sonora and the Transformation of the Border during the Porfiriato*, Berkeley, Calif., University of California Press, 1997.

Turcheneske, J.A., Jr., *The Chiricahua Apache Prisoners of War: Fort Sill, 1894–1914*, Niwot, Colo., University Press of Colorado, 1997. Published version of author's 1979 Ph.D. dissertation at the University of New Mexico.

Weber, D.J., *The Mexican Frontier, 1821–1846: The American Southwest Under Mexico*, Albuquerque, N.Mex., University of New Mexico Press, 1982.

Wellman, P.I., *Death in the Desert: The Fifty Years War for the Great Southwest*, New York, Pyramid Books, 1965. Popular history written with a novelist's eye.

Worcester, D.E., *The Apaches: Eagles of the Southwest*, Norman, Okla., University of Oklahoma Press, 1979.

Articles and chapters

Gates, J., 'General George Crook's First Apache Campaign (the use of mobile, self-contained units against the Apache in the Military Department of Arizona, 1871–1873)', *Journal of the West*, 1967, vol. 6, pp. 310–20.

Gatewood, Charles B. 'The surrender of Geronimo', in C.L. Sonnichsen (ed.), *Geronimo and the End of the Apache Wars*, Lincoln, Neb., University of Nebraska Press, 1990 [1986], pp. 53–70. Gatewood convinced Geronimo to surrender in 1886.

Greene, J.A., 'The Crawford Affair: International Implications of the Geronimo Campaign', *Journal of the West*, 1972, vol. 2, pp. 143–53.

Kenoi, Samuel E., recorded by M.E. Opler, 'A Chiricahua Apache's Account of the Geronimo Campaign of 1886', in C.L. Sonnichsen (ed.), *Geronimo and the End of the Apache Wars*, Lincoln, Neb., University of Nebraska Press, 1990 [1986], pp. 71–90. Kenoi's recollections of the Geronimo campaign were first published in 1938.

King, J.T., 'George Crook: Indian Fighter and Humanitarian', *Arizona and the West*, 1967, vol. 9, pp. 333–48.

King, J.T., 'Needed: A Reevaluation of General George Crook', *Nebraska History*, 1964, vol. 45, pp. 223–36.

Maynard, D.P., 'Manpower, Weapons, and Tactics of the Apache wars, 1871–1875', *Periodical: Journal of America's Military Past*, 1997, vol. 24, pp. 3–15.

Park, J.F., 'The Apaches in Mexican–American Relations, 1846–1861: A Footnote to the Gadsen Treaty', *Arizona and the West*, 1961, vol. 3, pp. 129–46.

Rothenberg, G.E., 'General George Crook and the Apaches, 1872–1873', *Westerners Brand Book* (Chicago), 1955, vol. 13, pp. 49–56.

Smith, R.A., 'Apache Plunder Trails Southward, 1831–1840', *New Mexico Historical Review*, 1962, vol. 37, pp. 20–42.

Smith, R.A., 'Indians in American–Mexican Relations before the War of 1846', *Hispanic American Historical Review*, 1963, vol. 43, pp. 34–64. Apache incursions.

Smith, R.A., 'The Scalp Hunt in Chihuahua – 1849', *New Mexico Historical Review*, 1965, vol. 40, pp. 116–40. Apaches were the target.

Smith, R.A., 'Scalp Hunting: A Mexican Experiment in Warfare', *Great Plains Journal*, 1984, vol. 23, pp. 41–79. Ditto.

Sonnichsen, C.L., 'From Savage to Saint: A New Image for Geronimo', in Sonnichsen (ed.), *Geronimo and the End of the Apache Wars*, Lincoln, Neb., University of Nebraska Press, 1990 [1986], pp. 5–34. His contemporaries wouldn't recognise him.

Stevens, R.C., 'The Apache Menace in Sonora, 1831–1849', *Arizona and the West*, 1964, vol. 6, pp. 211–22.

Turcheneske, J.A., Jr., 'Arizonans and the Apache Prisoners of Mount Vernon Barracks, Alabama: "They do not die fast enough"', *Military History of Texas and the Southwest*, 1973, vol. 11, pp. 197–226.

Utley, R.M., 'The Bascom Affair: A Reconstruction', *Arizona and the West*, 1961, vol. 3, pp. 59–68.

Utley, R.M., 'The Surrender of Geronimo', *Arizoniana: The Journal of Arizona History*, 1963, vol. 4, pp. 1–9.

Worcester, D.E., 'The Apaches in the History of the Southwest', *New Mexico Historical Review*, 1975, vol. 50, pp. 25–44.

BIBLIOGRAPHY

9 War on the Canadian prairies, 1870–85

Secondary sources

Books

Beal, B. and R.C. Macleod, *Prairie Fire: The 1885 North-West Rebellion*, Edmonton, Alta., Hurtig, 1984.

Berton, P., *The Impossible Railway: The Building of the Canadian Pacific*, New York, Knopf, 1972.

Bumsted, J.M., *The Red River Rebellion*, Winnipeg, Man., Watson and Dwyer, 1996.

Carter, S., *Capturing Women: The Manipulation of Cultural Imagery in Canada's Prairie West*, Montreal, McGill-Queen's University Press, 1997.

Dempsey, H.A., *Big Bear: The End of Freedom*, Lincoln, Neb., University of Nebraska Press, 1984.

Dunn, J., *The Alberta Field Force of 1885*, Calgary, Alta., Jack Dunn Publisher, 1994.

Flanagan, T., *Riel and the Rebellion: 1885 Reconsidered*, Toronto, University of Toronto Press, 2000 [1983].

Friesen, G., *The Canadian Prairies: A History*, Lincoln, Neb., University of Nebraska Press, 1984.

Giraud, M., *The Métis in the Canadian West*, 2 vols, tr. G. Woodcock, Lincoln, Neb., University of Nebraska Press, 1986 [1945].

Granatstein, J.L., *Canada's Army: Waging War and Keeping the Peace*, Toronto, University of Toronto Press, 2002.

Hildebrandt, W., *The Battle of Batoche: British Small Warfare and the Entrenched Métis*, rev. edn, Ottawa, Parks Canada, 1989.

Howard, J.K., *Strange Empire: A Narrative of the Northwest*, New York, Morrow, 1952. The saga of the Métis. A classic.

Jenish, D., *Indian Fall: The Last Great Days of the Plains Cree and the Blackfoot Confederacy*, Toronto, Viking, 1999.

Martel, G., *Le messianisme de Louis Riel*, Waterloo, Ont., Wilfrid Laurier University Press, 1984.

Miller, J.R., *Big Bear (Mistahimusqua)*, Toronto, ECW Press, 1996.

Milloy, J.S., *The Plains Cree: Trade, Diplomacy and War, 1790 to 1870*, Winnipeg, Man., University of Manitoba Press, 1988.

Morice, A.G., *A Critical History of the Red River Insurrection, after Official Documents and Non-Catholic Sources*, Winnipeg, Man., Canadian Publications, 1935.

Morris, J., *Heaven's Command: An Imperial Progress*, New York, Harcourt, Brace, Jovanovich, 1980 [1973]. Chapter 17, 'The Humiliation of the Métis: The Subjection of an Alien Culture', pp. 337–57, is magisterial.

Morton, D., *The Last War Drum: The North West Campaign of 1885*, Toronto, Hakkert, 1972. No longer the authoritative account, but still very good.

Morton, D., *The Canadian General, Sir William Otter*, Toronto, Hakkert, 1974. Biography by a descendant.

Pettipas, K., *Severing the Ties that Bind: Government Repression of Indigenous Religious Ceremonies on the Prairies*, Winnipeg, Man., University of Manitoba Press, 1994.

Preston, R.A., *The Defence of the Undefended Border: Planning for War in North America, 1867–1939*, Montreal, McGill-Queen's University Press, 1977.

Sharp, P.F., *Whoop-Up Country: The Canadian–American West, 1865–1885*, Minneapolis, Minn., University of Minnesota Press, 1955. There actually was a Fort Whoop-Up. The Mounties had their work cut out for them.

Sluman, N., *Poundmaker*, Toronto, Ryerson Press, 1967.

Sprague, D.N., *Canada and the Métis, 1869–1885*, Waterloo, Ont., Wilfrid Laurier University Press, 1988.

Stanley, G.F.G., *The Birth of Western Canada: A History of the Riel Rebellion*, Toronto, University of Toronto Press, 1992 [1936]. Long the standard history, now badly dated.

Stanley, G.F.G., *Toil and Trouble: Military Expeditions to Red River*, Toronto, Dundurn Press, 1989.

Stonechild, B. and B. Waiser, *Loyal Till Death: Indians and the North-West Rebellion*, Calgary, Alta., Fifth House, 1997.

Turner, J.P., *The North-West Mounted Police, 1873–1893*, 2 vols, Ottawa, King's Printer, 1950. The official story by an insider.

Warner, D.F., *The Idea of Continental Union: Agitation for the Annexation of Canada to the United States, 1849–1893*, Lexington, Ky., University of Kentucky Press, 1960.

Woodcock, G., *Gabriel Dumont: The Métis Chief and his Lost World*, Edmonton, Alta., Hurtig, 1975.

Articles and chapters

Caldwell, R.H., '"We're making history, eh?": An Inquiry into the Events that Occurred near Cut Knife Hill, North West Territories, 1–2 May 1885', in D. Graves (ed.), *More Fighting for Canada: Five Battles, 1760–1944*, Toronto, Robin Brass Studio, 2004, pp. 75–146.

Dobak, W.A., 'Killing the Canadian Buffalo, 1821–1881', *Western Historical Quarterly*, 1996, vol. 27, pp. 33–52. Indian overkill did it.

Fraser, W.B., 'Big Bear, Indian patriot', in Donald Swainson (ed.), *Historical Essays on the Prairie Provinces*, Toronto, McClelland and Stewart, 1970, pp. 71–88.

Macleod, R.C., 'Canadianizing the West: The North-West Mounted Police as Agents of the National Policy, 1873–1905', in R.D. Francis and H. Palmer (eds), *The Prairie West: Historical Readings*, 2nd edn, Edmonton, Alta., Pica Pica Press, 1992.

Madill, D.F.K., 'Riel, Red River, and Beyond: New Developments in Métis History', in C. Calloway (ed.), *New Directions in American Indian History*, Norman, Okla., University of Oklahoma Press, 1988, pp. 49–78.

Morton, D., 'Cavalry or Police: Keeping the Peace on Two Adjacent Frontiers, 1870–1900', *Journal of Canadian Studies/Revue d'études canadiennes*, 1977, vol. 12, pp. 27–37. The American and Canadian methods of dealing with Indians compared.

Mossman, M., 'The Charismatic Pattern: Canada's Riel Rebellion of 1885', *Prairie Forum*, 1985, vol. 10, pp. 307–25.

Stacey, C.P., 'The Military Aspect of Canada's Winning of the West, 1870–1885', *Canadian Historical Review*, 1940, vol. 21, pp. 1–24.

Stanley, G.F.G., 'The Last Word on Louis Riel – The Man of Several Faces', in F.L. Barron and J.B. Waldram (eds), *1885 and After: Native Society in Transition*, Regina, Sask., Canadian Plains Research Centre, 1986, pp. 3–22.

Tobias, J., 'Canada's Subjugation of the Plains Cree, 1879–1885', *Canadian Historical Review*, 1983, vol. 64, pp. 519–48.
Vandervort, B., 'Wolseley, Garnet Joseph, 1853–1913', in C. Messenger (ed.), *Reader's Guide to Military History*, London, Fitzroy Dearborn Publishers, 2001.
Warner, D.F., 'Drang nach Norden: The United States and the Riel Rebellion', *Mississippi Valley Historical Review*, 1953, vol. 39, pp. 639–712.
Winter, C.F., 'Surrender of Poundmaker', *Canadian Magazine*, 1911, vol. 36, pp. 411–19.

10 Indian Wars of the Porfiriato, 1876–1900

Secondary sources

Books

Alexander, R.T., *Yaxcaba and the Caste War of Yucatán: An Archaeological Perspective*, Albuquerque, N.Mex., University of New Mexico Press, 2004. Good up-to-date summary of historiography of the Caste War.
Balbas, M., *Cronicas de la guerra del Yaqui, 1899–1901*, Hermosillo, Sonora, Gobierno del Estado, 1985.
Balbas, M., *Recuerdos del Yaqui: principales episodios durante el campaña de 1899 a 1901*, Mexico, Sociedad de Edicion y Librería Franco Americana, 1927.
Clendenen, C.C., *Blood on the Border: The United States Army and the Mexican Irregulars*, New York, Macmillan, 1969.
Dabdoub, C., *Historia de el Valle del Yaqui*, Mexico, Libreria de Manuel Porrua, 1964.
Fuentes, G., *El ejercito mexicano*, Mexico, Grijalbo, 1983.
Gonzalez Navarro, M., *Raz y tierra. La guerra de castas y el henequen*, Mexico, El Colegio de Mexico, 1970.
Gregg, R.D., *The Influence of Border Troubles on Relations between the United States and Mexico, 1876–1910*, Baltimore, Md., Johns Hopkins University Press, 1937.
Gutierrez Santos, D., *Historia militar de Mexico, 1876–1914*, Mexico, Ediciones Ateneo, 1955.
Hatfield, S.B., *Chasing Shadows: Apaches and Yaquis Along the United States–Mexico Border, 1876–1911*, Albuquerque, N.Mex., University of New Mexico Press, 1999 [1997]. Apaches from US hid out in Mexico; Yaquis slipped over the US border. Uses Mexican sources.
Hernandez, F., *Las razas indígenas de Sonora y el guerra del Yaqui*, Mexico, Talleres de la Casa Editorial 'J. de Elizalde', 1902.
Paso y Troncoso, F., *Las guerras con las tribus Yaqui y Mayo del estado de Sonora*, Mexico, Tipografia del Departamento de Estado Mayor, 1905. Semi-official account of the Yaqui wars.
Rippy, J.F., *The United States and Mexico*, New York, Knopf, 1931 [1926]. An older witness to the difficulties of rapprochement.
Smith, C.C., Jr., *Emilio Kosterlitzky: Eagle of Sonora and the Southwest Border*, Glendale, Calif., Arthur H. Clark, 1970. Rurales leader; fought both Apaches and Yaquis.
Spicer, E.H., *Cycles of Conquest: The Impact of Spain, Mexico, and the United States on*

the Indians of the Southwest, 1533–1960, Tucson, Ariz., University of Arizona Press, 1970 [1962]. Fundamental.
Tinker Salas, M., *In the Shadow of Eagles: Sonora and the Transformation of the Border during the Porfiriato*, Berkeley, Calif., University of California Press, 1997.
Turner, J.K., *Barbarous Mexico*, 2nd edn, Austin, Tex., University of Texas Press, 1969 [1911]. Powerful polemic on deportation of Yaquis to slavery in Yucatán henequen fields.
Vanderwood, P.J., *The Power of God against the Guns of Government: Religious Upheaval in Mexico at the Turn of the Nineteenth Century*, Stanford, Calif., Stanford University Press, 1998.
Villa Rojas, A., *The Mayas of East Central Quintana Roo*, Washington, D.C., Carnegie Institution, Publication 559, 1945. Helpful on Cult of Speaking Cross.
Wells, A. and G.M. Joseph, *Summer of Discontent, Seasons of Upheaval: Elite Politics and Rural Insurgency in Yucatán, 1876–1915*, Stanford, Calif., Stanford University Press, 1996.

Articles and chapters

Corral, R., 'Biografía de José María Leyva Cajeme', in Corral, *Obras historicas*, vol. 1, Hermosillo, Sonora, Biblioteca Sonorense de Geografía e Historia, 1959. Our best source on the life of Cajeme.
Hillary, F.M., 'Cajeme, and the Mexico of his Time', *Journal of Arizona History*, 1967, vol. 8, pp. 120–36. Useful complement to Corral biographical sketch of Cajeme.
Janvier, T.A., 'The Mexican army', in Anon., *The Armies of Today: A Description of the Armies of the Leading Nations at the Present Time*, New York, Harper Brothers, 1892, pp. 361–96.
Kelley, J.R., 'The Education and Training of Porfirian Officers: Success or Failure?', *Military Affairs*, 1975, vol. 34, pp. 124–8. Good source on professionalisation of the Mexican military under Diaz.
Powell, T.G., 'Mexican Intellectuals and the Indian Question', *The Hispanic American Historical Review*, 1968, vol. 48, pp. 19–36.
Sims, H.D., 'Espejo de caciques: Los Terrazas de Chihuahua', *Historia Mexicana*, 1969, vol. 18, pp. 379–99.
Spicer, E.H., 'Mexican Indian policies', in W. Sturtevant (ed.), *Handbook of North American Indians*, vol. 4, *History of Indian–White Relations*, Washington, D.C., Smithsonian Institution Press, 1988, pp. 103–9.
Stabb, M.S., 'Indigenism and Racism in Mexican Thought, 1857–1911', *Journal of Inter-American Studies*, 1959, vol. 1, pp. 405–23.

Conclusion: Long shadows

Secondary sources

Books

Fitzgerald, F., *Fire in the Lake: The Vietnamese and Americans in Vietnam*, Boston, Mass., Little, Brown, 1972.

Hayden, T. (ed.), *The Zapatista Reader*, New York, Thunder Mouth Press, 2002.
Higgins, N., *Understanding the Chiapas Rebellion: Modernist Visions and the Invisible Indian*, Austin, Tex., University of Texas Press, 2004.
Slotkin, R., *Regeneration and Violence: The Mythology of the American Frontier, 1600–1800*, Middletown, Conn., Wesleyan University Press, 1973.
Weinberg, B., *Homage to Chiapas: The New Indigenous Struggles in Mexico*, London, Verso, 2000.

Articles and chapters

Hess, P., 'Feature: Raid in Iraq's "Indian Country"', *United Press International*, 8 August 2003.
Kaplan, R.D., 'War on Terrorism: Indian Country', *Wall Street Journal*, 21 September 2004.
Linn, B.M., 'The Long Twilight of the Frontier Army', *Western Historical Quarterly*, 1996, vol. 27, pp. 141–67.
Weigley, R.F., 'The Long Death of the Indian-Fighting Army', in G.D. Ryan and T.K. Nenninger (eds), *Soldiers and Civilians: The US Army and the American People*, Washington, D.C., National Archives and Records Administration, 1987, pp. 27–39.

Comparative

Secondary sources

Books

Belich, J., *The Victorian Interpretation of Racial Conflict: The Maori, the British, and the New Zealand Wars*, Montreal and Kingston, McGill-Queen's University Press, 1989 [1986].
Bois, J.-P., *Bugeaud*, Paris, Fayard, 1997. Most recent biography of the French general whose counter-insurgency strategy in Algeria in the 1840s was much admired by US contemporaries.
Cassidy, R.M., *British and American Peacekeeping Doctrine and Practice after the Cold War*, Westport, Conn., Praeger, 2004. Useful for comparing British and US military and strategic cultures as they evolved over the 19th and 20th centuries.
Connor, J., *The Australian Frontier Wars, 1788–1838*, Sydney, University of New South Wales Press, 2002.
De Moor, J.A. and H.L. Wesseling (eds), *Imperialism and War: Essays on Colonial Wars in Asia and Africa*, Leiden, E.J. Brill, 1989.
Gump, J.O., *The Dust Rose Like Smoke: The Subjugation of the Zulu and the Sioux*, Lincoln, Neb., University of Nebraska Press, 1996 [1994].
Kiernan, V.G., *Colonial Empires and Armies, 1815–1960*, Montreal and Kingston, McGill-Queen's University Press, 1998 [1982].
Moreman, T.R., *The Army in India and the Development of Frontier Warfare, 1849–1947*, London, Macmillan and King's College, 1998. Very suggestive, particularly on importance of counter-insurgency doctrine.
Porch, D., *Wars of Empire*, London, Cassell, 2000. US is part of the cast.

Strachan, H., *European Armies and the Conduct of War*, London, George Allen and Unwin, 1983. Helpful chapter on comparative impact of colonial warfare on modern European armies; includes US Army.

Vandervort, B., *Wars of Imperial Conquest in Africa, 1830–1914*, Bloomington, Ind., Indiana University Press, 1998.

Articles and chapters

Beckett, I.F.W., 'Low-Intensity Conflict: Its Place in the Study of War', in D.A. Charters, M. Milner and B. Wilson (eds), *Military History and the Military Profession*, Westport, Conn., Praeger, 1992, pp. 121–9.

INDEX

Aborigines, Australian 21
Adams, John Quincy 123
Adams–Onís Treaty (1819) 122
Adobe Walls: first battle of (1864) 100–1, 133; second battle of (1874) 167–9
Adowa, battle of (1896) xv, 249n11
Alberta 217, 219
Alberta Field Force 219, 226–7
Algeria 19, 21, 58, 60–1
Alligator 133–4
Anglo-Maori wars 11, 21
Apache Indians xv, 9, 31–3, 38–9, 41–2, 76–7, 97, 192–210, 248
Apache Pass, battle of (1862) 100, 192, 199–200
Apachería 31, 38, 194
Arapaho Indians, Northern 3, 6, 16, 173–4
Arapaho Indians, Southern 167, 169
Arickaree River 3–4
artillery 100–1, 132–3
artillery, quick-firing 98
Ash Hollow (1855), battle of 170, 269n55; *see also* Harney, William S.
Assiniboine Indians 215, 224
Australia 21; *see also* Aborigines, Australian

Bacalar 156, 241
Bacatete Mountains 33–4, 235, 236–9
Bacúm, incident at 147–8
Bad Heart 5, 12
Banderas, Juan 34, 84–5, 141–5
Barrera, José María 158
Barue kingdom 232–3

Bascom Affair 199
Bascom, George N. 199
batabs 35, 85
Batoche, battle of (1885) 224–6
Batoche, Métis capital 217, 224–6
Battleford , 'siege' of 218, 223
Bazaine, Achille-François 146–7
Beasley, Daniel 116–17
Beaujour, Félix de 23
Beecher, Frederick 4–5, 7
Beecher Island, battle of (1868) 3–16, 81
Belly (Oldman) River, battle of (1870) 255n51
Benteen, Frederick 46, 182, 184–5, 260n35
Benton, Thomas Hart 8, 60, 87
Big Bear 98, 112, 216, 217, 227–8
Big Hole River, battle of (1877) 190
Big Horn Expedition, the 178
Blackfoot Indians 30, 215–16, 219
Black Hawk 107
Black Hawk War (1832) 107
Black Hills 175
Black Kettle 173
Black Seminoles 122, 127, 128–30, 258n19, 278n87
Boer War, Second (1899–1902) 225–6
Bonaparte, Napoleon 58, 80
Bourke, John Gregory 178, 203
Boyer, Mitch 184–5
Bravo, Ignacio 240–1
'breechloader revolution' 46, 299n40
'British Band' 107; *see also* Black Hawk; Sauk and Fox Indians
British Columbia 106

INDEX

British Honduras (Belize) 35, 151, 157, 241
'Brown Bess' musket 99, 240
Bryce, Lord James 18
Buatachive, fortress of 235
Buell, George P. 204
buffalo (bison) 167–8, 170, 215, 255–6n52
'Buffalo Soldiers' 6, 31, 204; *see also* Ninth Cavalry, USA; Tenth Cavalry, USA
Bugeaud, Thomas-Robert 19, 61
Buli, Luis 239
Burnt Corn Creek, battle of (1813) 115

Cajeme (José María Leyva) 34, 84–5, 100, 144–5, 230–6
Calhoun, James 97, 185
California Column 100, 199–200
Callwell, Charles E. 19, 49–51, 57, 122, 135, 170
camels in US southwest 20, 252n9
Camp Grant massacre (1871) 291n35
Canada, Dominion of 17–18, 21–2, 211–12
Canadian Pacific Railway 211, 219–20
Canby, Edward R.S. 188–9
cantones 156
Capetamaya, battle of (1881) 233
captain-general 139, 144
Captain Jack (Keintpoos) 188–9
Carbo, Guillermo 207
Cárdenas, Lázaro 242, 244
Carleton, James 100, 200
Carr, Eugene 167, 204, 205
Carson, Christopher 'Kit' 100–01, 167
Caste War (1847–1900) xv, 22, 35–6, 149–60, 239–42, 244–5
cattle herding, Indian 48
Caudillos, Mexico 42, 89, 160; *see also Hacendados*, Mexico
cavalry, limitations on use 180–1
Chaffee, Adna R. 207
Chan Santa Cruz 157–60, 241–2
chaplains, US Army 68–9
Chasseurs d'Afrique 43, 57, 58, 258–9n21
Cherokee Indians 110–11, 119–21, 125–6

Cheyenne Indians, Northern 3–7, 12–15, 29, 172–87
Cheyenne Indians, Southern 165–7
Chi, Cecilio 85, 155
Chihuahua 108, 161–2, 194, 196–7, 204–5
Chivington, John M. 172–3
Choctaw Indians 123–5
Cibicu Creek Incident (1881) 205–6
Científicos 229
Clark, Ransom 132, 279n103
Clearwater River, battle of (1877) 190
Cochise 198–9, 200, 201
Colegio Militar xiii, 88–9, 229
Colerain, Treaty of (1796) 122
collective land ownership, Indian 76–7, 78–9, 110, 139, 141
Colt pistol 100, 194
Comanche Indians xv, 9, 27–8, 39–41, 43, 47–8, 66–7, 83–4, 161–4
Comanchería 27
Connor, Patrick 14, 173–4
conscription, Mexico 64
Cooke, William W. 90, 184
Corona, Ramón 230–1
Corral, Ramón 148, 196, 235
Corredor, Mauricio 205, 292n53
Council House Fight 162–4
counterinsurgency strategy, Mexico 236–8
counting coup 82
Crawford, Emmet 203, 292n53, 207
Crazy Horse 23, 28, 185, 187
Cree Indians 9, 22, 28–9, 215–18, 223–4, 226–8
Creek Indians 25, 39–40, 42, 48, 66, 83–4, 110–22
Creek War, First (1813–14) 40, 107, 110–22
Creek War, Second (1834) 107
cronyism 92
Crook, George 8–9, 31, 46, 51, 76–7, 136–7, 175, 178–9, 202–3, 206–8
cross-cultural comparative studies xi–xiii
Crowfoot 228
Crow Indians 42–3, 177–9
Cruzob 158, 242
Cuba 129–30, 151

331

INDEX

Curly 184
Curzon, Lord George N. 18
Custer, George Armstrong 6, 59–60, 159–60, 166–7, 177, 179–87
Cut Knife Hill, battle of (1885) 9, 101, 223–4

Dade, Francis L. 132
Dade Massacre (1835) 132–4
Davis, Britton 203
Davis, Jefferson 19, 20, 155
deportation: Apache 209–10; Yaqui 238–9
De Rudio, Charles (Camillo di Rudio) 90
Díaz, Félix 88
Díaz, Porfirio 148, 160, 204, 229–30, 240
doctrine, military 10–11, 72–4
Dodge, Richard Irving 45, 291–2n40
Dog Soldiers 4, 43, 85–6, 166–7
Dragoons 53, 56, 57, 134
Dull Knife 187
Dumont, Gabriel 220–3, 225–7

earthquake, New Madrid 112
École Polytechnique xii, 54, 88
Eight Towns 34, 142, 149; *see also* 'sacred pueblos'
ejidos 244–5
El Añil, fortress of 233–4
Elliott, Joel 167
Emathla, Charley 127
Emuckfaw Creek, battle of (1813)
Enes, António 209
Enotachopco Creek, battle of (1813) 40, 97, 118
Ethiopians xv
ethnogenesis 25, 254n29, 255n47
ethos, military: Mexico 78–9; USA and Canada 74–8
Everglades 108, 128, 134–6
exceptionalism xii, 61

fear 96–8
Fetterman Massacre 16, 165, 174–5
Fetterman, William Judd 16, 174–5
Fifth Cavalry, USA 167, 187

filibusters 156–7
Finerty, John G. 43
firearms, pyrotechnic value of 46–7
Fish Creek, battle of (1885) 221–3
flux, peripheral xiii–xiv, 105–6
Ford, 'Rip' 100, 164
Forsyth, George 3–6, 8–11, 251n24
Forsyth Scouts 3, 8, 16
Fort Abraham Lincoln 177, 180, 187
Fort Apache 205–6
Fort Brooke 132
Fort Fetterman 177
Fort Garry 213–15
Fort Gibson, Treaty of (1833) 127
fortification techniques, Indian 119–20
Fort Jackson, Treaty of (1814) 120–1
Fort Kearny 170
Fort King 132
Fort Laramie: 10, 170, 175; Treaty of (1852) 170; Treaty of (1868) 175
Fort Mims, massacre of (1813) 116–18
Fort Wallace 6
Forty-first Foot 109
Fourth Cavalry, USA 169, 187
Francis, Josiah 113
Free, Mickey (Felix Ward) 199
French Foreign Legion 90, 147
Frenchman's Butte, battle of (1885) 226–7
French military, US Army emulation of 53–6, 58–61, 261n66, 261–2n68
Frog Lake massacre (1885) 218, 227

gachupines 141–2
Gadsden Purchase (1853) 162
Gaines, Edmund Pendleton 87–8
Gall 28, 181, 186
Gálvez, Don Bernardo de 32
Gándara, Manuel María 146
García, Lorenzo 196
García Morales, Jesus 147–8
Garnier, Isidore-Théodule 146
Gatewood, Charles 203, 209
Gatling gun 98, 100–01, 223–4, 272n107
Gaza Nguni 209
genetical determinism 75
Geronimo 112, 205, 206–10, 256n56

332

INDEX

Ghent, Peace of (1814) 109
Ghost Dance 191
Gibbon, John 177–8, 179–80, 190
glory, pursuit of 55–6, 91, 131
Gold Rush, California 23, 145, 230
Gordon, Charles George 'Chinese' 24, 217
Grant, Ulysses S. 175
Gras-Kropatschek rifle 98
Grattan, John L. 10, 170
Grattan Massacre 10, 170
Gray, John 184–5, 288n64
Great Sioux Uprising (1862) 97, 171–2, 286n34
Grierson, Benjamin H. 204
Grover, Abner 4, 6
Guadalupe Hidalgo, Treaty of (1848) 162, 284n5
Guardia (Guard of the Saint) 158, 245
Gump, James O. xi, 28–9
gun trade 44–5, 259n30,
Gutiérrez, Dolores 144
Gwin, William M. 146

Hacendados, Mexico 89, 145; *see also Caudillos*, Mexico
Half Yellow Face 182
'hammocks' 134
Hancock, Winfield Scott 165–6, 284–5n19
Hardy, Robert 142
Harney, William S. 51, 53, 87, 91–2, 135, 136, 170, 269n55, 269n57
Harrison, William Henry 51, 108
Hatch, Edward 204
Hawkins, Benjamin 111–12
Henry rifle 185
Herron, J.S. 20
Hickock, James Butler 'Wild Bill' 166
Hidalgo, Father Miguel 141
High-head Jim (Cussetaw Haujo) 113
Hitchcock, Ethan Allen 92, 130–1, 269n57
'Home Guards' 29
Horse and Gun pattern of Indian warfare 6–7, 40–7, 258n18
horses, 'American' 56–7
horses, barb 57

Horseshoe Bend, battle of (1814) 118–21
Houston, Sam 120, 162
Howard, Arthur L. 'Gatling Howard' 101, 223
Howard, Oliver O. 69, 136, 190, 201–3
Hudson's Bay Company 18, 21, 29, 44, 211–12
Huerta, Victoriano 88, 268n39
Hurst, John 4–5, 10, 12

Indian policies: Canada 71; Mexico 70–1; Spain 71; USA 70–1
Indian Springs, Treaty of (1825) 114
individualism, possessive 124–5
Iraq War, Second 247–8
Isandlwana, battle of (1879) xv, 13–14, 133

Jackson, Andrew 40, 51, 86–7, 107, 118–21, 121–2
Jefferson, Thomas 123
Jeffords, Thomas J. 201
Jesuits 34–5, 140, 144
Jesup, Thomas Sidney 128, 130–1
Johnson, Richard Mentor 109–10
Jomini, Antoine-Henri 55
Joseph, Chief 191
Josephite Order 237
Juarez, Benito 60, 146
Juh 33, 200, 207
Julesburg 173
Jusacamea, Juan María 144

Kaplan, Robert D. 248
Kearny, Philip 58–60, 60
Kearny, Stephen Watts 58, 197
Keogh, Myles W. 90, 185–6
Killdeer Mountain, battle of (1862) 172
King, Charles 93, 203
Kiowa Indians 41
Kipling, Rudyard 96
Kirker, James 196–7
Kitchener, Horatio Herbert 77
Klamath Indians 188–9
Kosterlitzky, Emilio 233

Ladinos (Yucatán) 22, 149–52
Lamar, Mirabeau Buonaparte 162

333

INDEX

Lake Okeechobee, battle of (1837) 128
La Pasión, battle of (1865) 146
La Reforma 15–16, 145
Laurentian Shield 214, 219
Lava Beds (California) 189
Lawton, Henry W. 208–9
leadership: Euro-American military 86–92; Indian military 81–5
Lee, General Robert E. 262n73
Lerdo Law (1856) 145
Lewis and Clark 29, 170
ligeros 282n45
Little Big Horn, battle of (1876) xv, 179–87, 217
Little Crow 171–2
Llano Estacado (Staked Plain) 27, 167, 169
Lodge, Henry Cabot 18
logistics, Indian 48–9
Lost River Valley 188
Lozen 81

McClellan, George 20, 59
McDougall, James 182, 184–5
machete, as weapon 45, 152
McIntosh, William 114
Mackenzie, Ranald 169, 187
McQueen, Peter 113–14, 127
Mahan, Dennis Hart 54–6, 58
Mangas Coloradas 31, 197–8, 200–1, 290n18
Manifest Destiny 15, 22–3, 25, 156, 286n36
Manitoba 172, 213–15
Mapuches 254n31
Marcy, Randolph B. 19, 60
Marines, US 128, 134–5, 248, 278n89
marksmanship: Indian 46–7; US Army 46, 288n68
Marquín, José María 146
Martin, John (Giovanni Martini) 184
Martínez, Angel 234–5
Martini-Henry rifle 11, 13, 99
masewalob 149–60, 239–42
Mauser rifle 99–100, 240
Maximilian, Emperor 147
Mayan Indians 14, 35–6, 42, 45, 47, 48, 67–8, 69, 149–60, 239–42, 244–5
Mayo Indians 34, 141, 147

Mazocoba, battle of (1900) 238
'medicine' 82–3, 174
Medicine Lodge, Treaty of (1867) 167
Menawa 114
Mérida 35, 151
Métis 63, 213–27
Métis Republic: (1870) 213–15; (1885) 217–27
Mexican–American War (1846–8) 91–2, 151, 155
'Mexico Moon' 161–2
Michno, Gregory 182, 186
Middleton, Sir Frederick 88, 219–20, 221–3, 224–6
Midland Battalion (Ontario) 218, 225, 226
Miles, Nelson 9, 11, 87, 101, 136–7, 169, 187, 191, 208–9
Milfort, Louis Leclerc 40
military societies, Indian 85–6
militia: Canadian 7, 9, 63, 214–15, 218–20, 221–7; Kentucky 109; Mexican 7, 64–5; Tennessee 118; USA 5, 109, 118
miners 198
Minié ball 98
Moctezuma 141, 144
Modoc Indians 46, 188–90
Modoc War (1872–3) 188–90
Mohawk Indians 246
Mojave Indians 77
Monroe, James 122–3
Monteil, Paul-Louis 10
Mooers, John G. 3, 5
Moraviantown, battle of (1813) 109–10
Mordecai, Alfred 55
Morris, James 211
motivation: Canadian armed forces 62–3; Mexican armed forces 63–5; US Army 58–62
Moultrie Creek, Treaty of (1823) 126
mounted infantry: (Kentucky) 108–10; (Tennessee) 108
movement, strategy of 52
Murat, Joachim 58–60, 180

Nahuat 158–9
Nakai'-dokli'ni 205

INDEX

Napoleon Club 55
Napoleon III 146–7
Nash, Gary xiii
National Guard: Mexico 89, 160; Sonora 233–4; Yucatán 151, 240
'Native State' 108–9
Navy, US 127–8, 134–5, 278n89
Neolin 25, 68
New Spain 32, 78
Nez Percé Indians 46, 190–1
Nez Percé War (1877) 190–1
Nickerson, Azor 203
Ninth Cavalry, USA 31, 204; *see also* 'Buffalo Soldiers'; Tenth Cavalry, USA
North-West Field Force 218–20, 223–7
North-West Mounted Police 22, 71, 218, 219, 226–7
North-West Rebellion, Canada (1885) xiv, 217–28
Nowlan, Henry J. 90
numbered treaties (Canada) 215–16

Ojibwa Indians 28, 215
Opata Indians 32, 34, 141, 143–4, 197, 256n59
Orangemen 69, 264n13
Orange Walk, battle of (1872) 283n67
Ortiz, Peace of 236
Osceola (Asi-Yaholo) 114, 127, 277–8n81
Other Magpie 81
other ranks, US Army 92–101
Otter, William 223–4, 225, 295n45

pa (Maori fortifications) 232
Pacheco, Louis 132, 279n103
Pacíficos (Mayan) 157, 160
Palo Duro Canyon, battle of (1875) 9, 169, 181
pan-Indianism 25, 107
Papago Indians 197
Parker, Quanah 23, 167
Parkman, Francis 25
Parthians 23
Pat, Jacinto 85, 155
Pawnee Fork 166
Pawnee Indians 67, 86
Payne's Landing, Treaty of (1832) 126

peripheral flux xiii–xiv, 15–16
Pesquiera, Ignacio 146–8, 231
Pesquiera, José 231
Philippine Insurrection 136, 247
phrenology 75
physiognomy, US Army officer corps 90–2
Pima Indians 34, 141, 146, 197
'plan for civilisation' 111, 115
Plan of Iguala 138
Platte Bridge Station, battle of (1865) 173
political autonomy, Indian 110, 139–41
Polk, James K. 154
polygenesis 74–5
Pontiac 25, 68
Poundmaker 98, 223–4, 227–8, 294n14
Powder River campaign (1865) 173–4; *see also* Connor, Patrick; Roman Nose
Powell, Levin N. 134–5
Preble, George H. 135
Procter, Henry 109–10
professionalism, military, USA 7, 86–8
Puc, Juan de la Cruz 159

Quintana Roo 241, 245

rape 96
'red–black alliance' 118, 122, 128–9
Red Cloud 174
Red River Colony, Manitoba 21–2, 172, 213–15
Red River Expedition, Canada (1870) xix, 213–15
Red River War, Texas (1874–5) 9, 167–70
Red Sticks 112–15, 158
religion and war: European–American 68–9; Indian 66–8
Remington, Frederic 100
Remington rifle 99–100, 240
removal of US Eastern Indian tribes 22, 25, 107, 276n65
Reno, Marcus 182–4, 187
revitalisation movements 67–8, 112–15, 157–60, 191, 253n25
Reyes, Bernardo 89
Reynolds, Joseph J. 178

335

INDEX

Riel, Louis 213–15, 216–17
riverine warfare 134–6
Roman Nose 5, 14–15, 85, 166, 174, 284–5n19
Rorke's Drift, battle of (1879) 11
Rosebud, battle of the (1876) 179, 287n49
Royal Military College, Canada 88
Rupert's Land 211
Rurales 229–30, 296n1

'sacred pueblos', Yaqui 35, 84–5; *see also* Eight Towns
Saint Patrick's Battalion 91–2
San Carlos Reservation 203
sanctuaries, cross-border xi, 187–8, 190–1
Sand Creek massacre (1865) 165, 167, 172–3
Santa Anna, António López de 70, 164
Sappa Creek (Dark Water Creek) (1875), battle of 170, 285–6n29
Saskatchewan 215, 216, 220, 226–7
Satanta 23, 98
Sauk and Fox Indians 25, 107
'savagery', Indian 76, 96
scalp bounty 107–8, 196–7
scalping 96
Scott, Thomas 213, 215
Scott, Winfield 86–8, 125, 131, 267n33
scouts, Indian 8–9, 20, 169, 174, 178–9, 205–6
secondary empires xiv, 16, 28, 164
Second Dragoons, USA 134
Seminole Indians 25, 48, 108, 121–37
Seminole War, First (1818) 121–2
Seminole War, Second (1835–42) 25, 108, 126–37
Seventh Cavalry, USA 6, 166–7, 177, 179–87, 191
shamans 82, 112–13
Shawnee Indians 39, 66, 68, 84, 107, 109, 112
Sheridan, Philip 3, 9, 137, 175–8, 180, 206, 207–8
Sherman, William T. 126, 165, 167
Shlesinger, Sigmund 4, 96–7
Shoshoni Indians 177, 179

Sibley, Henry L. 172
siege tactics, Mayan 152–4
Sierra Madre Mountains 33, 203, 206–7
Sierra O'Reilly, Justo 154–5
'Singing of the Boundary' 33–4
Sioux Indians: Santee 28–9, 97, 171–2; Teton (or Lakotas) 4, 6–7, 28–9, 39, 43–4, 174–87
Sitting Bull 23, 28, 112, 178–9, 187–8
Sixth Cavalry, USA 205
Sixtieth Royal Rifle Regiment 62–3, 214–15
Sladen, Joseph A. 201
Slim Buttes, battle of (1876) 187
'small wars' 19, 49–53
Snider-Enfield rifle 99
Social Darwinism 251n24
Sonora 34–5, 138, 141–9, 192, 194–7, 230–9
Soyopa, battle of (1832) 144
Speaking Cross, Cult of the 85, 157–60, 242, 245
Spencer carbine 4, 11–12
Springfield rifle 236
Stanley, Henry Morton 166
static defence, strategy of 52–3
Stilwell, Jack 4, 12
Strange, Thomas Bland 'Gunner Jingo' 219, 226–7
Sully, Alfred 172
Summit Springs, battle of (1869) 86, 167
Sun Dance 178–9, 228

Taiping Rebellion 24
'Talking Tree, The' 34
Tallapoosa River 110, 118
Tall Bull 86, 166–7
Tarahumara Indians 197, 205
Tartars 23
Taylor, Zachary 131
technological determinism 15
Tecumseh 25, 107, 108–10, 115
Tenskwatawa ('The Prophet') 25, 68, 107, 115, 158, 253–4n27
Tenth Cavalry, USA 16, 31, 204; *see also* 'Buffalo Soldiers'; Ninth Cavalry, USA
Terrazas, Joaquin 31, 205

INDEX

Terrazas, Luis 207
Terry, Alfred 173, 177, 179–80
Tetabiate (Juan Maldonado) 236–8
Texas 23, 161–4, 204
Texas Rangers 164
Thayer, Sylvanus 54
Third Cavalry, USA 12–13
Third Colorado Volunteer Cavalry 172–3
Thirty-Ninth Infantry Regiment, US Army 118–19
Tirailleurs Sénégalais 281n34
Tocqueville, Aléxis 123–5
Topete, Bonífacio 207
Topete, Fausto 234
Torím, battle of (1875) 231
Torres, Lorenzo 238
Torres, Luis 148, 206
training: Canadian militia 93–4; Mexican army and militia 94; US Army 94–5
Tres Castillos, battle of (1882) 9, 205
Trevor-Roper, H.R. 24
Turner, Frederick Jackson 106
Two Leggings 83

Union Pacific Railroad 18, 175
United States as imperialist power (nineteenth century) 17–20, 260–1n54
Upton, Emory 61–2, 73

Vallodolíd (Yucatán) 153
Victorio 31, 200, 204–5
Vietnam War (1965–75) 72, 246, 247–8
Villa, Loreto 237–8
Virgin of Guadalupe 85, 141

Walch, Paddy 113
Wandering Spirit 217–18, 227
War of 1812 25, 62, 107–10

'Wars against nature' 53, 169, 192
Washita, battle of the (1868) 167, 181, 287n54
ways of war, Indian 39–48
weaponry: Canadian militia 99; Mexican army and militia 99–100; US Army 98–9
Weatherford, William (Red Eagle) 113, 121, 171
Weigley, Russell 72, 247
West India Squadron 127
West Point (US Military Academy) 10, 54–6, 86–7
White Bird Canyon, battle of (1877) 190
White Bull 185
Winchester rifle 99, 194, 236
Wolf Mountains, battle of (1877) 187
Wolseley, Garnet 9, 62, 92, 201, 208–9, 213–15, 217
Wood Lake, battle of (1862) 172
Wood, Leonard 192, 208–9
Wool, John E. 125
Worth, William Jenkins 135–6
Wounded Knee massacre (1890) 191

Yaqui Indians 14, 22, 31, 33–5, 42, 45, 48, 67–8, 69, 78–9, 84–5, 229–39, 243–4
Yaqui River 244
Yaqui Valley 244
Yellow Haired Woman 81
yoris 142
Yucatán xv, 22, 35–6, 149–60, 239–42, 244–5

Zapatista National Liberation Army 246–7
Zavala, Lorenzo de 78–9, 139, 280n43
Zona Indígena 243–4
Zulus xv, 11, 13–14, 24, 27, 133

eBooks – at www.eBookstore.tandf.co.uk

A library at your fingertips!

eBooks are electronic versions of printed books. You can store them on your PC/laptop or browse them online.

They have advantages for anyone needing rapid access to a wide variety of published, copyright information.

eBooks can help your research by enabling you to bookmark chapters, annotate text and use instant searches to find specific words or phrases. Several eBook files would fit on even a small laptop or PDA.

NEW: Save money by eSubscribing: cheap, online access to any eBook for as long as you need it.

Annual subscription packages

We now offer special low-cost bulk subscriptions to packages of eBooks in certain subject areas. These are available to libraries or to individuals.

For more information please contact webmaster.ebooks@tandf.co.uk

We're continually developing the eBook concept, so keep up to date by visiting the website.

www.eBookstore.tandf.co.uk

Routledge History

European and Native American Warfare, 1675–1795
Armstrong Starkey

Warfare and History series

'Starkey has given his readers a useful bibliographical guide and a thought-provoking analysis. The attractive paperback should find a place on many a student bookshelf.' John Oliphant, *The Journal and Imperial and Commonwealth History*

Challenging the historical tradition that has denigrated Indians as 'savages' and celebrated the triumph of European 'civilization', Armstrong Starkey presents military history as only one dimension of a more fundamental conflict of cultures, and re-examines the European invasion of North America in the 17th and 18th centuries. Combining the perspectives of ethno-history and military history, this book provides an evaluation of the evolution and influence of both Indian and European ways of war during the period. Significant conflicts are analysed including King Philip's war in New England (1675–1676) notable due to the number of armed Indians, the American War of Independence, and the conquest of the old Northwest, 1783–1815.

Hbk 1857285549   Pbk 1857285557

The War for Independence and the Transformation of American Society: War and Society in the United States, 1775–83
Harry M. Ward

Warfare and History series

The War of Independence had a substantial impact on the lives of all Americans, establishing a nation and constructing American identity. *The War for Independence and the Transformation of American Society* focuses on a conflict which was both civil war and revolution and assesses how Americans met the challenges of adapting to the ideals of Independence and Republicanism. The war effected political reconstruction and brought economic self-sufficiency and expansion, but it also brought oppression of dissenting and ethnic minorities, broadened the divide between the affluent and the poor and strengthened the institution of slavery. Focusing on the climate of war itself and its effects on the lives of those who lived through it, this book includes discussion of:

- ★ Recruitment and Society
- ★ The Home Front
- ★ Constraints on Liberty
- ★ Women and family during the war years
- ★ African Americans and Native Americans

This book is a fascinating account of the wider dimension to the meaning of the American Revolution.

Hbk 1857286561   Pbk 185728657X

Available at all good bookshops
For ordering and further information please visit:
www.routledge.com

Routledge History

Introduction to Global Military History
1775 to the Present Day
Jeremy Black

'A lucid and succinct account of military developments around the modern world that combines a truly global coverage of events with thought-provoking analysis. By juxtaposing the familiar with the previously neglected or largely unknown, Jeremy Black forces the reader to reassess the standard grand narrative of military history that rests on assumptions of western cultural and technological superiority . . . It should have a wide market on world history courses that are increasingly common parts of American, British and Australian university programmes.' Professor Peter H. Wilson, *University of Sunderland*

'Jeremy Black does an admirable job in distilling a tremendous amount of information and making it comprehensible for students.' Professor Lawrence Sondhaus, *University of Indianapolis*

'An excellent book. Too often, in military studies and histories, the land, air, and maritime aspects are dealt with in separate books. This work integrates all aspects of conflict in a reasonable manner.' Stanley Carpenter, *Professor of Strategy and Policy, US Naval War College, Newport, Rhode Island*

Hbk 0–415–35394–7   Pbk 0–415–35395–5

Rethinking Military History
Jeremy Black

'Jeremy Black has exercised his formidable powers of historical dissection, critical analysis, and creative cogitation to produce an exciting book…it should spark constructive debate about how historians may better practise their craft.' Theodore F. Cook, *William Paterson University of New Jersey*

'Jeremy Black provides timely arguments against a narrowly technological perception of military history, shaped by Western experience. His survey of five centuries of global warfare shows the shortcomings of this perspective and the necessity to understand the political and cultural aspects of warfare.' Jan Glete, *Stockholm University*

'Formidable.' Paul A. Fideler, *Lesley University*

This must-read study demonstrates the limitations of current approaches, including common generalisations, omissions, and over-simplifications. Engaging theoretical discussions, with reference to specific conflicts, suggest how these limitations can be remedied and adapted, whilst incorporating contributions from other disciplines. Additional chapters provide a valuable and concise survey of the main themes in the study of military history from 1500 to the present day.

Hbk 0–415–27533–4   Pbk 0–415–27534–2

Available at all good bookshops
For ordering and further information please visit:
www.routledge.com